CHRIST'S CHURCHES
PURELY REFORMED

CHRIST'S CHURCHES PURELY REFORMED

A Social History of Calvinism

PHILIP BENEDICT

Yale University Press / New Haven & London

Published with assistance from the foundation established in memory of
Oliver Baty Cunningham of the Class of 1917, Yale College.

Copyright © 2002 by Yale University. All rights reserved. This book may not be
reproduced, in whole or in part, including illustrations, in any form (beyond that copying
permitted by Sections 107 and 108 of the U.S. Copyright Law and except by reviewers for
the public press), without written permission from the publishers.

Designed by Mary Valencia
Set in Caslon 224 Book type by Tseng Information Systems, Inc.,
Durham, North Carolina.

Printed in the United States of America by Edwards Brothers,
Ann Arbor, Michigan.

The Library of Congress has cataloged the hardcover edition as follows:
Benedict, Philip.
Christ's churches purely reformed : a social history of Calvinism / Philip Benedict.
p. cm.
Includes bibliographical references and index.
ISBN 0-300-08812-4 (cloth : alk. paper)
1. Calvinism—Europe—History. I. Title.
BX9415 .B47   2002
284'.24—dc21   2002002411

A catalogue record for this book is available from the British Library.

The paper in this book meets the guidelines for permanence and durability
of the Committee on Production Guidelines for Book Longevity
of the Council on Library Resources.

ISBN 0-300-10507-X (pbk. : alk. paper)

10 9 8 7 6 5 4 3 2

CONTENTS

CONTENTS

CONTENTS

ILLUSTRATIONS

FIGURES

MAPS

GRAPHS

TABLES

ACKNOWLEDGMENTS

Three generous institutions provided financial support for the research and writing of this book: the National Endowment for the Humanities through both a Fellowship for University Teachers and one for the National Humanities Center; the John Simon Guggenheim Memorial Foundation; and the George A. and Eliza Howard Foundation. I began some of the research as a member of the Institute for Advanced Study and wrote a sizable portion of the book at the National Humanities Center. I would like to express my deep gratitude to all of these institutions. I would also like to express my thanks to the kind staffs of the Brown University Library and the Andover-Harvard Theological Library, with special thanks to Brown's interlibrary loan office, which filled endless requests for obscure books with efficiency and good cheer.

My gratitude is no less deep to the many friends, colleagues, and students (overlapping categories) who helped me over the years. So many people supplied bibliographic leads and factual guidance that I cannot recall them all. I can thank by name David Daniel, Bruce Gordon, Kaspar von Greyerz, Peter Lake, Bruce Lenman, Guido Marnef, Brendan McConville, Graeme Murdock, Henk van Nierop, Katalin Péter, the late Bob Scribner, and David Weir, while at the same time apologizing to those omitted from this list. George Deak, Witold Rodkiewicz, and Alexandru Vari provided invaluable research assistance with Hungarian- and Polish-language materials. Barbara Diefendorf, Mark Greengrass, Robert M. Kingdon, and Hugh McLeod all did the yeoman's service of reading and commenting upon early drafts of the manuscript. So too did the members of my Spring 1999 History 207 seminar at Brown University—David Denno, Charlotte Eichna, Jessica George, Melanie Gustin, Stephen Johns, Matt Kadane, and Philip Mead—as well as Lara Heimert at Yale University Press. The book is much the better for all of their helpful advice. Individual chapters also benefited from the critical and much-appreciated commentary of Tim Harris, Guido Marnef, Graeme Murdock, Henk van Nierop, and Judith Pollmann. An earlier version of part 4 was presented to Bernard Roussel's seminar at the Ecole Pratique des Hautes Etudes, Section des Sciences Religieuses. I must thank Barbara Diefendorf, Kaspar von Greyerz, and Judith Pollmann for allowing me to see and benefit from unpublished work of theirs. Calvin Tams helped greatly with last-minute fact checking. As always, my greatest debt is to my wife, Judy, for her prodding, patience, independence, love, and support.

CONVENTIONS

If an established English spelling exists for a foreign place-name I have used it. Otherwise, I have used the name that I believe best conveys the locality's linguistic and political complexion during the period under study here. For some east European cities that now bear very different names and might be more familiar to readers by their modern names, I have provided these as well on first mention.

As for matters of capitalization, I have tried to leave theological, ecclesiological, and political positions in the lowercase so long as they refer to individual inclinations, but to capitalize them when they refer to organized churches or clearly defined political groupings. Thus, presbyterian theologians advocated forms of church government by synod; Presbyterian theologians were attached to the distinctive Scottish and English churches of that name or to the English political grouping that emerged during the civil war. Similarly, I have capitalized the names of specific, well-recognized historical events but left contemporary ambitions in lowercase, for example, the Genevan Reformation but the ideal of further reformation. As it is often difficult to determine just when a current of opinion became a party or church, or when a set of changes amounts to a recognizable historical event, some choices I have made may be rather arbitrary.

INTRODUCTION

Although Martin Luther towered over the initial decades of the Reformation, Calvinism superseded Lutheranism within a generation as the most dynamic and widely established form of European Protestantism. Into the 1540s, the cause remained confined primarily to Switzerland and the neighboring regions of south Germany. Around midcentury it burst its fetters. Reformed churches took root and grew in defiance of the established authorities in France, Scotland, the Netherlands, Hungary, and the vast Polish-Lithuanian commonwealth. England's national church assumed a Reformed cast under Edward VI between 1547 and 1553 and permanently joined the ranks of Europe's Protestant kingdoms when Elizabeth I succeeded Mary Tudor in 1558. A growing number of princes within the Holy Roman Empire accepted the faith and imposed it upon their subjects. By the end of the sixteenth century, Reformed worship was established from Aberdeen to Alba-Julia and from Béarn to Brest-Litovsk. Soon, the colonizing efforts of England and the Netherlands would carry it to North America and South Africa as well.

This dynamic faith inspired extraordinary sacrifices and sparked extraordinary crusades. At its core was the conviction that God's holy word made clear the form of worship expected from his children. God would never abandon those whom he had created, sustained, and granted the gift of everlasting life. The gratitude they owed him in return should inspire them to serve him in all their deeds, to worship in the manner he had decreed, and to shun all false devotion and idolatry. Such convictions steeled hundreds to face a martyr's death. They repeatedly unsettled the political order by sparking the rejection of established rituals, the formation of illegal new churches, and resistance to princely innovations in worship believed to threaten the purity of God's ordinances. The political history of later sixteenth- and seventeenth-century Europe is incomprehensible without an understanding of the history of Calvinism and the reasons its spread proved so unsettling.

One reason the faith proved so compelling to so many was that it inspired dreams of a dramatic transformation of manners, morals, and the social order. "If the order set forth in this book were well observed among those who call themselves christians," proclaimed the preface to the most comprehensive mid-sixteenth-century set of rules for worship and government within a Reformed church,

> the world would not feel the wrath of God, as do and will increasingly those who do not amend their ways. Princes and magistrates would be more peaceful; wars would cease among the nobility; the ambition of prelates would be punished; and all would do their duty in their calling. Children would be instructed from a young age in holy discipline; doctrine would be purely preached; the sacraments properly administered; the populace held in check; virtue would be prized; vices corrected; true penance restored and excommunication pronounced on the obstinate and rebellious; God's honor would be advanced together with the proper invocation of his holy name; the most honorable estate of marriage would be restored to its original form; brothels would be abolished; the poor would be cared for and all begging eliminated; the sick would be visited and consoled; and the dead honored with an honest burial devoid of superstition.[1]

The Latin motto of many Reformed churches today, "Ecclesia reformata, quia semper reformanda" (The Reformed church because always reforming) was coined in the middle of the seventeenth century by the Dutch churchman Johannes Hoornbeeck. It captures perfectly the restlessness of a tradition that recurrently generated internal revitalization movements inspired by such hopes even after they had not been immediately realized—as inevitably they were not. Committed adherents always had to ask themselves if they were doing everything possible to serve God and to observe his strict ordinances of worship.

The history of Calvinism is not only central to the religious and political history of the early modern era; influential sociological and historical interpretations deem it the progenitor of essential features of the modern world. The most famous such interpretation asserts that Calvinism encouraged inner-worldly asceticism and the growth of capitalism. Elements of this interpretation may be traced back to the sixteenth century itself: to the self-perception of the Reformed that they had effected a particularly thorough "reformation of life," and to the polemical Protestant commonplace that Catholicism fostered idleness through its numerous saints' days. Holland's dramatic rise to commercial supremacy in the seventeenth century, Britain's leading role in industrialization, the disproportionate importance of Protestants among France's entrepreneurial elites, and the more prosperous character of the Protestant regions of Germany and Switzerland in the nineteenth century all lent further credence to this idea, even before the great German sociologist Max Weber offered the most celebrated explanation for it around 1900 in his *The Protestant Ethic and the Spirit of Capitalism*. This work quickly attained canonical status within the emerging discipline of sociology. Among scholars, it has sparked refutations, reiterations, and extensions down to the present day. Among the broader reading public, it cemented the association between Calvinism and disciplined work. When President Clinton had to spend a wedding anniversary apart from his (Methodist) wife in 1998, he joked with reporters, "Her Calvinism will let me work, but no golf."[2]

Another long-influential theory credits Calvinism with promoting democracy. Again, the association goes back to the sixteenth century, when hostile Catholic polemics depicted the Reformed as partisans of sedition eager to replace crowned heads with Swiss-style confederations. The Reformed initially threw this accusation back at the Catholics, charging the Jesuits with being the leading advocates of king killing. In the changed political circumstances of the eighteenth and nineteenth centuries, however, what had once seemed an insult became a point of pride. The deeply influential Whig view of history glorified the apparent connection between Calvinism, revolution, and liberty created by linking into a single chain the political theories of the Huguenot monarchomachs, the Dutch revolt, Britain's seventeenth-century revolutions, and the American Revolution. The self-governing structures of many Reformed churches were now identified as incubators of political self-determination. Calvin's vision of church and state acting as coordinate but separate instruments for the advancement of God's law was said to encourage the defense of mixed constitutions. No single historian or social scientist ever formulated as striking an explanation for the presumed link between Calvinism and democracy as Weber did for that between Calvinism and capitalism, but the desire to explore this apparent association stimulated much research into the history of political thought and of Reformed church organization.

This book surveys the history and significance of Reformed Protestantism in Europe from its origins until the end of the age of orthodoxy around 1700. No single author has attempted to tell this story since John T. McNeill completed *The History and Character of Calvinism* in 1954.[3] In the intervening fifty years, a dramatic two-part sea change has transformed historical writing about the European Reformation. First, Reformation historians, like their peers who write about other topics and periods, have incorporated the actions and aspirations of ordinary men and women into a tale that long privileged the role of elite actors. Drawing inspiration from the historical sociology of religion and from historical anthropology, they now examine crowd involvement in the Reformation and the history of parish-level religious practice with the same care that they once reserved for the ideas of the era's leading theologians. Second, broader transformations in the contemporary religious landscape have altered the relation between historians of this subject and their topic and have generated a new awareness of the many ways in which confessional blinkers and stereotypes long distorted historical writing about it. Until well into the twentieth century, most church history was written by members of the church in question eager to explore a critical moment in the formation of their religious tradition. Now, with the postwar growth of ecumenical concerns, the rapidly advancing secularization of mass culture, and the declining salience of denominational identity, specialists are far more likely to be aware of the history of all of the major confessional families that emerged from the Reformation and to have studied several of them. The most sympathetic and penetrating studies of Protestant theology are often written by Catholic scholars. Growing numbers of Reformation historians are agnostics of secular or non-Christian backgrounds. All this has led to a "deconfessionalization" of Reformation history and a tendency to see the features that united the various Christian churches in this era as well as those that divided them.

Both parts of this transformation have called into question the classic interpretations of Calvinism's significance for the advent of modernity. In alerting historians to the large gap that often existed between the parish-level practice of a given religion and its formal rules and doctrines, the new social or anthropological history of early modern religion has revealed how risky it is to infer the psychological experience and social behavior of the members of a given faith from its theology—essentially the method of Weber and many other pioneering historical sociologists of religion. The deconfessionalization of Reformation history has meanwhile shown specialists that the claims for Calvinism's unique historical meaning were often made in ignorance of comparable features of post-Reformation Catholicism or Lutheranism. For more than thirty years, historians of early modern Catholicism have emphasized the many features of that tradition's spirituality that promoted self-control, moral effort, and disciplined labor in the world—in short, something very much like a Protestant work ethic. Historians of Lutheran political thought have challenged the old stereotype of a politically passive faith by highlighting Luther's acceptance after 1531 of the legitimacy of resistance to the emperor, the ringing defiance of the Lutheran Magdeburg Confession of 1550, and the clear traces of this work's influence on subsequent Reformed resistance theory. The boldest macrointerpretations of the past three decades have depicted Catholicism, Lutheranism, and Calvinism as spurring parallel, not contrasting, transformations in European society, notably a process of "confessionalization" according to which all three promoted state integration and the production of disciplined, obedient subjects, even as they divided the Continent into mutually hostile religious camps through their reciprocal anathematization. And while these interpretations have all challenged the view that Calvinism offered the royal road to modernity, many of the best studies of the religious culture of specific groups of Calvinists have become quasi-ethnographic explorations that divorce their subject entirely from any of the master narratives that have traditionally linked the sixteenth century to modern times. The landscape of interpretation has changed dramatically since McNeill's time.

Four major concerns structure this work. Its first and most basic goal is to provide a clear narrative of the Reformed tradition's development that at the same time answers the most important analytic questions that arise from the narrative. What accounts for the exceptional dynamism of this variant of Protestantism? How and why, after an initial period of limited growth, were Reformed churches able to establish themselves across so much of Europe amid widely varying kinds of circumstances? What was Calvin's precise role in the definition and expansion of this tradition that ultimately came to be associated with his name? Given that he was a figure of the Reformed tradition's second generation, can he even be considered the most substantial shaper of the tradition? If so, how did he come to exercise such influence? How and why did the tradition change in the generations following his death?

A second goal is to assess in the light of current knowledge the classic theories that accord Calvinism distinctive importance in the broader development of Western society. This ambition is less self-evident than it might appear, for while Weberian themes have long shaped the general image of Calvinism's historical significance held by the educated public, they exercised surprisingly little influence on the research of most specialists in this field for the better part of the twentieth century; and interest in them has weakened further in the past decades as a result of the new emphasis on similarities among the post-Reformation confessions.[4] At an international conference on European Calvinism from 1540 to 1620 held a decade ago, a participant observed during the final session that Weber's name had not come up once in the course of three days' discussion. The consensus of those present was that this was for the best. Yet leading contemporary sociologists of religion still express confidence in the fundamental accuracy of Weber's views.[5] Students of economic development return to them whenever current events direct attention to the cultural dimension of economic performance.[6] Because these views remain vital in many parts of the academic world and beyond, readers coming to this subject have a right to expect an evaluation of them. Furthermore, I am convinced that an investigation of them usefully directs attention to key aspects of Calvinism's history that most recent historians have tended to overlook. This history will thus attempt not to lose sight of the issues such views raise.

A third theme emerged with increasing clarity as the book unfolded: the importance of church institutions and of struggles over church institutions within the story of the Reformed tradition. The history of church institutions has rarely excited historians of early modern religious life. No history of international Calvinism can escape this topic. Those who believe that Calvinism promoted a particularly thorough reformation of life have often attributed this to its exemplary institutional arrangements, epitomized most perfectly in Geneva, where a consistory of ministers and elders exercised vigorous disciplinary authority over all church members with the cooperative backing of the secular authorities. Those who believe that Calvinism promoted democracy have attributed this to the apprenticeship in self-government provided by congregational and presbyterial-synodal forms of church organization. Yet the institutions thus highlighted were not found in all Reformed churches, which raises the question of why they arose in some, but not others. Furthermore, bitter disagreements over institutional arrangements divided many Reformed churches. The two greatest centers from which Reformed influence subsequently radiated outward, Zurich and Geneva, each arranged moral discipline and the relation between church and state in different manners, which each city's theologians justified on scriptural grounds. As the movement spread and more churches established themselves amid diverse circumstances, the degree of institutional diversity increased. At the same time scriptural legitimation cast certain institutions as ideals to be struggled for and sparked agitation to establish them where they were lacking. Battles between partisans of church government by bishops and by presbyteries and synods were soon added to the battles between those who advocated the Zurich and the Genevan style of church-state relations. How a multivocal tradition interacted with diverse local circumstances to produce the initial institutional arrangements that characterized each national Reformed church is thus central to the history of Calvinism. So too is the story of the subsequent development of theories of *de jure* presbyterianism and episcopalianism and of the conflicts that these theories engendered. Last of all, the question of how each church's mature institutions influenced its capacity to effect a reformation of manners cannot be neglected.

Just as institutional diversity characterized Europe's Reformed churches, so too did mature Calvinist piety assume more than one style of devotion. The fourth major concern of this book is to trace the emergence of these modes of piety and to understand why they emerged and took root where and when they did. After the great luminaries of the early Reformation pass from the scene, the history of theology and worship typically joins the history of church institutions in the orphanage of historiographic neglect. But the classic sociological theories about Calvinism again direct one's attention to this topic, as does the newer concern to capture the character of lay religious practice. For Weber, the element of Calvinism that stimulated its rationalized self-discipline was the doctrine of predestination, which with each successive generation occupied an ever more vital place in Reformed dogmatics. The doctrine confronted believers with the stark question, Am I among those predestined to salvation or to damnation? and spurred them to live the upright life that devotional writers told them was evidence of their election. The religious culture of the best-studied of Calvinists, the Puritans of England and New England, unquestionably involved a carefully codified, deeply introspective style of precise piety that emerged at a moment when predestinarian themes were strongly emphasized. The exploration of mature Reformed devotional practices across seventeenth-century Europe reveals, however, that this style of piety was strikingly absent or muted in many Reformed churches, even though predestinarian theology was no weaker. Clearly these practices did not arise simply as a logical, if unintended, consequence of the doctrine of predestination. Additional features of historical context were necessary conditions of their emergence in England and of their spread beyond it. This book attempts to identify such features. More generally, it seeks to give theological and devotional developments of the generations after Calvin's death their due place in the history of the Reformed tradition.

Some features of the book's subtitle deserve a brief explanation. I label this a social history of religion, yet one trenchant recent critic has fairly criticized most of the social history of the Reformation of the past decades as a secularized historiography addressed to an audience of agnostics that reduces religious movements to instruments of putatively deeper historical forces and thus misses their *coeur religieux*.[7] This book seeks to exemplify an alternative kind of social history of religion. It is a social history insofar as it attends to the actions and beliefs of all groups within the population and draws upon methods pioneered by social historians. It does not assume that the religious can be equated with the social or is ultimately explained by it.

Particularly fruitful for thinking about the relation between religion and society are the ideas of Michael Mann, the paradoxical sociologist who argues that the very word that conventionally defines his discipline's subject should be avoided if possible. "There is no one master concept or basic unit of 'society,'" Mann has written. Rather, what are conventionally called societies are best thought of as overlapping networks of formal and informal systems of constraint that have arisen to satisfy basic human needs. These power networks are of four sorts: ideological, political, military, and economic. None is primary in the sense that it determines the others "in the last analysis." All interact promiscuously. When one changes, it will both shape and be shaped by the others.[8]

The Reformation unsettled Europe so deeply because it transformed its central institution of ideological power, one whose reach extended into every parish and home: the Christian church. In a religion of the book, religious power derives from the ability of individuals or institutions to convince others that they hold the key to interpreting its sacred texts. The Reformed tradition offered a new interpretation of Christianity's sacred texts. Inevitably, its emergence affected the other power networks in society, just as its articulation and institutionalization took place within constraints set by those networks. No history of the tradition will be true to its subject unless it recognizes the many ways in which those who built it were driven by the desire to live up to the demands that they believed the renascent Gospel placed upon them. No account of the long-term development of the churches that issued from the Reformation can neglect the internal dynamic of change that arises as insurgent religious movements transform themselves into established churches, codify their teachings, and confront the obscurities and internal contradictions that earlier generations were able to avoid. There is, in short, no gainsaying the force of belief systems in the story of the European Reformation. At the same time, no history of this subject can neglect the ways in which the various Reformed churches were shaped by the conditions of their birth and the intellectual formation of their early leaders. No account of the subsequent unfolding of the tradition can neglect the interplay across successive generations between the force of religious imperatives, the conditioning influence of other power networks, and the play of contingent events. Beliefs make history, but not under circumstances of their own choosing. They are also themselves the products of history. The interplay between the force of a religious tradition and the contexts in which it arose and took root lies at the heart of the approach adopted here.

Calvinism is an even more problematic word than *society*. Like its parallels *Lutheran* and *Zwinglian*, *Calvinist* was originally a label attached to certain theological positions by opponents eager to stigmatize them as inventions of fallible individuals. The specific viewpoints so labeled have always varied. The word emerged in the mid-1550s in the context of no fewer than three debates in which Calvin was then engaged, one over the proper interpretation of the Eucharist, the second over the proper ceremonies of the liturgy, and the third over whether or not the secular authorities had the right to punish heresy.[9] Several generations later, especially within the world of Anglo-American theology, *Calvinism* came most commonly to be used to connote a fourth viewpoint, the high predestinarian theology often summarized in five points captured by the acronym TULIP: Total depravity, Unconditional election, Limited atonement, Irresistible grace, and the Perseverance of the saints. None of these viewpoints, modern Calvin commentators would stress, suffice by themselves to capture what is most characteristic or most essential in Calvin's own thought. Still less can they be taken to identify the essential features of the larger tradition to which Calvin attached himself but of which he was not the sole spokesman. While a few of those attacked as Calvinists accepted the label for the purposes of public debate, most rejected it as the appropriate name for the party or church of which they were a part. They preferred to call themselves variously the evangelical, reformed, evangelical reformed, or reformed Catholic churches, the term *reformed* emerging as the most common label amid the broader process of confessional differentiation and hardening that characterized the long Reformation era. *Reformed* is thus for several reasons a more historically accurate and less potentially misleading label than *Calvinist* to apply to these churches and to the larger tradition to which they attached themselves. Up until this moment, I have used *Calvinist* and *Reformed* synonymously to make myself clear to nonspecialist readers who are more likely to recognize the former term. Henceforth *Reformed* will be this book's label of choice whenever reference is being made to the broad tradition that it examines and to any of the churches associated with that tradition. Use of the terms *Calvinist* and *Calvinism* will be confined to situations in which the ideas of modern interpreters who use these terms are being discussed, in which doctrines distinctive to Calvin as opposed to other Reformed theologians are at issue, or in which those views that subsequently came to be considered quintessentially Calvinist are being examined. In this last case, the word will generally appear in quotation marks. The Reformed tradition broadly understood, not Calvinism in any of the narrower senses of that word, is this book's precise subject.

In the delicate matter of determining just where to draw the boundaries of the Reformed tradition, I have tried to take my inspiration from the period itself and to foreground the historical process by which boundaries were demarcated at the time. Consciousness of a distinctively Reformed variant of Protestantism first took shape in the second half of the 1520s, as divisions emerged within the evangelical movement over the issue of the Eucharist, and Luther and his supporters refused fellowship with those who espoused a purely symbolic understanding of the Lord's Supper. The exact terms of the disagreement between the Reformed and the Lutherans subsequently shifted in subtle ways, but the antagonism that emerged in the 1520s was never effaced, even if in certain times and places Reformed groups insisted upon their fundamental agreement with the Lutherans, made alliances with them, and admitted them to communion. All of the churches included as Reformed here displayed their belonging to a common tradition by accepting one of a relatively narrow range of positions on the doctrine of the Eucharist, by endorsing one or more of a common set of confessions of faith, by inviting one another's theologians to their synods, and by sending future ministers for higher education to one another's universities. The changing ways in which they drew the boundaries separating them from other groups will remain part of the narrative throughout. Dissident groups born from theological disputes within these churches but anathematized by the dominant voices within them are included to the extent that their discussion is integral to the story of the larger family of the Reformed churches during the time period examined here.

The Church of England stood in a particularly complicated and fluid relation to the majority of Europe's Reformed churches in this period. Although one still encounters historical atlases with confessional maps of sixteenth-century Europe that tint England a hue of its own, as if a distinctive Anglican tradition was born with the Reformation, Reformed theology dominated the Church of England for at least a generation after it had clearly aligned itself with continental Protestantism. During this time virtually all of the church's most influential members considered themselves part of the larger Reformed family. Amid the debates that subsequently developed within the church, some English theologians began to depict their church as sui generis, neither Reformed nor Roman Catholic, but instead incorporating the purest traditions of the early church. This view gained ground with the advance of the Laudian party in the 1620s and 1630s, was cast out from the established church during the civil war and interregnum, but survived to return stronger than ever at the Restoration. Even at the height of its strength under the later Stuarts, however, it never so dominated the historical self-understanding of the English church that it eliminated the rival position that the Church of England was part of the larger Reformed family. Thus, a comprehensive history of the Reformed tradition must make room for the Church of England because it was the largest national church associated with the Reformed tradition and a net exporter of theological ideas from the end of the sixteenth century onward. Furthermore, even though many within it sought to dissociate it from the Reformed tradition, it does not make sense to eliminate these voices from the story told here and to include only those who met some doctrinal test of Reformed orthodoxy. To do that would be to silence half of the ongoing dialogue that defined the church's changing character. A substantial portion of this book is devoted to following the twists and turns of this long struggle to define the character of the Church of England, so that its changing relation to the main lines of Reformed doctrine and practice elsewhere may be understood.

In the fifteen years that I have been working on this book, I have had ample opportunity to learn why nobody else has written a general history of this subject for so long. It is not simply the vastness of the secondary literature in a wide range of languages that discourages the would-be synthesizer. Even more problematic is the striking inconsistency of emphasis and coverage within this literature. Both during and after the Reformation, the fate of Europe's Reformed churches varied dramatically. As a result, the historical imagination of later generations in each country has tended to fasten on different aspects of each church's history. The growing internationalization of historical scholarship in the past generation has narrowed such disparities between national traditions of scholarship. Still, the historian eager to follow themes or problems across the history of all of the major Reformed churches all too often discovers that what has been well studied in one national context has been neglected in another. I set out to write a work of synthesis based on secondary works and the most easily accessible published primary sources. I frequently discovered that it was also necessary to have recourse to manuscript materials and rare book rooms. This remains predominantly a work of integration and interpretation, but it also contains important elements of original research.

Limitations of time and linguistic competence have prevented me from covering every topic I would have liked to explore, especially with regard to central and eastern Europe. At their height, the Reformed churches of both Poland and Hungary were considerably larger than most general histories of the Reformation acknowledge, even if they remained on the periphery of the larger Reformed universe. I have tried to give these churches their due place, but I have been handicapped by the relative paucity of primary sources, by the thinness of the secondary literature in west European languages, and by my own lack of knowledge of either Polish or Hungarian. Little is said about these churches in the section of the book devoted to religious practice and church discipline, essentially for want of adequate studies. One can hope that the crumbling of old barriers between East and West will inspire further research into the fascinating history of these churches.

Finally, in a work like this, readers have a right to know the author's relation to the religious tradition under study. The opening sentence of McNeill's book included his recollection of memorizing the Westminster Assembly's Shorter Catechism as a child; mine can recount no comparable memory. I am a total outsider, an agnostic, nonpracticing Jew raised in a secular household. While I thus lack the easy familiarity with enduring elements of the tradition that a church upbringing offers and worry about my lack of formal instruction in theology and the Bible, I can only hope that I have been able to overcome some of these handicaps through that most basic of mental processes cultivated by historians: the effort to think one's way sympathetically into a distant and, to a degree, alien worldview.

PART I

The Formation of a Tradition

The Reformation began with the great burst of enthusiasm for social and ecclesiastical renewal that historians now call the evangelical cause to highlight its protean, ill-defined character. In this time of "magnificent anarchy," Martin Luther's criticism of papal authority at the Leipzig Debate of 1519 and his steadfast defense of his ideas at the Diet of Worms in 1521 galvanized intensifying aspirations for a reform of Christendom and inspired a tidal wave of treatises, broadsides, and sermons urging rejection of the authority of Rome and a return to the purity of the Gospel. The watchwords were broad. Even those theologians who would prove most central in shaping the evangelical cause had not yet articulated many of the positions they would ultimately espouse. The thousands of people who responded enthusiastically to their initial words understood them differently according to their experience, upbringing, and aspirations.

As events forced those who emerged as leaders in various regions to confront practical questions about what precise form a proper reformation of Christianity should take and who could legitimately carry one out, diverse understandings began to emerge. Some engendered local experiments in worship and church organization, gained political support, and ultimately gave birth to new church orders. Others inspired a measure of dedication but never became institutionalized or were soon suppressed. Forceful and influential reform spokesmen might find that the new church orders they endorsed were adopted by communities in neighboring territories as well, giving rise to regional families of church orders. By the later 1520s and early 1530s, the German-speaking portions of Europe from the Baltic states to Switzerland were dotted with both individual parishes and larger territories that had altered their worship and church life in ways that displayed more local variations and nuances than historians have yet been able to map. As they shaped and argued over these alterations, the leading evangelical theologians defined more clearly not only the positive details of their reforming vision, but also what they could not accept. Because all of these changes were enacted in defiance of both the pope and the emperor, they were legally and politically precarious.

The Reformed tradition can be said to have had two births. Most straightforwardly, it was born in Zurich out of the encounter between Huldrych Zwingli's reforming vision and the political culture of Switzerland's cities. Zwingli was an ardent Erasmian turned critic of Rome. His mature conception of a reborn Christianity included a strong concern for the moral betterment of the community and a desire to purge worship of all material and nonscriptural features. The civic authorities of the recently independent, militarily powerful Swiss Confederation had already begun to oversee the moral and religious life of the community. Soon after coming to Zurich in 1519 Zwingli emerged as the leading evangelical preacher in a city where agitation for change quickly developed. At once a herald and defender of reforming aspirations, Zwingli was also moderate and politically astute enough to win and retain the support of the city fathers. By channeling desire for change in a manner that preserved and reinforced the unity of the civic community, he molded in 1524–25 the first civic reformation in a region that would ultimately witness many. Essential features of the Zurich reformation included a consistently austere style of worship that sought to eliminate all features of medieval Catholicism lacking an explicit biblical basis; an insistence upon the prohibition against worshiping graven images and the consequent removal of altarpieces, paintings, and sculptures from the city's churches; a simple eucharistic service understood as a memorial of Christ's Last Supper; and a new civic-run morals court charged with implementing a reformed set of moral laws. Zurich and its theologians would remain loyal to this pattern of reformation, and the city became a center for its dissemination to other cities and territories, first in the surrounding region and then throughout much of Europe. The call to purge all nonscriptural elements from worship and the hostility to idolatry would henceforward permanently characterize the Reformed tradition. While the range of eucharistic theologies associated with the tradition would widen, all affiliated theologians and churches would follow Zwingli in rejecting the claim that Christ was physically present in the communion bread and wine.

Seen through a wider lens, the Reformed tradition was also born from the process of confessional definition within the larger world of emerging Protestantism that divided the primal ooze of the early evangelical movement into two rival varieties of Protestant state churches: the Lutheran and the Reformed. In this dialectic of boundary marking, the actions and decisions of Luther and his followers were at least as important as those of the early Reformed champions. Amid the profusion of prophets who sprang up across Germany and Switzerland in the early Reformation, none could match the charisma of the German Hercules whose initial outspokenness had launched the movement and whose copious writings flooded the region. The theological positions that Luther articulated as the movement developed were consequently of enduring significance. His downplaying of the importance of outward forms of worship and willingness to accept practices that might lack biblical sanction but nonetheless did not appear to him to contradict the essence of the Gospel; his commitment to a literal understanding of Christ's words to his disciples, "This is my body"; and his casting of those who favored a metaphorical interpretation of these words as "sacramentarians" in league with the devil were all fundamental steps in demarcating a boundary line that would leave the Saxon pattern of reformation on one side and the Zurich pattern on the other. His associate Philip Melanchthon espoused in his later years a eucharistic theology that blurred this line, but the majority of those who claimed Luther's legacy after his death in 1546 rejected this position and advocated instead a "ubiquitarian" understanding of the real presence that sharpened it.

The precarious legal situation of the territories within the Holy Roman Empire that had instituted local reformations gave Luther and later Lutheran theologians great political leverage in the empire. Innovations in worship were outlawed at the conclusion of the Diet of Worms (1521). Territories and localities that introduced a new church order consequently faced the threat of Emperor Charles V coming to Germany and punishing them for breaking the law. To protect themselves, they began to negotiate defensive political alliances, a project that took on special urgency when Charles V indeed returned in 1530. Luther denounced the sacramentarians so vehemently and worked so closely with the most powerful German Protestant ruler, the elector of Saxony, that when the largest and most important evangelical alliance took shape, the princes who joined it refused admission to territories that would not accept a confession of faith containing the eucharistic position they deemed orthodox. Even though Zwinglian and other sacramentarian ideas cir-

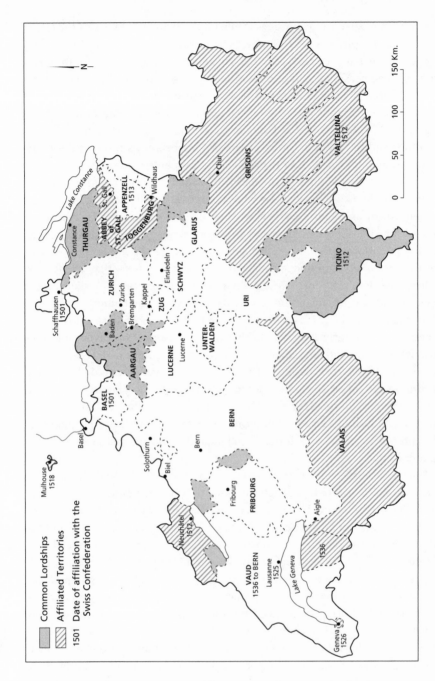

Map 1. The Swiss Confederation and Affiliated Territories

Common Lordships

Affiliated Territories

1501 Date of affiliation with the Swiss Confederation

Mulhouse 1518

Schaffhausen 1501

Constance

Lake Constance

THURGAU

ABBEY of ST. GALL

St. Gall

APPENZELL 1513

Wildhaus

TOGGENBURG

GRISONS

Chur

VALTELLINA 1512

ZURICH

Zurich

Bremgarten

Baden

Kappel

Einsiedeln

SCHWYZ

GLARUS

ZUG

URI

TICINO 1512

AARGAU

LUCERNE

Lucerne

UNTER-WALDEN

BASEL 1501

Basel

BERN

VALAIS

Solothurn

Biel

Bern

FRIBOURG

Fribourg

Aigle

Neuchâtel 1512

VAUD 1536 to BERN

Lausanne 1525

Lake Geneva

1536

Geneva 1526

0   50   100   150 Km.

N

Map 2. The Holy Roman Empire

culated alongside Lutheran ones in the empire and proved more attractive to ordinary townsmen when they were able to compete with them on relatively equal terms, the need to secure the protection of this alliance steadily pushed evangelical territories within the empire toward the Lutheran camp. Such was not the case on the other side of the still-fluid political boundary demarcated by the Swiss Confederation, where imperial law no longer held sway.

By the time Zwingli's life was cut short on the battlefield in October 1531, the political forces that would eventually mold the confessional pattern of the Reformation in Germany and Switzerland alike had already begun to reveal themselves. Zwingli's accomplishments were considerable. He played the central role in shaping the transformation of the ecclesiastical order within

Zurich and gained a powerful voice in the city's governing circles. Working closely with kindred spirits in nearby towns, he helped to ensure the triumph of nearly identical reformations in most of the larger cantons of Switzerland. Church orders that shared many features with Zurich's triumphed in quite a few south German free imperial cities. In the later 1520s, Zwingli was probably the most effective and outspoken clerical champion of an evangelical political action to defend and spread the cause of the reformation through the German-speaking world. Still, when Luther abandoned his previous reluctance to advocate political or military action in defense of this cause and the League of Schmalkalden took shape in the crucial years 1530–31, it quickly became apparent that the center of gravity in the emerging world of Protestant politics in Germany lay in Saxony, not in Switzerland. The disastrous outcome of the aggressive military policies that Zwingli advocated in the last months of his life capped the shift in the balance of power. For the next twenty-five years doctrines and patterns of worship closer in character to those of Zurich than to those of Wittenberg would, though never disappearing, retreat within the empire.

In Switzerland, the Zwinglian legacy also stood in peril after the death of its prophet, for in the aftermath of defeat Zurich's magistrates grew wary of listening to clergymen, while over the ensuing decades Bern and Basel each felt the temptation of aligning itself with the German Lutherans. Here, however, an energetic and effective disciple of Zwingli's, Heinrich Bullinger, assumed the elder preacher's mantle of ecclesiastical leadership in Zurich and became in many ways an even more effective church politician on a wider European scale. Within Zurich, Bullinger attained sufficient prestige to safeguard a measure of independence and influence for the city's pastors. On a larger stage, he defended the principles and extended the reach of Zwingli's theology with tenacity and vigor for upward of four decades. He so successfully cultivated potentially like-minded churchmen and political leaders through both personal contacts and a massive private correspondence that his web of connections came to reach as far afield as England, Poland, and Hungary and to include future leaders of the Protestant cause within each country. He reshaped and amplified Zwingli's central ideas in commentaries and expositions of doctrine that attained far wider dissemination than any of Zwingli's own writings, a task of theological elaboration to which several other skilled theologians who ended their days in Switzerland also contributed. Lastly, he played a central role in drafting a series of confessions of faith that defined a revised Reformed consensus on the eucharist and proved capable of winning the adherence of many churches both within and beyond Switzerland.

During these same years, Reformed churches also came to be established in a few regions on the fringes of Switzerland and the empire whose locations made them vital relay stations for the subsequent growth of the cause. During the 1540s, John a Lasco, a refugee Polish aristocrat whose theology placed him closer to Zurich than to Wittenberg, shaped the Protestant church of a little territory in northwestern Germany, East Friesland, whose chief port, Emden, was a short sail from the Netherlands. Between 1547 and 1553, a Lasco went to England, where he took charge of the church created in London for evangelical refugees fleeing the Netherlands and France. Both Emden and London became centers for corresponding with and sustaining like-minded souls who remained behind in those countries. Their churches became models for the organization of underground churches there—Reformed models. Still more potent models of a properly Reformed church came to be established in the French-speaking territories on Switzerland's western border that were drawn into political affiliation with the Swiss Confederation between 1512 and 1536, and where Bernese arms subsequently shielded evangelical expansion. The Reformed cause triumphed here in a series of cities including Neuchâtel and Lausanne, but it was the largest city of the region, Geneva, that ultimately captured the leading role in the cause's subsequent expansion.

The Genevan Reformation was not identical to the Zurich one, although it too was shaped by the encounter between the specific outlook of its most charismatic reformer and the distinctive features of its local political culture. Here, the reformer, John Calvin, was a supremely eloquent, supremely determined outsider who had grown up in the milieu of the pre-Reformation church courts and who believed that the Bible clearly specified the offices and disciplinary institutions of the Christian church. The city was a newly and precariously independent commercial crossroads with still weakly developed civic institutions and a strong need for the political reinforcement that both industrious immigrants and moral purity were believed to provide. After a long and closely contested struggle, Calvin was able to sway the Genevans to accept something that urban reformers elsewhere had sought vainly in the preceding decades: a church with an independent system of ecclesiastical discipline and excommunication controlled by the ministers and church elders rather than by the city fathers. Under Calvin's vigorous leadership, this system of consistorial discipline helped make Geneva a model of the successful reformation of manners and morals. The city became a magnet for immigrants, who stimulated its economy and multiplied the capacity of its printing industry. Calvin proved to be an even more prolific, captivating, and penetrating author of theological works than Bullinger. He was scarcely less assiduous than his Zurich counterpart in building networks of supporters and reaching out to politically influential figures far beyond his local power base. He cooperated closely with Bullinger even while differing with him on certain points of theology and ecclesiology.

When the Peace of Augsburg brought the first great phase of the Reformation's expansion to an end in 1555, Reformed variants of Protestantism were thus confined to a few small territories and cities on the fringes of Germany: parts of Switzerland, the affiliated French-speaking territories of Neuchâtel and Geneva, East Friesland, and a few refugee churches in northern Europe. Yet the cause stood poised on the verge of dramatic growth. Zurich, Geneva, and Emden were all centers for the dissemination of Reformed ideas and propaganda. Bullinger and Calvin had extensive networks of international correspondence. Bullinger, Calvin, and a Lasco all enjoyed great prestige among the increasing ranks of people in many lands who had grown convinced that there was something dramatically wrong with the Roman Catholic Church but as yet had no alternative to it in which to worship. Zurich, Geneva, and the refugee churches offered such people three distinct models of how such an alternative might be structured. Finally, and most important, the majority of the key features that ensured that it would be the Reformed tradition, not the Lutheran, that galvanized this diffuse dissatisfaction with the church of Rome into the second great wave of Protestant expansion had by now been articulated. The theological positions defined by its first-generation founders on the question of the eucharist, the reformation of worship, and the relation between personal salvation and moral and social renewal all placed the Reformed tradition more squarely in line with the chief impulses that attracted people to the Protestant cause than the Lutheran alternatives. The leading Reformed theologians of the second generation all emphasized far more strongly than their Lutheran counterparts that those living in Catholic countries who had seen the light of the Gospel had to separate themselves as completely as possible from the "abominations of popery." Calvin in particular argued that the Bible outlined many of the proper institutions of a Christian church and thus was prepared to suggest that believers create churches of their own with these institutions as an alternative to Rome. With Zurich and Geneva offering alternative models of how church and state fit together, the tradition could appeal both to rulers determined to exercise direct authority over sacred things and to ordinary believers in situations of persecution eager to establish a properly reformed church that could function independently of the state.

1

ZURICH CONTRA WITTENBERG

As a child, Calvin accompanied his mother to kiss a fragment of the body of Saint Anne treasured by a local abbey and saw statues of Saint Stephen bedecked with jewels to honor the saint on his feast day. Calvin's predecessor in reforming Geneva, Guillaume Farel, recalled going on his first pilgrimage as a boy to a mountain shrine near Tallard famed for restoring sight to the blind. There, the priest in charge of the simple cross believed to be made of wood from Christ's own cross awed the pilgrims by explaining that whenever a severe storm occurred, the cross trembled violently and shot off sparks, preserving the land from devastation. These actions of their childhood that the two reformers recollected in later years with a mixture of scorn and dismay were fundamental elements of Christian religious life at the dawn of the sixteenth century. The faithful believed that material objects were laden with supernatural power, prostrated themselves before such objects, and adorned them. Paraliturgical rituals proliferated to organize their worship and petitioning. No holy object came to be surrounded by more ornate rituals than the wafers used to celebrate the holy Eucharist that were transformed during the mass into the body of the living Christ and then were displayed in ornate golden monstrances or carried through tapestry-bedecked streets in grand processions. So intense was the attachment to such objects that when the call to cleanse and spiritualize Christianity by returning to the pure word of God convinced many that they were not holy and that their cult was groundless, those who had previously venerated them often turned angrily against them, desecrating or smashing them.[1]

The flamboyant diversity of late medieval religious life, however, resists characterization by a single theme or preoccupation. Alongside the profusion of collective paraliturgical rituals and the tendency to attribute supernatural power to material objects, powerful devotional movements encouraged individual believers to develop a direct spiritual relationship with God. The invention of printing promoted the circulation of devotional books in the vernacular that spread techniques of self-monitoring intended to help believers make their lives a continual imitation of Christ's virtues. The majority of theologians emphasized that the fate of each human soul hung in the balance until the very moment of death; that the traditions sanctioned over the centuries by the Holy Mother Church had no less force for Christians than those initially revealed in the Bible; and that, in the final balance sheet to be drawn up at the moment of death, people's sins could be counterbalanced not only by their good works, but also by the withdrawals made on their behalf from the storehouse of merit vouchsafed to the Church. But minority voices within the church upheld a doctrine of predestination, denied that the sanction of church tradition extended beyond those doctrines whose kernel could be found within the Bible, and expressed an Augustinian pessimism about the power of the will to contribute to salvation.[2] The Lollard and Hussite heretics of the later fourteenth and fifteenth centuries in England and Bohemia had challenged the doctrine of transubstantiation and the sanctity of the visible church. As the fifteenth century gave way to the sixteenth, textual scholars inspired by Renaissance humanism also called into question the monopoly that scholastically trained theologians had previously exercised over biblical interpretation. Their program of reading Holy Writ in its original languages and reexamining its most ancient manuscript versions to purify the text of errors introduced by copyists promised to renew its study. The Reformation would not be simply a reaction against central features of late medieval religiosity. It would also be the continuation and intensification of trends in religious life that had gained strength during the waning Middle Ages. It is no accident that later Reformed histories began the story of the Reformation not with Luther's protest against indulgences, but with the humanist recovery of the Gospel, and included Girolamo Savonarola and Jan Hus among the prophets of the true faith.[3]

In the eyes of the devout, abuses riddled the late medieval church. The wealth and territorial ambition of the popes were proverbial. The leading bishops were often great noblemen who accumulated church livings in reward for their services to the crown yet rarely visited their sees. The vast real estate portfolios of ecclesiastical institutions included bathhouses that everybody knew were brothels. Despite the proliferation of universities in the last centuries of the Middle Ages, most parish priests lacked university training and rarely dared to preach. Even though they received payment each time they administered certain sacraments, many had to supplement their livings with second jobs because the upper clergy diverted so much tithe revenue into its own coffers. Clerical concubinage was so widespread in parts of Germany and Switzerland that bishops profited from the practice by selling pardons for the offense. The nominal dedication of the mendicant orders to a life of poverty did not prevent certain Franciscan and Dominican convents from waiting until bad harvests drove up prices to sell their ample stores of wheat for maximum profit. Anticlericalism was rife.[4]

As always in the history of Christianity, however, the observation of shortcomings was accompanied by the call for reform. The reform of strict observance—requiring the members of religious orders to live according to the letter of their rule—advanced in many religious orders in the opening decades of the sixteenth century. Pastoral reformers among the episcopate convoked synods to remind parish clergymen of their obligations and ordered them to buy and read such books as Jean Gerson's *Three-part Work* or *Instruction for Curates in How They May Instruct the Simple Folk.* Some Spanish dioceses promoted teaching laymen the Ten Commandments and basic prayers of the church by means of printed *cartillas* read aloud every week. A few bishops shocked their colleagues by abandoning powerful positions at the papal curia or a royal court to return to their sees to preach and tend their flock. Exemplary clergymen inspired awe, gratitude, and worship.[5]

So powerfully contradictory were the various tendencies within Latin Christendom around 1500 that when a relatively obscure theology professor at the University of Wittenberg proposed for debate ninety-five theses that challenged key elements of established doctrine, an earthquake shook the established church to its foundations. Within three years, the critical, anti-Roman thrust of Luther's ideas had been sharpened through public debate, he had clearly enunciated the two fundamental Reformation principles of *sola fide* (justification by faith alone) and *sola scriptura* (the Bible as the sole source of religious authority), the pope had excommunicated him, and the so-called Luther affair was on the lips of people throughout Germany and beyond, forcing them to ask if they could remain loyal to the Church of Rome. Awareness of the issues was fostered by an avalanche of occasional publications in small, easily accessible formats addressed to laymen as well as clerics. Fewer than 100 such publications have come down to us from any year up to and including 1517; the corresponding number for 1520 is roughly 1,050 and for 1524, 2,400.[6] Preachers took up their message and spread it among still

11

wider strata of the population. Soon mass petitions and crowd actions sought concrete changes in worship and in social practices deemed un-Christian. The agitation had touched localities from the Baltic to the Alps even before the largest organized movements for change, the vast peasant bands of 1525, rose across south and central Germany with their demands for the abolition of servile dues, the communal election and payment of parish priests, and a broader renewal of society along Christian principles. Often, but not always, as a result of pressure from below, territorial rulers and city magistrates favorably inclined toward church reform then began to establish new church orders, whose precise features varied.

A major concern of recent Reformation scholarship has been to determine the reasons for the evangelical cause's remarkable appeal. Surviving volumes of sermons and sermon outlines from the period 1522–29 suggest that evangelical preachers most consistently articulated a cluster of interrelated themes: justification by faith alone; the need to return to the Bible, the one true source of authority in matters of religion; the ability of ordinary folk as well as the learned to understand Scripture; the corruption of the clergy; the abusive character of the numerous practices of the late medieval church, including pilgrimages, commissioned masses, and monastic prayer, whose logic exalted the performance of ritual actions over the inward experience of faith and whose biblical basis was uncertain; and the need for faith to manifest itself in works of love and charity. Many of these themes coalesced logically to produce a recharged anticlericalism. This was not the anticlericalism already widespread prior to 1517, bred by resentment against the wealth, privileges, and frequent immorality of the clergy. To this already existing resentment it added the explosive new accusation of fraudulence: once one grew convinced that indulgences, anniversary masses for souls in purgatory, or the prayers of cloistered religious were all worthless and nonscriptural, the most obvious explanation for the origin of these practices was that the pope and his monks had invented them to make money and increase their power. Broadsides and propaganda pieces flayed clergymen as merchants who swindled the simple with their false wares and *Totenfressers* who feasted on the wealth of the dead. The pamphlets written by laymen demonstrated a concern to apply the call for social renewal through Christian love and charity to concrete contemporary situations, but they rarely echoed Luther's central theological message of justification by faith alone. Crowd actions in the early Reformation years most often included iconoclastic attacks on formerly sacred objects and shrines, anticlerical violence directed especially at monastic houses, and demands for stronger measures against poverty, drunkenness, and prostitution.[7]

The spread of evangelical sentiment recharged anticlericalism and appealed to the wisdom of the laity, but—in less of a paradox than it might first appear—it also enabled individual clergymen to gain extraordinary political influence. The overriding appeal to Scripture bestowed vast persuasive possibilities on trained experts in biblical interpretation. With the established principles of worship, morality, and social organization all under intense scrutiny, preachers who convinced their audience that they spoke from Scripture to the issues of the day were eagerly listened to. Their charisma was most intense in small to midsized cities in which a high proportion of the population could hear them preach directly; but those whose reputation for wisdom or courage extended beyond the confines of a single city could exercise wider influence, for small cities often modeled their church orders on those of nearby larger ones, and rulers sought out the advice of prominent theologians when they had a church position to fill or needed advice on ecclesiastical matters.

As the implementation of the broad principles of the evangelical cause gave rise to different understandings of the proper form of Christian worship and belief, the charisma of the leading reformers proved critical in shaping the nascent Protestant movement into two larger blocs. The splintering of the evangelical movement into rival interpretations of the demands of the Gospel began under the impress of immediate events between 1521 and 1525. By the end of the decade, the dissimilarities were starting to be codified in formal confessions of faith. Although the process of confessional elaboration and differentiation would continue for several generations thereafter, the antagonism that had developed between Zurich and Wittenberg by Zwingli's death was so bitter that subsequent attempts to overcome it would prove vain.

Forty years ago, in his vastly influential *Imperial Cities and the Reformation,* Bernd Moeller offered what remains the most ambitious explanation of why a Reformed reformation emerged and gained at least temporary ascendancy in the cities of south Germany and Switzerland, while Lutheranism carried everything before it from Franconia northward.[8] Moeller explained this division as the outcome of the encounter in south Germany and Switzerland between a distinctive set of intellectual traditions and a distinctive sociopolitical environment. On the one hand, this was the region of the most intense intellectual development in pre-Reformation Germany. Humanism was stronger here than elsewhere in the empire, and this fostered an engagement with practical ventures of moral and social improvement in the civic arena that predisposed the region's reformers, all of whom emerged from a humanist background, to develop a theology that stressed personal sanctification and the amelioration of the community in ways that Luther's did not. On the other hand, guild representation in city government was prevalent here and urban politics consequently less oligarchic, with the result that the "corporate communalism" characteristic of the medieval commune survived more strongly. This envisaged the city as a sacred community collectively responsible for its residents' salvation. Such an environment at once helped to generate and proved highly receptive to the "distinctively urban" theology of the Swiss and south German reformers.

Four decades of research on the theme of the Reformation and the cities have not invalidated certain elements of Moeller's structural explanation. The great early prophets of the Reformed tradition were almost all humanists before they were reformers, and this intellectual formation left a clear stamp on the theology of many of them. Features of the Reformed message also appear to have resonated more with ordinary townsfolk than their Lutheran alternatives once the rivalry between the two traditions emerged, and the fact that the Reformed cause first triumphed in self-governing cities rather than in a territory subject to a prince meant that the reform priorities of the urban laity had more influence over its initial codification. The language of sacred community was particularly strong in the Swiss cities prior to the Reformation and infused Reformed rhetoric in its wake. As Moeller himself has admitted, however, his linkage of Reformed reformations with more broadly representative urban governing structures exaggerated the social harmony of those cities with guild regimes and downplayed the force of popular pressure for religious reform in those without them. Even where the guilds boasted direct representation in the city council, urban government was highly oligarchic, for those who represented the guilds came from the wealthier strata of urban society. Across the empire it was the rule that mass agitation was critical to the triumph of a new church order.[9] Furthermore, humanism was hardly unknown in north and central Germany. It shaped the outlook of leading allies of Luther in the eucharistic controversy as well as of most early Reformed theologians.[10]

What Moeller's stress on preexisting regional differences within the German-speaking world chiefly neglects is the importance of certain crucial decisions taken by Luther under the impress of immediate circumstances that subsequently became fixed principles of his outlook, notably his views on the Eucharist and on the presence of images within churches. These decisions assumed enormous sway because of Luther's exceptional charisma. They were further magnified by his political connections to the electors of Saxony and by the need for evangelical territories to accept whatever terms these powerful princes dictated for any Protestant alliance. Ultimately they defined magisterial Protestantism across most of the empire. The political boundary separating Switzerland from Germany, on the other hand, created a politically protected space within which a regional reformation of a divergent character could survive. After initially spreading its reach well into south Germany, this regional reformation would have to retreat behind this boundary during the generation after Zwingli's death; but the fact that it embodied from the start principles that appear to have resonated strongly with laymen ensured for it an enduring appeal that would ultimately carry it well beyond this boundary.

THE WITTENBERG REFORMATION AND THE ORIGINS
OF THE LUTHERAN-REFORMED DIVISION

Because decisions of Luther's were so central to the process that defined the Reformed tradition in opposition to the Lutheran, and because some of the most critical of these decisions were first taken in Wittenberg early in 1522, even before agitation for religious change had begun in Zurich, our story begins in Wittenberg. Here, the earliest steps were taken to transform the ideals of the evangelical movement into concrete changes in worship and religious organization in the fall of 1521, in the aftermath of the Diet of Worms, while Luther was in hiding at the Wartburg under the protection of his prince, Frederick the Wise of Saxony.

In Luther's absence, three of his colleagues took the lead in preaching evangelical doctrines and experimenting with new forms of worship: Andreas Bodenstein von Karlstadt, Luther's older colleague on the theology faculty; Philip Melanchthon, a young humanist professor of Greek; and Gabriel Zwilling, one of Luther's fellow Augustinian monks. In September, Melanchthon altered some features of the communion service, replacing Latin with German, removing references to the mass as sacrifice, and distributing the elements in both kinds to those present. Early in October, having lost faith in the value of private masses and the monastic rules, a number of members of the Augustinian order sought to quit the order or ceased saying commissioned masses. Faced with growing pressure for change, Frederick the Wise established a committee of theologians to investigate the actions of the Augustinians and to determine the proper shape for the liturgy. After a public disputation on the subject presided over by Karlstadt, the members of the committee associated with the theology faculty presented a report calling for major reforms in the liturgy. Conservative canons attached to the All Saints chapter argued that no changes should be made unless mandated by a general council.[11] Frederick postponed making any changes in the face of this division. While he temporized, the townsfolk and university students began to make their voices heard. In early December masses were disrupted and threats were uttered against the Franciscans. A few days later, a group of Wittenbergers presented six demands to the city council, calling for communion in both kinds, preaching from the Gospel alone, an end to private masses, the closing of taverns and brothels, and amnesty for those arrested after the disturbances of the preceding days. The elector responded by demanding that all petitions be presented to him as prince and ordering that all customary ceremonies be retained; but the evangelical theologians were emboldened to press ahead. On Christmas day, Karlstadt, dressed in plain clothes, celebrated the Eucharist at All Saints church in German and distributed both bread and wine to the communicants. Two weeks later, the Augustinian General Chapter gave leave to every member of the order to decide whether to stay or go. A few days later, those who remained, led by Zwilling, removed and destroyed all of the altars and images in the cloister chapel.

Faced with steadily mounting agitation for change, the Wittenberg city council decided on January 24, 1522, to adopt an ordinance drawn up with Karlstadt's assistance that ordered the changes in public worship initiated by Karlstadt to be adopted throughout the city, provided for the removal of all images from the city's churches, and ordered the income from discontinued religious endowments to be placed in a common chest for the relief of poverty. Several days later, Karlstadt published a little treatise entitled *On the Removal of Images* that attacked the decoration of churches with images of the Virgin and saints as contrary to the Second Commandment and dangerous because of the way in which it distorted the spiritual growth of ordinary believers. Even before the authorities could see to it that the images were removed from the city churches, a crowd of townspeople took care of the matter in an unauthorized iconoclastic rampage.

As would be the case in cities across the empire, religious change was thus institutionalized in Wittenberg after the preaching of evangelical preachers gave rise to growing pressure from a sizable fraction of the urban population. Demands for the transformation of worship focused on the celebration of the mass and the presence of images and altars in the churches, those two points of such intense devotion. The burghers of Wittenberg also demanded action against taverns and brothels, illustrating how the lay impulse to put the teachings of Scripture into practice generated concern for the moral purification of the community.

But the changes implemented in worship in Wittenberg under popular pressure placed the city dangerously afoul of imperial law, whose provisions neighboring princes were only too happy to seize upon as a pretext for intervening in the affairs of their rivals. On January 20, even before the Wittenberg civic ordinance was adopted, the imperial government, in a measure aimed at electoral Saxony, forbade all innovations in religion. Soon after the measure, Frederick sent an emissary to express his displeasure at the changes adopted. When the Wittenbergers moderated but did not repeal their changes, he made his objections publicly known. In this same period, the cautious Melanchthon began to express some doubts about the wisdom of the actions taken in the city. He now argued that the form of rituals was insignificant. Ideas that threatened "spiritual righteousness," such as the belief that the mass was a sacrifice, required correction, but the outward form of the rituals could be maintained without threatening the spiritual wellbeing of the population.

At this point, Luther decided to return to Wittenberg. Letters and a secret visit had kept him regularly informed of what was transpiring in the university town while he was in hiding, and it is clear that he generally approved of the actions of his fellow evangelicals until early January. Now he had himself fitted for a new monk's cowl to show that even if he had broken with the spirit of the old church order, he agreed that its outward forms could be maintained. He then delivered a series of eight sermons rebuking the Wittenbergers for going so far so fast and urging them to undo the changes. The Wittenberg Ordinance was the special target of his criticism. The outward forms of worship did not matter enough to be the subject of civic legislation. What was crucial was to preach the Gospel. In time old practices would wither away and new ones would take their place without explicit legislation. To move too swiftly to legislate new forms was to risk upsetting those who had not yet come to true faith.

The position of Luther and Melanchthon carried the day among the majority of Wittenberg's clergy and magistrates. All changes in worship decreed by law were repealed. But not all of the Wittenberg theologians were willing to accept this. Karlstadt argued that scriptural commandments positively required certain changes in worship, most obviously the rejection of all graven images. To restore statues to churches once they had been removed would be a manifest violation of the Ten Commandments. He spoke out against the latest changes and began work on a treatise setting forth his views. When Luther got wind of this, he convinced the town fathers to confiscate the treatise before it could be published and to forbid Karlstadt from preaching in Wittenberg. Karlstadt soon left for the rural parish of Orlamünde, where he devoted himself to pastoral work and instituted a radically simplified German mass. After two years of self-imposed silence, he published a series of treatises in 1524 that pushed his critique of established forms in worship in new directions, notably into attacks on the doctrine of the real presence and on the baptism of children too young to have come to faith. His tract *Shall We Go Slow and Respect the Consciences of the Weak?* returned to the argument engaged in Wittenberg in 1522 and claimed that the Bible obliged believers to carry through changes in worship wherever they could on the parish level without tarrying for any. Such views provoked the elector to order his expulsion from Saxony.

The significance of the events in Wittenberg for the early history of the Reformed tradition is threefold. First, the division of opinion between Luther and Karlstadt illustrates how as the Reformation unfolded its leading figures had to confront questions they had not anticipated, and how as that happened individuals who had previously collaborated could arrive at varying answers to those questions. Did the difference of opinion between Luther and Karlstadt follow logically from theological postulates they had already articulated? Did it result from decisions made for tactical reasons on the spur of the moment? The evidence is not detailed enough for us to be sure. Luther's relative indifference to the outward forms of worship can be plausibly related both to his formation as a monk and theologian, which may have left him less acutely aware of the meaning of ritual practice for lay religion than a parish priest would have been, and to the psychological weight of his personal discovery of the liberating power of the doctrine of justification by faith alone, which always remained for him the central Christian tenet requiring proclamation in the last days. At the same time, the fact that he did not speak out against the changes in Wittenberg until the elector made his displeasure clear argues for the importance of immediate tactical considerations. Whatever the case, political power then determined whose answers would triumph. In this instance the greater attractiveness of Luther's position to the civic and territorial authorities under the circumstances of the moment, together with his greater prestige, led to Karlstadt's banishment. The positions that Karlstadt advocated were nonetheless no less possible to derive from the broad watchwords of the evangelical movement than Luther's. As the movement spread, others would arrive independently at similar positions. In other circumstances they could carry the day.

Second, the viewpoint on the reform of worship first articulated by Luther and Melanchthon in these critical months became normative within the Lutheran tradition. This viewpoint deemed elements of worship inherited from medieval Catholicism acceptable so long as they did not contradict the principle of justification by faith alone. The biblical prohibition against graven images was understood to forbid the veneration of images but not their use in church decoration to illustrate doctrinal truths and scenes from sacred history. When, after several more years, Luther believed that Wittenberg was ready for mandated changes in organized worship and the violence of the Peasants' War had convinced him that it was too dangerous to leave this to congregational initiative and the spontaneous course of the Gospel, the guidelines he enunciated for the transformation of worship gave individual parishes and territories a great deal of leeway in deciding whether they wanted to perform the Eucharist in German or Latin and how many saints' days they chose to preserve. Later Lutheran church orders kept between ten and thirty-five special holidays or feast days, retained parts of the Roman liturgy, and permitted altarpieces and other decorations in church.[12]

Third, the manner in which Luther came to understand his disagreement with Karlstadt would shape his response to the news of a reformer in Zurich whose understanding of the Eucharist bore a close resemblance to that developed by Karlstadt at Orlamünde. Always inclined to understand the events around him as a struggle between God and the Devil in the last days before the apocalypse, Luther identified Karlstadt as one of the "false brethren" spoken of in Galatians. He saw him as an agent of Satan who had infiltrated the camp of Christian liberty in order to bring its followers back into bondage and as possessed of a "rebellious, murderous, seditious spirit."[13] When controversy over the doctrine of the Eucharist began to divide Wittenberg and Zurich, Luther cast the dispute in the same starkly polarizing terms. With the forces of God pitted against those of the Devil, he felt obligated to deploy his vast prestige to counter the spread of devilish sacramentarianism.

ZWINGLI AND ZURICH

It is a sign of how rapidly evangelical sentiment spread across the German-speaking world that within weeks of Luther's return to Wittenberg, agitation for change in religious practices began in Zurich, 350 miles to the southwest. Zurich was just one of many cities in the region in which preaching that its opponents deemed Lutheran had been heard by this time. Owing both to its character and to the eloquence and political savvy of its leading evangelical preacher, it would soon emerge as the epicenter of religious change in this corner of the Germanophone world.

Zurich stood just across the new and still fluid political boundary that separated the Swiss Confederation and its associated territories from the Holy Roman Empire. The confederation had emerged from a small, late-thirteenth-century defensive alliance of a few Alpine valleys to become by the later fifteenth century a force in European politics. Critical in this process were two developments: the addition of the urban-dominated territories of Bern, Lucerne, and Zurich and the emergence of the Swiss as Europe's finest mercenary soldiers during their long wars against the Habsburgs and Burgundians. During these conflicts, the Swiss established their de facto independence from the Holy Roman Empire, although that independence remained open to challenge; as recently as 1499 Emperor Maximilian had gone to war to establish that "the Swiss, too, must have a master." His defeat spurred additional territories to join the victorious confederacy—Basel and Schaffhausen in 1501, the rural district of Appenzell in 1513—or to enter into pacts of alliance (*combourgeoisie*) with individual cantons. This latter process would continue through the 1520s on the western marches of the confederation, where Germanic dialects gave way to Franco-Provençal. The Italian wars also offered the Swiss the opportunity to conquer the region around Lugano and Locarno from Milan and to place it under direct confederal lordship. The boundaries of what is Switzerland today thus encompassed in the sixteenth century a hodgepodge of self-governing rural cantons, urban cantons in which a single dominant city ruled over a surrounding *contado* that often vastly exceeded it in population, independent but allied cities and territories, and regions under the lordship of one, several, or all of the members of the confederation.

Mercenary service shaped much of Switzerland's economic and political history during these years. Of the cities attached to the confederation in 1517, only Basel, the mercantile gateway to the rich Alsatian plain and the home of a university and several printing houses, approached 10,000 inhabitants. Most Swiss towns housed from 2,000 to 5,500 people and were little more than overgrown cattle markets and modest stops on the long-distance trade routes that struggled across the Alpine passes, supplemented with textile production in the cases of Zurich, Saint-Gall, and Fribourg. Mercenary service was an attractive avenue to fortune in such a rugged environment, especially as Europe's crowned and tiaraed heads, led by the king of France and the pope, plied the leading captains with gifts and pensions to win their service. In the second decade of the century, however, changes in military technology challenged the dominance that the Swiss pike phalanxes had established on Europe's battlefields since the 1470s. By adding gunpowder weapons and using various forms of battlefield entrenchment, other armies found they could blunt the fearsome charge of the phalanxes and mow down the pikemen in their ranks. Mercenary service had always had its critics, for it sent young Swiss off to die on foreign battlefields; and if it brought in return employment and booty, much of the profit went to pensionlords whose luxurious mode of living contrasted with traditional Swiss simplicity in a manner that, in this era of the Helvetic Renaissance, evoked the Tacitean discourse of corruption. As casualty rates mounted, the criticism intensified.[14]

Within the modestly sized cities of this region, the civic authorities exercised substantial control over religious matters. Zurich's city council oversaw the finances of many religious foundations in the city, monitored the behavior of their members, and watched over their performance of worship. The jurisdiction of the ecclesiastical courts had been whittled back after long struggle, while clerics swore the civic oath like other burghers and often paid taxes. Civic legislation also sought to regulate many aspects of public morality so that, in the words of a Zurich ordinance regulating dancing, "the Lord God preserves for us the fruit in the field and gives us good weather." Basel had established a special city court in 1457 to punish adultery, blasphemy, and the desecration of feast days, citing the obligation of city governments to uphold God's honor and prevent "great sins and wickedness."[15] This was certainly not the only part of Europe in which urban authorities believed it their duty to protect the moral purity of the community so that God's wrath might be deflected; but the language of municipal deliberations suggests that it was a region in which the ideal of the city as a *corpus christianum* was taken most seriously.

The establishment of Reformed churches within large stretches of this territory depended upon the combined efforts of a group of interconnected individuals. At the outset of his reforming career, Zwingli saw himself as just one of a group of "learned and excellent men" working for the recovery of the Gospel, the "true bishops of the day" that also included the prominent early Swiss humanists Joachim Vadian, the city physician and frequent mayor of Saint-Gall, Heinrich Glareanus, a classicizing geographer and poet who was close to Erasmus when both men lived in Basel and who would finally remain loyal to Rome, and Oswald Myconius, a teacher who moved between Zurich, Lucerne, and Basel and who argued as early as 1518 that obedience was owed to Rome only so long as the pope expressed Christian truth.[16] Three years after Myconius helped to bring Zwingli to Zurich in 1519, Zwingli was joined by Leo Jud, an early protégé, fiery preacher, and translator into German of many of the Latin works of Erasmus and Luther. Central to the progress of the Swiss Reformation were a series of disputations at which partisans of reform argued side by side for their position. A collaborator of Zwingli's at these assemblies was Johannes Oecolampadius, a Swabian humanist who had worked for a while at Basel helping to prepare Erasmus's edition of the New Testament before deciding to enter a Brigittine convent, only to leave it after a year to emerge in Basel from November 1522 onward as a transfixing evangelical preacher. Berchtold Haller was another protégé and confidant in powerful Bern, which ruled the largest territory of any Swiss canton. Zwingli also corresponded frequently and collaborated actively with the leaders of the Strasbourg Reformation, Wolfgang Capito and Martin Bucer.

For all of the importance of these individuals, Zwingli was, as Haller called him, "the first in the Confederation to begin the amelioration."[17] He was evidently an appealing and successful preacher, for despite making enemies among leading figures in the Zurich Great Minster, he could report proudly to Myconius toward the end of his first year in the city, "We do not stand alone. In Zurich there are already more than two thousand more or less enlightened people who have up to now drunk spiritual milk and can soon digest solid food."[18] As the quotation suggests, he was also a cautious and adroit tactician of reform who often consciously refrained from revealing the full extent of his reservations about the established state of affairs until he felt that the ground had been properly prepared for him to speak out. Yet he also knew when to engage in open acts of provocation or defiance to push the pace of change along. Allies in the city council from his arrival in Zurich onward helped him retain his position and begin to campaign for changes in worship at a time when fellow evangelicals were being forced out of comparable posts in Basel, Bern, and Lucerne. As the pace of reform advanced, the council turned to him for advice on numerous questions of religious policy and placed him in charge of overseeing education and the censorship of printed matter in the city. A gathering stream of treatises and memoranda flowed from his pen from 1522 onward. In the second half of the decade he worked tirelessly to form a political coalition to advance the evangelical cause throughout the region and traveled to nearby territories to offer advice on the drafting of church orders. The exceptional power he had obtained by the end of the decade is shown by his presence within an informal, secret six-member inner council that advised Zurich's larger governing councils on policy.

Zwingli was born on January 1, 1484—six weeks after Luther—in the village of Wildhaus in the territory of Saint-Gall. His father was a wealthy peasant who had served as village *ammann*. Huldrych can thus be said to have been born into the ruling class of this peasant republic, a background that may have facilitated his acceptance by the members of Zurich's Rat and that predisposed him to see the political community as the proper agency for the promotion of God's law, to the point of accepting a virtual obliteration of the distinction between the church and the political community. As he would later write, "When the Gospel is preached and all, including the magistrate, heed it, the Christian man is nothing else than the faithful and good citizen; and the Christian city is nothing other than the Christian church."[19]

The Zwingli family's prosperity ensured Huldrych good Latin schooling at Basel and Bern and eight years of higher education at the universities of Vienna and Basel. He left Basel with a master of arts degree, having probably been most influenced by teachers trained in the tradition of the *via antiqua*. He continued his theological education after taking up a living as parish priest in Glarus by studying Duns Scotus's commentary on Peter Lombard's *Sentences*. Soon, however, he would turn his back on the "darkness of Scotus," for the crucial formative impressions on him were his initiation into the world of humanism through a correspondence with Vadian and Glareanus, his beginning the study of Greek, and his discovery of Erasmus at Glareanus's suggestion. The great humanist's works enchanted him. A fulsome letter he wrote to Erasmus early in 1516 expressed his awe at the splendor of his erudition and declared that he was giving himself over to him as he would never give himself to any other. Erasmus's call to renew Christianity through the study, dissemination, and internalization of the Gospel inspired Zwingli to vow in the same year to dedicate himself to preaching from the Bible and to guard himself from further sexual encounters. He kept the first vow better than the second.[20]

In later years, Zwingli always dated his embrace of the cause of reform to this decision of 1516. More recent historians have tended to place his crucial

"Reformation breakthrough" between 1519 and 1521, when he began to express a pessimistic, Pauline vision of human nature and to stress the role of divine grace in salvation. Because Zwingli's few earlier writings did not express any clear position on providence, grace, or free will, the identification of these views with a breakthrough on Zwingli's part rests on the assumption that, as an Erasmian partisan of a renaissance of Christianity, he must have previously believed in the freedom of the will. This assumption is highly questionable, however, given that Erasmus himself did not make his views on this topic clear until his debate with Luther in 1525 and that such prominent humanists of the preceding generations as Lorenzo Valla had emphasized the power of God's eternal will. It is certain that from 1516 on Zwingli regarded the Bible as the supreme authority in matters of faith and that this led him to alter the character of his pastoral work and to offer an increasingly outspoken Erasmian critique of existing religious and political practices. By his own admission, his study of Augustine around this time also deepened his sense of God's majesty and of the centrality of grace in salvation. When he moved to Zurich to take up his post there in January 1519, he substituted the systematic, chapter-by-chapter exposition of the Gospels for the traditional practice of preaching on selected fragments. Within the year he was questioning the veneration of the saints, the elaborate character of Corpus Christi day activities, and the principle of the tithe. The transition from Erasmian to reformer probably did not involve any dramatic change in intellectual outlook.[21] Erasmian ideas continued to shape fundamental aspects of his mature theology. Viewpoints that he absorbed from Erasmus included the convictions that true piety involved inward matters of the spirit; that the holy was not to be found in material things; that money spent on the ornate decoration of churches could better be spent on aiding the poor; and that the clergy should confine itself to preaching the word while Christian magistrates took responsibility for the moral improvement of community.[22]

The initial result of Zwingli's discovery of Erasmus was to confirm him as a critic of the mercenary business. Zwingli had accompanied his parishioners from Glarus on their expeditions into Italy in 1513 and 1515. The horrible defeat at Marignano that capped the second voyage only heightened the repulsion he had begun to feel at the trafficking in fighting men. He opposed further service on French behalf, a position for which the papacy, eager to monopolize Swiss troops, rewarded him with an annual pension. The attention paid in Erasmus's *Adages* to the proverb "Dulce bellum inexpertis" (War is sweet to those who don't know it) struck home. Zwingli's brief political poem of 1516, "The Labyrinth," drew an antiwar moral of an Erasmian cast. When Glarus signed a new pact to commit soldiers to the Valois monarchy, he left his parish there. These political opinions proved crucial in bringing him, after a two-year stay at Einsiedeln in his native Toggenburg, to Zurich at the end of 1518. The town council was seeking to crack down on the continuing private trade in mercenaries in order to forestall further trouble in the Zurich hinterland, where anger at the loss of life at Marignano had provoked revolt. Although Zwingli's admitted infringements against clerical celibacy tarnished his candidacy for the position of *leutpriester* (people's priest) at the Great Minster, his known opposition to mercenary service swung the critical votes in his favor. When his early sermons castigated the mercenary business effectively and named names of those who profited, he cemented the support of powerful allies in the civic leadership.[23]

Zwingli's later insistence on the reforming character of his work from 1516 on was always bound up with his intent to assert his stature as an independent reformer; he was no mere disciple of Luther's. This insistence appears justified insofar as he remained throughout his career a theologian whose language and ideas differed from Luther's on many points and owed obvious debts to Erasmus. Yet Zwingli's correspondence also makes it clear that he became aware of Luther and his writings before he received the call to Zurich, that he at once began to procure many of Luther's books and to follow the Luther affair with interest, and that he deeply admired Luther's courage in speaking his mind about the abuses of the church. His anger at what he came to perceive as the Roman church's unjustified persecution of Luther emboldened him to speak out against Rome himself. In 1520 he renounced his papal pension. By 1522 he had moved beyond Erasmus, for he was now willing to defend the viewpoint that all "invented, external worship" was worthless and should be discarded, even if it was sanctioned by the institutional church. Early in that year he defied one church law that he judged without standing by marrying. His first reformatory tract, "Concerning Choice and Liberty Respecting Food," of April 16, 1522, defended the violation of traditional church rules requiring fasting during Lent through a lengthy demonstration that these have no biblical basis but are purely human commandments.[24] Zwingli's progression into an active if always tactically cautious proponent of ecclesiastical change thus took off from the Erasmian call for the moral renewal of Christianity through the return to the Bible, but then added to this notes of Augustinian pessimism about human nature and a willingness to reject the authority and traditions of the established church, now seen as fatally corrupt under the stimulus of the Luther affair.

Whereas Luther's theology developed outward from the starting point of *sola fide,* the central kernel of Zwingli's reforming critique was opposition to all forms of false, external worship, as measured against the other great Reformation principle of *sola scriptura.* He tellingly entitled his fullest theological statement *Commentary on True and False Religion.* "Faithfulness," he wrote there, "demands, first, that we learn from God in what way we can please Him, in what manner serve Him. Next, it demands that we shall add nothing to what we have learned from Him, and take away nothing. . . . True religion, or piety, is that which clings to the one and only God." In the war between true and false religion, singular vigilance was necessary to guard against the marked tendency of human beings to conceive of God visually, to depict his image, and to worship the images they created. In doing away with all forms of worship that God had not explicitly requested, however, a measure of tactical prudence was in order: "The things . . . on which faith hinges should be brought out without delay; but the things that militate against it need to be demolished with skill, lest they do harm in their downfall and bury the little that has already been built up."[25]

The emphasis on serving God properly in turn was linked to energetic moral activism. Whereas Luther distinguished sharply between two components within Scripture, the law and the Gospel, and argued that the chief purpose of the biblical commandments was to bring people to knowledge of their sinfulness, Zwingli held that "the law is a Gospel for the man who honors God." As "the constant will of God" the commandments were a beacon for those with faith to follow. Given original sin, of course, they could never do so fully. Those with faith nonetheless enjoyed a measure of regeneration, a term that Zwingli used far more often than justification to express the consequences of faith. Christian life thus became "a battle so sharp and full of danger that effort can nowhere be relaxed without loss; again, it is also a lasting victory, for he who fights it wins, if only he remains loyal to Christ the head."[26]

Another cornerstone of Zwingli's theology was a powerful sense of God's all-controlling providence. He never left behind his early humanist enthusiasm for the ancients and for linguistic study. Amid flourishes of trilingual erudition, his *Sermon on the Providence of God* (1530) moved from the proof of God's existence as a first mover, to the proof that if God exists he must be intelligent, good, and all-powerful, to the proof that such a God must have determined from all time those who would be saved and have elected them for good reasons—not according to their merits but in order to display his mercy and power. Moses, Paul, Plato, and Seneca were all cited as witnesses. Although he did not use the term *predestination* frequently here or elsewhere in his works, the word did appear and the idea was certainly implicit in his philosophical vision of an all-powerful deity, for "predestination is born of providence, nay is providence."[27]

Just as Luther's example inspired Zwingli to break thoroughly with Rome, so the publication of a growing number of Luther's writings in nearby Basel reinforced Zwingli's preaching in inspiring elements in Zurich to begin to agitate for change. The occasion for Zwingli's treatise on freedom in the choice of foods was a public scandal provoked when, early in Lent 1522, a gathering in the house of the printer Christopher Froschauer ate sausages. When Froschauer was fined for this by the city council, Zwingli defended him, first from the pulpit and then in print. He convinced the council to reconsider the issue and to solicit the opinion of the Great Minster and the three people's priests. The bishop of Constance, in whose see Zurich was located, riposted by sending a delegation to urge the council to uphold the law. Ultimately, the council did so. But it declared its resolution to be provisional and asked the episcopal eminences to explain definitively how such a measure conformed to Christ's injunctions. The decision suggests that the council was beginning to grant legitimacy to the principle that laws dealing with religious matters should conform to Scripture. It also suggests that, having long been increasing its control over religious affairs in the city, the council was now willing to position itself as the appropriate judge of arguments advanced by clergymen about whether or not a given law did so conform. This was a position that Zwingli actively encouraged.[28]

In the months that followed, provocative actions challenged other traditional usages. In late June and early July, Zwingli and several other partisans of the evangelical cause, both clerical and lay, interrupted public sermons and charged that the preachers erred. In July a group of clerics petitioned the bishop to abolish the requirement of clerical celibacy. Then, in a published treatise in the vernacular, they addressed the same appeal to the ruling authorities of the confederation, again suggesting that it was up to the secular authorities to make the final judgment in such matters. In August a group of clergymen meeting in nearby Rapperswil asserted that Scripture should be the sole touchstone for Christian practice. The fall months were troubled by continuing reports of fasting rules being ignored, tithes refused, and members of religious houses throughout the vicinity seeking to leave their order. Faced with this agitation, the bishop of Constance once again called on the powers that be in Zurich to silence the novelties being preached in their town. The Confederal Diet, still dominated by partisans of the established order, took measures to prevent alleged Lutheran preaching in those territories subject to the common authority of the confederation. In December it appealed to all member cantons to prohibit new teachings in the areas under their governance.[29]

The Zurich authorities now had to make some decisions. In January 1523, they invited clergymen from throughout the region to assemble and discuss whether or not sixty-seven articles drawn up by Zwingli summarizing ideas he had previously set forth in his sermons conformed with the Gospel. After hearing the discussion, which has come to be known as the First Zurich Disputation, the city council adjudged that nobody present proved Zwingli's teachings to be heretical and accordingly that it should allow him to continue to preach. At the same time, it ordered all of the canton's clergy to stick to proclaiming "the holy Gospel and the pure holy Scriptures" in their sermons and to refrain from calling one another heretics. Although the decision did not order innovations in church practice, it can be seen as the magistrates' full assertion of their power to judge religious questions in consultation with local clerical experts.[30]

Pressure for change continued to mount, spearheaded less by Zwingli than by the recently arrived Leo Jud and growing numbers of laymen. In August, a vernacular baptismal liturgy was introduced at the Great Minster. In September the question of images came to the fore, as it had so quickly in Wittenberg. From his pulpit, Jud called for their removal from the city's churches, while a pamphlet by Ludwig Haetzer, *A Judgement of God Our Spouse Concerning How One Should Regard All Idols and Images,* collected the scriptural passages condemning idolatry and repeated arguments from Karlstadt's *On the Removal of Images.* Groups of men tore down a large crucifix and destroyed images in several nearby villages.[31] Once again, Zurich's magistrates decided they needed help in determining how to respond and called for a theological disputation to clarify the issues. This time laymen as well as clerics were invited to present their views. The Second Zurich Disputation dealt with a series of questions: Should changes be introduced in the liturgy? was the use of images in worship appropriate? did secular leaders have the authority to legislate about such matters? if they did, how soon were they obliged to proceed? In the end, the magistrates accepted the tactically shrewd suggestion of a rural priest that the meeting recognize the impropriety of the worship of images and urge the clergy to preach against it, but that it not take any stronger action for the moment so that public opinion might be won over to the cause of change.[32]

Such temporizing did not sit well with all Zurichers. A growing number felt that God's word was clear and that mere human laws should be discarded. The payment of the tithe was a sticking point in surrounding rural communities. During the preceding decades, several communities had petitioned for greater control over their parish life, which was often dominated by powerful religious houses or urban collegiate churches. The spread of the evangelical cause intensified the desire for parochial autonomy, for now Gospel preachers arrived in the countryside with a message and style of preaching that certain communities wished to hear. In one such community, Witikon, the inhabitants ousted their incumbent and installed in his place an evangelical preacher recently expelled from Basel, Wilhelm Reublin. Zwingli had asserted as early as 1520 that the Bible offered no support for the upper clergy's tithe rights, and a number of communities had begun to refuse to pay such tithes. In June 1523, six rural communities, apparently under Reublin's leadership, petitioned the council for the elimination of the tithe. Their appeal was denied.[33]

Two days after the rural communities brought their case before the council, Zwingli spelled out his position on the relation between God's law and secular law in a sermon called "Regarding Divine and Human Righteousness." Unlike Luther, whose doctrine of the two kingdoms distinguished sharply between the end of secular government, whose purpose was to maintain peace and order in this world, and the requirements of the Scriptures, which enjoined individual Christians to live in a certain manner, Zwingli made it clear in this sermon that he considered government to be an instrument of divine law responsible for bringing the behavior of the Christian community into as close conformity with that law as possible. The secular authorities were servants of God established to promote the divine will. At the same time, Zwingli emphasized that government was established largely to prevent the disturbances that result from the weaknesses of human nature. This justified actions that governments might take to maintain institutions and make laws necessary for the smooth operation of society, even if these lacked scriptural foundation. Until such time as peaceful efforts to have ungodly laws repealed bore fruit, obedience to such laws was a Christian's civic duty. These latter points drew upon the treatise on secular authority that Luther had published just a few months earlier.[34]

Many of Zwingli's fellow travelers saw these last views as a sellout. Evangelicals plunged ahead with parish reformations in several nearby communities, altering the order of services and tearing down altars in defiance of local officials, then defending themselves with arms when threatened with arrest. The divisions widened as certain groups of evangelicals, including a fraction of those Zurichers who had previously been among Zwingli's staunchest supporters, challenged the legitimacy of infant baptism and urged that it give way to the baptism of adult believers instead. Since there is no immediately evident New Testament foundation for infant baptism, it was inevitable that this issue would arise sooner or later in the course of the evangelical challenge; Zwingli himself contemplated accepting adult baptism for a while. Ultimately, however, he rejected it, for the consequence of reserving baptism for adult believers was likely to be that a segment of adults would never consider themselves, or be considered by others, worthy candidates for the sacrament, with the result that the civic community to which Zwingli was so attached would become divided between the baptized and the unbaptized. The forced analogy he used to justify infant baptism—that that sacrament was the New Testament equivalent to circumcision among the Jews as a sign of entry into the covenant with God and therefore that Christians should be baptized as infants just as Jews were circumcised at a young age—demonstrates his eagerness to defend the comprehensive Christian community. He carried the day at another disputation held in January 1525, and it was decreed that all un-baptized children be brought for baptism within eight days. A group led by Conrad Grebel and Jörg Blaurock remained adamant in rejecting infant baptism and proceeded to carry out their own ceremony of adult baptism. They were forthwith banned from the territory of Zurich, as were the rural radicals like Reublin, who had also questioned infant baptism. Thus was Swiss Ana-baptism born as a separate movement. It would develop into a notable presence in parts of the confederation, subject to ever harsher penalties until a law of March 1526 decreed death for anybody who rebaptized another person. Zwingli's later writings brim with long passages refuting Anabaptist errors. Henceforward Anabaptism would always be one of the negative poles on the left against which the Reformed would define themselves.[35]

Zwingli's wish to avoid shattering the unity of the civic community and his deference to the city magistrates as the ultimate arbiters of ecclesiastical law allowed him to maintain the confidence of the council throughout 1523–25. As evangelical preaching intensified, individual churches continued to alter their worship services, and participation in traditional feast day celebrations and processions declined, the city authorities waited. Then, in June 1524, they initiated a four-year process of transforming the laws governing matters religious in Zurich. These regulations established most of the enduring features of the city's new church order. Throughout, the magistrates drew heavily on Zwingli's advice.

Seven major changes were involved. The first council decree ordered the removal of all images from the city's churches. Those who had personally donated devotional objects were allowed to take them home; then a team of workmen supervised by a dozen council members went from church to church removing and destroying all statues, crucifixes, votive lamps, and paintings and whitewashing the murals of biblical scenes that covered much of the wall surface of many churches. Monetary bequests attached to the maintenance of church lamps or furnishings were diverted to the care of the poor. Seventeen altars had once stood in the Great Minster, but now Zwingli could exclaim, "In Zurich we have churches which are positively luminous; the walls are beautifully white."[36]

Second, between October and December 1524, as the city's religious houses quickly lost members, the civic authorities seized the property of the houses and prohibited the taking of new monastic vows. One convent was kept open for those who desired to remain in holy orders. The bulk of the property formerly controlled by these institutions was diverted to support hospitals and a new system of poor relief. In keeping with the era's latest ideas of welfare reform, this system replaced the previous mixture of casual alms-giving, guild-sponsored systems of relief, and hospital-administered care with a single civic agency. Officers in each parish oversaw the regular distribution of relief to the deserving poor. Begging in public was forbidden, and relief was denied those who "go to public places and pubs, play games and cards, and practice other such mischiefs and frivolities."[37]

Third, at Easter time 1525, the council voted by a narrow majority to abolish the mass and replace it with an evangelical communion service. Each congregation was given the liberty to devise its own. The new service Zwingli developed and had printed as a model was dramatic in its simplicity. The minister, dressed in his usual plain robe, led the congregation in several vernacular prayers, alternating them with readings from the New Testament on the institution of the sacrament and Christ's words, "I am the bread of life." The emphasis of the prayers was on receiving this bread with praise and thanks and accepting the obligation to live as befitted a member of Christ's body. Assistants then went out among the congregation to pass out ordinary bread and wine.[38]

Fourth, in April 1525, the council placed Zwingli in charge of the Great Minster schools, which he set about reorganizing. In the cloister school of nearby Kappel, the young Heinrich Bullinger had already initiated regular exegetical lectures on the Bible, followed by a general discussion of the text in question. Although designed chiefly to ensure the theological education of the monks, the lectures took place in the vernacular and were open to nearby residents. It is not known if this directly inspired Zwingli. In any event, he set up a similar system to serve both as theological training for current and future ministers and as a means of diffusing biblical knowledge among the laity. Ministers, canons, and students gathered five times a week to discuss a biblical text in its Latin, Greek, and Hebrew versions and to hear a Latin lecture on it. Then a vernacular sermon conveyed the essence of the session to any townsfolk in attendance. These assemblies were called *Prophezei* after 1 Corinthians 14.26–32, in which Paul encourages groups of prophets to gather, interpret, and teach one another. The Zurich Prophezei would subsequently be replicated with modifications in Geneva, Emden, Scotland, Poland, and the Puritan "prophesyings" in England.[39]

Fifth, in May 1525, the council rejected the jurisdiction of the episcopal court at Constance and established in its place an autonomous marriage court, or *Ehegericht*. Composed of two members of the Small Council, two members of the Large Council, and two ministers, this body originally confined its jurisdiction to disputes over promises of marriage and the like that had constituted the bulk of cases taken by Zurichers to the episcopal tribunal. Over the next several years, it extended its competence to the supervision of a broad range of morals offenses. Similar courts were framed throughout the rural parishes of the canton, with "two honorable men from among the elders in the name of the church" being joined to the tribunal by 1530. When the new evangelical Eucharist was established in Zurich, Zwingli opined that notorious sinners should not be allowed to participate. The creation of the Ehegericht and rapid extension of its jurisdiction permitted a new division of responsibilities. It was initially agreed that the magistrates and the ministers should each proceed against notorious sinners in their own way: the magistrates with such penalties as fines, imprisonment, or the stocks; and the church with excommunication. In December 1526, however, the magistrates decided to reserve the power of excommunication to themselves. Subsequent laws reserved the penalty of excommunication for those who rejected the teachings of the church. Sinners received purely secular penalties and were permitted to participate in communion—indeed, after 1532, positively required to do so because it was believed it might inspire them to improve. The rejection of the use of excommunication to sanction serious immorality and the subordination of moral discipline to magisterial control in time became principles associated with the Zurich church and defended by its leading theologians.[40]

Sixth, in March 1526, the council cut the number of holidays observed in the city to thirteen. Zwingli had advised that only Christmas, Annunciation, and three special new feast days in honor of all martyrs, all evangelists, and all prophets and church fathers be observed as days of rest alongside the fifty-two Sundays of the year. The council found this too dramatic an alteration of the traditional church calendar. The Zurich clergy would continue to criticize superfluous and unscriptural holy days as instances of false worship, and many quietly dropped the liturgical observance of certain of them. In 1550 a new council mandate cut their number back to six.[41]

Finally, in April 1528, Zurich's magistrates mandated twice-yearly synods to monitor and improve the parish clergy. Pre-Reformation bishops had summoned the curates under their authority to synods for centuries to proclaim ecclesiastical regulations. A few had also called more regular assemblies to monitor clerical behavior. These precedents were now regularized and slightly modified. The magistrates identified two purposes for the synods, which took place under the watchful eye of civic officials: the examination and, if necessary, censure of the moral and professional behavior of the parish ministers; and the mutual discussion by the ministers of problems they had encountered in carrying out their jobs. Lay delegates accompanied their ministers to the earliest synods, but they ceased to attend after 1532. In that same year, the magistrates added the office of church deacons and gave them the task of visiting each parish in their jurisdiction to check on the behavior of the minister.[42]

The new church order created between 1524 and 1528 thus stripped the churches of their former decoration; altered the form of the liturgy; eliminated most holy days; forbade the taking of monastic vows; gave the Zurich civic authorities control over all former church property; reorganized the town's systems of charity and education; placed the secular powers in charge of overseeing the clergy's performance of its duties; and created a civic morals board to urge more Christian behavior on the city's inhabitants. During these same years, a string of ordinances also tightened the regulation of behavior by limiting the number of guests at wedding feasts, forbidding people from going about masked, and barring all dancing that was considered indecent or took place either out-of-doors or at night. With the Peasants' War raging close by, the Zurich council also promised to investigate complaints about unfair tithe requirements or servile dues, although in the end it moderated the preexisting situation only slightly.[43] This pattern of local reformation differed from that set in motion at the same time under Luther's endorsement in Saxony. Its purge of images from the churches and of feast days from the calendar was more thorough; the civic institutions it created to promote community moral regeneration were novel. These features are at once explained by Zwingli's enduring Erasmianism and his intense and closely related sensitivity to the dangers of false worship and to the importance of putting Christian morality into practice; by the regional political culture that deemed the moral purification of the community a civic responsibility; and by the broader lay desire, expressed in Wittenberg in 1521–22 but failing to triumph permanently there, to uproot fraudulent forms of worship and do away with social evils. Although certain German territorial church orders would also create morals boards and legislate against a range of social evils, the variance between the early Zurich and Saxon reformations would continue as a general rule to demarcate the Reformed tradition from the Lutheran for generations and centuries. To the extent that this would remain the case, the Zurich Reformation may be said to have responded more fully than the Saxon to the aspirations for change that drove the urban laity to become involved in the struggles of the Reformation.

THE EUCHARISTIC CONTROVERSY

In themselves, the dissimilarities between the Zurich and the Saxon reformations need not have led to a division of magisterial Protestantism into two rival wings. Most early reformers were willing to grant local churches latitude in determining their worship and church government. What sparked open acrimony between the Swiss and the Saxons was the matter of how to understand the central ritual of Christian worship, the Lord's Supper.

The possibility of serious divisions opening up over this issue was first revealed by an episode that occurred around the time Luther returned to Wittenberg to speak out against the changes legislated in his absence. Whereas the doctrine of transubstantiation had reigned supreme among late medieval theologians, at least one reputed schoolman, the Frisian Wessel Gansfort, posited a view of the Eucharist that argued that, alongside the actual sacramental eating of the divine flesh that occurred when believers received the consecrated host, a spiritual communion with Christ occurred. In the first decade of the sixteenth century, Cornelisz Hoen, a Delft lawyer and member of a local circle of biblical humanists, encountered Gansfort's views and elaborated them in a way that emphasized the spiritual half of the equation to the exclusion of the physical. When news of the Leipzig Debate reached Dutch humanistic circles early in 1521, a group of those favorable to Luther decided that they might help him do battle against the Romanists by dispatching one of their number, Hinne Rode, with copies of Gansfort's and Hoen's works.[44] As presented in the version eventually published in Zurich in 1525, Hoen's argument was quite simple. Christ had spoken metaphorically when he told his disciples, "This is my body," just as he did on many other occasions. The "is" in the sentence really meant "symbolizes." Hoen's brief letter resonated at several points with central themes of the evangelical movement. He argued that transubstantiation had no basis in the early church but was a late development in the history of theology that fostered unwarranted clerical privileges, the excessively ornate decoration of churches, and the pointless "bellowing of monks in the choir."[45]

Hoen's symbolic understanding of the Eucharist was no grist to Luther's mill. As he later stated, "I am captive and cannot free myself. The text is too powerfully present, and will not allow itself to be torn from its meaning by mere verbiage." When he first spelled out his eucharistic doctrine in 1523 in his *The Adoration of the Sacrament,* he insisted that "one must not do such violence to the words of God as to give to any word a meaning other than its natural one, unless there is clear and definite Scripture to do that." If Christ said that the eucharistic bread and wine were his body and blood, that is what one must believe, for Christians must bend their belief to the word of God, not to their reason.[46]

Luther's rejection of the ideas set forth in Hoen's letter did not stop the document from circulating in evangelical circles. Rode lost his teaching position in Utrecht following his visit to Wittenberg and moved to Basel and then to Zurich. Here, he communicated Hoen's letter to Zwingli. Bullinger would later write that Zwingli told him that he had had doubts about the doctrine of the real presence for several years prior to 1524 but had refrained from expressing them until the time was ripe. The accuracy of this report cannot be verified. All that is clear is that Zwingli first articulated a symbolic interpretation of the Eucharist after Rode's arrival in Zurich in a letter of November 1524 ostensibly addressed (although never sent) to a colleague in Reutlingen.

The letter first circulated in manuscript and was then published in March 1525. It incorporated Hoen's argument about the metaphorical character of Christ's words of institution, emphasized that man knows and communicates with God through the spirit rather than the body (a theme already of import to Zwingli), and asserted that the sacrament serves to fortify faith by reminding believers of Christ's sacrifice.[47]

Zwingli was not the only prominent evangelical to whom a symbolic interpretation of the Eucharist appealed. Oecolampadius in Basel was of a similar mind. When Capito and Bucer in Strasbourg learned of Zwingli's letter, they too initially expressed a measure of agreement, as did two men in distant Silesia, Caspar Schwenkfeld and Valentin Crautwald. Then there was Karlstadt, whose doubts about the real presence had been known to those aware of his work in Orlamünde, including Luther, for some time. He made his views known publicly in treatises of November 1524, in which he argued that Christ was pointing to himself and not referring to the bread he offered his apostles when he said, "This is my body." It appears to have been the publication of Karlstadt's tracts that prompted Zwingli to set his own views down on paper, as a corrective to what he saw as Karlstadt's less persuasive exegesis.

In December 1524 Luther let loose a blast he had been working on for some time to rebut Karlstadt, *Against the Heavenly Prophets in the Matter of Images and Sacraments,* in which he called his former Wittenberg colleague a "mad spirit" bent on twisting the Bible to suit his fancy. Luther's correspondence from late 1524 and early 1525 makes it clear that he saw Zwingli and Oecolampadius as victims of the same madness. As he received word that their ideas were receiving a hearing in a growing number of localities, he grew sufficiently alarmed to address letters to several cities warning them against these blasphemous new interpretations of the Eucharist. Published controversy directed specifically at the ideas of Zwingli and Oecolampadius began in July 1525, when the Wittenberger Johannes Bugenhagen sought to rebut Zwingli in his *Open Letter Against the New Error Concerning the Sacrament of the Body and Blood of Our Lord Jesus Christ.* Johannes Brenz and thirteen fellow Swabian preachers joined the attack. Oecolampadius and Zwingli replied with defenses of their position. The controversy escalated over the next years into a sustained and increasingly bitter exchange of refutations and responses that reached a peak in 1527–28. By this time the central protagonists had become, on one side, the two Swiss theological confederates Zwingli and Oecolampadius and, on the other, Luther himself.[48]

Neither side gave ground theologically, but the experience of the debate was deeply polarizing. Luther's treatises contained numerous ad hominem attacks on his antagonists and cast the issue in a manner that showed he understood it as part of the larger battle between the forces of God and those of the Devil in the end time. Such a battle permitted no compromise: "Either they or we must be ministers of Satan." "I testify on my part that I regard Zwingli as un-Christian, with all his teachings, for he holds and teaches no part of the Christian faith rightly. He is seven times worse than when he was papist."[49] For their part, Zwingli and Oecolampadius protested their respect for Luther as one who had contributed mightily to the restoration of Christian truth but grew increasingly exasperated at his unwillingness to grant that he might be in error on this matter. The Strasbourg theologians, who sought from the start to find a common ground between the two positions and warned of the dangers that threatened the evangelical cause if it allowed itself to become divided, watched the debate with growing dismay.

The Strasbourgers were not the only ones to worry about the perils of division within the evangelical camp. The menace of imperial intervention against those territories that had defied imperial law by implementing changes in worship hung over all that had done so, especially as Charles V freed himself from his other entanglements and made plans in the late 1520s to come to Germany. Philip of Hesse, one of the first major German territorial rulers to reform his church, championed a defensive alliance among evangelical territories to counter this threat. The growing theological rift threatened to scuttle such a partnership. To forestall rupture, Philip invited the leading theologians on each side of the controversy to a colloquy. Zwingli responded relatively eagerly to this initiative, Luther far more begrudgingly. Late in September 1529, Philip was able to bring Luther, Melanchthon, Zwingli, and Oecolampadius together in his university town of Marburg. The meeting showed the vast areas of agreement that existed between the two camps, for they were able to reach agreement on fourteen major points. But no common ground could be reached on the question of the Eucharist. Zwingli boasted at one point in the debate that his chief proof text throughout the entire controversy, John 6.63 ("The spirit alone gives life; the flesh is of no avail."), would break Luther's neck. Luther replied that necks did not break as easily in Hesse as in Switzerland. Luther had recourse to the flourish of lifting aside the tablecloth to reveal the words "This is my body" chalked on the table. The Swiss were unmoved. At the close of the discussion, Luther told the Swiss that he could not allow them to be his disciples. Both sides told the other that they should pray to God for enlightenment. The Marburg colloquy did not definitively seal the division between Luther's supporters and the Reformed, for theologians and politicians continued to pursue the dream of mutual concession on this issue for years and even generations to come, but it made evident just how bitter and intractable the breach had become.

REFORMED EXPANSION AND THE POLITICS
OF EVANGELICAL UNION

The debates within the evangelical camp over the matter of the Lord's Supper hardly slowed the cause's expansion. During the four and a half years that elapsed between the implementation of state-supported reformations in both Saxony and Zurich and Zwingli's face-to-face meeting with Luther at Marburg, a growing number of other cities and territories across Germany and Switzerland mandated religious changes within their jurisdictions. For all the advances made by the cause in Switzerland and the neighboring regions of south Germany, however, it also encountered stiff opposition in certain parts of the confederation. If Zwingli responded eagerly to Philip of Hesse's invitation to discuss the religious differences dividing the evangelical cause, he did so because his attention had increasingly turned to the task of organizing political alliances between the territories committed to the cause. He aimed to advance its interests against those of its political enemies in Switzerland and the Holy Roman Empire who were also organizing.

The pattern of Zwingli's correspondence can be used to trace the geographic area within which he exercised his most direct influence. As map 3 shows, in his first years in Zurich, he corresponded with a few individuals in France, mainly Swiss friends studying in Paris and early French supporters of the evangelical cause. As the 1520s advanced, he also entered into correspondence with a few individuals in more distant German cities such as Frankfurt, Nuremberg, and Liegnitz (Silesia), primarily over issues related to the eucharistic controversy. But the vast bulk of his correspondence was exchanged with individuals residing in a region that reached from the southern and eastern confines of Switzerland into that part of the Holy Roman Empire located south of a line running from Strasbourg through Ulm to Augsburg. Within this area, which represents the geographic center of the early Reformed tradition, his most frequent correspondents were Myconius prior to his expulsion from Lucerne, Oecolampadius in Basel, Bucer and Capito in Strasbourg, Haller in Bern, Vadian in Saint-Gall, and Johannes Comander in Chur. By the later 1520s, he had developed in addition a dense network of correspondents in the smaller towns and villages of north central Switzerland and those parts of Germany just across Lake Constance, where many localities looked to him to recommend clergymen when they had vacancies and to guide them on matters ecclesiastical.

Preaching that challenged the traditional order had begun in much of this region almost as soon as in Zurich. In the same year that Zwingli arrived in Zurich, 1519, a young clergyman known to have been impressed by Luther received a church appointment in Constance. In Lucerne the following

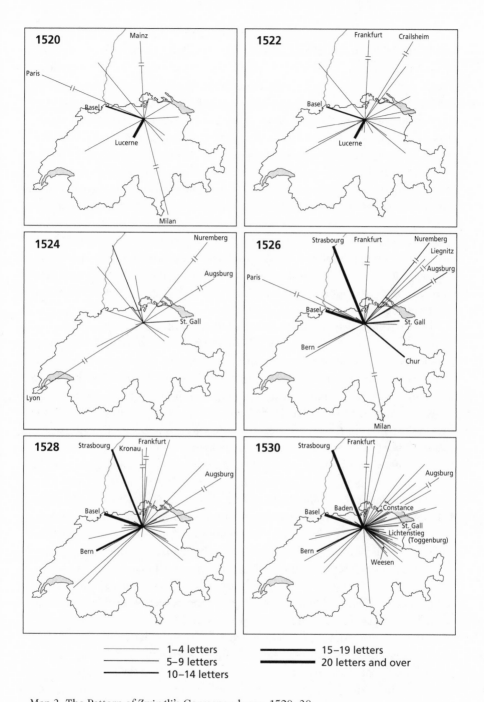

Map 3. The Pattern of Zwingli's Correspondence, 1520–30

1520

Mainz
Paris
Basel
Lucerne
Milan

1522

Frankfurt
Crailsheim
Basel
Lucerne

1524

Nuremberg
Augsburg
St. Gall
Lyon

1526

Strasbourg
Frankfurt
Nuremberg
Liegnitz
Augsburg
Paris
Basel
St. Gall
Bern
Chur
Milan

1528

Strasbourg
Kronau
Frankfurt
Augsburg
Basel
Bern

1530

Strasbourg
Frankfurt
Augsburg
Basel
Baden
Constance
St. Gall
Lichtensteig
(Toggenburg)
Bern
Weesen

1–4 letters
5–9 letters
10–14 letters
15–19 letters
20 letters and over

year a trio of young humanists received warnings not to teach or preach in a Lutheran manner. The Bern people's priest, Haller, was first drawn to evangelical teachings in 1520 when he read Luther's sermons on the Ten Commandments. On learning of Zwingli's preaching in Zurich later in the year, he traveled there to hear him and subsequently began a correspondence that was critical to his decision to imitate Zwingli's example of preaching strictly from Scripture. By 1523 evangelical sentiments were potent enough in Bern that carnival plays depicted the pope and his clergy conspiring to keep the Bible from ordinary laymen lest they discover the scams that brought the First Estate its fabulous wealth.[50] In contrast to the pattern that would typify the spread of the Reformation in most of Europe, the movement also reached quickly into the Swiss countryside, especially in canton Zurich and the regions to its east and south, often carried by evangelical clerics expelled from the cities. Rural communities began to demand a permanent preacher of the Gospel and even, as in Witikon, to take direct action to secure one.[51] This formed the background to the agitation of the Peasants' War, which touched much of the region.

The Peasants' War briefly slowed the advance of the evangelical cause in Switzerland, for the violence inspired the ruling authorities of many regions to crack down harder against the preaching of novelties. The cause was also hurt by a poor showing at a confederal disputation assembled at Baden in 1526 to determine whether or not a series of evangelical theses were heretical. Of the leading evangelicals only Oecolampadius trusted the promises of safety made to those invited and dared to venture into this common lordship territory, where several people had already been condemned to death for heresy. The Catholic champions, led by John Eck and Thomas Murner, adroitly deployed scriptural passages, church history, and even certain of Luther's arguments on the Eucharist to mount an unsettling rebuttal of Zwingli's and Oecolampadius's positions on this issue, the veneration of images, and intercessory prayer. The majority of cantons represented at the Diet voted to condemn their theses as heretical. Bern, Basel, and Schaffhausen tellingly did not.[52]

At the end of 1526, the affiliated city of Saint-Gall became the first town linked to the confederation to join Zurich in formally establishing a new church order. Long-standing battles against the powerful local abbey fueled antagonism against the established church in this linen-weaving center. Under Vadian's lay leadership, it purified churches of their images and instituted an evangelical Lord's Supper between December 1526 and April 1527.[53] Also in 1527, municipal elections tipped the balance of power in favor of the reforming party in Bern. When its municipal authorities called for a new disputation in January 1528 to consider ten theses, an all-star team of evangelical theologians including Zwingli, Oecolampadius, Bucer, Capito, and Ambrosius Blaurer of Constance made sure to attend. The smaller Catholic delegation was thoroughly overmatched. Immediately after the three-week debate, the local clergymen made their support known for the evangelical theses by a vote of 235 to 46, and the city fathers outlawed the mass and ordered all images removed from its churches. As in Wittenberg seven years previously, crowds of townsmen at once sprang to the task. Two days of iconoclasm followed during which children sang triumphantly, "We have been freed from a baked God"—a mocking reference to the host—while Zwingli exhorted the iconoclasts from the pulpit of the ransacked Minster, "Let us clear out this filth and rubbish! Henceforth, let us devote to other men, the living images of God, all the unimaginable wealth which was once spent on these foolish idols." One butcher threatened to kill anybody who tore down his guild's altar and complained that the destruction made the church look like a stable, a point that a dismayed member of the city council echoed symbolically by riding a donkey into it. Their actions availed little against the torrent.[54] In the subsequent months referenda were organized in the rural communities of Bern's large hinterland to see if they wanted to follow suit. The great majority of communities voted to do so, and the new church order was subsequently imposed on those that did not. This was a notable victory for the evangelical cause because Bern's extensive hinterland reached into French-speaking areas, and the city had recently formed pacts of combourgeoisie with Neuchâtel, Lausanne, and Geneva.

From Saint-Gall and Bern, agitation spread to the rural territories of the Abbey of Saint-Gall and to Glarus. In 1529 it was Basel's turn to be rocked by a series of iconoclastic riots led by guildsmen. These led to the resignation of traditionalist city council members and the adoption of a new church order, soon imitated in Basel's satellite of Mulhouse. Pressure from Zurich also tipped the balance in favor of reformation in Schaffhausen, where, in spite of an oligarchic city council that had blocked change, evangelical sentiment had taken root among much of the artisanal and agricultural population. Meanwhile, in those affiliated or subordinate territories under common confederal control, the religious divisions within the federal Diet resulted in a remarkable situation in which the choice of religious orientation was left up to each community. In many areas, notably Appenzell, Glarus, the Grisons, the Thurgau, and Toggenburg, parishes declared for the cause of church reform.[55]

By 1530, then, local reformations had been enacted within Switzerland in four urban cantons, Zurich, Bern, Basel, and Schaffhausen, in the affiliated city of Saint-Gall, and in many rural parishes. The new church orders of these localities drew heavily on the example of Zurich. Zwingli himself drafted most of Bern's new ecclesiastical ordinance while he was there for its disputation. It included provisions for both a Prophezei and community morals courts like the Zurich Ehegericht, here called *Chorgerichten*. In Basel, Oecolampadius pressed for a variant system of moral discipline. His biblical and patristic studies had convinced him that a true Christian church modeled on that of the earliest centuries after Christ included an autonomous system of ecclesiastical discipline that he believed should be jointly administered by the pastors and leading lay figures within the church and should have the capacity to pronounce sentences of excommunication against those who refused to mend their ways after a series of brotherly admonitions. Because Basel's city council had long battled to reduce the authority of the local church courts and itself exercised much supervision of morals, it refused to grant a body that might be dominated by clergymen powers of excommunication, just as Zurich's council before it had done. Modifying the proposal for a joint lay-clerical board of censors that Oecolampadius set before it, it established two institutions: an Ehegericht staffed like Zurich's, whose jurisdiction was confined primarily to marriage disputes, and a set of parish morals councils composed of two city councillors and one church member, whose successive admonitions could trigger excommunication. Two years later, the city council reserved for itself the prerogative to deliver the final warning that led to excommunication. In some of the rural territories of the Abbey of Saint-Gall, where Anabaptist groups that emphasized the use of the ecclesiastical ban were strong, local clerics also pushed for an autonomous system of ecclesiastical discipline. Zwingli spoke against this at synods in Rheineck and the Thurgau in 1529 and carried the day here for a system in which church officials warned the sinners and secular authorities laid down the punishment.[56]

While the cause of church reform advanced across Switzerland between 1525 and 1529, no less remarkable than its advance was the early and effective opposition organized by the governing authorities of the majority of the smaller Swiss cantons. The forest cantons of Uri, Schwyz, Unterwalden, and Zug had inherited a distrust of Zurich's imperialism from a series of wars they had fought in the fifteenth century to turn back attempts by the powerful city to extend its hegemony over rural inner Switzerland. They were scarcely predisposed to look kindly on a movement emanating from that city. The absence of monasteries in these cantons and hence of the anticlericalism that their landed wealth and tithe rights generated in other parts of rural Switzerland also made the ground less fertile for the evangelical cause here. Finally, the tenacious attachment that country dwellers everywhere in Europe felt to those Catholic rituals that promised protection against the vagaries of nature could find political expression more easily in these self-governing rural communities than virtually anywhere else on the continent. When the Zurich Rat invited the inhabitants of Obwalden to participate in the Second Zurich Disputation, it received a reply that mingled peasant mistrust of urban sophistication with powerful arguments for loyalty to Rome:

> We are happy at all times to be at your service; nevertheless we do not have particularly well-educated people, but rather pious and reverent priests who interpret the Holy Gospels and other Holy Scriptures for us, as they were interpreted also for our forefathers, and as the Holy Popes and Council have commanded us. This we will maintain and in this we will believe until the end of our lives, and for this suffer even death, until a Pope or a Council command otherwise, for we do not intend in so far as it is within our power, to alter what has been determined so regularly of old by the whole of Christendom, both spiritual and secular. Furthermore we do not believe that our Lord God has given so much more grace to Zwingli than to the dear saints and doctors, all of whom endured death and martyrdom for the sake of the faith, for we have no special information that he leads, as a result, a more spiritual life than others, but instead that he is disposed to agitation more than peace and quiet. Therefore we shall send no one to him, nor to anyone like him, for we do not believe in him.[57]

Such suspicion of Zwingli and the evangelical cause was matched by the leading citizens of Lucerne, who in the absence of much industry or trade were dependent upon the military business. The humanist evangelicals who appeared at an early date in this city and who echoed Zwingli's criticism of mercenary service were all expelled in 1522. The same carnival season of 1523 that saw plays mock the Roman church in Bern saw Zwingli's portrait burned in the streets of Lucerne. By 1524, Lucerne, Zug, Uri, Schwyz, and Unterwalden were consulting together to coordinate action against heresy on the federal level, while within their boundaries tough measures against heterodoxy kept the evangelical cause from ever developing into more than isolated incidents of individuals embracing or expressing the new belief. No less vigorous in its repression of heresy was Fribourg, which in 1527 became the first polity in Europe to require its inhabitants to swear fealty to the church of Rome. Solothurn also remained loyal to Rome, although the outcome was very much in doubt here for a while after a robust evangelical movement developed in the wake of the Bern disputation. Evidence of deep-rooted attachment to the traditional faith can also be seen in the Berner Oberland's violent although ultimately unsuccessful resistance to the Bernese mandate to abolish the mass throughout its territory. In no other part of the German-speaking world would as large a percentage of the population be preserved for the Catholic cause through the actions of largely self-governing communities as in Switzerland. As a result, a majority of the federal Diet always opposed innovations in religion. The Diet's power to intervene in the internal affairs of individual cantons was uncertain, but the issue was one that the Catholic cantons felt firmly enough about to appeal to the imperial mandates against heresy, creating the alarming prospect that the emperor might use the issue to reassert his dominance over Switzerland.[58]

In this climate of ongoing political struggle and uncertainty, Zwingli bent his energies to promoting a confessional alliance that could defend the evangelical cause against its enemies and provide a military shield for its continuing expansion. Notwithstanding his outspoken criticism of mercenary service, he was no pacifist. On the contrary, his moral activism and belief that Christian magistrates had a duty to uphold the divine will led him to advocate the use of governmental force to protect the proclamation of God's truth. His willingness to embrace the sword in this context contrasted dramatically with Luther's denial in these years that it could ever be lawful to oppose the emperor by force. Around 1525 or 1526, Zwingli drafted a long memorandum for presentation to the Zurich council in which he reviewed the city's position within the regional and European political and diplomatic setting and, addressing strategic and military factors, proposed measures for advancing the evangelical cause. His urgings helped spark the Christian Fortress Alliance with the free imperial city of Constance in December 1527. Bern, Saint-Gall, Basel, Schaffhausen, Biel, Mulhouse, and Strasbourg linked themselves to this alliance over the next three years. The Catholic cantons responded by forming a Christian Union with Austria.[59]

The presence of Constance and Strasbourg in the Christian Fortress Alliance highlights the bond that existed between the Swiss and south German evangelicals in this period. Constance and Strasbourg were both large enough and important enough to house their own theologians, so their local reformations did not simply follow Zurich's blueprint. Still, their leading reformers corresponded regularly with the Swiss and shared much of the same sensibility, above all the aversion to idolatry and the concern with communal sanctification. Strasbourg carried through a large-scale removal of church images in September 1524, three months after the whitewashing of Zurich's churches. The new liturgy put in place in most of the city's churches in 1525 included a dramatically simplified eucharistic service and the elimination of all holidays.[60] Constance's new church order, adopted in stages between 1527 and 1531, stripped all decoration from the churches and included a system of discipline by which civic *Zuchtherren* (Discipline lords) were empowered to issue fines and penalties to all who offended "against God, against the common good, or against their neighbor," although here twenty-four holy days were retained. Constance's ecclesiastical regulations in turn served as the model for the nearby free imperial cities of Memmingen, Esslingen, and Isny.[61]

When the eucharistic controversy broke out, the leading theologians of Strasbourg and Constance showed themselves generally inclined toward the positions defended by the Swiss, but, as indicated, they were still more mindful that the issue not rupture evangelical agreement. In Strasbourg, Bucer worked from the start to mediate between the two sides. Constance's chief reformer, Blaurer, argued that the interpretation of the Eucharist was a relatively minor matter: "We would still be Christians whether the supper of Christ would be completely removed or not."[62] The distinctive position of the churches of this corner of the empire was made evident when the first formal confessions of faith were drafted for presentation to the emperor at the Diet of Augsburg in 1530. The majority of evangelical territories within the empire aligned themselves behind the document drafted by Melanchthon that subsequently became known as the Augsburg Confession. Zwingli, eager to ensure that his ideas receive a hearing, drafted a personal account of his faith that was printed and given to the emperor. The cities of Strasbourg, Memmingen, Lindau, and Constance found both of these documents wanting. They submitted their own Tetrapolitan Confession, drafted by Bucer. This differed from the Augsburg Confession in rejecting the use of images in worship and declaring that nothing should be taught by the church except what was expressly contained in the Bible or could be fairly deduced from it. On the Eucharist, it attempted an ambiguous compromise between the Zwinglian and Lutheran positions.[63]

Slightly farther to the north and east, reforming impulses emanating from Zurich and Strasbourg battled for supremacy against those emanating from Wittenberg in the late 1520s and early 1530s in several large free imperial cities whose civic authorities hesitated for a long time before implementing a full reformation by statute. The conflict was most acute in south Germany's biggest and richest city, Augsburg. Because Augsburg depended for much of its trade on the Habsburg lands and court and because it was surrounded by Catholic territories, the city fathers were understandably reluctant to implement a reformation. Evangelical sentiment nonetheless developed rapidly in this bustling entrepôt, and many of its parishes came to be filled by advocates of religious change. When the eucharistic controversy heated up, the evangelical clerics divided between supporters of Luther's position and supporters of Zwingli's and battled in print and from the pulpit. Strikingly, the Zwinglians promptly became by far the largest religious party in the city, gaining wide support among the guilds but also winning supporters among the ruling elites. When the divisions between the two evangelical parties became so bitter that the city fathers feared disturbances unless one party or the other was silenced, they expelled the Lutherans as the weaker party. The eucharistic issue was the leading point of contention between the two groups of evan-

gelical preachers, but they also clashed over the form of the liturgy and the
degree to which they were willing to tolerate "civic and honorable pleasures
and ancient city customs." While the Lutheran Johann Forster defended dancing, his more censorious counterpart Wolfgang Musculus, a former secretary
of Bucer's, declared that he would rather see his daughter join a whorehouse
than attend a dance.[64] The Reformation followed a similar course in Ulm and
Frankfurt. In Kempten, likewise pulled between rival Swiss and Saxon tendencies, the burghers were polled in 1533 on whether to retain or eliminate
images. They voted to get rid of them by a margin of 800 to 174.[65]

The greater popular appeal of the Reformed positions than the Lutheran
ones in these towns where they competed on a relatively equal footing de-
serves emphasis. Why did the Zwinglian preachers draw larger followings than
the Lutherans? Probably because they offered a sharper and more psychologically satisfying alternative to the many forms of object worship that were
so central to late medieval religiosity but had now come under attack. Once
one came to believe that the worship of relics or prayer before a saint's image
availed nothing, the Zwinglian call to eliminate all graven images surely
seemed at once a more stirring battle cry and more psychologically prudent
than the Lutheran suggestion to cull simply those images that had become objects of veneration. Why play with fire and allow images to remain in church
when the Bible so clearly condemned idolatry, when human beings had repeatedly shown themselves so prone to seek the spiritual in the material and
to build cults around things, and when clergymen had shown themselves so
unscrupulous about taking advantage of this weakness? For those convinced
that paying to have a mass said had nothing to do with winning eternal salvation, and who had perhaps already wondered if repeating the words of the
liturgy could truly transform bread and wine into Christ's flesh and blood
when to all outward appearances they appeared unchanged, understanding
the Lord's Supper as a symbolic memorial of Christ's one true sacrifice must
likewise have seemed more plausible and more prudent than denying transubstantiation yet insisting that Christ was somehow physically present in the
elements.[66] Defending a doctrine of real presence could only appear to encourage just the sort of respect for the communion bread and wine that had led
so many idolatrous forms of worship to grow up around them throughout the
Middle Ages. The sterner call of the Zwinglians for the moral purification of
the community also may have touched a chord, for many of the early evangelical pamphlets written by laymen had stressed the theme of social renewal,
and hopes for a dramatic ethical transformation would reappear frequently in
future times and places where the Reformation cause suddenly gained a wide
following. Whatever the precise mix of considerations that went into it, this
greater appeal in situations of direct competition offers one important part of

the answer to the larger question of why Reformed Protestantism ultimately spread so much more widely across Europe than Lutheranism.

Communities like Augsburg and Ulm in which competing evangelical preachers debated one another for an extended period of time were, however, decidedly rare. Zwingli's writing obtained only limited circulation in north Germany. Just one of his books was translated into the region's Low German. Despite this, a number of preachers arrived independently at eucharistic views the local Lutherans condemned as sacramentarian. Ten such figures have been found among the evangelicals active in the region between Goslar and the north German coast in the first decade of the Reformation. In Silesia, Schwenkfeld and Crautwald jointly articulated a eucharistic theology that stressed Christ's spiritual, not physical, presence at the communion ceremony, entered into contact with Zwingli and came to view him as a kindred spirit. Yet whenever Wittenberg's theologians got news of such opinions, they hastened to warn the relevant authorities about the dangers of permitting "fanatics" in their midst, and their influence was such that they often obtained their prompt dismissal. Thus, on receiving one such warning, the city fathers of Goslar invited Luther to send a representative to debate the two most popular evangelical preachers in that city, both of whom upheld a symbolic interpretation of the Eucharist. Nicolas von Amsdorf, one of Luther's most trusted associates, made the trip and was able to convince the authorities to banish both men. Catholic leaders also found attacks on the real presence highly offensive. In Silesia, a harsh royal measure of 1528 decreed death for those who upheld the "new heresy against the holy sacrament of the real body and blood of our Lord Jesus Christ." Even though this decentralized territory was little more than a conglomeration of all-but-independent duchies, Schwenkfeld's erstwhile protector, Duke Friedrich of Liegnitz, had no choice but to expel him from his lands and to pursue a rapprochement with the other Lutheran and Catholic dukes, lest he risk being deprived of his lands. The task of remaking Liegnitz into a Lutheran territory briefly ran off the tracks when the nobleman brought in to oversee the reorganization of worship himself adopted Schwenkfeldian views. In Wismar and Emden, too, pressure to set a Lutheran cast on the local Reformation was resisted for a decade or longer. Such cases were the exception, however. Lutheran and Catholic hostility combined with the simple fact of the region's greater distance from Zurich to make north Germany decidedly inhospitable to those of a sacramentarian inclination.[67]

Despite the hostility of Luther and his associates to what Melanchthon called the threat of a "horrible mutation of the church," and despite the obstacles that this placed in the way of Reformed expansion in the northern half of Germany, patterns of reformation that can be classified as more Swiss than

Saxon had gained a tight hold across a significant part of the German-speaking world by 1530. Not only had they triumphed in the larger cantons of Switzerland and in certain free imperial cities closest to the Swiss border; they were advancing elsewhere in the south, the most densely populated and prosperous part of the land, as the 1520s drew to a close. Zwingli was the evangelical churchman most actively involved in building potential military and political alliances in defense of Protestantism, for Luther continued to maintain that under no circumstances was resistance to the emperor justified, even as Charles V disentangled himself from his other obligations and turned his attention to the empire. The Zurich reformer built good relations with the most active princely champion of evangelical alliance, Philip of Hesse, who had his eyes fixed on the restoration of his cousin Ulrich to the Habsburg-occupied southern duchy of Württemberg.[68] Had the prevailing circumstances not suddenly changed in 1530–31, it is possible to imagine scenarios in which the first great wave of Protestant expansion in Germany eventuated in a Reformed south and a Lutheran north or even a Germany as a whole more Reformed than Lutheran.

But the state of affairs did suddenly change in 1530–31. Specifically, three political and military events between December 1530 and October 1531 dramatically strengthened the relative influence of the Wittenbergers and ensured Lutheranism's subsequent domination of German Protestantism. First, as 1530 drew to a close, Philip of Hesse's long efforts to establish a basis for a grand evangelical alliance finally bore fruit, but the northern Protestant princes, led by the elector of Saxony, would agree to the formation of this Schmalkaldic League only on the condition that its members agree to subscribe to either the Augsburg or the Tetrapolitan Confession. Philip accepted this demand. The Swiss did not. The evangelical alliance that took shape within the empire thus became an instrument for imposing the hegemony of Lutheran eucharistic views.[69]

Second, ten months later, at a conference summoned by the elector of Saxony at Torgau, the elector's legal councillors convinced Luther that his commitment to the principle that the powers that be are ordained of God did not necessarily imply that the emperor could not be resisted. Within the constitutional structure of the empire, the elector's lawyers persuaded him, the territorial princes shared power with the emperor. Among their powers was the right to resist unjust imperial laws. Luther would henceforward endorse the possibility of armed resistance to the emperor in increasingly strenuous tones. Should Charles V ever seek to uphold by force the imperial legislation that forbade innovations in religion, the evangelical princes and magistrates could be confident that they were doing their Christian duty in opposing him.[70]

Finally, just as the political strength of Lutheranism increased within the empire, the course of action Zwingli championed in Switzerland ended in disaster. For two years prior to 1531, the reformer had gained increasing sway over the formulation of Zurich's foreign policy, which he sought to bend to the cause of promoting the expansion of the true faith. In 1529, the aggressive use of force produced a success that encouraged further such adventures. The backdrop was the surge of evangelical expansion within the confederation in the wake of the Bern disputation. This period saw a multiplying of incidents in which evangelicals encouraging iconoclasm encountered Catholic authorities demanding that sacrilege be duly punished. Vituperation mounted. The Zurich authorities schemed to find ways to prevent Catholic officials from assuming positions of ascendancy within those territories ruled jointly by several cantons. When those in command at Catholic Schwyz executed an evangelical minister whom they had illegally seized in a territory beyond their jurisdiction, Zurich marched a large force to the border of the forest cantons at Kappel, ignoring pleas for caution from the Bernese. The eager mediation of the cantons not immediately involved in the quarrel allowed this so-called First Kappel War to be concluded without a battle. The laconically worded peace treaty negotiated at Kappel constrained the Catholic cantons to dissolve their alliance with the Austrian Habsburgs and to allow the inhabitants of each community within the common lordships and affiliated territories to determine their own religious fate, thereby opening the way for the further advance of the evangelical cause in these territories.[71]

Even while the First Kappel War seemed to prove the value of using force to defend the interests of the evangelical cause, the negotiated outcome profoundly disappointed Zwingli, who had hoped to administer a crushing defeat to the Catholic cantons and to obtain a clear statement enabling the true Gospel to be preached everywhere in Switzerland. He continued to push for action even after his efforts to forge an alliance with Philip of Hesse and the German evangelicals foundered. He advanced schemes to bring the smaller cantons of the confederation under the control of Bern and Zurich and argued that the ambiguous wording of the first Kappel peace should be interpreted as permission for the free preaching of the Gospel throughout the common territories, even where the Catholics were in the majority. In the face of Bernese caution, Zurich agreed in May 1531 that for the moment it would fight the Catholic cantons only through economic means, namely, by imposing a blockade on the importation of foodstuffs. But noises of open war continued to sound from the city, alarming the Catholic territories further. Fatefully, these were not backed up with serious mobilization.

By October, the other Protestant cantons were eager to call off the blockade, but Zurich persisted. The understandably alarmed Catholic cantons chose this as the moment to declare war. Some seven thousand troops struck at Kappel. Zurich was able hastily to mobilize a force only half that size, including many of the canton's clergymen who believed they enjoyed no privileged status and took up pikes alongside their fellow citizens. In a short battle on October 11, the Catholic forces routed the Zurichers. Among their five hundred casualties were twenty-five clergymen, including Zwingli himself. It was a final testimony to his preeminence that the victorious Catholics sought out his corpse, ceremoniously quartered and burned it, and then mixed the ashes with manure. Were the Zurichers still inclined to honor relics of their saints, there would be nothing of him to venerate.

The defeat at Kappel completed the sequence of events that foreclosed the possibility of Swiss prominence in an evangelical political alliance within the empire. The peace that followed required Zurich to renounce all alliances beyond the confederation. Within Switzerland Catholicism was restored in several of the common lordships that had been the scene of greatest tension between the two religious camps in the preceding years. Reforming churchmen recognized that they had no choice but to renounce the dream of obtaining liberty for evangelical preaching everywhere in the confederation, and the rapid Protestant expansion of the preceding five years ceased. The Catholics still dominated in a majority of the cantons, even though the Protestants controlled the largest ones and thus comprised roughly three-fifths of the total population. Zurich's government took steps to ensure that no minister would ever again establish the influence over foreign policy that Zwingli had been able to accumulate. Five weeks after receiving the doleful news of the events at Kappel, the already ailing Oecolampadius also died. "Sacramentarianism" was now emarginated politically within the Holy Roman Empire and bereft of its leading theologians. Zwingli had lived long enough and worked successfully enough to oversee the triumph of Reformed reformations in much of Switzerland, but new leaders were desperately required if they were to survive and inspire similar transformations elsewhere in Europe.

2

THE SECOND GENERATION
Switzerland and Germany

I n the decades after 1531, a new generation of Reformed prophets stepped into the breach created by the deaths of Zwingli and Oecolampadius. Zwingli's post at Zurich's Great Minster was assumed by a talented young theologian, Heinrich Bullinger, who defended Zwingli's ecclesiastical legacy within the city, overcame the threat of isolation that menaced the Zurich church for more than a decade after the defeat at Kappel, and became the most prominent figure within a group of closely allied theologians who restated Zwingli's positions in a way that reached a far wider European audience than Zwingli himself had ever done. Although the quarter of a century after 1531 was a period of retreat and marginalization for Reformed currents within the Holy Roman Empire, one small territory in Germany's northwest corner, East Friesland, was sufficiently isolated to resist the forces promoting the triumph of Lutheranism elsewhere. Under the guiding hand of the refugee Polish aristocrat John a Lasco, this became a center for the dissemination of Reformed propaganda into neighboring areas. A Lasco also played a central role in shaping the institutions of the little churches established by French and Dutch refugees in London that likewise became a model for other new Reformed churches. Finally, the steady expansion of Bernese influence within the Francophone marches of western Switzerland combined with the arrival of another refugee of exceptional talents as both a church organizer and a theologian, John Calvin, to turn Geneva into a still more celebrated model of a godly Christian community and center for the diffusion of Reformed influences. Together, Bullinger, a Lasco, Calvin, and their associates and contemporaries enriched and codified the theological legacy of the first generation of Reformed thinkers, oversaw the creation of new Reformed churches that became centers for the dissemination of the cause, and established a network of contacts that reached from the British Isles to the fringes of the Ottoman Empire. In so doing, they laid the groundwork for the dramatic expansion of Reformed churches across Europe in the 1550s and 1560s.

The leading Reformed theologians of this period were all independent thinkers who did not see eye to eye on every point of doctrine, while the churches that became the source and model for the Reformed tradition's expansion differed from each other in crucial organizational features.Relations among key leaders of the second generation grew strained at times as a result of this disaccord. Yet, aided by political pressures that nudged them toward cooperation, they managed to build and preserve effective working relations with one another and to draw up a series of confessional statements that expressed their wide areas of agreement. This generation thus witnessed at once a widening of the range of views and institutional arrangements associated with the Reformed cause and a codification of the basic principles that came to define the tradition. If the next generation of Reformed expansion would be characterized by tension between the various models of church organization elaborated in these years, disagreements over these issues would never rupture the foundation of agreement. Indeed, the diversity of institutions that emerged in this period may be seen even as a source of future strength, for it enabled the cause to establish itself under an unusually broad range of political circumstances.

In 1976, Fritz Büsser, professor of ecclesiastical history at Zurich, published an article in the *Neue Zürcher Zeitung* with the bold title "Bullinger, Not Calvin."[1] His claim in the article was actually modest: Bullinger was a more influential biblical commentator than Calvin. Since the publication of his article, however, the assertion that Calvin was not the only second-generation Reformed theologian of influence, and that in one domain or another he was rivaled or outshone by another Reformed churchman of his time, has become a leitmotif of scholarship on this period. The most convenient English-language introduction to Bullinger's life and work insists that his chief publication, the *Decades,* was at least as important as Calvin's *Institutes* to the development of Reformed thought.[2] A leading historian of Reformed theology has suggested that the *Commonplaces* of two other authors of this generation, Peter Martyr Vermigli and Wolfgang Musculus, may have been more important models for later Reformed theology than Calvin's *Institutes*.[3] "If we were to identify one author and one book which represented the centre of theological gravity of the Elizabethan Church," the chief authority on that subject has written, "it would not be Calvin's *Institutes* but the *Common Places* of Peter Martyr. . . . And at least equally influential was Bullinger, whose view of the religious role of Christian magistracy was well adapted to political reality in Elizabethan England."[4] A major reason specialists insist upon speaking of the Reformed rather than of Calvinism lies with this growing recognition of the importance of second-generation theologians other than Calvin.

This chapter will trace the history of the Reformed cause within German-speaking Switzerland and the empire in the generation after Zwingli's death with emphasis on the work and ideas of the still fairly obscure and inadequately studied individuals who assumed leadership roles within it. The next chapter will look at Switzerland's French-speaking borderlands and at the far better known work of Calvin. By the end of part I, readers should have a firm basis for assessing the precise contribution of all of the major figures of the initial generations who together articulated the multivocal Reformed tradition.

BULLINGER AND GERMAN SWITZERLAND

Bullinger was born in 1504 in the Aargau, one of the regions close to Zurich under the common lordship of the confederation where evangelical worship was outlawed following the Second Kappel War. Clerical concubinage was not simply widespread there, as in so many other parts of Switzerland; it was unofficially sanctioned by the bishop in Constance, who waived all penalties against the offense in return for payment of an annual fee. As the fifth and youngest son of the dean of the capitular church of Bremgarten and his steady consort, young Heinrich anticipated a pattern that became common after the Reformation when he left home at twelve for a higher education intended to prepare him to follow his father into the clergy.[5]

Like so many other early spokesmen of the Reformed tradition, Bullinger found himself transported by his education from humanism to open revolt against the church of Rome. He was first sent to the distant but celebrated humanist gymnasium of Emmerich, in the duchy of Cleves. He moved on to the university of Cologne, where he arrived in 1519, just as the Luther affair was on everybody's tongue. Feeling that he had to decide for himself the issues that were leading the ecclesiastical hierarchy to condemn the Saxon monk as a heretic, he embarked on a systematic program of reading that started with Peter Lombard's *Sentences,* the standard medieval introduction to theology, then compared this with the church fathers whom Lombard cited and with the Bible, and culminated in an examination of Luther's Reformation treatises of 1520. Concluding that Luther's writings were more faithful to the original sources than Lombard's, Bullinger began "to abhor completely the papal

1. "The Light is Restored to the Candlestick." This Dutch print of the mid-seventeenth century illustrates how the Reformed viewed their cause not as having been inspired by one or two outstanding prophets and founding fathers, but as a collective effort to restore the pure Gospel that began prior to the Reformation with Wyclif and Hus and involved Lutheran as well as Reformed figures of the sixteenth century. In the foreground a pope, a cardinal, a monk, and a demon vainly try to blow out the candle of the restored light with false learning and pretty lies. The theologians discussing Scripture around the table are, clockwise from lower left, Jan Hus, Martin Bucer, Heinrich Bullinger, Peter Martyr Vermigli, John Knox, Philip Melanchthon, Jerome of Prague, Huldrych Zwingli, Martin Luther, Girolamo Zanchi, John Calvin, Theodore Beza, William Perkins, Johannes Oecolampadius, Matthias Flacius Illyricus, and John Wyclif. On the wall are portraits of still other, lesser Protestant theologians, historians, and political champions. (By permission Atlas van Stolk, Rotterdam)

teaching." Melanchthon's *Commonplaces,* encountered late in 1521, pleased him still more.[6]

Bullinger returned home to Bremgarten in 1522 a young "Martinian" who had renounced his previous intention of entering the Carthusian order and would accept the post offered him as head of the cloister school at Kappel only after negotiating special terms that exempted him from taking monastic vows or attending mass. At Kappel, he initiated a systematic program of Bible reading and exegesis for the benefit of those monks not destined for advanced theological training, open to all who cared to attend, that anticipated the Zurich *Prophezei.* He soon heard Zwingli and Jud preach and contacted them. By September 1524, he felt close enough to Zwingli to approach him with his ideas about the Eucharist, which had evolved, under the teachings of the Waldensians, toward a symbolic understanding of the ritual. In 1527, he spent five months in Zurich improving his mastery of ancient languages and regularly attending the *Prophezei.* He impressed the Zurich authorities sufficiently for them to send him along with their delegation to the Bern disputation, where he met Bucer, Blaurer, and Haller. The Zurich synod urged him to become a parish minister, and in 1528 he did so in Kappel following the secularization of the cloister.

In February 1529, Bullinger's father announced to his surprised parishioners in Bremgarten that he had been preaching false doctrines for years but now had seen the light. Although evangelical sentiment was spreading through the Aargau in the wake of the Bern disputation, a narrow majority of the congregation was still loyal to the old ways and decided to remove their suddenly heterodox priest. Several candidates were invited to preach trial sermons as possible replacements. The younger Bullinger was one, and his audition was literally smashing—his sermon was so powerful that the Bremgarteners stripped the images from their church and burned them. He got the job.

Bullinger was able to remain in his hometown for only two years before evangelical worship was prohibited throughout the Aargau following the Second Kappel War. His reputation was such that Zurich, Basel, Bern, and Appenzell all quickly offered him positions. This competition for his services gave him some critical leverage in dealing with the Zurich authorities, who had been convinced by the military disaster at Kappel that it was dangerous to allow ministers to affect government policy, and who had thus decreed that henceforward preachers would be required to refrain from discussing political questions. Bullinger refused to accept the position as Zwingli's successor at the Great Minster on these terms, arguing that the pastor's calling included the obligation to proclaim the Bible forthrightly, even if this might involve pointing out that policies and actions of the ruling authorities were un-Christian. The city fathers agreed to allow the ministers to set forth their criticisms of government policy privately in writing, and Bullinger accepted the post. Soon he was also put in charge of overseeing the other Zurich ministers and handling their communication with the city magistrates, responsibilities that would later come to be called those of the church's Antistes. He was just twenty-seven at the time, and would exercise these responsibilities for more than forty years until his death in 1575.

As the leader of Zurich's church, Bullinger quickly emerged as a staunch defender of the system of church organization and discipline established by Zwingli. Early in 1532, Jud proposed a purely ecclesiastical morals court for the city. Bullinger argued strongly against this and ultimately convinced Jud to alter his position. As the Genevan church emerged over the years as an alternative model of Reformed church organization, Bullinger would reiterate and amplify these arguments in private correspondence and in his *Treatise on Excommunication* (1568). Against the Genevan appeal to New Testament passages that suggest the existence of an independent system of discipline in the early church, he maintained that the necessity for such an independent system ceased when the civil magistrates became Christian. Where the magistrates were Christian, the institutions of ancient Israel offered the appropriate model, with pious kings overseeing the temple and punishing those who violated both tablets of Ten Commandments. Bullinger also denied that Paul's injunction in I Corinthians to put away wicked persons justified excluding them from the Lord's Supper. God ordered all Israelites to keep Passover, and Jesus did not exclude even Judas from the Last Supper. These were the arguments that convinced the Zurich authorities in 1532 to require those punished for morals offenses by the Ehegericht to take communion.[7]

While Bullinger accepted and justified magisterial control over the church, he also battled to defend a measure of clerical sway and authority. He was the chief draftsman of an ordinance accepted by Zurich's Rat in October 1532 that created a joint committee of magistrates and ministers to oversee the territorial church. Together, eight councilmen and all the city's pastors, under the joint chairmanship of a minister and a council member, exercised jurisdiction over the doctrine and behavior of the cantonal clergy and appointed new ministers, whose fitness was first determined by a commission composed of two ministers, two professors, and two members of the city council. Determining the penalties for clergymen censured by the synod was left up to the civic authorities. Bullinger and his fellow chapter members also successfully defended the continued existence and autonomy of the Great Minster, a capitular church. He somewhat less successfully opposed the civic use of confiscated church property for purposes other than supporting clergymen, schools, and the care of the poor, arguing, as did a growing chorus of Protestant theologians in these years, that to put church goods to profane and god-less uses was to commit sacrilege. (This argument would henceforward be a key theological underpinning of Protestant clerical assertiveness.) Finally he and his fellow ministers continued to seek to influence civic legislation, for he, no less than Zwingli, believed that the best "civil and politic laws" were those that "according to the circumstances of every place, person, state, and time, do come nearest unto the precepts of the ten commandments and the rule of charity." The many clerical petitions that survive in the city archives show the clergy pressing urgently for improvements in the system of poor relief, for stricter measures against drunkenness and blasphemy, and for a reduction in the number of holy days.[8]

For much of the 1530s and 1540s it appeared that the Zwinglian legacy might be either dissolved into a broader Protestant consensus or exposed to diplomatic isolation and potential annihilation. Luther saw the outcome of the battle of Kappel as a providential event that revealed God's hatred of the "fanatics." In its aftermath, as we shall see, he redoubled his warnings to German rulers and cities to avoid their errors. Within Switzerland, the other Protestant cantons had to pay reparations for the Second Kappel War and were angered by policies of Zurich that had precipitated the disaster. Probably the central development in the internal politics of the young Protestant movement in the 1530s was the tireless campaign Bucer mounted from Strasbourg to define a middle way between the eucharistic views of Luther and Zwingli in order to heal the rifts in the Protestant camp. His quest was furthered by the young Calvin, who first made a name for himself in 1536 with the publication of *The Institutes of the Christian Religion.* Calvin articulated a middle position often defined as that of a "spiritual real presence": when faithful Christians consumed the bread and wine of the Lord's Supper, Christ became truly present within them in spirit. Reunionist efforts gained further impetus from the willingness of Melanchthon in Wittenberg to accept a more spiritual interpretation of the real presence than was characteristic of Luther or most of Luther's allies in the eucharistic debates; in large measure Melanchthon assumed this stance thanks to Oecolampadius's and Bucer's historical arguments demonstrating that an explicit doctrine of a physical real presence was a relatively late development in the history of the church. If Luther could be induced to moderate his hostility to the Zurichers, the common ground Bucer, Calvin, and Melanchthon were beginning to define appeared to offer a good possibility of reuniting all of the territories that had instituted Protestant church orders.

In May 1536, Bucer's faith that goodwill and ambiguous words could reconcile people of contrary views bore fruit in his greatest triumph as an ecclesiastical diplomat: the negotiation of an agreement with Luther and Melanchthon known as the Wittenberg Concord that declared that Christ's body and blood were "truly and substantially" present in the Eucharist. In the flush of goodwill that followed, Luther declared that he was prepared to work with the Swiss and indicated his approval of a confessional document, the First Helvetic Confession, that the Swiss Protestants had drawn up as part of the diplomatic efforts aimed at achieving reunion. Bern received the Wittenberg Concord favorably and in 1537 appointed a new Lutheran minister, Simon Sulzer. From 1538 to 1542 Calvin worked closely alongside Bucer in Strasbourg, met a number of Lutheran theologians at the parleys of Haguenau, Worms, and Regensburg, and showed himself committed to Bucer's reunionist efforts. The Zurichers, however, remained suspicious of the document. Its assertion that Christ's body and blood were "substantially" present in the Lord's Supper sounded to them at once too vague and too similar to the scholastic terminology of transubstantiation that all Protestants had rejected. They had also been stung too harshly by Luther's hostility in the past to believe his new-found expressions of goodwill.[9]

Bullinger steered the Zurich church through this period of potential isolation without departing too far from the sacramental doctrine of Zwingli and Oecolampadius. Throughout the 1530s and 1540s, he dispatched a steady stream of letters to evangelical churchmen throughout Switzerland and Germany expounding and defending his understanding of the sacrament. Once again, the actions of Luther and his supporters contributed to maintaining barriers within the Protestant camp. Despite his conciliatory words of the later 1530s, Luther could not let go of his antipathy to the sacramentarians of Zurich. Between 1541 and 1544 he made increasingly intemperate remarks that culminated in his *Brief Confession Concerning the Holy Sacrament,* which lit into "Karlstadt, Zwingli, Oecolampadius, Stenkefeld [sic], and their disciples at Zurich and wherever they are." This lack of charity dismayed Calvin, who esteemed Oecolampadius and depended on Swiss support for Genevan independence. During the same years, Sulzer's attempts to remodel the Bernese church along Lutheran lines encountered resistance, for attachment to a Swiss-style reformation remained strong within the Bernese clergy, above all in the rural parishes. Finally, the political benefits of alliance with Germany's Lutherans began to look much less attractive to the Swiss when war erupted within the empire in 1546 and Charles V defeated the princes at Mühlberg in the following year. A year later the Bernese government ousted Sulzer and replaced him with a protégé of Bullinger's, Johannes Haller, signaling a return to a policy of ecclesiastical alignment with Zurich.

Calvin for his part wrote to Bullinger soon after Luther turned his back to the Swiss to see if their differences over the Eucharist could be worked out. Bullinger replied with a written statement of his views. Calvin expressed reservations and tried to nudge him into modifying them. He refused to do so. After five years of fitful correspondence, Calvin took it upon himself to go to Zurich, where in May 1549 he succeeded in negotiating a joint statement on the question, the Consensus Tigurinus. The text of this agreement stated that the celebration of the Eucharist involved both a physical and a spiritual eating. Christ was truly present, but the physical and the spiritual eating occurred separately from each other, not concurrently as Calvin had sought to maintain. The document thus both allowed for a real spiritual presence yet retained the Zwinglian position that Christ was speaking metaphorically when he said, "This is my body" and that the material world was distinct from the realm of the spirit.[10] The Consensus Tigurinus became the basis for an enduring rapprochement between the churches of Zurich and Geneva, one that saw the leaders of both work closely together, on occasion even keeping silent about the disparities of outlook between them in order to lend support to the other. The Bernese likewise accepted the Consensus Tigurinus, although Basel did not, since this relatively tolerant center of humanistic study and publishing distanced itself from Zurich and Geneva for several generations from 1550 to the early seventeenth century. In bringing together the churches of Geneva, Zurich, and Bern and defining a eucharistic position that permitted a range of emphases and understandings, the Consensus Tigurinus was a major event in the history of the Reformed churches, for it served to conjoin the troika of churches critical to the cause's survival in Switzerland and its expansion beyond. As we shall see, the consensus was soon followed by a bitter renewal of the eucharistic controversies that set both Calvin and Bullinger against the majority of Germany's leading Protestant theologians and cemented the division of magisterial Protestantism between Lutherans and Reformed.

Bullinger was also centrally involved in drafting some years later the second major confessional document that solidified the agreement of most of Switzerland's Protestant churches with Zurich: the Second Helvetic Confession of 1566. This originated as a personal statement of Bullinger's written in 1561 for presentation to the Zurich Rat on his death as a testament of his faith. He showed it to Vermigli and others. Amid the political crisis that broke out within the empire in 1566 after the elector palatine introduced Reformed elements into his territorial church (see chapter 7), Bullinger recognized that the document could be of use to the elector as a distilled statement of the basic Christian principles with which he was aligning himself. He circulated it among the Protestant cities of the region and rapidly obtained the signatures of the ministers of Zurich, Bern, Schaffhausen, Saint-Gall, Chur, Mulhouse, Biel, and Geneva. Within the next decade, the ministers of Neuchâtel indicated their approval, as did many of the Reformed churches founded elsewhere by this date, including those of France, Scotland, and Hungary.[11]

Bullinger's drafting of the Second Helvetic Confession was just a tiny part of his work as a theologian and author.[12] He completed his first notable treatise, *On the Origin of Errors* (1528), while still in Kappel. This added to Zwingli's psychological explanation of the impulses leading people into idolatry a compelling historical account of the gradual corruption of Christian worship through the introduction over time of new rituals. Perhaps more than any other work, it stoked the later Reformed suspicion of the least ritual innovation as a dangerous step down the slippery slope to popery. If the Reformed churches would be always reforming, and if their members would be quick to see small liturgical innovations as huge threats, it would be in large measure because Bullinger had taught them how easily and insensibly rot had infected the church in the past.[13]

Shortly after arriving in Zurich, Bullinger began to publish Latin commentaries on the various books of the New Testament, the first systematic project of commentaries attempted by a Reformed theologian. From 1533 on, these compositions sounded a theme that would become ever stronger in the writings of all of the main Reformed theologians of this generation, namely, that those who had seen the light of the Gospel sinned if they hid their true convictions and continued to take part in the rituals of the Catholic church. Commenting on I Corinthians, he took Paul's warning not to be an idolator like the ancient Israelites who ate with the daughters of Moab and bowed down to their idols as a warning against taking communion in the Roman church. Those who lived where the true faith was persecuted, he subsequently advised, should keep from ungodly assemblies, teach children the true faith at home, and profess their faith publicly as often as circumstances permitted. Once true worship was allowed they should dissolve all "private and domestical churches" and join in a common assembly.[14] It was a call for withdrawal from the church of Rome.

This advice made its way into his most important work, a collection of fifty sermons organized in groups of ten that came to be known in some parts of Europe as the *Decades* (its Latin and English title) and in others as the *Housebook* (its German and Dutch title). Published between 1549 and 1551, the sermons were originally intended for the edification of the clergy and for pulpit use as homilies. They soon were recognized to offer a valuable summary of doctrine for laymen as well (hence the bestowal upon the collection of the name *Hausbuch* by its first translator into German, Haller). Avoiding overt polemics yet rebutting key Catholic objections to Protestant doctrines, the collection began with a concise exposition of the nature of God's word, the doctrine of justification by faith alone, and the Apostle's Creed; devoted two full sets of ten sermons to explaining the implications of the Ten Commandments and the nature of God's law; and finally explored the nature and worship of God and of the holy catholic church, understood as the invisible community of the faithful of all epochs. The book proved such a good summary of doctrine that later Reformed church synods recommended its purchase to deficient ministers and advised groups of laymen in communities too small to support their own minister to read a sermon from the book each Sunday when a minister from a neighboring church could not come to preach.[15] Bullinger reworked the sermons into a more systematic exposition of doctrine in 1556, *The Sum of the Christian Religion.* He also wrote polemical and topical works against Anabaptism, anti-Trinitarianism, and Catholicism, more focused expositions of specific points of doctrine, and a practical guide to Christian marriage.

Zwingli's theological writings, with their classicizing and at times abstractly philosophical language, never succeeded in reaching a large audience; his best-selling single book was printed a mere six times. Bullinger's writings attained far wider dissemination. The *Decades* went through 32 editions and the related *Sum of Christian Religion* a further 30 by 1670. *On the Origin of Errors* was reprinted 17 times through 1621. The 401 total editions of works from his pen that his bibliographers have identified dwarf the 162 known Zwingli editions, even without counting the many reprintings of the confessions of faith and synodal decisions that Bullinger helped to draft.[16] The circulation of his works peaked in the 1550s and 1560s but continued for decades after his death (table 2.1). Beyond their original Latin and German versions, they proved steady sellers in English translation to the 1580s and appeared in more than forty French editions in the 1550s and 1560s. They attained their most enduring popularity in the Netherlands, where the *Housebook* continued to be printed throughout much of the seventeenth century and became a staple of pious households and one of two approved sources for homilies aboard the ships of the Dutch East India Company.[17]

Bullinger's theology remained largely faithful to Zwingli's, but the younger man often expressed his views in distinctive terminology and parted company with his predecessor in a number of ways. While vigorously upholding Zwingli's position that the sacraments were signs and that the words of the institution were spoken figuratively, he also accepted that the eucharistic eating entailed a genuine communion with Christ. He frequently had recourse to the image of the sworn covenant to emphasize the constancy and reliability of God's promises to man, a constancy that should in turn inspire men to make a pact to serve God. This covenant metaphor, which probably came easily to Bullinger, living as he did in a region where peasant leagues and confederations were so much a part of the political order, would be developed still more fully and systematically by later Reformed theologians. The one and eternal testament or covenant of God that Bullinger identified in his work of that title

TABLE 2.1

Editions of Bullinger by Language, 1520–1670

	Total	Latin	German	French	English	Dutch	Italian	Czech	Polish
1520–29	4	2	2						
1530–39	41	26	13		1			1	
1540–49	48	24	10	1	12	1			
1550–59	90	38	27	17	5	1	1		1
1560–69	80	31	14	24	4	7			
1570–79	35	12	12	2	9				
1580–89	33	8	11		7	7			
1590–99	19	5	10			4			
1600–70	47	9	12		1	25			
Uncertain date	4	1	3						
Total	401	156	114	44	39	45	1	1	1

Source: Joachim Staedtke, *Heinrich Bullinger Bibliographie, Werke*, part 1, vol. 1 (Zurich, 1972). The table omits confessions of faith, synodal decrees, and prefaces to other authors' works written by Bullinger.

(1534) was instituted between God and the ancient Israelites and renewed by Abraham, Moses, David, and Christ. This vision of a single covenant underlay his willingness to see the ecclesiastical institutions of ancient Israel as an enduring model for Christians. He expressed a strong sense of God's all-controlling providence and upheld the predestination of the elect, but he was hesitant to affirm the doctrine of double predestination (that is, that God also chose those whom he condemned to reprobation). When Calvin began to uphold double predestination in pamphlet controversies in the early 1550s, Bullinger admonished him in private letters that he was delving more deeply into God's mysteries than Scripture permitted.[18]

Other churchmen active in Zurich between 1531 and 1575 also carried on Zwingli's legacy and contributed to the city's importance as a center for the dissemination of Reformed ideas. Its school for training future ministers attracted prominent scholars, including Conrad Pellikan (1478–1556), an early Hebraist and the author of an eight-volume set of commentaries covering the entire Bible, and Theodor Bibliander (ca. 1504–64), a student of oriental languages who prepared one of the first Latin translations of the Koran. Rudolf Gwalther (1519–86), Bullinger's student at Kappel, followed him to Zurich and served as a pastor in the city for thirty-three years before succeeding him as Antistes. His Latin homilies on many books of the New Testament gained wide circulation.[19] The most distinguished theologian of all to settle in Zurich was the Florentine-born Peter Martyr Vermigli, who spent the last years of his peripatetic career on the banks of the Limmat. Born in 1499, Vermigli received an excellent education at Padua that was at once humanistic and scholastic and won renown within the Catholic church as a preacher, expositor, and prior of the Augustinian order. During stints in Spoleto, Naples, and Lucca, he became acquainted with such noted Catholic advocates of personal spiritual renewal as Gasparo Contarini and Juan de Valdés and encountered the writings of Bucer and Zwingli. By 1542, contact with circles of advanced evangelicals in Lucca led him to conclude that the rituals of the Roman church involved an intolerable idolatry; the reconstitution of the Roman Inquisition to deal with the problem of heresy in Lucca then prompted him to flee across the Alps. Already a mature scholar, he took up a post lecturing on the Old Testament in Strasbourg, where he soon earned a reputation as an expositor that eclipsed even Bucer's. The Augsburg Interim crisis forced him to Oxford for four years. After a second stay at Strasbourg, he succeeded Pellikan in Zurich in 1556.[20]

Vermigli had imbibed a strong doctrine of double predestination from his Paduan Augustinian teachers, who were loyal to this minority strand of late medieval theology. His views on this question troubled Bibliander, who believed that God wished to save all mankind. In the debate between them that ensued, Vermigli defended his views so successfully that the other Zurich churchmen relieved Bibliander of his teaching responsibilities. The space that had previously existed within the city to dissent from the doctrine of predestination was now eliminated. While in Zurich, Vermigli began to publish his lectures as a series of commentaries on the books of the Old Testament. Others took up the task after his death in 1562, then excerpted and reshaped his commentaries into a more systematic exposition of doctrine, the *Commonplaces,* that became a standard text for theological instruction after their 1576 publication. The work appeared in fifteen editions to 1656 and won praise from such paragons of learning as Justus Julius Scaliger, who deemed Vermigli one of "the two most excellent theologians of our times" along with Calvin. Not only did Vermigli espouse an independently formulated doctrine of double predestination similar to Calvin's; his doctrine of the Eucharist likewise accorded with that of Calvin and the Consensus Tigurinus. He lacked sharply defined views about the precise institutions of a properly reformed church.

The patchy survival of the Zurich school's matriculation registers leaves us ill informed about its student body. Those known to have studied there include Marten Micron, the eminent pastor of the Dutch refugee church in London who called the Zurich theologians "our fathers, teachers and guides in the reformation of the church." In the years between 1559 and 1610, for which matriculation records survive, an average of fourteen students enrolled per year to study theology.[21]

After flirting with Lutheranism between 1537 and 1548, Bern became no less a stronghold of the Reformed tradition than Zurich. From 1549 to 1560, its municipal secondary school housed another prominent expositor of Reformed theology: Wolfgang Musculus. Musculus was the austere Augsburg preacher who said he would rather see his daughter enter a whorehouse than attend a dance (see chapter 1). He left Augsburg during the Interim crisis, arriving in Bern just as the church of its recently conquered French-speaking territory, the Pays de Vaud, was being divided between partisans of a Genevan-style church with an autonomous system of consistorial discipline and defenders of a Zurich-style church under magisterial control. His major work, the *Common Places of the Christian Religion* (1560), was the first systematic exposition of Reformed doctrine arranged around the discussion of a menu of topics or commonplaces. The work was hailed as an effective introduction to theology, was translated into French and English, and went through ten editions in all, winning enthusiastic readers in lands as far afield as Poland and Hungary.[22] Perhaps its most noteworthy feature was its assertive defense of magisterial control over a state church, which Musculus had already advocated forcefully in Augsburg and which he now championed against the partisans of the emerging Reformed countermodel established in Geneva. In a properly structured Christian commonwealth, he claimed, the institutional church was an administrative agency of the state. Christian magistrates had the obligation to preserve God's honor and promote Christian piety. By virtue of their *merum imperium,* or absolute authority, over their territories—a concept he drew from Roman law—their duties extended to making ecclesiastical laws, appointing ministers, and generally seeking to advance true piety. So strong was his sense of the appropriateness of magisterial control over the ministry that he deemed instances of clerical usurpation of independence from the magistrate to be the mystery of iniquity spoken of in Paul's letter to the Thessalonians. Musculus's *Common Places* would be one of the chief sources for later theories of state control over the church within the Reformed tradition.[23]

Musculus's eucharistic theology partook of the effort of his early Strasbourg teacher and patron Bucer to define a middle ground between Zurich and Wittenberg. The words of the institution were not merely symbolic, but neither was Christ physically present in the eucharistic elements. Instead He was both sacramentally and spiritually present and was conveyed in the former manner to all who partook of the ritual but in the latter manner only to genuine believers. On predestination, Musculus espoused a cautious variant of double predestination.[24]

The wide dissemination achieved by the writings of Bullinger, Vermigli, and Musculus spread their ideas far beyond the original heartland of the Reformation. So too did a final aspect of their work, their letter writing. Letters were one of the major means churchmen used in this period to keep abreast of events unfolding throughout Europe, to advise and console kindred spirits in distant lands, and to win converts to their views. Their reach extended beyond the original recipients, for edifying letters were often copied and passed along to other potentially interested parties without the express consent of their authors, who wrote in full awareness of this possibility.[25] No Protestant reformer appears to have kept more couriers busy carrying letters to distant lands than Bullinger. Some fifteen thousand letters to and from him survive, more than ten times as many as survive for Zwingli and more than three times as many as for either Luther or Calvin, although it is impossible to know the fraction of each one's correspondence lost or destroyed. Like Zwingli, Bullinger conducted his most intense epistolary relations with correspondents in and around Switzerland, most notably with the cities of Bern, Basel, Chur, Geneva, Schaffhausen, Saint-Gall, Constance, Augsburg, Strasbourg, and Heidelberg. Unlike his predecessor, he also corresponded frequently with people in England, Poland, Hungary, France, and Italy.[26]

The very mass of Bullinger's correspondence has kept it from being as well studied as it deserves to be. A team of scholars began publishing it in 1973, but it is so vast that at their current rate of progress they will not finish until

2109. The studies of the unpublished letters attempted so far offer tantalizing glimpses of their significance as a vehicle of clerical influence. Bullinger exchanged upward of fifteen hundred letters with correspondents in the Grisons, that large affiliated region to the southeast of the confederacy in which evangelical ideas continued to advance at the local option of the largely autonomous communities of the area even after the Second Peace of Kappel. These reveal the Zurich Antistes dispatching copies of his writings, suggesting candidates for clerical vacancies, offering advice about political and ecclesiastical matters of all sorts, and informing his correspondents in the region about the latest ecclesiastical and political developments across Europe. The southernmost towns of this region, notably Chiavenna, came to house sizable numbers of Italian evangelical refugees, who brought with them an intensely questioning, often highly rationalistic or spiritualistic outlook that would lead many to emerge as spokesmen for a range of radical positions. Many wrote Bullinger with their questions and ideas. When Camillo Renato advocated an idiosyncratic reinterpretation of the Lord's Supper and denied the validity of Catholic baptism, Bullinger wrote him to defend Zurich's position on the Eucharist and prepared a statement about the sacraments that a regional synod used to end the schism that threatened to divide the Italian refugees in the region. When, in the wake of these events, the churches of the region decided that they should convene synods at regular intervals in the future in order to maintain agreement among themselves about doctrine and worship, he reviewed and commented upon a draft of the plan. If one historian has judged Bullinger "the virtual protector of the Protestant churches of the Grisons," his letters were a critical instrument of that protection.[27]

Farther afield, Bullinger sought propitious moments to influence the policies of influential churchmen and political leaders. Together with Bucer, he organized in 1536 a concerted letter-writing campaign by Swiss and south German churchmen to woo the new archbishop of Canterbury, Thomas Cranmer. In that same year, he entertained several English merchants of evangelical inclinations who visited Zurich. The next year Gwalther's son traveled to England. These events initiated a set of contacts between Zurich and early English Protestants that grew more frequent after Zurich became a refuge for the Marian exiles. Many of Queen Elizabeth's first generation of bishops had had direct experience of Zurich and kept in regular contact with Bullinger and his associates, writing urgently for advice about the issues troubling their church and receiving a steady stream of counsel in return.[28] From 1543 onward, Hungarian evangelicals also began to visit Zurich and solicit advice from Bullinger. They sought his opinion on confession, church goods, the Eucharist, and the use of images in worship, all of which he spelled out in letters. A long open letter to the faithful in Hungary that he dispatched in 1551 offered a synopsis of the principal points of Reformed doctrine and a criticism of the false claims and ceremonies of the Roman church. It concluded by stressing the obligation of true believers living among papists or Turks to refrain from participating in their worship or ceremonies, referring readers to the excellent writings of "our beloved and worthy brother" Calvin on this subject. The letter circulated widely in manuscript before being printed twice in 1559 in separate localities. It was also partly in response to requests from Hungary for guidance about liturgical and institutional matters that Bullinger's son-in-law Ludwig Lavater wrote *On the Rites and Institutions of the Zurich Church* (1559), which made the Zurich manner of proceeding widely available in print for imitation elsewhere.[29] Polish correspondents also entered into contact with Bullinger from 1549 onward. He exchanged letters with more than a score of Poles and was drawn into the disputes that split the Polish church over the doctrine of the Trinity sufficiently to publish two works on the subject.[30] Through his letters as through his books, the ideas of the Zurich reformation reached far beyond their cradle.

REFORMED CURRENTS IN THE EMPIRE

While Reformed ideas began to reach as far afield as England and Poland during the 1530s, 1540s, and 1550s, they suffered repeated setbacks during these years in the Holy Roman Empire. The ebbing of Reformed currents within the empire resulted from three causes: (1) Luther's aggressive hostility to sacramentarian ideas; (2) the Schmalkaldic League's policy that only those who rejected these ideas could be admitted to the alliance; and (3) the two-stage war of the Schmalkaldic League, whose first phase from 1546 to 1547 ended with Charles V imposing an interim church settlement whose heavy component of Catholic ritual was repugnant to evangelical churchmen inclined toward Swiss simplicity, and whose second phase from 1552 to 1555 ended with the Peace of Augsburg, which, while granting legal toleration to Protestant state churches, restricted it to those that accepted the Augsburg Confession. The advance of Lutheran currents at the expense of Reformed was not all-conquering, however. On the northwest fringe of the empire, the little territory of East Friesland, isolated by its marshes and dunes, sheltered a territorial church of a Reformed orientation. Elsewhere, individual evangelicals continued to be drawn toward ideas that were closer in character to those of the Reformed than of a Lutheran orthodoxy that grew more rigid after Luther's death. Although Reformed currents lost ground within the empire, they were not entirely driven out.

Luther pulled out all of the stops in his campaign against the sacramentarians after Zwingli's death in battle. Augsburg having expelled its Lutheran preachers earlier in the same year, Luther wrote to his followers there to celebrate their baptisms and marriages among the Catholics rather than the Zwinglians, for the errors of the latter were worse than those of the former, he proclaimed. When the city fathers of Frankfurt dismissed a Lutheran preacher late in 1532, he warned the town's inhabitants in an open letter that their preachers now taught differently from him and should be shunned or, if possible, expelled. Adding insult to injury, he included with this a copy of his open letter of 1524 to the people of Mühlhausen against Thomas Muntzer. Other letters in a similar vein were sent to the city fathers of Münster, whose foremost evangelical, Bernhard Rothmann, had embraced a symbolic view of the Eucharist, and to the duke of East Prussia, where Schwenkfelders fleeing persecution in Silesia had settled.[31]

The consequences that resulted when Germany's Protestant princes made acceptance of the Augsburg Confession a requirement for their political support were soon revealed in different ways in Württemberg, Augsburg, and Münster. The south German duchy of Württemberg was the scene of one of the greatest early political triumphs for the evangelical cause, when a surprise attack in 1534 restored Duke Ulrich to the throne from which the Habsburgs had displaced him for rebellion in 1519. The peace treaty negotiated by the elector of Saxony expressly excluded sacramentarian views from any church settlement that might be imposed on the territory. Swiss and south German influences were so strong in the southern part of the duchy that the restored duke thought it best to bring in Blaurer from Constance to oversee the reform process here, while the northern part of the territory was put under the supervision of a Lutheran professor from Marburg. The duke pushed the two men to work together and even managed to induce them to hammer out a compromise eucharistic formula. In Augsburg, as agitation mounted from the increasingly Protestant population to eliminate the city's remaining pockets of Catholic worship and to secularize the church's property, the city council recognized that it could take the risk of offending the surrounding Catholic territories only if it could recover the support of the Saxon theologians and the Schmalkaldic League. It initiated diplomatic overtures to Wittenberg and permitted Lutheran preachers to return to the city in 1535, four years after they had been expelled. Münster meanwhile afforded an alarming lesson in what might happen if a civic reformation proceeded along lines that the Wittenbergers did not sanction. Its most prominent evangelical preacher, Rothmann, espoused an eclectic theology that drew heavily on Swiss ideas. The city council refused to approve any church order that jeopardized the city's ability to attract evangelical allies to aid it in defying its prince-bishop. By late 1533, however, it dared not expel Rothmann, for he had acquired backing among the townsfolk. Into the breach created by this deadlock came a swelling number of Melchiorite Anabaptist refugees, whose ideas, advanced in a situation in which the threat of punitive action against the city grew steadily greater, soon won Rothmann over to the concept of believers' baptism. The radicalization of the Münster reformation that followed culminated in the communitarian, polygamous despotism of the inspired prophet John of Leyden and, in 1535, in the conquest of the city by troops subsidized by the Imperial Circles. The Münster reformation was crushed, and the prereformation religious order restored.[32]

The negotiation of the Wittenberg Concord furthered the advance of Lutheran influences in the localities that once had come most strongly under the sway of the Swiss and south German reformation. Although certain ministers in Augsburg expressed dismay on learning that the cities of the Tetrapolitan Confession had agreed to this document, they assented to sign the Augsburg Confession. This paved the way for the city council at last to outlaw Catholicism and set up a new church order. Ulm, Frankfurt, and Württemberg also accepted the Wittenberg Concord and moved in a Lutheran direction; Blaurer was forced out of Württemberg in 1538. Strasbourg adopted Luther's hymnal in 1541 and recruited graduates of Wittenberg and Tübingen to be its pastors. The range of opinions accepted in parts of the region remained broad. Vermigli taught in Strasbourg with Bucer's blessing, and Calvin also found shelter in the town between 1538 and 1542, while Augsburg's adoption of its new church order in 1537 precipitated an extensive stripping of the altars and institution of an austere church order. Still, the tide was now moving strongly in a Lutheran direction in Protestant south Germany.[33]

This tide crested after the Schmalkaldic wars. In the first phase of the conflict, Charles V defeated the allied Protestant princes and cities and imposed upon all of the previously Protestant territories except for resolutely defiant Magdeburg an essentially Catholic form of worship tempered only slightly by concessions to Protestant sensibilities. Some Protestant churchmen accepted this so-called Augsburg Interim or negotiated compromises with it. Those of a Reformed bent were most likely to reject it and flee elsewhere because of their concern for purity of worship. When the princes counterattacked in 1552 and won a succession of battles that forced Charles V to grant toleration for Protestant worship, they then specified that this toleration should extend only to those who accepted the Augsburg Confession. Constance, the one city that had not accepted the Wittenberg Concord, lost its independence and was absorbed into the Habsburg lands. When Protestant church orders were restored after 1555 in the south German cities in which austerity had been the rule before 1546, they followed a more purely Lutheran order of worship. The region remained open to its former ministers who had fled during the interim. Vermigli returned to Strasbourg when he was driven from England on the accession of Queen Mary. Several territories tried to lure Musculus back from Bern. But those of this temper soon discovered that an increasingly narrow and aggressive Lutheran orthodoxy made the region inhospitable. Strasbourg's ministers pressed Vermigli so hard to avow his approval of the Wittenberg Concord that he decided that he preferred to move to Zurich. In the first major Reformed-Lutheran dispute in which predestination, not the Eucharist, was a central point of contention, Girolamo Zanchi, a disciple of Vermigli from the convent at Lucca who had fled north in 1552 and likewise taught at Strasbourg, left in 1563 following bitter arguments with Johannes Marbach, the head of the city's company of pastors. The cities of south Germany that had once been home to a distinctive "upper German" form of civic reformation close in spirit to that of Switzerland had been squeezed into a Lutheran mold.[34]

Still, the political and military forces that pushed most Protestant territories in Germany toward Lutheran doctrine and practice could not reach into every cranny of this astoundingly variegated, decentralized polity; and neither could the arguments of theologians or the dictates of princes keep individual theologians from finding elements of Reformed teaching attractive. Because territorial cities often enjoyed considerable autonomy from their princes, the city council of Wismar was able to resist calls from its ruling duke and the Hanseatic League to silence its sacramentarian preacher Heinrich Never for over a decade before finally succumbing in 1541. Since the East Elbian *Junkers* enjoyed even more autonomy vis-à-vis their nominal overlords, they were able to protect Schwenkfeldian refugees on their land into the second half of the century.[35] The most notable exception to the trend toward Lutheran dominance was East Friesland, a region closely tied by trade and language to the neighboring provinces of the northern Netherlands and isolated from the rest of the empire by a barrier of marshes. The Reformation history of this territory had contained sacramentarian characteristics from the start, for the first evangelical preacher in its major port, Emden, had been a partisan of a symbolic interpretation of the Eucharist probably derived from Cornelis Hoen. When the ruling count Enno II decided late in the 1520s to implement a princely reformation along Lutheran lines under the direction of ministers invited from Bremen and Luneburg, the citizens of Emden successfully resisted features of the church order they tried to impose, especially the proclamation of Lutheran eucharistic doctrine. The church of the entire county then received a new direction when Countess Anna of Oldenburg assumed regency power in 1542 and soon named as superintendent of the church a recent refugee of distinction, John a Lasco.[36]

The itinerary that led a Lasco into his role as a Reformed church organizer was one of the more dramatic personal voyages of a century filled with such odysseys, revealing—among much else—that Reformed ideas continued to attract new adherents inside the empire even during the 1530s, when such ideas were on the defensive. No other reformer stemmed from as privileged a background as this Polish scion of a lesser noble family that had risen to the heights of political power thanks to the skills of John's uncle of the same name, a clerical diplomat and courtier who became a trusted secretary to King Sigismund and ultimately chancellor of Poland and archbishop of Gniezno. Born in 1499 in the family fief of Lask, the younger John a Lasco was ordained at the age of twenty-two and received the fancy foreign education at Bologna, Padua, and Paris that befitted a young man destined for high church offices. On his student travels, he passed through Zurich and met Zwingli. He lived for several months in Basel in 1524–25 in the house of Erasmus, from whom he later said that he received his "first notions of religion." There he also attended Oecolampadius's lectures on theology. The debate over the Eucharist was just then splitting Oecolampadius from Erasmus. A Lasco agreed with Erasmus that the sources Oecolampadius cited in support of his claim that the church of Rome had strayed from the teachings of the early church were not sufficiently compelling to justify rejecting that church and its traditions. Attractive ecclesiastical prospects still beckoned back home.[37]

Soon after John returned to Poland, the Laski family made a fateful political choice. When the Hungarian throne suddenly fell open following the disaster at Mohács in 1528, they precipitously entered the service of the claimant John Zápolyai. King Sigismund supported Ferdinand of Habsburg, who won control of most of the country. The bishopric promised John a Lasco in Hungary slipped from his grasp. The family lost favor in Poland as well. Further attempts to secure a bishopric came to naught. As his prospects for high ecclesiastical office dimmed, a Lasco entered into correspondence with Melanchthon, remembered fondly the pleasures of pious, learned conversation in evangelical circles to the west, and at last embarked on several journeys in that direction. On the second of these, made in 1539–40, he came into contact with one such circle in Louvain deeply influenced by the traditions of the Brethren of the Common Life. One member of this circle was Albert Hardenberg, a Franciscan soon to be removed from his faculty position for heterodoxy, after which he became an evangelical preacher in Bremen with a distinctive outlook owing strong debts to Zwingli, Bullinger, and especially Bucer.[38] Another was a weaver's daughter whom a Lasco decided to marry. His marriage declared his rupture with the Catholic church. He fled to East Friesland, known as a relatively safe haven for dissidents of varied stripes. A letter he wrote several years thereafter to his old Hebrew teacher, Pellikan, makes it clear that he had now embraced a position on the Eucharist similar to Bullinger's. After living in Emden for two years as a private individual, he was named superintendent of its territorial church. He thus gained in East Friesland the Protestant equivalent of the episcopal office he had been unable to obtain back home.

As a Protestant churchman, a Lasco showed himself in many ways to be the most Erasmian of reformers. Like Erasmus, he emphasized reform of life over abstract theology. Indeed, his theological opponents did not have much regard for his skills as a theologian, and he himself never published his longest work of doctrinal exposition, the *Summary of the Doctrine of the Church of East Frisia* (1544), after Bullinger and Melanchthon, to whom he sent copies, pointed out flaws in it. He rejected all confessions of faith as improper, a position that prefigured that of the Dutch Remonstrants eighty years later. Strikingly for a Protestant, he upheld the freedom of the will.

A Lasco's greatest strength lay as a church organizer. Soon after taking up his post in Emden, he wrote a tract entitled *On the Holding Aloof from Papal Services* that attacked excessive compromise with idolatry for the sake of the weak. He convinced Countess Anna to order the removal of all altars and images from the territory's churches. Shortly thereafter, he was able to put in place a system of ecclesiastical morals discipline by a joint board of ministers and lay elders, with powers to exclude individuals from communion for misbehavior and false belief. He also founded a ministerial *Coetus,* a weekly synodlike meeting of clergymen whose purpose it was to discuss issues of doctrine, review and censure one another's behavior, and examine candidates for the ministry. The *Coetus* was a powerful instrument for promoting uniformity of church practice and doctrine in an area where Anabaptist influences were strong and many church livings were still held by Lutherans. Participation was not made mandatory, however, so a range of theological positions continued to thrive within the territorial church. A Lasco in addition devoted himself to debating and writing energetically against the Anabaptists, prepared a catechism for the church, and encouraged the countess to publish a strict new *Polizeiordnung* that required attendance at Sunday services and punished blasphemy, excessive feasting, and usury.[39]

Between 1548 and 1553, the crisis created by Charles V's military victory over the Schmalkaldic League weighed heavily on East Friesland because the territory shared a border with Charles V's possessions in the Low Countries. To forestall the danger of Habsburg military intervention, Countess Anna agreed to accept a mitigated form of the Augsburg Interim that she negotiated. A Lasco rejected the compromises with idolatry that this entailed and emigrated to London. Here, Edward VI invited him to become superintendent of the churches that he had recently permitted to be opened for refugee French and Dutch evangelicals. The order of worship and institutions of those churches, shaped in good measure by a Lasco himself, provided the Polish nobleman with the basis for his most important written work, probably drafted with assistance from his fellow pastors in these churches. This was his *Full Form and Manner of the Ecclesiastical Ministry Established in the Strangers' Church of London,* the Latin version of which was published in Emden in 1555 and soon translated into French; a modified Dutch version prepared by Marten Micron appeared in 1554 and went through four further Dutch and one German editions.[40] An extended description and defense of the church's liturgy and institutions, this book offered one of the era's fullest published blueprints for properly reformed church practice.

Many features of the refugee churches spelled out in the *Full Form and Manner of the Ecclesiastical Ministry* replicated institutions that were first established a decade earlier in Strasbourg and Geneva and that will be discussed at greater length in the following chapter. They included the creation of a series of ministerial offices within the church said to be of divine institution (the offices of minister, elder, and deacon) and the autonomous exercise of church discipline by a body composed jointly of the ministers and elders, with full powers of excommunication. But the church order spelled out in this work differed from that enshrined in the Genevan ecclesiastical ordinances of 1541 in a number of ways that made the book an alternative to the model of a Reformed church represented by Geneva. First, the *Full Form and Manner of the Ecclesiastical Ministry* placed even greater importance on the need for properly organized church discipline than do any of the Genevan ecclesiastical ordinances, identifying discipline as one of the core aspects of a true church and stressing that all new members of the church must submit themselves to it. In this, a Lasco and the refugees in England were following Bucer, who had emerged as a preeminent theorist of the church in the 1530s and likewise held that the exercise of discipline was one of the essential marks of a genuinely Christian church.[41] Second, it identified the office of civil magistrate as one of the church offices of divine foundation, alongside pastors, elders, and deacons. Magistrates had the task of upholding with the sword the two tables of the law, the system of ecclesiastical discipline and the good order and tranquility of the church. The work declared as well that the superintendent's office was instituted by Christ himself. The duties of the office included overseeing the other ministers and representing the views of the church to its enemies and to the secular authorities. Finally, the *Full Form and Manner of the Ecclesiastical Ministry* allowed for a striking degree of congregational participation in various activities of the church. In the *Prophetie* of the Dutch church—modeled, as the name suggests, on the Zurich Prophezei—church members who had questions or doubts about points advanced by the pastor in his Sunday sermon could submit their questions to the elders for discussion at the next Prophetie. Ministers were chosen through a two-tiered system of congregational election in which the church members first chose by secret ballot those whom they considered best qualified, then the ministers and elders made the final selection from among those with the most votes.[42] A Lasco's espousal of congregational input in the selection of ministers probably derives from two sources: (1) East Friesland was one of the corners of late medieval Europe in which many parishes had the right to choose their own curate;[43] and (2) refugee churches could be assumed to consist of surpassingly committed and well-informed believers. This most aristocratic of reformers thus helped draft an exceptionally democratic church order.

In addition to spelling out the procedures for selecting and installing the ministers of a properly reformed church, the *Full Form and Manner of the Ecclesiastical Ministry* described in detail the rituals, sacraments, and prayers used in the London refugee churches. Baptism was administered publicly before the entire congregation "following the institution of Lord Christ" with a simple daubing with water in the name of the Father, Son, and Holy Ghost. No provision was made for the emergency baptism of sickly newborns by ministers or midwives because those chosen by God would enter heaven through his grace, and no further ritual was required. The Lord's Supper was likewise celebrated only publicly in regular church assemblies, without any of the "mystical, or rather magical, vestments such as they have in Popery, nor candles, torches, copes, chasubles or surplices." Before being admitted to the service for the first time, individuals had to declare their spiritual confidence that they were true members of Christ's church and pass a brief examination on the rudiments of the faith. For the ceremony a simple table was placed in the middle of the church. After reading Christ's words of the institution and breaking an ordinary loaf of bread into pieces, the minister passed these and the communion wine to those seated around the table for as many seatings as were required by the size of the congregation. Special days of fasting and thanksgiving were scheduled as necessary to implore God's assistance in times of tribulation or to acknowledge moments of good fortune. For funerals, the *Full Form* called for a procession devoid of "theatrical pomp" to accompany the body of the deceased to the churchyard where it would be buried, followed by a sermon about the triumph of faith over death and a brief prayer expressing confidence that the deceased's soul had been taken to heaven. The volume also made provisions for a simple marriage ceremony and specified procedures for visiting the sick. The French translation of the work opened with one of the fullest statements ever of the range of benefits that those drawn to the cause expected from the institution of a proper set of church ordinances and institutions:

> If the order set forth in this book were well observed among those who call themselves Christians . . . the world would not feel the wrath of God, as

do and will increasingly those who do not amend their ways. Princes and magistrates would be more peaceful; wars would cease among the nobility; the ambition of prelates would be punished; and all would do their duty in their calling. Children would be instructed from a young age in holy discipline; doctrine would be purely preached; the sacraments properly administered; the populace held in check; virtue would be prized; vices corrected; true penance restored and excommunication pronounced on the obstinate and rebellious; God's honor would be advanced together with the proper invocation of his holy name; the most honorable estate of marriage would be restored to its original form; brothels would be abolished; the poor would be cared for and all begging eliminated; the sick would be visited and consoled; and the dead honored with an honest burial devoid of superstition.[44]

In addition to being the place where a Lasco learned many of the lessons that went into the *Full Form and Manner of the Ecclesiastical Ministry,* East Friesland attained wider significance in the history of Reformed church building as a haven for people escaping the vigorous heresy hunting in the Low Countries and a center for the diffusion of Reformed ideas throughout northwestern Europe. Refugees from the Netherlands, many of them Anabaptists, had already begun to flee to Emden before a Lasco's arrival. They came in growing numbers in subsequent years, and a Lasco's establishment of a firmly Reformed church order guaranteed that the influences radiating back to the Low Countries would be predominantly of that character. Among the several thousand refugees drawn to Emden were enough printers to publish at least 230 books of a Protestant character between 1554 and 1569, including Bibles, devotional and catechetical works, theological treatises, and antipapal polemics. The great majority were intended for export to the Low Countries. Indeed, Emden, which housed not a single press before the advent of a Lasco, became the most important center for the printing of Protestant religious literature in Dutch during this crucial period of the faith's underground germination in the Netherlands. Correspondence reveals that evangelicals in the Low Countries also looked to Emden's church for advice about ecclesiastical matters and solicited it to send them ministers. For these reasons, Emden's church ultimately became known as the "mother church" of the Reformed movement in the northern Netherlands.[45]

Other refugee centers emerged in these years of importance for the subsequent dissemination of the Reformed cause. Between 1550 and 1553, and then again after Elizabeth came to the English throne in 1558, the English permitted groups of refugees from the Low Countries and northern France to settle and establish their own congregations not only in London, but also in several smaller towns. A few cities in the empire, notably Wesel, Aachen, and Frankfurt, also consented to shelter groups of refugees from the southern Low Countries. Strasbourg provided a similar haven for some of the growing numbers of French evangelicals who felt compelled by their conscience to look abroad from the 1520s onward. Calvin would briefly serve as the minister of its refugee French church. Geneva, of course, would ultimately become the most famous refugee center of all, admitting its many French-speaking refugees to the civic church but establishing separate congregations at times for Italian and English speakers. During a generation in which evangelical ideas were spreading outside the empire but failed to gain legal toleration except in Scandinavia and England, the little spaces of liberty that the Reformed cause was able to obtain from Switzerland through the empire into England would be enormously important to its expansion. The refugee churches incubated models of church organization that the ruling authorities were not yet willing to permit on a territorial scale and provided havens where militant minorities could work for the cause's advancement in the homelands they had left.[46]

One final set of developments of the period prior to 1555 was also significant for the ultimate fate of the Reformed tradition within the Holy Roman Empire, for they opened the door to its renewed advance in Germany after the Peace of Augsburg. They involved not individuals who can be unproblematically associated with the Reformed camp, but instead one of the leading Wittenberg reformers, Philip Melanchthon.

Melanchthon always remained a respected colleague and collaborator of Luther's, but he was an independent theologian in his own right, the author of his own set of *Commonplaces,* the century's most frequently reprinted single introduction to Protestant doctrine (115 editions through 1560 alone). His thought evolved over the years in a manner that departed from Luther's in several ways. Most important, he granted the will a measure of cooperation in the process of justification, and he embraced a more spiritual interpretation of the real presence. During the last decade of Luther's life, relations between the two men became guarded and at times even strained. Melanchthon also corresponded with Calvin and Bullinger and furthermore happened to be the author of the Augsburg Confession. As such, he was not averse to modifying that document when it seemed to him that God had granted him greater clarity of scriptural understanding. In 1540, he changed the article on the Lord's Supper to remove the suggestion of the original text that Christ was actually present in the elements and was conveyed to all who received them regardless of their faith. The phrase "with the bread and wine the body and blood of Christ are truly exhibited to those who eat in the Lord's Supper" now replaced "the Body and Blood of Christ are truly present, and are distributed to those who eat in the supper of the Lord." Following this change, it could seem more possible for those who accepted a spiritual real presence to see themselves as being in agreement with the Augsburg Confession. This in turn gave future rulers who might be inclined toward Reformed doctrines an argument they could use to claim the right to institute such worship under the terms of the Peace of Augsburg.[47]

For all of his prestige, however, Melanchthon did not speak for all, or even most, Lutheran theologians. The gulf that remained between the majority of Lutheran theologians and the Reformed became evident when a boatload of those associated with the Dutch church of London, forced to flee England after Mary's accession, made its way around the Baltic seeking permission to settle and to worship in their accustomed manner. One after another, the authorities of Denmark, Wismar, Lubeck, and Hamburg refused them permission unless they would conform to the practices of the local Lutheran churches. They rejected this and finally settled in Emden. A polemic over the issue of the Eucharist had already broken out between a Lasco and the Hamburg pastor Joachim Westphal. Now, the inhospitability of the Baltic Lutherans attracted the attention of the other Reformed theologians, notably Calvin, who laid into Westphal as a "brute barbarian" and a "son of the devil" in his *Defense of the True and Orthodox Doctrine of the Sacrament* (1555). The conflict grew into a major polemical battle, commonly called the second sacramentarian controversy. Many of those who entered the fray on Westphal's side began to insist that Luther's idea of ubiquitarianism—the view that Christ in his humanity is everywhere present in the world, and that this is how he could be physically present in the eucharistic elements—was an important dogma. By the quarrel's bitter end, it was clear that Westphal was no isolated figure, but was more representative of Lutheran opinion than Melanchthon.[48]

In part, this was because by this time Melanchthon's luster had dimmed as a result of his willingness to compromise during the interim crisis. Under pressure from the duke of Saxony, who had allied himself with the emperor and conquered the lands of his old rival the elector, Melanchthon and some other Saxon theologians accepted a modified form of the Augsburg Interim, the so-called Leipzig Interim, which preserved what they believed were the basic Lutheran theological positions but made concessions on many matters of worship that they defined as *adiaphora*. Melanchthon's stance in this crisis was little changed from the position he and Luther had taken when they agreed to restore elements of Catholic worship thirty years previously at the very dawn of the Reformation in Wittenberg in 1522; but the context had now changed. Many hard-liners among the Lutheran clergy saw his concessions as a sell-out. When the resistance they organized from Magdeburg and elsewhere led to the resurgence of Protestant arms in the second phase of the Schmalkaldic Wars, they felt that their position had been vindicated. For the next generation, German Lutheranism would be split between these self-styled Gnesio-Lutherans, or genuine Lutherans, and the Philippists. Their dissimilar interpretations of the Eucharist was one of the principal points of contention in this split. A corollary became whether the terms of the Peace of Augsburg required acceptance of the original edition of the Augsburg Confession drawn up by Melanchthon in 1530 (the so-called Invariata), or his revised version of 1540 (the Variata). For the rest of the century, the question of whether or not a territorial church could legally formulate eucharistic teachings in line with the Variata but not the Invariata remained murky and contested.

Across the empire, Reformed currents had thus retreated by 1555 to a few little pockets such as East Friesland and the refugee churches of the Rhineland. But the Melanchthonian tradition represented a variant of Lutheranism that was less sharply at odds with Zurich and Geneva than the emerging ubiquitarian orthodoxy, and there remained legal wriggle room for princes to adopt a Reformed reformation. For a while, it had seemed possible that all Protestant territorial churches might unite around a single eucharistic formula. This eventuality had foundered against the Zurichers' loyalty to a metaphorical understanding of the words of the institution and the increasingly aggressive attachment of the majority of Lutherans to a physical understanding of the real presence. By forging a virtually solid bloc of Reformed churches in Switzerland and its affiliated territories, Bullinger's combination of steadfastness and diplomacy had helped the Zurich church to overcome the isolation that threatened it in the later 1530s and early 1540s and to compensate for the retreat of Reformed influences within the empire. At the same time the broad international audience reached through the treatises and commentaries of Bullinger, Musculus, and Vermigli, together with Bullinger's extensive correspondence with figures in England, Hungary, Poland, France, and Italy, enabled Reformed ideas to reach well beyond Switzerland and the empire into much of the European continent. A Lasco's diplomacy likewise made Emden and London further outposts of Reformed influences. The work of these individuals has rarely figured at the heart of the story of the European Reformation, yet it is plausible to believe that, even if still another powerful theologian and urban reformer had not appeared in this same generation in the person of Calvin, the labor of these men would have sufficed to initiate the significant phase of Reformed expansion into England, the Netherlands, and eastern Europe that began toward the end of their lives.

3

THE SECOND GENERATION
Calvin and Geneva

For all of the importance of Bullinger or a Lasco, the strong-willed Frenchman who passed through Geneva in 1536 and unexpectedly found himself in charge of its church for most of his remaining twenty-eight years unquestionably merits the leading role traditionally assigned him in the history of the Reformed tradition. John Calvin's acuity as a theological expositor and elegance as a literary stylist earned his writings an audience that exceeded even Bullinger's. His success in instituting an independent system of church discipline in Geneva that others had sought vainly elsewhere contributed to a reformation of manners that helped make that city an even greater magnet for refugees than Emden or Zurich, with a printing industry of twice Emden's capacity and a theological academy that attracted three times as many students as Zurich's. Although the reach of Calvin's correspondence did not extend as far as Bullinger's, Calvin—sometimes at Bullinger's suggestion—more often assumed the leading role in international controversies than his Zurich counterpart and was more assertive about advising those all-important cradles of further expansion, the refugee churches. For all of these reasons, Calvin became the most forceful voice within the increasingly multipolar and multivocal Reformed world of the second generation, even when the other leading theologians of his time are properly acknowledged.

THE EXPANSION OF THE REFORMATION
IN FRANCOPHONE SWITZERLAND

Calvin's work in Geneva arose from the encounter of a brilliant, driven man with a newly independent city uniquely susceptible to being molded by such a person. The stage was set by Protestantism's expansion into Switzerland's French-speaking borderlands in the decade before Calvin's arrival in Geneva in 1536.[1] Even after the Second Peace of Kappel halted Protestantism's expansion in the core areas of the Swiss Confederacy, Bernese protection enabled the fiery Guillaume Farel to evangelize here. Farel, a native of the French Alps, had been an associate and disciple of the great French counterpart to Erasmus, Jacques Lefèvre d'Etaples, first at Paris and then at Meaux. Characteristically, he was the first of the "Bibliens" of Meaux to carry Lefèvre's Christian humanist critique of false worship to the point of outright rupture with the Roman church. After fleeing to Basel in 1524 and living for a while with Oecolampadius, he put his personal courage, impetuous oratory, and genius for provocation to work preaching without the permission of the local ecclesiastical authorities in communities from Switzerland to Lorraine. From 1526 to 1529, his chief base was Aigle, in Bernese territory, where he opened a small school under a pseudonym and, after the Bern disputation, took charge of implementing the local Reformation that made this tiny town the first Protestant city in French-speaking Europe. Over the next seven years, he crisscrossed the surrounding region, absorbing numerous banishments and at least one beating while gradually gaining hearers in a growing number of localities. A series of visits to Neuchâtel culminated in two days of systematic iconoclasm and the abolition of the mass there in 1530. The Bernese annexation of the Pays de Vaud in 1536 provided new military and political support. The Reformation quickly triumphed in the episcopal city of Lausanne, where Farel had previously encountered substantial opposition. Soon, a reformation on a Bernese model was imposed on the entire territory. In the areas under the common lordship of Bern and Fribourg, as in those parts of eastern Switzerland under a joint Protestant-Catholic condominium, the choice of religion was left up to the individual parishes, and Protestantism was embraced in many after aggressive evangelization. The most crucial victory of all, once again achieved in the face of strong opposition, came in Geneva.

By the 1530s, Geneva was no longer the great center of international trade it had been in the preceding century, but it remained a regional trading center of ten thousand inhabitants that was displaying a new spirit of municipal autonomy. Long governed by its bishop, it had by 1500 largely fallen under the sway of the dukes of Savoy, who possessed rights of legal jurisdiction over the city and had turned the episcopal see into a virtual family monopoly.

2. View of Geneva. By Matthias Merian, 1654. Geneva would have looked little different when Calvin first laid eyes on it in 1536, except that the city walls would have lacked the bastions seen here. After growing significantly between 1536 and 1566, the city's population gradually dwindled back to 1536 levels over the first half of the seventeenth century. (By permission of the British Library)

But the expansion of Swiss power in the early sixteenth century gave the city a new margin of maneuver. In 1519, Bern and Fribourg proposed a pact of combourgeoisie. For the next seven years, Geneva divided between partisans of Savoyard authority, who tended to come from old families that had made their wealth in the fifteenth century and now staffed positions around the ducal and episcopal courts, and champions of alliance with the Swiss, who tended to be wholesale merchants from newer families who resented the taxes and other impediments that the dukes put in the way of their trade with Switzerland and south Germany. After much struggle, marked by executions and banishments, the Eidguenot partisans of alliance with Switzerland carried the day and put in place not only a military pact with Bern and Freiburg, but also certain civic institutions "in the custom of the Swiss," notably a new Council of Two Hundred. Over the following several years, further new tribunals displaced the courts of the bishop and the duke. The bishop visited his city for the last time in 1533. Geneva had turned Swiss and gained its independence.[2]

The 1526 pact of combourgeoisie with Bern and Fribourg opened the door to Protestantism in the city, but the cause made little headway at first. Farel's first two preaching visits to the city, in 1529 and 1532, were spectacularly unsuccessful. On his second visit, he barely escaped with his life after city officials called him in for questioning and a crowd chanting, "Kill, kill this Lhuter!" gathered outside. Soon after this incident, however, a young Dauphinois acolyte and accomplice, Antoine Froment, set up shop in Geneva as a schoolteacher. Attracting students by promising that he would teach them to read and write within a month or they owed him nothing, he mixed religious lessons with his instruction and before long won a growing audience. During the Easter season of 1533, a stocking maker and lay evangelist in touch with Farel organized an evangelical communion service and preached publicly.[3]

For the next two years, turbulent incidents followed hard upon one another. The partisans of religious change, in the manner of the Zurich evangelicals a decade earlier, resorted to provocation to advance their cause. Their opponents came to blows with them on several occasions. The municipal authorities hesitated to embrace either side. On one occasion, a group of *évangelistes* howled like wolves to drown out the chanting of the priests in the cathedral. On another, marchers in church processions were hooted with the catcall, "Feed those braying asses thistles." Lenten and advent preachers were contradicted; images smashed.

In the midst of these events, Farel and the young native of nearby Orbe whom he had recently convinced to become an evangelical minister as well, Pierre Viret, came to the city under the protection of a Bernese safe-conduct, organized Reformed worship, and found themselves thrust by a mob into possession of one of the city's churches. For their part, the mendicant friars sent to the city preached vigorously against the "Lutherans" and denounced them as stooges of the Swiss, an accusation that set off two riots. When documents seized in connection with a criminal case suggested Fribourg's cooperation with the bishop to revive his power, Geneva ended its alliance with Fribourg, leaving Bern as its sole protector. A failed attempt to kill Viret by poisoning his spinach further inflamed anti-Catholic sentiment, as did moves by the bishop and his Savoyard allies to retake the city by force. In the summer of 1535, a disputation was organized, but four weeks of argument pitting Farel and Viret against a pair of Catholic opponents could not bring a hesitant city council to decide the religious issue. Finally, an outburst of iconoclasm that stripped the city's churches of most of their "idols" pushed it in August 1535 provisionally to abolish the mass and seize most church property.

The bishop and duke intensified their military pressure against the city, their small band of mercenaries now reinforced with Genevans who had opposed the alliance with Switzerland and the turn toward what they called the new religion. At this critical juncture, the Bernese intervened to disperse the besieging forces and take control of the neighboring Pays de Vaud. Soon thereafter, a general assembly of the city voted to "live henceforward according to the holy law of the Gospel and the word of God, and to abandon all masses and other ceremonies, Papal abuses, images, and idols." During these same months, many of the pieces of an austere civic reformation along Swiss lines were put in place. A radically simplified liturgy was instituted. All holidays and feast days were abolished. Revenue from seized church property was allocated for new schools and a reorganized system of civic hospitals. Edicts expelled prostitutes and ordered fornicators and adulterers to "abandon their wicked life" or face a whipping or banishment.

Such was the situation when a legally trained young French evangelical who had just made a striking theological debut with a work entitled the *Institutes of the Christian Religion* passed through Geneva in July 1536 bound for Strasbourg. Calvin expected to spend just one night, but Farel learned of his presence and realized how useful somebody of his training and talents might be. Our one account of the interview at which Farel convinced Calvin to stay was written by Calvin himself twenty years after the fact: "Farel detained me in Geneva, not so much by counsel and exhortation, as by a dreadful threat which I felt in the same way as if God had laid his mighty hand upon me from heaven to arrest me. . . . After learning that my heart was set upon devoting myself to private studies, for which I wished to keep myself free from other pursuits, . . . he proceeded to warn me that God would curse my retirement and the tranquility which I sought for my studies if I withdrew and refused to help when it was so urgently needed."[4] The account is clearly shaped by Calvin's concern to suggest that he was called to his prophetic office by providential forces that he dared not resist, but the story also fits with what we know of Farel's character. Undeniably less trustworthy is Calvin's oft-cited deathbed recollection of the work that had been accomplished in Geneva prior to his arrival: "When I first arrived in this church there was almost nothing. They were preaching and that's all."[5] A civic reformation along Swiss lines had in fact already been largely implemented. For most of the next thirty years, Calvin would confront the turbulence of Genevan politics and seek to establish a different model of church organization and a still more thorough reformation of manners.

CALVIN THE THEOLOGIAN

When Calvin arrived in Geneva, he had scarcely turned twenty-seven, but he had already written the first edition of what would become the century's most enduringly influential theological masterwork. Important elements of his theology emerged only under the pressure of events in Geneva, during his subsequent sojourn in Strasbourg from 1538 to 1542, and in dialogue with other theologians he respected, most notably Melanchthon. Still, much of his mature theological vision was already present in the 1536 edition of his *Institutes*. So too were the exegetical and rhetorical capacities that would assure his work a vast international audience. For these reasons, it makes sense to examine his theology before his work in Geneva, although the connection between the two should never be forgotten.

Calvin was a child of the world of the ecclesiastical courts. His father occupied a succession of posts attached to the cathedral of Noyon in Picardy that gave him good connections with the bishop and enabled him to arrange an excellent education for his son. At the tender age of eleven, the young Calvin received a chaplaincy that amounted to a de facto scholarship. Two years later he left for Paris and the Collège de la Marche in the company of a member of the bishop's family. He shifted to the more highly esteemed Collège de Montaigu, received his arts degree, and studied law at Orléans with the celebrated jurist Pierre de l'Estoile. After a brief sojourn in Bourges as well, he received his law degree in 1531.

Students of Calvin's thought have devoted attention to exploring the effect of this education on his mature theology. The regent of the Collège de Montaigu during his time there was the distinguished Scotist John Mair, and scholars have observed parallels between certain theological positions later advanced by Calvin and the views of Scotus and the *schola Augustiniana moderna*. As a student in the arts faculty, however, Calvin would not necessarily have been exposed to any formal training in theology. No direct reliance on any texts he might have read in Paris has ever been proven, and certain of Calvin's arguments that interpreters have highlighted for their similarities with late medieval theology do not appear until the later editions of the *Institutes*.[6] His legal education likely was more important for his later career, both because his legal expertise commended him to the ruling authorities in Geneva, who turned to him for advice about matters of legal procedure as well as help in drafting the ecclesiastical ordinances of the city, and because legal exegesis avoided allegorical interpretation and confined itself to reconciling passages in the law, in a manner that Calvin would follow in his Bible commentaries.[7] But the law would not prove his final resting place. He grew interested in humanism and in 1531 returned to Paris to follow courses at the new trilingual Collège Royal. When he published his first book in the following year, it was, in good humanist fashion, a commentary on a classical treatise, Seneca's *On Clemency*.[8]

The process that carried Calvin from the authorship of this work, which betrays no sign of commitment to the evangelical cause, to an open rejection of "the superstitions of the Papacy" is singularly ill illuminated by contemporary evidence; even Calvin's later autobiographical statements are of little help. We know that Luther's works were passed around in circles such as those in which he moved, that as the years passed he came into contact with a number of individuals who hoped for the purification of worship through a return to the essence of Scripture, and that the conservative theologians of the Sorbonne viewed such hopes as heretical and dangerous to the church, although many of those who embraced such views would have denied this. It also seems clear that by late 1533 Calvin could be counted among the admirers of Lefèvre d'Etaples's follower Gérard Roussel. At the end of the year he came under suspicion as a "Lutheran" and was forced to flee Paris because of his known friendship with the rector of the Sorbonne, Nicolas Cop, whose provocative oration to open the academic year, blending Erasmian and Lutheran ideas, prompted the authorities to seek the arrest of those known to be associated with him. The next year was a time of peregrination around France for Calvin: he resigned his benefice in Noyon in May 1534, and then, after the Affair of the Placards in October prompted another, harsher crackdown on heresy throughout the kingdom that would take at least one close friend to the stake, he fled to Basel. There, he set busily to work on an exposition of the true evangelical faith that he dedicated to Francis I to show him that this was not seditious, as its enemies charged. He also wrote a preface to Pierre Olivétan's translation of the Hebrew Bible, the first document from his pen to display an unambiguous rejection of the Roman church and its corruptions.[9]

The text of the *Institutes of the Christian Religion* that Calvin completed in just eight months in Basel was only the first version of a work that he would return to and expand throughout his lifetime. The full title of the first edition of 1536 declared that the work contained "almost the whole sum of piety and whatever it is necessary to know in the doctrine of salvation" and that it was a "work very well worth reading by all persons zealous for piety." Its structure was modeled after Luther's small catechism, with six chapters explicating the Ten Commandments, the Apostles' Creed, the Lord's Prayer, the true sacraments, the false sacraments of the Roman church, and the proper relation of church and state. Three years later, an expanded folio edition appeared with eleven new chapters. Now the stated goal of the work was also "to prepare and train students of sacred theology for the study of the word of God that they might have an easy access into it." Further expansions followed in 1543, 1550, and 1559. By the last edition, the original work of just 85,000 words had burgeoned to an opus of 450,000 words reorganized around four broad themes: the knowledge of God, the process of salvation, the character and consequences of faith, and the institutions and sacraments of the church. Calvin also prepared French editions of each revision after 1539.[10] As each revision enlarged existing sections with new arguments responding to issues that Calvin came to see as significant, the result was a work of complexity, motif lapping upon motif in sedimentary deposits in a manner that makes it best thought of as a treasury of more or less perfectly harmonized explications of individual points of doctrine, rather than a work of absolute logical and metaphorical consistency.[11]

Calvin's importance as a theologian derived in large measure from his ability to appreciate and to express cogently the insights of the leading magisterial reformers of the preceding generation while mixing in distinctive accents of his own. The modeling of the first version of the *Institutes* on Luther's catechism suggests his debt to the Wittenberg reformer. Calvin always saw himself as a defender of Luther's fundamental theological principles—principles that, in his view, the master sometimes lost sight of himself, carried away as he so often was by his formidable temper. On many issues concerning the process of justification by faith alone and the bondage of the will, his ideas echoed Luther's; this is particularly true of those sections of the *Institutes* that represent its earliest geological layers. Calvin was also close in spirit and ideas to his fellow humanist drawn into the orbit of theology, Melanchthon, whose *Commonplaces* was the most complete exposition of Protestant ideas prior to the appearance of the *Institutes*. Bucer, whom Calvin got to know well when he spent three years in Strasbourg between his first and second stays in Geneva, left a still deeper imprint. As we shall see, Calvin's sojourn in Strasbourg was instrumental in shaping his thinking about ecclesiology. Even before arriving in Strasbourg, however, Calvin knew Bucer's commentaries and was strongly swayed by them in his formulation of the doctrine of predestination. As for Zwingli, Calvin was sufficiently critical of his purely symbolic interpretation of the Eucharist that he told correspondents he avoided his writings for a long time; yet it is evident from the internal evidence of the *Institutes* that he had read *On True and False Religion* prior to 1536 and that at several crucial points where the Zurich reformer parted company with Luther, as on the matter of images, Calvin followed Zwingli and expressed himself in a way that hints at the mark left by the elder man.[12]

Although many passages in the first edition of the *Institutes* have been shown to be close paraphrases of ideas expressed by one or another of these authors, Calvin sifted what he read and organized his ideas around distinctive points of emphasis of his own. Perhaps the most frequently sounded note in his writings is his tightly conjoined emphasis on God's absolute control of all that occurs on earth and man's consequent obligation to serve and glorify the all-powerful God who created him. God is not simply the creator of all things, but their "everlasting Governor and Preserver" who "sustains, nourishes, and cares for everything he has made, even to the least sparrow." He is also the fount of all good—indeed, he was so good that he had his only son assume human flesh and purchase our redemption by suffering an agonizing death. In gratitude, human beings should bend all of their efforts to serving him: "We are not our own: in so far as we can, let us therefore forget ourselves and all that is ours. Conversely, we are God's: let us therefore live for him and die for him. We are God's: let his wisdom and will therefore rule all our actions. We are God's: let all the parts of our life accordingly strive toward him as our only lawful goal." And again: "The whole life of a Christian ought to be a sort of practice of godliness, because we have been called to sanctification."[13]

Because the key to serving God lay in subordinating the individual will to God's and in cleaving to his commandments, it followed for Calvin, as it had for Zwingli and Bullinger, that worship that deviated from the pattern commanded in the Bible was a grave lapse of duty. Even the first edition of the *Institutes,* written in a measured tone to convince Francis I that the evangelical faith represented no threat to order, cast the dangers of false worship in strong terms. Catholic eucharistic practices were "veritable inventions of the devil," "frightful abominations," "most wicked infamy and unbearable blasphemy" forged in the "shop" of the papacy. "The common cause of all believers, that of Christ himself" was set against "the order of the priests," whose practices were "veritable inventions of the devil." Although many details of worship are things indifferent, believers ought not to participate in rituals that are truly wicked, alleging their desire not to offend their neighbor, for then they will remain forever stuck in the mud, with no hope of escaping.[14] Calvin's strong sense of the foulness of Roman rituals led him to urge believers who had seen the light of the Gospel to flee them. He first sounded this theme in two Latin letters published in Basel in 1537, then gave it fuller and more forceful exposition in two tracts of 1543 and 1544, the *Short Treatise to Christians living among Papists* and the ironically titled *Nicodemites' Excuse.* Believers in Christ still living in Babylon must leave if at all possible for some region in which worship is pure. If they cannot do so, they must not be like Nicodemus, who came to Christ only at night, but must abstain from the mass, pray to God in private that he restore his church to a purer state, and instruct and edify their neighbors. In one of his most striking images, he compared those who continue to practice idolatry and false worship with latrine cleaners, who grow so accustomed to the stench in which they work that they cannot understand why others hold their noses in their presence. "Hardened by habit, they sit in their own excrement, and yet believe they are surrounded by roses." As we have seen, Bullinger and a Lasco similarly began to exhort believers to shun the abominations of popery in these years. The powerfully expressed abhorrence of false worship articulated by all of these men was fundamental in galvanizing the underground evangelical sentiment that existed in many parts of Europe by the middle decades of the sixteenth century into open withdrawal from Roman worship. Nobody expressed this abhorrence more vigorously than Calvin.[15]

Of the various elements of proper Christian worship, none was more essential than the Lord's Supper. Calvin's eucharistic theology, as already indicated, attempted to define a middle ground between the symbolic understanding of Oecolampadius and the Zurich theologians and the Lutheran doctrine of a real presence. Christ made himself truly present to believers in the ritual, but only in spirit—not as a real, substantial presence. Lutheran interpretations of the sacrament appeared to Calvin to imply a carnal and crass conception of God. Because Christ's spirit came to believers during the ritual, it had multiple benefits. It confirmed and refreshed their faith, inspired them to greater thanksgiving and love for God, and bound them to one another in concord and affection. Because of these benefits, Calvin recommended that the sacrament be celebrated weekly. Although the ritual was spiritual food for believers, however, it was deadly poison for those who lacked faith, for Paul had warned the Corinthians that those who partook unworthily ate and drank judgment upon themselves. For this reason, and to preserve the reputation of the community of believers gathered around the eucharistic table, the faithless should be kept away from the ceremony.[16]

The emphasis on keeping the eucharistic community pollution-free led in turn to a concern with church discipline. To be sure, the elect could not be recognized with full assurance here on earth, so all those who outwardly professed the true faith, did not live scandalously, and believed themselves worthy of admission to communion after personal self-examination should be admitted to the sacrament. The first edition of the *Institutes* nonetheless in-

dicated that excommunication had been instituted to bar the evidently un-
believing and unworthy. Additions to subsequent editions specified in ever-
greater detail how church discipline should operate and who should exercise
it. Jesus' words in Matthew 18:15–17 were a blueprint for shunning sinners
who refused to amend their ways after first private, then collective admonitions failed to move them. Farel, Oecolampadius, Blaurer, and the south
German Lutheran Johannes Brenz had all already inferred from this the desirability of an ecclesiastical system of moral supervision and excommunication alongside whatever civil instances might exist. Plans for such a system,
normally involving lay church members as well as ministers, were included
in draft church ordinances for Schwäbisch Hall, Basel, Constance, Ulm, and
Strasbourg, but the magistrates of these long-standing free cities all proved
unwilling to give church bodies the final say in excommunication. Calvin's
first proposed ecclesiastical ordinance for Geneva of 1537 followed these precedents, Oecolampadius's Basel writings being probably his direct inspiration.
Later editions of the *Institutes* stressed that discipline formed the sinews of
a rightly ordered church and encompassed the power of excommunication,
which served ends different from the state's suppression of criminal behavior.[17] This would always be contested by Bullinger and the Zurich theologians,
who argued, as we have seen, that where the governing authorities were Christian, they were ultimately responsible for discipline as part of their larger
oversight over church and community.

Not only did Calvin come to see the Bible as providing a clear model for
church discipline; he also became assured that Scripture spelled out the basic
offices found in any properly ordered Christian church. Here Bucer directly
inspired him. The Strasbourg reformer's *On True Pastoral Care* of 1538 located within the New Testament two fundamental orders of ministers that he
believed the Holy Spirit designated as appropriate for the church in every
age: "the pastors and teachers, and those servants who meet the needs of the
poor on behalf of the common church." Bucer also considered it "the Holy
Spirit's ordinance . . . that each church have a number of elders who are
all pastors and bishops, i.e. overseers who provide pastoral care and carry
out the pastoral office."[18] Calvin spent the years 1538–42 alongside Bucer in
Strasbourg. His 1543 revision of the *Institutes* incorporated Bucer's claim that
various forms of ministry had a clear biblical sanction and gave greater precision and consistency to the lists of ministers found in Bucer's work. Commentators have traditionally called the resulting product Calvin's doctrine of
the fourfold ministry. This identified four permanent ministries in a rightly
ordered church. The first were ministers of the word charged with proclaiming the Gospel and administering the sacraments. The Bible had called these
by a variety of interchangeable names: bishops, presbyters, pastors, minis-

ters. From this, Calvin, like Bucer, deduced that the Roman Catholic hierarchy that distinguished bishops from parish ministers was illegitimate. Some pastors could exercise a supervisory or oversight role, but all should preach and minister to a congregation at the same time. Teachers formed the second order. They were experts in scriptural interpretation but lacked the authority to apply Scripture to individual cases, to exhort, to administer ecclesiastical discipline, or to administer the sacraments. Elders charged with the censure of morals comprised the third order of ministers. Deacons responsible for the relief of the poor were the fourth. Calvin discerned two grades of deacons, those who collected and distributed alms and those who devoted themselves to the physical care of the poor and the sick. The latter group included the widows whom Paul mentions in 1 Timothy 5:9–10, and thus Calvin's disposition made room for deaconesses as well as deacons, a point much emphasized by recent commentators.[19]

In locating the outlines of the properly ordered church in the Bible, Calvin at once strengthened ministerial authority by claiming divine ordination for it and gave those who recognized the need to escape the pollution of Rome a positive alternative model of a true Christian church. The 1536 edition of the work already made strong claims for the power of pastors:

> They may boldly dare do all things by God's word, whose ministers and stewards they have been appointed; may compel all worldly power, glory, loftiness to yield to and obey his majesty; may for him command all from the highest even to the last; may build up Christ's household and cast down Satan's kingdom; may feed the sheep and kill the wolves; may exhort and instruct the teachable; may accuse, rebuke, and subdue the rebellious and stubborn; may bind and loose; and finally may launch lightnings and thunderbolts; but do all things in God's Word.[20]

His subsequent revisions of the *Institutes* further hardened his ecclesiology in a clericalist direction and augmented his claims for the scope of ecclesiastical discipline.[21]

In claiming that the ministers could "compel all worldly power," Calvin might appear to have set the clergy above even secular rulers, but he took strong issue with the Anabaptist view that true Christians should have nothing to do with government and was eager to deny the charge that the evangelical cause was a threat to the political order. Following Paul, he stressed that the powers that be were ordained of God. Christians could act as magistrates. Because government was divinely ordained, to resist the lawful ruler was to resist God: "We owe . . . reverence and . . . piety toward all our rulers in the highest degree, whatever they may be like." He did, however, add one qualification to this strong statement of the duty of obedience. If the local government made provision for magistrates to oppose unjust decrees, as it did for the ephors of ancient Sparta, these magistrates were duty bound to exercise that authority. Calvin also stressed that secular rulers were properly themselves instruments of the law, which God had created: "Nothing truer could be said than that the law is a silent magistrate; the magistrate, a living law."[22] Tension may thus be discerned in his thought between his call to respect the established political order and his strong sense of the majesty of the divine will, which all men were obliged to obey and which ministers had a duty to proclaim forthrightly.

Tension also characterized his discussion of the respective spheres of secular and ecclesiastical authority, another topic that successive editions of the *Institutes* examined at length. On the one hand, Calvin separated secular and ecclesiastical government far more sharply than the Zurich theologians ever did. The authority of the church extended over matters spiritual. Its charge was to combat sin, to aid believers in the process of their personal sanctification, and to guard the church against dishonor. Secular government watched over outward forms of behavior. It fostered peace and tranquility among men. Yet Calvin also assigned to the secular magistrates the responsibility of seeing to it that both tablets of the Ten Commandments were upheld. They were thus obligated to punish idolatry, sacrilege, and blasphemy. They also had the duty of seeing that ecclesiastical discipline was upheld and the ministers of the word were not mocked. Although separate in jurisdiction, secular and ecclesiastical government were "conjoined."[23]

The precise form of secular government was a matter of theological indifference; governments could be monarchical, aristocratic, or democratic. In the later editions of the *Institutes,* however, Calvin expressed a frank preference for aristocratic forms of government, since they were least likely to fall into tyranny. This was congruent with his views on church government, which favored the selection of elders not by direct election, but through nomination by the clergy followed by confirmation by both the magistrates and the congregation as a whole, although again this was a matter of earthly prudence, not divine decree.[24] Calvin's preference for aristocracy over monarchy might seem surprising on the part of one who was born a subject of the king of France and continued throughout his life to consider himself a Frenchman, especially in light of the many political treatises of the time that proclaimed the superiority of monarchies over all other forms of government. But he also peppered his sermons with cutting remarks about the wickedness and arrogance of individual kings, just as Erasmus's correspondence with his close friends reveals bitterness on his part about oppressive taxation and the excessive concentration of power in a few hands.[25] Sixteenth-century intellectuals may have seen less divinity hedging a king than is commonly thought.

Finally, and most famously, Calvin's theology included a strong statement of double predestination. He first addressed the topic directly in the 1539 edition of the *Institutes,* almost certainly in reaction against Melanchthon's 1535 revision of his *Commonplaces,* in which Melanchthon expressed worry about the moral consequences of a strict doctrine of predestination and introduced a measure of free will into his discussion of election. Bucer's statement of double predestination in his 1536 commentary on Romans also had a great effect. Calvin prefaced his discussion of the subject with a warning that predestination was one of the greatest mysteries of divine justice, and that imprudent speculation about this issue beyond the boundaries defined by Scripture was "foolish and dangerous, nay, even deadly." He was nonetheless equally adamant that, because God had revealed the doctrine, it would be improper to avoid discussion of it, as Melanchthon urged. "In actual fact," Calvin wrote, "the covenant of life is not preached equally among all men, and among those to whom it is preached, it does not gain the same acceptance either constantly or in equal degree." In a world governed by an omnipotent God, this can be for only one reason: "Eternal life is ordained for some, eternal damnation for others." To the fear that telling people their salvation derives from God's inscrutable will may destroy their motivation to live an upright life, Calvin replied, "Scripture does not speak of predestination with intent to rouse us to boldness that we may try with impious rashness to search out God's unattainable secrets. Rather, its intent is that, humbled and cast down, we may learn to tremble at his judgment and esteem his mercy. . . . Paul teaches that we have been chosen to this end: that we may lead a holy and blameless life. If election has as its goal holiness of life, it ought rather to arouse and goad us eagerly to set our mind upon it than to serve as a pretext for doing nothing." The proper use of predestination was to teach those with faith that their belief derives from God's eternal counsel and would endure through all tribulations. Used in this way, it was, Calvin insisted, a comforting and fortifying doctrine.[26]

Admirers and opponents alike recognized Calvin as a master stylist in both Latin and French, blessed with a "golden pen" and a superior ability to express complex theological issues in an easily understandable manner.[27] By constantly expanding and reorganizing his *Institutes,* he was able to create a work that was comprehensive but reasonably compact, appropriate for theological instruction yet also accessible to laymen. In addition to the successive Latin and French editions that he himself prepared, complete translations appeared during the sixteenth century in English, Dutch, German, Italian, and Spanish. No fewer than four theologians of the next generation, including the celebrated Kaspar Olevianus, prepared condensed versions, and a fifth, Johann Piscator, reorganized the volume as a set of theses for disputation by students of theology. The work went through seventy-six sixteenth-century editions in these various formats, not including separate publications of short extracts, placing it ahead of Bullinger's *Decades* and *Sum of the Christian Religion* (sixty-two editions combined) as the best-selling Reformed theological work of the century.[28]

The *Institutes* was hardly Calvin's only work of significance. Once he hit his stride in Geneva, he gave thrice-weekly lessons on the Bible, preached daily every other week, and composed commentaries on the major books of the Old and New Testaments that he began to publish from 1540 onward. Nearly eight hundred of his sermons found their way into print during his lifetime, and after 1557, he allowed his thrice-weekly lessons to be printed too. Doctrinal challenges, major events, and the need to offer believers edification about specific issues prompted him to write still more works. His speed of composition was remarkable; he completed one book of a hundred pages in less than a week. So too was his capacity for work. When his recurring migraines, gout, or hemorrhoids confined him to bed, he dictated from there.[29] His occasional publications ranged from a brief exposition of the Lord's Supper to treatises of advice to the faithful in France, Poland, and the Low Countries to attacks on a wide range of opponents and targets, including the Council of Trent, Anabaptists, anti-Trinitarians, astrologers, Lutheran ubiquitarians, and those "moyenneurs" who favored excessive compromise with the church of Rome. His most successful occasional work (twenty editions to 1622) was his *Announcement of the Value Christianity Would Receive from an Inventory of Relics* (1543), a lampoon of false worship that tabulated the body parts of the leading objects of veneration in Christendom's most famous shrines to show how many heads and feet certain saints would have to have had if all relics were genuine.

Just as the *Institutes* came to outsell Bullinger's *Decades,* so the total volume of Calvin's published works outstripped Bullinger's by the 1540s and continued to do so for most of the rest of the century (graph 3.1). His books appeared in French, German, Italian, Spanish, English, Dutch, Czech, and Polish as well as Latin. Although the vast output of his works in French narrowed to a trickle after the 1560s, the volume of translations into German and English increased noticeably in the last decades of the sixteenth century, an indication of the growing impact his thought would have after his death in England and certain German territories (table 3.1). Bullinger was more widely printed in German and Dutch, but Calvin's writings were more widely disseminated in all other tongues including Latin, the cosmopolitan language of the learned (cf. table 2.1, p. 60). Even his enemies testified to his impressive skills and eminence as a theologian and author. The greatest masterpiece of sixteenth-century Catholic controversial theology, Robert Bellarmine's *Disputations Against the Heretics of Our Time,* cited Calvin in

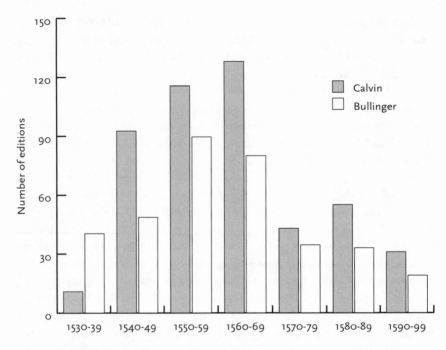

Graph 3.1. The Volume of Calvin's Publications Compared with Bullinger's, 1530–99

TABLE 3.1

Editions of Calvin by Language, 1530–99

	Total	Latin	French English	German Italian	Dutch Spanish	Czech Polish
1530–39	10	6	2 —	2 —	— —	— —
1540–49	93	29	45 9	3 4	— 1	2 —
1550–59	116	43	59 3	4 5	2 —	— —
1560–69	128	27	88 8	1 2	2 —	— —
1570–79	43	20	1 18	3 —	1 —	— —
1580–89	55	15	1 25	9 —	5 —	— —
1590–99	31	14	1 3	6 —	5 1	— 1
Total	476	154	197 66	28 11	15 2	2 1

Source: Calculated from Rodolphe Peter and Jean-Pierre Gilmont, *Bibliotheca Calviniana* (Geneva, 1991–2000).

order to rebut him more often than any other Protestant theologian, Lutheran or Reformed.[30] The vast diffusion of his works was one of the most powerful foundations of his influence throughout Europe.

CALVIN COMPLETES THE GENEVAN REFORMATION

The twenty-seven-year-old Frenchman who arrived in Geneva in 1536 was thus a theological expositor of unusual skill and productivity. His importance within the subsequent history of the Reformed tradition derived from more than this alone, however. No less significant was his success in helping to transform Geneva into a community that by 1560 had gained a reputation in evangelical circles as the very model of a reformed community and in Catholic eyes as the most dangerous lair of apostasy in Europe. In the twenty-five years that Calvin spent on the shores of Lake Leman, he succeeded in establishing the system of independent church discipline that other reformers had sought in vain. He spearheaded a reformation of manners promoted collaboratively by church and state that demonstrably transformed the political culture of the city and the behavior of its inhabitants. He oversaw the departure from the city of many political and intellectual rivals and witnessed the arrival of still more refugees drawn to Geneva by its reputation as a godly community—refugees who enriched Geneva's economy and printing capacities even more than did those who flocked to Emden in this period. All of these transformations contributed to making the city the greatest single fount for the subsequent dissemination of Reformed ideas. None came easily.

When Calvin gave in to Farel's adjurations and agreed to remain in Geneva, he initially consented to serve only as a doctor or reader of the holy Scripture, believing himself unprepared for a pastor's role. The success of his early lectures on Paul in the cathedral, the respect accorded his opinions when he took part in the Lausanne disputation a few months later, and the encouragement of such eminent churchmen as Bucer, who wrote to him to say that God had clearly blessed his ministry, all gradually convinced him otherwise. At the end of the year, he accepted a pastorate and in short order became the dominant figure among the city's clerics. Farel, although twenty years his senior, was keenly aware of his intellectual limitations and tended throughout his life to embrace the ideas of the stronger minds nearby. Calvin, on the other hand, possessed a series of attributes that commended him to Geneva's ruling councils and made him a force to be reckoned with in the close quarters of a sixteenth-century city. His legal training prepared him to draft ecclesiastical legislation. His theological acumen made him an effective advocate of the city's Reformation policies. His fellow ministers and earliest biographers, Theodore Beza and Nicolas Colladon, noted his exceptional recall of the Bible and "truly prophetic vehemence," which he was not averse to unleashing in the chambers of the city council. All these traits served him well in the face-to-face jousts of scriptural and legal argument that were so critical to carrying the day when key questions of ecclesiastical organization were under discussion. Colladon also praised his vigilance. He developed an extensive network of correspondents and informants both inside and outside the city that permitted him to remain abreast of events unfolding in Geneva's governing circles and to rally support from outside at sensitive moments. "Satan and his followers never caught him unawares, but he was always able to warn his flock before the blow."[31] Finally, he had no hesitation about acting ruthlessly when challenged. Although committed in principle to charity and reconciliation, and although capable of acting on these principles when dealing with senior Protestant theologians from other cities, he combined his high estimate of the ministerial calling with not only an awesome confidence that the views he defended represented the pure word of God, but also an apparent fear that the least concession might open the door to rampant disorder. Whenever his personal honor or the truth of his teachings was challenged locally, he demanded nothing short of total capitulation. Musculus called him an always-drawn bow.[32]

Calvin's first actions as spokesman for the city's ministers were anything but triumphs. He was almost certainly the author of a set of articles for the organization of the church that the ministers presented to the council early in 1537. These called for monthly celebrations of the Lord's Supper, the drafting of a brief outline of the faith individuals would be required to master before being admitted to the sacrament, and a system of ecclesiastical discipline exercised by "persons of upright life" that gave the ministers the power to bar unrepentant sinners from the table.[33] The council initially accepted most of these proposals, although it restricted communion to four yearly celebrations. An *Instruction and Confession of Faith Used in the Church of Geneva* followed from the pastors. But the city still held sharply divided opinions on religious matters, and implementation of the program ran into opposition. A sizable number of inhabitants balked at making the required confession of faith. Although in time they were induced to accept the statement, the effort involved convinced the city council to decree at the same time that nobody should be denied access to the Lord's Supper. After new elections brought to power a group of syndics hostile to the ideas of the ministers, relations between the city council and the clerics deteriorated. The city council ordered the clergy to reintroduce certain features of worship still used in Bern but abolished in Geneva, notably the use of special communion wafers instead of ordinary bread and the observation of four holidays. The ministers refused, less out of insistence upon the inalterability of the ceremonies at issue than out of a belief that the council should not dictate church practice. They then defied a ban against preaching against these actions and refused to celebrate communion during Easter 1538. For this provocative insistence on what they claimed to be their clerical prerogatives, they were dismissed and ordered to leave town within three days.[34]

Calvin made his way to Strasbourg, where at Bucer's invitation he ministered for the next three years to the new congregation established there for French refugees. This period of close contact with the author of *On True Pastoral Care* was critical to the maturation of his doctrine of the fourfold ministry. It also was among the most pleasant and productive periods of his life. He published his first French edition of the *Institutes* and first Bible commentaries. He made his debut into the wider world of European theology by accompanying Bucer to the Regensburg Colloquy. The refugee church to which he ministered attained the independent system of church discipline run by a consistory of ministers and elders and the autonomous administration of ecclesiastical poor relief by deacons that had become both Calvin's and Bucer's ideal. Strasbourg's magistrates were not prepared to give the civic church the authority to bar people from communion, but they thought it fine if immigrants regulated their own behavior and ran their own charities.[35]

While Calvin was in Strasbourg, Geneva's church floundered. The *Guillermins,* as Farel and Calvin's supporters were called, grumbled and balked at the way church affairs were now run. The city's new pastors were overwhelmed by the task of winning over the populace and proved to have little skill at defending their version of the faith. When the bishop of Carpentras, Jacopo Sadoleto, wrote an appeal to the Genevans to return to the Roman church, Calvin had to take on from Strasbourg the task of writing the reply that the city's ministers could not or would not produce. Many of the council members who had been Calvin and Farel's chief opponents fell into disgrace after they negotiated a settlement with the Bernese to a dispute over judicial rights in some nearby villages that ceded far more than most Genevans were willing to accept. Two of the city's new ministers abandoned their posts without requesting permission from the municipal authorities. Recognizing Calvin's utility to the city, the now more strongly *Guillermin* city council dispatched an envoy to Strasbourg in September 1540 to see if he could be induced to return. It took a year of entreaties to get him to take up once again this cross that he had told Farel he would rather die "a hundred other deaths" than endure. In the end, it appears to have been the intervention of the Zurich officials that persuaded him to return by giving him confidence that their support would enable him to overcome the opposition to his policies within Geneva. The authorities in Geneva and Zurich alike emphasized that Geneva's strategic location at the gates of France, Italy, and Germany would permit "this man blessed by God with such remarkable gifts" to "spread the reign of Christ more than if he taught in any other city in the world." Farel, for his part, chose to remain in Neuchâtel, where he had been given a pastorate after leaving Geneva.[36]

Immediately upon returning, Calvin set to work drafting a new set of ecclesiastical ordinances. These bear the clear imprint of his Strasbourg experience and show that the outcome of his first ministry in Geneva had not moderated his zeal to assert ecclesiastical prerogatives. The ordinances specifically invoked the four ministries that God was said to have established for his church. They placed the power to test and nominate candidates for pastoral positions in the hands of the sitting ministers, whose choice was then to be reviewed by the city government and finally put before the congregation—just the process of ministerial selection lauded in the 1543 revision of the *Institutes*. Elders were to be chosen by the city officials from the members of the various councils that made up the city government; on this score, the Genevan ordinances linked the consistory more tightly to the city government than would many later Reformed church orders. The title of deacon was bestowed upon the administrators of the city's hospital, again selected by the city fathers. The ordinances also made provision for a weekly gathering, or *conférence,* of ministers at which biblical passages were to be discussed in common "to preserve purity and agreement of doctrine," and for quarterly sessions of fraternal correction to ensure they did not succumb to a long list of vices deemed incompatible with their office. Parents were required to bring their children to weekly catechism classes, and no child was to be admitted to communion until he or she could recite the catechism. Finally, the regulations stipulated the oversight of ecclesiastical discipline by a consistory of pastors and elders. The delicate issue of just who had the power to pronounce sentences of excommunication was resolved with a circumlocution that named no names but seemed to suggest that this power lay with the consistory: if, after being admonished privately and then before the consistory, an offender did not mend his ways, "may he be forbidden from communion and may he be denounced to the magistrate."[37] Whether or not this phraseology was deliberate, Calvin undoubtedly felt he had to compromise in order to gain approval for the ordinances. As he wrote a ministerial colleague, the ordinances were the best that could be hoped for under the circumstances.[38]

Under Calvin's guidance, the consistory swung vigorously into action. The ecclesiastical ordinances instructed the elders to attend to those who expressed religious opinions contrary to the doctrines of the church, who were negligent about attending services, and who engaged in vice or crime. Somewhat more abstractly, Calvin assigned discipline several goals in the *Insti-*

tutes: to ensure that the church of Christ was not dishonored, to prevent the good members of the church from being corrupted by the bad, and to help the bad mend their ways.[39] Thanks to the full edition of the consistory registers now being prepared by a research team under the direction of Robert Kingdon, scholars have a far clearer picture of the action of the consistory than was previously available on the basis of the source that had shaped most discussion of the body: the extracts of particularly juicy cases made from the notoriously hard to read originals by the nineteenth-century local historian Frédéric-Auguste Cramer. In its first years of operation, the consistory busied itself prodding the tepid and the unconverted to attend the weekly sermon, to learn the new prayers and catechism, and to give up Catholic devotional practices to which they remained attached. In 1542, the body heard the already impressive number of 320 cases, of which 161 involved such religious irregularities as missing sermons and failing to master the rudiments of the faith. Several Genevans were reprimanded for using magical charms or called in on suspicion of possessing rosary beads. Others were told to acquire a Bible or hire a teacher to instruct them in the faith.[40]

As the consistory gained confidence and the Genevans accommodated themselves to the new religious order, the pastors and elders turned their attention to other matters. In 1550, the consistory took up 584 cases, of which only 86 involved suspected magical or Catholic practice, failure to attend sermons, and inadequate knowledge of the catechism. Eager to preserve amity among all communicants, the consistory now devoted a large part of its attention to reconciling interpersonal disputes (238 cases), especially family quarrels and domestic assaults. It also increased its oversight of a range of morals offenses, predominantly alleged sexual improprieties (160 cases), but also such matters as gambling, dancing, and false business practices (a further 34 cases). Finally, the consistory came to be used to defend clerical authority. Some 38 people were summoned in 1550 to answer reports that they had spoken ill of the church's ministers or the growing numbers of French refugees in the city. In these first years of operation, the body had recourse to three levels of punishment: private admonition before the consistory, usually delivered by Calvin himself; exclusion from communion; and referral of serious offenses against civic morals legislation to the secular magistrates. Later on, certain offenses were also deemed to require public reparation before the entire congregation.

The referral of wrongdoers to the secular magistrates for punishment reflected Calvin's view that, while temporal and spiritual government were separate domains with their own jurisdictions, the two kingdoms were nonetheless conjoined. He and his fellow ministers sought to establish a close working relation with the city government, so that civic justice reinforced ecclesiastical discipline, and they could turn to the magistrates for support when their authority was challenged. To their dismay, the Genevan ruling councils often hesitated to act as aggressively against immorality as they would have liked. Calvin preached many an angry sermon against the "brute beasts" who inhabited Geneva and the pusillanimous magistrates who ruled over them: "A stubborn mule needs a stubborn muledriver" was a proverb he often repeated.[41]

Through the ministers' persistence, and also because a large fraction of the population shared their belief in the need for moral reform—morals legislation had accompanied the initial implementation of the Genevan Reformation even before Calvin's arrival, it should be recalled—a stream of legal measures seeking to regulate the behavior of the city's inhabitants flowed from the ruling councils. A measure of 1544 issued in response to a complaint by Calvin prohibited the singing of dirty songs and forbade loitering in the streets during the Sunday sermon. A measure of 1546, abandoned after less than a month, required inhabitants who wished to drink or dine out to do so at one of five newly established "abbeys" overseen by members of the city government. No dancing or dicing was permitted; patrons were required to say a prayer before consuming what they ordered; and a Bible was made available to serve as the basis for edifying discussion. A more enduring law of the same year forbade parents to bestow on their children the names of the patron saints whose cult had been followed in the region, names belonging to God alone such as Emmanuel or Sauveur, and "absurd and stupid names such as Toussaint, Croix, Dimanche." A broad morals edict of 1549 added new penalties for confirmed blasphemers, prohibited speaking ill of God's word or the city magistrates, and enjoined that "nobody give themselves over to fornication, drunkenness, vagabondage, or foolishly wasting time, nor to debauching another, but that all work according to their capacity." Further police ordinances between 1550 and 1562 increased the penalties for blasphemy, gambling, and drunkenness and prohibited the sale or purchase of cards, dice, and objects of popery. Sumptuary edicts spelled out regulations to ensure modesty of dress "according to one's estate." Shortly after Calvin's death, a 1566 law imposing new penalties for sexual relations outside of marriage mandated the death penalty for cases of adultery involving two married people. Even before this law was passed, Geneva's courts had begun to exact the death penalty in certain cases of adultery, although when the consistory could persuade the offended party to forgive his or her spouse, the offense was rarely referred to the secular authorities.[42]

The new moral climate was accompanied by a transformation in Geneva's ministry and population. The initial six ministerial colleagues who greeted Calvin on his return from Strasbourg were more of a hindrance than a help, he told Myconius. Within five years all but one had died, been deposed, or been transferred to a rural parish, to be replaced by men whom he regarded as kindred spirits.[43] The local chronicler Michel Roset reported, "This year [1542] the foreigners began to withdraw themselves to Geneva, leaving France and Italy to enjoy the spiritual goods that the Lord daily bestowed on this Church." Statistical evidence about the number of refugees is not available until 1549, when a register began to be maintained to keep track of all those requesting permission to settle in the city. In the next eleven years, more than five thousand heads of household inscribed their names in this register, and several thousand more went unrecorded. These immigrants remained a distinctive and influential segment of the urban population, rarely intermarrying with native Genevan families.[44]

Not everybody in Geneva appreciated the flood of immigrants, harsher laws, and new consistorial oversight of their lives, especially since the ministers who promoted these measures were themselves outsiders who drew much of their support from the immigrants. (Not until 1594 would a native-born Genevan become a pastor of the city's Reformed church.) To many native Genevans it began to appear as if their reformation had been hijacked by foreigners. When some of the anti-*Guillermins* exiled in 1541 were welcomed back in 1545 to fill the population void created by intermittent bouts of the plague over the preceding three years, the anti-Calvin sentiment only grew. A faction that identified itself as the *bons Genevoysiens* formed and began to resist the ministers' efforts to regulate behavior and to exercise ecclesiastical discipline without magisterial oversight. The definitive triumph of the new ecclesiastical order over this opposition came only after a decade of struggle.

The conflict began in 1546 over the surprising issue of superstitious names. When a barber presented his son for baptism before the congregation and asked that he be christened Claude, the name of a popular regional saint, one of the new ministers refused and unilaterally bestowed on him instead the biblical Abraham. This unprecedented action sparked a "great and scandalous commotion" in the church. The governing council in the wake of this incident displayed its support for the ministers by promulgating the law forbidding inappropriate names; many within the city saw it as an unacceptable interference in one of the most basic matters of familial autonomy and continuity. Recurrent conflicts flared up over this issue for the next five years, and a rising chorus of complaint against the foreign ministers and their immigrant supporters was heard. A threatening note left in the pulpit of Saint-Pierre lit into the "buggered renegade priests who have come here to ruin us." People named their dogs Calvin and called Calvin Cain. Soon, some said, even the king of France would move to Geneva. When the consistory began to summon and reprimand those who spoke ill of the ministers, the hostility turned against it.

One inhabitant called the consistory "a new jurisdiction to bother people." A former syndic reportedly said that "he didn't care if he didn't participate in the Lord's Supper for seven years, and as for excommunications, they didn't bother him any more than the Pope's."[45]

At the eye of the storm was a prominent member of a leading family whose relation with the consistory grew more and more poisoned from 1548 onward: Philibert Berthelier. Originally a supporter of the Genevan Reformation, Berthelier's troubles with the consistory began when he was called before the body for allegedly telling somebody that he had once drawn his sword in Lyon to defend Calvin's reputation, but now he would not clip his fingernail for him. In subsequent years, a drunken swordfight, an engagement that he broke on finding out that the woman was not rich, an assault on several recent immigrants, and a report that he appeared to be too familiar with a widow brought him back before the consistory for increasingly unpleasant confrontations. In 1553, he decided he wished to take communion once again. Rather than appear before the consistory to express his regret for his past actions, he approached the body that he and others believed had control over access to the Last Supper, the Small Council. After hearing Berthelier out, the council, then under the control of a web of families hostile to Calvin's views about ministerial power, gave him permission to participate in the service. Calvin and his fellow ministers declared that they would leave town before they would admit Berthelier to communion. This was too alarming an eventuality for the council to countenance. It persuaded Berthelier not to present himself at church on communion Sunday.

Further adroit maneuvers enabled the underlying issue to be avoided for two more years as tension between the good Genevans and those whom they called the French reached a fever pitch. A minister was struck in the head while reproving a group of dancers. A gang of young artisans paraded through the city one night calling out a lewd parody of the verses sung in church prior to the recitation of the Ten Commandments—not "raise your heart, open your ears, obstinate people, to hear the voice of your God," but "raise your ass, open your thighs, girls, for the journeymen are here!" Such blasphemies seemed to the pious to bespeak the utter breakdown of morality. Amid this alarm, six people were convicted and executed for sodomy, further fueling fears of moral collapse. An elderly notary under sentence of excommunication partook at one of the quarterly communion services and afterward claimed in his defense that he thought the council's support of Berthelier's request to be allowed to take communion applied to all excommunicates. For thus profaning the communion table, his tongue was pierced with a hot iron and he was banished. Calvin watched each annual election anxiously to see how "our" party would do.[46]

The final showdown came in 1555. In that February's municipal elections, those whom Calvin's supporters labeled the faithful put their candidates in all four syndical seats. They appear to have been helped in this unexpected victory by the perception among the broad mass of Genevan bourgeois that the group hostile to Calvin had been clinging illegitimately to power by placing kinsmen on the councils in violation of the stigma against *parentèles* so central to urban political cultures in this era. Over the next few months, several members of this clan were purged from the Council of Two Hundred, and thirty-eight immigrants were admitted to the status of bourgeois, thereby reinforcing the voting strength of the faithful. As the *Enfants de Genève* complained about their slackening control of the city, trouble broke out on the night of May 16. Several encounters between members of the two factions led the cry to race through town that the time had come to kill the Frenchmen. Many inhabitants spilled into the streets with their arms. Leaders of the anti-Calvin faction helped to disperse the crowds after an hour, and nobody was injured. Calvin's supporters were nonetheless convinced of the existence of a treasonous conspiracy against the city. They used the ensuing investigation into the tumult to complete the defeat of their rivals. Orders were issued to arrest the leading good Genevans. Those who did not flee to Bernese territory were seized and interrogated under torture. The investigation claimed to uncover a larger conspiracy to "overturn ecclesiastical discipline and the holy Reformation." At least twelve death sentences were handed down, and although a majority of those condemned managed to flee, four leading Genevans were executed, one in so bungled a manner that the executioner lost his job and was banished from the city for a year for allowing his victim to languish for so long. Over the months to come, many more refugees were admitted to the Genevan bourgeoisie, members of the anti-Calvin group were removed from office, and those who spoke against such actions lost their posts or citizenship for doing so.[47]

The harsh measures taken in the wake of the May events silenced opposition within Geneva, but they cost the city valuable outside support. Calvin's friends among the ministers of the other Swiss cities warned him that the reports circulating about his role in these events were destroying his reputation even among those who supported him. He was said to have attended the torture sessions and to have approved all of the government's actions. He justified himself in a long letter to Bullinger several months later in which he denied that he had attended the sessions at which torture was used. In any event, he pleaded, the torture was moderate and its employment quite natural, for "the judges could not permit the plot to be denied when it was obvious."[48] Such an explanation may have satisfied Bullinger, but it did not mollify the Bernese civic authorities, who were moved by the tales told by exiled

Genevans to try to obtain safe-conducts allowing them to return to Geneva and defend themselves in the face of the charges made against them. When this was refused, the Bernese took a much harder line in the negotiations then under way on the renewal of their treaty of combourgeoisie with Geneva. A troubling standoff left Geneva without any formal allies.

In this crisis, Calvin demonstrated the skills that made him valuable to the Genevan city council. He involved himself actively in the diplomatic offensive the Genevans mounted, drafting many of the memoranda that set forth their position. As relations with Bern deteriorated, he used his connections with ministers in other towns in the confederation to advance the idea of the city becoming a full-fledged member of the confederation. Ultimately, however, the salvation of his party resulted as much from changing international conditions as from his actions. In August 1556, Philibert-Emmanuel of Savoy led the imperial forces to a smashing defeat over the French at Saint-Quentin. The duke then began to mass an army in Franche-Comté for a planned liberation of Savoyard territory from the French who had occupied it since 1536. In the face of this threat, the Bernese realized how much their common interest with the Genevans in resisting Savoyard territorial claims outweighed any rifts between them. Negotiations were reopened in a more accommodating fashion, and in January 1557 the treaty of combourgeoisie was renewed. The threat of isolation was over, and the triumph of the party favorable to Calvin in Geneva was secure.[49]

As Colladon observed about the tumult of 1555 and its aftermath, "the discovery of the conspiracy led to a great advance for God's Church, for the populace was rendered more obedient to the divine word, the holy reformation was better observed, and scandals were duly punished."[50] Not only was the right of the church to determine who would be admitted to communion without magisterial interference established beyond challenge; in 1561, the ecclesiastical ordinances were revised to state that excommunicates who did not seek to mend their ways and gain readmission to the service would be subject to civil penalties including banishment. Consistorial power was now backed by state authority. It turned dramatically stricter. In 1553, the consistory had pronounced sixteen excommunications. By 1560, it regularly handed down more than two hundred per annum. Roughly one adult in eight was summoned before the tribunal each year. Certain remarkable cases show just how closely behavior was now overseen. A carter was excommunicated for urinating in the street without turning his back. Nine individuals were penalized for failing to supervise their servants adequately during an epidemic and thus perhaps contributing to its spread. Two men and a woman were barred from the Lord's Supper for "scandal and disrespect to the institution of marriage" because they watched a man slice a loaf of bread during breakfast after his wedding night to show how many times he had had intercourse with his bride. A statistical breakdown of the full range of offenses for which city dwellers were excommunicated between 1564 and 1569 is informative (table 3.2).[51]

In the wake of the events of 1555, one chronicler wrote, "Everybody devoted themselves to the service of God now, even the hypocrites." The city's parish registers from this era reveal astonishingly low rates of illegitimate births and of prenuptial conceptions: 0.12 percent and 1 percent, respectively, probably the lowest rates ever reliably observed by European historical demographers. Some 30 percent of newborn children now received names drawn from the Old Testament, whereas a generation earlier the figure had been barely 3 per cent. Among the numerous contemporary testimonials to how thoroughly manners had been reformed, perhaps the most convincing, because of its source, comes from an Italian Jesuit who passed through the city in 1580: "What caused me some surprise was that during the three days I was in Geneva I never heard any blasphemy, swearing, or indecent language, which I attributed to diabolic cunning in order to deceive the simpleminded by having the appearance of a reformed life." The reformation of manners for which Geneva came to be celebrated by godly visitors appears indeed to have been achieved.[52]

The struggle to establish the church's ability to exercise independent powers of excommunication and to promote the reformation of manners was Calvin's longest-running battle in Geneva, but it was hardly his only one. His conviction that Christians owed strict obedience to God's word and that faithful ministers were the earthly spokesmen of that word led him to see challenges of any sort as nothing less than affronts to "the honor of Christ," affronts that demanded proper reparation. His sensitivity on this score is illustrated by the case of Pierre Ameaux, a member of the Small Council who opined at a dinner party in 1546 that Calvin taught falsely and exerted too much influence over the Small Council. When Ameaux's words found their way to Calvin, he demanded action from the council. It decided to have Ameaux apologize on bended knees to Calvin before the assembly of Two Hundred, but this was not a public enough penance to suit the minister. He refused to present himself for the ceremony and was not satisfied until the council condemned Ameaux to process through the city, kneeling at every major square or intersection to proclaim his regret at having dishonored the word of God, the magistrates, and the ministers.[53]

Silencing challenges to his teachings especially concerned Calvin. Three major battles during his lifetime defined the limits of Genevan orthodoxy. The first broke out in 1551 when Jerome Bolsec, a former Carmelite who had taken refuge in a village close to Geneva, sharply criticized his views on predestination at the city's weekly biblical conferences. Calvin responded so forcefully

TABLE 3.2
Causes for Excommunication in Geneva, 1564–69

Offense	Number	Offense	Number
"Scandals" and lying	347	Theft	62
Domestic quarrels	302	Ignorance of doctrine	53
Quarrels with others	258	Clandestine marriage	50
Fornication and lubricity	160	Business fraud	42
"Rebellion" to elders	151	Gambling	35
Quarrels with kin	126	Dances and "profane songs"	33
Drunkenness	102	Usury	27
"Superstition"	69	Gluttony and idleness	23
Blasphemy and swearing	66		

Source: E. William Monter, "The Consistory of Geneva, 1559–1569," *Bibliothèque d'Humanisme et Renaissance* 38 (1976): 479.

to the accusation that his doctrines made God the author of sin that a city official in attendance took Bolsec into custody on suspicion of blasphemy. At Bolsec's urging, the city consulted with the theologians of Basel, Zurich, and Bern before passing judgment. To Calvin's disappointment, the replies made evident the diversity of opinion that existed among the Swiss theologians on this question. The Zurich theologians warned that both parties in the debate seemed to have spoken immoderately on this thorny issue. Bern's counseled leniency. The court still found Bolsec guilty of "having risen too audaciously in the holy congregation of our ministers and having proposed a false opinion contrary to the sacred scriptures." He was banished from the city.

This was not the end of the affair. Genevans continued to discuss the issue in the streets and taverns, so Calvin turned to print to defend his views. His *Concerning the Eternal Predestination of God,* published in Latin and French, offered an extended justification. In June 1552 he complained to the council that a local lawyer and frustrated candidate for the ministry, Jean Trolliet, was going around the city's taverns saying that his book on predestination was hardly evangelical. Calvin wanted strong action against this slander. Farel aided him by returning to Geneva and reminding the council how fortunate it was to have such a man of God as Calvin in its employ. Trolliet countered adroitly by citing Melanchthon's views on predestination. In the end, the council released Trolliet without punishment but decreed that the *Institutes* contained "God's holy doctrine," that Calvin was a faithful minister of the word, and that henceforward nobody was to speak against him. This silenced Genevan tongues, but the controversy spread outside the city and split the clergy of the Pays de Vaud until its Bernese overlords stepped in and prohibited pulpit discussion of the topic. These were the first controversies over an issue that would move to center stage in Reformed doctrinal expositions and debates in the generations to follow.[54]

The second battle, precipitated by the burning of Michael Servetus in October 1553, centered on the issue of punishing heresy with death. Servetus was an Aragonese doctor who had earned a reputation as a notorious heretic when scarcely twenty with the publication of his *On Errors about the Trinity* (1531), which denied Christ's divinity. By assuming a new identity, he was able to practice medicine undisturbed in several French cities for thirteen years, but his passionate advocacy of his highly idiosyncratic millenarian religious vision finally cost him his safety, and Calvin was in the middle of his detection. In 1545 he sent Calvin a draft of his *Restitution of Christianity* in an effort to convince him of his views. When Calvin replied with a copy of the *Institutes* intended to set him straight, he returned the copy to Calvin with dismissive marginal annotations. Nine years later Servetus published the *Restitution* anonymously, but the trail he laid down in doing so allowed French authorities to detect and arrest him. When he denied that he had written the book, Calvin furnished the French ecclesiastical courts with the damning evidence of his earlier correspondence about the book. Servetus escaped from prison in Lyon but, like a moth drawn to a flame, passed through Geneva as he fled and attended one of Calvin's sermons, where he was recognized and arrested again. In light of his denial that God had ever assumed human substance in Christ, the issue of whether or not he deserved death for his teachings was scarcely controversial among either Switzerland's leading theologians or much of the Genevan population. Consulted again about what the city should do, the ministers and officials of Basel, Zurich, and Bern unanimously expressed their horror at his views. Some of Berthelier's allies rallied to Servetus's defense, but this only cost them support for their apparent willingness to tolerate views that the great majority of the population found shockingly blasphemous. Following the execution, Calvin published a *Refutation of the Errors of Servetus* that not only flayed the Spaniard's teachings but also defended the use of capital punishment in cases of serious heresy. This latter claim, however, offended certain of those who had fled persecution elsewhere to take refuge in Geneva. Several tracts published pseudonymously in Basel criticized the execution of Servetus and Calvin's justification of it. The most cogent of these issued from the pen of a former Genevan schoolmaster, Sebastian Castellio, whose writings on this topic are justly regarded as articulating one of the earliest principled defenses of freedom of conscience. Castellio's writings in turn sparked a longer justification entitled *Of the Punishing of Heretics by the Civil Magistrate* by Lausanne's Theodore Beza, who was emerging as a prominent ally of Calvin's. Just as the Reformed

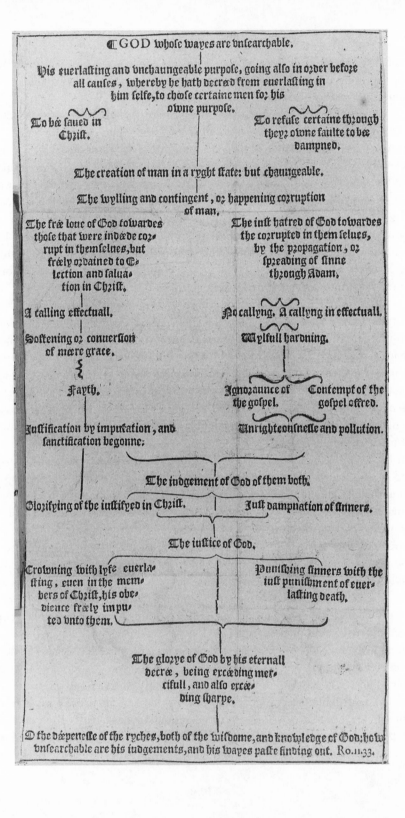

❧GOD whose wayes are vnsearchable.

His euerlasting and vnchaungeable purpose, going also in order before all causes, whereby he hath decreed from euerlasting in him selfe, to chose certaine men for his owne purpose.

To bee saued in Christ.

To refuse certaine through theyr owne faulte to bee dampned.

The creation of man in a ryght state: but chaungeable.

The wylling and contingent, or happening corruption of man.

The free loue of God towardes those that were indeede corrupt in themselues, but freely ordained to Election and saluation in Christ.

The iust hatred of God towardes the corrupted in them selues, by the propagation, or spreading of sinne through Adam,

A calling effectuall,

No callyng. A callyng in effectuall,

Softening or conuersion of meere grace.

Wylfull hardning.

Fayth.

Ignorance of the gospel.   Contempt of the gospel offred.

Iustification by imputation, and sanctification begonne:

Vnrighteousnesse and pollution.

The iudgement of God of them both.

Glorifying of the iustifyed in Christ.

Iust dampnation of sinners.

The iustice of God.

Crowning with lyfe euerlasting, euen in the members of Christ, his obedience freely imputed vnto them,

Punishing sinners with the iust punishment of euerlasting death,

The glorye of God by his eternall decree, being excæding mercifull, and also excæding sharpe.

O the deepenesse of the ryches, both of the wisdome, and knowledge of God: how vnsearchable are his iudgements, and his wayes passe finding out. Ro.11.33.

churches were about to enter the great phase of expansion that placed them frequently in situations in which their members faced prosecution for their beliefs, leading spokesmen of the cause issued perhaps its most forceful defenses of the legitimacy and even necessity of punishing confirmed heretics with death.[55]

Servetus's highly idiosyncratic vision of the restoration of Christianity inspired few direct disciples, but others followed him in questioning the doctrine of the Trinity. Italian evangelicals were especially prone to do so, for many had studied in Padua, and when the strong rationalizing tendencies of Paduan Aristotelianism encountered the Reformed imperative to winnow out all doctrines and practices unsupported by Scripture, the effect could be corrosive. Between 1555 and 1558, several Italians living in or near Geneva, most notably the Piedmontese doctor Giorgio Biandrata, an elder of Geneva's Italian church, approached Calvin with questions about the Trinity. Had the Father not preceded the Son and delegated power to him? Weren't words like *Trinity, person,* and *essence* papist inventions? In the eyes of those who raised these issues, the questioning of the doctrines codified at the fourth-century councils that had declared Christ coequal with the Father and at once both human and divine was just another step in shucking off unwarranted traditions on the voyage back to the purity of the apostolic age. In the eyes of Calvin and the other leading Swiss theologians, however, any suggestion that Christ was not at once both human and divine made his role in salvation incomprehensible. To nip this questioning in the bud, Calvin ensured that all members of Geneva's Italian church were made to sign a confession of faith proclaiming the essential and eternal unity of all three persons of the Trinity. At least one of those who signed this document, Valentino Gentile, quickly repented of doing so. He reportedly told friends that the terms *Trinity* and *essence* were postbiblical inventions and wrote a statement denying that the Father and Son were a single essence. For this, he was imprisoned and forced publicly to burn his written statement. He then left Geneva for eastern Europe, a favored place of refuge for Italian radicals. There he amplified his questioning of Trinitarian doctrine before returning to Bern, where in 1566 he was

3. Theodore Beza's Table of Predestination. The table sets forth the doctrine of double predestination in the form of a flow chart. Beza, a French noble refugee professor of Greek at Lausanne who would later come to Geneva and succeed Calvin as the city's chief pastor, drew it up in the midst of the debates over predestination touched off by the Bolsec affair. It was frequently printed from 1555 onward, appearing in Latin, English, French, and Dutch. This version is from *The Treasure of Trueth, touching the ground worke of man his saluation, and chiefest pointes of Christian Religion* (London, 1576), containing texts by Beza, John Foxe, and Anthony Gilby. (By permission of the Folger Shakespeare Library)

decapitated for his views. Biandrata likewise took his opinions to eastern Europe, where debates about the Trinity split the nascent Reformed movement. Calvin devoted three printed treatises between 1561 and 1563 to refuting Gentile, Biandrata, and other anti-Trinitarians in Switzerland and eastern Europe. The anti-Trinitarian tradition that emerged at this moment would henceforward join Anabaptism as one of the negative poles against which the Reformed defined themselves, and the Nicene doctrine of the Trinity became one of the most tightly guarded borders of Reformed orthodoxy.[56]

Gentile, Biandrata, and Bolsec were only three of many evangelicals who took refuge in Geneva for a while, only to move on after discovering they could not get along with Calvin or accept all of the doctrines and policies imposed there. Bolsec grew so embittered that he later returned to the Roman church and published a slanderous biography of his nemesis including a charge that Calvin had been deprived of his canonry in Noyon for homosexuality that would be a staple of Catholic polemics for generations to come. For every disillusioned refugee who found the bounds of Genevan orthodoxy too narrow, however, several more apparently agreed with John Knox's encomiastic description of the city as "the maist perfyt schoole of Chryst . . . since the dayis of the Apostillis," for by 1560 Geneva's population had swollen to twenty-one thousand inhabitants, more than twice the 1530 figure. Every aspect of the city had been transformed. According to the leading historian of Genevan government, the city fathers of this once tumultuous and faction-ridden town "had evolved from carefree demagogues into the grave and painfully honest stereotype of Calvin's ideal magistrate."[57] Not one of the twenty-five members of the Small Council sitting when Calvin first arrived in 1536 was alive and living in Geneva. The children of fully a third resided in exile. The thousands of new immigrants who had taken their place had introduced the fine textile and clock-making industries that would in time make the city's fortunes. The sizable number of printers and booksellers among them had enabled the output of the city's presses to increase from three titles in 1537 to forty-eight in 1561; by comparison, the output of Emden's presses peaked at twenty-five editions in 1555. Laurent de Normandie, the well-heeled former mayor of Calvin's home town of Noyon, had put into place a vast clandestine distribution network by which the output of these presses reached across France, Savoy, Lorraine, Alsace, and Poland. Among the books produced during these years were copies of Geneva's ecclesiastical ordinances in French and English, with additional excerpts from the city's secular laws in the English version so that readers could learn the full panoply of measures that had made Geneva "a Citie counted of all godly men singularly well ordered."[58] The Catholic polemicists who began to identify Geneva as the most dangerous lair of heresy in Europe around this time do not seem to have picked the wrong target.[59]

One of the most difficult questions about the Genevan reformation is how Calvin, an outsider, was finally able to wield so much power that he could overcome the opposition of some of the city's most prominent families, establish the independent structure of church discipline that other Swiss and German reformers had sought in vain, and oversee such a dramatic transformation of every aspect of city life. While much of the answer lies in his formidable personality and skills, much also lies in Geneva's character and historical situation. As a newly independent city, Geneva lacked the long-established traditions of self-rule and civic morals oversight that the burghermasters of the German free imperial cities or the Swiss urban cantons so jealously guarded. During the crisis of the Schmalkaldic wars between 1547 and 1552, and then again after 1557 when the dukes of Savoy reestablished their power on the city's doorstep after the interlude of French occupation, the city lived in fear of being attacked by imperial or Savoyard forces. In an era when so many were convinced that collective sanctification brought divine protection, this gave added urgency to the quest for moral purification, an urgency reflected in the preambles of the city's successive police regulations, in which the need to avert divine judgment through purity of life is increasingly underscored.[60] The precarious international context also was an incentive to shelter many refugees, despite the competition they represented to the city's native artisans and dominant families. Of pivotal import here too was the fact that guilds enjoyed no representation in Genevan government, as they did in Basel, where guild power was such that only foreigners with personal wealth were allowed to settle.[61] Finally, this predominantly mercantile city housed few learned men who could stand up to Calvin and his fellow ministers in face-to-face debates.[62] The potter was skilled. He also worked with malleable clay.

CALVIN'S INTERNATIONAL INFLUENCE

When the officials of Zurich and Geneva were trying to talk Calvin into returning to Geneva in 1541, they stressed that the town's location and trade connections made it a place from which he could exercise wide influence. Even while he battled to overcome opposition and to promote his vision of church reform within Geneva, he never lost his refugee's consciousness of the importance of events beyond the city. He encouraged like-minded evangelicals across the continent, spoke out on the great theological issues of the day, and dedicated his treatises to a wide variety of European rulers. As the mythic status that Geneva attained as a model of a godly community grew and copies of Calvin's writings proliferated, the reach of his influence grew as well. The final element of his influence derived from the attention he devoted to the larger European scene.

A mapping of Calvin's surviving correspondence between 1542, the first full year after his return to Geneva, and 1563, the last full year prior to his death, discloses the expanding reach of his authority (map 4). By the later years of his life, the geographic extent of his correspondence was comparable to that of Bullinger's. Examination of the contents of his letters and of the published works he directed at an audience beyond Geneva suggests that his sway exceeded that of his Zurich counterpart in many countries.

The great majority of Calvin's letters during the first half of the 1540s were exchanged with fellow reformers in Switzerland and its francophone borderlands. Viret in Lausanne and Farel in Neuchâtel were particularly faithful and frequent interlocutors in these years. The continuing collaboration among these men as well as the inevitable circulation of ministers and ideas throughout a region united by a common language and similar political circumstances meant that these nearby French-speaking areas that had embraced the Reformation became the first part of Europe where distinctively "Calvinist" currents took hold. The same arguments over predestination and ecclesiastical discipline that troubled Geneva found an echo here, many ministers pressing for the establishment of a system of consistorial discipline similar to that in Geneva. While the independent principality of Neuchâtel ultimately adopted an ecclesiastical order that largely replicated Geneva's, efforts in this direction in the Pays de Vaud ran up against the determination of the territory's Bernese masters to retain magisterial control over excommunication and to preserve the institutional uniformity of the territorial church. The passions aroused by this issue came to a head shortly after the showdown in Geneva. In 1558, the classis (a regional ecclesiastical assembly) of Lausanne proposed a set of ecclesiastical ordinances that would have set up a system along Genevan lines. The Bernese authorities, their distrust of clerical assertions of power heightened by the stories told by refugees from Geneva, rejected these. When a number of ministers insisted that it was their prerogative to examine church members' faith before admitting them to communion, they were told to accept the form of ecclesiastical polity decreed by the city fathers or resign. Approximately thirty did so, including Viret and Beza. The expulsion of these ministers from the Pays de Vaud was an event of no small moment for the broader history of the European Reformation, for it came just as demand for ministers was intensifying from newly formed churches in France. Many of the banished clergymen would be sent to organize the fledgling congregations there.[63]

Beyond the borders of Switzerland, Calvin initially focused much of his attention on the Holy Roman Empire, for his sojourn in Strasbourg and partici-

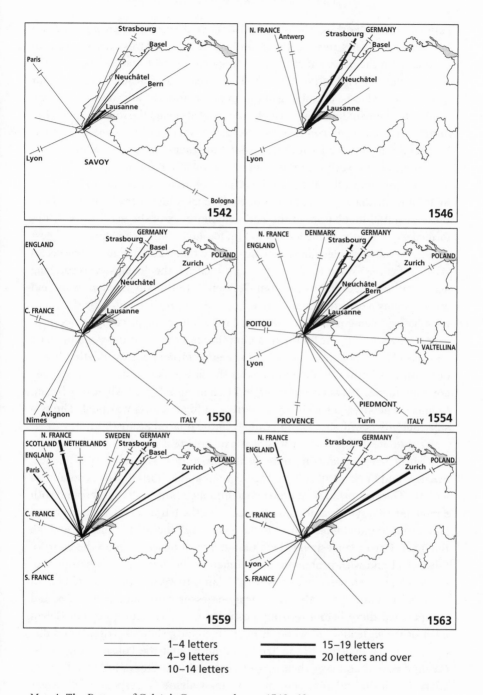

Map 4. The Pattern of Calvin's Correspondence, 1542–63

pation in the Regensburg Colloquy had awakened a strong interest in German ecclesiastical affairs in him. Urged on by Bucer, he addressed an appeal to Charles V on the occasion of the Diet of Speyer in 1544 that he titled *On the Necessity of Reforming the Church*. Three years later, when the Protestant cause appeared to be crumbling in the empire before the advance of Charles's armies, he kept anxiously abreast of affairs and attacked the interim in his *The Adultero-German Interim*. He also dedicated works to the rulers of Saxony, Württemberg, and the Palatinate, dispatching them along with letters urging the princes to persevere in their pursuit of a godly reformation. He devoted special attention to the affairs of the refugee churches, traveling to Frankfurt in 1556 to mediate a dispute within the French church there. In response, these essential incubators of the national churches of the great wave of Reformed expansion to come looked to him for advice and asked him to suggest pastors to fill vacancies far more consistently than they did any other ecclesiastical figure.[64] Much to the dismay of the Zurich theologians, who had long ago come to expect the worst from Germany's Lutherans, he and Beza held out for many years the ever-elusive hope of rapprochement with the more conciliatory elements within German Lutheranism, inspired by concern to gain diplomatic support for the new churches in France. At the same time, he was sharply outspoken in the second sacramentarian controversy that broke out with the Lutheran ubiquitarians in the late 1550s. Indeed, the copious correspondence between Bullinger and Calvin reveals that when this began, Bullinger encouraged Calvin to take the lead in attacking Westphal. The two subsequently coordinated their strategy in the quarrel against him.[65]

By the late 1540s, Calvin was also exchanging a growing number of letters with correspondents in more distant territories. The rulers of Denmark, Sweden, and England all received dedications and exhortations—generally, as with the German princes, to little effect, although Edward VI did respond with a monetary gift. Of greater consequence were the letters of advice and consolation sent to individuals known to have been well inclined to the cause. Like Bullinger, Calvin corresponded with a number of figures around the court of Edward VI and with prominent churchmen of the early Elizabethan period. He developed extensive contacts with Poland, thanks in part to the help of Francis Lismanino, the Minorite royal confessor who came to Geneva and was married there before returning to Poland; on his return, he sent Calvin a list of Polish leaders to whom it might be appropriate to write. When disputes over the doctrine of the Trinity began to split the Polish evangelicals, Calvin directed no fewer than three tracts to the "brothers in Poland" in an effort to halt the widening schism.[66] In sum, Calvin's correspondence reveals not simply a range of contacts comparable to that of the Zurich Antistes, but also an assertiveness about intervening in doctrinal debates and a recognition on Bullinger's part of Calvin's capacities as an advisor and polemicist that made him by the late 1550s the more visible figure of the two on the international ecclesiastical scene. Tellingly, Calvin's leading role in the second sacramentarian controversy encouraged the larger tendency that can be observed in these years for contemporaries to identify him as the leader of the European Reformed. At the outset of the controversy, Westphal referred to his opponents as the Zwinglians or sacramentarians. By 1558 he frequently called them Calvinists.[67]

As map 4 suggests, however, Calvin's closest attention came to be directed toward what he always called his *patria,* France.[68] When the explosion of church building took place there between 1555 and 1561, he was inundated with letters imploring him to dispatch ministers to reap the harvest, seeking his counsel about matters of doctrine, worship, and discipline, and reporting on events in ways that imply he was looked to as the chief administrative officer of the new churches.[69] The following chapters explore further the precise degree of control Calvin exercised over the development and policies of the Reformed churches in the various parts of Europe where such churches took shape. Suffice it to say for now that his relations with the nascent French churches were of an intensity and a character with few or no parallels in the history of Reformed church building, and were all the more significant because the French church in turn became a model to other churches.

One final development of Calvin's years in Geneva spread his influence beyond the city and above all in France: the foundation in 1559 of the Geneva Academy. The establishment of an institution of higher learning to train future generations of pastors was first broached in the ecclesiastical ordinances of 1541. For lack of money and teachers, however, the school was not established until Calvin's final triumph over his opponents enabled him to pry loose sufficient funding from the city government, and the Bernese expulsion of the partisans of independent ecclesiastical discipline from the Pays de Vaud brought a contingent of experienced professors from Lausanne. The Genevan Academy opened in the summer of 1559 under Beza's rectorship, with chairs in theology, Greek, Hebrew, and philosophy. It was immediately swamped with Frenchmen eager to gain a measure of theological formation so that they could return home and pastor to the churches springing up across their homeland. Within five years, Beza claimed, the academy had enrolled three hundred students. About forty-five new students matriculated each year, three times the number that did so in Zurich. Four-fifths were subjects of the Valois monarchy. The following decades would see the universities of Heidelberg and Leiden become still more prestigious centers of Reformed higher education, but the Genevan Academy would remain a magnet for students from other countries for more than a century. Among those who enrolled in it during its first twenty-five years were Philip Marnix van Sint-Aldegonde, subsequently a leading councillor of William of Orange; Karel de Zerotín, the governor of Moravia and a major patron of Protestant churches there; Georg, count of Sayn-Wittgenstein-Berleburg, who would introduce a Reformed church order into his territory; and Jacob Arminius, whose theological writings would inspire the Reformed tradition's greatest doctrinal battles.[70]

CONCLUSION TO PART I
Cooperating Allies, Contrasting
Models of Christian Community

The years between 1531 and 1555 can be seen in retrospect to have been ones of modest but strategic expansion for the Reformed churches. Within the Swiss Confederation and its affiliated territories, the movement gained new ground only in the large but sparsely populated region of the Grisons in southeastern Switzerland and in a few small French-speaking territories on the confederation's western borders between Geneva and Neuchâtel. Reformed doctrines and practices retreated within the Holy Roman Empire, holding onto footholds only in East Friesland and the small spaces of toleration created for refugee congregations in the Rhineland. Yet the consolidation of the movement in and around Geneva provided a base that was perfectly located for the movement's subsequent expansion into France, just as Emden was perfectly located for its growth in the Low Countries. Strong ties were also formed in these years between English Protestantism and Zurich, while the reach of Reformed influence began to extend into eastern Europe's expanding evangelical movements. Clearly, the small corners of the European continent that had embraced Reformed worship by 1555 would not have assumed the importance they did had they not become home to several talented and deeply committed theologians, men who were capable of writing a body of treatises that won them admirers and disciples across national and linguistic boundaries. The organizational and theological accomplishments of Bullinger, a

Lasco, and especially Calvin directly inspired the great explosion of Reformed churches that would follow.

These men were cooperating allies, but they were not advocates of a monolithic vision of how church and state related to one another. In Zurich and Bern, Bullinger and Musculus consolidated and defended the pattern of civic reformation first forged by Zwingli, the *ammann's* son, according to which church and community blended together, a civic court oversaw moral discipline, and excommunication was reserved for those who rejected established teachings. In newly independent Geneva, Calvin, the French child of the ecclesiastical courts, stressed the importance of excommunication as a tool of moral discipline and won independent powers of excommunication for a consistory of pastors and elders. John a Lasco's *Full Form and Manner of the Ecclesiastical Ministry* outlined a model similar to Calvin's in its appointment of elders to assist with an autonomous system of ecclesiastical discipline and of deacons to oversee the distribution of charity. At the same time it defined the civil magistracy as one of the church's ministries and allowed ordinary church members a role in electing pastors they did not have in either Geneva or Zurich.

Some crucial innovations in the organization of larger regional churches also took shape in these years in territories on the fringes of Switzerland that would subsequently prove to be of considerable importance. In both Zurich and Geneva, the churches of the surrounding rural areas stood under the tutelage of the main urban church in a manner that paralleled the larger subordination of *contado* to city in these polities. So dependent upon the city were the rural churches around Geneva that they did not even have their own consistories, although *gardes* were appointed from leading village families to ensure church attendance. Issues of church discipline were handled in the city, and mixed magisterial-ministerial visitation committees came out regularly from Geneva to inquire about the functioning of the rural churches. Oversight of the rural ministers in canton Zurich was exercised by the twice-yearly synods, presided over by the Antistes and a city magistrate; appointed deacons followed up the reprimands and regulations issued at these with regular visits to between four and twenty parishes clustered into units variously known as chapters or colloquys. Where the rural communities were less thoroughly subordinated to a single urban center, however, elements of a more participatory and egalitarian church structure took shape. In the decentralized allied valleys of the Grisons, where each community was permitted to choose between Catholicism and evangelical worship, the leader of the local Reformation, Johannes Comander, convinced the Diet in 1537 to found regular synods to forestall too much variety of belief and worship among the evangelical communities. These began to operate regularly and to examine potential candidates for the ministry from 1553 on, in the wake of the near-split occasioned by the ideas of Camillo Renato. In the seventeenth century, these synods would promote the establishment of parish-level consistories with disciplinary powers, a sign of the prestige the Genevan system of ecclesiastical discipline had obtained within the broader Reformed world by this time, even in territories located much closer to Zurich than Geneva.[1] In the Pays de Vaud, a three-tiered hierarchy of colloquies, classes, and synods took shape in the 1530s, with the classes headed by elected deans and serving as a venue for clerical examination and discipline alongside parish visitations by *jurés*.[2] These latter two systems would offer valuable models for the organizing of a territorial church when such churches began to be founded in large kingdoms without government authorization.

Just as leading Reformed spokesmen championed different ways of fitting church and state together, so too they advocated a range of theological opinions. Calvin's eucharistic doctrine of a spiritual real presence challenged Zwingli's purely symbolic understanding of the Lord's Supper. Subtle nuances separated Bullinger from Calvin on this issue even after the Consensus Tigurinus. A Lasco dissented from the dominant Reformed consensus that denied humans agency in their own salvation. Calvin and Vermigli's forthright advocacy of a doctrine of double predestination diverged from Bullinger's hesitation to delve too deeply into the mysteries of this thorny issue.

Although this was an era when theological disagreement often provoked angry ruptures, all of the leading Reformed churchmen retained enough respect for one another to cooperate in spite of their differences. To be sure, the battle over discipline in the Pays de Vaud prompted some to depart for Geneva and beyond. Many of those who crossed swords with Calvin in Geneva returned to the Catholic church or joined the separate anti-Trinitarian churches that were founded in Poland and Transylvania. A Lasco nonetheless had such respect for his peers' theological learning that he agreed not to publish his *Summary of the Doctrine of the Church of East Frisia* after Bullinger and Melanchthon raised criticisms of it. Bullinger and Calvin worked out in the Consensus Tigurinus a joint formulation on the explosive issue of the Eucharist that in turn made possible Geneva's acceptance of the Second Helvetic Confession shortly after Calvin's death. Both men agreed to disagree on fundamental issues of ecclesiology, for they both believed that the visible church allowed for diversity of institutional forms and worship according to time and place. Bullinger consequently supported Calvin in his conflict over excommunication with Berthelier, arguing that each church needed to use the system best suited for it, even though in other circumstances he advocated the superiority of Zurich's system of moral discipline to the Genevan. Calvin in turn rebuked a group within the French church of London pressing for strict conformity to the Genevan rites of worship, urging them not to make "an idol of me, and a Jerusalem of Geneva."[3] Such solidarity was founded upon the wide areas of agreement they continued to share about most basic questions of theology and worship.

As the Reformed confession of the era that gained the widest approval, the Second Helvetic Confession may be taken to be the most authoritative statement of these areas of agreement and thus of the essential theology of the Reformed tradition at the end of the second generation. This document deftly sidestepped many of the detailed questions about which Reformed theologians were beginning to disagree. It asserted that God had predestined from all eternity those whom he would save but said nothing about the relation between his will and the fate of those who would end up damned. It declared that church institutions should follow the model of the earliest centuries of the church without specifying these precisely. It stated that ministers should conduct church discipline but took no position on whether or not church disciplinary bodies had powers of excommunication. It explicitly rejected the argument that the churches that issued from the Reformation could not be the true Christian church if differences of practice and institutions existed among them. Unity does not reside in outward ceremonies and forms, but in the true preaching of the Gospel and the proper administration of the sacraments.

The largest portions of the confession were devoted to the nature of God and to the fall and redemption of mankind. Sinful human beings were made just in God's sight through the imputation of Christ's righteousness. At the same time God's chosen are regenerated by the Spirit and made capable of doing good. God alone was to be worshiped; there should be no veneration of the saints, much less of their relics. As God is spirit and by nature invisible and immense, images of him are lies, and people should be instructed in religion through the preaching of the Gospel. Fasting is commendable, but it should not be required at fixed times, and especially not during Lent, which has no foundation in the writings of the apostles. A few holy days relating to Christ's birth, life, and resurrection may be devoted to worship in addition to the Lord's Day, but feasts in honor of the saints are inappropriate. Worship should be in the vernacular. The sacraments are signs of sacred things, but alongside the physical eating of the eucharistic elements in the Lord's Supper believers partake of Christ's body and blood through a spiritual eating. The church is the invisible assembly of the faithful that has existed for all time, appearances to the contrary during certain eras notwithstanding, with the Israelites and the Gentiles sharing the same fellowship. Christ is its sole head. All erstwhile church property should be devoted to supporting ministers, schools, and the poor.[4]

One further point on which all of the leading Reformed theologians of this generation insisted was the impropriety—indeed, the polluting danger—of participating in the public rituals of popery. The magnitude of this principle can hardly be overstated in accounting for the Reformed movement's central role in the subsequent period of Protestant expansion, for it encouraged those living in Catholic lands who accepted it to separate from the established church. In 1554, furthermore, Calvin went one step beyond simply urging believers to withdraw from the Roman church. In two letters addressed to the faithful in France, he urged them to form assemblies of their own and advised that if a group of believers gathering for prayer and edification wished to administer the sacraments, they needed to follow certain procedures. First, they should elect a consistory. This in turn could select a pastor. In another letter written soon thereafter to a Piedmontese nobleman who had inquired what those living under the papal tyranny who sought to abstain from idolatry should do about baptizing their children, he encouraged the man to think about forming "some assembled flock that makes up a church body and a pastor," promising help in finding a minister if needed. That winter, two pastors went out from Geneva to preach among the Waldensians of the Piedmontese Alps, the first of more than 220 pastors dispatched over the next eight years to oversee the organization of worship in Piedmont and France.[5] This active encouragement of the formation of what would become known as "churches under the cross" (that is, churches formed secretly in defiance of local law) contrasted sharply with the counsel Luther offered those in similar circumstances. Not only did he tell his followers in Augsburg in 1532 that they could have their children baptized in the Roman church. He also advised them against holding private assemblies of their own to celebrate the Lord's Supper and reiterated this disapproval of private ecclesiastical gatherings in letters to his followers in Antwerp written around 1531 and 1544.[6]

By the 1550s, sentiment in favor of establishing an alternative to the Roman church was building in many parts of Europe beyond Protestantism's original epicenter in the empire and Switzerland. Already during the 1540s, small groups of believers had attempted to form conventicles for common Bible reading and prayer, or even assemblies with the regular administration of the sacraments, in a few localities in Scotland, France, the Low Countries, and Italy. These proved short-lived in the face of government repression. In 1554–55 assemblies reemerged in all of these countries except Italy, where the establishment of the Roman Inquisition in 1544 had unleashed a powerful weapon against organized heresy. We do not know the exact considerations that led Calvin to begin to encourage the formation of churches under the cross in 1554; neither can it be shown that the new assemblies of 1554–55 that appeared in Poitiers, Paris, Antwerp, and parts of central Scotland all owed their foundation directly to the advice contained in Calvin's letters. Over the next few years, however, ministers sent out from Geneva would play a major role in shaping the hundreds of new churches that soon sprang up in France. The political difficulties for the French crown created by the emergence of a strong movement for church reform in that country in turn prevented the French from sending to Scotland the sort of military assistance that in 1542–46 had been crucial in putting down a first wave of agitation for a Protestant church. Calvin's active encouragement of the formation of autonomous church gatherings thus became a further reason for the dynamism of the Reformed movement in this period.

Reformed doctrine had already shown a greater capacity to mobilize popular support than Lutheran ideas when the two were in direct competition in the cities of south Germany. Now it also offered compelling reasons for those drawn to it to separate themselves from the church of Rome. It offered a model derived from the Bible of how to form independent churches in the absence of governmental support. It was firmly ensconced in a number of enclaves that were well situated to serve as bases for wider expansion and that appeared to contemporaries to be admirable models of reformed communities. Its theologians had given expression to its basic tenets in a number of monuments of compelling biblical exegesis. With its diversity of ecclesiologies, it could justify magisterial control of a state church as well as the formation of independent churches under the cross, making it appealing to rulers who had already assumed the supreme headship within their territories. All of these considerations help to explain why the Reformed churches were poised for a dramatic period of expansion in 1555. They also help one understand why the processes by which that expansion occurred would prove to be strikingly varied, as would the institutional outcomes of the various Reformed reformations. For as this multivocal tradition encountered the great diversity of political, socioeconomic, and cultural circumstances that prevailed within the various regions in which Reformed churches were founded, the upshot would be an even wider range of church structures and worship traditions than that already established in the first two generations of the movement's growth.

PART II

The Expansion of a Tradition

The Reformation unfolded across Europe at differing speeds. Within the Germanic cultural world, including its economic and cultural outcroppings in Scandinavia and eastern Europe, the "Luther affair" quickly gave rise to a flood of sermons and publications and to excited public debate. Pressure to alter the established religious order grew so rapidly that the governing authorities of many territories were moved by varying mixtures of personal conviction and political expediency to implement changes by the later 1520s or early 1530s. Because of Bernese control of certain French-speaking areas of the Swiss borderlands, this same current of expansion also leaped easily over the linguistic boundary into a few territories affiliated with the Swiss in the 1530s.

As a rule, however, linguistic boundaries dramatically impeded the dissemination of evangelical propaganda, while rulers beyond the Holy Roman Empire typically showed less indulgence to heterodox ideas than those within it. Outside the German-speaking world, printed books, itinerant preachers, and locally influential teachers all gradually spread heterodox ideas of varied, often ill-defined provenance. Occasionally these won sizable bands of followers in one place or another in brief, localized bursts of enthusiasm. Not until the 1540s and especially the 1550s, however, did they give rise to enduring forms of worship independent of the Catholic church.

The Habsburg lands to the southeast of the empire, where German speakers lived scattered among those who spoke a variety of other tongues and where a powerful aristocracy curtailed government repression of heresy, were the first part of Europe outside the Germanic linguistic sphere to see such churches emerge. Here, starting in the late 1530s and early 1540s, evangelical ideas began to eventuate in local revisions of the form of worship through what might be labeled parish reformations. Gradually, these spread to more and more parts of this region; the parishes affected grouped themselves into larger territorial synods; and these took on a clear confessional complexion. Next touched was England, where Henry VIII's rejection of pontifical authority in 1533–34 had created a situation in which well-placed groups of reform-minded individuals could push a now-autonomous Church of England into a Protestant mold. During the reign of Edward VI (1547–53), the worship and theology of the church were altered in ways that were unmistakably Protestant. Queen Mary restored Catholicism after Edward's death, but five years later, after Mary's death, Elizabeth I brought England back into the Protestant camp. Also in the second half of the 1540s, the first efforts were made to organize evangelical churches in the Polish capital of Cracow. Over the next two decades, continuing efforts at expansion and organization spread Protestant churches across much of the vast territory of the Polish-Lithuanian Commonwealth.

The pace of change quickened after 1555. In short order, groups of believers formed networks of churches under the cross in three important west European polities, the rulers of which had set their face firmly against Protestantism. In Scotland, a political revolution soon made the new churches the established religion of state. In France and the Netherlands, the churches had to wage a long struggle to survive. Ultimately they gained legal toleration in France and became the public church of those northern provinces of the Netherlands that won their independence from Habsburg rule. In all of these countries, conflicts touched off by the organization of the new churches became central political struggles of the latter part of the sixteenth century. The second wave of Protestant expansion thus built up slowly, but it eventually engulfed most of Europe north of the Iberian and Italian peninsulas. By the end of the sixteenth century, firmly established and legally recognized Protestant churches stretched from the Atlantic to the borders of Muscovy and into the recently conquered Hungarian fringes of the Ottoman Empire.

This second wave of Protestant expansion unfurled overwhelmingly under the sign of the Reformed. In the German- and Slovak-speaking parts of Hungary and the German-dominated cities of Polish Prussia, Lutheran influences dominated once the churches of these areas assumed distinctive confessional coloration. Small organized Lutheran and Anabaptist churches also took shape alongside the Reformed in the Netherlands, and anti-Trinitarianism became salient in Poland and Hungary. Everywhere else outside Germany and Scandinavia, Protestantism would be virtually synonymous with Reformed Protestantism for generations, if not centuries, to come. Reformed currents advanced even within the Holy Roman Empire, where they had been in retreat over the previous generation. In a string of territories from the Rhineland to Prussia that had already embraced the Reformation, the ruling princes, now deciding they found this variant of Protestant theology more compelling than the increasingly contentious Lutheran orthodoxy, carried out second reformations that implanted Reformed worship in place of or alongside the Lutheran.

Generations of historians have explained the sudden prominence of Reformed currents across Europe with the patently tautological observation that Calvinism was the most dynamic of the Reformation's various creeds after the death of Luther. Many of the reasons for the faith's particular dynamism have already revealed themselves. The expansion of Reformed churches across Europe would reveal still more. Institutional features of those churches that developed in opposition to the governing authorities turned out to equip them well to organize the political and military defense of their interests against hostile rulers. The consistory proved to be able to double as a valuable information gathering and fund raising body. The network of regional and national synods that the Reformed first set up in France and soon replicated elsewhere could coordinate resistance on a broader scale. In short, the combination of a theology that urged separation from the abominations of Rome with church institutions that proved to be helpful in coordinating resistance enabled the Reformed to carry through "revolutionary reformations" in opposition to hostile rulers in situations in which the Lutherans rarely could do the same. Yet even while its implacable hostility to impure worship infused the Reformed cause with a destabilizing zeal, and even while Calvin's political theory justified resistance by lesser authorities to ungodly commands, Reformed political theology continued to insist on the need for ordinary subjects to obey the duly constituted authorities and to appeal to princes to step forward to uphold God's holy decrees. In its Zurich variant, it even offered those in power religious sanction for supervising both the nomination of the clergy and the exercise of moral discipline. The movement was thus as capable of appealing to rulers as it was of galvanizing revolutionary reformations. The dominant strain within Lutheranism being represented by an ever more precisely defined orthodoxy aggressively intolerant of dissent, pious rulers eager to perform their obligations as Christian princes not only might grant Reformed ideas a hearing as a potential alternative without fearing that their authority over their subjects would be reduced if they embraced it; they might also often find these ideas compelling. This was especially likely to happen when they had been raised in a Melanchthonian milieu, fought alongside Reformed allies, or relied upon clerical advisors inclined toward Reformed views. The patterns of international migration that brought such advisors to these courts thus also contributed to Reformed success. In short, the dynamism evidenced by the remarkable geographical expansion of Reformed churches in these years arose from an accumulation of specific theological features, organizational attributes, and historical circumstances that all helped the cause win supporters among princes and people alike, then defend itself tenaciously in those instances in which it expanded in defiance of the ruling authorities.

The variety of the processes by which the diverse Reformed churches took shape further augmented the variety of liturgical forms, institutional structures, and patterns of church–state relations that already marked the churches of Zurich, Geneva, and Emden by midcentury. Not only were some of the emerging national churches more closely modeled on one or the other of these churches as a result of the human and epistolary connections between them. The distinctive configuration of political and social conditions found in each territory in which the new Reformed churches took root, the process by which the churches were brought into being, and the place they obtained within the political community all also shaped central features of each new national church. The result of the great phase of Reformed expansion was a family of churches that recognized a degree of kinship with one another, yet displayed considerable variety in their institutions and worship practices and were able to exercise varying degrees of control over the behavior of their members.

For all the variety that would characterize these churches, recurring patterns did shape their early history. One of these was the rising response Calvin's theological writings and the Genevan model of church organization received across the continent. The initial extent of direct Genevan influence varied widely from one national Reformation to another, being most pronounced in France and least pronounced in Hungary. In time, it augmented everywhere.

Another pattern was the growing attractiveness of the presbyterian-synodal system of church organization first developed in France. Each generation brought the Reformed tradition new problems and new debates. In this era of rapid expansion, a pressing issue became that of how to organize national churches and maintain unity among local congregations when these arose within large polities whose rulers were unsympathetic. The presbyterial-synodal system solved this problem by linking local churches all deemed equal in authority into a hierarchy of local, provincial, and national assemblies that in turn determined policy for the church as a whole and played a role in appointing new ministers. Such a system had the further merit, in the eyes of clerics and pious laymen suspicious of government interference in church affairs, of providing a method of ecclesiastical governance that was largely independent of the secular authorities. In this era when few church settlements were as yet stable and waves of believers regularly moved across borders following the accession of a new monarch, the revocation of a grant of religious toleration, or the outbreak of a civil war, ideas and institutions elaborated in one country quickly became known in others. The presbyterial-synodal system became a model for elements within virtually all of the new Reformed churches. Often, it was opposed by others who articulated defenses of the existing system. Its ultimate impact tended to be greater in those Reformed churches that evolved independently of the political authorities than in those that owed their existence to royal fiat. At the same time, the international debate over these questions of church order led a number of of those who championed one or another of these forms to claim biblical sanction for institutions that were initially defended on the basis of expediency alone. Thus were born in this generation the first arguments for *jure divino* presbyterianism and episcopalianism.

Part II examines in turn each major region in which Reformed churches became established during Protestantism's second wave of expansion. Because the advance of the presbyterial-synodal system is such an important theme in the history of all of the Reformed churches across Europe, the survey will begin with the country in which this system first took shape, France. It will then examine the other two closely related cases of west European Reformed churches that materialized, like the French, in opposition to the established political authorities and came to be characterized by church orders incorporating a strong presbyterial-synodal element: Scotland and the Netherlands. Next will come the cases of England and the German states, where the triumph of Reformed theological influences depended far more on the decisions of the ruling authorities and where presbyterian-synodal forms were often rejected or accepted only in part. Finally, the rather different cases of eastern Europe, where presbyterian-synodal influences arrived late or never, will be taken up. For each area, the story will be carried down to that point late in the sixteenth century when the national church in question had obtained a stable position of legal toleration or establishment and relatively enduring institutional structures. The goal in each case will be to narrate and account for the distinctive course of each national reformation, the features of each set of Reformed churches, and the diverse ways in which these fit into the larger societies of which they were a part. In many cases, this first generation of a national church's history gave rise to internal tensions that shaped the history of the church in question for generations to come.

4

FRANCE

*The Construction and Defense
of a Minority Church*

rance was sixteenth-century Europe's most populous kingdom. At midcentury, approximately eighteen million subjects lived under the authority of kings whose powers made them appear to contemporaries to be the very models of absolute monarchs. Such national identity as France possessed in this period was bound up with pride in a "most Christian" monarchy that had been ever vigilant in the fight against heresy. But with Charles V's inheritance of more than a half dozen of Europe's most important crowns, the French kings found themselves in the unwonted position of being surrounded by the lands of a still mightier ruler. In their rivalry with the Habsburg emperor, they availed themselves of any potential ally, including the Protestant princes of Germany, whose diplomacy led them to be less severe in their repression of the new Protestant heresies than they might otherwise have been inclined to be. Francis I, moreover, was well disposed to new humanist scholarship and protected certain biblical scholars and critics of the ecclesiastical establishment whom the strictest defenders of Catholic orthodoxy viewed as dangerous heretics. In such a situation, evangelical ideas spread widely enough so that when Calvin began to encourage the formation of churches under the cross and to dispatch ever-growing numbers of pastors into the country, and when the accession of two youthful kings within eighteen months of one another after 1559 seriously weakened the force of royal authority, new Reformed churches materialized in greater abundance than in any other European kingdom around this time. These new churches quickly assumed what would be their enduring institutional contours, linked in the presbyterian-synodal manner that would be so widely emulated.

As the churches proliferated, many of those drawn to them dared to dream that Catholicism might soon topple in France. Such hopes were cruelly disappointed. Although the Reformed won the support of a fraction of the great nobility, the three sons of Henry II who successively mounted the throne after 1559 all remained loyal to the Roman faith. The defenders of Catholic orthodoxy rallied much of the population around the faith of their ancestors. A series of bloody civil wars broke out. Through dogged resistance, the Reformed were able to avoid total defeat in all of these wars, even though they formed only a minority of the population. Still, massacre and defection thinned their ranks. A second moment of hope emerged when the vagaries of dynastic succession brought the Protestant Henry of Navarre into line to ascend to the throne after 1584. By this time, however, Catholic militance had become so powerful and well organized that massive opposition forced him after eight years of struggle to renounce his faith in order to assure his accession. Except in the little principality of Béarn, where the Reformation was imposed by the ruling house of Navarre as an act of state, the Reformed church thus became the legally tolerated faith of only a small fraction of the population in France. Through its tenacious resistance, this minority nonetheless preserved rights of legal toleration for its form of worship against recurrent challenge throughout the civil wars. Because of the country's considerable overall population and its traditional importance within European culture and higher education, this minority church would retain a key role in the international Reformed world well into the seventeenth century.

Although new Reformed counterchurches began to multiply in a sustained fashion only after 1555, sentiment in favor of some transformation of the established church along lines similar to those characteristic of the German and Swiss Reformations began in France almost from the moment Luther's name became known. Indeed, aspirations for a humanist Christian Renaissance of the sort that fed into the early Reformed movement in Switzerland were developing in France even before the publication of the ninety-five theses. In Paris, Jacques Lefèvre d'Etaples was at the center of a group of scholars whose editorial work on the Bible and reading of the church fathers were by 1517 leading to a critique of long-observed devotional and sacramental practices. When Luther began to criticize Rome, Parisians paid attention. His Latin writings could be purchased in Paris by February 1519. A Swiss friend of Zwingli's studying there reported the following November that "no books are purchased

Map 5. France

with greater avidity." Over the next five years, six Frenchmen are known to
have been moved by their reading to travel to Wittenberg to study with Luther. A preacher in Grenoble advocated communion in both kinds and clerical marriage. The most significant changes came in Meaux, where in 1521
the reforming bishop Guillaume Briçonnet had placed Lefèvre and a number
of his students in pivotal positions in the diocese. By 1524, members of this

group were in epistolary contact with Zwingli and Oecolampadius and had embarked upon liturgical experiments to incorporate the vernacular exposition of the Bible more centrally into church services. Those on both ends of this correspondence could easily have seen themselves as fellow workers in the common cause of evangelical renewal.[1]

But the cause of a humanistic Christian Renaissance could not evolve into a local reformation in a city like Meaux, part of a larger centralized kingdom, in the same manner it did in Zurich, part of a loose confederation. France housed the most authoritative theology faculty in Latin Christendom, the highly conservative University of Paris. In 1521, the doctors of that institution condemned Luther's works as heretical. Laws forbade the purchase and ownership of his books. Francis I rejected the arguments of those "Sorbonistes" who sought to equate the *secte fabrisienne* with the *secte luthérienne* and showed himself willing to protect biblical scholarship of a humanist cast, but he supported the measures against Lutheran doctrines and reacted strongly against all incidents of iconoclasm and sacrilege. Furthermore, his protection was vulnerable to disruption, for his prime concern was war against the Habsburgs. When he was taken prisoner after the battle of Pavia in 1525, his queen, Louise of Savoy, and the Parlement of Paris initiated heresy proceedings against the Meaux circle, forcing its members to flee for safety to Strasbourg. After Francis regained his freedom and returned to his kingdom, he permitted the members of this group to return as well. Most did so—one who did not was Guillaume Farel—and many gained influential church positions through the patronage of the king's evangelically inclined sister Marguerite of Navarre. But the experiments in worship they attempted were narrowly circumscribed as a result of the laws against Lutheran doctrine. They and like-minded evangelicals could continue to hope that reform might someday come from within the church. No immediate transformation was forthcoming.[2]

The early French Reformation thus became a matter of the clandestine circulation of heterodox ideas. As is inevitable with currents of opinion whose adherents sought to escape detection, the precise growth of adhesion to these ideas is difficult to trace. The number and geography of heresy trials and of reports of attacks on Catholic holy objects, as well as the volume of Protestant literature in the local language, nonetheless offer rough guides to the force and extent of the underground dissemination of such ideas, permitting comparisons between regions and countries. In France, the geography of heresy trials and of public manifestations of hostility to the church of Rome indicates that by 1525 fewer than a dozen cities had been touched by the so-called contagion of heresy. But by 1540 virtually every region of the country except Brittany and Auvergne had become infected. Within the large judicial circumscription

TABLE 4.1

Heresy Trials before Two French Appeals Courts, 1521–60

Parlement of Toulouse*		Parlement of Paris**	
1521–30	8		
1531–40	121		
1541–50	257	1540–49	797
1551–60	684	1550–59	290

*Estimated total population of jurisdiction: 2,000,000
**Estimated total population of jurisdiction: 8,800,000
Sources: Raymond Mentzer, *Heresy Proceedings in Languedoc, 1500–1560* Transactions of the American Philosophical Society 74 (Philadelphia, 1984), pp. 169–70; E. William Monter, "Les executés pour hérésie par arrêt du Parlement de Paris (1523–1560)," *Bulletin de la Société de l'Histoire du Protestantisme Français*, 142 (1996), 200. Population estimates derived by extrapolation from the figures in Jacques Dupâquier et al., *Histoire de la population française*, II, 68, 76.

of the Parlement of Toulouse, the number of heresy trials increased steadily with each decade from the 1520s through the 1550s, while in the still larger portion of the kingdom subject to the jurisdiction of the Parlement of Paris, the number of cases attained an impressive peak in the 1540s (table 4.1). The intensification of persecution visible in an upsurge of trials before the latter court in the second half of the 1540s also fueled a growing movement of flight to Geneva. Late in 1549, the Genevans established their *Livre de Bourgeoisie* to keep track of all those requesting to be allowed to settle there. In the following year, 122 Frenchmen had their names recorded.[3]

The growing number of heresy trials and rising tide of emigration stemmed not only from the advance of heterodox sentiments, but also from a hardening of the line between orthodoxy and dissent. On the one hand, the contours of permissible religious belief were set ever more clearly and narrowly in the decades after 1525. A particularly important step came in 1543, when an aging Francis I instructed the Sorbonne to draft a set of articles of the faith that came to define orthodoxy. The articles defended not only the central doctrines of Catholicism whose rejection defined magisterial Protestantism, most notably the importance of works in salvation, but also the value of such practices as pilgrimages and prayers to the Virgin that were contested by a broad range of humanist as well as Protestant critics.[4] On the other hand, criticism of the established church became more and more outspoken, and sacramentarian views increasingly pronounced in the works of evangelical propaganda circulating within France. The most successful early evangelical books in the vernacular, such as the oft-reprinted *Book of True and Perfect Prayer,* mixed excerpts from the Bible with devotional meditations and prayers by a variety of authors from Luther to Erasmus to Farel. The dominant note was a broad, theologically ill-defined call for a return to the lessons of Scripture. Luther's writings were reprinted more often in translation than any other foreign Protestant author, though even Luther's voice, it must be added, was far more muted than in Germany: just 22 editions of his work were published in French during his lifetime, as against 2,946 in High German, a measure of how substantially the combination of the linguistic barrier and governmental persecution slowed the diffusion of Protestant ideas.[5] But from the time that divergences over the interpretation of the Eucharist emerged among the reformers, the majority of French evangelicals in touch with the disputes in Germany seem to have sided with Zwingli. Farel's ideas took on a strongly Zwinglian cast after his flight to Switzerland. Because his *Summary and Brief Declaration* (1529) was the most important statement of evangelical theology by a native French author prior to Calvin's *Institutes,* eucharistic views in line with those espoused in Switzerland found their way fairly quickly into French evangelical propaganda. With the triumph of the Reformed cause in Neuchâtel and Geneva and the rapid establishment of printing presses there, outspokenly Reformed notes then began to dominate the printed propaganda for religious change that circulated within the country. It is a measure of how swiftly Geneva came to dominate the production of evangelical religious propaganda for the French market that of the forty-three vernacular titles listed in 1542 on the first French index of prohibited books, fully 70 percent came from Geneva. Calvin's writings were by far the most numerous among the works listed on this and successive indexes. Viret's ran a distant second. Through their outspoken attacks on the corruption of the Roman church, on the abominations of the mass, and on the unholy compromises of Nicodemism, these works urged their readers to make their rejection of the old forms of worship plain.[6]

As evangelical propaganda of a Reformed cast circulated ever more widely through the kingdom, those attracted to such ideas chose various courses of action to give expression to their beliefs. In at least one case that is well known to us because it is reported in *The Ecclesiastical History of the Reformed Churches in the Kingdom of France,* efforts were made to establish regular worship. This occurred in Meaux in 1546, when a group of individuals inspired by the example of the French church of Strasbourg—Calvin's old church—chose one of their members to preside over their gatherings and deliver sermons and administer the sacraments in a private home. According to the *Ecclesiastical History,* three to four hundred members led by a wool carder deeply versed in Scripture were soon involved in the clandestine worship. So large a group could not avoid detection by local judicial officials. Sixty members were seized in a raid; fourteen of the leaders were executed; others were banished to nearby cities, where some of them in turn became the kernel of new, informal prayer groups.[7]

The organization of informal gatherings for Bible reading and mutual edification was a more common course of action. Two such groups are known to have existed in Lyon in 1551. One, organized by Claude Baduel, met secretly and worked quietly to propagate evangelical ideas while maintaining an outward show of Catholicism; the other was composed primarily of artisans given to such public acts of bravado as singing psalms while parading through the streets with arms. In still other cases, individuals simply abandoned certain traditional Catholic practices and let their hostility to them be known, but were then led by a brush with the law to conform to the practices of the established church. In the little town of Saint-Seurin d'Uzet in the western province of Saintonge, Jean Frèrejean convinced his father in 1541 that he should stop commissioning a mass for the family dead at Christmas and no longer invite the clergy of the town to the annual family banquet. Shortly thereafter, a priest asked him if he believed in purgatory and received the reply that the only true purgatory was that of Jesus Christ on the cross. Frèrejean was denounced to the ecclesiastical authorities and, after interrogation, fined 100 *livres* for his heretical views: "As a result of this persecution which caused us the loss of a large part of our goods and great fear . . . , against our conscience we subsequently attended mass, vespers, and other superstitions of the papal church until the year 1560, when the church of God began to establish itself and reform the present land of Saintonge."[8]

The fate of these various individuals and groups reveals a great deal about the legal repression of heresy in France. Although thousands of people were tried for this crime in the first six decades of the sixteenth century in France, only 14 percent of those tried by the Parlement of Paris and 6 percent of those tried by the Parlement of Toulouse paid with their lives. The death penalty tended to be reserved for those who committed flagrant acts of iconoclasm and those who played leading roles in organizing regular worship gatherings, as in Meaux. For people who simply expressed wicked opinions, the most common penalty was a public confession of guilt or conditional liberation. In all, the number of executions for heresy within this vast kingdom between 1523 and 1560 was about five hundred.[9] Repression at this level could break up the most ambitious endeavors to organize regular Protestant worship and scare many people into outward conformity, but it could not prevent small groups of evangelicals from assembling for prayer and the reading of Scripture. Across the kingdom there were pockets of people whose disenchantment with the Roman church offered a valuable base on which to build when Calvin began suggesting they set up churches of their own.

The key import of the churches that began to be created with Calvin's encouragement from 1555 onward was that they provided an institutional basis that gave shape and direction to the longings for evangelical reform that had spread through the kingdom by that time. All had the attributes of a proper church as defined by Calvin: a consistory, a minister, and regular celebration of the sacraments. The first such churches were erected in Paris and Poitiers. As evangelicals in other nearby towns got wind of them, they formed similar churches under their guidance or sought ministers from Geneva. By 1559, at least seventy-two churches had been founded.[10] Then, political events presented these fledgling churches with ideal conditions under which to grow. The proliferation of Reformed churches throughout the kingdom so alarmed King Henry II (r. 1547–59) that he offered the Habsburgs concessions for peace in order to free his hand to deal with the scourge of heresy at home. The peace concluded, however, he died in a jousting accident in the tournament celebrating it. He was succeeded by the sickly fifteen-year-old Francis II, whose reign lasted for eighteen months; then by the ten-year-old Charles IX. The accession of each touched off intense maneuvering for control of the young monarch and of the regency government that ruled in Charles's name. A crisis of authority ensued. "The kingdom was as if without a king," one chronicler recorded. "Justice lost all its force."[11]

In many regions, the new Reformed churches, which previously had gathered in secrecy, now began to assemble publicly, in some cases seizing public markets or churches for their use, in others, as private homes grew too small for their gatherings, renting barns. The exportation of propaganda and devotional literature from Geneva was conducted on a massive scale—so massive that when a barge was seized on the Seine with forbidden books aboard in 1562, it took eight booksellers to inventory the full cargo. The ground had been well prepared, and this literature touched a chord. Ministers sent from Geneva to help frame the new churches reported back in wonderment that their new flocks grew breathtakingly and that dozens of surrounding communities also begged for ministers. "Pastors are demanded from all parts. . . . But our resources are exhausted," Calvin said worriedly, adding in a comment that reveals a great deal about his social attitudes, "We are reduced to searching everywhere, even in the artisan's workshop, to find men with some smattering of doctrine and of piety as candidates for the ministry."[12] The most careful estimates are that approximately 1,240 churches were "planted" in the kingdom between 1555 and 1570, the great majority of them between 1559 and 1562.[13] In addition to the 220 pastors that Genevan records show to have been sent to France, the Pays de Vaud and the county of Neuchâtel also contributed to the effort, detaching a number of their ministers temporarily from their duties so they could tend the growing flocks. One who left permanently was Pierre Viret, who pastored successively to churches in Nîmes, Lyon, and Béarn. Theodore Beza made several voyages to France between 1559 and 1564 to act as a spokesman for and advisor to the new churches.[14]

With so many clerics coming from the Swiss borderlands to take charge of the organization of the new French churches, they naturally shaped them along Genevan and Vaudois lines. Most French churches adopted the Genevan liturgy and catechisms. A consistory of elders and ministers overseeing ecclesiastical discipline and admission to communion became the rule. The French Reformed confession of faith adopted at the first national synod of 1559 was evidently written in Geneva, rushed to Paris for the gathering, and accepted with only minor changes. It includes many distinctively Calvinist touches, including insistence upon the power of God's all-controlling providence, a patent statement of double predestination, and an affirmation of Christ's real but purely spiritual presence in the eucharistic elements. Because many ministers came from the Pays de Vaud rather than Geneva itself, certain characteristic features of that territory's church order also were adopted in parts of the country. Thus, in Languedoc and Dauphiné churches were initially divided into classes that chose a dean to visit each local church to oversee the local pastor and ensure conformity of practice, precisely as was done in the Pays de Vaud. These practices, however, did not obtain the approval of the churches' national synods once these began to assemble regularly and so disappeared.[15]

The dominating presence of so many ministers from the francophone Swiss borderlands did not mean, however, that the French churches were cast entirely in a Swiss mold. The distinctive situation of a religion established without the approval of the governing authorities forced the churches to improvise. French consistories came to act as administrative as well as disciplinary bodies, supervising congregational finances and defending the church's legal interests. The deacon's office gradually vanished, and the consistory oversaw the relief of the poor. Above all, the proliferation of independently established churches across a broad kingdom in the face of governmental persecution suggested to those involved that they needed to cooperate with one another to maintain unity of doctrine and discipline. This imperative gave rise to the most critical independent initiative of the French churches: the development of the presbyterian-synodal system. The most significant step was taken at the first national synod of 1559, which was convoked by several leading French churches without Calvin's prior approval, in apparent continuation of earlier trials in Poitou to work out a system for maintaining fellowship among the churches springing up across the region. The first decision taken at the initial national synod was that no church could claim domination or precedence over any other, a principle of equality that contrasts sharply with the subordination of rural churches to the metropolis in such territories as Geneva and

Zurich. Also approved were provisions for the regular reassembly of provincial and national synods, presided over by a moderator chosen exclusively for that gathering and composed of both lay and clerical delegates, to which the individual churches were to refer all doctrinal and disciplinary questions of more than purely local consequence. In subsequent years, a third level of regional assembly, the colloquy, was added. It was specified that new elders were to be coopted by the sitting consistory, and that ministers were to be named by the regional synod, colloquy, or gathering of ministers and elders from neighboring churches. The resulting system thus involved a federation of churches of equal status, independent of secular authority, with the fundamental powers of ecclesiastical decision making and ministerial appointment vested in a regional and national hierarchy of synods rather than in individual churches. It was a system that would appeal as well to many in other countries who were eager to see a church with a measure of autonomy vis-à-vis the civil magistrates yet possessing mechanisms for preventing each local congregation from following its own course.[16]

The plan was not instituted without challenge. Early in 1562, Jean Morély, a Parisian landowner who had moved back and forth between France, Switzerland, and England after first being drawn to Protestant ideas at Bordeaux's Collège de Guyenne, proposed a radically different schema in his *Treatise on Discipline and Christian Government*. The wondrous growth of the church in France, Morély argued, was an opportunity for the divinely ordained form of church government to be restored: one in which all decisions concerning discipline, doctrine, and the nomination of ministers were taken by the full assembly of each local church. If the church was rightly ordered in this manner, he was convinced, the Holy Spirit would animate all of its decisions, and Christ would truly be its head. In some regards, Morély's proposals for the congregational election of pastors and for open discussion of doctrinal issues in a congregational *prophétie* resemble the practices of the strangers' churches of London, which he knew. But he went well beyond a Lasco in his faith in the indwelling of the Spirit within the visible church. Indeed, Morély's proposals seemed dangerously impractical, anarchic, and democratic to Calvin and Beza, who now rallied strongly to the defense of the system established in France—on prudential rather than jure divino grounds. The *Treatise on Discipline and Christian Government* was burned in Geneva as harmful to the church. Morély was excommunicated. The French national synod of 1562 condemned the book for its "wicked doctrine tending to the dissipation and confusion of the church." This was not the end of the affair, for Morély held onto his ideas even as he sought and gained readmission to the church, and he was able to gain further hearings for them at several provincial and national synods down to 1572. Support for his views was limited, however, and the sympathy he was able to awaken arose not so much from acceptance of his arguments as from dismay at the ardor the Genevans displayed in seeking to drive him from the church. His ideas anticipate later congregationalism in ways, but no direct connection has been found.[17]

The success of the new Reformed churches in attracting members stunned contemporaries: to the alarmed Blaise de Monluc, "every good mother's son wanted a taste." Monluc exaggerated. The most probable estimates would put the total number of those who committed themselves to the Reformed cause in these years between 1.5 and 2 million, or about one good mother's son in ten.[18] Still, this already impressive level of success was made more significant yet by the fact that the movement took deeper root in certain areas than in others, most importantly in an arc of provinces sweeping from Dauphiné across Languedoc and Monluc's native Gascony up the west coast to Poitou. The cities, so strategically vital at the time, were, except for Paris, deeply touched. By the early 1560s, the Reformed made up the majority of the population of Nîmes, Montauban, and La Rochelle and between a fifth and a third of the population of such leading provincial metropoles as Rouen, Orléans, and Lyon (map 6). Most of the countryside remained steadfast to the old ways, but a few regions of active rural industry, notably the Cévennes mountains in Languedoc, the countryside around Niort in Poitou, and the Pays de Caux in Normandy, also became centers of Protestantism. Their numbers and strength concentrated in outlying regions of the kingdom, the new Reformed churches would be difficult to uproot, even if most people remained loyal to the Roman church.

Who joined the new churches? Local studies show that members were recruited in roughly equal proportions from the social and wealth strata that made up the urban population, with the noteworthy exception of the vine dressers and other agricultural laborers who made up a sizable fraction of the population of many towns: they tended to remain overwhelmingly Catholic. The literate were disproportionately represented within the ranks of the new churches, as were the geographically mobile. These patterns imply that the capacity to examine the Bible independently and detachment from local devotional traditions both helped to induce individuals to break with the Roman church.[19] Strikingly, husbands and wives often chose opposite sides when faced with this decision. In keeping with the patterns just outlined, women, who were less often literate and tended to migrate over shorter distances, opted less often to join the new church.[20] More striking yet—indeed, probably the most crucial feature of all of the sociology of the early French Protestant movement—the cause was virtually as strong among the nobility as it was in the cities, although again there were regional variations. Estimates of the noblemen drawn to the cause in ten regions range from 10 to 40 percent of the

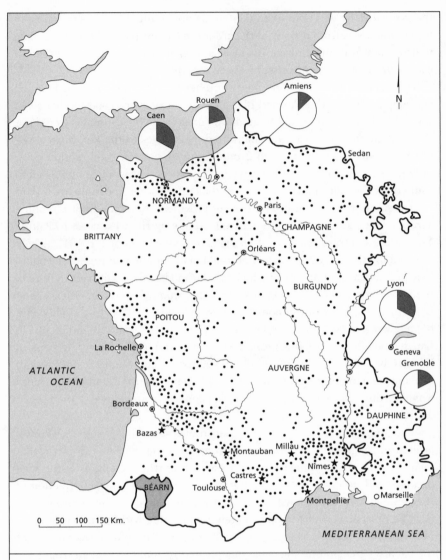

- Localities where a Reformed church is known to have been established during the sixteenth century

★ Localities where the mass was abolished and Reformed services made the sole local form of worship prior to April 1562

o Major cities

▨ Territory where Reformed worship was imposed by law in 1571

Pie graphs indicate approximate Reformed strength as a percentage of the total population in the early 1560's where this is known

Map 6. The Reformed Churches of France ca. 1562

Second Estate.[21] Among the aristocrats who converted were such prominent figures as Louis, prince of Condé; Gaspard de Coligny, admiral of France, and Jeanne d'Albret, queen of Navarre and Francis I's niece. In 1558, even Jeanne's husband, Anthony of Bourbon, the first prince of the blood, attended the Reformed services that were held publicly in the Pré-aux-Clercs in the suburbs of Paris, giving rise to the impression that he had embraced the faith.

Although no new convert is known to have reported why he or she joined the faith in anything other than the most formulaic and unrevealing of terms (for example, "I saw the light"), the abundant verbal and visual propaganda that survives from France conveys a revealing idea of what the cause represented to those who joined it. When a group of five young painters and printers was surprised and arrested by royal sergeants as they walked the vineyards outside Troyes in 1557 reading aloud and discussing two works of evangelical literature, the books seized with them were an attack upon the Catholic mass and the *Antithesis Between Christ's Deeds and the Pope's,* a frequently reproduced reworking of Lucas Cranach's *Passional of Christ and the Antichrist* in which sixteen paired woodcuts contrasted the simplicity, humility, and charity preached by Christ with the arrogance, pretension, and twisted rituals of the papacy. Songs and satires mocked the consecrated host that Catholics worshiped as nothing more than a piece of dough consumed and ultimately deposited in the latrine like any other piece of food. In woodcuts and pamphlets, the church was depicted as a bazaar of false wares and a stewpot of cooked-up rituals invented by a scheming clergy to line its pockets. The con game required that laymen be kept in the dark about the Bible. If word got out about its true message, the game was up. Idolatry in all of its forms was recurrently criticized. More positively, pamphlets emphasized the need to replace the mass with a simpler eucharistic service, to preach the saving message of justification by faith alone, and to give all believers direct access to the Bible. But the cause did not represent simply a call for new, simplified ways of worship consonant with the Bible message of justification by faith alone and an attack on the wealth, pretensions, and false doctrine of the clergy, with emphasis on the improbability of transubstantiation and the wickedness of idolatry. Many of the pamphlets of the era urged that the wealth of the church be directed to other, more socially useful ends, such as reducing the tax burden, repurchasing alienated portions of the royal domain, and rewarding outstanding royal servants. Many called for stronger action against a range of moral failings said to be prevalent. The movement thus embodied hopes for moral and social renewal. Indeed, its early chroniclers recurrently reported that those who embraced the faith soon manifested an extraordinary amendment and purity of life.[22]

The dramatic growth of the new faith and its success in attracting noble

La Verité à du tout renuerſee
L'hypocriſie, & la marmite auſſy,
Elle ne peut plus eſtre redreſſee
Par ſeducteurs auec tout leur ſoucy,
Vn chaſcun d'eux y met la main auſſy
Que vous voyez, mais en vain il ſefforce,
Car Verité deſcend du Ciel icy
Qui va briſant de leur Canons la force,

4. "The Overturning of the Great Marmite." This colored woodcut that circulated widely in France early in 1562 expresses the optimism felt by many recent converts in that year that the Catholic Church's days were numbered. It compresses into a single image many common themes of the printed propaganda for the cause: that a corrupt Catholic clergy kept believers in the dark the better to profit from their ignorance, that the restored light of the Gospel could overcome this, and that the blood of the martyrs was the seed of the church. From the tetragrammaton in the upper right—a symbol for God used by Reformed artists from the 1520s onward to avoid depicting the divinity in human form—the Bible descends borne by the Holy Spirit to topple the stewpot filled with the false wares of the Roman church (papal bulls, indulgences, cardinal's hats, etc.). The suffering of martyrs in the fire beneath the stewpot also helps to crack it. In vain, an array of churchmen strain to keep it aright-when they are not fishing more benefices from it or turning away to caress their womenfolk. In the upper left, other churchmen keep the laity blindfolded and fenced off from the truth. At the very top left corner, the Pope topples from his throne. (Cliché Bibliothèque Nationale de France, Paris)

converts brought its adherents face to face with the same sorts of moral and political dilemmas that the first enthusiastic converts to the evangelical cause in the Swiss and German cities had confronted a generation earlier. What were the obligations of individual believers in seeing to it that false worship and idolatry were eliminated when the ruling authorities continued to uphold traditional practices? Could ordinary citizens take it upon themselves to remove the roadside crosses, street corner Virgins, and church altarpieces that were so much a part of the contemporary landscape? Could they defend themselves against government officials who sought to arrest them for seeking to worship God purely, free brethren from jail who had been imprisoned for their beliefs, or even seek to depose rulers who defended the false church of Rome and its idolatrous practices? After the death of Henry II, the accession of a teenage king raised additional constitutional questions. The adolescent Francis II looked for advice to his uncles by marriage from the house of Lorraine, the cardinal of Lorraine and the duke of Guise, but his reliance on their guidance upset the balance that the previous Valois had maintained at court among the great noble families of Guise, Bourbon, and Montmorency, breeding resentment within the latter clans. Much of the second-level nobility was likewise alienated when the crown was forced to revoke many military commissions and pensions in cost-saving measures necessitated because of severe financial plight. The precedents that argued in favor of the view that kings could rule without the tutelage of a regency council from their thirteenth year on were not beyond challenge; and there was no agreement about who had the right to name the members of a regency government in the event one was required. Resentment at the extent of the influence that the Guise exercised over Francis II soon led to assertions that they had improperly usurped their authority and that such a young king required a regency council led by the first prince of the blood. Resentment burned intensely within the ranks of the Protestant nobility. "We are often asked whether it is permitted to rise against those who are enemies not only of religion but also of the realm," Beza wrote to Bullinger in September 1559.[23]

As noted, Calvin wrote his initial edition of the *Institutes* to demonstrate to Francis I that the true evangelical faith was not the seditious creed that its enemies made it out to be. He insisted in that work that secular rulers are God's vicars on earth who must be obeyed even when they act unjustly, but he also included the qualification that when a territory's political arrangements included officials appointed to restrain the willfulness of kings, such as the ephors of ancient Sparta, these officials were obliged to oppose manifestly unjust orders. During the years of dramatic church growth and concurrent political crisis that ran from the accession of Francis II through the First Civil

War of 1562–63, Calvin seems to have been pulled in opposite directions by his fear of disorder, his excitement at the possibility of the imminent triumph of God's word in his homeland, his dismay at the successive French kings' continued deafness to that word, and his outrage at the persecution the faithful continued to suffer. In letters to congregations and ministers in the country, he repeatedly warned them against taking the law into their own hands and expressed dismay on receiving news of incidents in which this was done. His sermons from this period nonetheless flayed France's rulers in scathing terms. The country was governed by murderers, blasphemers, voluptuaries, and thieves, he declared from the pulpit in December 1562. One should spit in the face of princes who disregard God's law, for they are not worthy of being considered men, he said on two other occasions. In 1559–60 he latched eagerly onto the questionable legal argument that Francis II was not of age to rule and urged the first prince of the blood, Anthony of Navarre, to take the lead in forming a regency. Some of the Protestant nobles wanted to go even further: to seize control of the young Francis II by force and bring the leaders of the house of Guise to trial. Calvin's attitude toward these conspiracies has been debated ever since the events themselves and is difficult to resolve with confidence; conspiracies necessarily involve dissimulation, and the failure of these enterprises led the Genevans to deny involvement, for fear their cause would appear seditious. Calvin appears to have opposed the most famous of these plots, the Conspiracy of Amboise, whose premature detection led to the capture of dozens of conspirators as they assembled in the woods near the royal castle. Scarcely had many of these conspirators been hung from the castle ramparts, however, when a second plan to assemble fighting men and coordinate risings across southern France began to be bruited about among even higher-ranking noblemen, including Anthony of Navarre and the prince of Condé. Coded letters in the correspondence of Calvin and Beza disclose that Calvin was more actively involved in this abortive conspiracy, to the point of helping collect the funds necessary for the enterprise. The possible participation of Anthony of Navarre in the project appears to have been what legitimated it in his eyes.[24]

Others drawn to the Reformed cause in these heady years, moved by anger at the persecution of the faithful and by zeal to drive out the abominations of popery, took yet more vigorous direct action. From 1559 onward, increasingly well organized efforts sought to free from captivity those arrested on account of their religious beliefs. Individual churches began to mount armed guards around their clandestine assemblies to protect them against the threat of Catholic violence or turned to local noblemen for such protection. By 1561, what the churches always presented as defensive imperatives had led them to create a paramilitary organization in certain provinces by which individual churches formed a squadron of troops who were grouped into larger units by colloquies and synods. Provincial synods played a central role in these military preparations and in the process revealed the utility of presbyterial-synodal forms for the mobilization and defense of an underground church. But defensive considerations alone hardly account for all of the militancy of those who came to be known in the wake of the Conspiracy of Amboise as Huguenots—a name evidently derived from a ghost said to haunt the region of Amboise at night and applied by their enemies to the Protestants because of their nocturnal gatherings and evil doings. A number of ministers and churches are known to have taken part in raising money and troops for the conspiracy of Amboise. Even after the defeat of this enterprise and the subsequent "affair of Maligny," militant impulses to purge the idols from the temple, rid the land of useless religious, and do away with the "stinking" mass welled up locally in many areas whenever the ranks of the movement began to swell toward a position of local dominance. Scattered attacks on Catholic shrines and holy objects in the years 1557–61 gave way in the summer of 1561 to systematic church purification campaigns across large stretches of Languedoc and Gascony as the cause gained strength in those regions. In many of the same regions, members of the religious houses either began to leave their convents voluntarily or were harassed into doing so. In some of the greatest urban strongholds of the cause in the Midi—Montpellier, Castres, Bazas, Nîmes, Montauban—the growth of the Reformed movement had culminated by late 1561 in full municipal reformations, with the local churches stripped of their images and the mass eliminated, sometimes by authority of the city government and sometimes independently of it. Ministers or consistories almost never took public responsibility for the removal of images and altarpieces without the approval of the civil authorities, but Viret defended the forcible liberation of prisoners of conscience and consented to preach in the cathedral of Nîmes four days after it was taken by force.[25]

Faced with the growing force and aggressiveness of the Protestant cause, Francis II's government struggled to arrive at an effective response, relaxing the enforcement of the laws against heresy but then dispatching officials to break up church assemblies that began to gather openly. When Francis died in December 1560, Catherine de Medici assumed the central place in a regency government established for the undeniably underage Charles IX. She drew inspiration from a group of men known to contemporaries as *moyenneurs,* who sought to repair the widening religious breach within the kingdom through a moderate reform of the existing church that they hoped would lead those who had left it to rejoin. One leader of this group was the jurisconsult François Bauduin, who had previously been Calvin's boarder and personal secretary in Geneva. In September 1561, Catherine invited the leading Protestant theologians to address an assembly of bishops then meeting at Poissy in the hope that a middle ground would be found to reunite the divided churches. Beza came from Geneva and Vermigli from Zurich, but the event only revealed the gulf between the two sides. Having failed to reconcile the two parties, Catherine then sought to resolve the religious problem by decreeing toleration. By the Edict of St. Germain of January 1562, commonly known as the Edict of January, the Reformed were granted freedom to assemble for worship anywhere in the country except within walled towns.[26]

The achievements of the Reformed by early 1562 were little short of remarkable. Within just a few years, hundreds of congregations had assembled across the kingdom. A set of national church institutions had been defined that would endure for more than a century with only minor modifications. Reformed worship had obtained legal toleration. In a few locales, it had even displaced Catholicism. But the toleration granted the Reformed was unstable. As contemporary poems and prints evince, the swelling ranks of those drawn to the new churches viewed the granting of toleration as simply a further step in the providentially inspired growth of a cause that would soon culminate in the abolition of Catholicism throughout the land. Many of those who remained loyal to Rome viewed the same decree as an abdication of the sacral monarchy's fundamental responsibility of protecting the Roman church. Some Parisian preachers went so far as to suggest that if the crown did not reverse its policy, it would forfeit its claim to its subjects' obedience; resistance theories could just as easily be formulated within the Catholic tradition as outside it. Within three months of the promulgation of the Edict of January, civil war erupted.

The precipitant of the conflict was the massacre of dozens of Protestants worshiping in a barn in the small town of Vassy by troops under the command of the duke of Guise. In the weeks that followed, the maneuverings of the leading Protestant and Catholic noblemen heightened the tension. Called to court to account for his actions, Guise proceeded instead to Paris, where he received a hero's welcome and the promise of men and money from the city government. Catherine urged the prince of Condé to take the young king, then at Fontainebleau, under his protection. Condé, apparently mistrusting the queen mother, declined. Instead, Guise and other leading noblemen, including Anthony of Navarre, who had by now embraced the Catholic cause, went to Fontainebleau with a large body of retainers and pressured Catherine and Charles to return to Paris. With this, the Protestants decided that the time had come for them to take up arms to defend, in Beza's words, "the authority of the king and the liberty granted the Churches by the recent edict." The subsequent Huguenot mobilization again revealed the utility of the presbyterian-synodal system for organizing the military and political defense of a minority church. Word was passed through the network of communication that existed within the church encouraging risings, and by early April some dozens of cities were secured for the faith. From Orléans, Beza oversaw the raising of money and troops from the other churches of the realm.[27]

Although the Protestants initially took many of France's leading cities, they could not overcome their numerical inferiority, and the war went poorly for them. Inside such Huguenot-controlled cities as Rouen and Orléans, events followed a pattern that would be repeated a decade later in many parts of the Low Countries. Initially, the new Protestant masters proclaimed a commitment to religious toleration and allowed Catholic worship to continue. Soon the polarizing effects of warfare swept aside the voices of moderation. The churches were purified of their altars and statues in great waves of iconoclasm. Catholic services ceased as priests fled in fear for their lives. Church property was seized and used for the war effort. Where the Huguenots controlled wider areas, they assumed control of local tax collection as well.[28] But even assistance from their fellow Protestants in England could not prevent them from losing city after city to the combined force of royal and Catholic arms, although the Catholics lost many of their leading commanders in battle or by assassination. After eleven months of fighting Catherine brought the conflict to an end with a new religious peace that limited Reformed freedom of worship to the lands of the faith's noble adherents and a circumscribed number of cities. Many ministers, including Calvin, denounced the Protestant nobles who negotiated these peace terms for selling out the cause, but only a providentialist faith that God would not abandon those who cleaved to his path could support the illusion that better terms might have been obtained by fighting on. The war was a disaster for the young churches. The uprisings that started it seemed to confirm the claims of the faith's Catholic opponents that it bred sedition and violence. In the aftermath of the conflict, the Reformed churches discovered that they had lost the ability to attract the flocks of new converts who had been joining the church before the fighting.[29]

The next thirty-five years were a time of tribulation for the French Reformed. New civil wars broke out in 1567, 1568, 1572, 1574, 1577, and 1580. In each one, the Protestants were able to gain control of only a fraction of the kingdom's territory. Where they were unable to secure their control, their services were outlawed, and they were subjected to numerous vexations. Many fled to nearby Protestant strongholds. Although each of the wars ended with a new edict of pacification that renewed a measure of freedom of worship, the provisions of the edicts were difficult to implement. Many of these interludes of nominal pacification witnessed bloody episodes of anti-Huguenot popular violence, culminating in the frightful Saint Bartholomew's Massacre of 1572. After a failed assassination attempt on Admiral Coligny led the Protestant noblemen gathered in Paris for the wedding of Henry of Navarre to speak threateningly of revenge, a panicked Charles IX was prevailed upon by his closest councillors—just which ones is still debated—to order the summary killing of many leading Huguenots. To that fraction of the Catholic population that nursed the deepest grudges against the Reformed, the order appeared to be the king's long-awaited chastisement of those heretics whose seditious spirit had prompted three civil wars and countless plots. Thousands of ordinary men joined in the killing. Thousands of Protestants were butchered in Paris and a dozen provincial towns; many thousands more were frightened into swearing humiliating oaths of abjuration, marking their reintegration into the Catholic church. By the later 1570s, the once buoyant Huguenot minorities that had taken control of cities like Lyon, Rouen, and Orléans in 1562 amounted to at most a few hundred families. Many of the smaller, more isolated Reformed churches had been extinguished.

That any churches survived was owing to resistance by Protestants in the "Huguenot crescent" from Poitou to Dauphiné, where members of the faith exercised numerical and political domination in perhaps half of the major towns. As the cause lost ground elsewhere, its leaders here realized that their viability depended upon securing permanent military control of their strongholds and taking steps to enable them to put an army in the field when necessary. After the Second Civil War in 1568, a number of Protestant-dominated towns, including La Rochelle, Montauban, and Castres, refused to submit to the military authority of their royal governors. In the wake of the Saint Bartholomew's Massacre, these cities became bastions against a royal effort to outlaw Protestant worship entirely. At the same time, delegates from Huguenot-controlled parts of Languedoc met to fix a common system for raising taxes and administering seized church property. This grew into a regular framework of regional councils and national political assemblies. In this manner, and with irregular assistance from the Palatinate and England, the Huguenots were able to mount a defense of the faith that preserved freedom of worship for its adherents throughout the country.

In the changed circumstances after 1572, Protestant mobilization could no longer be justified simply as a matter of protecting royal authority against evil Catholic councillors, for the crown openly assumed responsibility for the liquidation of many leading Protestant noblemen in the Saint Bartholomew's Massacre, and there could be no doubt that the king's will stood behind the orders the Huguenots defied. To justify such disobedience, a number of Reformed spokesmen, including Beza, now issued unambiguous statements of the rights of lesser magistrates to resist a tyrannical king. Two of these works proved especially resonant over the subsequent centuries: Beza's anonymously published *On the Right of Magistrates Over their Subjects* (1574), which was reprinted ten times in French before 1581 and at least seventeen times in Latin between 1576 and 1649; and the anonymous *Vindication of Liberty against Tyrants* (1579), which had twelve Latin printings, a French edition in 1581, a partial English translation in 1588, and full English translations in those years of revolution 1648 and 1689. In part because the Huguenots in this period sought the support of moderate Catholics, these works had the novelty, when compared with earlier works of Protestant resistance theory, of couching the grounds for political resistance in essentially secular terms. Lesser magistrates, they argued, did not just have a duty to resist the commands of rulers who oppressed the true religion, as the *Magdeburg Bekenntnis* had earlier maintained. They could also resist rulers who acted tyrannically or had broken their implicit contract with their subjects. That said, Catholic resistance theories of this period were more radical yet in that they granted not only lesser magistrates but also the populace as a whole the right to disobey royal tyrants who failed to protect the faith.[30]

Ironically, the nonconfessional character of these Huguenot statements of resistance theory would soon make them grist for the Catholics' mill, for in 1584 the dynastic status was profoundly transformed by the death of the duke of Alençon, the last surviving brother of the childless Henry III. The Huguenot leader Henry of Navarre now became the heir apparent to the throne. Hope rekindled in Reformed breasts that God's wondrous providence might yet decree that theirs would be France's religion of state. The kingdom's Catholics had other ideas. Elements within the Catholic church and nobility had organized an ever more militant defense of the faith as the Wars of Religion progressed. By the 1580s it was unquestionably the most important element within French political culture. These men revived the sworn association of the Catholic League, first formed in 1576, to militate for the extermination of heresy and to defend the principle that only somebody loyal to the church of Rome could accede to the throne. In 1585, the legal toleration of Protestantism was repealed. By 1588, the league's ability to dictate policy to Henry III had grown so great that the king decided that the only way he could reassert his authority was to have the duke and cardinal of Guise summarily killed. But the killing of these Catholic champions prompted a vehement backlash. The doctors of the Sorbonne declared Henry a tyrant and the population absolved of its obligations of obedience. Cities across the kingdom rose in revolt. In August 1589 the Dominican friar Jacques Clément assassinated the king. In the long and bitter battle for succession that ensued, Navarre, now Henry IV, found that for all his military genius, he could subdue those who opposed his claims to the throne only by converting to Catholicism. His decision to do so in 1593 guaranteed that the Bourbon dynasty that would rule France for the next two hundred years would be a Catholic dynasty.

The Edict of Nantes that Henry IV issued in 1598 at the close of this last and longest civil war granted the king's former coreligionists slightly more generous terms than the edicts of pacification that had preceded it. The Huguenots were permitted to gather for worship in approximately 700 localities. Special courts to adjudicate contentious matters involving them were set up. Their rights of access to royal offices, schools, and charitable institutions were reaffirmed. Special brevets accorded them military control of roughly 150 strongholds and modest royal subsidies for their schools and pastors. The churches that now reconstituted themselves were clustered more strongly in the Huguenot crescent than they had been in 1562. The better documentation available for this period allows one to estimate their total membership with some accuracy at just under a million souls.[31]

Three dozen years of conflict had thus reduced the ranks of the French Reformed between a third and a half. The movement that came through the fire nonetheless remained a sizable one, and one that epitomized more unmistakably than any other a Reformed church that regulated its internal affairs and carried out its disciplinary tasks independently of the secular authorities. The early organizers of the church had hoped to see it gain the support of the regime and work together with the secular magistrates; a redaction of the "discipline" of the church of Saint-Lô from 1563 had even listed the magistrates as one of the four varieties of ecclesiastical ministers. In that small fraction of French localities where the Protestants formed the overwhelming majority of the population around 1600, the secular and ecclesiastical authorities cooperated in overseeing poor relief, education, and moral discipline, to the point that the consistory and village council appear in places to have been the same body. But in the majority of communities in which the new faith took root, the events of the Wars of Religion taught the churches to rely on their own resources to survive. At successive national synods, they increasingly marked their distance from the secular authorities. Synodal decrees warned against selecting magistrates to serve as elders, forbade consistories to denounce church members discovered to be guilty of heinous crimes to the secular judges, and declared all consistory proceedings secret, even those in which consistory members were insulted in manners that might be actionable before the secular courts.[32] All this was a far cry from the sort of defense of consistorial authority that Calvin sought and obtained from the Genevan magistracy. The French Reformed churches thus became the enduring model of a network of churches that maintained purity of doctrine, quality control over local clergy, ecclesiastical discipline, and reasonable uniformity of practice with a minimum of reliance on secular authorities.

BÉARN: A PRINCELY REFORMATION ON GENEVAN LINES

In one small corner of France's modern boundaries, Béarn, the outcome of the Reformation was very different. This still independent Pyrenean principality of perhaps one hundred thousand people was ruled jointly by Anthony of Navarre and his wife, Jeanne d'Albret, until late 1562, when Anthony died and Jeanne became sole ruler. If Anthony of Navarre never lived up to the great expectations that the Genevans briefly had for him and ended up casting his lot with the Guises and the Catholic church, Jeanne proved a lasting convert to the Reformed faith. Displaying both strong religious conviction and considerable political sagacity and aided by the timely intervention of a Huguenot army in her hour of greatest peril, she oversaw a gradual reformation from above of her little territory that culminated in 1571 in the abolition of Catholicism, the legal requirement that all inhabitants attend the new worship on pain of fine or imprisonment, and strong legislation in support of a reformation of manners.

Some changes in worship may have begun in the region well before Jeanne publicly forswore Catholicism at Pau on Christmas day 1560. One hostile Catholic source writing after the fact declares that the midcentury bishop of Oloron, Gérard Roussel, a former member of Lefèvre d'Etaples's Meaux circle, introduced a series of innovations into his diocese that included an end to the elevation and adoration of the host, the distribution of communion in both kinds, and clerical marriage. When the ruling house of the territory began in 1557 to assume an interest in the new religion then taking shape in France, a number of Béarnais noble families renounced Catholic worship and sent to Geneva for a pastor. Still, the inhabitants of this largely rural territory were slow to take to the new churches coming into being throughout the region. Even after Jeanne cast her lot publicly with the Reformed, she thus had to proceed gradually—especially since just across her southern border lay the territories of Philip II, whose ancestors had already seized the better part of Navarrese territory. In 1561 she dispatched ministers to the leading cities with instructions to the local authorities to provide them hospitality and tolerate their preaching, which often reached out to the surrounding countryside as well. In 1564 she felt that the cause had advanced enough to order the first state-mandated changes in worship. Images were ordered removed from several churches; Catholic processions were prohibited outside the confines of church buildings; and the principle of freedom of conscience was proclaimed with the unbalanced proviso that wherever Catholic worship ceased, it could not be reestablished. The Reformed clergy exhorted Jeanne to follow the example of the great Israelite kings and eliminate what remained of Roman idolatry at one fell stroke, but the dangers of moving too precipitously were soon revealed. The *jurats* of various towns protested that abandoning the annual Corpus Christi processions "greatly scandalized" their inhabitants. When the queen took the next step and ordered the secularization of all ecclesiastical property in 1566, a band of leading noblemen and clerics entered into a conspiracy to seize her person, restore the old church structure, and do away with the Reformed religion. Indiscreet lips sank the conspiracy.[33]

Only after French intervention in the principality backfired and resulted in the dispossession of many Catholic noblemen was a full reformation by law implemented. At the outset of the third French civil war in 1568, Jeanne placed herself at the head of the Huguenot troops massed in La Rochelle, where many leading partisans of the Protestant cause, fearing a royal strike against them, had gathered. In response, Charles IX sent an army into Béarn, asserting that the Protestant rebels had captured its queen and that it was his sovereign obligation to protect it. His army took control of much of the principality, obtaining support from local Catholic noblemen and abolishing Reformed worship wherever it went. But it stalled before the great Albret fortress at Navarrenx, within whose walls more than fifty ministers had sought shelter. When a Huguenot relief force from the Protestant strongholds of southwestern France came to the town's rescue and drove out the invaders, Catholicism had been discredited through its association with an attack on the territory's independence. The Béarnais noblemen who had sided with the French were stripped of their lands, and the mass was soon abolished. In 1571, a set of "ordinances for the police of the church in which God's Majesty shines forth" capped the implementation of the Béarnais reformation.

Well before the final abolition of Catholicism, a synod of delegates from the region's churches had approved in 1563 a form of ecclesiastical constitution for the principality drawn up by the Genevan-trained Pierre Merlin. As Merlin proudly reported to Calvin, this followed Genevan example closely with one noteworthy exception. Asserting on the basis of both Scripture and the example of the early church that all goods given to the church ought to be administered by people with a legitimate calling within it, it established a nine-member council to be chosen by the ecclesiastical synod to seek out ecclesiastical property, administer it, and ensure that it was not dissipated or absorbed into the royal treasury. (In Geneva, the municipal authorities had largely incorporated the property formerly belonging to the Catholic church into the civic treasury.) The discipline also called for a system of consistorial discipline, annual synods with powers of appointment to clerical vacancies, and smaller regional colloquies that served as clerical gatherings for the discussion of Scripture and chose a *surveillant* to visit annually the churches that composed it.[34] The 1571 ordinances for the police of the church reiterated all of these provisions, including the independent administrative board to oversee ecclesiastical property. Stating that it was the queen's intention to fulfill a Christian prince's obligation to eliminate idolatry and promote true piety, the measure insisted that all inhabitants receive consistorial admonitions "without bitterness or complaint" and fixed a sliding scale of fines for those who failed to attend church services, culminating in imprisonment for the third offense. All inhabitants were instructed to make themselves worthy of admission to communion by mastering the articles of the faith, with banishment decreed for those who abstained from the sacrament without the approval of the church. Additional clauses prohibited games and amusements on Sundays so that the Sabbath could be consecrated to worship, commanded six honest days of labor a week to stave off poverty and debauchery, and castigated dancing, drunkenness, magical healing, superfluity of dress, immodest songs, gambling, and loans at excessive rates of interest.[35] The church order established in Béarn must be judged the purest realization of the aspirations of the Genevan ministry for a new church that would at once preserve much of the autonomy and resources of the Roman church yet enjoy the backing of secular authorities.

5

SCOTLAND
A Revolutionary Reformation

A national Reformed church took shape in Scotland at almost exactly the same moment as in France, once again against the backdrop of a contested regency government. Here, however, the conflict spawned by its growth had a very different outcome. The military aid of the neighboring English combined with a more fortuitous series of domestic political events to allow the partisans of reform quickly to savor the elimination of popery. Replacing the old order with a settled, effective new system of church administration proved far harder. The institutions first adopted, quite dissimilar from those in France, never proved capable of functioning as intended. The young queen who ruled in the wake of the change accepted the Protestant religious settlement but herself remained loyal to Catholicism, creating a situation in which the ruler could not be accepted as a godly prince and opening a breach for clerical initiative in shaping the further evolution of the church. Continuing political turmoil further complicated matters. As regents, rulers, and clergymen all strove to develop a more effective system of church government, struggles erupted between them, laying the foundations for a tradition of ecclesiological conflict that would be one of the most enduring features of subsequent Scottish church history. Not until the end of the century was a relatively stable compromise attained between the rival visions of the proper church order that emerged in the generation after 1560.

The close diplomatic connections epitomized by Francis II's marriage to Mary Queen of Scots bound Scotland's political history closely to France's, but the two countries differed greatly. Whereas France was Europe's most populous country, with rich agriculture, a well-developed commercial economy, and powerful institutions of central government, Scotland was a small, poor, factionalized kingdom in which the formal institutions of government counted for far less than sworn bonds among men. Edinburgh, the country's capital and largest city, reminded a French visitor at midcentury of nothing grander than Pontoise. The kingdom's total population of less than 750,000 in 1550 was scarcely that of a good French province. Scotsmen were known to attend church in armor with weapons in hand, and even a native earl could address a letter to the elector palatine with the apologetic remark that he was writing from "almost beyond the limits of the human race."[1]

The early growth of Protestant sentiments in Scotland is shrouded in uncertainty. The sources from this period are generally sparse. The ecclesiastical court records have disappeared, depriving us of the transcripts of heresy trials that typically provide the most revealing information about the underground spread of heterodoxy. The ideas of the Reformation reached this peripheral kingdom less quickly than they did more centrally located territories on the Continent, and they initially appear to have circulated slowly. The first statute against Lutheran heresy was promulgated in 1525, four years after Francis I had issued like measures. Not until the 1530s is there evidence of sympathy for Protestant ideas in several parts of the country, including Dundee, Saint Andrews, Edinburgh, and Ayrshire, where several incidents of iconoclasm occurred in 1533. King James V (r. 1513–42) was a concerned opponent of the new ideas, but during his reign just thirteen people are known to have been executed for heresy. In sharp contrast to the pattern in France and the Netherlands, the number of executions fell off in the next two decades. Just eight more people are known to have died for their beliefs down to 1560. In all, fewer than ninety heresy convictions are known to have been handed down in the country. Such evidence as survives does not suggest the same gradual percolation of evangelical ideas through every stratum and region as occurred in France.[2]

Small groups of militant converts drove the Scottish Reformation in concentrated bursts of evangelization. This pattern first manifested itself after another of the troubled minority successions that Scotland so often drew in the lottery of dynastic succession followed James V's death in 1542. James's sole child, Mary, was scarcely five days old. The first prince of the blood, James

Map 7. Scotland

Hamilton, second earl of Arran, assumed power within the new regency government and was inclined at first to seek alliance with England and to favor the Protestant cause. Arran legalized reading of the Bible in English and chose as his chaplains two evangelicals, Thomas Gwilliam and John Rough. They preached openly across central Scotland, winning many to their views, including a young, Saint Andrews–educated notary apostolic and tutor named John Knox. Friars soon found themselves heckled, mendicant houses were attacked, and images were smashed in the localities that had emerged as centers of Protestant opinion: Perth, Dundee, and the neighboring counties of Angus and Fife on the country's east coast.[3]

The bullying imperiousness of Henry VIII's efforts to profit from the situation in order to protect his northern border prevented this first upsurge of Protestant momentum from triumphing. Henry sought not only to arrange a marriage between Mary and his son Edward, but also to ensure that he could take immediate control of the Scottish castles along the border. His techniques of "rough wooing" included seizing Scottish shipping and sending English raiders across the border. Long-standing Scottish suspicions of the "auld enemy" were revived, Arran backed away from the English alliance, and a war ensued in which those favoring alliance with the French, led by the queen mother Mary of Lorraine (the sister of Francis, duke of Guise, and of the cardinal of Lorraine), gained ascendancy. Arran felt compelled to reconcile himself publicly with the Catholic hierarchy and to remove Gwilliam and Rough as chaplains. The war was a civil war as well, as a faction of Scotsmen continued to champion the alliance with England and the Protestant cause. With the protection of members of this faction, the fiery George Wishart preached openly across much of the central Lowlands in 1545–46, coming at times within thirty miles of Edinburgh, before he was captured and executed. A year later, a group of Protestant magnates stormed into Saint Andrews castle, killed the archbishop who had seen to Wishart's execution, and took control of the town. Their tenure lasted more than a year and was marked by worship and celebration of communion in a Protestant manner. Knox was among those in Saint Andrews at the time, and it was here he began to preach, devoting his first sermon to demonstrating that the church of the Rome was the Antichrist. Ultimately, Saint Andrews was retaken by a group of soldiers dispatched from France, and all those within the city who surrendered were sent into exile there, Knox to row in the galleys. The child queen was betrothed to the heir to the French throne, and Arran granted the French duchy of Châtellerault. After a brief span of open, militant proselytization, Protestant sentiments were once again driven underground. The new archbishop of Saint Andrews, John Hamilton, noted confidently in 1552 "how many frightful heresies have, within the last few years, run riot in many divers parts of the realm, but have now at last been checked . . . and seem almost extinguished." He may have been overconfident. After a brief voyage across the border in 1551, a Swiss student at Oxford could write to Rudolf Gwalther in Zurich that it was generally thought that more Scotsmen were "rightly persuaded as to the true religion than here among us in England."[4]

The theological contours of early Scottish Protestantism were shaped in large measure by English Reformation literature, most importantly Tyndale's New Testament, but a displacement of early Lutheran influences by ones closer in spirit to the Reformed may also be discerned. Patrick Hamilton, the country's first martyr—he was roasted slowly for six hours in Edinburgh in 1528—had visited Wittenberg and Marburg and seems to have held views close to those of Melanchthon. Five years later, a printer in Malmö produced several Lutheran works in Scots for export across the North Sea. Wishart, however, had visited Switzerland, was a strong opponent of all ceremonialism, and translated the First Helvetic Confession. Knox accompanied him on much of his preaching tour of 1545–46 and should probably be placed in the same theological tradition until his visits to the Continent in the 1550s.[5]

The first surge of Protestant militancy in the 1540s was broken as a result of Henry VIII's lack of political finesse and the intervention of French troops. Beginning in the mid-1550s and building to a climax between 1558 and 1560, a new wave of evangelization arose. Its ultimate triumph was no less a product of foreign intervention, royal personalities, and the play of political contingency than was the failure of the 1540s.

Throughout most of the 1550s, the increasingly powerful Mary of Lorraine, an adroit politician, placed political advantage above the unrelenting enforcement of Catholic orthodoxy. Mary Tudor's accession to the English throne in 1553 not only restored England to obedience to Rome, but also brought it into the Habsburg orbit by virtue of Mary's marriage to Philip II. Protestant preachers with good connections in England began to appear to Mary of Lorraine to be potentially useful as irritants to the stability of the Tudor-Habsburg regime. She was also eager to maintain the support of as much of the political nation as possible, for her overriding preoccupation in these years was to negotiate and gain approval for terms of Mary Stuart's marriage to the French dauphin by which the future Francis II would share in ruling Scotland during Mary's lifetime. She therefore refrained from acting vigorously when a number of Scottish ministers who had fled to England in 1546 returned home following Mary Tudor's accession and renewed their contacts with Scottish noblemen inclined to Protestantism. At the same time, fiscal problems impelled her to impose unpopular new taxes, while the growing prominence of Frenchmen at court caused predictable unhappiness. A politically favorable moment of reduced repression, comparable to conditions in France after the death of Henry II, thus presented itself to Scotland's Protestants.

Among the ministers who returned to Scotland were the two men who would exercise the greatest leadership over the emerging Reformed churches: John Willock and John Knox. Willock is the lesser known of these two today, in large part because he never published anything, but he was regarded by many in the late 1550s as the leading Protestant spokesman in Scotland. An erstwhile Franciscan who had abandoned holy orders in 1541, he had lived in England as chaplain to the duke of Suffolk, fled to Emden when Mary Tudor came to power, and made preaching tours through Scotland in 1555 and 1556 before returning for good in 1558. Knox's authorship of the *History of the Reformation in Scotland,* the fundamental source for all accounts of this period, has guaranteed that his prominence in upcoming events would not go unrecognized. After serving his time in the king of France's galleys, he had taken up a church living in the north of England and participated in the debates over the Second Book of Common Prayer. Fleeing to Frankfurt when Mary Tudor was crowned, he became one of the leaders of a group that worked out an austere order of service devoid of such features of the prayer book as kneeling at communion and ornate church vestments. He made his first visit to the city he found so inspiring, Geneva, after being expelled from Frankfurt for the politically imprudent but utterly characteristic act of comparing Charles V to Nero. Upon his return to Scotland in 1555–56 he preached in much of central Scotland, developing close connections with a number of committed lairds with whom he corresponded after returning to Geneva.[6]

Although Knox came to Scotland from Geneva at just the moment Calvin was beginning to encourage believers in other countries to form churches of their own, he does not appear to have advocated the founding of churches in the manner that Calvin advised the faithful in Poitou to follow, namely, with a permanent consistory that appointed a minister. Instead, he preached and in some localities "ministered the Lord's Table" to groups in noble households and towns from Ayr to Edinburgh without establishing consistories. In December 1557, a small group of Protestant noblemen followed the common Scottish custom of formalizing ties of mutual obligation through a sworn oath and banded together "to strive in our Master's cause, even unto the death . . . to maintain, set forward and establish the most blessed word of God and his Congregation," to obtain faithful ministers, and to keep and defend them. Shortly thereafter, a council of "the Lords and Barons professing Christ Jesus" vowed to see the English Book of Common Prayer used for public worship in all parish churches. They also sought to institute evangelical preaching and the interpretation of Scripture "in quiet houses, without great conventions of the people thereto," but again did not seek to establish functioning counterchurches complete with consistories. Only in 1558, according to Knox, as groups of the faithful aspired to "have the face of a Church amongst us," were elders elected to administer church discipline in certain localities.[7] By 1559, organized churches existed in at least seven and possibly numerous other communities. In Dundee, the assembly had the protection of the town council, which granted a stipend to the minister and prohibited any expressions of contempt for him or the church. At no point prior to the Protestants' political triumph do the various "privy kirks" set up in defiance of the queen regent ever seem to have assembled in synods such as that which gathered in Paris in 1559, nor do the churches appear to have mobilized troops or coordinated their resistance through the network of consistories, as would be done in both France and the Low Countries. Noblemen acting as patrons and protectors of the cause were far more exclusively the leading political champions of the Reformation than was the case in either continental country.[8]

Both Knox and Willock encouraged militancy on the cause's behalf, for like many committed English Protestants they had been radicalized by the Marian restoration and were willing to countenance armed resistance even by individuals against rulers who threatened to undo properly constituted forms of worship. Of the two, Knox's views are better known, for he wrote several pamphlets that were published during his second Genevan exile and is presumed to be the author of additional letters and declarations reported in his *History of the Reformation in Scotland.* He embraced with unusual zeal the role of the godly minister as Old Testament prophet, required to speak truth to power:

> The ministers, albeit they lack the glorious titles of lords and the devilish pomp which before appeared in proud prelates, yet must they be so stout and so bold in God's cause that if the king himself would usurp any other authority in God's religion than becometh a member of Christ's body, that first he be admonished according to God's Word, and after, if he condemn the same, be subject to the yoke of discipline, to whom they shall boldly say, as Asarias the high priest said to Uzzias the king of Judah . . . , "Pass out, therefore, for thou hast offended."[9]

More adamantly opposed even than Calvin to any concessions to Roman ceremonialism, he viewed with uncommon abhorrence the restitution of idolatry in any locality in which it had been abolished, an action that, in Old Testament fashion, he viewed as certain to bring down God's wrath upon the offending community. His *First Blast of the Trumpet against the Monstrous Regiment of Women* of the spring of 1558 was directed at his adopted homeland of England, where precisely this had happened after the accession of Mary, and about whose affairs he believed himself entitled to speak as minister to the refugee congregation in Geneva. In his view, Mary had broken a covenant with God through her restoration of the mass. The *First Blast* not only advocated resistance against her: it took the impolitic tack of categorically denying women the right to rule, deploying an array of biblical and classical references to demonstrate that such rule was against nature and Scripture alike. What made this so impolitic, of course, was that Mary Tudor would soon be followed to the English throne by an equally female but committedly Protestant ruler, while Scotland too had a young queen and a woman regent. Knox later protested apologetically to both Elizabeth and Mary Stuart that he had not meant to attack them in this treatise, but his apologies hardly mitigated their dislike for him and his views, especially as his apology to Mary was so grudging: "If the realm find no inconvenience from the regiment of a woman, that which they approve shall I no further disallow than within my own breast, but shall be as content to live as Paul was to live under Nero."[10]

For Scotland, his stance to begin with was less radical because the nation had not yet carried through a proper reformation, but he still went well beyond Calvin in the forms of direct action he was willing to endorse. Three pamphlets addressed to Scottish audiences in July 1558—open letters to the queen regent, to the nobility and estates, and to the "commonalty," respectively—called upon Mary of Lorraine to embrace the cause of the reformation and to overturn the actions of false bishops. In the likely eventuality that the queen regent did not see the light, Knox left leeway for ordinary believers to advance the reformation of worship. Not only did the civil authorities have the obligation to oversee the reformation of religion, he asserted, but "the whole body of that people and every member of the same" shared the responsibility to punish idolatry. Thus, Knox took a stance comparable to Karlstadt's in his encouragement of lay action against the false worship of images. Furthermore, the common people could maintain preachers of God's word if their superiors would not provide these for them, defend these preachers against all who would persecute them, and justly refuse to pay tithes to support false bishops and clergy.[11]

While Protestant militancy increased, Mary of Lorraine temporized, confident she could deal with the challenge of heresy once the affair of the crown matrimonial was resolved. Bishops who wished to see stronger action against the Reformed were told that such action would occur as soon as Parliament had approved the grant of future power to the French dauphin. The Protestants were told that they could "devise ye what ye please in matters of religion" once the issue was favorably settled. When Parliament ratified the dauphin's rights in November 1558, Mary kept her word to the bishops. By then, however, the Protestant movement had strengthened. More important yet, the international situation had changed. Mary Tudor died that same month, returning a Protestant ruler to the English throne and raising the possibility that the movement might receive backing from south of the border.

On January 1, 1559, the doors of religious houses were placarded with the Beggars' Summonds, which charged the mendicant orders with housing able-bodied men who had perverted God's word in a way that defrauded the genuinely poor of much charity that was rightfully theirs. The orders were admonished to surrender their property by Whitsun or face forcible expropriation.[12] As the deadline drew near in May, Knox returned to the country. The report of an eyewitness makes it clear that the importance traditionally accorded Knox in the history of the Scottish Reformation rests on more than just the self-promotion of the *History of the Reformation.* Knox was "able, in one hour, to put more life in us than five hundred trumpets continually blustering in our ears," he wrote. A sermon in Dundee "vehement against idolatry" touched off two days of iconoclasm and pillaging of the city's religious houses after a priest tried to celebrate mass before the high altar in the wake of the sermon.[13] Mary sought to summon all Protestant preachers to Stirling for trial, but the Perth congregation appealed to "all brethren" to protect them, and many noblemen and congregations rallied to their defense. In the ensuing test of strength, the queen regent could not raise enough troops to force the issue and was compelled to grant terms that allowed Protestant worship to continue where it had been instituted. She soon broke the terms of the peace, prompting the defection of a number of leading noblemen. The weakening of her support seemed less threatening to her after July, however, for the sudden death of Henry II that month brought her son-in-law to the French crown and her Guise relatives to supremacy in the French royal council. Augmented French military assistance soon followed.[14]

Faced with French reinforcements, the Lords of the Congregation looked south of the border for help. Although Queen Elizabeth had hardly forgotten the intemperate remarks about woman sovereigns in Knox's *First Blast* and was troubled by the idea of endorsing rebellion against a lawful monarch, the prospect of French domination in Scotland outweighed such considerations. With English assistance, the young earl of Arran, recently converted to Protestantism while living in France, was secretly transported back to Scotland via Geneva and Emden.[15] His father, Châtellerault, placed himself at the head of the opposition. In October, both Knox and Willock told a gathering of the regent's opponents they could see no reason the born counselors, nobility, and barons of the realm might not deprive the regent of her authority. The reasons they adduced in support of that judgment mingled time-honored justifications for aristocratic resistance with religious motifs of a novel stripe. Mary had failed to preserve Scottish liberties against foreign advisors, had refused to allow God's word to be preached openly, was "a vehement maintainer of all superstition and idolatry," and scorned the counsel of the nobility.[16] The insurgents declared the regent suspended from her duties and vested power instead in a "great council of the realm" led by Châtellerault. Some eleven thousand English troops came to the aid of those who favored this proclamation.

The course of events that ensured the insurgents' triumph was such, Knox boasted, that even their enemies had to confess God fought for them. The French undertook to send a further forty-five hundred men to Mary's aid, but winter storms drove them back from the Scottish coast. Once spring arrived, the troubles brewing at home with the Conspiracy of Amboise convinced Francis II not to send the ships forth again. Then, in June 1560, Mary of Lorraine suddenly died. From France, Francis II and the now-eighteen-year-old Mary Stuart made no effort to rally those who had stood by their regent. Instead, by the treaty of Edinburgh of July 6, 1560, they agreed to withdraw all French troops and to accept government by a council to which they appointed seven men while the Parliament appointed seventeen. All questions of religion were referred to an upcoming parliament.[17]

The hastily assembled Parliament dominated by the Lords of the Congregation met the next month and voted to abolish the mass and eliminate all previous statutes "not agreeing with Goddis holie worde"—a sweeping, if vague, decree. It also adopted a new confession of faith drafted by a committee of six clergymen and considered, but did not accept, rules for the government of the church drawn up by the same men at the behest of the great council of the realm. This set of proposals was modified and presented again to an assembly of clergymen summoned by Knox in December. Apparently adopted there— a gap in the meeting's records makes it impossible to be sure—this document was distributed throughout the kingdom as a constitutional blueprint for the Church of Scotland. It came to be known as the First Book of Discipline. To put in place a common liturgy for the new church, church assemblies in 1562 and 1564 ordered the adoption of the Book of Common Order, the form of services drawn up by Knox and several other Marian exiles in Frankfurt that the English refugee community there had rejected as excessively austere, but that subsequently served the English church in Geneva. The triumph of the Lords of the Congregation had produced a new religious order. One observer wrote of Knox, "He ruleth the roast, and of him all men stand in fear."[18]

Given Scotland's distance from Geneva, this new church order, notwithstanding the antecedents of its liturgy, was far less dependent on direct Genevan example and influence than the French Reformed church order. Knox knew Genevan theology and institutions firsthand, but he was an independent thinker, and for all his power was only one of six people who drew up the confession of faith and the First Book of Discipline. None of the other five Johns who helped to draft these documents—Willock, Spottiswoode, Winram, Row, and Douglas—ever visited Geneva or corresponded with Calvin. All we know about their theological formation is that several remained loyal to the established church until just before 1560 and that those who had broken with the church had gone to England and Emden.[19]

The Scottish confession of faith was broadly Reformed in character, but few of its features can be said in any meaningful sense to have been Calvinist. In contrast to the Gallican confession of faith, the document sidestepped the matter of predestination. In the tradition of Bucer and a Lasco but not Calvin, it identified three marks of the true church, including the proper exercise of ecclesiastical discipline. In keeping with the central theme of so much of Knox's preaching, it emphasized the obligation of the civil magistrates to suppress idolatry and superstition, tellingly citing the Old Testament kings who distinguished themselves in this enterprise in the same order that Bullinger cited them in his *Decades*. It is distinctive among Reformed confessions in the extent to which it depicts, with apocalyptic undertones, the church of Christ locked in an ongoing struggle against Satan. Perhaps its most clearly Calvinist feature is its explicit rejection of a Zwinglian understanding of the sacraments as naked signs and its emphasis instead on Christ's genuine spiritual presence in the elements of the Eucharist and within those who rightly partake of them; but here too its wording is sufficiently ambiguous about the precise nature of Christ's presence to stand in alignment with a broad range of Reformed theologians.[20]

In that Knox's group in Frankfurt drew its liturgy from Genevan models, the new patterns of worship embodied in the Book of Common Order were more directly Genevan in inspiration. Calvinist tones were also furthered by the inclusion of Calvin's catechism in virtually every known published edition of the Book of Common Order. The calendar of worship ordered by the First Book of Discipline made no mention of any holidays and went so far in its program for rooting out "the superstition of times" as to suggest the Lord's Supper be celebrated on dates other than Easter Sunday and the other major church festivals. Yet, quite unusually among the Reformed, civil legislation of the era reiterated with seemingly no criticism from reforming ministers pre-Reformation prohibitions against eating meat during Lent and on fixed days during the week. Perhaps in consequence, Lent also continued to be a period when marriages were avoided.[21]

The institutional arrangements outlined in the First Book of Discipline are best seen as an early Reformed attempt to devise rules for the administration of a church on the scale of a large kingdom, slightly later in date than, but largely independent of, the decisions of the first French national synod. Whereas the problems the French churches faced were those of promoting cooperation and maintaining unity among a growing number of churches founded independently of the secular authorities, the drafters of the First Book of Discipline needed to lay down rules for a new style of worship within an established church they had taken over. In this enterprise, they drew inspiration from the pre-Reformation church, from post-Reformation German territorial church orders, from Geneva, and from the refugee churches in England and the empire. The document ordered the suppression of all monasteries, chantries, capitular churches, and other ecclesiastical bodies except for parish churches and schools, but intended to retain the pre-Reformation system of glebe lands and tithes for the support of the schools and parish ministry. It also denounced the seizure of such lands and dues by certain gentlemen "now as cruell over their tenants, as ever were the Papists"—a problem that would continue to bedevil the implementation of its provisions. In the manner of many German territorial reformation mandates, it ambitiously called for a Latin and grammar school in every parish and a secondary school in every principal town, spelling out their curricula and regulations in detail. Perhaps most strikingly, it created ten to twelve regional superintendents to oversee the process of setting up properly reformed church practices throughout the kingdom. The office of superintendent, of course, was to be found in many German church orders. In his *Full Form and Manner of the Ecclesiastical Ministry,* a Lasco had also defended it as being of divine origin, although the functions he assigned to the office varied enough from those in the First Book of Discipline to allow the inference that this was not its direct source. The Scottish superintendents were to be appointed by the Great Council of the Realm for the first three years and then elected by the ministers of their region and the superintendents of the neighboring areas. Their first task was to travel throughout their jurisdictions to "plant and erect Kirkes" that would operate according to the new dispensation. They were then to return regularly to preach at and to monitor the functioning of these churches. To improve the clergy's biblical knowledge, the First Book of Discipline instituted prophesyings similar to those of Zurich and the refugee churches of England and East Friesland. Ministers and others deemed gifted in the interpretation of Scripture were to assemble regularly in the main town of each region for sessions in which one of their number would gloss an individual passage of the Bible. Discussion would follow.[22]

At the parish level, the First Book of Discipline called for the congregational election of ministers, who were to be vetted by the ministers and elders of the nearby principal town to certify their capacity for the office. If a congregation had not selected a fit minister within forty days, the superintendent could name one. Lacking any candidates with sufficient knowledge of doctrine, the parish was to be served instead by a reader, who could read the common prayers and the Bible in church assemblies but could not administer the sacraments. Elders were likewise to be elected. They supervised the administration of ecclesiastical discipline jointly with the minister. Deacons, who received the rents of the church and collected and disbursed alms, might also assist in this task, as they did in certain French congregations. Finally, the document not only specified the schedule for weekly public assemblies and quarterly eucharistic celebrations, but also commended morning and evening prayers and regular instruction in the basics of the faith by the head of the household in private houses. Those who could not say the Lord's Prayer, the Apostle's Creed, and the Ten Commandments were not to be admitted to the sacraments.[23]

This new church order hardly commanded the enthusiasm of the entire population. Reacting—perhaps overreacting—against a national historiography that long identified Protestantism with the national will, several recent historians have drawn attention to the substantial evidence of antipathy to or apathy about the changes wrought by the Reformation. In Edinburgh, only a quarter of the adult population presented itself for communion in 1561. In Aberdeen, where little sign of any heterodox sentiment manifested itself prior to 1560, the city's first Protestant minister was not named until August of that year, and many former Catholic clerics not only remained in town well after that date, but presided over secret assemblies of worship that enjoyed de facto toleration into the 1570s. The often delicate evidence of will formulae turns up only five indisputably Protestant wills among twenty-seven drawn up by lairds in the region of Angus and the Mearns between 1550 and 1575, while distinctively Protestant formulae do not appear in the wills of commoners until the 1590s.[24] The social makeup of the hard core of support for the new Protestant order appears to have come primarily from the urban population and the lesser nobility, notably in the region from Stirling to Montrose and Saint Andrews in the northeast part of the belt stretching across Scotland's waist that formed the most populous part of the country. Those enthusiastically committed to the cause probably represented only a minority of the population. Many barons, especially in the north, remained well intentioned toward Catholicism, providing a potential basis of support for Mary Stuart if she chose to rally opposition against the new church settlement, as some urged her to do.[25]

Furthermore, the system of church government sketched out by the First Book of Discipline neither received the formal approval of either crown or parliament, nor came to be systematically implemented in toto. Its proposals for the reorganization of ecclesiastical property remained a dead letter, and the pre-Reformation system of church benefices lived on, with beneficed clergymen in place retaining the right to their income. If these clergymen accepted the new Confession of Faith and were deemed qualified, they could continue to officiate at the services of the new Reformed church; if not, they simply collected their revenues. Old rights of ecclesiastical patronage likewise remained intact, precluding the implementation of congregational election of ministers in many parishes. Between 1562 and 1566, a series of statutes directed some of the income of old church benefices to support the new ministers, giving the officiating clergy a modest economic foundation that was supplemented in certain areas by stipends from the local authorities. But these changes did not deprive the former incumbents of most of their revenues. Meanwhile, the office of superintendent never developed as the drafters of the First Book of Discipline had hoped. An initial group of eight superintendents was appointed in 1561, including three incumbent bishops, but the office was never filled in two regions. After 1561, no further superintendents received appointment, and at least one, Willock, found the demands of the job so aggravating that he preferred to devote his time to the quieter satisfactions of a parish living across the border in Lancashire. New bishops meanwhile continued to be named. Much of the old church hierarchy and system of benefices thus survived the revolution of 1560.[26]

The structures that ultimately came to prevail within the Scottish church emerged out of thirty more years of institutional improvisation and political conflict in a context of recurrent turmoil. Mary was a most reluctant queen of Scots, only returning to the kingdom (in May 1561) after six months of fruitless negotiation for a new royal husband following Francis II's death. When she came, she made the critical decision of accepting the new Protestant order, insisting only upon the right to have mass said wherever her court was located. This nonetheless offended the keen sensitivities of the hottest Scottish Protestants about the reestablishment of idolatry. Her insistence on keeping her claim to the English throne violated the terms of the treaty of Edinburgh and guaranteed English mistrust. Then her precipitate and disastrous decision in 1565 to marry Lord Darnley—an irresponsible drunk and a Catholic to boot—alienated many of the powerful lords at court. Her heightened reliance on the Italian ex-musician David Rizzio disaffected still more. A series of noble intrigues and factional conflicts followed, highlighted by the murders of Rizzio and Darnley, Lord Bothwell's abduction and forcible marriage of the queen, and finally, in July 1567, her disputed deposition, which sparked six years of intermittent civil war between the partisans of her claim to the throne and parties who advanced the cause of her infant son, James VI. With English assistance, the adherents of the young James at last carried the day, and a powerful member of the House of Douglas, the earl of Morton, restored order as James's regent. Morton's ascendancy lasted from 1572 to 1578, when a new round of faction fights and murders broke out. More permanent stability came only when the now-teenaged James asserted his own authority in the mid-1580s.

This domestic unrest shaped the politics of Scottish church building in crucial ways. The weakness of central authority allowed the country's leading aristocratic families to increase the control they already had over church benefices and property. This set them against churchmen who insisted that erstwhile church property be used exclusively to support the clergy, schools, and poor relief. As both Morton in the early 1570s and King James after 1583 struggled to impose a measure of authority, they recognized the utility of ecclesiastical patronage for rewarding supporters, bribing onetime enemies, and diverting a fraction of ecclesiastical revenues into their own coffers. They became proponents of retaining and restoring the power of bishops. For their part, the strongest ministerial partisans of a purely reformed church quickly learned to act autonomously in defense of the church's interests because so long as Mary ruled they could not acknowledge her as a proper protector of the faith. Within the power vacuum created by the incessant political conflicts, they found they could gain a political voice by wielding the moral authority inherent in their office. A self-assured and stiff-backed group of clerical reformers thus came to confront noblemen and rulers eager to benefit from what they believed to be their right to control the church.

The institution that arose as the forum for articulating church interests was the General Assembly of the Church, composed of representatives of the three estates in a manner analogous to the Scottish Parliament. The first General Assembly was convened in 1560 to discuss the planned church constitution embodied in the First Book of Discipline. Further gatherings soon began to meet frequently, either at a date fixed at the close of the preceding assembly or in response to a summons from Knox or the subsequent ministers of Edinburgh. From 1563 onward, regional synods of ministers and elders, possibly modeled on those in France but equally possibly drawn from the traditions of the pre-Reformation church, also began to assemble twice yearly in certain areas. In the absence of superintendents, the General Assembly took charge of the planting and oversight of parish churches by designating commissioners to carry out these tasks.[27]

Morton was a champion of the Protestant cause who admired and envied the authority that England's rulers had secured over their church and was eager to take advantage of the prerogatives he believed accrued to a godly ruler in a Reformed state. He reinforced the supremacy of Reformed dogma in 1573 when, as part of his effort to impose order, he decreed that all benefice holders had to subscribe to the Scottish confession of faith. His presentation two years previously of several new bishops of questionable capacity but undoubted connections nonetheless touched off controversy over whether or not the church should play a role in vetting or selecting bishops. The matter was resolved with an agreement signed at Leith that reaffirmed the offices of bishop and archbishop, placed alongside them in each see a chapter of learned ministers, recognized their subordination to the General Assembly, and provided that they would be nominated by the king but examined for fitness by the chapter prior to final appointment. Such constant improvisation of new offices satisfied no one, however. As Morton observed, no settled polity had been established in the church "partly through want of the allowance of the authority at the first reformation, and partly because the benefices of cure were of long time suffered to be possessed by persons repugnant to the [Reformed] religion." In 1574, he summoned a conference to consider whether the supreme magistrate should not head the church as well as the state. This proposition encountered stiff clerical opposition and was beaten back. In March 1575, he set up a commission to draft new articles for the administration of the church. The letter that one well-intentioned privy councillor, Lord Glamis, wrote to Geneva soliciting advice from Theodore Beza reveals the questions and apprehensions seen as most in need of resolution. Were bishops appropriate in a Reformed church? Was there a continued need for the General Assembly now that a godly prince ruled the country, and, if so, who properly summoned such an assembly? Could church revenue be assigned to the prince's service?[28]

Scotland's turn to the churches in Switzerland for advice brought the divergences between the ecclesiological traditions of Geneva and Zurich into sharp relief—not for the first time, we shall see—and prompted the Genevans to articulate a more uncompromising position on episcopacy than before. In earlier letters of pastoral advice to residents of countries like England and Poland, Calvin and Beza had refrained from condemning outright the preservation of elements of episcopal hierarchy within a Reformed church. Beza now responded to Glamis's questions with a letter that explicitly repudiated episcopacy, arguing that experience had proven it detrimental to the good order of the church and asserting the principle of equality among ministers. He also stated the need for regular national church synods, while denouncing the presence of bishops in parliament, "for the bishop hath nothing to do in ordering of mere civil affairs." Zurich's new Antistes Gwalther learned of the discussions and hastened to defend the tradition that blended rather than separated secular and ecclesiastical government. A dedication to the young King James was affixed to his *Homilies on Galatians* (1576), and copies of this work, which argued for royal headship of the church, were dispatched northward.[29]

A series of committees labored over the reorganization of the Scottish church and finally produced in 1578 its second major proposed constitution, the Second Book of Discipline. This document makes it clear that Genevan principles had become dominant within the Scottish church by this date. Included in it were both a definition of the four categories of ministers and a delineation of the distinctive but nonetheless mutually reinforcing attributes of the civil and ecclesiastical powers drawn straight from the *Institutes.* Neither superintendents nor bishops were retained. Instead, the document recommended a presbyterian-synodal system of church government whose model appears to have been the French church, with four ascending levels of ecclesiastical assemblies: those of the individual church, the region, the nation, and international councils. Concern about the control of ecclesiastical property also animated the document's drafters. Any diversion of church revenue for private or profane uses was condemned as a detestable sacrilege, and church officials were designated to take over from the crown the collection of ecclesiastical revenues. Andrew Melville, a young theologian who had spent six years in Geneva before taking up a teaching post at Glasgow in 1574, was the most outspoken advocate of the document and the presbyterian-synodal system it framed. Contrary to an important interpretation, however, the Second Book of Discipline was the product of more than a new generation of clergymen importing foreign presbyterian principles into a church that before had respected episcopacy. Among the roughly thirty churchmen responsible for its drafting were many veterans of 1560. The evident failure of the system outlined in the First Book of Discipline and the appeal of presbyterian principles to both ministers and godly laymen who had learned to mistrust the alliance of bishops and magnates must be reckoned the chief reasons this proposed church constitution differed so from the first.[30]

Just as the majority of churchmen had defeated Morton's attempt in 1574 to have the prince declared the head of the church, so now the regent and much of the nobility found the Second Book of Discipline excessively assertive in its claims for clerical autonomy and control of ecclesiastical property. Footdragging by the regency council prevented the document from ever being formally accepted by a parliament. The church therefore took it upon itself to put its features in place, mounting an agitated campaign against episcopacy and lay control over the church. Between 1576 and 1580, the General Assembly sought to impel all bishops to take up a parish ministry as well. In 1580 it condemned episcopacy as unscriptural. When, in the unsettled political climate that followed Morton's downfall, the new regent desired to impose on the recalcitrant chapter of Glasgow a candidate for archbishop of whom they did not approve, rioting university students prevented him from entering the cathedral, and the General Assembly excommunicated him. In 1581 the General Assembly drew up a pilot plan to establish thirteen assemblies intermediate between the individual consistory, or kirk session, and the larger regional synod, as an "exemplatour to the rest that may be established heirafter." How quickly these assemblies, known as presbyteries, went into operation is unclear, but in time they became the most energetic link within the chain of Scottish ecclesiastical assemblies. They carried out visitations within their district, worked to depose incompetent readers, and chose representatives for the General Assembly.[31]

By 1582, ecclesiastical conflict was beginning to dominate national politics. Fears that the appointment of the new archbishop of Glasgow betokened an attempt to restore Catholicism contributed to the palace revolution known as Ruthven's Raid. This brought to power a faction that decreed the church's right to hold its own assemblies at its own discretion. When King James escaped from the clutches of the Ruthven raiders and a faction headed by the earl of Arran took control, a backlash followed. An aggressively antipresbyterian formulary required all members of the clergy to admit to the royal supremacy over the church and declared invalid all jurisdictions and judgments not approved by parliament. Twenty-two ministers refused to sign this document and lost their positions, while others had already fled into exile in England with the fallen Ruthven group. Pamphlets began to fly. The archbishop of Saint Andrews, Patrick Adamson, defended the king's authority over the church and his right to choose the form of government he wished in *A declaration of the kings majesties intention and meaning toward the late acts of parliament.* An anonymous *Answer to the declaration of certain intentions set out in the kings name,* probably written by Melville from exile in Newcastle, replied that no minister should have supremacy over any other and accused the bishops of aiming to usher in a "new Popedome in the person of the king."[32]

In the wake of Arran's fall, the active young King James forestalled the deepening polarization of Scottish opinion between propresbyterian and proepiscopalian parties through an ingenious compromise worked out following consultation with Melville and other leading ministers. The "Black Acts" of 1584 were revoked. Both presbyteries and bishops were retained. The bishops, who were required to hold a parish ministry, were made permanent moderators of the presbyteries, but the final authority of the presbyteries over many questions of discipline and doctrine was acknowledged. Powers of ecclesiastical visitation were placed in the bishops' hands. James took another step toward mending relations with the church when he attended a General Assembly in 1590 and lauded the Church of Scotland as "the sincerest Kirk in the world." A parliamentary statute of 1592 gave secular legal recognition to the powers of synods and presbyteries and to their prerogative to approve candidates for church positions, although it left intact patronage and the system of benefices. Between 1590 and 1592, most presbyteries—forty-seven existed by this time, covering virtually all of the Lowlands—formally subscribed to the Second Book of Discipline. These steps did not resolve all of the troublesome issues of church governance that had arisen over the preceding decades. Ecclesiology would be the recurring bone of contention throughout Scottish church history from the Reformation onward, and soon the still-unresolved issue of whether or not General Assemblies were needed would arise as a further point of conflict. But the basic features of a system blending bishops and presbyteries that would largely define the Scottish church polity for the next forty years were put in place by the Jacobean via media of the late 1580s and 1590s. Under James's continuing leadership, a fairly effective system of church administration began to function smoothly.[33]

Over these years during which church, crown, and nobility fought their three-cornered battle to determine the shape of a settled ecclesiastical constitution, the "planting" of the new church order also made great strides at the parish level, although a persisting shortage of adequately trained ministers and continued attachment to elements of pre-Reformation worship prevented the transformation from being as complete as the partisans of reform would have wished. In the heart of the Lowlands as well as in the peripheral bishoprics of Galloway and Orkney, whose incumbents accepted and promoted the Reformation settlement, Protestant worship was established in most parishes by 1563 and in nearly all by 1567. Elsewhere, the transformation of the liturgy often did not come until Morton decreed in 1573 that all incumbents had to accept the Scottish confession of faith; some isolated parishes lacked ministers or readers loyal to the new church order even after that date. Attendance at communion quickly picked up in Edinburgh. Whereas only a quarter of all potential communicants took part in the Lord's Supper in 1561, a majority did so by 1566. It took far longer to obtain a well-trained ministry, however. Many parishes were served at first by readers, with occasional visits from the ministers of nearby localities. In 1567, probably no more than 250 of Scotland's roughly 1,000 parishes had an accredited minister. Thirty years later, 539 ministers were in place across the country, leaving upward of 400 parishes still in the hands of readers.[34] The absence of written parish records from the Gaelic-speaking Highlands has long led historians to believe that the Reformed church remained essentially missionary there until well into the seventeenth century, but it now appears that the new order was in place and staffed by as high a percentage of ministers as in the Lowlands by 1574. Worship followed the Gaelic translation of the Book of Common Order made in 1567; readers translated the Bible into Gaelic from English or Latin as they read it aloud for up to an hour of a Sunday; and many ministers came from the ancient bardic orders that had long been the bearers of the classical verse traditions of this oral culture.[35]

The establishment of Protestant worship throughout the kingdom hardly brought the immediate elimination of all traditional forms of Catholic church practice. The observance of holy days and pilgrimages continued in many parts of the Lowlands into the 1580s and even beyond. Around Dumfries, the General Assembly complained in 1588, there was "no resorting to the hearing of the Word; no discipline; superstitious days kept by plain command, and . . . all superstitious riotousness at Yule and Pasche." Two years earlier a visitation of the diocese of Dunblane found evidence of people visiting holy wells and observing the ancient saints' days. That same visitation, however, identified only five individuals whom it classified as obstinate papists.[36] Generally, organized recusancy, as opposed to the survival of Catholic traditions, was rare. A few Jesuit missionaries and seminary priests came to Scotland late in the century to try to organize Roman worship, but the endeavor paled in comparison to that which preserved and strengthened the old faith so successfully in the post-1572 United Provinces. If perhaps as many as a fifth of the magnate families of 1560 remained committed to Catholicism down to the end of the century, some sheltering priests, they found few followers among the rest of the population. At no point in the seventeenth century do professed Catholics appear to have exceeded 2 percent of the population.[37]

A final assessment of the place the Reformed church had assumed in Scottish society by the end of the sixteenth century must be nuanced. On the one hand, the absence of qualified ministers in a substantial minority of parishes and the continuing strength of pre-Reformation beliefs and rituals suggest that parish-level religious practice was still far from fully protestantized. On the other hand, the confusion of Scottish politics and the weakness of royal authority during so much of the later sixteenth century had enabled the Reformed church to take its place among the governing authorities of the realm and to gain a good deal of sway over secular legislation and the language of politics. In this localized society with weak formal institutions, the establishment of kirk sessions created the first system of nationwide judicial bodies that sought with any degree of success to uphold an impersonal set of moral standards. In this politically divided society in which contenders for power often needed to reinforce their legitimacy, the prestige attendant upon showing oneself a godly magistrate or prince led at least some ruling authorities, particularly among the lesser lairds and urban magistrates, to embrace this role and cooperate closely with the ministers. Ministerial outspokenness rarely incurred severe punishment.

Studies of the functioning of local churches have stressed the cooperation that developed between the kirk sessions and secular authorities in many areas. Not only did the personnel of the kirk sessions and secular governing bodies overlap—in Perth and Glasgow, the provost, or bailie, was always a member of the kirk session—but the punishments levied by the church often included fines collected through the offices of the civil authorities. Legislation passed in the wake of the Reformation laid down strict moral rules. Between 1563 and 1592 Scotland's parliament made notorious adultery a capital crime, enacted stiff penalties for the "fylthie vice of fornication," and increased penalties for blasphemy. It lent its support to godly worship by requiring attendance at Sunday services, obliging all gentlemen, "substantious yeomen," and burgesses above a specified level of income to acquire a Bible and psalmbook and outlawing such superstitious behavior as the singing of carols. The boldness with which leading ministers asserted the power to censure the ruling officials meanwhile attained a level rarely matched in the Europe of this era. In 1596, a year when clerical denunciation of the vices of every estate rose to a crescendo, the General Assembly reprimanded the king in March for swearing and the queen for "not repairing to the word and sacraments, night walking, balling etc.," while Melville had an audience with the king in September at which he lectured "God's silly vassal" on his subordination to the church.[38]

The nominal rigor of the laws should not deceive. Parliamentary statutes in Scotland were more in the nature of pious wishes than binding decrees, and few secular courts enforced the legislation concerning adultery or blasphemy in this period. A subsequent chapter will likewise show the limits of Scottish church discipline at this time. What the Reformation created was not an ordered, puritanical society, but a political culture in which the language of the godly magistrate, the obligation of the ruler to combat idolatry, and the pretensions of the clergy to moral guardianship over the society all gained substantial resonance, and in which, as in Geneva, an independent system of church discipline worked with the backing of the state. Initially, the royal and the ecclesiastical courts alike were weak, but as they gradually consolidated power over the centuries, the full consequences of the situation would slowly reveal themselves.

6

THE NETHERLANDS
Another Revolutionary Reformation

The establishment of Reformed churches in the Netherlands bore important parallels to the course of events in both France and Scotland. As in France, the churches adopted a presbyterial-synodal structure during an initial period of growth in the face of opposition from the established authorities. As in Scotland, the Reformed faith ultimately became through struggle the legally privileged religion of state. But whereas Scotland witnessed the rapid nationwide victory of a "revolutionary reformation" followed by a long tug-of-war to define and put into place the institutions of the new national church, the victory of the Reformed church in the Netherlands came slowly, amid the upheavals of the Dutch Revolt, while the structure of the church was largely determined prior to the first victories of the rebellious Sea Beggars in 1572. Furthermore, the church's triumph was only partial. Not only was it confined to the seven northern provinces that broke away from their Habsburg overlords to form the independent United Provinces. These provinces were ones in which the movement was at first weak, and even after its triumph in them only a fraction of the population was deeply committed to it. Its strongest partisans were nonetheless loath to abandon the presbyterial-synodal form of church government and consistorial system of church discipline established during the difficult years of the 1560s. They ultimately preserved these features for the Reformed church of the region at the cost of abandoning the ambition of encompassing the entire population within it. The Reformed church became the state-supported public church while claiming only a minority of the population as full-fledged members and allowing large numbers of citizens to live outside its discipline and communion.

This exceptional outcome may be in turn linked to the exceptional length of the Dutch Reformation. The Netherlands was one of the first parts of Europe to be touched by Protestantism but one of the last to witness the establishment of a Protestant church. Thanks to the linguistic similarities between Dutch and Low German and the intense commercial links connecting the region to the Baltic, the Rhineland, and south Germany, the Netherlands felt the full force of the initial expansion of the evangelical movement across the Germanic world as neither France nor Scotland did. It was in Antwerp in 1521 that Albrecht Dürer first obtained a copy of Luther's *On the Babylonian Captivity of the Church,* a gift from no less a personage than the municipal secretary. At least thirty of Luther's works had been translated into Dutch by 1530, when just three had to English and twelve to French.[1] As the example of Cornelisz Hoen and his circle at Delft suggests, certain humanist cenacles in the region were already moving prior to 1517 toward a critique of the doctrines of the established church that would subsequently contribute to the elaboration of Reformed theology. The message of Luther and his contemporaries then fell on receptive ears in this region of high urbanization, high literacy, and numerous poetic societies, or chambers of rhetoric, that often proved well disposed to these ideas. The Augustinian houses of Antwerp and Tournai emerged as centers of Lutheran influence. By the winter of 1523–24, lay evangelicals were gathering regularly for mutual edification in Antwerp and Amsterdam. The execution of Europe's first Protestant martyrs at Brussels in July 1523 did not deter the continued circulation of the new ideas. Heresy trials and other types of evidence suggest that by 1530 these ideas had gained adepts in at least twelve cities in Flanders alone, and soon evangelical Bible discussion groups were meeting openly in village taverns in this province's extensive regions of rural industry. Between 1530 and 1534, the millenarian ideas of Melchiorite Anabaptism also swept like wildfire across much of the region, culminating in the departure of thousands of inhabitants for the New Jerusalem at Münster. Holland and Friesland were the centers of this movement, but a rash of trials in 's-Hertogenbosch, Maastricht, Antwerp, Liège, and Deventer shows that it found adherents elsewhere as well.[2]

What differentiated the Habsburg Netherlands from most of the Holy Roman Empire of which it technically remained a part was the determination with which the ruling prince sought to repress these ideas. In most of the empire, Charles V had to rely on largely uncooperative princes or city councils to

Map 8. The Netherlands

Legend:
1609 border between the Dutch Republic and the Spanish Netherlands following the Dutch Revolt

N

GRONINGEN
Emden
Groningen
Leeuwarden
Franeker
FRIESLAND
Sneek
DRENTHE
Enkhuizen
Hoorn
OVERIJSSEL
Alkmaar
Deventer
Haarlem • Amsterdam
GELDERLAND
Leiden
UTRECHT
Delft
Utrecht
HOLLAND
Gouda
Dordrecht
's Hertogenbosch
Wesel
Zierikzee
Breda
Venlo
ZEELAND
Middelburg
Goes
Roermond
Flushing
BRABANT
Rhine
Turnhout
Maas
Antwerp
Bruges
Eeklo
BISHOPRIC OF LIEGE
Maastricht
Ghent
Hasselt
FLANDERS
LIMBURG
Brussels
Steenvoorde
Ypres
Liege
Kortrijk
Tournai
Lille
Wattrelos
HAINAUT
Namur
ARTOIS
Douai
Mons
Arras
Valenciennes
LUXEMBOURG

0   25   50 Mi.
0   25   50 Km.

TABLE 6.1

Heresy Trials and Executions in Six Regions of the Netherlands, 1521–66

	Flanders		Zeeland		Holland	Friesland	4 W T*	Antwerp
	Tried	Executed	Tried	Executed	Executed	Executed	Executed	Executed
1521–30	82	4	13	2	6	0	1	
1531–40	128	30	57	16	292	13+	13	
1541–50	169	30	4	1	57	10	33	
1551–60	589	102	21	4	43	13	28	98
1561–66	1347	92	33	5	3	0	68	17

*4 W T = Four Walloon Towns (Lille, Mons, Tournai, and Valenciennes)

Sources: Johan Decavele, *De dageraad van de reformatie in Vlaanderen* (Brussels, 1975), 2:52–57; Alistair Duke, *Reformation and Revolt in the Low Countries* (London, 1990), 99; Clasina Rooze-Stouthammer, *Hervorming in Zeeland* (Goes, 1996), 457; Guido Marnef, *Antwerp in the Age of the Reformation* (Baltimore, 1996), 84; J. Woltjers, *Friesland in Hervormingstijd* (Leiden, 1962), 109–10, 117–18.

implement the provisions of the Edict of Worms. In the Netherlands, he could act directly. He issued his first placard against Lutheran heresy in September 1520, even before Diet of Worms condemned Luther. In 1523 he received papal approval to appoint a general inquisitor whose jurisdiction was the investigation and trial of heresy cases. Long-established secular and ecclesiastical tribunals also pursued the crime, especially in the wake of the Anabaptist scare of 1534. The special inquisitorial judges became particularly effective against heresy from 1545 onward, when an energetic circuit-riding judge for the region of Flanders, Lille, and Tournai, Pieter Titelmans, built up a network of paid informants and initiated nearly a hundred cases a year. The pattern of the repression varied from region to region (table 6.1). In the centers of early Anabaptism, such as Holland, trials and executions peaked in the wake of 1534. In Flanders and the Walloon towns, where Titelmans was active, they multiplied after 1545. But what was most noteworthy about the repression of heresy in the Netherlands was its sheer scale: more than thirteen hundred people were executed for their beliefs between 1523 and 1566, in a region of approximately two million inhabitants. In no other part of Europe would the extinguishing of heresy claim nearly so high a toll of victims. Relative to each country's total population, the roughly five hundred people executed in France (with nine times the population) and twenty-one in Scotland (with a third) represented less than one-twentieth the Netherlands' death toll. More than anything else, it was the intensity of the repression during the years before 1555 that prevented the powerful early evangelical impulses in this region from eventuating in the establishment of Protestant churches as they did in so much of the Holy Roman Empire. So extreme was the repression, indeed, that by 1560 many among the local political elites began to recoil at the bloodshed and to worry about the toll it was taking on the region's commerce. In both Holland and Antwerp, the number of executions declined sharply after 1560, while in Flanders and Zeeland the percentage of heresy trials ending in capital sentences dropped.[3]

The theological currents that molded heresy in this region were also unusually diverse. The strength of Melchiorite Anabaptism has already been mentioned. Reorganized and revitalized by Menno Simons in the middle decades of the century, it long continued to attract new converts. The character of early non-Anabaptist Protestantism has been the subject of divergent judgments from recent historians. One leading specialist has pointed out that the chief influence on the printed evangelical literature in Dutch appears to have come from Wittenberg rather than any center of Reformed thinking. Of 170 vernacular pamphlets of a reforming character published in Dutch between 1520 and 1540, roughly 40 percent were written by Luther and his German followers.[4] Yet sacramentarian opinions, including jibes about the consecrated host as a "white God" or "baked God," appear in the transcripts of heresy trials from several locales as early as 1525—far earlier than in France or Scotland—and recur with considerable frequency thereafter, indicating a tradition of attack on the real presence that may even have antedated the Reformation. By 1529, an evangelically minded priest in Tournai was in correspondence with Farel and Bucer, and the brief statement of evangelical views by Cornelis van der Heyden printed in Ghent in 1545 and reissued in both Dutch and French, the *Short Instruction,* expressed a symbolic interpretation of the Eucharist.[5] The spiritualist ideas of Caspar Schwenkfeld and Sebastian Franck also gained a force in the Netherlands they lacked in Germany. With their emphasis on the insignificance of the outward forms of religion and the importance of inner rebirth through direct spiritual communion with God—which allowed believers to conform to the established church even while pursuing their central religious experiences independently of clerical mediation—these ideas were most attractive to evangelicals living under conditions of intense repression. David Joris, Dirk Volckertsz. Coornhert, and Hendrik Niclaes and his many prominent secret adherents in the Family of Love all expressed influential variants of these mystical and spiritualist ideas.

Throughout the period of Protestantism's underground growth to 1566, direct Genevan input was modest. Calvin exchanged only four letters with inhabitants of the Netherlands during his lifetime, and only fourteen of the ministers known to have played a pivotal role in the construction of Reformed churches in the region visited Geneva prior to 1566.[6] But the refugee churches of the empire and England were an indirect channel for Calvin's influence as well as for that of John a Lasco. As in France and Scotland, the groups of secret Protestants that took shape in parts of the Low Countries occasionally grew large and bold enough to seek to institute regular services. In 1544, several citizens of Tournai appealed to Bucer to send them somebody capable of organizing a church. The mission was given to Pierre Brully, a former Dominican of Metz and Calvin's successor at the head of the French church of Strasbourg. Brully preached and seems to have set up functioning churches in Tournai, Valenciennes, Lille, Douai, and Arras before he was captured after two months in the region and executed. Small conventicles continued to gather after his death in Tournai, but Brully's execution stopped the creation of churches under the cross for the subsequent ten years and spurred many of those in the early churches to flee abroad. In the very next year the first refugee church founded by people fleeing the Low Countries took shape in the lower Rhenish town of Wesel. The English refugee churches followed after 1550, and growing numbers of émigrés sought shelter in Emden. These provided clearly Reformed models and centers of direction for the varied currents of underground heterodoxy within the Low Countries. Calvin's solicitude for the refugee churches of the lower Rhine made them vital relay points of Genevan influences to the nearby Walloon regions. A Lasco was the great influence in the coastal and more northerly regions because these received books, guidance, and, later, pastors from Emden and London.[7]

While forceful repression long succeeded in preventing the heterodox currents that swirled through the Low Countries from giving rise to organized, enduring forms of Protestant worship, it could not prevent—indeed, it probably fostered—growing disenchantment with the traditional practices of the Catholic church. Delft boasted several Marian shrines that attracted pilgrims and rewarded them with miracles at the beginning of the century, but between 1520 and 1535 the offerings given these shrines dropped by 60 percent or more. The proceeds from indulgences, the volume of legacies to the church, and the number of those entering holy orders in Antwerp likewise tumbled from the 1520s onward. In Dokkum in Friesland, barely half of the eligible population presented itself for Easter communion in 1560. Statistical studies of trends in participation in various Catholic practices in the parts of Europe touched by underground Protestant propaganda in this period remain unfortunately rare, but when more comparable studies are available they will likely show that the abandonment of Catholic practices was particularly pronounced in the Low Countries. An anonymous clergyman complained in 1568 of "an almost universal feeling of hatred . . . in the hearts of the majority of the people against the clerical estate, as if we were the cause of the rigors and executions carried out for a long time for the sake of religion." The early Reformation in the Low Countries was a rich stew of theological ingredients that fed disaffection from the Roman church well before permanent alternatives took root.[8]

Renewed efforts to organize individual congregations under the cross began in 1554–55 in the great commercial metropolis of Antwerp. To impede the detection and denunciation of its members, the new church divided itself into sections of eight to twelve members; only a few sections would gather at a time to hear the sermons of the church's ministers, who served for brief periods before returning to a place of exile such as Emden. In 1557 a Reformed church with a consistory was founded in the small Zeeland port of Flushing; another may have taken shape in Zierikzee. The dramatic growth of the Huguenot movement in France between 1559 and 1562 spilled across the border and led to the organization of churches in several Walloon communities, most notably Tournai and Valenciennes, which in short order became the greatest centers of Reformed strength in the Low Countries in this period. By early 1566, regular congregations are known to have been formed in at least sixteen communities between Zeeland and Hainaut, none north of the great rivers of the Rhine and Maas.[9] In the same period, as many as twenty-five itinerant preachers evangelized the countryside of industrial West Flanders. The number of underground churches was far smaller than in France, but the way in which the movement developed was similar.

The range of Reformed theological influences shaping these new churches remained broad. A Nieuwkerk surgeon interrogated for heresy in 1560 told his judges that four highly noteworthy prophets of God's word had risen in recent times: Zwingli, Calvin, a Lasco, and Marten Micron. The refugee church in London was the mother church of the earliest congregations in Zeeland and West Flanders. The imprint of Genevan patterns of theology and French models of church organization nonetheless grew stronger. Guy de Bray, a native of Mons who studied in Geneva and Lausanne in 1557–58, was the driving force behind the reestablishment of church assemblies in and around Tournai. Soon after he returned to the area, he drafted a confession of faith that he tossed into the chateau of Tournai with a letter announcing defiantly it was too late to extinguish the pure light of the Gospel, for thousands of believers were prepared to die for it. De Bray circulated his writing to several other ministers in the region for their approval. Published in French in 1561 and in Dutch in 1562, this Belgic confession of faith, as it came to be called, derived much of its structure and wording from the 1559 French confession, while taking several articles directly from a confession that Theodore Beza drafted in Lausanne. It reiterated the French confession's exposition of the eternal decrees of election and reprobation and of a spiritual real presence in the Eucharist, imparting a clear Genevan flavor to the document. At the same time, reflecting the intense local competition with rival Anabaptist and Lutheran currents of reform, it contained extensive expositions of the doctrines of baptism and of the Eucharist rebutting Anabaptist and Lutheran views. Eager to show that the Reformed were no less concerned than the Anabaptists about maintaining the purity of the church community—and in line with the tradition of a Lasco and the Dutch church of London—it included discipline among the essential marks of the true church.[10] During these same years, the first steps were also taken to bring the nascent churches of the region into association with one another. In 1563, drawing inspiration from the presbyterial-synodal system erected in France, three protosynods met in Antwerp. Among their decisions was that all would-be church members be required to sign the Belgic confession of faith. A largely Genevan-inspired confession of faith thus became one of the foundational documents of the young Netherlandish churches.[11]

While a structured network of Reformed churches began to take shape in the Netherlands, a broader movement of opposition to the territory's Habsburg rulers also developed. The proud nobility of the region that had enjoyed such favor at the court of Charles V had been alienated by its growing exclusion from the critical circuits of decision making under the reign of Philip II, Margaret of Parma, and Cardinal Antoine Granvelle. Early in 1564, it won a major political triumph when its opposition to a proposal to reorganize the region's bishoprics provoked Granvelle's dismissal. Many of the leading aristocrats now resumed an active role in the Council of State for the Low Countries. One of the goals for which they militated was moderation of the persecution of heresy. Although not Protestants themselves, several had Lutheran wives. Others feared that the harsh enforcement of the placards against heresy threatened to bring all authority into disrespect and harm the region's trade. In distant Madrid, Philip II saw matters otherwise. He rejected an appeal to moderate the laws. The arrival of his letters to this effect in Brussels prompted more concerted protest action. Late in 1565, a group of nobles of varying religious sympathies drew up a petition that called for the abolition of the inquisition, moderation of the placards against heresy, and the granting of freedom of conscience. Between Christmas 1565 and April 1566, they circulated the petition and persuaded about four hundred of the regional gentry to sign it. Pamphlets and engravings attacked the inquisition and the "bastard" Margaret of Parma. Finally, in April 1566, the signers of this "Compromise of the Nobility" rode into Brussels in an imposing procession, to the applause of a sympathetic crowd assembled with the aid of printed handbills, to present it to the regent. Powerless to resist, Margaret instructed the local authorities of the region that, pending the final approval of the king, nobody was henceforward to be troubled for their religious beliefs, although the prohibition on public worship outside the auspices of the Catholic church remained in force.[12]

In Reformed eyes, freedom of conscience that tolerated Anabaptist ideas while forbidding the proper worship of God was a troubling mixture of license and unwarranted proscription. From Geneva, Beza expressed dismay at a petition that would have granted liberty to "so many horrible . . . hateful sects that pullulate in those lands" while precluding the open exercise of true religion. Individuals in the Low Countries realized, however, that the moderation of persecution presented an opportunity for proclaiming their faith in ways that had not previously been dared. On May 28, a young Augustinian, Carolus Daneel, fled the convent in Ypres and began preaching in the area. As the spring days lengthened, many others imitated his example. The open-air "hedge preaching" attracted crowds in the thousands. The Ghent magistrate Marcus van Varnewijck observed with wonder the good order that prevailed at the gatherings. Men, women, and young girls each sat in separate sections with their own teachers. From time to time, psalms were sung from the psalters that were on sale for a stuiver apiece. The preachers who spoke "gave the impression that now for the first time the truth had been revealed and the Gospel preached aright because the preachers especially cited the Scriptures

most valiantly and stoutly. They let the people check each passage in their testaments to see whether or not they preached faithfully." Public expressions of
anti-Roman sentiment multiplied. When a priest came to administer extreme
unction to a dying man in Brussels, a weaver's wife uttered one of the better
anti-Roman jibes of the era: "They're bringing the oil, but there's no salad in
the house."[13]

As it did so often in Europe since 1517, open and enthusiastically attended
evangelical preaching led to attacks on the holy objects and altarpieces of
Catholic worship. On August 10, those who had attended a sermon at Steenvoorde in the Flemish Westkwartier were incited by a former monk in the
audience to attack a nearby chapel and strip it of a number of statues and
paintings. Over the following days, the raiders turned their attention to nearby
churches. Soon, the iconoclasm swelled into a phenomenon of a character
and scale unmatched in the history of the European Reformation. Most of
West Flanders was affected the next week, then the large towns of the Scheldt
region, the northern Netherlands, and finally, in the early fall, cities as far east
as Maastricht and Venlo. A final episode shook Hasselt, in the prince-bishopric
of Liège, in January 1567. In many localities, the movement was largely spontaneous, and hundreds of people were caught up in the excitement. In Ghent,
crowds of psalm-singing men and women lent support to those who did the
actual work of stripping bare the churches. Elsewhere, the iconoclasm was
the work of relatively small groups of paid men, who often appear to have
been put up to the task by leading elements within the local Reformed church
seeking to demonstrate their movement's strength and to speed up the course
of ecclesiastical change. Certain towns, notably Lille and Bruges, prevented
destruction through determined action by the local officials and municipal
guard. More commonly, however, the civic militia disregarded orders to protect the local churches—a sign of how thoroughly the Catholic church had
lost support by this time. "We will not fight for church, pope, or monks," the
militia leaders of Middelburg declared.[14]

In the aftermath of the iconoclasm, the leading evangelical preachers in
many cities petitioned the authorities for permission to preach within the
town walls; or they simply took over the stripped-down churches for their own
use. In Antwerp, celebration of the mass was temporarily forbidden for fear of
inciting even more disorder, while Protestant sermons were permitted in the
city under an agreement brokered in September by William of Orange. Similar accords took shape in most of the towns of Flanders, Brabant, Hainaut,
and Holland. Two months later, the Antwerp Reformed took the further step
of beginning to administer the sacraments at their assemblies, although the
September accord permitted only preaching. Farther north in Leeuwarden, a
group of burghermasters already inclined toward the Protestant cause fore-

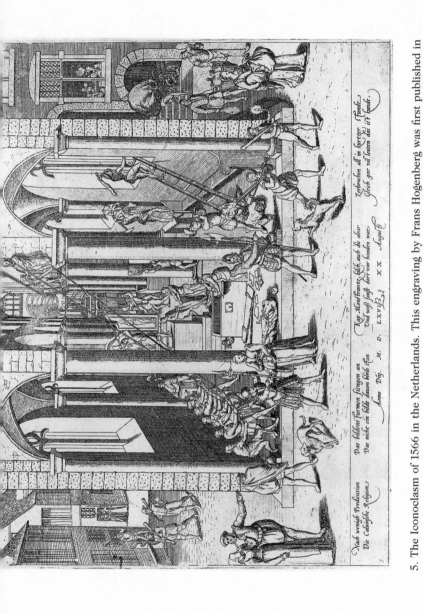

Within the engraving:

Nach weinig Predication
Die Culsinische Religion.

Das bildern furmen fiengen an
Das mehr ein bildt dawn bleib ftan.
Anno Dij. M. D. LXVI.[?] xx Augusti

Kay. Matt Frantz felst, auch die altar
Und welt fonst dort vor handen war.

Zerbrochen all in forryer Stunde,
Gleich gar vil newen das ist funde.

5. The Iconoclasm of 1566 in the Netherlands. This engraving by Frans Hogenberg was first published in Cologne in 1570 as part of a larger series of prints recounting the recent history of the Low Countries in pictures. In the church in the center, a team of iconoclasts pulls down statues, breaks stained glass windows, hacks apart an altarpiece, and tears up ecclesiastical garments. Other men and women carry goods away from a sacristy on the right. In its cellar broken barrels of wine can be seen to gush wine. The German caption asserts that the destruction began "after a little preaching of the Calvinist religion." (Hamburger Kunsthalle Kupferstichkabinett, photo by Elke Walford, Hamburg).

IIS· AL· VERLOREN· GHEBEDN· OFT· GESCHETEN
ICK· HEB· DE· BESTE· CANSE· GHESTREKEN
1566

LÆT ONS WEL BIDDEN SONDER OPHELDEN | LÆT ONS RAS KEREN EN WORDEN NIET MOE⌒
OCH DAT ONS HEILCDOM TE MEER MACH GELDEN | WANT ÆLE DEES CREMEKIE HOORT DEN·DVYEL TOE

6. Emblematic Print of the Iconoclasm. This Netherlandish print contemporary to the events of 1566 depicts the Beggars on the right (many wearing at their belts the beggar's bowls adopted as the symbol of the cause) engaged in what is presented as a cleansing operation. The statues, chalices, and other objects of the church that they pull down and sweep away are said by the caption to belong to the devil. On the left Catholic clergymen pray to the pope, seated like the whore of Babylon atop a seven-headed beast, to preserve their sanctuary, but above them the devil carries away more crucifixes, croziers, and censers and admits in the caption that the game is up, whether they pray or shit. (Rijksmuseum, Amsterdam)

stalled any iconoclasm from below by taking all precious church objects under their protection, then permitted evangelical preaching after a poll of the inhabitants revealed a majority in favor of this. Finally, when the new ministers announced they would not continue to preach in churches that still contained idols, they purged the churches of all decoration and outlawed any other services. The entire process was controlled by the city fathers.[15]

The dramatic events of the Wonderyear of 1566 should not be associated exclusively with the Reformed cause. Those who preached were of various confessional orientations, insofar as their views had any identifiable confessional orientation at all. In the northern and northeastern provinces, the new forms of worship devised in this period often lacked a clear confessional character. Some assemblies, for example, Amsterdam's, consciously tried to encompass adherents of both Lutheran and Reformed inclinations. The church there persisted in admitting to communion adepts of both the Augsburg and the Belgic confessions even after Antwerp's Reformed dispatched a deputation to persuade them to change. In Antwerp and, on a far smaller scale, Breda, Lutheran assemblies took shape alongside Reformed ones. The Antwerp Lutherans appealed to nearby German Lutheran territories for additional preachers and a number responded to the call, among them such prominent figures as Matthias Flacius Illyricus and Cyriacus Spangenburg. Since at least 1564, meanwhile, leading figures among the noble opposition, including William of Orange and his brother Louis of Nassau, had been convinced that the key to obtaining enduring rights of Protestant worship lay in uniting all shades of Protestant opinion around the Augsburg Confession and had actively promoted the general acceptance of that document.[16] By doing so they hoped to obtain diplomatic and military support from Germany's Lutheran princes.

Ministers and institutions of an unmistakably Reformed orientation nonetheless did more to give shape to the dramatic surge of anti-Catholic sentiment than any others. Many of the hedge preachers of 1566 were men who returned from exile in such Reformed centers as Emden and England. Consistories of a Reformed sort were established to direct many of the new Protestant assemblies, and these were often in contact with the refugee churches abroad and the leading Reformed churches within the Low Countries. By the end of the year congregations with consistories functioned in at least eight towns in the county of Holland alone, where there had been no regularly functioning church under the cross prior to 1566. (No accurate estimate has yet been made of the total number of such churches across the seventeen provinces of the Low Countries in this period.) Early in the year, Catholic observers spoke vaguely of sectaries or "those of the new religion." By the summer government correspondence was filled with references to "the Reformed religion," "Calvinist" services, and worship "à la huguenote."[17] The political

TABLE 6.2
Approximate Strength of the Reformed in
Eleven Localities of the Netherlands, 1566 (%)

Greater than 50	25–33	10–15	Less than 10
Tournai	Antwerp	Ghent	Amsterdam
Valenciennes		Roermond	Breda
Kortrijk		Eekloo	Turnhout
		Bergen-op-Zoom	

Sources: *Algemene Geschiedenis der Nederlanden* 6:179; Geoffrey Parker, review of J. G. C. Venner, *Beeldenstorm in Hasselt* in *English Historical Review* 106 (1991), p. 396; Decavele, *Eind van deen rebelse droom*, p. 28; Marnef, *Antwerp*, pp. 101, 104.

arguments marshaled to sway the Reformed to embrace the Augsburg Confession proved unpersuasive, in part because Beza made known to his correspondents in the Low Countries the objections to the document held in Geneva. The powerful Antwerp church militated actively against the Martinists.[18]

Estimates of the fraction of the population that participated, whether out of curiosity or conviction, in the hedge preaching and church assemblies of the summer and fall of 1566 range from five-sixths of the inhabitants of the great Reformed center of Valenciennes to under one-tenth of the population in Amsterdam, Breda, and Turnhout (table 6.2). Examination of those brought to justice for their involvement in the movement in Ghent, Antwerp, and Hasselt reveals a sociological pattern very similar to that of French Protestantism at its high tide: the movement cut across age, wealth, and status, although within artisanal ranks it displayed a moderate tendency to recruit members disproportionately from the literate and skilled trades. A range of sociological patterns nonetheless characterized the Protestant movement in the Low Countries. Across West Flanders and in Kortrijk, the movement retained a decidedly proletarian cast, recruiting overwhelmingly from poorer textile workers and the propertyless. As in France, it was generally far stronger in the cities than in the countryside, although it took on considerable force in regions of rural industry—most spectacularly in West Flanders. The extent of noble affiliation with the Reformed movement is less clear. Just under 20 percent of the gentry families of the county of Holland either adhered to the Reformed or proved tolerant of heresy in this period, but many of these may have been more inclined to tolerate or encourage the movement than actually join it. Even such leading members of the noble opposition to Philip II to whom the Reformed looked for support as Hendrik van Brederode, named protector of the faith late in 1566, appear not to have made a public profession of the creed; Brederode's personal library was remarkably devoid of Calvinist books. It seems that the Reformed cause did not attract as many converts among the nobility of the Low Countries as in France and Scotland.[19]

Although the Protestant cause swelled to impressive proportions in the region's cities and industrial villages as the Wonderyear advanced, its legal status grew more insecure with each provocative step beyond the bounds specified in Margaret of Parma's moderation of the placards against heresy—themselves conditional concessions that Philip II never approved. As Margaret recovered from the shock of the iconoclasm and took the measure of the opposition, she regained her nerve and began to assemble troops to reassert the laws of the land. Faced with growing evidence that force might be used against them, the Lutherans and the Reformed sought to collaborate to obtain freedom of worship. Late in the fall, representatives of the various Protestant churches presented the Habsburg government with a singular offer: they would give the king three million guilders if he would grant them freedom of worship. The leading cities of Royal Prussia had obtained a *jus reformandi* through a cash payment to their ruler, the king of Poland; this precedent, undoubtedly known in the Netherlands thanks to its intense trade with Danzig, may have inspired the suggestion. Philip II was not to be bargained with like a king of Poland. Unsurprisingly, he rejected the offer.[20]

From the early 1560s onward, the Netherlandish Reformed, perhaps even more than their brethren in France and Scotland, had been divided over questions of the bounds of legitimate resistance to persecution. The issue of whether or not imprisoned brethren might be freed by force was much debated in the Dutch refugee churches. Amid the events of the Wonderyear, several Reformed consistories collected funds to pay bands of iconoclasts and hire troops for their eventual protection. The most crucial step toward legitimizing resistance came in late November, when a synod in Antwerp known to have been attended by representatives from Valenciennes, Ghent, Ypres, Friesland, and Gelderland adopted the position that subjects "may resist by force their magistrate, if it breaks and does not observe the privileges and commits wrong or open violence." At the same gathering, councils were set up to take charge of the military defense of the cause and to raise money to pay for this; again, synods were being used to rally armed resistance. The three-million-guilder request was circulated through Reformed gatherings with instructions to assemble the money at once. If the king did not agree to the request, at least one assembly was told, the money would be used to pay for troops that the confederates had begun to raise in Germany.[21] The Antwerp Lutherans took a very different course. They rejected any recourse to force and urged believers not to "look at the thunder nor at the billows of the sea but at Jesus Christ, our keeper who is with us in the ship, and will not let his ship be wrecked."[22] This policy cut them off from the most aggressive political forces, whose militance would in time prove critical to the institution of independence and Protestant worship in the northern half of the region. In this part of Europe, at least, the Lutherans showed themselves more respectful of existing authority and less revolutionary in behavior.

By late November Margaret felt strong enough to dispatch garrisons to the "wicked towns" of Tournai and Valenciennes to punish them for permitting the celebration of sacraments and to forestall other troubles. At the urging of certain ministers and, in all probability, the Valenciennes consistory—according to a judicial investigation, the city council decided nothing of import without consulting the consistory—the cities refused to admit the soldiers. Now they were in a position of open rebellion against the government. The consistories of Flanders raised troops for their defense, but the relief force was surprised and routed at Wattrelos, prompting ministers to flee West Flanders and Tournai to open its gates. Valenciennes resisted for three more months, but several further attempts to mobilize troops for its defense also came to grief. Among those in the city when it surrendered in March was Guy de Bray, who paid with his life. Throughout the crisis, Germany's Lutheran princes refused to intervene, for they did not want to risk upsetting the religious peace within the empire; any possibility that the German princes might guide the Reformation in the Low Countries in a Lutheran direction was thus foreclosed.

The first wave of open revolt in the Low Countries consequently ended far less propitiously for the Protestant cause than had been the case in Scotland or even France. After the fall of Valenciennes, all public Reformed worship ceased throughout the seventeen provinces. The noblemen most compromised in the resistance fled abroad, as did many ministers and hundreds of ordinary believers. In his last sermon in Antwerp before public worship ceased, the preacher Isbrand Balck mournfully likened those reborn in Christ to birds that fly over all the world. A kernel of true believers remained behind in a number of cities and continued to meet for secret worship in the years that followed, but the membership of these reconstituted churches under the cross was tiny. Sporadic guerrilla resistance to the reimposition of Catholic worship continued in the Westkwartier until 1568. But across most of the region, order had been restored and Protestant worship eliminated less than a year after the first appearance of the hedge preachers—even before the "iron duke" of Alva arrived in the Low Countries at the head of ten thousand Spanish troops.[23]

The duke had been sent to the Netherlands to ensure the firm repression of rebellion and heresy. One of his first acts upon arrival was to impanel a special tribunal, the Council of Troubles, to hear cases arising out of the late disorders. This court tried no fewer than twelve thousand people and executed

more than one thousand of those it could get its hands on; most of those in-
dicted fled. During Alva's tenure as governor-general in the Low Countries,
he also implemented the crown's new bishoprics plan and moved to impose
a series of new taxes, overriding the traditional liberties of the region as necessary to do so. He beat back several invasions from abroad by William of
Orange and his supporters. The refugee churches resumed their previous role
of succoring their brethren in the Low Countries by dispatching books and
ministers, but Alva's success in rooting out organized heresy within the seventeen provinces is indicated by the records of the important ecclesiastical gatherings that met in Wesel in November 1568 and in Emden in October 1571.
The acts of the Emden assembly refer to twenty-eight "fugitive" churches
operating in Germany and England and just sixteen churches under the cross
still functioning within the Netherlands.[24]

The assemblies at Wesel and Emden, which in time came to be viewed as
the first national synods of the Dutch Reformed Church, were distinctive in
two regards. First, they aligned the institutions of the Netherlandish churches
more closely to Genevan and French models, specifying Calvin's four orders
of ministers, calling for regular meetings of regional, provincial, and national
classes and synods, and echoing the principle of the French church that no
individual congregation could claim superiority over any other. At Emden,
the few surviving churches of the northern Netherlands also assented to the
policy already followed in the south in 1566 that linked admission to communion to the profession of Reformed faith and the acceptance of consistorial
discipline. Second, the Emden synod announced the Palatinate's emergence
as a major center of authority within the Reformed world. The refugee congregations in Heidelberg and Frankenthal took the initiative in assembling the
synod, and it adopted the Heidelberg Catechism for use in the Dutch-speaking
churches, while recommending Calvin's catechism for the Walloon churches.

Under the circumstances of the moment, the Wesel and Emden gatherings represented a remarkable expression of faith in the future on the part of
the Reformed. To most contemporaries in October 1571, the situation in the
Low Countries must have seemed proof that a policy of force could repress
religious dissent. But Alva's sovereign disregard for the region's time-honored
privileges had badly alienated political opinion. Just how badly would be revealed when, on April 1, 1572, a group of Sea Beggars—exiled Netherlanders
who had taken to preying on Spanish shipping in the English Channel and
North Sea—landed in the Holland port of Brill after they had been expelled
by Queen Elizabeth from their base in England. They had expected simply to
raid the town to replenish their supplies, but, finding no Spanish garrison, decided to remain and to seek to liberate some of the neighboring towns. Over
the next month, they moved from success to success. In virtually all of the

towns of Zeeland and Holland, they were able to find small numbers of supporters willing to open the gates to them from inside. The vast majority of the population was sufficiently disaffected by "Spanish tyranny" not to put up any resistance. By the end of the summer, all of the cities of Holland and Zeeland except Amsterdam, Middelburg, and Goes were in Beggar hands. Orange proclaimed that he had been unlawfully removed from his position as stadtholder of Holland, and a gathering of the provincial estates assembled on local initiative accepted his authority.

In certain cities of the region, the rebel triumph initiated an immediate religious revolution. On the same day that Enkhuizen went over to the Beggars, a preacher—probably an inhabitant of the city who had previously kept silent about his religious beliefs—began to speak publicly in the fish market. On the following day, the city's Grote Kerk was taken over with the aid of the civic militia, images were removed, and a new pattern of worship was instituted by the incumbent priest, who now declared himself in favor of the new order. A new group of magistrates chosen for the city included a number of former exiles. The new city council "purified" all of Enkhuizen's remaining churches and precipitated the flight of those clergymen who remained loyal to Rome.[25]

More often, the establishment of Reformed worship led more slowly to the abolition of Catholicism. The numbers of those who initially joined the Reformed churches in Holland were small; just 156 people took part in the first communion services in Enkhuizen, 180 in Delft, and 368 in the most resolutely Reformed of the province's six major cities, Dordrecht. Zeeland was a greater center of early Reformed strength, having witnessed the founding of churches under the cross before 1566; 660 people partook of the Lord's Supper shortly after Middelburg came over to the side of the revolt. Even this was only a fifth of the adult population of the city (table 6.3).

Before opening their gates to the Beggars, many cities had negotiated deals whereby their churches and cloisters were to be left undisturbed. Meanwhile William of Orange hastily decreed a policy of toleration for both faiths that, unusually for the era, now had deep purchase in the political culture of the region because the long campaign against the inquisition and Alva's policies had relied heavily on the argument that religious persecution was inimical to the land's liberty and prosperity. Yet the Beggar soldiers were avid for revenge against an ecclesiastical power structure that had forced them into exile and killed so many of their fellows. These defenders of the rebellious towns disrupted processions, ransacked cloisters, and killed more than forty Catholic clergymen. The counteroffensive mounted by the duke of Alva in the fall of 1572 spread panic throughout the rebellious districts, especially after the slaughter of Naarden's inhabitants in December demonstrated that even towns

TABLE 6.3

Reformed Church Membership in Twelve Localities of the Northern Netherlands, 1572–79

Figures indicate the number of people admitted to communion in the church. Figures in parentheses indicate the approximate percentage of the population represented by this total, where the local population is known.

	1572	1573	1574	1575	1576	1577	1578	1579
Holland								
Delft	180 (3%)		617 (9%)					
Dordrecht	368 (6%)		536 (9%)					
Enkhuizen	156 (4%)							
Naaldwijk		28						
Alkmaar					156 (4%)			
Haarlem						27 (0.3%)		
Gouda							50 (0.8%)	
Kampen								181
Zeeland								
Middelburg			660 (20%)					
Zierikzee					114 (4%)			
Goes								200 (20%)
Friesland								
Sneek						177		

Sources: Abels and Wouters, *Nieuw en ongezien*, 1:230–39; Elliott, "Protestantization," 148, 167; Duke, *Reformation and Revolt*, 211; Spaans, *Haarlem*, 89; J. Briels, "De Zuidnederlandse immigratie 1572–1630," *Tijdschrift voor Geschiedenis*, 100 (1987): 335; Bergsma, *Tussen Gideonsbende en publieke kerk*, 111–13. Urban population estimates drawn from Jan de Vries, *European Urbanization 1500–1800* (Cambridge, 1984), 271, using the figures for 1550 but reducing them to take into account the population decline between that date and the 1570s; the number of those of age to take communion has been placed at 60 percent of the total population.

that surrendered to the Iron Duke could expect no mercy. Rumors of Catholic plots ran rife, and the least Beggar setback or triumph could be the occasion for anti-Catholic violence. Early in 1573 the States of Holland outlawed Catholic worship. Parish churches that had not already been seized were handed over to the Reformed, and a portion of the ecclesiastical revenues that had already been inventoried by the magistrates to support the war effort was assigned for the support of Reformed ministers. Orange himself formally joined the Reformed church and took communion in 1573.

After riding the Beggars' coattails into a privileged position, the suddenly dominant Reformed churches had to negotiate their precise relation with the civic community. The hard core of Reformed supporters, encouraged by the majority of the newly designated ministers, desired to preserve the consistorial discipline and synodal organization that they had known in the refugee churches and that the assemblies of Wesel and Emden had declared to be normative for the Netherlandish church. Consistories and regional classes were formed. The classes took in hand the installation of Reformed ministers in rural parishes. In 1574 a provincial synod assembled at Dordrecht and asserted the rights of consistories and classes working together to appoint new ministers and decreed that all schoolmasters should sign the church's confession of faith.[26] The great majority of the population, however, did not warm to the austere practices the church sought to maintain, nor did the city fathers of many towns wish to pay for an evangelical minister without retaining the dominant voice in his selection and oversight. It took some years of tug-of-war to work out a stable modus vivendi governing the relation between ministers and magistrates.

The points of contention were several. Some ministers refused to accept the decisions of church synods on the topic of worship. Their insistence upon pursuing an independent course in turn raised the question of whether or not the synodal assemblies had the power to depose dissident ministers. One who dissented was the Leiden minister Caspar Coolhaes, a Cologne-born former Carthusian who had previously served as a minister in several nearby German territories and in Deventer, where the city fathers had appointed him as preacher in 1566 on the condition that he share a church with the Catholics and leave its furnishings undisturbed. He denounced decisions of the Dordrecht synod of 1574 that called for the elimination of all feast days and funeral sermons as needless meddling in minor matters of church practice about which no rules were justified. After further disagreements divided Coolhaes from his fellow ministers in Leiden and led to his being summoned to defend his views before a synod at Middelburg in 1581, the Leiden authorities forbade him to attend as an official delegate, although he chose to answer the summons personally in order to defend his views as a brother speaking to brothers. He was excommunicated by a subsequent synod and left his post. Another dissenter was the Gouda pastor Herman Herbertszoon, who fought a running battle with the regional classis during the 1580s over his refusal to recognize the binding authority of the confession of faith and to preach regularly from the approved catechism. Gouda's city fathers likewise believed that regional church assemblies had no authority over local churches and represented an unwarranted attempt to create a "new Popery." Unlike Coolhaes, Herbertszoon retained his position until his death in 1607. While certain city governments that were well intentioned toward the Reformed cause recognized them as having the power to make decisions that were binding on local church gatherings, others continued to deny them any authority unless they had specifically consented to allow their ministers to take part in their deliberations.[27]

A second, related point of contention focused on the degree of magisterial participation in the selection of ministers and elders. The city fathers of many towns refused to accept the procedures outlined by the Dordrecht synod of 1574 that asserted the church's independence from magisterial control. In 1576 the States of Holland proposed its own set of church ordinances that invoked the guardianship exercised over the church by the rulers of ancient Israel and vested the prerogative to choose the clergy squarely in the hands of the secular authorities. Additional proposals and counterproposals for a church constitution continued to be advanced by synods and secular assemblies right down through the celebrated synod of Dort of 1618. These were accompanied by a vigorous pamphlet debate, a central role once again going to Coolhaes. After leaving Deventer, Coolhaes had spent nearly six years in the Palatinate, which, as we shall shortly see, was the site during just these years of the most important debate of this generation between partisans of independent ecclesiastical discipline and government and defenders of a church subordinated to the ruling authorities on the model of Zurich. Coolhaes defended this latter model in a series of treatises published between 1580 and 1585 that amplified and adapted to the Dutch situation the arguments advanced during the Palatine controversy by the great spokesman of magisterial authority over the church, Thomas Erastus. While Coolhaes's views were shared by many regents, they did not convince the great majority of his fellow Reformed clergymen, who were willing to concede to the secular officials nothing more than a right of "approbation and approval" of the appointment of ministers and elders chosen by the church. Ultimately, none of the various constitutions for the church advanced by either ecclesiastical synods or secular political gatherings ever succeeded in being instituted throughout Holland. The precise arrangements for the selection of ministers and elders came to be worked out on a city-by-city basis, through systems that often involved a complicated mixture of civic and ecclesiastical committees. In Dordrecht, for example, a church committee narrowed the range of candidates for each ministerial vacancy to three men, who were presented to the city council for its approval. A second committee composed of equal numbers of burghermasters and church representatives then made the final selection, which in turn required the ratification of both the full city council and the local classis. Patronage rights survived in many rural parishes, adding still another voice to the process. Congregational election of elders survived in some places.[28]

The linked issues of ecclesiastical discipline and access to the sacraments had been the subject of the most intense conflicts between ministers and magistrates in the cities of Switzerland and south Germany, but in Holland these themes were resolved with relatively little strife through an ingenious compromise. The Netherlandish churches had framed strong, independent systems of church discipline during the years of exile, but the majority of the population of Holland and Zeeland, while it had grown disaffected with the Roman church, balked at accepting consistorial oversight of individual behavior. This sentiment was shared by many among the ruling authorities, who also retained a lingering attachment to the idea that the church should encompass the entire community. The States of Holland drafted instructions for William of Orange in 1574 insisting that no consistories be established without the approval of the appropriate town council or provincial assembly. The draft church ordinance adopted by the States two years later proposed that all adults be allowed to partake at the four annual communion services. But the churches' defense of their disciplinary mechanisms thwarted these proposals. Instead, the equation between the civic community and the church community gave way. Only those who made formal profession of the Reformed faith, who were deemed to be of upright character, and who subjected themselves to church discipline were allowed to become full church members and be admitted to communion. Church discipline applied only to these people. No laws, however, required attendance at communion or a role in any of the other activities of the church, nor did the secular authorities add any civil penalties to an ecclesiastical sanction of excommunication. As the state-supported church, the Reformed church was expected to permit everyone to attend its sermons and receive the sacrament of baptism. Even the children of "whoremongers, excommunicates, papists and other such" could not be known for certain to be outside the divine covenant, the 1578 synod of Dordrecht declared in justification of this latter. Those seeking to marry could choose between a church ceremony and a kind of civil marriage. It soon became clear that many inhabitants of Holland and Zeeland were content to become sympathizers (*liefhebbers*) or auditors (*toehoorders*) who attended Reformed sermons without signing up for the full-credit course and taking part in the Lord's Supper. Twenty-three of Leiden's twenty-eight magistrates fell into this category in 1579. The Reformed thus retained their prerogative to control access to communion at the expense of any pretensions to counting all of the inhabitants of the region among their members. A significant fraction of the population began to practice a brand of personal Christianity that did not include regular observance of any form of communion.[29]

The sympathizers were not the only group that came to live outside the boundaries of full membership in the Reformed church. Once the threat of Spanish reconquest receded, the regents of most towns ceased to enforce the prohibition of Catholic worship enacted in the heat of the revolt. In some cities, secret Catholic worship went on without interruption; in many others it was restarted by missionary priests dispatched by a papal vicar-general first named in 1583. Soon, Catholics would be a sizable minority in many parts of Holland and a majority in certain rural areas. A good number of Anabaptists and several groups of Lutherans also set up churches of their own.[30]

During the first years that followed the Beggar conquest of most of Holland and Zeeland, negotiating the boundary between the church and the civic community was hardly the most pressing matter facing the rebellious regions. Sheer survival against the threat of Habsburg reconquest topped all other concerns. The Beggar advance in Holland and Zeeland in 1572 was promptly followed by the seizure of Mons and Valenciennes in the south, but these were retaken by Alva's troops after an attempt to secure French intervention and spark a general rising aborted miserably amid the bloodshed of the Saint Bartholomew's Massacre. For the next four years, only the dogged resistance of Leiden, Haarlem, and Alkmaar and the desperate cutting of the dikes prevented Alva and his Spaniards from driving the prince of Orange into the watery grave he feared would be his when he fled north of the great rivers in 1572. Trade withered and water overspread as much as two-thirds of Holland's land. But Philip II was waging war against the Ottomans in the Mediterranean at the same time that he had to put down the rebellion in the Netherlands. The burden of war on two fronts forced him to suspend interest payments on his public loans, led his financiers to cease their transfers of funds to the Low Countries, and triggered a series of mutinies by troops left without pay in the Netherlands that culminated in the sacking of Antwerp in the "Spanish fury" of November 1576. The Spanish governor-general's untimely death in the midst of this crisis gave the local authorities little choice but to act on their own to restore order. The States of Brabant and Hainaut convened an assembly of the States-General that became the occasion to express the grievances against Spanish misrule that had been building up over the preceding decade. The States-General drew up the terms for a general pacification of the region, the Pacification of Ghent, and negotiated their begrudging acceptance by the new Spanish governor dispatched to the region, Don John of Austria. By the terms of this document, all edicts against heresy were suspended. It was forbidden to disturb or attack the Roman Catholic religion outside the provinces of Holland and Zeeland, while Reformed Protestantism remained the only faith allowed in those two provinces.[31]

Once again, the slackening of persecution inspired Reformed public worship and attempts to topple the Catholic stewpot. As in 1566, Flanders and Brabant were at the epicenter of militancy. Exiled ministers promptly returned to the regions of the southern Netherlands where they had been so numerous in 1566. Where churches under the cross had struggled on, they came out into the open. In July 1577, Don John of Austria grew tired of having to negotiate with the States-General and the nobility of the region, fled Brussels, and captured the citadel of Namur, openly manifesting his antagonism to William of Orange and the regime of the States. This prompted Orange to place Protestant partisans whom he believed would be loyal to him within the municipalities, while they in turn backed his efforts to gain the provincial governorship. A coup in October brought the Reformed to power in Ghent. The Gentenaars soon exported their revolution to many of the region's smaller towns, taking them by surprise, removing their Catholic magistrates, and replacing them with men inclined toward the Reformed cause. As he had in Holland, Orange tried to implement religious toleration in order to maintain as broad an anti-Spanish front as possible, but he was powerless once more to cool off an overheated atmosphere of hatred and suspicion of the Roman church. Cloisters were closed and plundered after they refused escalating demands upon them to lodge soldiers. Reports of sodomy in the religious houses touched off a wave of trials, torture, and execution of mendicants during the summer of 1578 that in turn broadened into a new surge of hedge preaching, iconoclasm, and municipal revolutions. By the end of 1578, the Reformed of Ghent had been granted four churches to hold all of the worshipers attending their now officially sanctioned services; a Protestant academy had been opened in the city; and only Orange's repeated intervention forestalled the total prohibition of Catholic worship. Across Flanders, at least fifty preachers were active, and fifteen classes had been established. The situation was comparable in Brabant. Agitation in support of the Reformed also spread to Tournai. In Amsterdam, Holland's last bastion of loyalty to Catholicism and the Habsburgs, several months of growing agitation culminated in the municipal putsch, or *Alteratie,* of May 1578 that led to the outlawing of Catholicism and a purge of the city council.[32]

Whereas the initial surge of Reformed strength in 1566 lasted less than a year, this period of the "Calvinist republics" in Flanders and Brabant endured for seven, but ultimately it too succumbed to the reassertion of Habsburg authority. Much of the Walloon nobility was more alarmed by the recrudescence of heresy than by the policies of the Habsburgs, and these men found their leader in Emmanuel de Lalaing, baron of Montigny. Alessandro Farnese, the future duke of Parma, who succeeded Don John as governor-general in 1578, recognized that he could build upon this sentiment to combat the Orangists. After negotiating an agreement with the so-called Malcontents, he made the southernmost provinces his base for a military campaign against the towns that had defied the terms of the Pacification of Ghent. Gradually increasing his military strength, he took Tournai in 1581, the chief ports of Flanders in 1583, and then, one by one, the great towns in the interior of Flanders and Brabant. When Antwerp fell in 1585, the era of the Calvinist republics was over. The Protestants of the recaptured cities were given up to four years to reconcile themselves with the Catholic church. Thousands did, while still more decamped for the rebellious provinces to the north. Little gatherings of secret Protestants continued to assemble in a few Flemish and Brabant towns, and the Antwerp assembly would even gain a measure of de facto toleration after 1652; but Parma's reconquest marked the effective end of Protestantism within this region in which it had once been so strong. In short order, Flanders and Brabant became bastions of Catholicism under the impact of one of the Continent's most successful Counter-Reformations.[33]

In the northeastern provinces, the Reformed were initially less numerous and less aggressive following the Pacification of Ghent, but here the forces of war worked in their favor. In Friesland, it took fully two years for the first organized Reformed church to resume regular worship after 1576. A middle group that approved of neither the militant defense of Catholicism nor efforts to institute Reformed domination controlled local politics. But this center could not hold in the face of the polarizing forces pressing upon the region from outside. The decisive event was the "treason" of the stadtholder of the northeastern provinces, Georges de Lalaing, count of Rennenberg. Like all of the leading noblemen of the Netherlands, Rennenberg found himself caught in these years in a fearsome struggle of conscience and calculation, as Reformed aggressiveness undermined the religious peace decreed by the Pacification of Ghent and Parma reasserted the authority of the king of Spain. In March 1580, he cast his lot with Parma, secured Groningen for a Spanish garrison, and called on Catholics throughout the region to rise and acknowledge their legitimate sovereign. But few rose. Instead, Rennenberg's betrayal of the terms by which he had been granted the stadtholderate led to the convocation of an emergency assembly of the States of Friesland restricted to "those prepared to set their lives and goods against the Spaniards, their supporters, and malcontents." After rejecting Rennenberg's authority, and with the Roman church now discredited as the ally of Spanish tyranny, this body went on to abolish the mass, close all convents, seize church property, and create Reformed churches and schools across the province. Variations upon this pattern produced the proscription of Catholicism and the establishment of Reformed worship in Utrecht, Overijssel, and Gelderland. With Parma's attention focused on the great cities of the south and then attracted elsewhere by the enterprise of the Armada and Spain's intervention in the French struggles over Henry IV's succession, the rebellious provinces of the northeast were able to complete their hold on the region by capturing Groningen in 1594. The military effort was led by two stadtholders who were perhaps the most convinced partisans of the Reformed cause within the house of Nassau, John of Nassau and his son William Louis. When William Louis oversaw the implementation of a Reformed church order in Groningen in 1594 and in Drenthe in 1598, the Reformed cause had triumphed across all of the northern provinces in which it had been relatively weak in the 1560s.[34]

Church practice in most of the northeastern provinces was modeled explicitly on that used elsewhere in the Low Countries, but the secular authorities tried to enforce greater participation in church rituals than was required in Holland. The option of civil marriage was not made available in Gelderland, Groningen, Drenthe, and Overijssel. All children in Overijssel were required to receive Reformed baptism on pain of monetary penalties. De facto toleration came later and more begrudgingly in these provinces for Catholics, Anabaptists, and Lutherans, who consequently were less numerous.[35]

In Utrecht, the aspirations for a broad church capable of encompassing the entire community that had manifested themselves across much of the north in 1566 survived with enough strength to eventuate briefly in an alternate model of a Reformed church. An alternative to Catholicism first took shape here when the eloquent, spiritualistically inclined curate of the Jacobskerk, Herbert Duifhuis, declared his intention "to preach in the manner of the reformed religion" and carried out a parish reformation in 1578 with magisterial approval. Duifhuis established no consistory, used no catechism, and admitted to communion all who cared to present themselves. His actions dismayed a second Protestant of a more orthodox Reformed stripe, the Geneva- and Heidelberg-educated Werner Helmichius, who vainly enlisted the aid of ministers from the larger region to convince Duifhuis of the error of his ways. His appeals to the politicians to remove Duifhuis went unheeded, and Utrecht became divided between the "Reformed of the Consistory" and the "Preachers of the Old and New Testament" for close to a generation. The latter defended open access to communion and carried on the traditions of the Jacobskerk after Duifhuis's death, but they found it more and more difficult to recruit new clergymen of acceptable quality once the region's universities became dominated by theologians who upheld the necessity of consistorial discipline and the authority of the church's synods. The political authorities of the republic at last forced an end to the split in 1605. Among those who grew up in Utrecht at the time and attended sermons by ministers of both orientations was the future Remonstrant Johannes Uytenbogaert. Strikingly, he sided with the Reformed of the Consistory, who would later excommunicate him, believing that "the church should not be without order and discipline."[36]

As in Scotland, it took some time for the Reformed churches in the provinces that ultimately won their freedom from Spain to begin functioning according to the regulations of the new churches. In the desolate sandy soils of the Veluwe, a few recalcitrant noblemen were said still to be thwarting the formation of consistories as late as 1685! In Utrecht, the divisions over worship prevented a provincewide synod from assembling until 1606, and classes did not come into existence until the church order was settled in 1619. Elsewhere, classes and synods began to assemble regularly within a year of the movement's triumph, but it could take some time for the network of classes to cover the entire province. The Frisian classis of Zevenwouden was not established until sixteen years after the Reformed attained dominance in 1580, soon collapsed, and did not begin to function regularly until 1601. Once classes were created, qualified ministers for every parish had to be found and consistories charged with overseeing church discipline. Three of the ten villages in the classis of Dordrecht still had no consistory when they were visited in 1589, sixteen years after the formation of the classis. Ministers appear to have been located more readily than willing elders, and far more quickly than was the case in Scotland. By 1583, fifteen of the sixteen parishes of the classis of Rotterdam had ministers.[37]

As the Reformed church settled in as the legally privileged, state-supported church of the region, the number of those who sought and gained admission to communion grew, but full members of the church remained a definite minority of the population in all regions studied to date. In Delft, the number of communicants increased from 617 in 1574 to 3,500 in 1621. In Haarlem, where just 27 people took communion in 1577, 4,000 did so in 1617. In Sneek, the number of communicants tripled over the same period.[38] Some of the growth resulted from the movement northward of perhaps as many as 100,000 refugees fleeing the fighting and eventual restoration of Catholic worship in the southern provinces. Some resulted from the desire to be associated with a church that increasingly consolidated its place as one of the pillars of respectable society. Despite such growth, full members of the Reformed church accounted for between 12 and 28 percent of the adult population in the nine regions or localities in Holland and Friesland for which we possess reliable estimates of both the number of churchgoers and the total population around 1600.[39] Much of the population remained outside the communion of any church. The pattern of religious practice in the United Provinces is perhaps best captured by an extraordinary religious census from 1640 for the Baarderadeel region of Friesland, which makes room among its categories not only for full members of the Reformed church, Reformed sympathizers (*liefhebbers*), Catholics, and Mennonites, but also for "doubters" and the "neutral."[40] The sociology of religion in the modern Netherlands long encouraged scholars to equate Calvinism with the little people, but a careful study of Delft in 1609 has shown that full members of the church represented a nearly perfect cross section of the population. The governing regents of Holland were not as uniformly hostile to the church and its pretensions as was once thought. Fully a quarter of the members of Delft's Council of Forty between 1590 and 1609 also served as church elders or deacons, while 42 percent of the new aldermen in strongly Reformed Dordrecht in these same years likewise had filled these church offices.[41] The one way in which church membership was most strikingly not a cross section of the population was that women joined in disproportionate numbers, accounting for about 60 percent of church members from the 1570s through the 1610s in all cases in which the sex breakdown of the congregation is known.[42] In the first years of an insurgent Reformed church, as we have seen in France, men may have been more likely than women to embrace the cause, but once matters settled down, the more general tendency in late medieval and early modern Europe of women to show themselves the more pious sex in the ordinary devotions of the various churches reasserted itself.

The place the Reformed church came to assume within the seven United Provinces of the Netherlands was different from that of any other established church in Europe. On the one hand, the Reformed church was the public church. Its ministers were paid from the tithe and the proceeds of seized church property. It provided the chaplains who accompanied the republic's armies and navies. In some localities, it controlled poor relief and vetted all schoolmasters. One major version of the national myth depicted the Netherlands' struggle for independence as a crusade to establish and preserve the true worship of God, likening the Dutch to the people of ancient Israel and their ministers to the Old Testament priests and prophets. The Reformed clergy also spoke out on government affairs in the manner of their colleagues in Zurich and Geneva. Successive provincial synods of Zeeland, for instance, urged rulers to stop the profanation of the Sabbath, to end dancing, *kermissen,* and prostitution, to punish those who had recourse to magic or divination, and to bar Jews from settling in the region. Where close and cooperative relations linked civil officials and the church, as in Zeeland or the city of Dordrecht, these appeals were often heeded. Following the call of the national synod of Middelburg (1581) for stronger laws against public sin and leisure activities during hours of worship, the States of Zeeland enjoined public drunkenness, adultery, fornication, and failure to observe Sunday rest. Even in less strictly Reformed regions, the authorities regularly announced days of fasting and repentance.[43]

On the other hand, across the republic as a whole the Reformed enjoyed neither the numerical preponderance nor the degree of ideological hegemony that Europe's legally dominant churches normally exercised. For every author who likened the Dutch struggle for independence to the liberation of ancient Israel from the yoke of Egypt, another depicted the long war for independence as a battle to preserve the traditional liberties of the region against tyranny, including ecclesiastical tyranny. Secular government commissions administered former church property and paid out ministerial salaries, and the civil authorities claimed the power to convene national synods and set their agenda. Many cities administered autonomous civic systems of poor relief alongside the Reformed diaconate or in place of it and allowed teachers to run schools even if they had not signed the Belgic Confession of Faith. The consistories and synods learned before long to moderate the severity of their demands for moral purity, and the measures regulating public morals generally fell far short of the strictness of those promulgated in Zurich, Geneva, and Scotland.[44] Last of all, ecclesiastical discipline was not backed up by civil sanctions as in Geneva and Scotland. The revolutionary reformation of the Low Countries was thus revolutionary for its reconfiguration of the relation between church and state and for the degree of freedom it obtained for inhabitants of this region to live their lives outside the institutions and rituals of any organized church, even while it gave birth to a Reformed church that was at once privileged and pure, an established church and a little company of the elect.

7

THE EMPIRE
Further Reformation by Princely Fiat

I n the Holy Roman Empire, where the powerful Reformed currents of the first burst of evangelical expansion had been pushed to the fringes between 1535 and 1555, churches of a distinctively Reformed cast also multiplied in the half-century after the Peace of Augsburg. A few developed in towns or regions close to the empire's Swiss, Dutch, Frisian, and Polish borders. A few were minority churches established by refugees fleeing the Low Countries. But by far the largest and most important of these emerged in already Protestant principalities whose rulers now implemented "second reformations"—transformations of their territory's liturgical practices, confessional documents, and (less often) church institutions along lines that went beyond the initial reformation settlement and brought them closer into line with the Reformed churches in western Europe.

The process by which these second reformations were implemented differed dramatically from that which led to the birth of Reformed churches in France, Scotland, and the Low Countries, where the Reformed first established themselves independently of the political authorities and then swept into power or obtained a measure of toleration as the result of their ability to mobilize a critical fraction of the territorial population. Germany's second reformations depended above all on decisions taken by territorial rulers in consultation with their leading councillors and most influential theologians. Insofar as wider political mobilization accompanied the second reformations, it most commonly took the form of resistance to them, resistance that increased as the period advanced. By the first decade of the seventeenth century it was so strong that rulers who themselves embraced Reformed ideas had to abandon the goal of transforming their entire territorial churches in accordance with their personal beliefs.

That churches with Reformed characteristics were founded in the German principalities by princely fiat rather than by aristocratic or popular mobilization means that the quest to account for the dynamism of the Reformed tradition after 1550 must take into account factors beyond those that appear so critical in the French, Scottish, and Dutch cases; that is to say, the urgency with which the Reformed called on believers to separate themselves from Rome and to form and defend churches of their own, the mass appeal and galvanizing power of the Reformed attack on idolatry and the "baked God," and the manner in which the presbyterial-synodal church structure facilitated the organization and military defense of the church. Bullinger and Calvin always hoped that Europe's crowned heads might embrace their version of the Gospel and addressed letters and treatises to them urging them to do so. That a growing number of German princes now did so, just as Jeanne d'Albret in Béarn and Edward VI and Elizabeth in England had done before them, shows that their hope of converting rulers was not misguided. Under the right circumstances, the Reformed cause could appeal to princes wanting to act as faithful protectors of true doctrine; Germany's second reformations often hung on the judgments of individual rulers that the Reformed theologians were more persuasive or less needlessly quarrelsome expositors of Scripture than were the proponents of Lutheranism's emerging orthodoxy who dominated the region's Protestant universities. These judgments were hardly made in a vacuum. They were likely to be made by the rulers of territories whose post-Reformation churches were marked by traditions of Melanchthonian or eirenic Lutheranism, whose upper administration was heavily staffed with men recruited from regions inclined toward a Reformed reformation in the first half of the century, or who were led by their own family ties or personal ambitions to fight alongside the Protestants in France or the Low Countries.

The revival of Reformed strength in Germany in this period can be understood only within the context of contemporary developments within the majority Lutheran churches, the growing political assertiveness of German Catholicism, and the continued evolution of local traditions of a Reformed character, traditions that were at times given new strength by the arrival of refugee and immigrant groups from the Low Countries. The midcentury split between the self-styled genuine Lutherans and the followers of Philip Me-

lanchthon dominated the politics of German Lutheranism for over a generation. The Philippists were numerous in Silesia, Pomerania, and at the university of Wittenberg, Germany's largest in this era. They tended toward an
antidogmatic, morally reformist style of piety strongly indebted to humanism.
Many were educated laymen. The Gnesio-Lutherans had their strongholds at
the universities of Jena and Tübingen, in the cities of north Germany, and in
Württemberg and Mecklenburg. They were characterized by a strong apocalyptic consciousness, assertiveness about the clergy's authority to determine
theological issues, and a concern to reach the populace through various sorts
of improving literature like the "devil books" that spread through Germany in
such profusion in this period, depicting Satan as the force behind some prevalent vice. Their chief spokesmen, notably Westphal and Flacius Illyricus, were
virtually all clerics.[1]

From the late 1550s onward, a group of theologians, pushed by the rulers
of Saxony, Brunswick, and Württemberg, began to work on devising a theological formula capable of ending the quarrels. Their efforts culminated in
the Formula of Concord of 1577. Circulated by the Saxons and soon adopted
in no fewer than eighty-six territories within the empire, this document was
taken by those who embraced it as the authoritative explication of the Augsburg Confession—a matter of political significance under the terms of the
Peace of Augsburg, which granted legal toleration only to churches that accepted that document. The formula used the original Invariata version of the
Augsburg Confession and taught Christ's physical presence in the communion elements. Many Philippists thus hesitated to accept it. The campaign to
promote its acceptance forced people and territories to make explicit confessional choices they often would have preferred to avoid.[2]

The Gnesio-Lutherans castigated the Philippists as crypto-Calvinists. As
we have seen, Melanchthon indeed shared certain ideas with Calvin, including a spiritual understanding of Christ's presence in the Eucharist, but he also
rejected predestination and considered external forms of worship largely as
matters indifferent. Some of his students unquestionably went beyond him
and drew closer to Calvin and other leading Reformed theologians on these
latter issues. Melanchthonian influences were very strong in the 1560s and
early 1570s at the court of the elector August of Saxony. Here, Melanchthon's
son-in-law Kaspar Peucer was court physician. The Wittenberg-educated jurist Georg Cracow occupied a critical role in council. The Wittenberg-educated
theologian Christoph Pezel was court preacher. These men corresponded with
theologians in Geneva and Heidelberg and read their works with appreciation. In 1574, a Leipzig publisher brought out under a false imprint an anonymous treatise that expressed a clearly Calvinist position on the Eucharist and
called for toleration for the Reformed. Having already forbidden sacramen-

tarian opinions and the possession of Calvin's works, the elector reacted strongly. Peucer, Cracow, and Pezel were all accused of harboring dangerous, heretical views and cast into prison, where Peucer would languish for twelve years. Other like-minded intellectuals fled the country. As part of the duke's celebration of his triumph over heresy, an effigy of Calvin was publicly hung from the gallows. The repression had unforeseen consequences. While in prison, Pezel discovered the consoling power of Calvin's doctrine of predestination and drew closer to him in his views. Philippism was not identical with Calvinism, but for at least some Philippists, the charge of Calvinism became a self-fulfilling prophecy.[3]

The harshness with which Saxony treated "Calvinism" reflected the mistrust and ill will that built up between Lutheran orthodoxy and the Reformed in Germany during the second half of the sixteenth century. The second sacramentarian controversy of 1555–62 revived the venom of Reformed–Lutheran controversy that had been forged by Luther's depiction of sacramentarians as seditious spirits and cast Calvin as the greatest sacramentarian of them all. Thereafter Lutheran polemicists mounted an ongoing campaign to demarcate the boundaries between the two currents, to defend Lutheran doctrines and practices, and to stigmatize those of the Reformed. The volume of printed polemic and the level of verbal violence only increased as more and more princes opted for Reformed second reformations. In 1613, when Elector Johann Sigismund of Brandenburg signaled his intention to alter his territory's church order by taking communion according to a Reformed rite, more than a hundred polemical works poured off Saxon, Pomeranian, and Prussian presses within just two years.[4]

In addition to the matter of the Eucharist, the polemicists on both sides battled over issues of predestination, worship, and the nature of Christ. Although Luther's *On the Bondage of the Will* (1525) expressed a vision of divine sovereignty that seems logically to imply the doctrine of double predestination, the Lutherans of this generation viewed predestination as a dangerous overinterpretation of the biblical word that bred despair among ordinary folk because they could not be sure that Christ had died for all. They claimed to find Arian and Nestorian errors in Reformed Christology. The Reformed custom of breaking the bread used for the Lord's Supper and distributing the pieces among the faithful, the fractio panis, became a flashpoint because it expressed symbolically the Reformed view that Christ was not physically hidden in the bread. The gesture shocked the sensibilities of the Lutherans, whose liturgies continued to surround the consecrated elements with strong marks of respect. One disgusted Lutheran likened a Lord's Supper with the fractio panis to throwing a dog a morsel of food, and satirical writings jeered at the Reformed as *Stutenfressers,* roll eaters. The matter of exorcism in baptism,

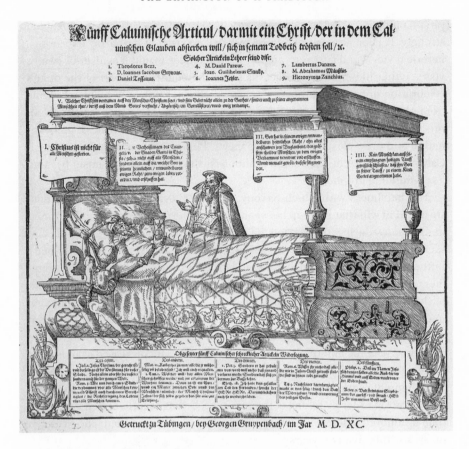

7. "The Five Calvinish Articles" This 1590 woodcut by the Tubingen artist Jacob Lederlein attacks the lack of comfort offered by Reformed teachings about predestination. Above a dying man are five "Calvinish" principles set forth in the works of a list of Reformed theologians and expounded by the minister at the bedside. Among them: Christ did not die for all men; the majority of humanity is condemned to damnation; Christian baptism offers no assurance that one is a child of God. The text beneath the bed offers biblical citations that counter these articles. (Kunstsammlungen der Veste Coburg/Germany)

which the Reformed, in their desire to remove all unscriptural ceremonial accretions, eliminated, was another flashpoint, for without it, Lutherans feared, the devil would not be driven out of a newborn's body.[5]

The interconfessional quarrel also involved disagreements about recent history and current politics. Reformed polemics asserted the continuity of their views with those of Luther's, arguing that they simply wished to complete the labor of purifying the church that the great Wittenberg Reformer had carried only halfway. The preachers of what they called the Flaccian cohort were quarrelsome dogmaticians who spurned the hand of Christian friend-ship just when unity among all Protestants both within and beyond the em-pire was most needed. The greatest threat to the restored Gospel, they were convinced, was an international conspiracy of Catholic powers led by Rome. The Gnesio-Lutherans by contrast pointed to current events in France and the Netherlands as evidence of Calvinism's seditious character. They depicted those German theologians who proclaimed their loyalty to the Augsburg Con-fession while rejecting the tenets of the Formula of Concord as hypocrites de-ceptively trying to gain access to the sheltering mantle of the Peace of Augs-burg. The best defense of evangelical truth, they argued, lay in scrupulously upholding the terms of that peace. When Christopher of Württemberg asked his leading theologian, Johannes Brenz, if it was proper to make an alliance with Zwinglians, Brenz told him absolutely not because "the spirit of their dogma is a blasphemy in Christ," and they are inclined to "iconoclastic ram-pages, the alteration of ordinary and useful ceremonies, and the deposition of ordained magistrates."[6]

German historians have typically attributed the resistance that sprang up in so many areas to the liturgical changes introduced by the second reforma-tions to long-standing and deep-rooted popular attachment to the rituals that the changes swept away. Because elsewhere in Europe a similarly intense de-fense of these rituals cannot be observed when Reformed reformations were implemented, it seems more convincing to attribute this to the success of the Lutheran propaganda campaign. Resistance to the changes was consistently strongest among the better-educated and higher-status elements within the lay population, just those whom one would expect to be most conversant with the controversial literature.[7]

If the bitter ongoing polemics built up a powerful current of suspicion of the Reformed among much of Germany's Protestant population, native Re-formed theological traditions were not thoroughly extinguished. Where these were strong, they could rally broad support of their own, especially because they were reinvigorated in this period by the arrival of publications and refu-gees from neighboring Reformed strongholds. Bucer's old home of Strasbourg, once so hospitable to Calvin, was one place where Reformed sentiments lived on. Although Lutheran orthodoxy increasingly dominated its church, the rec-tor of the city's prestigious Latin School, Jean Sturm, continued to defend the principles of the Tetrapolitan confession, championed close ties with the Huguenot cause in France, and made the school a center for ideas that ortho-dox Lutherans regarded as beyond the pale. Their opposition to him finally forced him out in 1581. Farther south in Alsace, Colmar carried through a late civic reformation in 1575 that was shaped by the city's close contacts with Basel. While its leaders initially sought to avoid any sharp confessional defi-

Caluinisch Deckmantel.
Daß ist:

Warhaftig Abbildnus des iez einreissenden Caluini/wie sich derselbig

vnder dem schein Augspurgischer Confession in die Kirch des Herrn eindringt:

Allen betrübten Christen/welche mit triffenten Augen solchen gantz schädlichen Inbruch sehen müssen zu einem richtigen beispiel abgerissen / vnd in einer kurzen Summa warhafftig für Augen gestelt.

8. "The Calvinish Cloak." This single-sheet print and accompanying text from ca. 1610 warn against the false claims of Reformed theologians to profess the pure Gospel and to benefit from the provisions of the Peace of Augsburg. The light of Christ shines down from above a church building on the left and illuminates the Bible, which is held by Luther, Melanchthon, and Brenz. While Lutheran theologians kneel before it, those associated with the Reformed camp (identified by the key) variously cover their eyes and ears, flee from it, pretend to honor it but carry a mask, or dispute needlessly at a nearby table. The extensive text highlights the differences of opinion between the Lutherans and the Reformed over the eucharist, cites instances or passages where the latter rejected or dismissed the Augsburg Confession, and echoes the Formula of Concord's warning that those who do not accept its principles cannot be considered brothers. (Herzog August Bibliothek Wolfenbüttel: Cod. Guelf. 31.8 Aug. 2o, Blatt 648)

nition for their church, the debates around the Formula of Concord led them
to reject that document and to incorporate certain features more typical of
the Reformed into their church order. In a similar fashion, Albert Hardenberg,
John a Lasco's old companion from Louvain days, enduringly molded theological opinion in Bremen along Reformed lines when he served as that city's
cathedral preacher from 1547 through 1561. He finally lost his post when the
city council bowed to complaints from the city's Lutheran ministers and pressure from nearby rulers about his sacramentarian errors; but his supporters in
the city soon mobilized against the Lutheran hard-liners within the council,
drove them from office, and brought in as church superintendent a student
of Melanchthon's who sought to find a middle way between Hardenberg's disciples and the orthodox Lutherans. After 1577 Bremen rejected the Formula
of Concord, undertook closer ties with the Reformed in the Low Countries,
and modified its ceremonies in a Reformed direction under the supervision of
the man formerly imprisoned for crypto-Calvinism in Saxony, Pezel. A similar
sequence of events occurred in East Friesland, where a Lasco's superintendency had already given the local church an even stronger Reformed imprint.
Two brothers of differing religious opinions jointly ruled the territory from
1558 to 1591: Edzard II, a champion of Lutheran orthodoxy, and John, who
protected the Reformed ministers and *coetus* in the administrative districts
he oversaw. Following John's death in 1591, Edzard attempted to impose a Lutheran church order throughout the land. In response, the burghers of Emden
banded together to defend their long-standing control of local church appointments "against the princely servitude." In 1595 a civic revolution swept new
burghermasters into power and outlawed Lutheran worship in the city. Military assistance from the neighboring Dutch republic allowed the town to defend itself until Edzard II died in 1599 and his successor, Enno III, ratified a
compromise church order permitting both Reformed and Lutheran *coetuses*
to function. East Friesland would henceforward be divided between Lutheran
and Reformed parishes, with the roughly forty Reformed parishes clustered
primarily in the region around the mouth of the Ems near the Dutch border.[8]

Churches of a distinctly Reformed character also sprung up along the lower
Rhine, close to the Netherlands. Prior to 1555, the rulers of Jülich, Cleves,
Berg, and the Mark searched for a middle way of moderate reform within the
confines of loyalty to Rome, while allowing their subjects leeway in matters
of conscience and giving shelter to Wesel's refugee church. The number of
refugee churches multiplied with the persecutions of the 1560s in the Low
Countries, and Reformed ideas spread beyond their confines. In Duisberg, the
adopted home of the great Flemish geographer Gerard Mercator, Reformed
exiles dominated the Latin School faculty from 1559 onward and shaped the
outlook of successive generations of students. Certain already established

evangelical civic churches, such as that at Wesel, became unmistakably Reformed in character. In other towns, such as Aachen, separate Reformed congregations were founded, and these attracted a fraction of the German-speaking population. From the 1570s onward, the scattered congregations of this region became linked in a synodal church order that emerged out of the same process that led to the triumph of the presbyterial-synodal system in the Low Countries, with the Emden synod of 1571, at which Aachen, Wesel, and Cologne were all represented, being a landmark in this process. Synods first met regularly in Jülich and Cleves. They were extended into Berg in 1589 and the Mark in 1611 as the dispersed churches of these areas struggled to protect themselves against the increasingly vigorous Counter-Reformation in the region. These regional synods agglomerated in 1610–11 into a single system bringing together delegates from all four territories for regular general synods, a system that endured into the nineteenth century. Early in the seventeenth century, roughly eighty congregations were attached to this system.[9] Trade links through the Baltic also led to the formation of immigrant English, Dutch, and Walloon Reformed communities in Hamburg, Stade, and Altona.[10]

The revival of Reformed strength in the empire thus did not depend entirely on princely fiat. Still, the greater part of this revival did stem from decisions made by territorial rulers. As I have suggested, patterns of education and alliance left their imprint on these choices. Second reformations were most often decreed by rulers educated by Philippist tutors and hailing from areas that had promoted conciliation between Lutheran and Reformed currents in the first half of the century, or whose experience fighting alongside the Huguenots in France and the Beggars in the Low Countries had led them to see the Reformed in a positive light. Once personally convinced of the truth of Reformed doctrines, they commonly waited for some time before trying to implement changes in church life they knew would spark opposition. When they finally decided to go ahead, the impetus to do so time and again resulted from the arrival of Melanchthonian or Reformed theologians fleeing persecution in another territory, who provided not only persuasive exhortations to grasp the nettle, but also the expertise and authority needed to implement the changes. Princely decision making in favor of or against a second reformation also involved a calculation of where the greatest risk to the order and security of the empire and its Protestant churches lay—in the threat of international Catholicism, as the Reformed argued, or in sacramentarian subversion of the Peace of Augsburg, as the Lutherans claimed. As militant Catholicism gathered force within the empire, the Reformed argument acquired increasing conviction. At the same time, the polarizing consequences of the endeavor to promote the Formula of Concord pushed some princes to feel greater kinship with the Reformed than with the Flaccian cohort. Yet if a variety of factors could affect the likelihood that a given ruler might embrace Reformed ideas and seek to alter the religious footing in his territory, there is ultimately no escaping the fundamental import of individual decisions of princely conscience in the story of Reformed advance in later sixteenth-century Germany. Many of the region's rulers were deeply conscientious about exercising their *cura religionis*. They studied the issues with care, and their decisions were as unpredictable as the human mind. It was not uncommon for brothers to come down on opposite sides of the confessional divide.

The unpredictability and importance of princely decisions of conscience are nowhere more evident than in the events that made the Palatinate the first major German territory to witness a second reformation and the greatest bastion of the Reformed cause within the empire for most of the next six decades. The first state-mandated elements of a reformation here had come late, between 1546 and 1556, and had eventuated in a fairly undogmatic, Melanchthonian territorial church noteworthy for its strict legislation against the use of images. The preoccupation with purifying the churches of their images was telling: the Palatinate was located astride the trade routes of the Rhine, and many of its chief administrators came from the patrician families of the free imperial cities of the German southwest, where Reformed ideas had been so strong.[11] In 1559, the succession to the territory passed to a member of a collateral branch of the ruling family, Frederick III. Raised a Catholic, Frederick had been drawn to Lutheranism through his first wife, Maria of Brandenburg-Ansbach. During the First Schmalkaldic War, he fought with the emperor, which estranged him from most of the Protestant princes. His accession to the Palatine electorship brought him face to face with the escalating theological divisions within Germany that particularly shook the territorial university of Heidelberg because of the Palatinate's openness to influences from so many directions. A devout man who in future years regularly rose at night to consult his Bible when mulling over a matter of state, Frederick felt that the position to which God had called him obliged him to resolve the disputes for himself. He first undertook systematic personal study of the Bible, then arranged for a disputation at court between several orthodox Lutherans dispatched from Saxony and Pierre Boquin, a French-born, Wittenberg-educated minister with Reformed inclinations. Finally, he read some of Luther's later writings, notably his *Brief Confession of the Holy Sacrament* (1541) written against Zwingli and Schwenkfeld. This course of study led him to conclude that the Reformed position on the Eucharist was truer to the Bible and that the Lutherans were prone to unfounded invective.[12]

Boquin was one of a number of theologians of a Reformed inclination who had arrived in Heidelberg before Frederick's new theological orientation was clear. Once it became evident that he was willing to shelter Reformed theologians, others followed. The roll call of distinguished new Heidelberg faculty members is also a record of the many areas in which Reformed ideas had won followers who could not worship safely there. Zacharius Ursinus, a disciple of Melanchthon and Vermigli, was driven from his native Breslau as Lutheran orthodoxy strengthened its hold in Silesia. Kaspar Olevianus hailed from Trier and followed Calvin's path through the law faculties of Orléans and Bourges before going to study theology in Geneva. Petrus Dathenus had galvanized crowds in Ypres during the Wonderyear before having to flee his native Flanders; after a decade in Heidelberg, he would return to head Ghent's church during the period of Reformed domination from 1577 to 1584. Zanchi, the former Bergamo Augustinian who had followed Vermigli to Strasbourg, came to Heidelberg after crossing swords with Marbach over predestination. These were only the most illustrious of the new faculty members who would enable Heidelberg's venerable university to eclipse Geneva as the most important center of Reformed theological instruction between Calvin's death and the flowering of the new university of Leiden in the last decades of the century.

In 1562, Frederick III implemented his first major piece of reforming legislation, a *Polizeiordnung* that required attendance at church services and called for unsparing punishment for blasphemy, drunkenness, excessive banqueting, and magic. A year later a new church order instituted simple baptismal and eucharistic services including the fractio panis, cut the number of church holidays to five, and contained a confessional document destined for a great future: the Heidelberg Catechism. Drafted by Ursinus and Olevianus— experts dispute each one's respective role—and approved by a larger committee of leading ministers and theologians in whose activities Frederick himself may have played a role, the Heidelberg Catechism expounded the basics of the faith, the Credo, the Lord's Prayer, and the Ten Commandments in 129 succinct questions and answers. The work was unequivocally Reformed in its assertion of a strictly spiritual divine presence in the Eucharist and its exegesis of the Second Commandment as prohibiting all images in churches. It was carefully silent on the matter of predestination. Not only did this pithy summary come to be used as a basic catechism and a confession of faith in most German territories that implemented second reformations. It was translated almost immediately into Dutch and, as we have seen, adopted as the catechism of the Dutch-speaking congregations within the Low Countries at the Emden synod of 1571. The Polish and Hungarian Reformed, too, would embrace it.[13]

Bullinger hailed the Heidelberg Catechism as "the best catechism ever published," but the same features that inspired his enthusiasm provoked the denunciation of Lutheran ubiquitarians and initiated a process of debate and appeal that culminated with Frederick being summoned before the imperial diet of 1566 to defend his church order against the charge that it fell outside the protection of the Peace of Augsburg. The rulers of several nearby Lutheran territories, closely advised by their court preachers and university professors, asserted that Frederick had embraced the false teachings of the "damnable sect" of Zwinglianism and Calvinism and should be excluded from the peace of the empire. In a dramatic speech before the emperor, Frederick swore that he had never read Calvin's writings and hardly knew what it might mean to be a Calvinist. He had simply aspired to follow the word, on the basis of which he would gladly revise any opinions of his that might be proven to him to be in error. Furthermore, he stressed, he had signed the Augsburg Confession and the conclusions of divers theological gatherings held since its drafting to explicate its meaning. This reply proved satisfactory to the elector of Saxony and to several other leading evangelical rulers, who feared that a condemnation of Frederick would precipitate a grave political crisis within the empire that could only profit the Catholics. The shelving of the question at the Augsburg diet thus opened the way for the legal establishment of Reformed doctrines within the empire, although the status of such doctrines would remain contested under the law until the Peace of Westphalia explicitly granted legal recognition to Reformed worship in 1648.[14]

Although Frederick may never have read Calvin's writings, the leading Swiss theologians in Geneva rallied to his side during the crisis occasioned by his summons to Augsburg. The diplomatic preludes to the Diet included vigorous Palatine essays to demonstrate that the doctrines for which Frederick was being threatened with punishment enjoyed wide backing beyond the empire. These efforts were a major step in creating among Europe's various embryonic Reformed churches a sense of belonging to common cause. The receipt of Palatine letters urging the Swiss Protestants, the English, and the young churches in France and the Low Countries to draft a common confession of faith was what prompted Bullinger to take out the document he had written for himself a few years previously and to seek endorsement of it from the other Swiss cities as the Second Helvetic Confession. With the assistance of Beza in Geneva, it was sent on to the churches of France, Scotland, the Low Countries, Poland, and Hungary, from whom it received approval. The support Frederick received from so many churches outside the empire in this crisis was one reason he henceforward became a resolute ally of Protestant movements across the continent and one of the most ardent promoters of diplomatic efforts to forge pan-Protestant alliances. Although he had rejected appeals for help from the French Huguenots in 1562, he now came to believe they were truly evangelical Protestants threatened by the same papal and Habsburg diplomats who had united to bring him down at Augsburg. During France's Second Civil War of 1567, his son John Casimir led an army of intervention to aid the Huguenots. Another son, Christopher, was sent to Geneva to study late in 1566 and would die in 1575 in an ill-fated relief expedition to aid the Dutch rebels.[15]

The Palatinate became more than a center of Protestant diplomatic initiative in the heart of Europe. As a home to refugees whose outlook was shaped by all of the various currents within the Reformed tradition, it also became in the late 1560s the scene of the greatest debate between partisans of the Zurich and the Genevan patterns of ecclesiastical discipline and church-state relations. On arriving in Heidelberg in 1560, Olevianus began to militate for an independent consistorial system of church discipline such as he had known as a student in Geneva. The church ordinance of 1564 instituted a system of church discipline closer to that of Zurich or Basel than Geneva. It empowered a board of government officials and ministers to exercise discipline through admonition and exhortation, but it did not create a separate body of elders for each church, and it granted a governmental council, the elector's *Kirchenrat,* the power to pronounce sentences of excommunication.[16]

Public controversy broke out over the question of church discipline in 1568 when an English student at Heidelberg, George Withers, proposed for debate the thesis that a consistory with full powers of discipline was a necessary component of a true church. (Ironically, Withers had initially sought to defend a set of theses against the use of clerical vestments, the issue just then agitating the English church, but he was urged by his professors to select another, less controversial topic.) Opposition to the theses that Withers defended was led by the man whose name would become associated with the doctrine justifying state control over the church: Thomas Erastus, a professor of medicine whose extensive theological knowledge had gained him a position within the Palatine Kirchenrat. Erastus had corresponded with the great Bernese champion of magisterial authority over the church, Wolfgang Musculus, prior to Musculus's death in 1563. Musculus had also dedicated his *Common Places* to the elector palatine. In a series of theses and in the *Explanation of the Weighty Questions Concerning Excommunication* (1569) that circulated widely in manuscript, Erastus argued that it was inappropriate to have two heads to one body and warned of the danger that the church might oppose the state and exercise a tyranny of its own. He also argued—in a highly revealing observation about the extent of support for the new church order—that the unity of the church might be ruptured by the *Disziplinisten's* eagerness to control access to communion in a situation in which scarcely 30 per cent of the population knew and confessed the essentials of the faith.[17]

Erastus's writings were hardly the sole, or even the most important, contributions to the Palatine debate. Bullinger wrote privately to Dathenus to warn him against taking Geneva as a model in all things and entered the discussion publicly with his *Treatise on Excommunication,* which he couched as an argument with the Anabaptists so as not to disrupt good relations with Geneva. The work's denial of any biblical sanction for the exclusion of believers from the Lord's Supper so embittered the Heidelberg Disziplinisten that they spurred a movement to ban the sale of Bullinger's writings, including his popular *Decades.* Also from Zurich, Gwalther defended magisterial responsibility for moral discipline in no fewer than three biblical commentaries. From Geneva, Beza weighed in with a manuscript refutation of Erastus's theses, the *Pious and Mild Treatise on True Excommunication and a Christian Presbytery.* It asserted the independence of the church and its discipline with unprecedented strength, claiming that the internal life of the church is subject only to Christ and his word, not to the oversight of a Christian magistrate. Even while forthrightly stating their divergent conceptions of the proper form of church discipline, Bullinger, Beza, and Gwalther redoubled, in their correspondence, their assertions of mutual respect and eagerness to cooperate with one another. Neither Erastus's nor Beza's treatise was published at the time; both found their way into print in 1589–90 when disputes within the English church once again made the question of discipline topical. One reason the doctrine of state control of ecclesiastical affairs came to be associated with Erastus rather than with its true initial champions, Zwingli, Bullinger, Gwalther, and Musculus, probably was the concern of the Genevans not to identify Zurich as the source of the rival tradition.[18]

Perhaps half of the most prominent Palatine clergymen were Disziplinisten. Their opponents made up a clear majority of the elector's leading lay councillors and included almost as many ministers, among them the court preacher Johann Willing. The final resolution of the dispute decreed by Frederick went a long way toward meeting the desires of the Disziplinisten, for Frederick thought the arguments of this party compelling. The church order of 1570 established a body of elders within each church charged with overseeing all of its operations and exercising ecclesiastical discipline. The body could admonish sinners privately and, after 1571, suspend them from the sacraments. If these actions did not produce the expected signs of repentance and reconciliation, the matter was turned over to the secular authorities, to whom the final sentence of excommunication was reserved. Also founded were regular gatherings of all ministers within a circle of eight to ten parishes for the discussion of Scripture, mutual criticism of one another's preaching, and collective *censura morum.* Crucial components of consistorial discipline and a measure of clerical self-policing thus came to be inserted within what otherwise stayed a classic German territorial church under princely supervision, with a central Kirchenrat and regional superintendents.[19]

Although Frederick succeeded in transforming the core of his possessions along the Rhine into a Reformed stronghold of continentwide significance, he never converted all of his own family to his views. His eldest son, Ludwig, was already fully grown when his father chose the Reformed path and never abandoned the Lutheranism in which he had been raised. As *statthalter* of the outlying Upper Palatinate, near Bavaria, he delayed the implantation of the new church order in that territory. When Ludwig succeeded to the electoral title on his father's death in 1576, he restored Lutheranism throughout the electorate and required that all university professors sign the Formula of Concord after its appearance in the following year. But Frederick knew his son's convictions. By his will, he carved out a separate inheritance for his younger son, John Casimir, the adventurous champion of the Huguenot cause in France and a committed Reformed partisan. John Casimir's cluster of territories around Kaiserslautern, especially the academy that he started at Neustadt, soon sheltered many of the leading Reformed councillors and theologians forced out of Heidelberg, including Ursinus, Zanchi, and Dathenus. Ludwig's restoration of Lutheranism also proved short-lived, for he died after just seven years on the throne. Under the provisions of imperial law, John Casimir became the regent for Ludwig's young son, Frederick IV. He surrounded the boy with Reformed tutors, reconstituted Frederick III's church order, and made Heidelberg once again a bastion of Reformed higher education and a center for pan-Protestant diplomatic initiatives. Each of these changes in the confessional orientation of the Palatine church was accompanied by the resignation or removal of the majority of the clergy in place at the time.[20]

Although the Palatinate was the only German principality of any size to establish a territorial church of a patently Reformed cast for two decades after the Augsburg Diet of 1566, a couple of tiny territories lying between Heidelberg and the Dutch border rapidly followed suit. Resonances from the Palatinate and the Netherlands gave the Protestant movement in Wied a Reformed cast by the mid-1560s. The territory accepted the Heidelberg Catechism in 1564 and formed a presbyterian-synodal church order in 1575. Count Ludwig of the adjacent Sayn-Wittgenstein was a keen student of theology, capable of reading the Old Testament in Hebrew. After meeting Beza and Bullinger on a voyage through Switzerland, he corresponded regularly with Reformed theologians and gave his territory's church order a Reformed tint as early as 1563. He entered Frederick III's service, then introduced the full set of Palatine church ordinances and ceremonies in 1577, when the Lutheran restoration in Heidelberg impelled him to return to his residence at Berleburg and enabled him to bring along Olevianus, who oversaw the restructuring of the church. Family connections helped introduce the cause in Moers: the ruler was married to a sister of William of Orange.[21]

The most consequential of the petty princelings of the lower Rhine who were led by their contacts with Switzerland, the Palatinate, and the Netherlands to champion the Reformed cause during these years was John VI, count of Nassau-Dillenburg from 1559 to 1584 and leader of the Wetterau *Grafverein,* an association of rulers of neighboring territories to which Wied and Sayn-Wittgenstein also belonged. John was the younger brother of William of Orange and Louis of Nassau. His debt-ridden territory of about fifty thousand souls located midway between Frankfurt and Cologne was a meager inheritance, but he played a central role in promoting the Reformed cause in both the Rhineland and the Netherlands. The principal event shaping his destiny came when he committed himself to aiding his brothers in the developing protest against Philip II in the Low Countries. He took charge of raising and commanding one of the military units that William sought to place in the field against Margaret of Parma in 1566. Prior to this expedition he had expressed dislike of "Calvinismo and other erroneous opinions," but his experience in the Low Countries led him to see the insurgents for religious change there as "poor Christians." Dillenburg became a place of refuge and a point of muster for his brothers, and John was gradually led toward the Reformed church, whose doctrines he embraced at some point between 1572 and 1574.[22]

Like the count of Sayn-Wittgenstein, John proceeded cautiously in introducing changes into his territorial church and needed the assistance of outside theologians forced into exile by events elsewhere in the empire. Pezel, who arrived in Dillenburg in 1577 shortly after being released from prison in Saxony, played the main role in encouraging John to act. Only in that same year did John have the Eucharist celebrated with the fractio panis in his chapel. The next year a general synod for the county accepted a new, manifestly predestinarian confession of faith written by Pezel, specifying that it recognized the Augsburg Confession "inasmuch as it agrees with the confessions of the other evangelical reformed churches outside Germany." Three years later, the order of services implemented in the Palatinate in 1563 was taken over, and after the Dutch national synod of Middelburg drafted a plan for a fully autonomous presbyterial-synodal church order for the Low Countries in 1581, this was adopted for use in Nassau-Dillenburg in 1582 with modest refinements. John spearheaded its extension throughout the Wetterau counties four years later at the general synod of Herborn, creating a common church system for Nassau-Dillenburg, Wittgenstein, Solms-Braunfels, and Wied. These little principalities thus all came to adopt a presbyterial-synodal system of church organization very close to the French and Dutch model, with independent consistorial discipline and the selection of ministers by the local classis or presbytery, although the territorial rulers retained the right to approve all clerical nominations and to name inspectors who oversaw church visitations and ministerial synods. The changes did not sit well with the local population, which had grown deeply attached to Lutheran rituals. When the new service for the Lord's Supper was introduced in Herborn, the parishioners stampeded from the church rather than take part. A year later, in October 1578, only 17 people joined in the ceremony. The recalcitrant were gradually won back, and by 1583 the number of communicants had climbed to 545, but reconciliation took longer in the town of Siegen and in some rural parishes, where as late as the 1590s village schoolmasters and even church elders occasionally boycotted communion. Town council members and other educated members of the local elites were the most stubborn resisters.[23]

John required perseverance to induce his subjects to reconcile themselves with the new church order, but he possessed that quality in abundance. He continued throughout his life to offer as much military aid to his older brothers in the Low Countries as his precarious finances allowed, and from 1578 to 1580 served as stadtholder in Gelderland, where he advanced the interests of the Reformed church in the wake of Rennenberg's reconciliation with Philip II. During the Lutheran interlude in the Palatinate, he stepped forward as the leading princely champion of the Reformed cause in the empire. When Bremen found itself under pressure to accept the Formula of Concord, he offered diplomatic reinforcement and dispatched Pezel to the city to stiffen its theological resistance. Together with the Lutheran counts of Mansfeld, he and his fellow Wetterau counts were the chief backers of Gebhard Truchsess von Waldburg in the war he waged between 1583 and 1587 to defend his right to the prince-bishopric of Cologne—a war that would have resulted in the Protestantization of that politically pivotal territory had Truchsess von Waldburg won. As one of three regents for the young count Philip Ludwig of Hanau-Munzenberg, he joined with Ludwig of Sayn-Wittgenstein to ensure that the count received a Reformed education that in turn inspired him to carry through a second reformation after he came of age in 1591.[24] John was also an important patron of higher education. The academy he founded at Herborn in 1586 soon boasted of one of the empire's most distinguished faculties. Among its early luminaries were Pezel, Olevianus, the legal and political theorist Johannes Althusius, and the theologian Johann Piscator, whose translation of the Bible (1602) competed with Luther's in Germany's Reformed territories—with only partial success because of its relative lack of literary grace.[25]

The pace of second reformations picked up in the 1580s for two reasons: 1) the drafting and promotion of the Formula of Concord propelled those who could not recognize their understanding of the Gospel in that document toward the Reformed camp; and (2) political and military developments both inside and outside Germany made Catholicism appear increasingly threatening. Inside the empire, Catholic military action with assistance from Spain secured not only the prince-bishopric of Cologne, but also that of Münster, in the mid-1580s. Other prince-bishoprics like those of Würzburg and Paderborn witnessed the introduction of the Jesuits and intensified efforts to force the territories' inhabitants back into the Roman church. Abroad, the cities of Flanders and Brabant fell one by one to Parma's troops in the first half of the decade, and pressure from the Catholic League forced Henry III to revoke Protestant rights of worship in France. These episodes prompted rulers in eastern as well as western Germany both to ally against the Catholic threat and to implement changes in their church orders. Most of these second reformations revolved around matters of liturgy and doctrine, but not around the reorganization of church institutions, as had occurred in the Palatinate and the Wetterau counties.

For a brief while, it appeared that electoral Saxony, the cradle of the Reformation and Germany's most powerful territorial state, would lead the way. In 1586, a young ruler shaped by the crypto-Calvinism of the 1570s, Christian I, acceded to the Saxon throne. He had been tutored until the age of fourteen by a preceptor who lost his post in the crackdown of 1574, and in time he grew close to Nicolas Crell, a Wittenberg-educated jurist secretly inclined to Reformed ideas. His own tendencies in this direction were confirmed by his reading of the controversial literature of the time, so that upon his accession he was already identified by foreign diplomats as a Calvinist even though he himself always rejected party labels. On taking the throne, he released his former tutor from house arrest, elevated Crell to the chancellorship, and began to modify the ecclesiastical status quo within his territory in gentle steps. The requirement that clerics sign the Formula of Concord was removed. Orthodox Lutherans were gradually replaced within the universities, and the leading administrative posts of church and state were assigned to partisans of Philippist or Reformed ideas. Theological polemic was outlawed. A new prayer book, catechism, and edition of the Bible with marginal commentary of a decidedly Reformed theological cast (the Crell Bible) were introduced. Finally, in 1591, the formula of exorcism was removed from baptism. After long resisting the entreaties of Palatine and French diplomats that he join an evangelical alliance to side with Henry of Navarre, Christian also swung around and embraced this project once the death of Henry III made Navarre the legitimate king of France in his eyes. In 1591, electoral Saxony, the Palatinate, Brandenburg, Hesse, and Anhalt entered an alliance to aid Navarre. The excitement the alliance ignited among Germany's Reformed was vividly recalled thirty years later by the Heidelberg court preacher Abraham Scultetus:

> I cannot fail to recall the optimistic mood which I and many others felt when we considered the condition of the Reformed churches in 1591. In

France there ruled the valiant King Henri IV, in England the mighty Queen Elizabeth, in Scotland the learned King James, in the Palatinate the bold hero John Casimir, in Saxony the courageous and powerful Elector Christian I, in Hesse the clever and prudent Landgrave William, who were all inclined to the Reformed religion. In the Netherlands everything went as Prince Maurice of Orange wished, when he took Breda, Zutphen, Hulst, and Nijmegen. . . . We imagined that *aureum seculum,* a golden age, had dawned.[26]

Fate dashed the great hopes that Scultetus and the Reformed placed in Christian I. An avid hunter, he insisted on saddling up despite feeling poorly in September 1591 and caught a fatal illness. The events of the Palatinate in 1584 were quickly replayed in the opposite direction. Christian's brother stepped in as regent for a young heir, reversed the territory's religious course, and reimposed the Formula of Concord. As in 1574, the crackdown on the "Calvinists" was harsh. Twenty leading clerics and advisors were jailed. After ten years in prison, Crell was tried and executed for the crimes of stirring up misunderstandings with the emperor, threatening the public peace with pernicious schemes of alliance with France, propagating Calvinist errors, and falsifying the meaning of Luther's Bible.[27]

Although Saxony's second reformation died in its infancy, two other territories that signed the pact of 1591, Anhalt and Hesse, enacted ecclesiastical changes. Anhalt was a long-standing Philippist stronghold whose location on the Saxon border made it a refuge for those fleeing the crackdowns of 1574 and 1591 in the electorate. From 1586 through 1603 it was ruled by John George I in consultation with his younger brothers, before being divided among the five brothers in 1603. Its second reformation began in 1590 when John George decided to eliminate the ceremony of exorcism from baptism. In doing so, he appears to have been doing little more than following the trajectory that had led so many Saxons from Philippism to a Reformed belief in the positive danger of certain of the ritual remains of popery. The change, he stressed, was one that Luther would have approved had he been alive. But the measure brought clerical protests that in time pushed him deeper into the camp of change. He was encouraged in this by his accomplished and energetic younger brother, Christian of Anhalt, who was the greatest champion during this and the subsequent decades of the apocalyptically tinged version of militant Protestantism that German historians term "political Calvinism." Christian had served at the Saxon court during his namesake's five-year reign and had come strongly under Crell's sway. He led the expeditionary force of 1591 sent to aid Navarre and openly embraced the Reformed religion while in France. He would afterward enter the service of the Palatine electors, who made him *statthalter* of the Upper Palatinate, where he battled to implement the changes in worship that the inhabitants of that region had so intransigently resisted under Frederick III, and in whose service he became the leading architect of the Protestant Union and the ill-fated Palatine intervention in Bohemia that unleashed the Thirty Years' War. He brought the same ardent spirit to advising his brother to enact more changes in Anhalt's church order, as John George did shortly after marrying the daughter of the equally ardent John Casimir of the Palatinate. The *Reformationwerk* (1596) stripped Anhalt's churches of images, crucifixes, and altars and instituted a eucharistic service with the fractio panis. The Heidelberg Catechism and Palatine liturgy were adopted in parts of Anhalt over the next decade.[28]

Hesse, divided among four heirs on the death of Philip in 1567, experienced the polarizing effects of doctrinal disputes with disproportionate force. Philip, the sponsor of the Marburg colloquy of 1529 and the greatest early champion of reconciliation among evangelicals in order to promote a powerful Protestant coalition, had given his territory a church order with both synods and elders to assist with ecclesiastical discipline that was quite unusual among Lutherans. Several of his sons, especially Ludwig of Hesse-Marburg, came of age at courts that promoted a narrower, ubiquitarian understanding of Lutheranism. Their efforts to impose this doctrine throughout the Hessian church via its synods pushed their more moderate brother Wilhelm of Hesse-Cassel into opening his territories to anti-ubiquitarians of all stripes. His son Maurice (r. 1592–1627), a humanist and Maecenas of exceptional gifts, was drawn into conflict with Spain during the protracted maneuvering over the Jülich-Cleves succession that began when the last member of the ruling dynasty went mad in 1590. In 1603 he married Juliana of Nassau and accepted her Reformed faith. Once he had secured his share of his contested inheritance following the death of his childless uncle Ludwig in 1604, he introduced a limited second reformation structured around five "points of improvement," most notably the introduction of the fractio panis, the elimination of images from the churches, and the use of the Heidelberg Catechism. Five years later, to improve his oversight of church affairs, he introduced a governing *Konsistorium* on the model of those found in most Lutheran state churches.[29]

Fear of an increasingly aggressive Catholicism, close ties to other Reformed princes, and resentment at efforts to impose a narrow version of Lutheran orthodoxy also combined to produce second reformations between 1587 and 1605 in three smaller territories: Bentheim-Steinfurt-Tecklenburg, Zweibrücken, and Lippe. The first was a small constellation of territories near the Dutch border whose count, Arnold II (r. 1573–1606), had been personally drawn to Reformed ideas ever since he had studied at Strasbourg and visited some French Reformed assemblies in the early 1570s. After refraining for over a decade from altering more than the form of worship services in his castle chapel, he was spurred to align his church policy with that of the United Provinces by the installation of a counterreforming bishop in neighboring Münster and the return of sundry other nearby counts to the Roman church. In 1587 he introduced a radically simplified liturgy along Reformed lines, consistorial discipline, and the Heidelberg Catechism.[30] Zweibrücken's transformation followed the conversion of a pious ruler, John I (r. 1569–1604), who had initially favored the Formula of Concord but swung over to Reformed ideas during a period of intensive theological study and consultation between 1577 and 1580; apparently he was put off by what he perceived as the arrogance of the Lutheran theologians and their unwillingness to contemplate a general synod of all German evangelicals, which a number of rulers proposed at the time as the best means of clarifying the theological puzzles that continued to stir so much debate. He oversaw catechism revisions that ended with the adoption of the Heidelberg Catechism and the introduction of some synodal elements into the government of the church. The territory already had a system of lay censors who assisted the authorities in exercising moral discipline; this was not changed.[31] Simon VI of Lippe (r. 1563–1613) was educated by a Melanchthonian tutor, fashioned close ties with a number of the Reformed-oriented lesser counts of the northwest, and corresponded with such Reformed theologians of the region as Pezel and Alting. After Maurice of Hesse-Cassel introduced his points of improvement, Simon did the same, introducing the fractio panis, eliminating exorcism in baptism, and purifying the churches of their altars and statues. Like Maurice, he took care to fortify central control over the church by establishing a Konsistorium and superintendents.[32]

The changes involved in most of these later second reformations were less dramatic than those implemented earlier in the Palatinate and the Wetterau counties, and they were generally accepted by the great majority of the parish clergy, but they nonetheless encountered intense lay resistance. When Christian I of Saxony eliminated the rite of exorcism from baptism, just 50 of roughly 1,400 parish ministers resigned or lost their posts because of opposition, but much of the population was outraged. Parents avoided baptizing their newborn or threatened ministers with physical violence to get them to include the exorcism ceremony. Following Christian's death, Leipzig students staged a mock trial of the most outspoken professorial champion of further reformation, Christoph Gundermann, and called for his head. Eighteen months later, what became known as the *Calvinistensturm* erupted in the same town, as students and artisans ransacked the houses of the most prominent burghers suspected of continuing to sympathize with the cause.[33] In Hesse, where the great majority of the clergy also proved willing to go along with the liturgical changes of 1605, the ministers sent to Marburg to carry out the first innovations were attacked and badly beaten within the church itself when the rumor spread that they were about to take down its images. Commissioners sent to Eschwege in 1608 found that 571 of 746 inhabitants expressed opposition to the now-three-year-old changes. In both instances Maurice came in person to the troubled town with troops at his back, lectured the inhabitants on their duty of obedience, and got the bulk of the population to conform to the new church order.[34] In Lippe, however, Simon VI had less luck in dealing with the semiautonomous Hansa town of Lemgo. After a divided city council agreed in 1609 to allow him to enter the city to oversee the implementation of the new church order, the bulk of the populace rose to reject this agreement. An insurrectionary town government was formed, the newly introduced clergymen were expelled, and eight years of military and legal skirmishing followed that ended with Lemgo winning a judgment from the imperial courts that preserved both its old styles of worship and its traditional liberties. It was the mirror image of the Emden Revolution of 1595, a Lutheran city now resisting a Reformed prince.[35]

These repeated instances of resistance were so sobering to princes contemplating second reformations that, following his conversion, the elector John Sigismund of Brandenburg (r. 1608–19), the last major German ruler to embrace Reformed ideas, soon abandoned his efforts to alter worship throughout his territory and restricted changes instead to those milieux he controlled most directly. Maurice of Hesse-Cassel visited Berlin shortly before these events. His stories of the difficulties he had encountered doubtless contributed to the decision.

The initial Brandenburg reformation had instituted a liturgically conservative brand of Lutheranism, but the growing Catholic-Protestant tensions in the empire drove the Hohenzollerns into the arms of those who advocated militancy against Catholicism when the Catholic rulers charged John Sigismund's father with acting illegally in his capacity as administrator of the diocese of Magdeburg and had him barred from the imperial diet of 1582. Although still Lutherans, the Hohenzollerns joined the alliance of 1591 and offered asylum to a number of clergymen driven from neighboring lands for their refusal to sign the Formula of Concord. John Sigismund then proved that early educational ken was not always determinative. His tutor was a strong anti-Calvinist, but he vexed his princely pupil. On a visit to Heidelberg, the future ruler encountered the sermons and polemical writings of divers Palatine theologians and grew convinced that the doctrine of ubiquity was a "false, divisive, and highly controversial teaching." By 1606, he appears to have been secretly won to the rites and ideas he encountered there. Seven year later, to "give his conscience peace," he first had communion celebrated with the fractio panis in a special ceremony on Christmas day 1613 in the Berlin cathedral.[36]

With the advice of Scultetus, dispatched from Heidelberg to advise on ecclesiastical policy, and in consultation with his privy council, which was composed largely of "political Calvinists" from outside the territory, John Sigismund mapped out a series of steps for additional reform: a ban on polemics from the pulpit, the gradual replacement of Lutheran with Reformed faculty members in the territorial university of Frankfurt a/d Oder, a reorganization of church government to place it under the control of a lay Kirchenrat, the elimination of exorcism from baptism, and the permanent establishment of Reformed worship in a purified Berlin cathedral. The drumbeat of clerical criticism was so insistent that the ban on polemics could not be enforced, however, while the old church Konsistorium continued to meet and ignored the decisions of the Kirchenrat. In a letter to Maurice of Hesse-Cassel of October 1614, John Sigismund wrote despondently that barely thirty people joined him for communion according to the new rites. A year after it was announced that the Berlin cathedral would become a Reformed place of worship, his more assertive younger brother, with the elector away hunting, dared to order the reorganization of the church furnishings. The action precipitated a tumult. One of the city's Lutheran ministers denounced it from the pulpit. Crowds massed to protect the minister from arrest. The houses of the court preachers were stormed. When the margrave came to break up the fracas, he was greeted with the cry, "You damn black Calvinist, you have stolen our pictures and destroyed our crucifixes; now we will get even with you and your Calvinist priests!" Rocks hailed down. The estates of Brandenburg extracted an agreement from the elector allowing all who so chose to remain attached to the Invariata Augsburg Confession and the Formula of Concord and compelling the elector to declare that he "in no way arrogates to himself dominion over consciences and therefore does not wish to impose any suspect or unwelcome preachers on anyone, even in places in which he enjoys the right of patronage." Theologians inclined to Reformed views continued to be presented to faculty positions at Frankfurt and to court preacherships. For long, however, the parish clergy were exclusively Lutheran, and the faith of the electors was shared by few of their subjects. By the second decade of the seventeenth century, it would appear, confessional identity had taken such deep root within Germany's various territorial states that rulers who changed their faith could no longer translate the principle of *cuius regio euis religio* into political reality.[37]

By the eve of the Thirty Years' War, the wave of second reformations had thus run its course. Reformed territories remained far less numerous than Lutheran ones within the empire, but the roll of Reformed churches was not inconsequential: upward of a dozen state churches in princely territories large and small; five civic churches in free imperial or largely autonomous towns (Emden, Bremen, Wesel, Mulhouse, and biconfessional Colmar); two constellations of associated churches in the confessionally mixed areas of Cleves-Mark-Jülich-Berg and East Friesland; and a number of smaller minority congregations. A highly approximate estimate of the Reformed population of Germany might be a million souls, out of a total population of sixteen million.[38] Two of the empire's seven electors, those of Brandenburg and the Palatinate, were personally committed to Reformed doctrines. If Herborn is accorded the status of a university, as it soon would be, the Reformed controlled four of twenty-six universities (Heidelberg, Frankfurt a/d Oder, Marburg, and Herborn). These enrolled one matriculant in eight.[39]

As the product largely of princely conversion, the churches created by Germany's second reformations usually differed from those in Geneva and western Europe in their organizational structure and theological shading. In the Wetterau counties and among the small territories and scattered churches close to the Dutch border, the churches closely resembled those of France and the Netherlands, whether established by princely initiative or independently of the political authorities. Frederick III's willingness to embrace the arguments of the Disziplinisten also led him to imbed inside his territorial church a system of consistorial discipline like that found in Geneva, France, the Netherlands, and Scotland, and he did so despite the opposition of much of his Kirchenrat to this potential rival to state power. In the territories in which a second reformation was implemented after 1585, however, the transformation initially involved little more than liturgical changes and the introduction of the Heidelberg Catechism. (As the seventeenth century progressed, efforts would be made to introduce elders and church discipline to Lippe and Zweibrücken.) In Bremen efforts to institute consistorial discipline were defeated by a city government that, like those of most of the Swiss and south German towns in the initial decades of the Reformation, was loath to surrender the oversight of manners and morals to an ecclesiastical board.[40] In several territories, the second reformation reinforced princely control over the church through the creation of a central Kirchenrat or Konsistorium. Descending systems of church government thus dominated many German territorial churches and coexisted with the ascending system of presbyteries and synods in others. Only a minority had independent systems of ecclesiastical discipline.

The absence of efforts to ordain consistorial discipline in many second reformations also reminds one that, although the accusation of Calvinism sprang quickly to the lips of contentious Lutheran theologians, the impetus behind these transformations came as much from the radicalizing dynamic of the era's theological polemics on those raised in the Melanchthonian tradition as it did from the influence and example of Genevan or west European Reformed ideas or institutions. German Reformed theology stood poised between Melanchthon and Calvin throughout the second half of the sixteenth century, the importance of the former increasing as one moved eastward. Only twenty editions of works by Calvin appeared in German between 1560 and 1599, and the geography of their place of publication tracks a noticeably westerly course—from Heidelberg in the 1560s and 1570s, through Herborn and Strasbourg in the 1580s, to Heidelberg, Herborn, Hanau, Neustadt, and Strasbourg in the 1590s. Even in a western part of the empire, Zweibrücken, a study of the contents of parsonage libraries in the opening decade of the seventeenth century reveals Melanchthon to have been the most widely owned author. Ursinus, Erasmus, Brenz, Bullinger, and Luther all rivaled Calvin in popularity.[41] Late in the century Herborn earned a reputation alongside Geneva as one of "the two principal fountains of the Calvinistical Predestination," while early in the next, Nassau, the Palatinate, Hesse-Cassel, Emden, and Bremen all sent delegates to the Synod of Dort, and all but Bremen supported the emerging predestinarian orthodoxy defined there. Anhalt's theologians, however, were not invited to attend, apparently because they were well known for their hostility to strict predestination. Brandenburg's chief Reformed divines politely declined an invitation, fearing that the synod would only be detrimental to their prepossession, Lutheran–Reformed reconciliation.[42]

The most influential recent interpretations of the second reformations have linked them to the process of state building in the territorial states of the empire. According to this argument, the Reformed tradition's emphasis on church discipline and the reformation of manners helped mold a disciplined and obedient subject population, while the reorganization of ecclesiastical administrative structures that accompanied the liturgical and theological changes encouraged the consolidation of state authority.[43] The changes in certain territories, such as Lippe and Hesse, were undoubtedly accompanied by a reorganization, centralization, and laicization of princely control over the church. This change, however, was necessitated in large measure by the opposition that the religious transformations sparked—opposition that reminds one that in practice religious innovations shook the loyalty of princely subjects rather than promoting it. Furthermore, little regard for advancing a reformation of manners is evident in many of these second reformations. In a broader comparative perspective, perhaps the most striking feature of Germany's second reformations was the willingness of godly rulers in the Palatinate and Nassau-Dillenburg to cede power to a largely independent system of ecclesiastical discipline and, in Nassau-Dillenburg, to a transterritorial, strongly autonomous system of church administration.

Rather than attempting to link the enactment of second reformations to calculations of functional utility, a more illuminating approach might recognize that many rulers tried to act as conscientious Christian princes and then undertake to identify the conditions under which some found the arguments for such changes convincing. Partisans of Lutheran orthodoxy commanded most of the strongholds of ideological authority throughout Protestant Germany and aggressively stigmatized Calvinism as the cause of iconoclastic rampages, the alteration of useful ceremonies, and the deposition of ordained magistrates—charges that were surely given greater plausibility by reports of what was going on at the time in both France and the Netherlands. Nonetheless, the powerful strands within Reformed political theology that emphasized the sanctity of established governments and cast magistrates as Christian ministers gave Reformed spokesmen a basis for rebutting these charges and appealing to rulers. In spite of the drumbeats of denunciation, Reformed champions were likeliest to get a fair hearing in those corners of Germany where Reformed or Philippist ideas had gained a strong early foothold, in those courts and cities that were hospitable to refugees from such areas and whose geography and family ties led their rulers to fight alongside the Reformed in France or the Low Countries. To those with such backgrounds or with these kinds of experiences, the Formula of Concord could appear to be a Trojan horse for unscriptural claims about Christ's ubiquity. The elimination of exorcism from baptism and the fractio panis could appear to be a continuation of the original Reformation endeavor to restore the pure worship of the original church. The institution of consistorial discipline could appear to be an instrument for the reformation of manners that had also been so significant a part of the evangelical cause from the start, and that certain rulers, notably Frederick III, had identified as one of the goals of their initial ecclesiastical legislation. In short, the Flaccian faction, not the crypto-Calvinists, might look like the dangerous innovators dividing the evangelical cause with their unnecessary dogmatism just when Rome, the Jesuits, and Madrid threatened to undo the gains of the Reformation.

If much thus hinged on the factors of education, experience, and personal decision making that led certain of Germany's territorial princes to this view of the situation, no less hinged on the patterns of education and recruitment that brought a critical mass of like-minded churchmen and counselors into their inner circle. Such a cadre of high officeholders was critical to the implementation of second reformations, not only because rulers looked to their main advisors for guidance, but also because they relied upon them to carry through major ecclesiastical changes. Years often intervened between the moment rulers of little territories personally accepted a Reformed understanding of key rituals and the moment they implemented changes in these rituals. Only once the winds of exile or the solicitude of like-minded rulers brought churchmen with the theological expertise and eloquence necessary to sell the changes to the local clergy could the actual process of making the changes begin. The recruitment of many key Palatine officials from the south German cities where Reformed currents had been powerful before 1555, the moderate traditions of the Hessian territorial church, and the presence of many Wittenberg graduates in Saxony and Anhalt are all crucial to understanding the second reformations and near-misses in those areas.

Sweden's Reformation history offers added support for this point by revealing what happened when such a cadre of theologians was lacking. The initial Swedish Reformation was more purely a product of princely calculations of economic and political benefit than virtually any other, and it took a long time for the Swedish church to assume either a clear confessional orientation or a detailed Protestant church order. When these began to emerge, much of the impetus came not from the crown but from Wittenberg-educated bishops and the larger body of clerical opinion as expressed by church synods. The king who presided over the first phase of the Reformation, Gustavus Vasa, was so unconcerned about doctrine that he unwittingly contracted for the tutoring of his son and successor, Erik XIV (r. 1560–68), a French evangelical, Dionysius Beurreus, who had passed through Switzerland and absorbed views of a decidedly Reformed cast. After Erik succeeded to the throne, he encouraged the immigration of skilled refugees from the Low Countries and East Friesland and allowed Beurreus to advocate views similar to those of the recent French Reformed confession of faith. Beurreus's views, however, sparked such intense and effective opposition from the archbishop Laurentius Petri and the rest of the church hierarchy that Erik had to reverse course, prohibit Reformed propaganda, and restrict immigration. Charles IX (r. 1604–11), who likewise had been educated by a Reformed tutor, supported further reformation, viewed the world as a political Calvinist, and inclined toward a symbolic view of the Eucharist. During the tumultuous decades that preceded his acquisition of power as a middle-aged man, however, the upper clergy had written the Lutheran orthodoxy that it had absorbed at its university strongholds around north Germany into established church law. When Charles sought to introduce portions of the Heidelberg Catechism into the catechism used by the Swedish church, to modify baptismal ceremonies in a Reformed direction, and to establish a Konsistorium that might wrest control of the church away from an ecclesiastical establishment that had become one of the most autonomous in the Protestant world, clerical foot-dragging defeated him at every turn. Neither Erik XIV nor Charles IX were long-lasting rulers, but their reigns show that the theological formation and recruitment patterns of a region's clergy could weigh more heavily than the personal inclinations of the ruling head in determining the course of a territorial church. After 1593 "Calvinism" was anathematized by name in Sweden, and the Walloon Reformed immigrants protected by successive rulers who were so important for the early development of its extractive industries enjoyed only a narrow margin of *de facto* toleration for the practice of their religion.[44]

8

ENGLAND

*The Unstable Settlement
of a Church "But Halfly Reformed"*

ngland's Reformation history displays important similarities with the
German princely territories that instituted second reformations.
Most obviously, the English Reformation, like many German territorial reformations, was first and foremost an act of state. Indeed, in
no other country that eventually became Protestant except Sweden was the
initial rupture from Rome so thoroughly an act of state as in England. As with
the German second reformations, the key to understanding why England's
Protestant state church assumed a Reformed rather than a Lutheran cast thus
lies in determining what shaped the confessional orientation of foremost decision makers. We also find, as in such territories as the Palatinate or Saxony,
siblings of differing religious orientations within the same ruling family, and
the sudden swings in religious policy that could ensue as one rapidly followed
another in this age of high mortality rates for rich and poor alike. But the theological orientation of the Church of England in a Reformed direction came
earlier than it did in the German principalities and was essentially fixed during the short reign of Edward VI (1547–53). Furthermore, because Edward
was only a boy, the principal decisions were largely taken by those around
him. This orientation thus depended less on the ruler's own experience and
religious decision making than on the inclinations of key councillors and
churchmen. The patterns of migration and personal connections that brought

English churchmen into the orbit of Reformed thought and foreign theologians into England at critical moments are particularly important in explaining why English Protestantism became more Reformed than Lutheran.

Although the enduring contours of England's Protestant church order were determined decades earlier than in those German principalities that underwent second reformations, not until nearly the end of the century was it clear that these contours were immutable. Henry VIII did little more than reject papal authority, decree royal supremacy over the national church, and seize a great deal of ecclesiastical property. Edward VI oriented the doctrine of the church in a patently Reformed direction, but worship was only partially shorn of the practices that most Reformed churches rejected as unbiblical, and plans for altering the canon laws and institutions of the pre-Reformation era came to naught. Leading historians believe that only the brevity of Edward's reign halted the process of innovation in midstream and prevented Edward's reformation from being as thorough as those carried out in the cities of Switzerland and south Germany.[1] The heirs of those who had led these changes certainly were convinced of this. After the Catholic interlude under Mary, Elizabeth held to the Edwardian settlement as the surest rock of stability in an increasingly polarized religious milieu, but advanced Protestants tried to revive the unfinished business of Edward's reign and soon added further demands for consistorial discipline and a presbyterial-synodal church order as the debates and developments of the 1560s made these come to seem essential elements of the best reformed churches. Throughout the first three decades of Elizabeth's reign, successive waves of agitation sought ever more sweeping programs of additional change. Only the resolute repression of the agitation of the 1580s for a presbyterian church order finally enshrined the permanence of the Edwardian–Elizabethan settlement. If, from one point of view, the critical period of definition for England's Reformation was unusually brief, from another point of view the English Reformation was uncommonly long. Even the stability achieved in the 1590s proved short-lived. The campaigns for further reformation of the late sixteenth century sparked defenses of the established church order that by the 1590s were beginning to foreshadow the subsequent movement of the church out of the mainstream of the Reformed tradition toward something distinctively Anglican. For at least another generation, these new voices represented no more than a minority view. Nonetheless, while the Church of England remained predominantly Reformed —indeed, Calvinist—in its theological orientation as the sixteenth century drew to a close, its mingle-mangle of austere doctrines, unreformed ecclesiastical courts and administrative hierarchies, and half-reformed rituals at once placed it in a distinctive position in relation to Europe's other Reformed churches and made it singularly unstable. The conflicts about and innovations in church polity, doctrine, and practical piety generated by this mix would prove exceptionally important to the history of the Reformed churches throughout Europe—all the more so in that, with its total population of 2.75 million people in 1541 and more than 4 million in 1600, England was the largest country whose national church took on Reformed hues.

The religious history of sixteenth-century England has been largely rewritten in the past generation by two movements of revisionist scholarship. The first, associated with Christoper Haigh, J. J. Scarisbrick, and Eamon Duffy, has wanted to exorcise the ghosts of the Protestant national myth that equated the cause of the Reformation with the will of the people. The sequence of religious changes implemented by England's monarchs from Henry VIII to Elizabeth I, they stress, was anything but the necessary consequence of a contemporaneous upsurge of evangelical sentiment among a population alienated from the late medieval church. On the contrary, change was imposed from above on a largely hostile or indifferent populace.[2] The second movement, associated especially with Patrick Collinson, Nicholas Tyacke, and Peter Lake, has more gradually and less polemically undercut the long-established projection onto the first generations of the Elizabethan and Jacobean church of the Church of England's later self-image as a distinctive church tradition representing a via media between Catholicism and continental Protestantism. A salient Anglican theological tradition of this sort did emerge in the wake of the Reformation, these historians would agree, but not until the last decade of the sixteenth century; it did not come to dominate the church until some point in the seventeenth. Prior to that time, the church drew its theological inspiration from continental theology and was fundamentally Reformed in outlook.[3] This second reinterpretation is particularly convincing because it has broken free of the insularity that characterizes so much English historiography and situated its subject within the range of contemporary European possibilities. The same is less true of the early Tudor revisionists, who display a much more limited awareness of the larger world of European Reformation scholarship and of its implications for their topic. These scholars' work has even so been valuable in underscoring the importance of contingency and elite decision making in the history of the English Reformation.

If one compares Protestantism's early growth in England with that elsewhere in non-Germanophone Europe, the evidence about its relative strength and speed is decidedly ambiguous. Echoes of the Luther affair quickly crossed the channel: two correspondents informed Luther that his works were selling in England as early as February 1519, and an evangelical discussion group formed at Cambridge's White Horse tavern in the early 1520s around the prior of the Augustinian house, Robert Barnes. By the second half of the decade, a number of English scholars, including Barnes, William Tyndale, and John Frith, had been driven to the Continent, had visited Wittenberg to study with Luther, and were publishing evangelical literature in English on Antwerp presses. Incidents of iconoclasm appeared quickly in England, perhaps because of the survival of the ideas associated with the medieval heretical movement of the Lollards, who also objected to the cult of images. Images on Worcester's high cross were defaced in 1522. All this seems very much like France. On the other hand, the number of executions for heresy fell off to close to zero in the 1520s, even though, because of the continuing presence of Lollardy, an effective machinery for the repression of heresy was in place in 1517, actively burning, and Henry VIII promptly made known his opposition to Lutheran doctrine. The first person to pay with his life for heretical views more Lutheran than Lollard did so in 1530, a relatively late date in comparison to neighboring lands. At that date, far fewer of Luther's writings had made their way into English than into French or Dutch.[4]

As "the king's great matter" began to drive Henry VIII toward his break with Rome, the evangelical cause profited, for Henry needed intellectuals to justify his actions, and the high church officials in place opposed what he did. Both Anne Boleyn, Henry's mistress by 1527 and queen from 1532 to 1536, and Thomas Cromwell, the chief advisor from 1530 to 1540, patronized and protected evangelicals. As their stars rose at court, men whose convictions had previously placed them in fear for their lives suddenly found the road to preferment leading to the very center of power—a recurring pattern in the story of the English Reformation. At least seven of the ten bishops appointed between 1532 and 1536 were reformers of one stripe or another and Boleyn clients. Writers and printers subsidized by Cromwell were now able to produce evangelical propaganda in London itself, including several vernacular editions of the Bible, translations of early German *flugschriften,* and a *Treatise declaryng and shewing dyvers causes that pyctures & other ymages ar in no wise to be suffred in churches.*[5]

The declaration of the royal supremacy in 1534 was followed by a tug-of-war among rival pressure groups at court to define the course of the now-autonomous Church of England. Cromwell and the new archbishop of Canterbury, Thomas Cranmer, wanted an open Bible, an end to certain forms of Catholic devotion, and liturgical and doctrinal change. They were opposed by a more conservative group headed by the duke of Norfolk and Stephen Gardiner, bishop of Winchester. Late in 1535, Henry began negotiations with the Protestant princes of the Schmalkaldic League. In those rare moments when Charles V was able to free himself from the numerous other conflicts to which his far-flung empire condemned him, he threatened to seek to avenge the honor of his repudiated aunt Catherine of Aragon and to implement the papal bull of deposition against Henry. The price for Schmalkaldic allies, of course, was acceptance of the Augsburg Confession.

The English church moved somewhat in the direction of religious innovation between 1536 and 1538. Royal injunctions in 1536 abrogated saints' days and ordered the provision of Latin and English Bibles for people to consult in church. A gathering of theologians in 1537 drafted an explication of doctrine given provisional approval for three years. It largely confirmed medieval orthodoxy but emphasized the role of faith in justification and of Scripture in matters of authority while censuring the idolatrous use of images. Further injunctions in 1538 ordered the removal of images to which offerings and pilgrimages had been made. Most important, in spite of the conservative rising of the Pilgrimage of Grace, probably the most remarkable mobilization in defense of the old faith in the initial decades of the Reformation anywhere in Europe, the monasteries were dissolved in stages between 1536 and 1540. Then, however, Henry broke off negotiations with the German princes late in 1538 and made it clear that he intended no modification of the church's dogmatic core, not even of those doctrines and practices that many moderate Catholics were willing to contemplate changing. Six articles reaffirmed transubstantiation, communion in one kind, vows of chastity, votive masses, clerical celibacy, and auricular confession. Denial of transubstantiation was to meet with death, with no possibility of recantation. Several reform-minded bishops resigned their sees, and such partisans of more thorough change as John Bale and John Hooper left for the Continent. Robert Barnes, who had returned to England in 1531, went to the stake in 1540, the same year that Cromwell fell from grace and also paid with his life. In 1543, more stringent royal injunctions restricted Bible reading to members of the upper ranks of society and explicitly commended the use of images. Writing soon after Barnes's execution, Luther summarized the recent course of events in bitter words: "But when we had deliberated at great length, and at great expense to our noble Prince Elector of Saxony, we found in the end that Harry of England had sent his embassy, not because he wanted to become evangelical, but in order that we in Wittenberg would agree to his divorce. . . . Harry is Pope, and the Pope is Henry in England."[6] He was a Catholic pope.

The deadly factional intrigue at Henry's court produced one final turn of the wheel of fortune before he died in 1547. Late in 1546, the duke of Norfolk and his conservative allies fell from grace. The causes of their disgrace reveal both how precarious a place was the court of a choleric king and how apparently trivial the causes of momentous events could be: Bishop Gardiner angered the king by refusing a proposed swap of estates and was removed from the list of those who would participate in a regency council for Henry's

young son in the event of his death; and Norfolk's son aroused the king's suspicions that he might be plotting against Edward's succession—by quartering Tudor heraldic symbols in his coat of arms—and brought his father down
with him. The regency council that came to govern after Edward's accession
thus turned out to include a majority inclined to religious change. The man
who first came to dominate it, Edward Seymour, earl of Somerset, possessed
enough evangelical conviction to express confidence in his prayers that he
stood among those "listed in the book of life . . . written with the very blood of
Jesus," even though he ultimately tired of ministerial admonitions, including
some by letter from Calvin in Geneva, and took to skipping sermons delivered in his chapel. The transformation of the church in a Protestant direction
that he initiated continued after his fall in 1549 under the government of his
successor, John Dudley, duke of Northumberland, a more discreet evangelical
but enough of one to be smitten for a time with John Knox. The key player
within the church was Cranmer, who skillfully negotiated his way through
Henry VIII's later years of growing religious conservatism without abandoning his conviction of the need to transform the church if and when its royal
head saw fit. By the later years of the brief reign, the preteen on the throne
had absorbed the convictions of his evangelical tutors and become more than
a cipher.[7] Somerset, Northumberland, Edward, and above all Cranmer each
played crucial roles in shaping the Edwardian religious settlement. Although
a generation passed before it was plain that the documents they put in place
would prove enduring, these would define the features of the Church of England for centuries to come.

Some of the earliest measures of Edward's reign dismantled the barriers
impeding the proclamation of Protestant ideas. The first Parliament of the
reign repealed all heresy and treason statutes promulgated since the end of
the thirteenth century. A surge of publishing activity followed. Between 1547
and 1549, the number of books printed in England increased from roughly 100
to 225. Three-quarters of those published between 1548 and 1550 concerned
religion, virtually all being of an evangelical cast, including previously banned
works by Luther, Bullinger, Calvin, Wyclif, Barnes, Frith, Hooper, and Tyndale. At court, Somerset patronized reform-minded preachers, some of whom
denounced the scandal of images in churches. Acts of iconoclasm followed to
remove objects from churches in London, Oxford, and Southampton.[8]

Scarcely three months into Edward's reign, Charles V defeated the Schmalkaldic League at Mühlberg. The ensuing interim crisis drove several leading
reformers to seek refuge in England, where their arrival proved important in
shifting the doctrinal orientation of English Protestantism toward a Reformed
stance. The learned heterodoxy of Henry VIII's reign had been open to many
influences, Erasmian, Lutheran, and Reformed. Its greatest debt was probably

to Luther, whose writings were by far the most frequently translated of any continental reformer in this period; moreover, Luther left a deep imprint on Tyndale, the leading native publicist and Bible translator. Swiss opinions were also known from early on, and these accorded well with native Lollard traditions of skepticism about the real presence and the cult of images; assorted English evangelicals had parted company with Luther by the early 1540s because of their sharp hostility to the cult of saints and images, symbolic understanding of the Eucharist, and intense Old Testament moral legalism. Frith, who came from a region of traditional Lollard strength, acknowledged a debt to Oecolampadius. Gwalther and Basel's Simon Grynaeus both visited England briefly during the 1530s, opened contacts with Cranmer, and encouraged English students to come to Zurich. Hooper took refuge there after fleeing to the Continent and subsequently became an outspoken advocate of a reformation in the Swiss manner.[9] Still, England's confessional die was not yet cast in any irreversible direction, as is evident from the invitations that went out to theologians in Germany after the Augsburg Interim was imposed. Melanchthon, the strongly anti-Zwinglian Württemberg Lutheran Johannes Brenz, Bucer, a Lasco, and Vermigli all were approached. Significantly, the last three accepted the invitation; the first two were willing to stay in Germany.[10] The more intense conviction of the latter figures that no compromise could be justified with popery, and the especial precariousness of both Vermigli's and a Lasco's situation as foreigners within Germany, cast them into exile just at the moment when the future shape of English Protestantism was about to be determined. This would be vital in shaping the theology of the Edwardian church, for these men possessed a learning and prestige unmatched in England.

Vermigli arrived first and was named to the regius chair in divinity at Oxford, where his students included at least six men who later became bishops. His teachings on the Eucharist soon outraged many within that university's largely conservative divinity faculty and led to a public disputation on the question. Since only Vermigli's version of the proceedings gained the official approval needed for publication, the debate came to be widely seen as a rout of transubstantiation. Bucer arrived a year later to take up a similar position at Cambridge. His prestige became such that three thousand people were said to attend his funeral when he died in 1551, and he too trained many future leaders of the English church. A Lasco, it will be recalled, took charge of London's strangers' church, which was permitted to arrange its own system of discipline and worship in order that these might serve as models of a truly reformed church. All three served on crucial Edwardian ecclesiastical commissions and advised the crown about ecclesiastical legislation. All three spent time in the household of Archbishop Cranmer.[11]

On the key theological matter of the Eucharist, Cranmer's views shifted critically between 1546 and 1548. Previously he had accepted an essentially Lutheran understanding of the sacrament. Now he became convinced that Christ's presence in the communion ceremony did not take the form of a localized presence in the bread and wine; instead Jesus was "effectually present, and effectually worketh not in the bread and wine, but in the godly receivers of them, to whom he giveth his own flesh spiritually to feed upon." The change cannot be credited exclusively to discussions with the continental theologians. At his trial in 1555, Cranmer attributed his new understanding of the Eucharist largely to the influence of Nicholas Ridley. He in turn claimed to have been convinced by the ninth-century theologian Ratramnus of Corbie, whose defense of a spiritual rather than a physical understanding of Christ's eucharistic presence was rediscovered and published by a variety of Protestants from 1531 onward. Still, it is known that Cranmer wrote to Bucer about the matter of the Eucharist late in 1547 and received a response that seems to have been significant for his change of views. Vermigli brought with him to England a copy of a text by the church father John Chrysostom that argued that the Eucharist remained bread after consecration and much excited Cranmer and Ridley when Vermigli showed it to them.[12] Cranmer's change of views was so important because he wrote his new convictions into the central doctrinal statements of the church.

Somerset's first injunctions concerning religion in July 1547 were largely conservative, although they condemned the superstitious abuse of images, allowed Bible reading for all, and abolished processions. As the repercussions of the new evangelical teaching and publication began to be felt, the laws were progressively modified in a Protestant direction. In 1548, a set of *Homilies* that included an expression of justification by faith was issued, confraternities were abolished, all images were ordered to be removed from churches, and the ceremonial of the mass was altered by inserting a section in the vernacular and permitting communion in both kinds. A committee under Cranmer's direction drew up a new book of common prayer, which was approved by Parliament in 1549 and issued for use throughout the kingdom. The document transformed the liturgy into the vernacular, cut the number of sacraments to two, eliminated the elevation of the host from communion, and specified that the officiating minister should break the communion bread before distributing it; at the same time, it retained many traditional practices in order not to offend the conservative inclinations of the bulk of churchgoers in a manner similar to the Lutheran liturgies of north Germany and Denmark that were among its chief sources.[13]

Precisians such as Hooper found the prayer book "very defective and of doubtful construction, and in some respects indeed manifestly impious."

Hooper refused to accept the bishopric of Gloucester offered him unless he was allowed to do so without putting on the "Aaronic habits" that bishops were still required to wear and without swearing his oath of office in the name of the saints and holy Gospels. A pamphlet war soon broke out around the issues of ecclesiastical vestments and kneeling at communion. Bucer and Vermigli, significantly, judged these issues to be *adiaphora* and advised Hooper to accept the ceremonies in place, even while they also expressed to Cranmer reservations of their own about the prayer book. A Lasco and Knox, then in England, backed Hooper. Ultimately, Hooper conformed. The First Book of Common Prayer, as this document became known, nonetheless proved short lived, for its rubric on the Eucharist allowed conservative churchmen to continue to celebrate the mass and claim the sanction of the document in so doing. Discussions about how to modify it began almost as soon as it was adopted, and it was replaced in 1552 by the Second Book of Common Prayer, which incorporated many of Bucer's suggestions for improvement and substantially restructured the communion service, eliminating many of the resemblances with the Roman ritual that remained in the first edition. Regular bread replaced the unleavened communion wafers. A table in the body of the church took the place of the altar. The vestments the officiating minister was required to wear were simplified, although not entirely eliminated. The words of exorcism were removed from the baptism ceremony. Communicants continued to kneel when receiving the communion elements, but an addendum was added stating that no adoration of the elements was thereby implied.

The Edwardian legislation was completed in 1553 with the promulgation of forty-two doctrinal articles drafted by Cranmer. In the matter of election, a lucid statement of predestination strongly indebted to Vermigli's terminology was softened by the omission of any mention of reprobation. In the matter of the Eucharist, a spiritual real presence was asserted and Christ's ubiquity rejected. On the question of whether or not discipline was a necessary mark of the church, the document identified just two marks, the correct teaching of doctrine and the proper administration of the sacraments. An apologia was inserted for the diversity of traditions and ceremonies according to the diversity of times and places. "Whosoever through his private judgement willingly and purposely doth openly break the traditions and ceremonies of the Church, which be not repugnant to the word of God and be ordained and approved by the common authority" was declared worthy of rebuke.[14]

Although nobody knew it at the time, the Book of Common Prayer of 1552 and the Forty-Two Articles of 1553 represented the furthest point the Church of England would advance down to the road to a Reformed reformation during the sixteenth century. Doctrinally, its eucharistic theology and doctrine of predestination now clearly affiliated it with the consensus of Reformed the-

The Ninth Booke containing the Actes and thinges

done in the Reigne of King Edward the fixt.

The Ship of the Romiſh church

Burning of Images.

¶ Ship ouer your trinkets & be packing you papiſts.

the Temple well purged.

The Papiſtes packing away their Paltry.

The comunion Table.

9. "Actes and Thinges Done in the Reigne of King Edward the Sixt." This woodcut illustration first inserted into the 1570 edition of John Foxe's *Acts and Monuments* depicts the highlights of King Edward's reign as recounted in this classic of English Protestant historiography. At the top the papists pack away and ship off their "paltry" as the churches are purged of all images. In the lower left the king seated on his throne gives the Bible to his prelates, who kneel before him as the standing lords watch. The lower right depicts worship reorganized around the preaching of the word, a relocated communion table, and a simplified baptismal service inside a church stripped of all adornment. (Brown University Library)

ology at the time and differentiated it from the doctrines that would be enshrined in Lutheran orthodoxy. In instituting the fractio panis and eliminating the ceremony of exorcism from baptism, it located itself on the Reformed side of the symbolic divide that later emerged over these issues in Germany. The sharpness of its rejection of idolatry and of the misuse of images paled before no Reformed church. Still, its worship remained only partially transformed when judged against the standards of the most austere Reformed churches on the Continent. The Book of Common Prayer formally sanctioned the emergency baptism of gravely ill newborns by midwives, the churching of women after childbirth, clerical vestments, and kneeling at communion—all practices abolished by this date throughout the Reformed territories of Switzerland and its borderlands and that later would be rejected by virtually all other Reformed churches as well. The Forty-Two Articles made it an article of faith that local traditions that did not run counter to Scripture ought to be accepted, even if they did not have positive scriptural foundation. An act of Parliament of 1549 preserved abstinence from meat during Lent and on Fridays, while an act of 1552 "for the keeping of holy days" retained twenty-seven such days, more than even many Lutheran churches observed. The prohibition of marriage during Lent and Advent passed unmentioned in the Edwardian legislation and would be retained under Elizabeth despite attempts to do away with it in 1562 and 1575. It is no wonder that Calvin opined that English worship lacked "that purity which was to be desired," even while he nevertheless judged all of these blemishes to be tolerable.[15]

The polity of the English church meanwhile went entirely untransformed. No hint of the doctrine of the fourfold ministry appears in any of the major Edwardian documents. A moderate rewriting of the ecclesiastical laws was undertaken by a committee of churchmen and lawyers but foundered against Northumberland's opposition when brought before Parliament, largely, it appears, because the duke was angered by a recent spate of sermons denouncing the diversion of ecclesiastical wealth to other than pious uses.[16] Consequently, no alterations were made in the hierarchy of church offices, the administration of the church, or the structure of canon law beyond Henry's initial proclamation that the king was the supreme head of the church. Bishops stayed in place, as did the pre-Reformation system of ecclesiastical discipline relying upon diocesan courts—no proper discipline at all in the eyes of many Reformed theologians. An important detail of this unreformed system was its retention of a requirement that appears to have been formalized early in the fifteenth century to control Lollard evangelization, whereby a license from the bishop was required to preach. Only a fraction of parish incumbents were deemed to be so qualified.[17]

Might Edward have pushed the reorganization of the church still further and altered any of these practices had he lived to maturity? We will never know, although it seems reasonable to believe he would have. Even before the clergy could subscribe to the Forty-Two Articles he was dead of tuberculosis. His successor was his Catholic sister Mary.

The successful Catholic restoration under Mary demonstrates that, even though the official face of the English church had briefly become Reformed under Edward, deep Protestant conviction had taken hold among just a a small fragment of the population. Northumberland and a few allies acted to block Mary's accession and to convey the throne to the Protestant Jane Grey; but this first of many sixteenth- and seventeenth-century endeavors to alter the rules of hereditary succession in the name of preserving the true religion garnered little support and was quickly crushed. In the House of Commons, a minority of close to a quarter of the membership opposed the repeal of the Edwardian religious legislation in November. When it became obvious soon thereafter that the queen intended to marry Philip of Spain, some Protestant gentry organized a rising in the name of opposition to foreign domination. The Wyatt rebellion in the southeast, however, was no more of a crisis than the rising that had greeted the introduction of the first Edwardian prayer book in the West Country six years earlier. In most localities throughout England, the mass was restored and altars resurrected as dutifully as they had been eliminated. Relatively few parish incumbents refused to accept the new church order and were deprived. Most strikingly of all, the number of new clerical ordinations, which had dropped off sharply in the preceding years, picked up. The imperial ambassador noted with satisfaction in 1555 how obediently Londoners took their Easter communion according to Roman rites.[18]

Yet the minority of committed Protestants contained individuals of exceptional dedication. Upward of 280 demonstrated the ultimate commitment, facing and accepting martyrdom. Their ranks included such leading churchmen as Cranmer, Hooper, Latimer, and Ridley; but the vast majority were layfolk of more modest status, disproportionately urban, male, and for the most part relatively young, which suggests that their convictions were shaped during the period of officially supported Protestant proselytization under Edward. London, East Anglia, Kent, Sussex, Bristol, and Gloucestershire produced the greatest number of martyrs, a pattern that conforms to what is known about the larger geography of early Protestant conviction. Not only do the most committed Protestants seem to have been found primarily in the south. At least initially, they may have been somewhat wealthier than their more tepid or conservative counterparts: the average tax payments of Londoners tried for heresy under Mary was well above the city norm, although the gap was smaller in Canterbury. The new ideas also took root more strongly where the pre-Reformation clerical establishment was small, so that conservative holdovers would not counter the message spread by the new evangelical preachers appointed under Edward; Protestant conviction was far stronger by the end of Edward's reign in Hull, which had just two parishes and a small clerical contingent prior to 1520, than in York, the ancient ecclesiastical capital of the north, with fifty parish churches and numerous religious houses.[19] In London, Suffolk, and parts of the north, the hard core of committed Protestants is known to have gathered secretly in churches under the cross for exhortations and the sacraments during Mary's reign.[20]

Approximately eight hundred other Englishmen, many of them gentry, clergymen, and young men preparing for the ministry, chose exile rather than accept the restoration of Catholic worship. As Germany's Lutheran territories proved by and large inhospitable to the English refugees, the emigration further reinforced the links between English Protestantism and the continental Reformed; refugee churches were established in Emden, Wesel, Frankfurt, Strasbourg, Zurich, Basel, Geneva, and Aarau. The debate begun under Edward about how fully worship ought to be reformed continued to divide the émigrés. Most of these churches based their worship on the Second Book of Common Prayer, but, as noted earlier, the Frankfurt church, whose leaders included Knox, drafted its own, more austere order of worship. After a group within the church demanded and gained an order from the city government requiring conformity to the Book of Common Prayer, many within the church moved on to Geneva and used it there. From the safety of exile, the refugees directed a steady stream of exhortation and consolation to their brethren in England. Seventy-two vernacular works of religious devotion and polemic were published abroad under Mary, including the anti-Nicodemite writings of Calvin and Bullinger.[21]

English historians, by quantifying the clues in wills of the era, have devoted considerable energy to detecting how the beliefs of the bulk of the population evolved amid the numerous transformations of official worship. The largest number of such studies have looked at the language of will preambles and have attempted to classify these as traditional, neutral, or Protestant, depending upon whether the testators commended their souls to the Virgin and saints or expressed confidence in their salvation through the merits of Christ's sacrifice. This method, it is now realized, has serious pitfalls because wills were often drawn up according to standard formulae that reflect the habits of the scribe as least as much as the desires of the testator. The evidence of such studies shows that in most areas only about 15 percent of wills from either Edward's reign or the first decade of Elizabeth's state the testator's belief that he or she will be saved through faith in Christ alone; no study has yet to find such a view in more than 33 percent of all wills from this period. Fewer studies have looked at the percentage of will makers who left money to endow masses

for the benefit of their soul after death, although the initiative for this gesture undeniably lay with the individual testator. In East Sussex and the West
Country, significantly, only 19 and 18 percent of all testators, respectively,
asked for such prayers under Queen Mary, whereas 70 percent had done so
in the 1520s.[22] This suggests that much of the population had lost its faith in
rituals fundamental to pre-Reformation Catholic piety, even if it was not prepared actively to resist the restoration of Catholic worship or insist upon a
clearly Protestant will preamble.[23] The attention of English historians to tracing religious change at the parish level illuminates what appears to have been
the norm in many parts of Europe that were contested between Catholicism
and Protestantism in these years. Those deeply committed to either Catholic orthodoxy or some brand of Protestantism both formed a minority of the
population. In between stood a broad middle group willing to adjust its practice in whatever direction the ruling powers deemed appropriate.

In such a fluid situation, it would once again be an accident of royal demography that determined the shape of England's established church. With each
passing year of Mary's reign, the writings of the Marian exiles grew more radical, as the restoration of Catholicism appeared increasingly firm. In Strasbourg, the exiled Edmund Grindal prudently studied German in anticipation
of a lengthy stay. But in 1558 the exiles' prayers were answered. Mary suddenly began to languish and died. Her sister and successor, Elizabeth, would
prove to be Henry VIII's only long-lived child, and thus the one who would
determine the final contours of a long-lived church order.

Elizabeth was raised a Protestant in the household of Catherine Parr and
could hardly do otherwise than reject the authority of Rome, in that to accept it would have been to grant the illegitimacy of her parents' marriage
and of her claim to the throne. The historian William Camden described her
as being very religious, praying daily, attending chapel on Sundays and holy
days, and listening carefully to Lenten sermons. The description suggests a
style of piety more attuned to the scrupulous performance of basic obligations
than deeply evangelical. She was no theologian and little inclined by either
temperament or training to take direct responsibility for defining the doctrines of the church placed under her care. Still, the direction of the changes
that would follow her accession was augured clearly enough by her first actions as queen. A returned exile preached the initial sermon in her chapel.
Shortly thereafter, she told the clerics officiating at Christmas mass, "Away
with those torches, for we see very well," then left the ceremony early so
as not to be present at the elevation of the host. Yet she also resisted entreaties that she remove the crucifix from her chapel. In the end, she revealed
herself to be firmly committed to the terms of the religious settlement enacted in 1559 and suspicious of all innovations, no matter how strong their

justification in evangelical principle and their precedents in other Reformed churches.[24]

After many "tossings and griefs, alterations and mutations" during its drafting, the settlement enacted in 1559 replicated the Edwardian church order of 1552–53 with minor modifications. To make it acceptable to as much of the population as possible and to minimize offense to the rulers of France and Spain—for as long as possible, Elizabeth sought to assure Europe's Catholic powers that her church was not incompatable with their beliefs—the Second Book of Common Prayer was preferred over the more austere service books of Frankfurt and Geneva advocated by some. Its Reformed character was toned down even more by its retention of those vestments restored under Mary and emendation of the words of administration at communion in a way that permitted a Catholic understanding of the sacrament. Even with these modifications, the Elizabethan Act of Uniformity barely obtained ratification by a majority of a House of Lords purged of four of its most strongly Catholic members. Royal injunctions ordered the use of special unleavened communion wafers and condemned only the superstitious abuse of images, although most of the visitors charged with implementing this latest remodeling of parish worship enforced the removal of all images. Elizabeth proclaimed herself the supreme governor of the church, not its head, in deference to those who stressed that Christ was its only proper head. In 1562, a new commission charged with preparing a set of doctrinal articles compressed the Forty-Two Articles into thirty-nine with minor modifications. Elizabeth did not allow these to be ratified by Parliament and made binding on all clergy until 1571, after her final excommunication from Rome.[25]

Elizabeth's initial ecclesiastical appointments showed the alignment of her church with Reformed theology. More than half of the initial set of Elizabethan bishops were returning Marian exiles. Her first archbishop of Canterbury, Matthew Parker, had been the executor of Bucer's will. His successor, Grindal, had carried Bucer's coffin at his funeral. The most notable early defense of the church, John Jewel's *Apology of the Church of England* (1564), came from the pen of a bishop who had been Vermigli's secretarial assistant while a student at Oxford and had lodged in his house while in exile in Strasbourg and Zurich. Three other books that appeared between 1560 and 1570 and that would shape English religious culture still more profoundly for generations to come reinforced the Reformed orientation of the church: the Geneva Bible, with its abundant marginal annotations of a largely Calvinist timbre, reprinted more than a hundred times in full or in part following its appearance in 1560; John Foxe's *Acts and Monuments,* published in English in 1563 and ordered in 1570 to be placed in all churches, with its edifying history of England's martyrs and their central role in the apocalyptic struggle between the church of Christ and the Roman Antichrist; and Alexander Nowell's catechism of 1570, which combined a defense of magisterial control over the church with a theology derived from Calvin and the Heidelberg Catechism. When Oxford revised its statutes in 1578, Nowell's catechism was prescribed for all students alongside that of Calvin, the Heidelberg Catechism, and the *Elements* of Hyperius, an eclectic Hessian theologian attacked in the 1560s as a crypto-Calvinist. Those wishing to study more theology were advised to read Bullinger, Calvin's *Institutes,* and Jewel's *Apology.* During these same decades, the leaders of the English church looked to both Zurich and Geneva for advice and kept up a sustained correspondence with each city's leading theologians.[26]

Not only was the dominant theology of the early Elizabethan church manifestly Reformed; with time it grew distinctly Calvinist. Soon after his return, Jewel exclaimed nostalgically, "O Zurich! Zurich! how much oftener do I now think of thee than ever I thought of England when I was at Zurich!" The city on the Limmat was a greater model than Geneva, and England's church leaders carried on a more intensive correspondence with it than they did with Geneva. But no author would be as frequently printed in England over the course of the second half of the century as Calvin. The peak years for Calvin editions came between 1578 and 1581, when six to eight of his books appeared each year. By the last decades of the century, his works had eclipsed those of all other theologians in the library inventories of Oxford and Cambridge students. They did the same in the library of the Puritan earl of Bedford, who owned eight works by Calvin but none by Bullinger and just one by Martyr—a striking disproportion given that he had spent a winter in Zurich during his student years but had never visited Geneva. Beza also obtained growing popularity, fifty editions of his works being printed in England. Here is a compelling illustration of the larger point that one of the reasons for Geneva's unique centrality within the larger Reformed world lay in the extraordinary skills of its leaders as expositors and writers. Even where direct connections were not as close as with Zurich, their writings came ultimately to predominate.[27]

In light of the unequivocal dominance of Reformed theology, many features of English worship and church government could only appear wanting to principled believers, especially in that so many of England's church leaders had direct acquaintance with continental Reformed churches. Still, although Knox urged returning Marian exiles "not to justify with our presence such a mingle-mangle as is now commanded," the overwhelming majority both of former exiles and of the committed Reformed Protestants for generations to come believed that one could take up a living within this church in good conscience because it was pure in the essentials of doctrine and worship and might yet be ameliorated from within. Elizabeth's style of rule also made it easy to retain hope for change from within. She kept her deepest convictions to herself, rarely defined unambiguous policy guidelines for her subordinates, and employed many trusted councillors who could be classified in German terms as "political Calvinists" and who protected and encouraged churchmen who wanted to create a more purely reformed church.[28] Agitation for the further reformation of the church from within welled up three times in her reign, growing at each upsurge more ambitious in its aims and better coordinated in its organization.

The partisans of further reformation in the English church long were said by historians to be animated by the ideology of Puritanism. Even more than most -isms of the early modern era, the concept of Puritanism is an ex post facto creation whose use by historians suggests far more coherence and consistency of viewpoint among those designated by this term than actually existed. Like most party labels of this era, the word *Puritan* was originally a term of abuse coined by hostile opponents. Its first known appearance dates to 1567, when the London topographer John Stow wrote of people "who called themselves puritans or unspotted lambs of the Lord" gathering for worship in the Minories Without Aldgate. Stow was writing of a group that desired a form of worship pure of unscriptural vestments or rituals. By the later part of Elizabeth's reign, the term was more often applied to those who pursued a strict reformation of manners; Puritans were hypocritical killjoys like Ben Jonson's Zeal-of-the-Land Busy in the play *Bartholomew Fair* (1614). In the 1620s, enemies of high predestinarian theology would also call that viewpoint Puritan. The best studies of those to whom the label was applied have found that most so-called Puritans indeed saw themselves as a separate group within the church, a godly minority of true believers set amid a sluggardly mass of unredeemed and benighted sinners. Their aspirations, however, extended to a wider range of issues than was implied by any of the above uses of the term; many, for instance, wanted to encourage the development of a learned parish ministry and to refute the errors of Catholicism. Furthermore, their aspirations evolved over time.[29] In light of this, it seems wisest to attend above all to the specific agendas of reform promoted by those to whom the term was applied and to be sparing in the use of the term *Puritan,* although it remains a useful form of shorthand for referring in various contexts to the godly partisans of the austere programs of further reformation.

The matter of vestments and rituals sparked the first, relatively mild agitation for further reform, as it had already sparked complaints under Edward VI and during the Marian exile. At the very first Convocation (clerical assembly) of the church following Elizabeth's accession, in 1563, the partisans of purification of the liturgy urged a reduction of saints days and the elimination of distinctive dress for the clergy, of kneeling at communion, of emergency baptism of sickly newborns, and of organs in churches. Their initiative failed to carry the day, but individual clergymen saw fit to implement such alterations or to introduce other minor changes in the manner of worship in their parishes. At Cambridge, George Withers denounced the abuse of stained glass in the churches, precipitating the revocation of his fellowship and his fateful move to Heidelberg, where his provocative questioning set off the quarrel between Erastus and the Disziplinisten. William Fulke's preaching against vestments inspired undergraduates to leave off wearing their surplices to chapel and to hiss those who did. Faced with the proliferating diversity of rites and practices, Elizabeth ordered Archbishop Parker to act. A set of *Advertisements* soon prescribed uniformity in matters of church apparel. A chorus of protest greeted the measures, and the partisans of change dispatched letters and envoys to Zurich, Geneva, and Scotland enumerating the defects plaguing the English church and seeking aid in eliminating them. Bullinger responded with a letter that Bishop Grindal printed without his knowledge or consent, admonishing the English partisans of further reformation to cease displaying "a contentious spirit under the name of conscience." Beza found the English reports more alarming, exclaiming to Bullinger in a private letter, "Where did such a Babylon ever exist?" and telling Grindal frankly of his opposition to emergency baptism and unnecessary rites. He nonetheless thought it best not to intervene too aggressively in English church matters lest he offend Elizabeth and diminish her willingness to help the French Protestants. Finally he grew exasperated by the continuing appeals of the English precisians and came to see them as unnecessarily quarrelsome. As might be expected, the idolatrophobic Scots were the most sympathetic. After thirty-seven London clerics were suspended for refusing to wear the prescribed vestments, the General Assembly of the Scottish church conveyed a protest against this action to their English brethren. Despite the Scottish protest, the suspensions stood, and the majority of those deprived finally conformed. One small group in London, recalling the secret congregations of the Marian period, chose to set up in 1569 its own assembly using the Geneva service book, the first instance of separatism directed against the Protestant Church of England. This assembly persisted in the face of persecution for a number of years.[30]

A second wave of agitation for reform advanced in the early 1570s and focused more on issues of church polity and discipline. Three closely spaced events around 1570 put an end to the equivocation of Elizabeth's early ecclesiastical policy and led her to reinforce Protestantism's situation in England. In 1569 the northern earls mounted an alarming revolt in which they tore up the Prayer Book and called for a return to the Catholic faith. In 1570 Pope Pius V excommunicated Elizabeth and loosed her Catholic subjects from their obligation to obey her. In 1571 the Ridolfi plot to depose her in favor of Mary

Stuart was discovered. As the queen in response introduced legislation to re-quire all clergymen to subscribe to the Thirty-Nine Articles, to force laymen to take communion at least once yearly in their home parish, and to make it a treasonable offense to declare that she was a heretic or schismatic, those who hoped to move the church farther in a Protestant direction realized that this might be the moment to act. Foxe and Cranmer's son-in-law Thomas Norton, perhaps acting with the support of Parker and Burghley, oversaw the printing of the previous manuscript plan of 1552 for the reformation of England's ec-clesiastical laws and proposed it in Parliament. Elizabeth killed the measure.[31] The failure of this moderate reform of the church structure was followed by more drastic proposals after the bishops followed up the formal adoption of the Thirty-Nine Articles with an oath of subscription that obliged the coun-try's ministers to assert that not only these articles, but also the use of the Book of Common Prayer and the wearing of the surplice, were all compatible with Scripture. Conscientious partisans of a purely reformed church might wear vestments or participate in rituals lacking biblical sanction if these were so ordered by their divinely appointed ruler, but could they swear that such practices were biblically justified? A bill was introduced into the next Parlia-ment that would have permitted bishops to license deviations from the Prayer Book, but it was defeated. Two London ministers, Thomas Wilcox and John Field (a literal resident of Grub Street), then wrote a ringing *Admonition to Parliament.* Assuming the voice of a larger group—the pamphlet was likely encouraged by a regular gathering of young ministers in the city—the *Admo-nition* declared that "we" long accepted the Book of Common Prayer, "being studious of peace and of the building up of Christ's church." Now being obliged to subscribe that the book conformed to Scripture, "we must needs say . . . that this book is an imperfect book, culled and picked out of that popish dung-hill," marred by many features ranging from the persistence of private baptism to public rites "full of childish and superstitious toys." The pamphlet looked to France and Scotland for its models of properly reformed churches: "Is a refor-mation good for France and can it be evyl for England? Is discipline meete for Scotland and is it unprofitable for this realme?" By contrast, "we in England are so far off from having a Church rightly reformed, according to the precept of God's word, that as yet we are not come to the outward face of the same." The tract went on to attack the lordship and pomp of bishops and to call for the creation of a proper system of consistorial discipline.[32]

In challenging the authority of bishops and calling for a system of consis-torial authority, Field's and Wilcox's *Admonition* introduced the same sort of issues that had troubled Scotland and the Palatinate. Other initiatives of these years reinforced the scrutiny of the church's institutions and disciplinary sys-tem. In 1571, a former Marian exile to Geneva, Percival Wiburn, spurred the local authorities of Northampton to draft a plan for the local reformation of manners that included weekly gatherings of the mayor and city council "assisted with the preacher, mynister, or other gentlemen" for "the correction of discorde made in the towne, as for notorious blasphemy, whoredome, drunkeness, raylinge against religyon, or the preachers thereof . . . and suche lyke" in order that ill life might be corrected, God's glory be set forth, and "the people brought in good obedience." The intervention of the local bishop hastily put an end to this experiment.[33] More important yet, Cambridge had been thrown into a "hurly-burly and shameful broil" in 1570 when a talented new divinity professor, erstwhile opponent of vestments and future anti-Roman polemicist, Thomas Cartwright, had delivered a series of lectures on the model of the primitive church as set forth in the Acts of the Apostles. Just how far Cartwright used the example of the early church to criticize the structure of the Church of England in his initial lectures is unclear because the lectures do not survive. Yet the response to his lectures points directly at the inference that he advocated the elimination of the offices of bishop and archbishop as then constituted in the church and the desirability of having in each church a preaching minister in whose appointment it had a voice. For such ideas, Cartwright lost his Cambridge post. He went to Geneva, where he taught in the academy and made it a point to sit in on a consistory session. By the time of his return to England two years later, his encounter with Calvin's doctrine of the fourfold ministry and with the critique that Beza was just then evolving of "pseudepiscopi" in his correspondence with Knox and the Scots had led him to discern in the Bible a far more elaborate blueprint of a properly reformed church.[34]

Cartwright joined the controversy sparked by the *Admonition* with his *Replye to An Answere made of M. Doctor Whitgift Agaynste the Admonition to the Parliament* (1573), which declared that a properly reformed church contained the classic four orders of ministers, exercised its own ecclesiastical discipline to which even rulers were subject, and permitted no minister permanent jurisdiction over any other. A *Second Reply* claimed that Calvin "misliked" even the "small preheminence" of being permanent moderator of the Genevan Company of Pastors. (There is no evidence this was in fact the case, but in 1578 Beza would oversee a change in the functioning of that body, ceasing to act as permanent moderator and insisting that the office henceforth be rotated, a sign that the idea of equality among ministers first articulated in the initial French national synod was now becoming a fixed principle of Genevan ecclesiastical organization.) The *Second Reply* also spoke of a hierarchy of presbyteries and synods, as did the *Full and plaine declaration of Ecclesiasticall Discipline,* of Walter Travers, likewise published in 1574. These works were the first fully elaborated theoretical statements of the program that would later be dubbed presbyterianism—a program that added the Franco-Genevan principle of the equality of all ministers to the insistence upon the necessity of consistorial discipline of Calvin, a Lasco, and the Palatine Disziplinisten, while holding up the hierarchy of synods of the French church as the model church structure for a larger polity. (Beza combined all of these principles into a single work for the first time four years later in his *On the Order Among the Pastors Serving the Church of Geneva* [1578].)[35] For expressing their views in print, Field and Wilcox were imprisoned for a year, while Cartwright fled once more to the Continent—to Heidelberg this time, where the later works in the controversy first appeared. Elizabeth ordered the formation of commissions of enquiry to enforce the required subscription to the basic articles of the church. Ultimately, however, the number of nonsubscribers these turned up proved so great that church leaders had to back off the strict enforcement of the order lest too many zealous combatants against the Catholic enemy be lost. Many ministers were allowed to subscribe with reservations.

For the next eight years controversy about the proper ordering of the church abated but did not disappear. The reform-minded Grindal was elevated to the archbishopric of Canterbury in 1575. One small group of partisans of further reform around Robert Browne broke off communion with the main body of the church in 1581, citing its "dumb [that is, nonpreaching] ministry" and its lack of proper discipline as reasons for not accepting the legitimacy of the church. After forming their own congregation in Bury St Edmunds, they were forced into exile in the Low Countries, where Cartwright encountered them while serving as minister to the Merchant Adventurers at Middelburg. He tried to convince them that while the English church might be flawed, the flaws were not so great as to require separation, the view that continued to be held by the great majority of partisans of further reformation. In some shires, the licensed preachers moderated discussions among the ministers of the vicinity in "exercises of prophesying" roughly modeled on the Zurich Prophezei and its reincarnation in the refugee churches of London. Here ministers mulled over "profitable questions" and occasionally discussed such matters of moral reform as how to stop "playes of Maietree" and the misuse of the Sabbath. These aroused the queen's mistrust and sparked a drama when she ordered Grindal to oversee their suppression. He refused, arguing that Paul's suggestions in his letter to the Corinthians that those who prophesy and speak in tongues (1 Corinthians 14) should gather regularly for mutual edification offered irrefutable biblical sanction for such gatherings. For this he fell into disgrace and was placed under virtual house arrest. Many of the clerical assemblies survived or reconstituted themselves after being temporarily suspended.[36]

Controversy grew more intense again after Grindal died in 1583 and was succeeded as archbishop of Canterbury by a man of a very different stripe, William Whitgift, the chief polemical opponent of the presbyterians in the controversy touched off by the *Admonition to Parliament.* Whitgift, too, stood at least partially in the traditions of Reformed thought, but those of Zurich rather than Geneva, France, or Scotland. "I make no difference betwixt a Christian commonwealth and the church of Christ," he exclaimed, echoing Zwingli. He believed that no blemishes marred the English church's beauty: "God be thanked, religion is wholly reformed, even to the quick, in this church." If it differed in its forms of worship from continental Reformed norms, this was simply an instance of the legitimate variety of practices found in different territorial churches. At the same time, he deeply feared subversion, was haunted by the specter of Anabaptism, and linked the maintenance of ecclesiastical hierarchy to the preservation of the political and social hierarchy. "I am persuaded," he wrote, "that the external government of the church under a Christian magistrate must be according to the form of government used in the commonwealth—a principle that James I would later express more pithily as "No bishop, no king."[37] Strong measures were needed to assure respect for the existing forms of the church, he believed, and he drafted a formulary requiring all clergy to swear that the Prayer Book contained nothing contrary to the word of God and that they would use it in public worship.

By the early 1580s, the more self-consciously godly ministerial conferences and exercises in prophesying had become occasions for discussing plans for further amelioration of the church and had entered into correspondence with one another. Whitgift's accession coincided with the brief ascendancy in Scotland of the earl of Arran, whose Black Acts had driven many of the partisans of the Second Book of Discipline, including Andrew Melville, into exile in England. Conferences with some of these exiles increased the resolve of the godly to resist the developments threatening the purity of both churches and to assert presbyterian principles. Ably led by the coauthor of the *Admonition to Parliament* Field, the self-styled "faithfull ministers that have and do seek for the discipline and reformation of the Church of England" produced a new surge of pamphlets. Allies introduced into Parliament in 1584 a bill to replace the Prayer Book with the Genevan liturgy and to install a system of church government with parish consistories and synodal assemblies for each shire. In support of this reform, the collaborating clerical conferences sought to assemble information demonstrating the continuing inadequacies of the ministry.[38]

When this new campaign to reform the church through parliamentary initiative gathered little support in Parliament and failed, a number of partisans of change, including Field, Travers, and Cartwright (now back in England and running a hospital in Warwick thanks to the patronage of the earl of Leicester and Lord Burghley), decided the time had come to draft a proper order for the English church comparable to Scotland's Second Book of Discipline. Travers drew up the order, which was circulated for discussion and went through a series of revisions. It contained provisions for parish consistories and three levels of ecclesiastical assemblies, ranging from local conferences of both ministers and elders for administrative purposes and clerical edification through provincial synods to a national synod. Called the Book of Discipline, it was circulated to an array of county conferences late in 1586 with a formulary that members were asked to sign indicating their acceptance of it. Here was the most ambitious assay yet to transform the English church from within. A few ecclesiastical conferences dared to accept the document and began to style themselves classes or synods. The great majority refused to subscribe to so radical a reshaping of the church. In anticipation of the Parliament of 1586, at which another bill would be introduced to replace the Prayer Book with the Genevan order of service, the communicating conferences also launched a drive to elect well-intentioned representatives. Again, the effort met with little success.[39]

As the work of reshaping the church continued to founder, frustration mounted among the partisans of further reformation. It finally burst forth in the intemperate polemics of the Martin Marprelate tracts of 1588, which blasted "our vile servile dunghill ministers of damnation, that viperous generation, those scorpions," the bishops. The defeat of the Spanish Armada in the same year removed the threat of Catholic conquest, freeing the hierarchy to act against the precisians in its midst. Field's death, also in 1588, cost the cause its best leader. Most of the prominent privy councillors who had so often sheltered partisans of further reformation also passed from the scene around this time: the earl of Bedford in 1585, the earl of Leicester in 1588, and Sir Francis Walsingham in 1590. These concurrent happenings all facilitated the most determined crackdown yet against the left wing of the church, which Richard Bancroft, Whitgift's former chaplain and successor as archbishop of Canterbury, organized with fastidious efficiency. After gathering information about the network of Puritan conferences and deploying this to present the network as more tightly organized and seditious than it really was, he won permission to oversee its dismantling. Cartwright and eight other ministers were imprisoned for more than eighteen months and subjected to an intimidating trial before the Star Chamber. The clerical conferences were broken up. Once again, a few precisians withdrew from the established church and formed separatist congregations in London and Norwich, now complete with a fourfold ministry on the Genevan pattern, if not, because there were too few churches to permit it, a full-fledged presbyterian-synodal organization.

After fifty-six members of one of these churches were arrested in the woods near Islington in 1593, a harsh new law against sectaries was enacted. The separatist ministers John Greenwood and Henry Barrow were executed. Remnants of these groups sought exile in the Netherlands, joining the mix there that would give rise to the Pilgrims of Plimouth Plantation and the earliest English Baptists. Fifty years later, when the onset of the civil war shattered the established order and reawakened hopes of all sorts for the reorganization of church and society, the Book of Discipline drafted by the presbyterians of 1585–87 would be revived and proposed as the platform for a new and temporarily successful reshaping of the English church. For the moment, the most highly organized effort to date to amend the shape of the Elizabethan settlement was scattered to the winds.[40]

Not the least of the consequences of the presbyterian agitation of 1584–88 was the theological response it generated among defenders of the status quo. The earliest response to the strong new assertion of the equality of ministers by Beza, Melville, and Cartwright had been to argue, as Whitgift and Scotland's Patrick Adamson did, that the nature of the ecclesiastical polity was a matter on which Scripture offered no clear guidelines and that as a result could be determined in whatever fashion seemed most expedient for the polity in question. Beginning with John Bridges' *Defense of the government established in the church of England for ecclesiastical matters* (1587), a series of authors began to claim apostolic origin for the institution of episcopacy, "so that we must needs confess that it is of God also." Here were the origins of *jure divino* episcopalianism. A still more ambitious defense of the status quo of a disparate character was undertaken by a learned ex-protégé of Jewel's, Richard Hooker, in his *Laws of Ecclesiastical Polity.* In the first four volumes of this work, published in 1593, Hooker denied that Scripture contained sure rules of church polity, argued that natural law represented a critical source of rules for human action alongside the Bible, and maintained that rites and institutions were not necessarily bad simply because they conformed to Roman usage. Like Whitgift, he followed the Zurich reformers in refusing any discrimination between the church and the commonwealth in a Christian kingdom. If he thus positioned himself on this issue in the tradition of Zurich and Erastus— Erastus's *Explanation of the Weighty Questions Concerning Excommunication* was in fact published amid the debates of these years, as was Beza's *Pious and Mild Treatise on True Excommunication and a Christian Presbytery* in reply—his great novelty lay in his appreciation for the rites of the English church that had been so recurrent an object of precisian attack. His long fifth book, published in 1597, defended the practices of the Prayer Book as having a "sensible excellency correspondent to the majesty of him whom we worship." They were not simply *adiaphora,* but positive aids to proper worship.

With this move, Hooker became the first to defend the Church of England as a golden mean not between the extremes of Rome and Anabaptism, as earlier defenses like Jewel's had done, but between Rome and Geneva. As one of his modern editors has written, his fifth book "in effect created Anglicanism as a self-consciously distinctive form of religious life."[41]

Although the first five books of Hooker's *Laws* would go through eight editions to 1639, his vision of the English church would not achieve its greatest impact until the second half of the seventeenth century. Most Englishmen, under James as well as under Elizabeth, continued to see their church not as occupying a distinctive phylum in the classification of Europe's newly diversified ecclesiastical kingdom, but as one of the Reformed churches.[42] The defeat of the presbyterial initiative of 1585–87, as of the earlier movements for further reformation of the 1560s and 1570s, nonetheless guaranteed that it would remain an idiosyncratic Reformed church. After 1590, attempts to change it significantly to make its polity and worship conform more closely to normative Reformed models ceased for a full half century. Instead, it began to change in other ways. On the one hand, the need to defend partially reformed rituals and an unreformed church polity would lead growing numbers of English churchmen away from the broader consensus of Reformed theology on certain issues. On the other hand, the failure to found an effective system of ecclesiastical discipline would spark those who still aspired to an ample reformation of manners to experiment with voluntary techniques for promoting individual and communal sanctification. In sum, by the 1590s, it was at last clear that the Elizabethan church settlement would not be radically changed during Elizabeth's lifetime. It was also manifest that the peculiar nature of that settlement had created a most unstable and dynamic national tradition.

9

EASTERN EUROPE
*Local Reformations
Under Noble Protection*

As the sixteenth-century traveler left the Holy Roman Empire and moved east, the population grew sparser and the power and privileges of the aristocracy increased. The great political entities of this region, Hungary and Poland-Lithuania, were imposing in their territorial extent, but they lacked the judicial, administrative, and tax collecting capacities of the west European monarchies, and the enshrinement in just these years of the principle of elective kingship hamstrung their potential for consolidation by forcing successive monarchs to strike debilitating bargains with those who elected them. Culturally and economically, these kingdoms were more closely tied to western Europe than ever before. The demographic and economic expansion of the sixteenth century stimulated the region's trade with Germany and the Low Countries in grain, forest products, livestock, and minerals. Pockets of German merchants and burghers throughout the region made German an urban lingua franca. Italian artists and intellectuals were drawn to the courts of the region. Thanks to these connections, evangelical ideas penetrated these kingdoms in short order, and forceful Protestant movements would ultimately win the allegiance, at least briefly, of an impressive fraction of each one's political elite. But as befits this politically and socioeconomically distinctive region, the process by which these movements came about and gained legal toleration was quite unusual. Religious change was neither accompanied by the violent political upheavals that attended the reformations from below in France, Scotland, and the Netherlands, nor accomplished by the controlling governmental hand of the princely reformations of England and many German territories. It resulted instead from generally nonviolent local reformations, protected and promoted, especially in the Polish-Lithuanian Commonwealth, by the powerful nobility of the region.

One key to the distinctive course of religious change in these regions was the relative weakness of monarchical authority, which afforded the evangelical movement unusual freedom in which to disseminate. It spread quickly through the German-speaking towns of the region, where it was overwhelmingly Lutheran in cast, then hurdled the language barrier to take root among Slavic- and Hungarian-speaking nobles, burghers, and clerics, who more often inclined to Reformed views. By the 1540s, localized changes were transforming parish-level religious practices in portions of both kingdoms. Attempts by the bishops and crown to suppress these in Poland sparked prompt resistance in the name of defending aristocratic privileges and quickly led to the establishment of legal toleration. Here, the movement's expansion was stalled by internal divisions and by an early, determined movement of Catholic renewal. In Hungary, the Catholic church virtually collapsed from within after the shattering Ottoman triumph at Mohács in 1526 and was too weakened even to pursue the suppression of heresy for most of the century. Only when the eastern branch of the Habsburg family that ruled a portion of Hungary embraced a more aggressively Catholic set of policies around the end of the century did the Protestants of this region feel the need to gain codification for their rights of worship. By that date, the face of worship was transformed across the country, and the political elite was almost entirely Protestant.

The distinctive pattern of the Reformation's progress in this region adds still another element to the question of why Reformed rather than Lutheran churches were more successful during the second wave of Protestant expansion. In both countries, the first expansion of the movement among the burghers of such enclaves of German domination as the cites of Polish Prussia and the Saxon mining towns of Transylvania eventuated in Lutheran domination of the local Protestant movement. The growth of the movement in other areas and among different sectors of the population led predominantly, although not exclusively, to the establishment of Reformed churches. Historians of the region tend to ascribe this pattern to an impulse toward ethnic differentiation presumed to be deeply rooted in the region, as if the Poles and Magyars embraced Reformed ideas precisely because they were not associated with Germanness, as Lutheranism was. The ethnic factor cannot be neglected, but one must wonder if ethnolinguistic rivalry was as yet a powerful enough force in the region to fully explain this phenomenon. The confessional divisions did not always follow linguistic fault lines with precision: Lutheranism predominated among the Slavic speakers of northwestern Hungary and Habsburg Carinthia, Styria, and Carniola (today's Slovenia); in the Polish-Lithuanian commonwealth, some cities came to have separate German-language Lutheran churches and Polish-language Reformed congregations, but others housed a single confession, Lutheran in numerous cases and Reformed in others, that offered worship in both languages. Clues that hint at the reasons Reformed churches came to outnumber Lutheran ones are scarce. The consistent attractiveness of Reformed ideas to those of humanist or Melanchthonian educational formation appears to provide one part of the explanation, but in the end the greater appeal of the Reformed is easier to observe than it is to account for here.

POLAND-LITHUANIA

At the close of the Middle Ages, the 815,000 square kilometers of the dynastic union of Poland and Lithuania composed the most religiously diverse polity ruled by a Christian king owing obedience to Rome. Three major territorial units of quite disparate character existed within this loose amalgam; they would be bound into a tighter union having a common representative institution by the Union of Lublin of 1569.[1]

The smallest of the three Jagiellon possessions, Royal Prussia, had been wrested from the control of the Teutonic Knights in 1454. Straddling the lower Vistula, the highway to the Baltic for grain exports from the interior, this was the most urbanized part of the commonwealth and the territory most akin to western Europe. Richly privileged, Danzig (modern Gdansk) was the commonwealth's greatest port and by far its largest city, an emporium for imported luxuries of all sorts with a population of roughly thirty thousand people in the late fifteenth and fifty thousand in the late sixteenth century. Elbing (Elblag) and Thorn (Toruń) ranked among the Polish-Lithuanian Commonwealth's eight largest cities. These three towns sent representatives to the upper house of the territorial estates; the smaller cities were represented in the lower house. The region had been exclusively Christian and loyal to Rome ever since the Teutonic Knights had first conquered it and forged a dense parochial network. Its cities were predominantly German speaking and kept their municipal records in that language.

The historic core of the Polish state and its most populous part, the kingdom of Poland properly speaking, was rapidly evolving during the sixteenth century toward the "nobleman's paradise" of the next two centuries. Although some nine hundred localities possessed urban privileges by the end of the sixteenth century, scarcely ninety lived primarily from manufacturing or com-

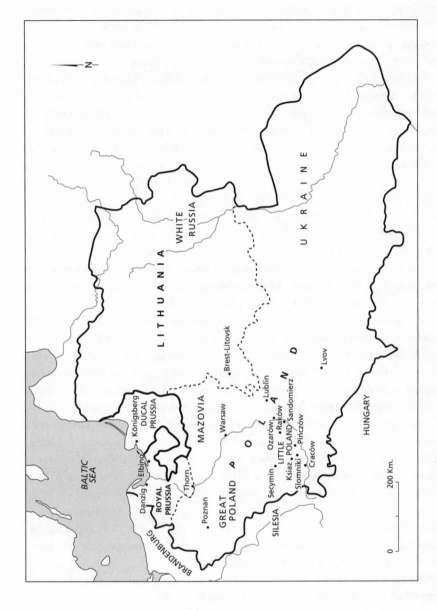

Map 9. The Polish-Lithuanian Commonwealth

merce, the rest being overgrown farming communities. Few exceeded three thousand inhabitants; according to Jan de Vries's calculations (which exclude Lithuania and Hungary), this was the least urbanized region of Europe except for Ireland.[2] The larger towns contained sizable numbers of German, Italian, and Scottish merchants and craftsmen, a bridge to a wider world in a region in which literacy rates were lower than in the west. German-speaking clerics, in particular, would prove an important conduit for evangelical ideas. Polish speakers nonetheless predominated in these cities, and the language of municipal deliberations in most had switched from German to Polish by the beginning of the sixteenth century. The smallness of these cities as well as their political weakness impeded their ability to offer an autonomous basis for a powerful reformation movement. Lay or ecclesiastical lords exercised proprietary control over the great majority of towns. Even the largest of the self-governing royal towns, such as Cracow, Poznań, and Lublin, were unrepresented within the Sejm (Diet) and were increasingly subject to the oversight and control of the royal agents, or *starostas*. Furthermore, commerce was regulated more and more in a manner that undercut domestic urban manufactures and monopolized much of the trade for the nobility and the German merchants of the great trading towns outside the territory's borders. Those possessing noble status made up no less than 8 to 10 percent of this territory's four million inhabitants. Such a large class inevitably contained vast gradations of wealth within its ranks, but in law and ideology all nobles were equal. Most displayed a fierce commitment to the defense of their "golden privileges" and an equally fierce contempt for all who lacked noble birth. A small but wealthy and politically influential fraction of these noblemen sought and obtained higher education. The kingdom's sole university in Cracow being in apparent decline, a growing number of the nobility traveled abroad to Leipzig, Frankfurt a/d Oder, and above all Wittenberg—another conduit for Protestant ideas. Poles of lesser birth, by contrast, continued to look predominantly to Cracow for a university education.

Although the kings of Poland had embraced Christianity since 966 and although concern about heresy was not unknown in late medieval Poland (at least a dozen people were executed as Hussites in the fifteenth century), considerable religious diversity was tolerated. The incorporation of southern Ruthenia into Polish territory had brought a substantial number of Orthodox Christians under the rule of the Polish crown, while attention to populating the vast expanses of the realm had led to permission being granted to an exotic mix of peoples to settle, including Moslem Tartars, Monophysite Armenians, Crimean Karaites, and Ashkenazic Jews. The Teutonic Knights, long-standing rivals of the Polish crown, denounced this willingness to accept infidels. To rebut the theological and legal claims that the knights advanced to justify their invasions, Polish canonists formulated justifications for the toleration of other faiths. Direct continuity cannot be observed between these ideas and those that would be put forth during the second half of the sixteenth century to justify the unusual toleration for Christian dissidents that came to exist in Poland in the wake of Protestantism's growth. But there can be little doubt that the experience of religious diversity helped prepare the ground for this. When such partisans of religious unity as the Jesuit Peter Skarga argued in the late sixteenth century for strong measures against heresy because "where people are not held by a common faith no other bond will hold them together," the argument could hardly seem convincing.[3]

Lithuania, the largest but least densely populated part of the Jagiellon dynastic union, stretched even farther beyond the pale of Latin Christendom. This land of forests and bogs, more thinly urbanized yet than Poland, was the last region of Europe to receive Christianity: its pagan kings converted only on concluding their dynastic alliance with Poland in 1385. At the turn of the sixteenth century, the Christianization of its ethnically Lithuanian regions was but superficial. Paganism flourished in much of the countryside, and the network of parishes was so loose that many parish churches lay fifty kilometers from one another and were expected to serve several dozen villages. The Orthodox Ruthenians who occupied much of the eastern expanse of the grand duchy employed the Cyrillic alphabet and were loyal to the patriarch in Moscow. Lithuania's first permanent printing press did not arrive until 1574. Insofar as the Reformation grew out of spiritual aspirations and dissatisfactions within late medieval Christianity that were most intense in areas where cities were numerous, the rituals and practices of flamboyant Christianity flourishing, and literacy and education widespread, few parts of Europe could have seemed less promising soil than Lithuania. But the region's great nobility, whose possessions commonly dwarfed in scale the holdings of the leading Polish nobles, was at the cutting edge of a gradual Polonization that was radically changing the customs and language of the grand duchy's elite in a manner that opened it up to western cultural and educational influences. The conversion of certain of these Polonized magnates would lead to the establishment of a surprisingly large number of Protestant churches.

The close trade links to Germany brought word of Luther's ideas quickly to the portions of the commonwealth near the empire and set off immediate agitation, centered around the Baltic, where demands for social and political reforms widely accompanied the call for evangelical renewal. King Sigismund I showed himself to be anything but tolerant. His first decree banning the importation of Luther's writings into Poland was issued at the relatively early date of July 1520. In 1523, he decreed death as the penalty for anybody who adopted or spread Lutheran ideas, while requiring all books printed in the kingdom or imported from abroad to be submitted for censure by the rector of Cracow, also on pain of death. Measures of 1535 and 1540 forbade Poles from studying abroad at heretical universities. Such harsh decrees were at least partly inspired by the alarming strength of the early evangelical movement throughout the Baltic and the rapid upgrowth of a Protestant bastion on the country's border in the former lands of the Teutonic Knights secularized by the Hohenzollerns in 1525. Evangelical sentiment mounted so precipitously in Danzig that supporters were able to force the authorities to set aside a church for evangelical preaching in 1522. In 1525, a popular uprising overthrew the city council and closed the monasteries. Evidence of comparable, if less intense, agitation has been discerned in twenty-six other cities as well in 1525, in Poland proper as well as in Royal Prussia.[4] Sigismund himself went to Danzig to restore the old religious and political order and to punish the rebellion's ringleaders. The agitation of 1525 died down. But as occurred elsewhere in Germany and around the Baltic, it was followed throughout the German-speaking areas of Royal Prussia by a second period of advance of evangelical sentiment, politically chastened in content, that led to renewed initiatives, with the assistance of the new Lutheran citadel of Koenigsberg, to refashion worship on a piecemeal basis in many localities. By 1555, as many as half the communities of Royal Prussia may have altered their worship in a Lutheran manner.[5]

The language barrier delayed the transmission of evangelical sentiments beyond the German-speaking burghers of the towns by approximately a decade. The first known evangelical sympathizer of Polish origin was Jacob Ilza, a member of the arts faculty at Cracow who fled the country in 1534 rather than renounce his ideas. In 1544, Jan Seklucjan, a native of Bamberg who had preached for a while in Poznań, began to publish the first Polish-language evangelical works from a press in Koenigsberg. His works included a number of translated satires against the clergy and the purchase of anniversary masses, a catechism after Melanchthon, hymns, domestic postils, and a translation of the Bible. A noteworthy evangelical circle also formed in the mid-1540s in the capital, Cracow, around two men: Francis Lismanino, the provincial of the Franciscan order known to have been drawn to the ideas of Erasmus and Bernardino Ochino; and Felix Cruciger, a Cracow graduate who resigned his church living in 1546 because of his growing disagreements with the Roman church. As a seventeenth-century account relates the story, Cruciger was summoned to the bishop's court on heresy charges and asked if he followed Calvin's views. This was the first time he had heard the name. He procured various Calvin works and became a follower. Whether or not the story is accurate, reliable evidence that Swiss theologians were beginning to have an effect on Polish evangelicals by 1546 survives in the epistolary traces of a

visit to Zurich in that year by Johann Maczinski, who had studied in Wittenberg and would correspond in future with Pellikan, Vadian, and a Lasco. Three
years later Calvin received his first letter from a Polish correspondent and replied to its advice by dedicating his commentary on Hebrews to the new Polish
ruler, Sigismund II.[6]

Agitation for religious change and the transformation of worship in the
localities was gathering steam by the end of the 1540s in Great and Little
Poland. Often, the critical role was played by noblemen who offered evangelical clerics shelter on their estates or in their compounds within the royal
cities. In certain towns essential protection and support came from prominent merchants. The leading lay champion of the cause in Cracow was Johann
Boner, a wealthy merchant and city councillor. Although of German origin,
his financial and commercial services to the court and the resident nobility
tied him closely to the aristocracy, and he must have been a fluent Polish
speaker in this city now dominated by that language. Such a pattern of connections helps to explain why Cracow Protestantism, always strongest among
the urban elite, would be exclusively Reformed in character for the next two
generations. Local reformations of worship, whose precise details are rarely
known, began to multiply between 1547 and 1553, most strongly in the region between Cracow and Lublin, which would become the heartland of Polish
Protestantism. Lithuania was affected as well in 1553, when no less a figure
than Nicolas Radziwiłł, the powerful chancellor of the Grand Duchy and one
of the most thoroughly Polonized magnates of the region, began to shelter
Protestant preachers. His theological inclinations moved from an initial set of
views close to Lutheranism toward a more unmistakably Reformed outlook
under the sway of the Cracow-educated Simon Zacius. His example was followed by other leading Lithuanian nobles.[7]

The most important initial effort to give fixed shape to the proliferating
changes in worship came from Francisco Stancaro, a Mantuan-born Christian
Hebraist whose evangelical leanings led him to flee Padua and then Vienna.
With six other heretical clerics, he established in 1550 a new order for the
church in Pinczów (in Little Poland) on the estate of Nicolas Oleśnicki. The
monks there had recently been driven from a cloister and the church purified of its images. The order was based closely on Herman of Wied's proposed
Cologne Reformation, drawn up jointly by Bucer and Melanchthon. Stancaro's
Canons of the Reformation of the Polish Church would be published in Frankfurt a/d Oder in 1552 and serve as the basis for other church foundations
carried out after the Italian exile was forced to flee Pinczów. The existing regional ecclesiastical synods within the Roman church provided a ready model
as the need to promote cooperation and unity of practice on a wider territorial
basis came to be felt; so too, as in Scotland, did the German Lutheran inno-

vation of the church superintendent. In 1554 a gathering of several ministers took place in the region of Słomniki, near Cracow, in what later synodal protocols would record as the first synod of a Reformed church. Cruciger, now serving as the pastor of Secymin, was chosen to head the church and before long was signing letters "Superintendent of the renascent Church of Christ in Little Poland, in the name of all the ministers and nobles united in the faith of Jesus Christ."[8]

As efforts to instill Protestant worship spread, the ecclesiastical hierarchy discovered the difficulties of enforcing the harsh laws on the books against heresy in a land in which assertive noblemen jealously guarded their honor and privileges. A clerical synod of the Roman church appointed an inquisitor for every diocese in 1551. A few bishops took action against priests who had married and at the noblemen who sheltered them. Because accused noblemen had the troublesome habit of turning up at the bishop's court with armed retinues, many sentences were handed down without a hearing. Some condemned the accused to forfeit their property. This inspired a united front of protest at the next Sejm by the assembled gentry, who saw such actions as abuses of judicial power. An eloquent defender of noble privileges, the Protestant Raphael Leszczyński, was elected president of the Chamber of Deputies; Protestants would likewise preside over every Sejm through 1565. The Catholic Jan Tarnowski, commander of the royal armies, was no less eloquent in his denunciation of the actions of the episcopal courts, which he saw as an intolerable attack on Polish liberties, all the more egregious in that the edicts against heresy had not been voted by a Sejm and thus violated the statute of 1505 that declared no new law could be proclaimed without the Diet's accord. A one-year suspension of ecclesiastical jurisdiction was obtained. Oleśnicki was meanwhile called before a royal tribunal, where he was reportedly bitten by one of the royal dogs but defended himself so ably against his accusers that he was released without punishment.[9]

The hierarchy tried to renew its punishment of heretics and their supporters as soon as the one-year suspension of ecclesiastical jurisdiction expired, concentrating its energies on plebeian violators. Once again its efforts foundered on aristocratic resistance. Three burghers of Poznań were sentenced to death for heresy in 1554, but after one escaped the other two were freed from prison by a posse of armed nobles. Another sentence followed against a cobbler. To the dismay of the bishop, who asked why noblemen should concern themselves with a simple artisan, a delegation of more than a hundred members of the gentry demanded and gained his release. "It's not that we care about the cobbler," Jacob Ostroróg told the bishop, "but we realize that if you got your way with him, you might do the same tomorrow to Marszewski, Tomicki, Ostroróg and others." At the Sejm of 1555 and then more permanently at that of 1562–63, ecclesiastical jurisdiction over laymen was once again suspended.[10]

A significant modification was made to this suspension in 1557 when it was decreed that "the royal towns and others since they cannot equal the gentry either in freedom or in dignity, should not be included in this permission." The crown would subsequently push its local officials to act against the Protestants in the towns under their jurisdiction, although some of these officials were themselves inclined toward the movement and refused to do so. This measure applied only to Poland. The already predominantly Lutheran towns of Royal Prussia ensured their ability to shape religious life within their walls as they desired by purchasing recognition of their rights of *jus reformandi* for the hard cash that the threadbare royal treasury always so desperately needed—thirty thousand florins plus a further loan of seventy thousand florins in the case of Danzig. The leading Protestant magnates of Lithuania extracted similar privileges for the churches in the Grand Duchy's royal towns in 1562, when the king needed their aid for a campaign against Muscovy.[11]

Although the establishment of Protestant churches continued to involve violation of the law and a measure of political risk in the royal towns of Poland, by the mid-1550s the nobility had won effective freedom to modify worship as its members saw fit on their domains. The culmination of endeavors to guarantee this freedom came with the Warsaw Confederation of 1573, drafted to ensure that the newly elected Henry of Valois, widely suspected of having tainted his hands in the Saint Bartholomew's Massacre of the preceding year, would not introduce religious strife "such as we clearly observe in other realms" on taking up the Polish throne. The measure, which Henry swore to uphold, pledged the nobility not to spill blood or invoke penalties of confiscation, imprisonment, or banishment against one another "for difference of faith or church" and to oppose anybody who tried to do so. At the same time it reaffirmed the authority of lords over their subjects and their powers to repress revolts on pretext of religion. Debate would follow for a generation over whether or not the protections guaranteed by this document extended to the towns and to commoners, and work to guarantee that they would was vainly undertaken at later Sejms. In practice, the upshot of this document was the triumph of a principle that could be summarized as *cuius dominatio eius religio*.[12]

Because of the rapid suspension of ecclesiastical jurisdiction and the weakness of the royal and ecclesiastical courts prior to its suspension, the Polish Reformation was a reformation without martyrs. The one known execution for a crime of belief in the sixteenth-century commonwealth was of an eighty-year-old woman, apparently a convert to Judaism, who was put to death in 1539 for denying the divinity of Christ. Her extreme unorthodoxy did not preclude several Protestant histories from claiming her as a martyr for the faith, nor did the general paucity of martyrs prevent a reworking of Crespin and Foxe, the *Story of the Cruel Persecution of God's Church,* from appearing from the Radziwiłł-subsidized press in Brest-Litovsk in 1567; the depiction of the Roman church as bloody and tyrannical was seemingly too much a part of the Protestant outlook and too effective a tool for rallying support to be foregone, even in lands whose national experience offered no grounds for such a view.[13]

As elsewhere, the greatest hope of Poland's Protestants was not simply to institute their own church and obtain legal toleration for it, but to implement a reformation of the national church. Hopes of this sort ran high in the mid- and late 1550s. The king since 1548, Sigismund II, was known to have read Protestant literature at court in the company of such evangelicals as Lismanino. After Lismanino broke openly with the Catholic church and married while in Geneva on a book-buying mission in 1554, he encouraged Calvin to write the king to urge him to reform his church. Calvin followed up with a series of letters to the king and leading noblemen. The Sejm of Piotrków in 1555 not only suspended the authority of bishops over laymen, but also declared that the king possessed ultimate authority in matters of religion; issued a call for a national council; outlined a possible agenda for such a council that permitted a vernacular liturgy, communion in both kinds, and clerical marriage; and decreed that until the council met, lords could introduce into their estates and houses any scriptural mode of worship they chose. Sundry Protestant confessions were presented to the king for his approval, while the affiliated churches of Little Poland held two assemblies. One worked out an accord of cooperation with the roughly thirty churches of the Czech Brethren that had been recently established in Great Poland after their members had been driven from Moravia. The churches agreed to collaborate on any proposals to be advanced at the national council, although each retained its own liturgy and confession pending final agreement on matters of ritual and the theology of the Eucharist. The other, held without any representatives of the Czech Brethren at Pinczów, urged that Calvin, Beza, and Etienne du Quesnoy, a philosophy professor at Lausanne, be called to Poland to participate in the council, a sign that Geneva had now come to be identified among the "ministers and nobles united in the faith of Jesus Christ" as a home of most admirable theologians. The invitation was not accepted—indeed, Calvin kept the Poles waiting nearly a year for his rejection. But he did commend John a Lasco, whom both Lismanino and a gathering of ministers and nobles had also urged to come. A Lasco accepted the call and returned to his homeland late in 1556 after sending ahead a letter urging the king to put away all foreign gods, as the prophets had commanded the kings of Israel. He was able to obtain audiences with the king, but Sigismund II kept delaying the proposed national council and never did himself accept a change of faith, fearing that this would bring "either damnation or the contempt of the Lord." There would be no reformation from above.[14]

In addition to urging Sigismund to reform the national church, a Lasco sought to introduce to the synods independently set up by the evangelicals institutions typical of the Reformed churches of western Europe but duly modified to suit the distinctive conditions of this noble-dominated commonwealth. Here he had greater success. The election of lay elders chosen from among the nobility was introduced into a number of churches. In August 1557 a Lasco summoned together the independently organized churches of Little Poland, Great Poland, and Lithuania for the first general synod of the Polish-Lithuanian churches. Little Polish synods of the same year agreed to adopt the Genevan catechism and the practice of excommunication in the manner of Geneva, while restructuring the school founded by Oleśnicki at Pińczów along the lines of that of Lausanne under the direction of a native of Lorraine. A Lasco also introduced into this church a practice akin to the prophesyings of the London church: the practice of monthly conventions of clerical superiors. True to his Erasmian heritage, he resisted codification of the church's doctrine in a confession of faith, asserting that the Bible was the only document necessary. This was at least in part a strategy to preserve as broad a front as possible among the assorted Protestant currents within the commonwealth. His aristocratic background and international prestige gave him a moral authority that no future Polish minister would match. Thus fortified, he led clerical protests against aristocratic seizure of church property and urged that the increasingly heavy obligations imposed on enserfed peasants be limited to two days of corvée labor per week, issues that would before long disappear from the agenda of reform.[15]

In the late 1550s, the Reformed cause appeared to be gaining ground rapidly in Poland-Lithuania, but the momentum of its growth was promptly disrupted by schism. The forging of cooperation with the Czech Brethren proved problematic, partly because of differences over the liturgy and lay elders, partly because the church of the brethren was hierarchically organized and subordinated to a bishop in Moravia, which fit awkwardly with the synodal system in use among the Reformed in Poland. Far more divisive yet was the challenge of anti-Trinitarianism, which proved strong in Poland because so many expatriate Italians were prominent within its Protestant movement. Francis Stancaro, in many ways the founding father of the Polish Reformed church, began to flirt with Arian views soon after drafting the first formal church order for newly independent congregations. In 1559, he returned to Poland after a six-year stay in Transylvania more convinced than ever of such views and proselytizing for them vigorously. Giorgio Biandrata, the erstwhile court physician to Queen Bona Sforza who moved to Geneva in 1556 but quickly alienated Calvin with his troublesome questions about the Trinity, likewise returned to Poland, in 1558. Both men were such effective spokesmen for their views that other prominent evangelical leaders, notably Lismanino and Nicolas Radziwiłł, soon embraced them. A Lasco dedicated much of the last year of his life to combating them, but his death in 1560 deprived the party that one might call the Nicene Reformed of its most prestigious spokesman. The three treatises that Calvin addressed to the brothers in Poland and two by Bullinger could not snuff out the brushfire from a thousand kilometers away. Synods and pamphlets continued to dissect the manifold complexities of this most mysterious of Christian mysteries well into the 1570s. By 1562, Cracow's church was in the process of dividing in two, and many noble supporters of the Reformation cause were growing alarmed by the spread of these ideas that prominent foreign theologians labeled horrible blasphemy. Since Anabaptist ideas also began to circulate at this very moment, they were willing to cooperate with the pro-Catholic forces in the Sejm on measures taken against foreign heretics. A law of 1564 commanded their expulsion, depriving the anti-Trinitarians of many of their leading spokesmen. Still, the damage had been done. The majority of native Protestant ministers in Poland and Lithuania alike had embraced the anti-Trinitarian position. The majority of Protestant noblemen remained loyal to the traditional doctrine of the Trinity. The schism culminated when the "brethren in Poland and Lithuania that have rejected the Trinity" organized their own synod in 1565. Their church became known as the Minor Reformed Church of Poland. In brief order it adopted some of the baptismal and pacifistic doctrines characteristic of strands of Anabaptism. Along with a sister church that developed in Transylvania in these same decades (see below), it is the church to which modern Unitarians trace their roots.[16]

The bitter battles fought out within Poland's Reformed church over the issue of the Trinity had three notable consequences. First, they contributed to the loss of momentum for the Protestant cause visible by the late 1560s. At least one nobleman, Nicholas Gostynski, is known to have been so dismayed by the quarrels within the Reformed camp that he removed the Protestant minister and restored Catholic services on his domain.[17] Others probably did so as well. An effective rallying of Catholic sentiment also contributed to Protestantism's loss of momentum. The majority of the episcopate militated effectively against all compromises with the Protestants in the critical years of the late 1550s and early 1560s. Fresh from presiding over the final session of the Council of Trent, Cardinal Stanislaus Hosius, bishop of Warmia, introduced the first Jesuit college to Braunsberg in 1565. Others followed. Incidents of Protestant derision of the symbols of Catholicism dot the chronicles of the 1560s. In 1564, for instance, a nobleman stopped a Corpus Christi procession in Lublin, ordered a priest marching in it to recite the Lord's Prayer, then snatched the pyx from his hand and threw it to the ground, exclaiming, "You said truly that God is in heaven. Then he is not in the bread, and not in your pyx." Although the nobleman escaped punishment, the Catholics began to celebrate their ceremonies accompanied by what a Protestant historian called the instruments of war. By the 1570s, the Catholics were initiating most incidents. By this time, the Protestant movement appears to have reached its peak strength in Poland and perhaps even to have begun its decline.[18]

Second, the alarm felt by so many about anti-Trinitarian views, together with the revival of Catholic aggressiveness, led the Polish Reformed to see their Lutheran and Czech Brethren counterparts as kindred spirits with whom it was advantageous to form a political alliance. The effort to forge a union with the Czech Brethren that had foundered by 1558 was renewed in the mid-1560s and led in 1565 to an agreement in the region of Cujavia. In Lithuania, the Reformed were able even to reach accord on the question of the Eucharist with the small Lutheran churches established in a few parts of that territory, mostly in cities where German merchants were numerous. In Poland, a conference of representatives of all three groups at Sendomierz in 1570 could not find a similar eucharistic formula satisfactory to them all, but the groups did agree that although each church would retain its own organization, liturgy, and beliefs, they would discuss all vital matters of religion at joint councils to be held at least once every five years. Ensuing agreements between the Reformed and the Czech Brethren pledged them to refrain from engaging in polemics against one another, to permit ministers of each confession to fill in for the others when necessary, and to allow members of any of the churches to take communion at any other while traveling. This Sendomir Consensus was a model for a similar compact reached in 1575 between the various post-Hussite and Protestant churches in Bohemia, where a separate Reformed church never took shape but where Calvin's ideas penetrated the circles of the Czech Brethren and a nobility that included many pious souls drawn toward a nonconfessional, meditative brand of Christianity. It would be cited by advocates of intra-Protestant irenism in the empire and beyond throughout the seventeenth century. As the contrast between the success of such initiatives in Poland and the bitter polemics between Lutherans and Reformed in the empire shows, cooperation between the two major branches of magisterial Protestantism was easier to stimulate when both groups were in the minority and Arianism loomed to the left.[19]

Third, the defection of so many Reformed ministers to the Minor Reformed

Church prompted those who remained loyal to the major church to tighten their links with the Swiss. Christopher Tretius, the Geneva- and Strasbourg-educated head of Cracow's college, traveled to Geneva and Zurich to consult with Beza and Bullinger and sent many of his best students on to Heidelberg or Switzerland for further study. In preparation for the Sendomierz synod a Reformed assembly accepted the Second Helvetic Confession as the best expression of its beliefs. Published three times in Polish over the subsequent decade, this became the basic confessional statement of the Polish Reformed churches. Zanchi, Zurich's Josias Simler, and Beza all dispatched treatises against the anti-Trinitarians back to Poland.[20]

The first major history of the Polish Reformation, Stanislas Lubieniecki's *History of the Polish Reformation,* was written late in the seventeenth century amid the death throes of Lubieniecki's Minor church. The book branches away from the Reformed movement at the point in the narrative where a separate Minor church takes shape. More recent historians of the Polish Reformation have been attracted above all to the place of the movement in Polish political history, to the doctrinal struggles fought out around the issue of the Trinity within the larger context of the so-called Radical Reformation and the origins of Unitarianism, and to the exemplary history of the coexistence of so many religious movements within the commonwealth, with its evident relevance to Polish national self-understanding and to contemporary international focus on multicultural coexistence. Given the few tiny Reformed churches surviving in the country at present, curiosity about the church practices of denominational ancestors, by contrast, has been relatively weak. As a result, while a great deal is known about the growth of the Reformation and the political struggles to which it gave rise over issues of toleration and church reorganization, the internal life, worship, and administration of the Polish Reformed churches, once established, remain very poorly understood.[21] It appears that by the last decades of the century the "church of the Helvetian confession" was divided into three provinces, those of Little Poland, Great Poland, and Lithuania. Each was in turn divided into districts, each district assembling in synod four times annually and each province once per year. In Great and Little Poland, although not in Lithuania, each province was headed by a superintendent elected for life by the lay elders or seniors. The superintendent in turn nominated clerical seniors, who oversaw each district and carried out visitations, while so-called political elders elected by the patrons of the churches also had a role in watching over the conduct of the ministers and congregations. Communion was taken either standing or kneeling, but sitting at the Lord's Table had been condemned by a synod as an Arian error "contrary to the general custom of all the Protestant churches of Europe"—a remarkable instance of possibly willful misinformation on the part of the synod itself. A recent study has shown that nonnobles filled the overwhelming majority of elders' posts in the church of Vilna, despite the provisions laid down in the time of a Lasco that elders were to be drawn from the nobility (perhaps applicable only to Little Poland).[22] A great deal of research needs to be conducted, however, before the worship, discipline, and administration of the Polish church can be confidently compared to those of its counterparts elsewhere.

Thanks to a pioneering statistical study of the number and geography of Protestant churches in the commonwealth, there is far better information about the movement's extent and strength at its height in the later sixteenth century. The greatest center of Reformed strength was Little Poland, where 265 Reformed churches are known to have existed at one point or another in the century, alongside another 100 or so churches born of its anti-Trinitarian offshoots. Many of these churches, however, existed only briefly. Another 229 Reformed churches were established in Lithuania, whose few large cities typically housed German-language Lutheran churches besides the Reformed churches that worshiped in Polish. Great Poland, where German-language Lutheran churches were common, housed just 15 Reformed congregations, plus 40 churches of the Czech Brethren and another 40 Polish-language Lutheran churches.[23] Protestantism in Royal Prussia likewise remained overwhelmingly Lutheran, but a congregation of Scottish peddlers in Thorn and a handful of elite townsmen in Danzig and Elbing who followed the path of other Germans in the late sixteenth century from Philippism to Calvinism furnished nuclei for Reformed churches to develop in all three of the province's chief towns. All three adhered to the Consensus of Sendomir in 1595 and even began to characterize their churches as Reformed, before opposition to liturgical change on the part of the majority of the Lutheran citizenry provoked a revolt against the Danzig city council and drove all three back toward Lutheran orthodoxy. Small but elite Reformed congregations survived the receding tide. Indeed, one of the most prominent Reformed theologians of the early seventeenth century, Bartholomaus Keckermann, taught at Danzig's Gymnasium Illustre.[24]

Most striking about Polish Protestantism was its elite nature. Around 1570, approximately one-sixth of the nobility of Poland-Lithuania, Royal Prussia excepted, embraced a form of Protestant belief. Among the political elite represented by those who held the highest administrative posts in the land and sat in the Senate of the Sejm, Protestants were in the majority, with twenty-eight Reformed, seven Lutherans, and one member of the Czech Brethren outweighing twenty-five Roman Catholics and seven Orthodox Catholics. In Mazovia, a region of poor soil, few cities, and smallholding noblemen, Protestant inroads were so feeble that a papal nuncio reported that the region was "as Catholic as Italy." But where the soil was more fertile, agriculture more export oriented, and noble possessions more extensive, churches were more numerous. In the royal cities, where their legal situation was more precarious, churches managed to come into existence in virtually every town of consequence except Lvov, but the scant evidence about their size suggests they were often small, at least in Poland proper. In Cracow, the church had about seven hundred members at its peak, most from the city's wealthier families, out of a total population of twenty-five thousand. As for the rural population, a recent study has suggested that no more than 10 percent of the peasants who lived on domains whose lords established Reformed worship may actually have attended it. Synods urged lords to "forbid people to attend papist churches, to go to confession, take communion, pray before pictures or have any dealings with papist priests." Some noblemen did try to compel their serfs to attend Reformed services on pain of a fine or whipping, but most who embraced the cause appear to have been hesitant to compel their serfs to enter. They instead allowed them to attend nearby Catholic services or even to support their own chapel, with the outcome that ministers complained of situations in which the lord and his household were the only ones to turn up for Protestant services. Even within aristocratic families, the patriarch himself was sometimes the only family member to convert. Jan Firley's wife remained loyal to Catholicism and secretly taught the faith to the children.[25] Together with the political weaknesses that hamstrung the movement's ability to take secure root in Poland's cities, the result was that even where Protestant churches were numerous, few were probably very large. Despite the movement's success in winning converts within the upper ranks of the political class and the substantial number of Reformed churches established in the sixteenth century, it is likely the faith remained restricted to a fairly small percentage of the population. Such lack of social depth would make the cause vulnerable to erosion in later generations.

HUNGARY

Hungary shared many of the characteristics of Poland and Lithuania, including the same ruling house of Jagiellon from 1490 to 1526; but the crushing defeat of its last Jagiellon monarch by the Ottomans at Mohács caused the Reformation to unfold here amid circumstances that were far more favorable to its diffusion. Like the Polish-Lithuanian Commonwealth, Hungary was a multiethnic, multilingual kingdom, a mosaic of Magyars and Slovaks, Vlachs and Croats, Saxons and Szeklers. German speakers abounded in the privileged towns. In the eastern voivodship "beyond the forests," Transylvania, Orthodox Christians lived alongside the dominant Latin Christian groups. Also like Poland-Lithuania, Hungary's economy was built overwhelmingly around the production and export of agricultural commodities, in this case primarily live-

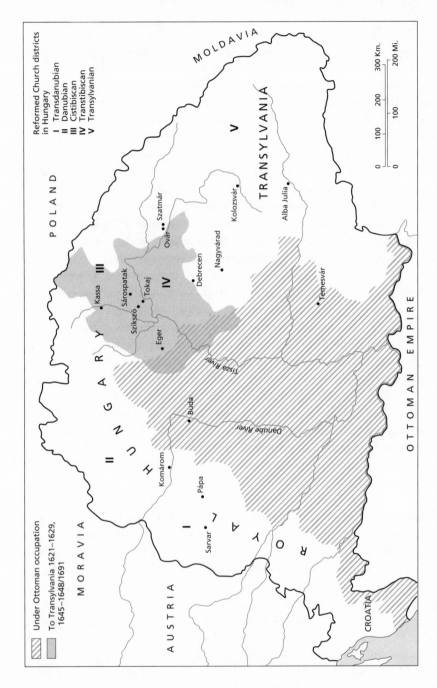

Reformed Church districts
in Hungary
I   Transdanubian
II Danubian
III Cistibiscan
IV Transtibiscan
V   Transylvanian

Under Ottoman occupation

To Transylvania 1621–1629,
1645–1648/1691

MOLDAVIA

POLAND

TRANSYLVANIA

V

Szatmár

Óvár

Kolozsvár

Alba Julia

III

Sárospatak

Kassa

Tokaj

IV

Nagyvárad

Debrecen

Szikszó

Eger

Temesvár

Tisza River

HUNGARY

Buda

Danube River

II

Komárom

Pápa

ROYAL

I

Sarvar

MORAVIA

AUSTRIA

CROATIA

OTTOMAN EMPIRE

300 Km.

200 Mi.

200

100

100

100

0

0

Map 10. Hungary

stock and wine. Here, too, the growth of demand and the intensification of market relations sparked by the demographic expansion of the sixteenth century led the powerful nobility to extract growing quantities of forced labor from a largely subjugated peasantry. Still, substantial parts of the country, notably the livestock-raising areas of the central Hungarian plain and a few leading wine-producing areas, remained dominated by freeholding peasant proprietors and the privileged burghers of small agrotowns. Agrotowns and small mining settlements dominated the kingdom's urban hierarchy. Skilled craftsmen were even less numerous than in Poland, the cities smaller, and not one printing press was active in 1517. Hungary possessed a recognized university at Buda, but after that institution ceased to function following the Ottoman conquest, Hungarians of all stations seeking a higher education had no choice but to study abroad. Wittenberg, where more than a thousand Hungarians enrolled between 1522 and 1600, was one of the favored destinations.[26]

The Luther affair rapidly awakened the same excitement among the German speakers of Hungary's cities that it did in Polish Prussia, while early support within university and court circles gave it further strength. Simon Grynaeus, the talented young humanist who became caught up in the evangelical movement and ended his university career as a professor of theology at Basel, spent several years in Buda after being driven from Vienna in 1521 and was only the most prominent of the humanists around the royal court drawn to the movement. Even the young queen, Mary of Habsburg, found Luther's ideas plausible enough to entertain for more than a decade the possibility that they might be correct. During this time the chief tutor and advisor to the teenage Louis II was Georg of Brandenburg, whose personal enthusiasm for the emerging Protestant cause is attested by his prompt completion of one of the earliest territorial reformations following his inheritance of Brandenburg-Ansbach in 1527. But with the menace of the Ottoman armies looming across the border and the papacy championing Hungary's cause by subsidizing its defense and urging Christendom's rulers to assist it, the middling Magyar nobility saw dalliance with heresy as a political and moral danger to the kingdom's well-being—all the more so in that the movement appeared to be gaining support from the large and inevitably resented retinue of German knights who had taken up residence at the court of Louis II and Mary. Alarmed Diets passed strong measures against Lutheranism in 1523 and 1525, the latter instituting the death penalty for the offense. Grynaeus was forced to flee, and executions appear to have taken place.[27]

Then came Mohács. Among the thousands who perished before the smashing onslaught of the Ottoman *timariot* was King Louis II, who fell from his horse while fleeing the battle site and drowned in a marsh. Ferdinand of Habsburg and John Zápolyai both stepped forward to claim the throne, rival elections were held, and a succession struggle began that would breed intermittent conflict for decades. Ferdinand initially carried the field, but Zápolyai was able to turn to the sultan for support and to retain control of the southeastern portion of the kingdom as a tribute-paying vassal of the Porte. The sultan intervened anew following his death in 1541, captured Buda, and, after new campaigns between 1543 and 1545, organized direct Ottoman rule over the central Hungarian plain, while placing Transylvania under the infant John-Sigismund Zápolyai. For the next 150 years, Hungary would be divided into three portions roughly corresponding to preexisting economic and geographic divisions: Habsburg-controlled Royal Hungary, which curved in an arc inside the kingdom's western and northern borders from the Adriatic to the Transylvanian frontier and encompassed the chief mining centers and the areas of most intensive agriculture; Transylvania, which already had a high degree of autonomy and its own diet and now proclaimed its independence; and Ottoman Hungary, stretching across the livestock-raising central Hungarian plain. The borders between these regions remained contested and fluctuating, with constant skirmishing across them encouraging the proliferation of military men claiming noble status in the border towns.

The defeat at Mohács shattered Hungary's ecclesiastical hierarchy as well as its political unity. Seven of the kingdom's sixteen bishops perished in the melee.[28] Many of their sees remained unfilled, as powerful magnates took control of the temporal. Two Transylvanian bishoprics likewise remained unfilled after 1542 and 1556, the prince usurping their income. Not only was the church largely decapitated; in the central portions of the kingdom, much of the parish clergy fled before the Ottoman onslaught, leaving nearly four-fifths of the localities in Ottoman-controlled regions without parish priests.[29] Finally, the new rulers of the portions of the kingdom had neither the liberty nor the inclination to pursue the campaign against heresy. Ferdinand was so busy with his military campaigns that he had little time to concentrate on the problem of heresy within his lands. Furthermore, he depended heavily on Protestant support within the empire for tax revenue to help fight the Ottomans, which prompted him to favor negotiation over repression in dealing with the problem. The Ottoman authorities looked for religious leaders who might cooperate with them as they strove to organize their control over their recently conquered territories and stem the flight of the population from the region. They were thus prepared to give evangelical preachers a free hand to proselytize so long as they respected Ottoman authority. The papacy showed its support for Ferdinand by excommunicating the Zápolyais, which naturally guaranteed their hostility to Rome. Thus was ruptured the association between Catholicism and the defense of the national homeland that had led so many Magyar nobles initially to defend the Roman faith in the 1520s. On the contrary, many came in future generations to see the purification of the church from the corruption that had infected it over the centuries to be the way to counter the divine chastisement the Turks represented.[30]

Protestantism's growth in Hungary has yet to be explored by the kinds of detailed local studies that have so enriched our understanding of the Reformation in other countries over the past thirty years. Evidence about the subject comes primarily from the letters that local evangelists wrote to their counterparts outside the kingdom and from the surviving copies of the books that appeared from the evangelical printing presses making their appearance in the region from 1529 onward. Such evidence suggests that Protestant sentiments spread steadily and vigorously in the decades after Mohács, first among the aristocracy and in the predominantly German-speaking privileged cities and mining centers, then during the troubled 1540s into market towns and villages as well. Melanchthon's correspondents from this decade sent him such enthusiastic reports about the freedom afforded them to preach the Gospel and about their success in organizing churches that he entertained the possibility of moving to Hungary during the darkest days of the interim crisis if the situation deteriorated further. In the Ottoman-controlled regions, wandering preachers had a free hand. Mihály Sztárai (d. 1575), a Paduan-educated ex-Franciscan who was the chief evangelist of the western portion of Ottoman Hungary, reported to a Viennese correspondent in 1551 that he had been able to preach throughout the region for the previous seven years. In the process, he claimed, he and his fellows had founded some 120 congregations. In Royal Hungary and Transylvania, the Christian authorities placed slightly greater obstacles in the way of the movement. Matyás Dévai Biró (1500–45), educated at Cracow and Wittenberg, preached in Buda and Kassa in 1531, in the counties of Sárvár in 1536, in Szikszó in 1541, and on the lands of Gáspár Drágffy in the region of Szatmár and Szilágy around 1544–45, with periods of imprisonment and exile accounting for the intervals between these dates. Six or seven homegrown evangelists of this sort spread Protestant ideas widely in Christian as well as Ottoman Hungary. Links to printing shops amplified the importance of certain of them, for example, Gál Huszár (1512–75), a man of uncertain educational formation who not only preached and ministered across much of northern Hungary between 1554 and 1575, but also oversaw a nomadic printing operation successively in Óvár, Kassa, and Debrecen that published both his sermons and others' works of edification and polemic. In all, five evangelical presses are known to have been opened in Hungary, producing by 1571 roughly 160 devotional and satirical works of a Protestant character. Noble converts patronized the creation of Protestant schools, as the count of Temes did in Temesvár between 1547 and his death in 1550. By the late 1540s, the movement was strong enough that when Ferdinand I tendered new laws against heresy in the wake of Charles V's victory at Mühlberg and during a lull in the battle against the Ottomans, pro-Lutheran sentiment was powerful enough in the Diet that sanctions were decreed only against sacramentarians and Anabaptists.[31]

Although noble support was often crucial to the movement's success, many nobles did not use their extensive rights of patronage to impose clergymen who shared their opinions, instead allowing their tenants a measure of autonomy. In many, if not most, of the locales where transformations of worship along Protestant lines were introduced, breakaway churches were not formed; instead, clergymen simply changed the form of the services within the parish church. Much of the clergy in place appears to have been inclined to accept some alteration of the liturgy, an end to clerical celibacy, and other reforms. When this did not come about from within the Catholic church, many abandoned their loyalty to Rome. Illustrative here is the biography of Andreas Dudith, a humanistically educated clerical diplomat who served as one of the Hungary's representatives at the Council of Trent, where he argued for the extension of the chalice to the laity. When the outcome of the council made it clear that reforms of the sort he desired would not be forthcoming, he resigned his bishopric and married. His later life was divided between diplomatic activity and scholarship in Poland and Silesia. He corresponded regularly with Beza even while conforming outwardly to the Lutheran church and inclining personally toward the anti-Trinitarianism of Biandrata.[32] Because there were relatively few religious houses in the country, there was also relatively little of the anticlericalism directed at idle monks and nuns of the sort that so often accompanied the Reformation elsewhere.

As the old episcopal structure of the Catholic church crumbled, a new framework of ecclesiastical organization rose from the rubble to take its place. A network of priestly fraternities covered Hungary at the end of the Middle Ages. These continued to meet as evangelical ideas spread, and they gradually mutated into ecclesiastical districts under clerical seniors. The districts in turn banded together in the Christian-controlled territories into six, later five, provinces, all but one of which were headed by elected superintendents generally accorded the title of bishop. By 1551, a church province with an elected superintendent or bishop had also formed in Ottoman Hungary (see map 10.) These ecclesiastical provinces formed the basic institutional units of most later Hungarian Protestant churches, of whatever confessional coloration they assumed.[33]

The theological influences shaping the early Hungarian reformation were multiple, often uncertain, and seasoned with a heavy dash of Erasmianism that led many to aim to avoid all narrow confessionalism. Much historical energy has been dedicated to determining the theological orientation of the prominent native spokesmen of the movement; the proposed solutions have not always generated universal assent. The close connections with Wittenberg meant that Lutheran and Philippist currents were powerful. The first essays to organize a Protestant church order on a regional scale, undertaken in the mid-1540s in the privileged Saxon towns of Transylvania, received Luther's direct approbation. Melanchthon carried on a copious correspondence with Hungary and frequently was able to place his protégés in ministerial or teaching positions. But Reformed ideas were also strong enough early on in the movement for a monitory letter of 1530 to name Oecolampadius and Zwingli as heretics to watch out for. Grynaeus sided with the Swiss once controversy broke out over the Eucharist. Students of his like the Transylvanian reformer Matyá Dévai Biró passed through Switzerland on their wanderings and later spread views denounced as sacramentarian. Even though the edict of 1548 condemned sacramentarian views but exempted Lutheranism from punishment, Reformed ideas gained ground in the 1550s. This was the period of Bullinger's most intense epistolary contact with Hungary, during which one of his extended letters of pastoral advice circulated so widely throughout the country that it was published in two localities in 1559, eight years after it was sent.[34]

Although many clergymen resisted the attempt to codify Christianity in strict formulae and would continue to do so for at least another generation, the law of 1548, by forbidding sacramentarianism, highlighted the issue of eucharistic doctrine and thus unleashed pressures toward confessionalization that would culminate by the end of the 1560s with Reformed doctrines being set as normative in several ecclesiastical districts. A canon in the town of Debrecen, Martin Sánta Kálmáncsehi, was denounced under the law for preaching sacramentarian ideas and was condemned in 1552 by a district synod of the Transtibiscan church province, in the northeast of the country. Kálmáncsehi's fate became caught up in one of the recurrent flare-ups of the long struggle between Habsburgs and Zápolyais. Initially protected by a local magnate, he was driven out of the region when Ferdinand's troops pushed into it. Three years later, as the military tide turned, he was able to return to Debrecen. He defended his views ably, and when an ecclesiastical synod gathered shortly thereafter, it was persuaded to adopt clearly Reformed eucharistic views and to choose Kálmáncsehi district superintendent. He was followed in this post in 1562 by Péter Méliusz Juhász, the leading defender of Reformed views of the subsequent generation. In 1567, a district synod in Debrecen definitively fixed a confession of a firmly Reformed cast and a system of church organization overseen by district superintendents. Debrecen's school added theological instruction in 1588 and would in time acquire the reputation of the Hungarian Geneva.

Driven out of Debrecen in 1553, Kálmáncsehi took refuge across the Transylvanian border in Kolozsvár, where he again began to preach. The Saxon clergy here cried, "Sacramentarian!" too, but with reinforcement from Méliusz, enough of the Magyar-speaking clergy were won over to his views for the church to divide essentially along ethnic lines in 1563–64. The Magyar-speaking ministers elected a new superintendent/bishop, Francis Dávid, and hastily adopted Beza's confession of faith and the Heidelberg Catechism. Confessional conflict likewise spread to the Cistibiscan church province to the north, where it touched off fighting between partisans of the divergent orientations in the militarized region near the Ottoman border. The soldiers, nobles, and townsmen of the region gathered in the fortress town of Eger swore an oath of loyalty to a Debrecen confession of faith in 1561 in a manner akin to the almost contemporaneous covenanting of noble partisans of the cause at the other end of the continent in Scotland. Over the next five years, synods of this district adopted Beza's confession, Calvin's catechism, and a system of church discipline controlled by the superintendents, although a breakaway minority pledged its loyalty to the Augsburg Confession. Confessionalization would not occur in the western portions of Habsburg Hungary for another generation, until the Lutheran crusade against crypto-Calvinism within the empire spilled across the border between 1591 and 1595 and prompted the establishment of distinct Lutheran and Reformed churches in both the Transdanubian and Danubian church districts. In Ottoman Hungary, the cause of church reform assumed an overwhelmingly Reformed tint early on and never gave rise to comparable struggles between partisans of different eucharistic positions.

The confessional battles in the east were further complicated in 1563 by the arrival of the anti-Trinitarian Biandrata at the Transylvanian capital of Alba Julia, where he became court physician to John Sigismund's new Polish wife, Isabella Jagiellon. Biandrata won over the local bishop Dávid, and the main body of Transylvania's fledgling Reformed movement veered toward Arianism. From Debrecen, Méliusz rallied support against Dávid. He launched a stream of polemical writings intended to rebut anti-Trinitarian ideas and spearheaded the assembly of a joint synod of the Transylvanian and Ottoman churches in 1566, followed by a great disputation in 1568. Far from healing the rift, however, the disputation convinced John Sigismund of the rightness of Dávid and the anti-Trinitarians. He embraced their viewpoint, and for a brief period until his death in 1571, Transylvania became the only country in European history ever governed simultaneously by an anti-Trinitarian bishop and an anti-Trinitarian prince. Anti-Trinitarianism also made inroads in both the Transtibiscan district and Ottoman Hungary, where one remarkable disputation in 1574 pitted Reformed and anti-Trinitarian champions who agreed in advance that whoever was judged to present the weaker case would be put to death—as was duly done.[35]

Amid these doctrinal quarrels, the Transylvanian diet adopted an exceptionally broad regime of religious toleration. Measures enacted between 1557 and 1571 extended rights of worship alongside those of Roman Catholicism to the Religion of Kolozsvár (the Reformed), the Religion of Szeben (Lutheranism), and the Creed of Francis Dávid (anti-Trinitarianism). Each congregation obtained the right to retain the services of any preacher of whose doctrine they approved, thereby effectively annulling the power of the church superintendent and instituting a legally protected system of congregational autonomy.[36]

In the Habsburg-controlled portions of Hungary, no formalization of Protestant rights of worship seemed necessary for most of the century, for after the short-lived effort of the late 1540s to outlaw sacramentarian and Anabaptist ideas, successive Habsburg rulers all but abandoned the repression of heresy. This changed dramatically in 1599, however, when a palace revolution encouraged by the papal nuncio at the court of the moody Emperor Rudolf II carried a set of strongly Catholic advisors into the imperial council. Habsburg armies were then at the height of their success in still another war with the Ottomans, the "long Turkish War" of 1593–1606. Having gained military control of Transylvania, the Habsburg administration proclaimed the legal reannexation of the territory in 1602, confiscated the lands of Protestant nobles, and restored Protestant churches to Catholic use. In Royal Hungary, an imperial right to decide the religious affiliation of the royal free towns was asserted, church buildings under Protestant control were confiscated, and Catholic priests were installed. These policies so alienated Protestant noblemen throughout Hungary that they provoked the rebellion of Stephen Bocskai and caused the reconquest of Transylvania to unravel. By the Peace of Vienna (1606), which ended the conflicts, the Habsburgs agreed to recognize the freedom of noblemen, burghers, and soldiers serving in border garrisons to worship as they pleased within Royal Hungary "so long as this does not harm the Catholic religion"—a disturbingly vague qualification that was removed at the diet of 1608. This diet also won Protestant peasants the right to worship as they chose, even if their landowner was Catholic.[37]

By this point, a clear majority of the population had become Protestants of one sort or another. All but three of the approximately three dozen magnates who sat in the upper house of the Hungarian Diet were Protestant. The most recent estimates of the population as a whole, extrapolating from what is known about the number of churches controlled by the respective confessions, place the percentage of Protestants within a total population of approximately four million people (Croatia excepted) at 75 to 80 percent. With more than two thousand churches, the Reformed composed the largest group, accounting for perhaps 40 to 45 percent of the population. Just as the faith had taken root in the Scottish highlands, so here it claimed the allegiance even of the shepherds of the mountain valleys on the Transylvanian border who lived in extended families headed by a paterfamilias who was at once judge and religious leader. The Saxon towns of Transylvania and the German- and Slovak-speaking regions of Habsburg Hungary were the strongholds of the Augsburg Confession, which claimed roughly a quarter of the population. What remained was divided among Unitarianism, Orthodoxy, and Roman Catholicism. This last had eroded to a tiny remnant except in Croatia, its ultimate bastion. According to a report sent to Rome by an apostolic nuncio, barely three hundred clergymen in all Hungary remained loyal to the Catholic church. Whereas there had been seventy Franciscan houses with fifteen hundred brothers in 1500, there now were just five houses with thirty residents.[38]

That individual Reformed church districts adopted such documents as Calvin's catechism, the Second Helvetic Confession and the Heidelberg Catechism reveals the essential doctrinal agreement between the Hungarian churches and their Reformed counterparts to the west. The style of worship varied from region to region. In the Transtibiscan district, Ludwig Lavater's *Rites and Institutions of the Zurich Church* (1559), written expressly to assist the Hungarians in setting up their church, guided the transformation of the liturgy. The churches were stripped of their images and altars; clerical vestments were eliminated; and the number of holidays was reduced to six. The Reformed churches of the western districts retained more Catholic elements in worship.[39] Church discipline was enough of an issue that from relatively early on Bucer declared amid otherwise pessimistic remarks about this topic in his *De Regno Christi* (1550) that in Hungary "there are now quite a number of churches which accept a solid Christian discipline along with a pure Christian doctrine and observe it religiously." The initiative for instituting disciplinary cases lay with the parish ministers or with bishop/superintendents carrying out ecclesiastical visitations; there were no elders. The secular authorities also had a role to play. In cities under Turkish rule, punishments were administered by the kadi, in Habsburg-ruled territories by the local lords, and in parts of Transylvania by the bailiff.[40] That Hungary's Reformed churches had been organized according to a variant chronology and pattern in each church district thus meant that in parts of the country the reformation of worship was less thorough than was the norm among Reformed churches, while the institutions of the church owed little to the example of either Geneva or the presbyterial-synodal model as it unfolded in western Europe. As in England, but at a still later date, agitation would be felt to reform these institutions further in accordance with these models.

CONCLUSION TO PART II

The Reformed Churches
at the End of the Sixteenth Century

The expansion of Reformed churches across Europe during the second half of the sixteenth century was nothing short of remarkable. In 1554, regularly assembling, legally sanctioned Reformed churches could be found only in parts of Switzerland and its affiliated territories and in a few localities within the Holy Roman Empire. At that date, as yet legally unsanctioned congregations were beginning to multiply in Little Poland and Lithuania, and the worship of some Hungarian parishes was coming to assume a clearly Reformed cast. Elsewhere, the cause was simply an unorganized current of heterodoxy—troubling to the Catholic authorities, to be sure, and increasingly influential within secret evangelical circles in many areas, but more a vision of how European religious life might be transformed than a set of churches and a body of believers dedicated to actualizing that vision. By 1600 it had become such a body of believers across Europe from Britain to Transylvania. The established churches of Scotland, England, Béarn, and roughly a dozen German principalities were all now Reformed. So, too, was the legally privileged church of the by-now effectively independent United Provinces of the Netherlands. Large networks of legally tolerated minority Reformed churches existed in France, Hungary, Poland-Lithuania, and the Rhineland. In all, perhaps ten million people worshiped in Reformed churches in 1600, whereas scarcely half a million had done so in 1554. If the great bloc of Lutheran state churches across north Germany and Scandinavia meant that the Reformed still may not have equaled the Lutherans in raw demographic strength, their political and cultural significance for the continent as a whole was at least comparable. A half century earlier, their relative political weakness had been palpable.

As part II has shown, the dramatic expansion of Reformed churches in the second half of the sixteenth century did not follow a single course across Europe. In some areas, the churches established themselves in defiance of the law, then triumphed or gained legal toleration thanks to their own activism and support from powerful members of the political nation. In these areas, the success of the Reformed cause can be attributed to its mass appeal, to its proclivity to galvanize and give shape to the growing dissatisfaction with the Roman church aroused by evangelical propaganda of all stripes, and to its organizational features that facilitated mobilization and self-defense. In other areas, the ruling political authorities willingly embraced Reformed doctrine and altered the territorial church accordingly. Here, the cause's success can be attributed to its persuasiveness to conscientious Christian rulers and their key theological advisors in instances in which the primary exposure of these men to Protestant ideas was to those emanating from Zurich, Geneva, and Strasbourg, or where their initial education and early experience placed them at some distance from strict Lutheran orthodoxy.

Just as the manner by which Europe's Reformed churches came to be established varied, so too did their character. Each national confession of faith had its nuances and points of emphasis. The Scottish and Dutch churches identified discipline as one of the marks of the true church, but the French mentioned only doctrine purely taught and the sacraments properly administered. The Belgic and French confessions of faith included lucid statements of double predestination; the Heidelberg Catechism avoided the question. The Scots insisted on the obligation of rulers to uproot idolatry and on the perennial conflict between Christ's church and the devil. Worship likewise varied. The English knelt to receive communion from a surplice-wearing minister; the French filed by their minister, who was dressed in a simple gown; the Dutch and Scots sat at a table as the elders passed around the bread and wine. While the Scots uncompromisingly eliminated all holy days, they continued to abstain from meat on Fridays and from marrying during Lent. The latter was an English practice as well, but most Reformed churches eliminated all required fast days or closed periods for marriage.

Already at midcentury, Zurich, Geneva, and Emden offered differing models of church government. As churches became established in a wide range of territories with a great variety of government systems and social structures, by means ranging from princely *diktat* to armed insurrection, the diversity of systems of church government increased. Two forces counteracted this tendency to a degree. First, many Reformed churches were shaped in direct imitation of neighboring churches by people who had learned about the institutions of a properly reformed church in exile. Second, a number of Reformed theologians articulated ever more detailed programs of the specific ecclesiastical institutions they believed the Bible mandated. Nearly half a century after Oecolampadius had discerned a scriptural basis for a system of ecclesiastical excommunication such as that Calvin succeeded in introducing into Geneva, and four decades after Bucer had found in Scripture evidence of certain essential church offices that Calvin systematized into the doctrine of the fourfold ministry, Beza, Melville, and Cartwright together built a case for the biblical foundations of the presbyterian-synodal system of church governance. This became an appealing program for recasting existing church formats to those convinced that the survival of bishops impeded the realization of their fullest hopes for reform. While these forces moderated the tendency of church institutions to vary from locality to locality, they could not prevent a wide range of systems from evolving.

Although the presbyterian-synodal system ultimately came to be justified in biblical terms, it began as an improvised solution to the problem of maintaining unity among scattered congregations established without government support, and it operated somewhat differently in each country. The system could function either independently or with some measure of governmental control and participation. Power and authority flowed both upward and downward. The individual churches delegated lay and clerical representatives to the regional assemblies, which in turn dispatched representatives to the assemblies above them. The larger regional and national assemblies then determined the principles according to which the local churches were to operate, specifying the boundaries of permissible variation in doctrine and worship, vetting ministerial candidates, and overseeing the exercise of parish discipline and the behavior of the ministry. The exact hierarchy of assemblies and their precise powers were not specified at the first French national synod of 1559, at which the system first was outlined. In two provinces close to Switzerland, Languedoc and Dauphiné, institutions directly borrowed from the Vaudois church order briefly took shape, notably a hierarchy of colloquies and classes, with the classes led by elected deans. The system that finally prevailed throughout France consisted of a four-step hierarchy of assemblies running from the local consistories through colloquies and provincial synods up to national synods. This structure served as the template for the other large west European territorial churches that adopted a similar system—Scotland, the Netherlands, Béarn, the Rhineland, and Nassau and the Wetterau Counties—as well as for the proposed revision of England's church order that was defeated in the 1580s. As table 9.1 shows, the names given to the cognate

TABLE 9.1

The Hierarchy of Assemblies in Reformed Churches with Presbyterian-Synodal Features

Pays de Vaud	Grisons	France	Netherlands	Scotland	Nassau & Wetterau Counties	Poland
Consistory (after 1558)	consistory (develops slowly)	consistory	*kerkeraad*	kirk session	presbyterium	
Colloquy	colloquy (later 16th century)	colloquy	classis	presbytery	*klassen-konvent*	particular synod
Classis		provincial synod	provincial or particular synod	synod	provincial or regional synod	district synod
				provincial assembly		provincial synod
Synod	synod	national synod	national synod	General Assembly	general synod	general synod

church bodies often varied confusingly from territory to territory, but most of these churches had the same four levels of assemblies.

Examination of the surviving records of these bodies shows that, while each level of assembly exercised roughly comparable duties, noteworthy disparities also emerged. In France, where the local churches were the building blocks of the system and colloquies did not begin to assemble regularly in some areas until the 1580s, the colloquies did little other than serve as occasions for ministerial exercises, solve minor conflicts between or within local churches, and adjudicate issues of pastoral appointments. The consistories, by contrast, assumed financial responsibilities that their counterparts in the Netherlands or Scotland did not have, since France's was a minority church that depended primarily upon internal fund-raising mechanisms, not benefices or government payments, to remunerate its ministers. In Holland, on the other hand, the classes took shape in many areas before ministers could be found for all rural parishes, and *kerkeraads* were even slower to be formed in many localities. Hence the classes became the linchpin of the church edifice, taking the lead in appointing ministers to many rural churches, electing visitors from their ranks to carry out parish visitations, and hearing difficult discipline cases. Dordrecht's classis even set up a standing committee to handle business that arose between its regular meetings. Scotland's presbyteries were equally central cogs in its church system, even if they were relieved of a part of their power of parochial visitation and ministerial appointment by the strengthening of bishops in the early seventeenth century. They handled the more serious discipline cases, pronounced sentences of excommunication, and, instead of meeting quarterly or twice yearly like the other assemblies of the same level, met every week or two.[1] Scotland's church was slightly dissimilar to the other synodally organized ones in two additional regards: (1) a fifth sort of assembly variously bringing together the bishops, clergy, and presbyterial representatives from an archiepiscopal province is known to have met a few times between 1612 and 1627, although no minutes of these meetings have survived and little is known about them; and (2) the delegates to its General Assemblies were chosen through processes comparable to parliamentary selection from among the groups represented in Parliament (the clergy, the barons, and the burgh commissioners), rather than being assigned by the provincial synods or assemblies.[2]

To the east, in Poland and Hungary, another kind of synodally organized church developed independently of the west European model. A hierarchy of area, district, and national synods ordered these churches, but they lacked parish-level consistorial assemblies. In both, as in Scotland, the existence of the office of superintendent or bishop also meant that important elements of top-down control existed alongside the collegial decision making ensured by

the hierarchy of synods. The superintendents of the Polish church were originally elected for life by the ministers of each district; in 1573, their terms were
shortened to run from synod to synod. While exercising a regular ministry
in one location, they convened district synods, visited the churches of their
jurisdiction, and helped approve new ministers. The Hungarian superintendents or bishops had similar powers but seem not have exercised a parish
ministry as well. They were selected by the district synods with major input
from powerful aristocratic patrons. The Hungarian church also retained archdeacons, who oversaw smaller territorial units with powers of visitation and
correction over the parish clergy.[3] In Scotland, the superintendents created
by the First Book of Discipline soon disappeared, but the revival of episcopal
authority promoted by James VI and I engendered a new mix of ascending and
descending principles of governance. Between 1606 and 1610, the bishops became the constant moderators of the presbyteries in their jurisdiction, took
over from the presbyteries much of the power to ratify candidates presented
to benefices, became the regular visitors of the parish churches in lieu of the
presbyterially appointed commissioners and visitors of the kirk who had been
instituted in 1593, and gained the power to approve all sentences of excommunication.[4]

Still different, and still more hierarchical, systems of church governance
prevailed in England and the Reformed churches of the larger German territories that implemented second reformations. Hesse-Kassel is a well-studied
example of such a church. Church policy here was determined by the *Konsistorium*, an administrative council presided over by the duke himself. This
body appointed the superintendents and, beneath them, "metropolitans" who
carried out the day-to-day oversight of the church and undertook parish visitations. Several levels of synods and classical assemblies also existed, but
these were strictly clerical, convened and run by the superintendents and
metropolitans as instruments of ministerial oversight and amelioration.[5] The
Church of England, of course, was unlike all of the other churches in retaining a virtually Catholic form of ecclesiastical organization, even as it entered
theological communion with the Reformed churches. Here, the full hierarchy
of secular clerical offices, including bishops, archdeacons, deacons, prebends,
and parish clergy, survived. Pre-Reformation church courts and the preexisting system of benefices did likewise. Individual bishops had to define as they
saw fit the proper balance between their traditional role as diocesan administrators and political figures in Parliament with newer Protestant conceptions
of their pastoral obligations. As a broad generalization, it can be said that
the more the establishment of any given Reformed church depended upon
princely initiative, the stronger episcopal or other descending systems of
church authority were likely to remain within it. Still, there were exceptions

to this rule because the rulers of Béarn and a few small German territories surrendered control over most of the operations of their churches to a network of synods, thereby demonstrating the influence of regionally prestigious models and theologians within small territories. The more the founding of any given church depended upon the initiative of either princes or the city councils of free imperial cities, the less likely it was as well to include a system of discipline by lay elders or a consistory. Yet, again, exceptions should be noted: the Palatine church joined Béarn, Nassau-Dillenburg, and the Wetterau counties in allowing consistorial discipline within a church of princely creation, while the Hungarian Reformed churches, wherein Genevan influence was weak, did not name parish elders and depended for moral oversight on the ministers or on parochial visitations by the superintendents.

To a few precise Englishmen, the absence of a proper system of consistorial discipline and the use of liturgical practices lacking explicit scriptural sanction so blemished a church that separation from it was required, but this was emphatically a minority view. By far the greatest number of Reformed churchmen persisted in emphasizing that local variations in worship and government were permitted and should not be grounds for destroying the fellowship among all true churches. As William Bradshaw wrote in 1606, "All Churches and all members of the Church, in what Country so ever they be, are not to be acounted Forreyners one to another, because they are all Citizens of heaven, and we all make one family or body."[6]

The solidarity among the various Reformed churches was expressed in several ways. One was mutual aid in times of affliction. When the duke of Savoy mounted a campaign to retake Geneva in 1589–93, collections to raise funds for the defense of the besieged city were organized in Scotland, England, France, Bohemia, Poland, and Hungary—including by some Lutheran and anti-Trinitarian congregations in eastern Europe. The elector Palatine, the count of Wittgenstein, and the estates of Holland, Friesland, and East Friesland, also sent funds, as did private residents of Frankfurt and several Swiss cities. Some of those who aided may have recalled Geneva's own earlier charitable collections for those seeking to leave the Palatinate following the Lutheran restoration of 1577 and for the brethren of Montpellier stricken by plague and famine in 1580. When funds were lacking, prayer might help. The Church of Scotland ordered a fast day to be held in 1595 to implore God's protection against "the barbarous crueltie and great bondage exercised and brought upon our dear and worthie brethren . . . specially in Poland, England, Saxonie, and diverse parts of Germanie."[7]

Plenty of raw human mobility also wove the disparate Reformed churches into a larger international community. During the troubled years of the sixteenth century, many leading ministers were cast by events from country to country. A vivid example is that of Jean Taffin, one of the most eminent devotional authors of the late sixteenth century. Born in Tournai, Taffin initially entered the service of Cardinal Granvelle, but was drawn to the Reformed cause after being assigned the task of judging the soundness of books suspected of containing heretical ideas. He briefly assisted the young church under the cross in Antwerp before going to Strasbourg and Geneva to complete his preparation for the ministry. After serving the refugee church in Aachen for a year, he was called to the important church of Metz, the erstwhile free imperial city recently come under the protection of the French crown. He ministered there until the Wonderyear, when he hastened back to Antwerp. The high hopes of that year soon gave way to a bitter period of reversals. After Marguerite of Parma shut down the church in Antwerp, he had to return to Metz, only to see Metz's church in turn outlawed and closed during France's Third Civil War in 1569. Heidelberg offered him refuge for several years; there he wrote his most important book, *Of the Marks of the Children of God, and of their Comfort in Afflictions,* which exhorted believers to persevere in the open profession of their faith no matter what reverses might shake their assurance. In 1574 he returned to the maelstrom of the Netherlands to become William of Orange's chaplain and was able to serve William for nearly a decade, until the prince's assassination. He then returned to Antwerp to serve that church once again, but this stint lasted no longer than the previous ones, for within a year of his arrival Antwerp fell to the duke of Parma. Like many others of its inhabitants, he then headed north, served as pastor of the Walloon church of Haarlem, and finally moved to Amsterdam in 1587, where he was able to live in peace for fifteen years before dying in 1602.[8] Even after most of Europe's Reformed churches settled into relatively undisrupted operation during the first decades of the seventeenth century, the movement of ministers and theologians across national boundaries continued. No fewer than nine of the twenty professors who taught at the Reformed academy of Saumur between 1599 and 1625 came from outside France. In the second quarter of the seventeenth century, when Leiden was the largest and most prestigious university in the Protestant world, more than half of its students hailed from beyond the Netherlands: 3,016 from war-torn Germany, 672 from England, 621 from Scotland, 434 from France, 354 from Poland, and 231 from Hungary.[9]

Finally, the divers Reformed churches demonstrated their solidarity by consulting with one another about theological questions, confirming one another's confessions of faith, and attempting to draft documents that could indicate the fundamental consensus among them. Sharing so similar and uncertain a history during the later sixteenth century, the Reformed churches of France and the Netherlands forged particularly close links. After the synod of

Emden in 1571 approved the French as well as the Belgic confession of faith for use in the churches of the Low Countries, the French churches reciprocated at their national synod of 1579 by approving the Belgic confession. Several Dutch clergy attended the French national synod of 1583, where both churches promised mutual assistance in time of need. It was decided even that each would henceforth send deputies to the national synods of the other, although this failed to materialize.[10] On matters of doctrine, both churches consulted more widely yet. When the French national synod of 1598 took up the controversial theses of one of its ministers, it invited the churches of Bern, Zurich, Schaffhausen, Heidelberg, the Hague, and Amsterdam to send representatives. A subsequent French national synod, having condemned several theses on justification of Herborn's Johann Piscator, wrote to the universities of England, Scotland, Sedan, Geneva, Basel, Heidelberg, and Herborn asking them to join in this condemnation. The synod of Dordrecht that would gather in the Netherlands in 1618 to resolve the great Arminian controversy (see below) would include attendees from England, Scotland, Geneva, Basel, Bern, Schaffhausen, Zurich, and many of the German Reformed territories; no French delegates attended only because the crown forbade their participation.[11] The exclusion of the Hungarians and Poles from these theological consultations is noteworthy. Lacking prestigious universities, the Reformed churches of these countries evidently stood in a semiperipheral relation to their sister churches to the west.

The most vital attempt to demonstrate the essential doctrinal unity and political solidarity of the Reformed churches during the latter part of the sixteenth century came in the face of the Lutheran efforts in Germany to promote the Formula of Concord. In response, John Casimir of the Palatinate and Wilhelm of Hesse convoked representatives of the churches of France, Hungary, Poland, and the Low Countries as well as delegates of the English crown, the prince of Condé, and the king of Navarre to a gathering at Frankfurt in 1577. After initially assigning Zanchi and Ursinus the task of drawing up a confession of faith to rebut the Flaccians, the representatives of the various churches and individuals decided simply to underscore how many churches espoused the same, nonubiquitarian doctrines. The result was the *Harmony of Confessions,* published in Geneva in 1581, in which the articles of eleven confessions of faith were arrayed under a series of headings to highlight their numerous points of agreement. The tract incorporated not only such leading Reformed statements as the Basel Confession of 1534, the First and Second Helvetic Confessions, the French and Belgic Confessions, and the Thirty-Nine Articles, but also the Augsburg and Tetrapolitan Confessions, the confession of the Czech Brethren, and the Saxon and Württemberg confessions of 1551–52. This document was formally approved by the churches of France, the Low

Countries, and Bremen. At the same time its attempt to proclaim the unity of these churches contained a measure of pious hope. The English authorities refused to approve the vernacular translation of the *Harmony* published in 1586 because a number of its glosses proclaimed that discipline was properly in the hands of presbyteries or consistories. The Czech Brethren were miffed that their confession was included without their permission.[12]

As this episode illustrates, the boundaries of the Reformed community were fuzzy around the edge, and there were limits to Reformed solidarity. The inclusion of the Augsburg, Saxon, and Württemberg confessions in the *Harmony of Confessions* was just one example of the conviction of many Reformed that the bonds of brotherhood ought to encompass the Lutheran churches as well. Those who had taken part in Lutheran services were allowed to attend the Lord's Supper at Geneva without undergoing the rite of public contrition required of those who had attended a Catholic mass; and the French Reformed decided in 1631 to admit visiting Lutherans to their communion services without impediment, asserting that the churches of the Augsburg Confession agree with "the other Reformed churches" on the fundamental points of true religion. A Haarlem minister spoke in 1615 of "the Reformed churches, as in France, Switzerland, England, Scotland, Denmark, Sweden, in the Palatinate, in Hesse, at Geneva and elsewhere," a list, it will be noted, that included the Lutheran states of Scandinavia but not the German states that had accepted the Formula of Concord—and that also excluded once again the Reformed churches of eastern Europe. While these actions or assertions bespoke a broad definition of Reformed fellowship, when it came to theological consultations, the French, Dutch, and Swiss sought the advice only of what Geneva's Company of Pastors called at one point "the orthodox universities of Germany," that is, those that fit a narrow definition of proper Reformed doctrine.[13]

Attachment to the Reformed cause also did not dictate a single course of political action as the sixteenth century drew to a close. "Political Calvinism," the apocalyptically tinged belief that only a foreign policy dedicated wholeheartedly to the defense of Protestantism could save the true faith from the machinations of the Roman enemy, shaped the world view of such leading ministers of state as the earl of Leicester in England, Christian of Anhalt in Germany, and Philippe du Plessis-Mornay in France.[14] It helped shape foreign policy decisions at key moments, as when Queen Elizabeth sent aid to the Dutch rebels in the 1580s and again, more disastrously, when Frederick V of the Palatinate accepted the offer of the Bohemian crown in 1618 and touched off the Thirty Years' War. Because of the force of this world view, Reformed princes were more inclined to involve themselves in Protestant–Catholic religious struggles around 1600 than were their Lutheran counterparts. Still, for every Frederick V who took up the calling he believed God had placed upon him to fight for the Protestant faith, there was a James VI and I, who resisted the call and worked for peace.[15] The endeavors of the political Calvinists to make international Protestant solidarity the keystone of foreign policy were limited by most contemporary policy makers' recognition that a complex mixture of dynastic, strategic, and religious factors shaped the behavior of their rivals and ought to shape theirs as well. International Reformed solidarity could not efface dynastic and national rivalry, any more than could Catholic or Lutheran.

Although the numerous Reformed churches established across Europe thus displayed significant differences of worship and church government, although Reformed rulers viewed the world of international politics in more than one way, and although the very term *Reformed church* was infused with ambiguities around 1600, the sense of fellowship and solidarity among these churches was powerful. They shared personnel, eucharistic fellowship, and crucial elements of political outlook; they consulted with one another on issues of doctrine; and they offered one another their prayers and financial solidarity in time of need. The events of the next century would test that solidarity.

PART III

The Transformations of a Tradition

Religious traditions present themselves as expressions of timeless verities, but they never cease to change, both as the world around them changes and as a result of their internal tensions. Although biographers of Calvin often end their accounts of his life with broader reflections on Calvinism's historical significance and contemporary meaning—as if whatever they understand by this -ism had disclosed its full potentialities and assumed its mature shape by the time of his death—many of the doctrines and practices that later generations have commonly associated with Calvinism and that would most profoundly shape the experience and aspirations of those raised within different strands of the mature Reformed tradition in fact were forged after the great reformer's death. The high predestinarian orthodoxy encapsulated in the acronym TULIP, the disciplined pious praxis of the Puritan way of godliness, and the militant covenanting defense of a self-governing church with no king but Christ are just some of the elements of the Reformed tradition that originated in this period. The generations from 1590 to 1700 were profoundly creative ones.

Many of the changes of this era arose out of the internal dynamics of the tradition's development. We have already seen how, at certain moments in the movement's early history, the course of events drew attention to questions that had not previously been perceived and sparked intense debate about them, for example, the question of whether or not a Reformed church could have bishops. As the various national churches passed from being insurgent causes to settled institutions and grappled with the problem of transmitting their doctrines to upcoming generations in as coherent and efficient a manner as possible, the discovery of new conundrums and new points of contention intensified. Positions first articulated in constant dialogue with the Bible and with strong doses of ecclesiastic polemic and moral critique now had to become system. The tools of formal logic that had seemed so useful for this purpose to the medieval scholastics but that the early reformers had rejected as alien to Scripture now came back into vogue. The need to instill a rationalized system of orthodoxy ended up altering the manner in which doctrine was presented, highlighting new problems and generating new debates. The matter of predestination proved particularly contentious. A series of synods and creeds from 1618 to 1675 sought to resolve these debates. What they accomplished above all else was to produce ever more detailed systems of orthodoxy that might temporarily quiet debate in a given region but rarely lasted for long without being contested anew.

Although powerful, the impulses that encouraged neo-scholasticism and the systematization of orthodoxy could never entirely overwhelm countervailing impulses toward a humanist, historicizing biblicism. These were embedded in the Reformed tradition from the outset because so many of its great theologians of the first generations had initially been humanists, because instruction in the three biblical languages quickly became a staple of Reformed higher education, and because the great early histories of the cause tended to trace the origins of the Reformation back to the humanist recovery of the original biblical text. First weakening as neo-scholasticism advanced, these impulses gained new vigor as a result of technical advances in biblical philology in the seventeenth century. As this occurred, the world of the Old Testament came to seem increasingly distant and historically alien to that fraction of Reformed theologians whose thought was shaped by these currents. The powerful sense of identification with ancient Israel weakened. At the same time, new philosophical currents challenged the tools and categories of Aristotelian thought that were so important to scholasticism. No sooner had orthodoxy been defined than it began to unravel under the twin challenges of biblical scholarship and the new philosophy. A new theological rationalism was reshaping Reformed doctrine in many regions by the end of the seventeenth century.

Other changes arose out of the tensions that came to exist in parts of the Reformed world between the institutions established at their first reformation and the ideal model of a scripturally reformed church articulated by successive generations of Reformed theologians. English churchmen aspiring to a thoroughgoing reformation of life felt keenly their lack of a church- or parish-based system of discipline on either the Genevan or Zurich models. As it became apparent toward the end of the sixteenth century that efforts to alter the church's institutions were not going to bear immediate fruit, some began to elaborate voluntary techniques for promoting moral improvement and a life of personal devotion. Hungarian churchmen were likewise troubled by episcopalian survivals and the absence of parish-based discipline in their church. Dutch *dominees* were upset by their limited influence on public affairs. Campaigns for further reformation arose within these churches, drawing heavily upon English inspiration. It was in the midst of one of these campaigns that Hoornbeeck coined the tag, "The Reformed church always reforming."[1]

External political events prompted still other changes. These were of three sorts. First, where churches existed in a situation of de jure or de facto religious pluralism, the attitude of the ruling authorities toward them had a great effect on their size and internal evolution. The Dutch and Transylvanian churches, which enjoyed a favored political status, gained members. Under such protection, individuals within the churches who believed the initial reformation had fallen short of its goals were encouraged to mount campaigns for further change. Where Catholicism remained the royal religion, notably in France, Hungary, and Poland-Lithuania, the footing of the Reformed churches grew ever more precarious. Only a few lonely voices upheld religious toleration as a positive ideal in this period. With most of Europe's rulers commanding greater resources and larger and more powerful armies, the Catholic rulers could take bolder measures to win over the Reformed, ranging from granting Catholics preferment at court to revoking outright legal toleration of the Reformed faith. When toleration was revoked, the members of the churches had to face stark choices: convert? emigrate? or resist? Even while legally protected by a royal grant of toleration, the churches rarely had the luxury of pursuing internal disagreements or programs of further reform to the point of open division.

Second, the winds of religious change switched direction about 1590 and began to blow toward Rome. The lure of Catholic thrones, the force of educations received in Catholic courts, and the appeal of the Roman church's combination of tradition, hierarchy, and splendor to an age that prized baroque display all tempted Protestant rulers and great nobles to convert. About a half dozen small principalities that were entirely Reformed by law at the beginning of the period passed under Catholic or Lutheran control between 1590 and 1700. In some of these cases, the new Catholic or Lutheran rulers decreed toleration for their faith and thus set the scene for their subjects to choose the church in which they wished to worship. In others they worked for the elimination of the Reformed church. In either event, these changes tested the loyalty of those who were members of the Reformed churches, just as the actions of the Catholic rulers of Poland, Hungary, and France had. The response in these various cases would vary considerably depending upon how the churches had been set up to begin with, the social composition of their membership, and how long Reformed domination had been established within those that were state churches.

Third, in the British Isles the union of the crowns of England and Scotland in 1603 brought two rather different churches under the rule of a single king. The Stuart monarchs soon attempted to impose greater uniformity upon them along lines defined by an English church that increasingly diverged from the main body of the Reformed tradition. This offended the religious sensibilities of the Scots and prompted open resistance. The crisis soon spread to England as well, where umbrage at Charles I's religious policies was the precipitant of the constitutional confrontation that followed the summoning of the Long Parliament. As England plunged toward civil war, episcopacy came under attack. Alternative models of structuring the English church were advanced. Individual congregations began to restrict admission to communion to those who could testify to the workings of grace within their souls. The unity of the church shattered, and none of the attempts made between 1645 and 1689 to put it back together again could do so. Sharp divisions also emerged within the Scottish church over the political course to which the nation had pledged itself by virtue of its national covenant with God. Here, too, neither the restoration of the Stuart monarchy in 1660 nor the Glorious Revolution of 1688 could produce a new church settlement capable of regaining the loyalty of the entire population of either country. Only the ultimate recognition that peace could come to each land only if several Protestant churches were allowed ended the intense, creative religious battles that racked both from the 1630s until the end of the seventeenth century.

The result of these changes was that by 1700 the world of Reformed thought and worship was even richer, more variegated, and more internally divided than it had been a century earlier. The cause was also more heavily concentrated in those lands that are now thought of as its enduring bastions, Switzerland, the Netherlands, and Britain, although the question of just which portions of England's diverse church landscape belonged within the Reformed family was contested and controversial.

10

THEOLOGICAL DISPUTES
IN THE AGE OF ORTHODOXY

istorians of Reformed theology have devoted most of their attention to the great figures of the first two generations, especially Calvin. This is understandable in light of the impulses that have long
motivated so much church history, for the urge to commemorate
the struggles and triumphs of the founding fathers, as well as the desire of
future generations in any religious tradition to come to grips with its great
early prophets, both direct the historian's attention to its first generations.
Within Europe's Reformed churches, late nineteenth- and early twentieth-
century internal renewal movements that encouraged a far more pervasive
self-identification of church members as "Calvinists" than would ever previously have been the case intensified this preoccupation with Calvin's thought
and legacy. But the theology and religious culture of the Reformed churches
did not cease to evolve once certain fundamental contours had been defined
amid the upheavals of the first generations. When a Scottish divinity student
reported in 1670 to the presbytery of Inverness on the content of his studies,
he declared that he had read "Calvins Institutions and Wendeline his Theological Systeme, . . . Pares and Ursins Catecheticks, and Willets Synopsis Papismi and Sharpes Course"—a mixture of famous and now obscure authors
active between the middle of the sixteenth century and the middle of the
seventeenth centuries.[1] With each new generation, new theological authori-

297

ties joined the founding fathers in shaping the outlook of Reformed ministers. Lay religious practice likewise continued to unfold. The worship of the mature Reformed churches of the later seventeenth century revolved at least as much around practices or concerns that had presented themselves in the generations following Calvin's death as around those defined in the first generations.

Furthermore, the historical import of late sixteenth- and seventeenth-century elaborations of Reformed thought stretches beyond this period alone. The history of Reformed theology from the eighteenth century to the present may be conceptualized as an ongoing struggle between a series of broad currents or impulses: modernism, biblical literalism, evangelical revivalism, and neoorthodoxy. The origins of the first three of these can all be located in the experience of the generations between Calvin's death in 1564 and 1700: modernism in the writings of those late seventeenth-century theologians who adapted the tools of anti-Aristotelian philosophy and biblical criticism to help them understand the Bible and in the process began to challenge some fundamental aspects of Reformed belief; biblical literalism in the doctrine of defenders of orthodoxy from Franciscus Gomarus through the authors of the Helvetic Consensus; and evangelical revivalism in the preaching to conversion and intense focus on the psychology of grace originated by the English practical divines from the 1590s onward and given highly emotional, temporally concentrated expression in the communion fairs of seventeenth-century Scotland. Even neoorthodoxy, although most often appealing to Calvin himself, was not without its debts to the theologians of this era, as evidenced by the fact that the most prominent Dutch neoorthodox theologian-politician of the generation around 1900, Abraham Kuyper, saw fit to reprint the academic theses of the most renowned defender of orthodoxy of the mid–seventeenth century, Gijsbert Voetius. The late sixteenth and seventeenth centuries may fairly be called the age of Reformed orthodoxy, but this orthodoxy was neither monolithic nor sterile. On the contrary, this was a period of theological ferment of the utmost significance.

THE ADVANCE OF REFORMED SCHOLASTICISM

The first half of the 1560s witnessed the passing of a generation. John a Lasco and Philip Melanchthon died in 1560; Peter Martyr Vermigli in 1562; Wolfgang Musculus in 1563; Calvin in 1564; and Guillaume Farel in 1565. Of the most celebrated Reformed churchmen of the second generation, only Bullinger and Viret survived into the 1570s.

Already during Calvin's lifetime, there were tendencies within Reformed theology toward a more systematic exposition of doctrine and the recuperation of the tools of scholastic logic rejected by most early reformers. The scholastically trained Vermigli was prone to cite the "very wise men among the scholastic theologians" and to rely on the logical tools of scholasticism.[2] The situation in which the Reformed churches found themselves after 1560 encouraged the blossoming of these tendencies. As churches became institutionalized across Europe, they faced the problem of transmitting their doctrines to coming generations of theology students in a clear, logically organized, coherent fashion. Furthermore, Catholic controversial writing became notably more sophisticated in the second half of the sixteenth century. To rebut the force of Roman arguments, Reformed theologians found the tools of logic increasingly useful both to expose flaws in the positions of the enemy and to defend themselves against the charge of internal contradiction.[3]

Reformed theologians of the third and fourth generations divided over the most useful methods of logic for the theological enterprise. The recuperation of the techniques of scholastic logic and exposition begun by the Paduan-educated Vermigli was furthered by his disciple Zanchi, also formed in the traditions of Padua before his flight from Italy. In the German-speaking Reformed world, the influence of Melanchthon, the author of impressive commentaries on Aristotle and a champion of the importance of logic within the Protestant university curriculum, also promoted these tendencies. Ursinus studied with both Melanchthon and Zanchi and was another Reformed theologian who made ample use of Aristotelian categories in his theology. Another of Zanchi's leading students was Franciscus Gomarus, the Dutch theologian who would play a main role in the Arminian controversy. Beza, too, relied heavily on scholastic terminology.[4]

While these figures promoted the revival of scholastic logic, a Huguenot professor of philosophy in Paris, Peter Ramus, championed a radically simplified, anti-Aristotelian logic that advocated presenting material through an ever-branching progression from the general to the particular via the division of each topic into two parts. Beza and Ursinus blocked Ramus's appointment to a teaching post at both Geneva and Heidelberg after he was forced to flee France when Protestant worship was temporarily proscribed in 1568. He obtained a post in Lausanne, however. Two years later, he returned to Paris. His death in the Saint Bartholomew's Massacre wreathed his methods with a martyr's halo that probably facilitated their adoption by a number of leading Reformed theologians of the younger generation, notably the Englishmen William Perkins and William Ames.[5]

Whether the logical aids used by Reformed theologians were Aristotelian or Ramist, the study of philosophy assumed a steadily more noticeable place in the curriculum as the sixteenth century gave way to the seventeenth. The humanistic disciplines had originally dominated new Reformed institutions of higher learning. The Geneva academy opened with chairs of Greek and Hebrew to prepare students for the study of theology, plus an arts professor who taught physics in the morning and rhetoric in the afternoon. Over the course of the late sixteenth century, the teaching of rhetoric waned, while the arts professorship evolved into one, then two, chairs of philosophy. Along with the advance of philosophical instruction came a tendency toward theological systematization. In Lausanne, the curriculum was transformed in the 1590s by Guillaume Du Buc, an emerging scholastic authority whose textbook of theology earned sufficient esteem to be printed in Geneva, Bern, Bremen and London. Where earlier theological education had been built around the successive exposition of books of the Bible, Du Buc required all students to take a course in systematic theology before beginning to study the individual books of the Bible, so that they could see how these fit into a larger doctrinal whole. Across the Continent, expositions of Reformed doctrine became longer, more systematic, and more organized around the intensive discussion of a series of distinct theological loci.[6] The recuperation of the logical distinctions and expository practices employed by the medieval scholastics and the publication of systematic expositions of doctrine for classroom use represent the central features of what is commonly labeled the growth of Protestant scholasticism.

THE PERPLEXES OF PREDESTINATION

Historians of theology continue to debate vigorously the extent to which the appearance of Protestant scholasticism refashioned the content as well as the form of the Reformed message. Many nineteenth- and early twentieth-century historians of dogma postulated a unified system of Reformed orthodoxy whose aim to deduce all points of doctrine from a few basic principles betrayed the original, less tidy biblicism of the Reformation. These authorities underestimated the sheer diversity of views found among late sixteenth- and seventeenth-century Reformed theologians. The same historians of dogma also depicted predestination as the overriding principle from which all doctrines were deduced. But few Reformed theological *summae* from this era elevated predestination to the rank of a basic article of belief or deduced the greater part of their theology from this doctrine.[7] Nonetheless, the more systematic discussion of critical points of theology, recirculating many of the logical distinctions introduced by the scholastics, undeniably altered the manner in which leading theologians presented key doctrines. Ambiguities or potential contradictions previously elided were now confronted and vigorously debated. Logical distinctions derived from late medieval commentaries rather than the biblical texts themselves were reintroduced into the discussions with the intent of resolving apparent contradictions. New complications were perceived, and new disputes arose.

A good example of how quarrels could push theologians to embrace novel views is the early seventeenth-century discussions of the authority of the

Bible. During the late sixteenth century, debates between Protestants and Catholics became more numerous, and a new generation of Catholic controversialists appeared to defend the Roman church. These men saw that the differences of interpretation among Protestant theologians formed one of the most powerful weapons in their armory. The Protestants appealed to the principle of *sola Scriptura* when challenged as to the grounds for their faith—but did not the variety of messages Protestant theologians discerned in the Bible prove that it offered no unambiguous, secure grounds for a single truth? Indeed, in light of the confusing jumble of early manuscripts on which modern editions of the Bible were based, could one even be sure of the exact words of Scripture unless the Holy Spirit had given the institutional Church the inspiration required to determine the best text of the Bible and the proper interpretation of it? Luther, Zwingli, and Calvin had not argued that every word of the Bible was divinely inspired; they simply believed that the essential salvific message and key historical details of the Bible were unarguable and assured. The Holy Spirit had conveyed these accurately to the scribes who recorded the books of the Bible, who put these truths in terms of their own choosing. In addition, the first generations of Reformation theologians saw themselves as reaping the harvest of the recovery of the pure Gospel text initiated by such textual scholars as Valla and Erasmus. Experts in the relevant languages could judge the reliability of disparate versions and adjust the text as necessary to account for their discoveries. So, when the Jewish scholar Elia Levita argued in 1538 that the vowel points found in the Masoretic Hebrew text of the Old Testament—a rendering most Protestant theologians accepted as the best version of that portion of Scripture—were added by its editors as an aid to the reading of the text, leading Reformed Hebraists like Sebastian Munster readily accepted his arguments. But these views changed under the pressure of controversy. In 1617 the esteemed Basel professor Amandus Polanus von Polansdorf attacked Levita's position in the course of trying to prove in debate with a Catholic opponent the superiority of the Masoretic codices to the Vulgate. The vowel points, he argued, were part of God's original revelation of the word to Moses, made in that oldest and most perfect of all languages, Hebrew. The Basel Hebraist Johannes Buxtorf soon offered a fuller scholarly defense of this position. Around the same time, the distinguished Leiden theologian Franciscus Gomarus began to proclaim that not only the message, but also the precise wording of the best editions of the Bible was divinely inspired. Controversy with Catholicism and the need to defend established positions had produced the doctrine of the literal inerrancy of the biblical text.[8]

The import of this change in outlook would not reveal itself for some time. Not so for the thorny matter of predestination. How are Christ's promises of salvation for all to be reconciled with the fact that in the end few are chosen?

How reconcile God's omnipotence and his goodness? Had God determined that some would be saved and others damned even before he determined Adam's fall? or was this decision logically posterior to the fall, in which case it might be asserted that people were damned for their sinfulness rather than according to God's mysterious but nonetheless just will? Could one fall from grace once one had received it? These questions also came to the fore in Reformed discussions of doctrine, and they quickly provoked controversies that were as bitter and long-lasting as they were complicated.

The changed manner in which the doctrine of predestination came to be treated in the third generation can be observed by comparing Calvin's discussion of the subject with Beza's. Calvin never explored the precise relation of the decrees concerning Adam's fall and those concerning individual election. Beza expounded the position that came to be known as supralapsarian, that is, that God chose some for salvation and others for damnation before he envisaged Adam's fall. Whereas Calvin had treated predestination within the broader context of his discussion of Christ and his work of justification, Beza foregrounded it under the topic of the doctrine of God, the topic usually taken up first in scholastic expositions of doctrine. His oft-reprinted table of predestination even set forth the doctrine in the form of a flow chart, drawing attention immediately to the differing fates of those two basic categories of humankind, the elect and the reprobate, once their destinies assumed divergent courses at the initial moment of divine triage. This in turn was reproduced as an "ocular catechism to them which cannot read" in the introduction to the *Golden Chain* of Cambridge's Perkins (1558–1602), an eminent, widely disseminated theologian of the succeeding generation and a man whose supralapsarian treatment of predestination was deeply indebted to Beza. The high predestinarianism of Beza and Perkins did not carry all before it in the late sixteenth and early seventeenth centuries. Even at Geneva, Beza's teachings on predestination were opposed by a band of his colleagues on the theology faculty of the academy, notably Charles Perrot. No voices, however, were more loudly heard than those of Beza and Perkins. The effect of their writings was to focus attention yet more sharply on the doctrine of predestination. For ordinary believers, the effect of emphasizing the doctrine of predestination and situating its discussion under the topic of God was to encourage them to ask at once if they were among the elect or the reprobate. For curious students of theology, the effect was to spark increased speculation about the precise order in which God devised and executed his eternal decrees.[9]

In according greater prominence to the doctrine of predestination, men like Beza and Perkins moved onto sensitive ground. As the disputes that predestination had already aroused in Geneva and Strasbourg had revealed, the issue was fraught with pastoral and psychological implications. Marbach first objected to Zanchi's teaching of the doctrine, he stated, when students lodged in his house complained that it made them worry they might be among the reprobate and could do nothing about their fate. This would continue to be a recurring objection to the doctrine, born of pastoral experience in many times and places. Bolsec objected to Calvin's teachings on the subject on the grounds that the doctrine turned God into a tyrant by making him the cause of so many people's damnation. Yet Calvin insisted that because the Holy Spirit had patently stated the doctrine in Scripture, it was meant to be openly proclaimed. What is more, as the Genevan chronicler Michel Roset indicated, many of those to whom he promulgated it found it a source of comfort rather than a spur to anxiety, as it suggested that God would never abandon his children, even in the darkest of times:"Great and small spoke of the subject. . . . Here is to be noted a singular grace and counsel of God, who by this means made this subject of predestination (previously obscure and almost inaccessible to the most part) most familiar in this church to the consolation and assurance of its children, who know that their salvation is founded on his eternal and unchangeable judgement." The prison experience of Christoph Pezel similarly led him to appreciate the consoling aid of Calvin's teachings on predestination.[10]

By the 1580s, the growing imprint of Calvin's and Beza's conceptions of predestination was beginning to arouse controversy in territories where Genevan theological traditions had earlier shared the stage with the views of such theologians as Bullinger, who were more reserved about the doctrine of double predestination. England's Thirty-Nine Articles mentioned only God's predestination of the elect to salvation, but in the mid-1580s members of several English clerical conferences began to argue they should be revised to note reprobation also, as well as to deny the possibility that individuals might fall from grace once they possessed saving faith. Others reacted strongly against these doctrines. Samuel Harsnett preached a sermon at Paul's Cross in 1585 that attacked double predestination as a Genevan error that made God the author of sin. Archbishop Whitgift ordered him not to preach on such subjects.[11]

In Bern, Beza's vigorous presentation of his version of predestination at the Colloquy of Montbéliard (1586) kindled similar argumentation. The colloquy brought together Beza and the aggressively ubiquitarian Jacob Andreae of Tübingen at the urging of Count Frederick of Montbéliard, who hoped to resolve the conflicts troubling his little French-speaking territory subject to the dukes of Württemberg, where local church traditions stemming from Geneva clashed with pressures for adherence to Lutheran orthodoxy emanating from Stuttgart and Tübingen. The colloquy could scarcely have been less successful. The two men argued so bitterly over the Eucharist, the nature of Christ, and predestination that they refused to shake hands at the end. Samuel Huber, a long-standing opponent of the Bernese church leader Abraham Musculus, seized upon Musculus's support for Beza at Montbéliard to criticize him for going beyond the traditional Bernese teachings in embracing Beza's doctrines of double predestination and limited atonement. Huber's reiterated repetition of these charges in the face of orders for silence from the Bernese government led in 1588 to the convocation of a second colloquy to deal with the charges that he raised, the Colloquy of Bern, attended by representatives from all of Switzerland's Protestant cantons. Huber shocked the gathering by calling predestination blasphemous. The delegates from Zurich replied with less than perfect historical accuracy that the positions Musculus had supported at Montbéliard were anything but novel and had been those of Zwingli, Bullinger, and Peter Martyr. Huber was condemned and eventually banished from Bernese territory. The colloquy demonstrated that all of Protestant Switzerland considered predestinarian teachings normative.[12]

Echoes of the Bern colloquy rippled outward. Huber took refuge in Tübingen and published a set of theses intended to demonstrate the universality of grace. From Heidelberg, Jacobus Kimedoncius responded with a detailed refutation in 1592. The Dane Neils Hemmingsen weighed in with his *Treatise on Universal Grace*. Cambridge became troubled by these issues. Andrew Willett criticized Huber and Hemmingsen in his *Summary of Papism* (1594), the work Scottish theology students were still reading in 1670. Whitaker lectured against those who averred universal grace. William Barrett replied with a series of sermons that denied that faith conveyed assurance of salvation. Continuing perseverance in grace was needed, and this depended upon an effort of the will. Here he was expressing views similar to those of his teacher, the Huguenot refugee and professor of divinity Peter Baro, who maintained that by his antecedent will God created all to universal life, although by his consequent will he sentenced to damnation those who rejected the grace he offered—a lucid example of the sort of scholastic distinctions now increasingly driving thought on this question. The Cambridge discussions prompted the convocation of an assembly at Lambeth palace in which a series of assertions on the issue were approved by the archbishops of Canterbury and York in an effort to define the limits of acceptable teaching. Although the original wording of individual questions proposed by Whitaker was modified to permit a wider range of opinions on the question, the final Lambeth Articles still appeared strongly predestinarian. From eternity, they stated, God has predestined some to life and others to death, not because of any actions or characteristics of those chosen, "but only the will of God's good pleasure." The number of souls predestined had been fixed once and for all, and genuine saving faith would never leave those who possessed it. When Baro continued to insist against the articles that Christ had died for all, he lost his Cambridge professorship.[13]

The Arminian Controversy in the Netherlands

The English and Bernese disputes were confined to clerical and university circles. In the Netherlands, a new round of arguments came to agitate the entire land. The trouble began when two Delft ministers penned a treatise against Beza's supralapsarianism. As their manuscript circulated among theologians, it was sent to a young Amsterdam minister, Jacob Arminius, who, because he had recently studied in Geneva with Beza, was thought to be likely to do a good job of refuting it. As Arminius examined the issue in greater depth, however, he articulated a position quite different from Beza's—whose views, in fact, he probably never shared. By late 1591, the content of his sermons engendered complaints to the consistory from his elder colleague Peter Plancius. Arminius was able to satisfy the consistory that he taught nothing improper, but he continued to grapple with the complexities of predestination for the rest of the decade. His fullest exposition of his thoughts on the question took the form of a two-hundred-page critique of William Perkins's *On the Order and Mode of Predestination* (1598), completed in 1600 but not published until 1612.[14]

Arminius's *Examination of Perkins' Pamphlet on the Order and Mode of Predestination* illustrates well how the detailed examination of specific points of doctrine could breed divisions where none had existed before. The English debates had raised the issue of the perseverance of the saints: Could those with genuine saving faith ever lose that faith over the course of their lifetime? Perkins had adduced seven reasons why they could not. Although Arminius, on taking up this question, pronounced it an issue that should be approached cautiously, his point-by-point consideration of Perkins's arguments found them wanting, and by the end of his discussion he was arguing unmistakably in favor of the possibility of falling from grace. Arminius's writings also demonstrate how elaborate the speculation about the nature of God's will had become by this time. Leaning heavily on syllogistic reasoning and scholastic distinctions, he postulated the existence of no fewer than four divine decrees on salvation: a first in which God appointed his Son as redeemer; a second by which he promised to receive into his favor those who believe in Christ; a third by which he provided the means necessary for faith; and a fourth by which he chose to save or damn those individuals who he knew in advance would accept and persevere in this faith. His mature thought discriminated between divine foreknowledge and predestination. It expressed the infralapsarian view that the decision to grant saving faith to individuals followed that which determined the Fall. It suggested that individuals could lose grace, and it implied that an act of will was involved in accepting and retaining saving grace, although grace alone procured salvation.[15]

When Arminius was named professor of theology at Leiden in 1603, the predestination issue exploded. Plancius warned another Leiden theologian, Franciscus Gomarus, that Arminius held dangerous views. The two publicly began to defend rival theses at university disputations, Gomarus asserting a position similar to Beza's. Students promptly began disputing the issues as well. The ministers of the region expressed alarm about what was being taught their future colleagues. The classis of Dordrecht demanded that something be done about the controversies in the university. Sentiment that a national synod was necessary to deal with the matter spread.[16]

If the Arminian controversy began as a disagreement about predestination, the call to examine the orthodoxy of a professor added levels of complication, for it reawakened all of the unresolved disputes over the control of church affairs that had troubled the Dutch church in its early years: Who had the authority to examine and remove an unorthodox teacher? Who should assemble and set the agenda for a national synod? Arminius's wife belonged to an influential Amsterdam regent family. When summoned before the Amsterdam consistory, Arminius refused to appear unless the burghermasters or their representatives attended as well, aligning himself with the view that civil authorities rightfully oversaw the church. In subsequent actions and petitions, he and his supporters defended the ability of city governments to control ecclesiastical appointments without interference from local classes or synods. They argued that the States should set the form and agenda of a national synod. The fullest and most extreme exposition of the political theories of the pro-Arminius party, Johannes Uytenbogaert's *On the Office and Authority of a Higher Christian Government in Church Affairs* of 1610, was judged by the like-minded Hugo Grotius to stand directly in the tradition of Wolfgang Musculus. Against this, Arminius's opponents insisted on the autonomy of the church and its competence in all matters regarding the setting and oversight of doctrine.[17]

Contention also broke out over the precise subject matter that the national synod ought to take up. Even though Arminius was convinced that his doctrines stood in accord with the fundamental confessional documents of the Dutch church, the Belgic Confession of Faith and the Heidelberg Catechism, he and his supporters insisted that these were time-bound materials whose reconsideration should be one of the items on the agenda of any national synod. The Gomarists judged it both unnecessary and dangerous to discuss any revision of the documents that "now for forty years have been openly preached in the Netherlands and for which so many pious martyrs have paid with their blood."[18] Another new issue had arisen with the passing of time: Were the confessions of faith adopted by the churches in the mid–sixteenth century and hallowed by the blood of martyrs definitive codifications of correct belief? or did Scripture alone remain the touchstone for deciding all questions?

All of the ingredients for deadlock and division were thus present. The secular authorities summoned Arminius and Gomarus to conferences at which they discussed their views, but no reconciliation resulted. The powerful regents of Holland, led by the grand pensionary Johan van Oldenbarnevelt, a stout supporter of Arminius, would summon only a national synod whose agenda and membership were controlled by the States and that would weigh the revision of the church's basic confessional tenets. The church's synods opposed this. As disagreements recurrently postponed the calling of a national synod, individual classes and provincial synods refused to allow the faith to be corrupted by what many perceived as novelties. They insisted on their powers to vet candidates for the ministry and even to coerce all ministers in place into signing the Belgic Confession of Faith—powers that the secular magistrates stoutly denied. The sorts of political conflicts that could ensue were revealed in Alkmaar between 1608 and 1610. The local classis suspended five pastors after they refused to sign the Belgic Confession. The civic authorities defended them, and the States of Holland denounced the act as an improper anticipation of issues yet to be decided by a national synod. At the next renewal of the city council, the stadtholder Maurice appointed several new regents known to support the removal of "innovating" ministers. Fearing that troops were on their way to the city to turn out the offending pastors, the civic militia secured the city's gates; the States took the unprecedented and legally dubious step of overturning the election and installing a new *vroedschap;* and that body in turn chose a new consistory. When one of the city's ministers refused to accept the purging of the consistory, he was deprived of his position and began to hold services in a nearby village. Many town residents chose to attend those rather than the services in the city churches. The classis of the region split in two. This was not the only such split to occur.[19]

Arminius died in 1609, but the Arminian controversy was now larger than any one man. Platforms around which a divided public opinion could rally were set out over the next two years. In 1610, forty-four ministers signed a formal Remonstrance to the States of Holland drafted by Uytenbogaert. It affirmed three key theological points: (1) the election of those who believe by the grace of the Holy Spirit and who persevere in their faith; (2) the universality of Christ's atonement, the salvific consequences of which are nonetheless restricted to those who believe; and (3) the resistibility of grace. It also certified the authority of the secular magistrates over the church, called for reflection over the revision of the Belgic Confession, and said that no actions should be taken against any ministers in place by lesser church assemblies until a national synod had been assembled. In March 1611, a group of Gomarist ministers responded. Their Counter-Remonstrance proclaimed the rival positions of limited atonement and the perseverance of the saints, who could, however, pass through periods of weak faith or temptation.[20] From 1609 onward, furthermore, a growing volume of publications in both Latin and Dutch began to set the ideas involved in the disputes before a broader public, adding to the volatility of the state of affairs.

The Remonstrants' appeal to the States of Holland revealed the relative weakness of their party within the clergy. Only a third of the ministers in South Holland and a quarter in North Holland supported their petition. Not one of the province's fifteen classes could rally a majority, although nine split over the issue. Outside Holland, the Remonstrant cause was still weaker. Yet thanks to the protection of Oldenbarnevelt and the regents of the majority of Holland's towns, the Remonstrant ministers were able to block all attempts to force them from office or to convoke a clerically dominated national synod. Oldenbarnevelt and his allies sought to calm the waters by issuing placards forbidding ministers to treat the offending questions in their sermons, blocking the convocation of provincial synods, and requiring the toleration of all views on the contested issues until a national synod had spoken. But such measures proved inadequate to the task and indeed appeared to the Gomarists to be but new examples of the secular magistrates' intolerable invasion of the sacred precincts of the temple. Many ministers continued to proclaim the disputed doctrines that in their eyes were central tenets of the faith. Some were removed from office for doing so, the ultimate proof of the government's spiritual bankruptcy in Contra-Remonstrant eyes: loyal ministers of the Reformed faith being silenced by the same authorities who turned a blind eye to gatherings of Lutherans, Anabaptists, and even papists! The deprived ministers began to hold assemblies in nearby villages. Their supporters trooped out to join them, awakening memories of the early hedge preaching and earning them the label mud-beggars. The pamphlet wars escalated, from roughly fifty publications in 1613 to three hundred in 1618. Meanwhile, Oldenbarnevelt's acquiescence in the Spanish seizure of Wesel in 1614 fostered additional doubts about his zeal for the defense of the true faith. So too did his unwillingness to interfere in the affairs of Leiden University and suspend Arminius's controversial successor in the chair of theology, Conrad Vorstius, whose views were widely accounted dangerously Socinian.[21]

The greatest early historians of the strife over Remonstrancy were themselves all Remonstrants, and their depiction of the social and ideological roots of the clash long dominated understanding of the matter. In their eyes, it was a battle between a tolerant regent oligarchy and the lower orders of the towns stirred up against their betters by immigrant preachers bearing theological innovations alien to the original, broad spirit of the Dutch Reformation. Recent study of the party divisions has failed to reveal sharp sociological divisions between the partisans of either side among the population at large. Most laymen followed the lead of their minister. If Remonstrants made up a sizable fraction of wealthy burghers within the great Contra-Remonstrant stronghold of Amsterdam, thus dissenting from the views of that city's ministers, substantial burghers also figured prominently in the Contra-Remonstrant minorities discernible in Remonstrant Gouda and Schoonhoven.[22] Immigrants from the south indeed leaned strongly toward the Contra-Remonstrant cause, and few of this party's leading ministerial spokesmen were born within Holland. But the Remonstrant ministers were not the long-established devotees of an older church tradition; on the contrary, they appear to have been noticeably younger than their Contra-Remonstrant counterparts.[23]

The division between the two parties was no less bitter for the absence of clear sociological differences among the rank and file. In the eyes of the Remonstrants, their "Calvinist" opponents were schismatics and evil spirits whose doctrines made God into a tyrant and bred desperation and immorality among ordinary believers. Popular pamphlets lampooned their ideas through the mouth of a "predestined thief" who quoted amply from high predestinarian divines as he confidently prepared for the scaffold. More learned treatises presented the Contra-Remonstrants as descendants of the same Flemish and Brabantine fanatics whose actions at Ghent and elsewhere had sabotaged William of Orange when he undertook to reach an earlier religious peace. The Contra-Remonstrants for their part saw the Arminians, with their talk of peace and toleration, as the new Joabs of the Book of Samuel, outwardly professing friendship while hiding swords behind their backs. They were nominal Christians who issued placards against the true Reformed religion. A widely reprinted hymn of the mud-beggars forthrightly affirmed the consoling aspects of predestination:

> God's dear Elect, what Creature shall deceive?
> Who shall me of the love of Christ bereave?
> In his Almighty arms, secure I lie;
> Nor death, nor Hell, nor deadly Sin shall prove
> So mighty to deprive me of his love:
> Possest of this, I fraud and force defy.

People argued about the issues on passenger barges and sang partisan songs in front of the houses of prominent members of the opposite faction. In the Remonstrant stronghold of Alkmaar in 1617, leading Contra-Remonstrants were ridden through the streets in a wheelbarrow and forced to pay for the ride.[24]

The mounting tension came to a head when the leader of the house of Orange, Maurice of Nassau, cast his lot with the Contra-Remonstrants. In July 1617, the Contra-Remonstrants of The Hague, who had established their own consistory after the dismissal of the town's leading Contra-Remonstrant minister, occupied an abandoned church for their services without government permission. Two weeks later, Maurice, a committed but theologically unsophisticated Reformed communicant, publicly showed his colors by attending services with the squatter congregation. Oldenbarnevelt and the States of Holland, fearing the spread of such acts of defiance, issued a "Sharp Resolution" empowering cities to hire mercenary troops, subject to no authority higher than that of the individual cities or the provincial states, to ensure respect for the resolutions on religious affairs. This was a direct challenge to Maurice of Nassau's authority over all troops as captain-general. After prudently reinforcing his power base throughout the other provinces, he obtained a resolution from the States-General the following summer ordering the dismissal of these special troops, known as *waardgelders,* and granting him extraordinary powers to preserve the state. He then moved with his own forces from one Remonstrant stronghold to the next, dismissing the auxiliary troops and purging supporters of Oldenbarnevelt from the town councils. Oldenbarnevelt himself was arrested, as were several of his leading supporters, including Grotius. A jerry-rigged court sentenced Oldenbarnevelt to death for having "dared to jeopardise the position of the faith and greatly to oppress and distress God's Church; . . . making hateful the true brethren in the faith . . . with the names of foreigners and Puritans, who want to imitate the Flemings and stir up the subjects against their rulers; and . . . attempting to cast the governance of these lands into disorder and confusion."[25] Grotius was condemned to life imprisonment but escaped two years later by hiding beneath his dirty laundry in the trunk in which his wife had his books and clothes transported to and from the prison; he spent most of the remaining decades of his life in Paris.

The purge of pro-Remonstrant regents from the city councils removed the chief obstacles to the national synod that the majority of provinces had long desired. The assembly met in Dordrecht in November 1618, charged with examining the five theological points advanced by the Remonstrants. The pure word of God was to be the sole standard against which these were evaluated, but revision of the church's basic confessional documents was not on the agenda. The Contra-Remonstrant party dominated overwhelmingly. But the synod was more than a purely Dutch affair. The other west European Reformed churches were invited to attend as well. The eight voting colleges of British, Swiss, and German delegates who came acted as a moderating force on the eleven colleges representing the Netherlands' nine provincial synods, their Walloon churches, and the theology faculties of their universities.[26]

The synod dragged on for more than six months and veered at times toward farce. A group of Remonstrant ministers was summoned to present their views and to receive the synod's judgment of them. They mounted so many procedural objections that they were finally sent away and their party's views examined on the basis of its printed works. The moderator of the synod and a few associates controlled affairs so tightly that one English observer likened the synod to a watch: the mechanisms that moved the hands were all hidden from sight. The final decisions of the synod nonetheless combined statesmanlike moderation with a manifest rejection of the foremost Arminian positions. "Arminius and his party" were predictably condemned as the instigators of all of the church's troubles, but the synod refused to enshrine as orthodoxy the full supralapsarianism of Gomarus. Instead, its canons on the divine decrees avoided extensive discussion of reprobation and simply declared that God chose for redemption, of his pure grace before the foundation of the world, a number from within a human race that had fallen of its own fault and was justly condemned to damnation. This election was in no way contingent upon God's foreknowledge of any actions or attributes of the individuals chosen. Whereas Remonstrant propaganda had claimed that to restrict the merits of Christ's death to a predetermined group of individuals was to make it impossible to believe in a Savior who had stated that he had come for all humankind, the synod held that God's counsel had attested that the saving efficacy of Christ's death extended just to the elect, although "as many as are called by the Gospel are unfeignedly called. . . . As God himself is most wise, unchangeable, omniscient and omnipotent, so the election made by him can neither be interrupted nor changed, recalled nor annulled." Above all, the decrees stressed the force of divine grace and the consoling aspects of the doctrine of predestination. All those granted true faith could attain assurance of salvation they could not lose. The Remonstrants had nonetheless been wrong in charging that this doctrine bred carelessness and immorality: "This certainty of perseverance . . . is so far from exciting in believers a spirit of pride, or of rendering them carnally secure, that on the contrary it is the real source of humility, filial reverence, true piety . . . and of solid rejoicing in God; so that the consideration of this benefit should serve as an incentive to the serious and constant practice of gratitude and good works."[27] This was the great codification of the five points of TULIP: Total depravity, Unconditional election, Limited atonement, Irresistible grace, and the Perseverance of the saints.

The decision of the synod was accepted by the States-General and sent to the provincial synods for the signature of all clergymen. Approximately two hundred refused to sign and were deprived of their livings. The most outspoken Remonstrant ministers were immediately escorted out of the country in a convoy. Remonstrant gatherings were outlawed. About forty deprived ministers in time reconciled themselves to the church; the unreconciled who were willing to live quietly as private citizens (about seventy) were allowed to remain in the country; the remainder were banished.[28]

Matters had not yet been brought to a close at Dort when the leading Remonstrant clergymen concluded they would no longer be accepted within the main body of the Dutch church and resolved to hold gatherings "like the Martinists and Mennonites" if forbidden to use the public churches. Following the banishment of the party leaders, a group met in Antwerp in September 1619 and formalized what came to be known as the Remonstrant Brotherhood. (The name *church* was deliberately avoided to underscore that this was an association of people unjustly driven from the public church.) The brotherhood committed itself to supporting the communities of believers left behind with preaching and the administration of the sacraments; it also set up a system of clandestine fund raising to enable it to pay stipends to ministers inside the country and in exile. In the following year, Simon Episcopius, who was becoming its chief theological spokesman, drew up what would remain the brotherhood's essential confession of faith until the late eighteenth century. It was a kind of anticonfession in that it advised in the preface acceptance of its precepts only insofar as they could be confirmed by conscience and Scripture; they should not be cited in conferences or disputes as authoritative. While recognizing the need for synods to discuss issues of doctrine, worship, and manners concerning many churches and inviting the participation in these of the Christian magistrate, it rejected imposing the decisions of such synods on anyone by law and defended the right of believers to assemble on their own for worship. Not surprisingly, the confession was sharply critical of double predestination, emphasized God's mercy rather than his justice, and pressed the notion that believers needed to persevere in faith in order to be saved. Its rejection of Lutheran and Catholic doctrines of the Eucharist, critique of idolatry as a violation of the Second Commandment, inclusion of a system of church discipline, and designation of elders and deacons as ministers of the church nonetheless marked its adherence to Reformed tradition. It understood that tradition eirenically and carefully avoided pronouncing on such matters of infra-Reformed disagreement as Christ's spiritual presence in the Lord's Supper or the exact structural details of church organization prescribed by Scripture.[29]

The brotherhood struggled to establish itself for nearly a decade, for the outbreak of the Thirty Years' War in 1618 and the renewal of war with Spain in 1621 heightened official suspicion of a cause that had been associated with inaction against the Catholic enemy during the Twelve Years' Truce, and led the governing authorities vigorously to enforce the placards against Remonstrant assemblies. Exiled ministers returned to hold clandestine gatherings that moved from one private home to another, but those who were caught faced imprisonment, and many seem to have lost heart after a while. Gradually, events created a space for the Remonstrants to win the de facto toleration already obtained by Holland's other religious minorities: the death of Maurice of Nassau in 1625 and his succession by the thoroughly *politique* Frederick Henry; the improvement after 1628 of the republic's military situation; and the retreat of the Catholic cause in Germany after Sweden's entry into the Thirty Years' War were of primary import. In 1630, the Remonstrants were able to build their first permanent house-church (*schuilkerk*) in Amsterdam. Four years later, they opened a small seminary, with Episcopius as professor of theology.[30]

The movement was now far smaller than it had been. Between the 1630s and 1700, the number of functioning Remonstrant congregations oscillated between thirty and forty. Rotterdam had easily the largest church with about seven thousand members in 1670. Amsterdam, the second pillar of the movement, housed roughly fifteen hundred church members throughout the century, less than 1 percent of the city's population by century's end. Haarlem's church was probably more typical yet in size with scarcely a hundred members. In all, the Remonstrants numbered barely twenty thousand to forty thousand souls, concentrated chiefly, as previously, in South Holland. But many of the church members came from substantial families, and the movement's possession of a seminary guaranteed it an intellectual importance out of proportion to its limited membership.[31]

The Arminian Controversy Beyond the Netherlands

Outside the Netherlands, the other Reformed churches closely followed the debate between the Remonstrants and Contra-Remonstrants, and many accepted the Dort decrees. Until the synod had spoken, "continual riots" between student supporters of the two parties racked the Huguenot Academy of Sedan; the 1623 decision of the national synod of the French Reformed churches to accept the Dordrecht canons brought the brawls to an end. The overwhelming majority of French ministers complied with the synod's imperative that they swear their approval of the Dordrecht decisions, although a few ministers refused and lost their posts, most notably the Sedan professor Daniel Tilenius, a product of the Melanchthonian traditions of Silesia, and Etienne de Courcelles, who later taught in the Remonstrant seminary in Amsterdam. The Genevan Company of Pastors similarly voted to require all ministers to subscribe to the Dort decrees a generation later in 1647. Although not formally adopted in either Scotland or German-speaking Switzerland, they were no less revered there. Scottish theologians almost uniformly lauded what they called "the sacred Synode of Dort." One Basel theologian who had attended it reportedly doffed his hat for the remainder of his life at any mention of it.[32]

While the great majority of French, Swiss, and Scottish Reformed clergymen supported the decisions taken at Dordrecht, English theologians reacted differently. Men such as Peter Baro and William Barrett had already anticipated many of Arminius's theses, although they had been in a clear minority among their peers, and Baro's dismissal from Cambridge in 1596 had taught them the danger of expressing their views openly. During the 1620s, shifts in royal policy allowed these ideas to be expressed once again, and a movement often labeled Arminianism turned into a powerful force within the English church. English Arminianism was hardly identical with its Dutch namesake, as those associated with the movement in England generally cared more about matters relating to worship, the sacraments, and the status of the clergy than about the doctrine of predestination. For this reason, full discussion of most aspects of this movement will be reserved for chapter 12. Insofar as the hostilities in England did focus on predestination, they were less a repetition of the Dutch quarrels than of indigenous English theological debates. Still, the Dutch dissensions inflected the English controversies in two ways. First, Arminius's writings confirmed the opinions and perhaps—although this has not yet been well investigated—enriched the arguments of the English followers of Baro and Barrett. Second, the condemnation of Arminius at Dort gave the opponents of this tradition a stigmatizing label to pin on it.[33]

Baro had left behind at Cambridge a number of loyal, if cautious, disciples, notably Lancelot Andrewes and the Regius professor of divinity John Overall. These men pricked up their ears when the collision between Arminius and Gomarus began to agitate Leiden and contacted Remonstrants who came to England between 1611 and 1614 to lay their ideas before King James. James's support for the synod of Dort reminded them to hold their tongues, but as the Thirty Years' War heated up, a shift took place in royal ecclesiastical policy in England. James's vision of Protestant kingship included supporting theological conclaves and predestinarian doctrine, but it did not extend to committing troops and money to the Bohemian gamble of his Palatine brother-in-law. He sought instead to dissipate the gathering clouds of war by encouraging mediation and seeking a marriage between his son and the Spanish Infanta. A segment of zealous Protestant opinion in England saw the conflict in Germany as the long-expected showdown between the forces of Christ and of the Antichrist and urged intervention. Even the archbishop of Canterbury, George Abbott, lobbied against the Spanish match. Furthermore, James's favorite during his last years, Buckingham, patronized a circle of clergymen around Bishop Richard Neile whose closely held private views appear to have tended toward certain of the positions associated with Arminianism. James was thus spurred by the opposition to his foreign policy to draw nearer to that important current of opinion within the English church that had long maintained that the Puritans formed an uncontrollable and potentially subversive element within the realm, just when some who held that position were also willing to extend the protection of the church to antipredestinarian arguments.[34]

This changed context explains how in 1624 a previously obscure Cambridge scholar, Richard Montagu, obtained royal permission to publish his *A New Gagg for an Old Goose*. Written to rebut a Catholic opponent, this work defended the Church of England by denying that it actually taught many of the doctrines that Montagu's Catholic antagonist attacked, including such doctrines as unconditional election and the perseverance of the saints; these were simply, it declared, the views of a "Puritan" minority. The work also opined that the pope was not Antichrist and that fallen humanity retained enough free will to concur with God's grace. Montagu had not read Arminius's writings, but he would subsequently do so and pronounce them admirable.[35]

Montagu's *Gagg* provoked a host of printed rebuttals from those who were shocked both by the substance of his theology and by his claim that the English church did not teach that the saints persevered in grace or that the pope was Antichrist. The equation of these latter doctrines with Puritanism particularly stung. "This is the first time that ever I heard of a Puritan doctrine in points dogmatical, and I have lived longer in the church than he hath done," wrote George Carleton. "I thought that Puritans were only such as were factious against the bishops in the point of pretended discipline." Leading noblemen pushed for and obtained a conference between theologians of the divergent inclinations at York House in 1626, but this resolved nothing. Whereas James's licensing of Montagu's work may have been only a tactical move against such critics of his policies as Abbott, his successor from March 1625 onward, Charles I, was committed in principle to the views of the circle around Neile. Within a year, he had named Montagu to a post as royal chaplain. In the manner of Oldenbarnevelt, Charles aimed to bring peace to the church by forbidding discussion of predestination in 1626, but his decree was initially no more successful, and episcopal appointments of men suspected of Arminian sympathies heightened the fear that Roman doctrines were being reintroduced into the English church—this against the alarming backdrop of the victorious advance of Catholic arms throughout the first decade of the Thirty Years' War. The Parliament of 1629 witnessed tumultuous scenes, the speaker of the House of Commons being held down in his chair while three resolutions were introduced, the first of which read, "Whosoever shall . . . seek to extend or introduce Popery or Arminianism or other opinions disagreeing from the true and orthodox church, shall be reputed a capital enemy to this Kingdom and Commonwealth." But open talk about predestination did recede, if not disappear, in the wake of a royal decree late in 1629 ordering the strict implementation of the ban on religious controversy. The king of England had the power to still theological contention that Oldenbarnevelt and the States of Holland lacked.[36] If silenced, though, the rival currents of thought remained vital. From this era onward, positions now bearing the labels Arminian and Calvinist would wage a continuing and roughly equal struggle for supremacy within English theology.[37]

Amyraut

Yet another chapter in the debates about predestination opened in France in the 1630s. In 1634, a theology professor at the Academy of Saumur, Moyse Amyraut (1596–1664), published a vernacular *Brief Treatise on Predestination* for the benefit of a recent convert from Catholicism who was horrified by the suggestion that God created the majority of people in order to damn them. In the treatise, Amyraut's thrust was to accentuate God's mercy yet avoid the errors censured at Dort. Building upon the ideas of his Saumur teacher John Cameron (1580–1625), who had set forth a different scheme of the divine decrees from that approved at Dort, Amyraut espoused a would-be middle ground commonly labeled hypothetical universalism. Christ's sacrifice, it held, was made not just for the elect but for all men, on condition that they believe. Of course, belief required the ingrafting of faith. This was granted to the elect only by a second decree confirming the original conditional offer of salvation to all. Amyraut also insisted that the doctrine of predestination be handled with circumspection, to the dismay of those who saw it as a central, consoling article of faith that deserved forthright proclamation. He, like Calvin, treated the issue under the topic of Christ and his saving work, not under that of the divine will.[38]

Although Amyraut's position was far from that of the Arminians on many points—he did not argue that individuals played a role in their own salvation or could fall from grace—his teachings nonetheless troubled many of his fellow Reformed theologians. Pierre Du Moulin, the leading French dogmatician of the preceding generation and an active participant in the polemical battle against Arminius, declared that however much Amyraut might claim to avoid the Dutchman's errors, he in fact embraced "at least two-thirds of Arminianism, from which all the remainder logically follows." Far from resolving any difficulties, Amyraut's doctrines made God appear less admirable in that they implied he was confused about his own will and underplayed the righteousness of his justice in condemning the great mass of humanity to deserved perdition. Amyraut was summoned to defend his views at the national synod of Alençon in 1637, which he did with sufficient dexterity to escape formal censure, although the gathering did suggest that the novelty of his ways of expressing his views ought to be avoided.[39] Controversy arose anew after one of Amyraut's correspondents discovered in 1644 that the theologians at Leiden were encouraging their students to defend theses hostile to his outlook. Polemics flew back and forth again among Amyraut, Du Moulin, and Leiden professors, including Du Moulin's son-in-law André Rivet. The Bernese were alarmed enough to forbid students from the Pays de Vaud to study at Saumur. Inside France, the provincial synods of Poitou and Bas-Languedoc briefly imposed prohibitions on admitting Saumur graduates to the ministry. In a rare example of princely or aristocratic intervention succeeding in calming a theologians' quarrel, the Huguenot duke of La Trémouille was able to bring Amyraut and various of his leading French opponents together in 1649 and broker a reconciliation that proved enduring.[40]

Throughout the course of the controversy and for decades thereafter, Amyraut's views on predestination enjoyed wide support among the leading ministers of the regions north of the Loire, especially among the *crème de la crème* of the French pastorate, the ministers of the Paris congregation of Charenton. They also proved influential in England among ministers searching for a middle ground in the continuing discord over predestination. The Geneva Company of Pastors nonetheless thought them so dangerous they forbade the Genevan clergy to teach the doctrine of universal grace; at Bern the ban preventing residents of its territories from studying at Saumur was enforced until Amyraut was safely dead. The sway of the French professor in the Netherlands was negligible.[41]

PRACTICAL DIVINITY

The remarkably fertile milieu of late sixteenth- and early seventeenth-century Cambridge not only gave rise to Cartwright's and Travers's calls for a presbyterial church order, to Whitaker's and Willett's anti-Catholic controversial writings, and to the tradition of Baro and Barrett out of which English Arminianism flowed. By far its most influential contribution to the history of early modern Christianity came within that branch of theology that contemporaries called practical theology, encompassing both moral theology and the practice of devotion. In the last decade of the sixteenth century and the first decades of the seventeenth, a circle of theologians and parish ministers in and around Cambridge devised a distinctive pastoral strategy and style of pious living, elaborated in a series of extremely popular devotional treatises in the vernacular, that sought to awaken laymen to the Gospel message of salvation and to instruct them about how to lead a godly life. These came to be diffused across much of Europe, outside as well as within the confessional boundaries of the Reformed tradition. The style of piety and the specific devotional practices set forth in this literature shaped Reformed religious life as few other developments of this period. The works of these "Puritan physicians of the soul" also generated theological disputation and, via certain of their offshoots, new separatist impulses.

It seems no coincidence that the first noteworthy body of Reformed practical divinity took shape in England at precisely this time. Although few of those who first developed this literature were directly involved in the efforts to institute consistorial discipline and a presbyterian form of church government, their works began to appear just as these efforts were being crushed. They appeared to offer a set of voluntary means for inspiring upright living and a more intense form of Christian life that must have appeared particularly appealing as hopes that institutional transformation might effect the same changes were being decisively shattered. As Patrick Collinson has written, "the theological achievement of the Puritans, from William Perkins onwards, can be roughly interpreted as the adaptation and domestication of Calvinism to fit the condition of voluntary Christians, whose independence of the ordered, disciplined life of the Church Calvin would have found strange and disturbing."[42] In the absence of a full preaching ministry and a regular system of consistorial discipline, zealous English preachers and spiritual writers were drawn to highlight the prophetic element in their calling; they had to be agents of salvation for people from many miles around. Voluntary techniques for teaching and reinforcing upright behavior offered an alternative to the prodding that a consistory might have provided had those who called for their establishment in England carried the day. Furthermore, Cambridge divines were active in the polemical confrontation with Catholicism. From the late sixteenth century onward, a vast new corpus of Catholic devotional literature began to take shape offering guides to the laity for pious behavior, associated most famously with such names as Luis de Granada and François de Sales. Part of this corpus was aimed in translation at the English Catholic market. Many of the first Cambridge works of practical divinity were written in response to this publishing offensive, to furnish a Protestant counterpart to this literature and thereby to stop the mouths of those who "cast in our teeth, that we have nothing set out for the certaine and daily direction of a Christian, when yet they have published (they say) many treatises of that argument."[43] Rivalry, as always, bred emulation.

At the fountainhead of the Cambridge tradition of practical divinity stood a group of interconnected university men and country pastors whom William Haller dubbed "the spiritual brotherhood." The patriarch of the group was Richard Greenham, rector of Dry Drayton from 1570 to 1591, who often took into his parsonage young men preparing for the ministry and shared with them his experience in healing afflicted consciences. Perkins was the central theological influence. He was not only England's first systematic Reformed theologian to attain international stature, but also, in the words of the great mid-seventeenth-century Dutch theologian Gijsbert Voetius, "the Homer of practical Englishmen to this day." He was also the first of the spiritual brotherhood to publish his works, and his shorter vernacular treatises such as *A Graine of Musterd-Seede* and *A Treatise Tending unto a Declaration Whether a Man be in the Estate of Damnation or Salvation* attained even more extraordinary success than his weighty Latin tomes destined for his professional peers. More editions of works from his pen were published in England between 1590 and 1620 than of any other author, and 372 editions of his writings ultimately appeared from both English and continental presses prior to 1700. If contemporary influence be the criterion, Perkins was easily the most preeminent English churchman and theologian of his remarkable generation.[44]

Others followed his lead. Richard Rogers, "another Greenham" according to his editor, offered the first worthwhile practical devotional manual systematically to cover all aspects of a Christian's life, the 1603 *Seven Treatises*. Arthur Dent engagingly set out *The Plain Man's Pathway to Heaven* through a dialogue set beneath an oak tree between a minister, an honest man, an ignorant man, and "a notable Atheist and caviller against all goodnesse" (25 editions between 1601 and 1638). William Ames carried Cambridge's focus on practical questions to the Netherlands, where he taught for many years at Franeker and published the most extensive work of applied moral theology or "Puritan casuistry," *Of Conscience* (18 editions in four languages between 1632 and 1700). The greatest single publishing success of the early seventeenth century came from an Oxford man, Lewis Bayly, whose *The Practice of Piety: Directing a Christian How to Walke that He May Please God* offered an extensive selection of prayers, meditations, and rules for living that covered all of the basic aspects of a Christian life and a pious death (164 known editions in 11 languages). These were only the most successful of a host of writers who devoted themselves to genres intended to awaken and reinforce a quickened piety among a broad audience. In the second half of the century, such immensely popular authors as Richard Baxter, Richard Allestree, and John Bunyan carried on the tradition.[45]

Experimental Predestinarianism

From a transconfessional point of view, the tradition of practical divinity forged by the Cambridge divines may be seen, as it has been by German historians of spirituality, as simply the Reformed manifestation of a larger phenomenon of these years: a "new piety" illustrated as well by the vogue for Granada and de Sales in Catholic lands and by the publication in 1605 of Johann Arndt's *True Christianity,* a staple of Lutheran devotion for centuries to come.[46] Yet while this literature shared features with its Lutheran and Cath-

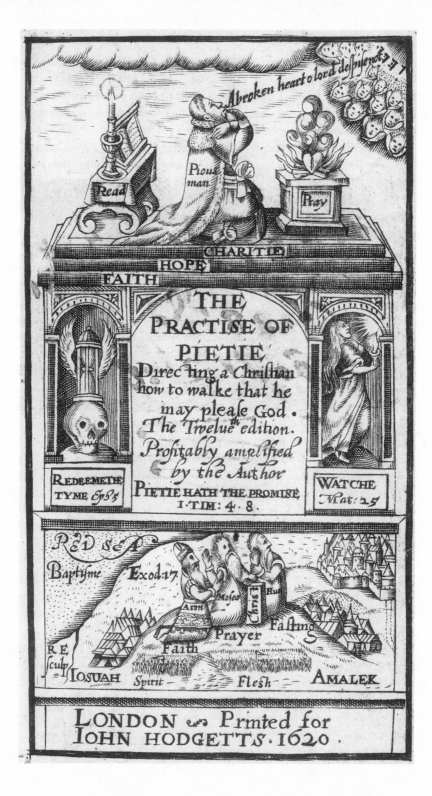

A broken heart o lord despise not

Read

Pious man

Pray

CHARITIE

HOPE

FAITH

THE
PRACTISE OF
PIETIE
Directing a Christian
how to walke that he
may please God.
The Twelue^th edition.
Profitably amplified
by the Author

REDEEMETH
TYME Eph 5

PIETIE HATH THE PROMISE
I. TIM: 4. 8.

WATCHE
Mat: 25

RED SEA

Baptisme   Exod:17

Aron   Moses Christ Hur

Prayer   Fasting

Faith

RE
sculp

IOSUAH   Spirit   Flesh   AMALEK

LONDON Printed for
IOHN HODGETTS · 1620 ·

olic equivalents, it also expressed distinctive themes and motifs drawn from the theological traditions and milieu from which it sprang. From the time of William Tyndale onward, the English Protestant tradition displayed an unusual degree of concern with the issue of attaining personal assurance of salvation. Perkins, of course, was a supralapsarian predestinarian who placed great weight on the division of the world between the elect and the reprobate. Most of the early English practical divines not only had connections to one another and to Perkins' Cambridge, but were also pastors of rural parishes. As such, they had to face the problem of delivering to an audience whose grasp of doctrinal abstractions was often shaky the Protestant message of justification by faith alone, more and more often set within a theology of predestination, in a church about whose liturgical practices and disciplinary mechanisms many of them had reservations. The pastoral strategy that many of these authors adopted involved calling people to salvation by initially expounding the full, infinitely demanding implications of the divine Law, then announcing the Gospel's promises of salvation for even the greatest of sinners. Central too was what Richard Kendall has called the "experimental predestinarian tradition"—the view that individuals could know from experience if they possessed saving faith, and indeed that ensuring they possessed this faith ought to be the Christian's chief goal. "Give no rest to yourselves, till you can prove that you be in the estate of salvation," Rogers exhorted his readers, and generations of English spiritual writers echoed this call.[47] In line with this emphasis, the "Puritan physicians of the soul" devoted much attention to exploring the process of growth in faith and its mysterious ebbing and flowing. They also supplied lists of marks of election, or "glasses of godliness," against which people could measure themselves in order to answer that foundational question they were exhorted to keep in the forefront of their minds: am I a child of God or no? By exhorting their readers to look to their experience and behavior to find evidences of saving faith, these authors hoped to exploit the consoling aspects of the doctrine of predestination because if the believer could find even the tiniest degree of faith—the grain of mustard seed of one of Perkins's titles—this could be taken as evidence of possessing that divine gift that the doctrine of perseverance taught could never be taken away. Once believers

10. Title page of Lewis Bayly, *The Practice of Piety.* The "Pious man" kneeling at the top between two tables marked "read" and "pray" implores God (depicted by the tetragrammaton), "A broken heart o Lord despise not." At the bottom the armies of the spirit and the flesh do battle between the Red Sea of baptism and the walls of Jerusalem. This work quickly became a classic of pious literature. It was first published around 1612; this edition of 1620 is already the twelfth. (By permission of the Folger Shakespeare Library)

had been brought to a degree of assurance of salvation, it was then necessary to guide them as to how they should order their new behavior. Hence the numerous volumes of cases of conscience, tracts on "domesticall duties," and guides to prayer and meditation.

The emphasis on making one's election sure drew attention to a question that would become a recurring point of discussion among English and Anglo-American predestinarians for generations to come: what kind of behavior or experience best evidenced saving faith? The answers given by individual devotional writers invoked different signs, often within the pages of the same book. *The Plain Man's Pathway to Heaven* specified no fewer than four lists of probable marks of election. Some of these, for example,

"reverence of God's name
keeping of Sabbath
truth
industrie
sobrietie
compassion
humility
chastity
contentation"

emphasized the outward evidence of virtuous behavior. Others, for example,

"assured faith in the promises of God
sincerity of heart
the spirit of adoption
sound regeneration and sanctification
inward peace
groundedness in the truth
continuance to the end"

highlighted personal sentiment and inward experience. Although most prominent ministers followed Dent in trying to include both forms of evidence, a dialogue arose between those on opposing sides. At one extreme, the popular devotional writer John Downame wrote that the proper method of gaining assurance was to begin with sanctification and work backward to election. At times his tracts veered dangerously close to the Catholic doctrine of justification by works, as when he urged charitable giving in *The Plea of the Poore* because "by these works of mercy we are furthered notably in the way to salvation." At the other extreme, the relatively obscure Suffolk vicar John Eaton, author of *The Honey-Combe of Free Justification by Christ alone* (published 1642 although written earlier) was so taken by his discovery of Luther's writings on justification that he denied that sanctification had any connection to assurance and accentuated instead the free imputation of Christ's righteousness. Shortly after the first major wave of Puritan emigration to Massachusetts, Anne Hutchinson and her supporters in the Bay Colony likewise criticized those who turned for comfort to the performance of "duties," favoring immediate communion with the Holy Spirit. This position alarmed many churchmen, for it seemed to suggest that the opponents of predestination may have been correct when they warned that the doctrine undermined morality. Those who espoused it were charged with Antinomianism, the belief that to the pure all things were pure, and that those who felt the stirrings of the Spirit within them could behave as they pleased. Eaton was deprived of his living, while Hutchinson's avowals touched off an altercation that roiled Massachusetts from 1636 to 1638 and led to her being driven from the colony.[48]

From about 1640 onward, the specter of Antinomianism thus began to haunt English theology. Fear of it may have driven some theologians away from predestinarianism entirely, encouraging the advance of Arminian conceptions of grace that would become so visible at the Restoration. Those who remained committed to predestinarian teachings can be separated in the second half of the century between two camps. The first was that of the "moderate Calvinists," figures like Richard Baxter and John Goodwin, who searched out a middle ground between Arminianism and Antinomianism. These men were receptive to Amyraut and his concentration on universal grace. They depicted both justification and sanctification as gradual processes and held that assurance was to be found in contemplating the signs of sanctification within oneself, notably in holy living. Against them were arrayed the "high Calvinists" like John Owen and Thomas Goodwin, who feared that the emphasis the former group placed on moral effort veered so far in the direction of Pelagianism that it was an even greater menace than Antinomianism. These men remained strict double predestinarians, defended the decisions of Dort, and adduced the inward stirrings of the Spirit as evidence of election.[49]

As those English theologians who explored the anatomy of conscience refined their skills in discerning the evidences of saving grace, they did not simply debate one another about the marks of assurance. Some gained enough confidence they could identify those with saving faith that they began to restrict full church membership to those who could present testimonies of their possession of it. Reformed churches had long charged individuals with demonstrating an adequate mastery of doctrine and the catechism before being admitted to communion, and some, such as the Dutch, demanded that newcomers present attestations of upright living. But all previous Reformed theologians had insisted that the visible community of church members in this world could not be equated with the invisible community of saints destined for salvation in the next. The division between the elect and the reprobate cut through the membership rolls of the Reformed churches. Around 1633, however, assorted Massachusetts churches began to stipulate that those who wished to be admitted to communion not only be of good character and demonstrate a mastery of the basics of the faith, but also be able to testify to the congregation or its governing elders about the action of grace in their hearts and why they felt they were among the saved. The custom of restricting membership to those "visible saints" who could provide this sort of testimony passed over to the English church in Rotterdam by 1637. Amid the upheavals of the civil war and interregnum, sundry English congregations adopted this practice as well. It is the most distinctive feature of what would become known as the Congregational churches.[50]

In the first years of the Reformation in Zurich, one of the initial schisms in the young evangelical movement occurred over whether baptism should be administered to all children at birth or restricted to adult believers. Zwingli, moved by his vision of the city as a Christian community and his fear that the restricting of baptism to believing adults would divide that community, had opted for infant baptism. If, however, the elect could be identified from evidences of saving faith, and if only that fraction of the community was to be admitted to full church membership, logically it might be appropriate to replace infant baptism with adult baptism. In 1633 a group of separatists in London replicated the act of many preceding groups of Anabaptists from within a Reformed theological outlook when they instituted the practice of adult baptism. The practice fit well with the early Congregationalists' restriction of full church membership to those who could claim the possession of saving grace and so propagated in these circles during the civil war and interregnum. These early Baptist churches separated themselves into two clusters along the theological fault line between predestinarians and antipredestinarians, creating the Particular Baptists, who taught that grace was destined only for the elect, and the General Baptists, who taught that it was offered generally for all. Here lie the origins of the modern Baptists.[51]

The Practices of English Piety

Although English devotional writers' cultivation of the experimental predestinarian tradition was of signal importance both to the flowering of Anglo-American theology and as the matrix out of which the Congregationalists and Baptists grew, it would be misleading to place the entire corpus of English practical divinity beneath the sign of experimental predestinarianism. The writings of William Ames betray little emphasis on the division between the elect and the reprobate and do not stress the need for believers to make their election sure. Predestinarian themes are similarly muted in Bayly's *Practice of Piety*. Because of the style of voluntary piety and the menu of ascetic practices that English practical divinity served to promote, the full corpus of such divinity was of no less importance than that fraction of the corpus that elaborated the themes of experimental predestination.

The style of piety expounded by the English practical divines emphasized first of all the centrality of preaching. It was through the preached word that individuals were brought to belief and confirmed in their faith. Thus, the brief *A Garden of Spirituall Flowers,* culled from the writings of Greenham, Rogers, Perkins, and others, urged a special regimen for Sunday sermon attendance. The godly head of household should lead his family to church and fix his attention firmly on the preacher. He should mark the daily text, note the preacher's discussion of each division within it, and find and dog-ear the scriptural passages alleged in support of the exegesis, in order to be able to review them more carefully later. Once back home, he should discuss the sermon with his family after the midday meal and then head out in the afternoon to a second sermon.[52]

The intense focus on the preached word, together with the long-standing Puritan hostility to the Church of England's surfeit of holidays, gave rise to one of the most important theological novelties introduced by the English practical divines: their strict doctrine of the Sabbath. Earlier Reformed theologians had often battled to see that no secular amusements or activities interfered with full attendance at Sunday services. A few of them, notably Zanchi and Franciscus Junius, had linked the Sabbath to the moral law. Béarn's ecclesiastical ordinances forbade all Sunday work and recreation. But Calvin and Bullinger alike judged the Fourth Commandment's injunction to keep the Sabbath day holy part of Jewish ceremonial law, no longer binding on Christians; Sunday set aside as a day of rest and worship was simply a practical application of the larger obligation to worship God with seemliness and order. Most leading Reformed theologians of earlier generations did not object to church members engaging in sober amusements after services. Calvin himself occasionally bowled on Sunday afternoons. It was thus a notable novelty when conferences at Cambridge and within the Dedham classis in the 1580s elevated strict Sabbath observance into nothing less than "the main groundwork upon which [to] build the practice of all other pious duties," "the training day of military discipline" containing "the sum and substance of all religion." The fully elaborated Puritan view of the Sabbath was published by Greenham's stepson Nicholas Bound in *The Doctrine of the Sabbath* (1595), which drew upon views earlier advanced by Greenham and Lancelot Andrewes. According to Bound, the Fourth Commandment was the most salient of the decalogue. Its injunction to keep the Sabbath holy was part of the eternal moral law, binding on Christians as well as Jews. It entailed the obligation to give the entire day over to worship and to acts of charity and consolation, except when extraordinary circumstances necessitated such work as protecting one's crops and possessions against a flood. It also made the dedication of any other days to divine worship, except for occasional days of fasting and mortification to implore God to divert his apparently impending wrath, serious acts of disobedience to the divine will. Bound's book was quickly called in by Archbishop Whitgift, but the view of the Sabbath it expressed became a staple of the literature of the practical divinity, and the question of whether or not lawful recreations were permitted on Sunday became a point of political and theological contention alike between "precise people" and anti-Puritans in England and later in the Netherlands.[53]

In addition to emphasizing careful attention to sermons and the dedication of a full day each week to worship and the service of God, the literature of practical piety promoted a rich diet of private devotions. One's first action on awakening, the *Garden of Spirituall Flowers* suggested, should by a holy and divine meditation on God's kindnesses and one's own sins. Prayer should follow, with the family gathered together if possible. Bible reading and psalm singing should be part of each day, and the day should end with more prayers and meditations. Bayly suggested reading one chapter of the Bible each morning, afternoon, and evening; this would permit completion of the entire Holy Writ each year by squeezing in six chapters on December 31. His *Practice of Piety* offered a generous provision of specific prayers and meditations for occasions in life: for morning and evening, before and after supper, on the Sabbath, before and after receiving the Lord's Supper, before taking physic, on death's doorstep, and so on. These, like many other published meditations, were often in the first person, tendering to the reader a virtual blueprint of the thoughts and emotions deemed appropriate for the moment. As the century advanced, magnified attention was devoted to encouraging meditation on the ways in which the features of the natural world bespoke the God who created them. "Every herb, flower, spire of grass, every twig and leaf, every worm and fly, every scale and feather, every billow and meteor speaks the power and wisdom of their infinite Creator," wrote Joseph Hall. Meditative Christians who moved through the world could thus be inspired to ring mental changes on everything they observed. Cotton Mather did so on spotting a tall man, which moved him to pray, "Lord, give that Man, High Attainments in Christianity; let him fear God, above many." Even in the act of urinating he could find an occasion for such meditation:

I was once emptying the cistern of nature, and making water at the wall. At the same time, there came a dog, who did so too, before me. Thought I; "What mean and vile things are the children of men. . . . How much do our natural necessities abase us, and place us . . . on the same level with the very dogs!"

My thought proceeded. "Yet I will be a more noble creature and at the very same time when my natural necessities debase me into the condition of the beast, my spirit shall (I say *at that very time!*) rise and soar. . . ." Accordingly, I resolved that it should be my ordinary practice, whenever I stop to answer the one or other necessity of nature to make it an opportunity of shaping in my mind some holy, noble, divine thought.[54]

The life of inward devotion was meaningless if not joined to strenuous moral effort. "Christianitie is like to a trade or occupation, wherein no good will be done, nor profit arise, except it be thorowly followed and with great diligence," Rogers wrote. Individuals would be called to account for time idly spent, added *A Garden of Spirituall Flowers.* This did not mean they should be excessively heedful of profit. Those "in prosperity" should use their means "soberly, and to the good of Gods children." All should avoid "cards, dice, and other kinds of gaming, wherein worldlings do take their felicitie." The more detailed manuals of Puritan casuistry spelled out an extraordinarily thorough code of conduct: in a relatively late work like Richard Baxter's *A Christian Directory: or, a Summ of Practical Theologie, and Cases of Conscience,* 1,143 folio pages were needed to cover "Christian Ethicks (or private Duties)," "Christian Oeconomicks (or Family Duties)," "Christian Ecclesiasticks (or Church Duties)," and "Christian Politicks (or Duties to our Rulers and Neighbours)." The work's abundant "directions for walking with God in a life of faith and holiness" included rules for the government of one's thoughts, passions, senses, tongue, and body.[55]

To help structure and reinforce the lessons of this methodical piety, the English devotional writers promoted specific practices of self-discipline. One such was maintaining spiritual diaries as a means of self-monitoring and self-improvement. Evidence of diary keeping for that purpose in fact predates this period in England. An account from 1574 of the Marian martyr John Bradford notes,

He used to make unto himself an ephemeris or journal, in which he used to write all such notable things as either he did see or hear each day that passed. But whatsoever he did see, he did so pen it that a man might see in that book the signs of his smitten heart. For if he did see or hear any good in any man, by that sight he found and noted the want thereof in himself, and added a short prayer, craving mercy and grace to amend. If he did hear or see any plague or misery, he noted it as a thing procured by his own sins, and still added *Domine miserere me,* "Lord have mercy upon me." He used in the same book to note such evil thoughts as did rise in him. . . . And thus he made to himself and of himself a book of daily practices of repentance.

The first surviving diaries of this kind originate in the Cambridge circle of the 1580s and 1590s. Rogers kept one, and Perkins urged his readers to do likewise; they constituted "catalogues and bills of thine own sins," he wrote in his *Graine of Musterd-Seede.* Later English writers echoed and amplified this suggestion. John Beadle urged believers to mark the time, place, and person by whom the journal keeper was first converted, the mercies vouchsafed by divine providence, and all prayers that had been answered.[56]

One early diarist from this circle, Rogers, also recorded the first known case of private covenanting, which he publicized in his *Seven Treatises.* According to his report there, a group of individuals in Wethersfield who met for mutual edification decided in 1588 to draw up a compact "for better living." Acknowledging they had failed to use "the long and continued peace and libertie of the Gospell to the end for which God did send both," they vowed they would strive to glorify God's name more eagerly, to feel the miseries of others more sharply, and to intensify their exertions to grow in grace and detach themselves from worldly pleasures. To assist in this undertaking, they pledged to set aside a time each day for prayer and meditation. To monitor their progress, they would communicate regularly about their "estate" with "some faithfull brother."[57] Less novel ascetic practices long part of the Western armory of such techniques were also encouraged by this literature, notably the recommendation that individuals review their day's actions at the end of the day.[58]

No vision of what Calvinism entailed has become more widely disseminated than the picture of the faith sketched in Weber's *The Protestant Ethic and the Spirit of Capitalism,* which in fact drew its story of Calvinist religiosity largely from works of English practical divinity from Bayly to Baxter and Bunyan. According to this account, the emphasis on predestination that over time became pronounced within Reformed theology in the generation after Calvin bred anxiety about election. This encouraged in believers the systematic pursuit of virtue in order to prove to themselves that they were among the elect. Thus arose a uniquely rationalized style of piety. Many features of the English literature of practical divinity substantiate this reading. The literature evolved at a time and in a milieu in which predestination was a strong presence and pointedly urged people to consider whether or not they were among the children of God. Much of it suggested that virtuous behavior could be taken as evidence of assurance. The style of piety it promoted, although drawing upon a common stock of ascetic practices, was undeniably thorough and systematic. But qualifications of this picture are called for. As we have seen, few authors made the evidence of moral behavior the sole or even principal ground for assurance; the inward working of the spirit was paramount for many. As well, the years around 1600 were the high-water mark for predestination in English theology. From the 1620s onward, the supralapsarianism of Beza and Perkins was in retreat, as supposed "Arminian" and Amyrauldian views gained ground. Later seventeenth-century English devotional writers, however, still urged readers to make their election sure and still offered them glasses of godliness in which they could look for signs of assurance. In fact, those most inclined to do so and to emphasize the evidence of works as marks of grace in this period were generally those least "Calvinist" in the matter of predestination.[59] The distinct characteristics of English practical divinity were not knit into a whole by any necessary predestinarian logic. As the history of their reception would prove, they composed a bundle of important themes, motifs, and practices that could be separated from one another.

THE CHALLENGE OF THE NEW PHILOSOPHY AND BIBLICAL PHILOLOGY

By reinforcing the doctrines of the first generations of Reformed theologians with the logical tools and expository methods of late medieval scholasticism, the architects of Reformed orthodoxy hoped to construct a firm edifice of dogma that could be effectively transmitted to upcoming generations. The effect was to stir up unanticipated conflicts about predestination, to move discussion of the order of the divine decrees to a new level of complexity, and to engender certain of the doctrines regarded by later observers as most characteristic of Calvinism. The last decades of the sixteenth and first decades of the seventeenth centuries also witnessed the initiation of what would become the English tradition of practical divinity, which defined a pattern of life that likewise would often be taken in later centuries to be synonymous with Calvinism. But no sooner had the dogmatic positions of high orthodoxy come to be staked out than changes in those fields of study that were the propaedeutic to the academic study of theology, that is, philosophy and the sacred languages, began to challenge these views.

Cartesianism and Its Consequences

From within philosophy came the challenge of René Descartes. Descartes's novelty was many-layered. His epistemology focused on systematic doubt, the analytic division of all questions into their simplest constituent parts, deductive logic, and the truth criterion of clear and distinct ideas in the mind. His scientific writings offered a mechanistic narrative of the operations of the natural world incorporating and claiming to explain the fruits of the most recent findings in the natural sciences, including Copernican astronomy. Al-

329

though he always identified himself as a loyal son of the Catholic church and although many contemporaries hailed his writings as the perfect antidote to the libertinism and unbelief of the age, his proofs of the existence of God seemed novel and dangerously unpersuasive to others. His programmatic statements and prefaces in both Latin and the vernacular boldly announced the bankruptcy of Aristotle and all other previous philosophers and positioned his ideas as the solution to the sceptical crisis of the era in a vivid, rhetorically effective autobiographical manner. Such ideas attracted many and alarmed no fewer. The most radical converts of the subsequent generation—notably Lodewijk Meijer, author of the *Philosophy the Expounder of Holy Scripture* (1666), and Baruch Spinoza, whose *Theological-Political Treatise* was published in 1670—went so far as to question the reliability of the Bible and of all the many portions of Christianity they believed could not meet the standard of offering patent, distinct truths to the mind. Descartes himself, however, distinguished between the truths and methods of philosophy and of theology, and supporters of his ideas seized upon and underscored this distinction as a means of reconciling continued commitment to the elemental beliefs of the Reformed tradition with a certain liberty of philosophizing. But even these individuals were obliged by Descartes's Copernicanism to oppose the literal inerrancy of the Bible and to accept instead that the authors of the Bible had sometimes accommodated their histories of miraculous phenomena to the prevailing beliefs of their time. They also rejected the categories and arguments of Aristotelian and scholastic philosophy. Even those Cartesians who viewed themselves as loyal heirs of the Reformed tradition thus were led into conflict with the tendencies of thought that had been reinforced by the rise of Protestant scholasticism.

From within philology came a less self-advertising but equally consequential challenge. Although the study of the sacred languages and the chapter-by-chapter exegesis of the Bible receded within Reformed institutions of higher learning in the generations around 1600, they never fully disappeared before the advance of philosophical training and doctrinal exposition. On the contrary, professors who taught these subjects continued to argue in good Erasmian fashion that the close philological study of the early editions of the Scriptures was one of the best means of promoting both the knowledge of God and true piety. Meanwhile, the march of classical erudition pressed on. By 1600, such titans of learning as Joseph Scaliger and Isaac Casaubon had mastered a wide range of ancient Near Eastern languages and glimpsed the possibility of understanding details of biblical history still more accurately by drawing upon secular historical sources and utilizing the early Chaldaic and (recently discovered) Syriac translations of the text. Over the course of the next hundred years, learned laymen like Scaliger, Grotius, Daniël Heinsius, and Isaac

Newton would prove vital in cultivating the *annotationes* tradition of biblical exegesis that examined each book historically and comparatively. They
were particularly daring besides in questioning such long-standing opinions
as Moses' authorship of the first five books of the Old Testament. Catholic
scholars as well, most famously Richard Simon, played a prominent role in
explicating the historicocritical approach to the Bible, encouraged by the belief that the variability of biblical editions might be an Achilles heal of Protestantism. But Reformed scholars, too, most notably at the Huguenot Academy
of Saumur, championed the utility of critical biblical scholarship, even while
striving to defend the basic points of Reformed theology against Remonstrants, anti-Trinitarians, and Catholics alike. In adopting such an approach,
these scholars promoted a more fully historical approach to the Old Testament, one that weakened the sense of identification with the world of ancient
Israel that had been so powerful for the Reformed tradition up until this time.
They implied in addition that the knowledge of divine revelation was progressive, advancing as the study of sacred philology advanced. Since that pillar
of orthodoxy Gomarus had just begun to maintain the doctrine of the literal
inerrancy of the Bible, this too deeply unsettled it.

The shock of Cartesianism was felt first and most disruptively in the Netherlands, where Descartes himself lived from 1628 to 1649. Even between 1633
and 1637, when he had completed the elaboration of his mature philosophy
but hesitated to publish it in the wake of Rome's condemnation of Galileo, his
manuscripts circulated among friends there. Within two years of the publication in 1637 of the first sections of his work, disciples in the philosophy faculties of Utrecht and Franeker were defending his ideas. By the 1650s, some
theologians as well were convinced Cartesians.[60]

Many Dutch theologians meanwhile feared anything that threatened the
Reformed church's already imperfect hold on their society. Gijsbert Voetius
(1589–1676) was orthodoxy's greatest defender. One of the most learned and
combative theologians of the age, he spent the first forty-five years of his long
life on the front lines in the wars against both Catholicism and Arminianism.
Born in the Brabant fortress town of Heusden, close to the unstable border
with the Spanish Netherlands, he was still a boy when his father died in battle
against the Habsburgs. Later, after serving as a military chaplain in the army
of Frederick Henry, he was given the task of introducing Reformed worship to
's-Hertogenbosch when that city was taken from the Spanish. This drew him
into a sharp pamphlet war with the celebrated Louvain Catholic theologian
Cornelius Jansenius, who tried to warn the inhabitants against the dangers of
Protestant teachings. As a scholarship student at Leiden just as the Arminian
controversy was beginning to divide the university, Voetius had forthrightly
championed Gomarus's views, for which he nearly lost his scholarship since

the principal of his college was a leading Remonstrant. His initial ministry in Heusden likewise embroiled him in the Arminian issue, for the city's other minister was another prominent Remonstrant.[61]

While a student in Leiden, Voetius absorbed not only the neo-Aristotelianism, high predestinarianism, and biblical literalism of his master Gomarus; he also gained exposure to the English tradition of practical theology, which inspired numerous imitators in the Netherlands. His publications included a set of pious exercises for students and a translation of Bayly's *Practice of Piety* with marginal annotations. When called in 1634 to Utrecht's recently founded Illustrious School, soon to be upgraded to a university, he expressly affirmed in his inaugural lecture the necessity of combining knowledge with piety. For his remaining forty-two years he promoted both with exceptional vigor in his capacities as professor of theology and minister. In the university, he supplemented his regular classes with special disputations held each Saturday at which points of theology bearing upon the questions of the moment were debated in front of all who cared to attend. During Voetius's lifetime, Utrecht became a leading university, attracting numerous students from abroad, most notably from Hungary. In the city, he and his fellow ministers, many his ex-students, encouraged the intensification of consistorial oversight of church members, the promulgation of stricter municipal laws against immorality, the enforcement of anti-Catholic legislation, and the elimination of carryovers from the medieval church, notably the capitular offices preserved for the benefit of prominent patricians of this erstwhile cathedral town. The same city that before had been split between the Reformed of the Consistory and the Preachers of the Old and New Testament witnessed during the 1650s and 1660s some of the Netherlands' sharpest conflicts between partisans and opponents of an austere and clericalist vision of a godly reformation. Pope Gijsbert, as his enemies called him, was convinced that piety and belief wanted strong reinforcement if the Netherlands was ever to become the watery Israel it was called to be. His unstinting pursuit of that goal, combined with his vast learning, made him the most towering figure within the Dutch Reformed Church of the seventeenth century.[62]

When Cartesian ideas began to attract support from members of Utrecht's philosophy faculty, Voetius reacted speedily. As early as 1639, several of his students defended theses against atheism directed at Descartes without mentioning him by name. Two years later, a defense of Cartesian ideas in public disputation by a member of the medical faculty set in motion the first endeavors to prohibit the teaching of such ideas and touched off a battle of pamphlets and petitions between Descartes and the Utrecht philosophy professor, Martin Schoock. The controversy ended with an order from the Utrecht authorities not to publish anything "pro or contra Descartes," but not before the feud had migrated to Leiden as well, where other publications followed, among them the first of Voetius's five volume of *Selected Theological Disputations*.

Voetius listed more than forty specific errors of Cartesianism in his disputations, but his primary objections were twofold. First, he saw Descartes's writings as examples of "indirect atheism." One side effect of the earlier disputes about predestination had been to inspire many Reformed theologians to teach with renewed conviction Aquinas's old arguments that humankind possessed an innate conviction of God's existence and of the fundamentals of the moral law—the better to punctuate people's inexcusable culpability in their damnation and thus to defend a predestinarian God against the charge of injustice.[63] In line with this trend, Voetius considered genuine disbelief in the existence of God to be impossible, so profoundly was the idea of God rooted in every person's mind. But if genuine disbelief was impossible, the closest cousins to atheists were those who shook people's faith by encouraging doubt and scepticism. Just as doctors who used bad medicines were guilty of murder, Voetius argued, so philosophers who encouraged their students to forget all they knew and who prized their own ideas above the knowledge of God and the natural law implanted in them were guilty of indirect atheism.[64] Descartes's incorporation of Copernican ideas into his natural philosophy was objectionable to Voetius as well on philosophical and biblical grounds alike. The objections on philosophical grounds were part of the broader exchange, vital in the history of science of the era, between partisans of the long-dominant Ptolemaic-Aristotelian understanding of the cosmos and those who championed innovative hypotheses about the motions of the solar system. The scriptural objections grew from Voetius's conviction that the sacred books allowed for no mistakes even in details that had nothing to do with the faith. Hence, a passage like Joshua 10:12–14, in which Joshua commanded the sun to stand still, demonstrated that the sun ordinarily moved around the earth; it was no mere metaphor employed to avoid a lengthy explanation of astronomical principles unknown to the ancient Israelites, as Cartesians were prone to see it. The fact that many of Descartes's early supporters included prominent Remonstrants—the translator of the *Discourse on Method* from French to Latin was none other than the pastor who had fled France because of his objections to the canons of Dort, Etienne de Courcelles—only added to the objectionable character of Cartesian ideas in Voetius's eyes.

Fighting over Cartesian philosophy and the authority of Scripture intensified in the 1650s with the publication of *Two Dissertations*, by the Leiden philosopher Christopher Wittich, which maintained that the language of the Bible was adapted to the prejudices of its audience: Holy Writ was not a manual of physics. This time the engagement spilled over into the vernacular when in Utrecht the patrician Lambert van Velthuysen joined the fray with a Dutch-language *Proof that the belief of those who teach that the immobility of the sun and the movement of the earth do not contradict God's Word* that jabbed sharply at theologians who meddled in matters in which they have no business. The discord grew intense enough to induce the classis of The Hague to complain that the polemics were calling Scripture into question and to appeal to the States of Holland to do something. But, amid the first stadtholderless period, when that long-standing pillar of support for the Reformed church, the House of Orange, stood at the nadir of its power, the political climate was hardly auspicious for ecclesiastical appeals for the protection of religious orthodoxy—especially since the influential Jan de Witt was an interested student of mathematics and science and a relative by marriage of one of the leading Cartesians. De Witt took charge of engineering a carefully worded resolution that, while appearing to chastise the offending Cartesians by ordering philosophers to avoid matters of scriptural interpretation, left them free to teach what they wanted within the domain of philosophy, so long as they avoided questions taken from Descartes that gave offense. The enforcement of this decree was left in the hands of the curators of the university, who insisted they had no intention of initiating an inquisition against Cartesianism.

Over the ensuing fifteen years, while de Witt reinforced his power, Cartesians enjoyed their greatest period of patronage for faculty appointments, despite the substantiation that the publication in these years of Meijer's *Philosophy the Expositor of Holy Scripture* and Spinoza's *Theologico-Political Treatise* appeared to offer for the Voetian claim that Cartesianism inevitably led to grievous error and atheism. Church synods and classes across the Netherlands and in neighboring Cleves-Mark-Jülich-Berg protested in vain against the dangers of Cartesianism and admonished candidates for the ministry to avoid the lectures of known Cartesians. Reaction to the return to power of the House of Orange in 1672 culminated in a decree of 1676 by the curators of Leiden University that forbade the public or private teaching of sixteen Cartesian propositions. By this time, however, Cartesians were well entrenched in many faculty positions. When Pierre Bayle arrived in the Netherlands five years later, he found Wittich not only still teaching philosophy at Leiden, but attracting more students than any other professor there. In addition, the vernacular pamphlet debates about Cartesianism had brought the question of the authority of Scripture to the attention of a broad Dutch audience.

Nowhere in the Reformed world did Cartesianism touch off public controversies as intense as those in the Netherlands and its neighboring German territories; but English university students, too, began to read Descartes regularly by the 1650s, prompting university philosophers there to try to counter its materialism. His ideas reached Lausanne in 1662 and were defended by the students of a young philosophy professor at Saumur, Jean-Robert Chouet, by 1667. In 1670, Chouet accepted a call to Geneva. Yet in the changing English and Genevan theological climate of the late seventeenth century the advent of Cartesianism was just one part.[65]

The Development of Biblical Scholarship

The question of just how the Bible was to be understood and whether or not every word of it was literally true came to the fore as the seventeenth century advanced, not only as a result of the skirmishes around Cartesianism, but also because of advances in the study of sacred languages and biblical criticism. The Netherlands was once again a center of such study. Among the formidably learned classical scholars who built the reputation of the University of Leiden in the historical and humanistic disciplines were such leaders as Scaliger and Heinsius, who were noted for their application of the rules of criticism and the study of Oriental languages to the *annotationes* tradition. The value of the humanistic disciplines in the formation of ministers also found a defender against the rising tide of neoscholasticism in Franeker in the person of Sixtinus Amama (1593–1629), professor of Oriental languages. Amama's *Antibarbarus Biblicus* (1628)—the title recalls Erasmus's early *Book Against the Barbarians*—deplored the reappearance of excessive theological curiosity among the doctors of the Reformed church in the latter days, urged in good Erasmian fashion that more attention be devoted to the reform of life and less to the discussion of idle subtleties, and suggested that a means for doing so was remedying the lamentable ignorance of the sacred languages among young candidates for the ministry.[66]

Perhaps still more vital to the expansion of Reformed biblical study was the Huguenot Academy of Saumur, where Louis Cappel (1585–1658) taught Hebrew for forty-five years. Unusually for a French Protestant, Cappel followed his studies at Sedan with a few years abroad at both Leiden and the Oxford of Isaac Casaubon, where he absorbed an interest in the technical problems of biblical exegesis. In 1624, he stirred up a storm within the small world of Reformed Hebraists with his *The Secrets of the Vowel-Points Revealed,* which directly attacked the Polanus-Buxtorf position that the vowel points were part of the original language spoken by God to Moses and made a strong case that these could not date from earlier than the sixth century A.D. Cappel followed this with a fuller discussion of the problems of biblical hermeneutics, the *Critica Sacra, or Six Books on Variant Readings of the Books of the Old Testament,* which was so explosive it could not be printed until sixteen years after its completion in 1634, and then only by a Catholic press in Paris. The great novelty of Cappel's biblical exegesis was not simply that he regarded the vowel points of the Masoretic text as a late addition—earlier Reformed theologians had believed that as well—but that he combined this conviction with the methods Scaliger had timidly begun to explore of correcting passages in the Masoretic text on the basis of other early translations and even nonbiblical texts, yielding a number of new readings of specific passages. Cappel was quite explicit about seeing the understanding of the Bible as something that evolved progressively. The interpretations of individual exegetes were never anything more than the best interpretations possible at any given moment, but this did not mean, as Catholic controversialists argued, that Scripture interpreted without the assistance of an authoritative tradition was impossibly obscure; on the contrary, so long as the text was properly "chastened" where necessary through philological and comparative methods, the message emerged clearly.[67]

Remonstrant exegetes like Grotius, Episcopius, and de Courcelles went well beyond Cappel in the daring with which they used the methods of historical criticism to question the authorship of divers books of the Old Testament; they in turn were exceeded by such men as Hobbes, Spinoza, and Simon. By the later decades of the seventeenth century, the defenders of orthodoxy were thus faced with the challenge of replying to a series of critics who offered strikingly novel and unsettling readings of large portions of the Bible. Those Reformed churchmen who found the methods of biblical criticism a useful tool for understanding theology rather than an innovation to be anathematized rarely went as far as a Hobbes or a Spinoza. Cappel, for instance, defended Moses' authorship of the Pentateuch, and he and his fellow Saumurois wrote rebuttals of the Remonstrant catechism and of the Socinians, so they remained firmly within the time-tested traditions of Reformed doctrine even while accepting a more historical and critical approach to the Bible. Acceptance of the utility of historicocritical methods for biblical study, in other words, did not necessarily breed the sort of radical questioning of the authority of scriptural texts found in the writings of the most extreme exponents of this method. Yet even in the hands of those eager to remain within the mainstream of Reformed thought, a shift in attitude toward the Bible followed: any discussion that altered the relation of interpreters to Scripture cut to the heart of the theological enterprise.

The clearest illustration of this is the changed view of the institutions and prophets of ancient Israel of those touched by these trends. Few convictions were more central to the early prophets of the Reformed tradition than the belief that the events, prophecies, and institutions of the Old Testament contained lessons of the utmost topicality for their own times. The debates between the partisans of a Genevan and a Zurich understanding of the relation between magistrates, ministries, and the proper exercise of ecclesiastical discipline revolved in large measure around disputes about the precise relation between the kings of Israel and the rabbis of the Sanhedrin at the time of the first Temple. In a prefatory letter to Calvin's lectures on Ezekiel addressed to the great Huguenot champion Gaspard de Coligny, Beza urged the assiduous study of the prophets for anyone involved in the political defense of the true faith, for the maxims of political wisdom set forth there were even more assured and unvarying than the truths of mathematics.[68] The result of adopting the historical and critical approach to the Old Testament of a scholar such as Cappel was to widen the sense of distance between ancient Israel and contemporary Europe. No longer was it as easy to see the institutions of that distant world as normative for the Christian church. No longer did the example of King Josiah purging Judah of idolatry seem quite as insistent a model of Christian rulership. The political thought of Cappel's Saumur colleague Amyraut manifests some of the implications of this changed stance toward the Old Testament. Amyraut denied that government was a divinely ordained institution whose obligations included protecting and promoting the true worship of God in the manner of the kings of ancient Israel. Instead it derived from human agreement and was dedicated to purely human aims. Such a view carved out a space for the toleration of more than one religion by a Christian prince and thus was perfectly suited to the political circumstances of the Huguenots in this period, but it was strongly at variance with the earlier traditions of Reformed political thinking that had insisted upon the obligation of rulers to protect true religion and justified the execution of heretics.[69]

The net result of the dissidence engendered by the advance of Cartesianism and the bolder new historical methods of biblical criticism was to bring a new agenda of questions to the forefront of theological discussion. The logical resolution of the tangles of predestination receded in urgency. Issues of the authority of Scripture and the extent to which Old Testament obligations were binding on Christians took on new importance. Furthermore, both Cartesianism and the advance of historical criticism could be seen as lending new power to the claims of reason within Christianity's centuries-old discussion of just how reason and revelation properly coexisted: Cartesianism through its call to subject all beliefs to systematic doubt and to retain only those that could meet the standard of clear and evident truth in the mind, historical criticism through its suggestion that the very text of Scripture required tools of critical reasoning in order to be properly established. The numerous scientific advances of the seventeenth century further burnished reason's claims. In this context, theologians felt themselves obliged to explore the issues of which parts of Christianity were truly compatible with reason and how Christianity could best be demonstrated to what was believed to be a multiplying legion of unbelievers. Others clung to a defensive confessional orthodoxy. The theological confrontations of the second half of the seventeenth century were very different from those of the first.

COCCEIUS, RATIONAL THEOLOGY, AND THE RETREAT OF ORTHODOXY

While Cartesian philosophy and biblical philology altered the terms of discussion of Reformed theology across Europe, the specific issues confronted within each national church differed more and more as the seventeenth century advanced. At the risk of slight oversimplification, three main circles of debate can be identified during the latter part of the century.

The first was centered in the Low Countries with extensions into the German Reformed territories and Hungary, linked to the tendency for pastors from these regions to study in Dutch universities. The attacks against Arminianism and Cartesianism had entrenched within the Dutch church a potent faction of precisian clergymen committed to high orthodox theology and the literal inerrancy of the Bible, while driving out anti-predestinarian views and the bolder strains of biblical criticism. Here the focus of controversy became the ideas of Johannes Cocceius (1603–69), one of the most eminent and original systematic theologians of the era, whose ideas appeared to the guardians of orthodoxy to challenge the literal word of the Bible and echo the dangerous ideas of Descartes. The opposing voices of Cocceius's supporters and opponents divided the Dutch Reformed for fully two generations.

Matters were different in England. Here, the midcentury splintering of the previously unified Church of England and the resulting emergence of a Babel of competing churches, tendencies, and individual prophets (see chapter 12) encouraged antidogmatic forms of theology that tried to reunite all believers through the appeal to reason. From the Interregnum to the aftermath of the Glorious Revolution, a style of rational theology that in the Netherlands remained confined to Remonstrant circles moved closer and closer to the mainstream of the English church, gaining strength from the conviction that it offered an antidote to atheistic implications latent in the new philosophy. In so doing, it opened the way for deism and anti-Trinitarianism, those still stronger variants of theological rationalism that set the terms of theological debate by the last decade of the century.

The third circle of theological debate encompassed Switzerland and the French Reformed churches, Geneva being the point of intersection between Cartesian and Salmurian inclinations coming from France and the high Reformed orthodoxy enshrined within the Swiss Confederation. Here predestinarian theology and scriptural literalism initially reinforced their domination in response to the new developments of the century's middle decades. By century's end, however, a dramatic transformation of the theological landscape was under way. The overlap between these debates was modest, but their outcome was everywhere similar: various forms of rational theology gained ground, forcing orthodoxy to retreat.

Cocceius

Johannes Cocceius was at once one of the most learned Hebraists of his age and a systematic theologian in the tradition of covenant theology, which, while it did not deny the doctrine of predestination, downplayed its importance. Born into a leading patrician family of Bremen, he received the most crucial portion of his education at that city's Gymnasium Illustre, whose leading light, Matthias Martini, was a master of the ancient languages, a covenant theologian in the tradition of Bullinger and Olevianus, and one of the Bremen theologians who had been most outspoken at Dort in opposing the stricter supralapsarians. Cocceius then moved on to Franeker, where he studied with Amama and William Ames. He won notoriety while still in his twenties by publishing a commentary on the Talmud and a highly esteemed dictionary of Hebrew. Ascending the rungs of an academic career that in due course took him to a chair in theology at Leiden, he published his most important work of systematic theology there in 1648, the *Doctrine of the Covenant and Testament of God*.[70]

Although difficult and repetitive, the *Doctrine of the Covenant and Testament of God* has been appreciated by seventeenth-century and modern theologians alike as one of the richest and most original statements of covenant, or federal, theology. While Cocceius's readings of the Bible were profoundly shaped by interpretive schema derived from this tradition, he nonetheless, true to the antischolastic thrust of his education, pointed up the need for an exegesis that stuck as close as possible to the text of Scripture and avoided unnecessary philosophical terminology. His strong historical sense was discernible in an approach to the covenants that stressed the progressive unfolding of God's salvific design through time. As Cocceius understood the twofold covenant God had made with humankind, the first part had taken the form of a covenant of works, by which God had inscribed the essence of the moral law in Adam's heart, promising eternal happiness in return for obedience to this law. After the Fall, a second pact had been established between the Father and the Son by which those who believed in Christ would be saved despite their sins. This covenant of grace had a twofold "economy." It was initially founded with Abraham and his descendants in expectation of Christ and announced through the many prefigurations of Christ evident in the Old Testament. Its precise features were then revealed with Christ's coming and the revelation of the New Testament, which instituted a new set of sacraments and permitted believers to grasp more firmly the essence of the moral law. Cocceius's conviction that the covenant of grace was already revealed, albeit obscurely, to Abraham and his descendants encouraged him to advance many allegorical and typological readings of Old Testament passages, which he saw as everywhere prefiguring the later work and teachings of Christ. Thus, according to him, even the colors of the curtain of the tabernacle described in Exodus 26 were meaningful: the blue was an emblem of grace, the scarlet a sign of humility.[71]

His sharp distinction between the two economies of the covenant of grace also led him to downplay the importance for Christians of the institutions and laws of ancient Israel. Thus, he notably saw the injunction to keep the Sabbath as simply an adaptation for the Jews of the larger moral principle that one must honor and serve God in all actions, imposed upon them because of their limited understanding and rebellious character, but not binding on all believers. Cocceius's theology contained a strong apocalyptic element too.

Cocceius's learning was impressive. Nothing in his theology manifestly contradicted the basic confessional documents of the Dutch church. His call to recover the true sense of the Bible and avoid unnecessary philosophical terms echoed original Reformation principles. For these reasons, he attracted many pupils and followers. Yet many features of his theology awakened the suspicion of Voetius and his allies. The criticism of scholastic terminology naturally stung. The allegorical readings of so many scriptural passages seemed not only too clever by half, a reversion to Catholic traditions of exegesis, but also yet another example of deviation from the transparent, literal sense of the Bible comparable to the Cartesians' twisting of Joshua 10:12–14. Furthermore, among the principles that Voetius and his fellow precisians had absorbed from the English practical divines and made their own was the insistence on keeping the Sabbath holy. The situation was thus ripe for division over Cocceius's ideas. To a certain extent, the Voetian–Cocceian divisions of post-1655 represented a continuation of the struggles around Cartesianism, insofar as both Cartesianism and Cocceianism challenged literal readings of the Bible and appealed to those traditions in Dutch political culture allergic to excessive clerical assertiveness. What is more, certain Cocceians embraced Cartesian ideas within the realm of philosophy. The Leiden theologian Salomon van Til (1643–1713) began a tradition of dividing the exposition of theological principles into two parts, natural and revealed theology, using the Cartesian proofs of God in the section on natural theology and Cocceian methods for revealed theology. The God known by reason, he further asserted, was the same as the one known by Scripture. Most Cocceians, however, were strongly critical of Lodewijk Meijer's application of Cartesian principles to re-

vealed theology, and there was no necessary connection between the Cocceians and the Cartesians, even if many Voetians lumped them together in a
broader crusade against "shameful novelties."[72]

For a battle that endured for more than a half century, the Voetian–Cocceian struggle has been remarkably little studied and remains obscure on
many points. Controversy began over the issue of the Sabbath, with a volley of
published treatises between 1655 and 1658. Positions rapidly polarized. The
more extreme Cocceians urged their auditors to resume their normal daily
activities when they got home from Sunday worship. The strictest precisians
condemned even sitting on one's front stoop on the Sabbath.[73] The synods
of Holland and Friesland grew so bitterly divided that the States had to forbid all discussion of the Sabbath question. New bouts between Voetians and
Cocceians took place irregularly throughout the succeeding decades, often
obliging the secular authorities to step in. Leiden University's overseers outlawed the teaching of seven Cocceian assertions in the same decree of 1676
that banned sixteen Cartesian theses. William III purged the city council of
Middelburg that same year after it chose a Cocceian parish minister unacceptable to the local classis. Twenty-two years later, he blocked the contentious
appointment of a Cocceian professor of theology to the University of Utrecht.
The division between the two camps over doctrine and lifestyle was strong
enough that the partisans of each tendency were said to be distinguishable by
the cut of their clothes and the style of their wigs.

The Dutch church had learned the dangers of schism, however, and the
conflict was never allowed to become a full rift. Amsterdam's ministers
showed the way toward a peaceful accommodation of the differences when
they worked out an agreement among themselves in 1677 to recognize their
agreement on the cardinal points of doctrine, to seek out future ministers
of a "moderate and peaceful humor," and not to enquire too far into where
and with whom candidates for the ministry had studied. Elsewhere, partisans of the rival tendencies adopted a policy of alternating appointments between the two camps. Through measures like these, the conflicts were contained, although squabbling between the parties did not fully die down until
the 1730s.[74]

Many German Reformed territories and Hungary as well witnessed conflicts between Cocceians and anti-Cocceians, the high point in Hungary coming in the 1670s. By contrast, Cocceius was so little read in either France or
England that one Huguenot minister in exile in the Netherlands after the revocation of the Edict of Nantes wrote an explanation of the points at issue between the two parties in order to explain to his bewildered refugee compatriots what all the fuss was about.[75]

The Latitude Men and Rational Theology in England

The England of the 1650s was a very different place from the Netherlands. Over the preceding decade, two civil wars had been fought, the king had been killed, and the monarchy abolished. While the king lost his head, the established church splintered. Partisans of episcopal, presbyterian, and congregational church government defended their respective positions with new dogmatism. Preachers and pamphleteers expounded a dizzying array of views without fear of censorship. Students of the prophetic books of the Bible announced the coming of the millennium. Quakers exalted the direct inspiration of the Holy Spirit. Prominent clergymen applied lessons from Old Testament history to present political circumstances, often with disastrous results. Many left their parish churches to worship in gathered congregations. Amid all the upheaval, not only did Descartes's works begin to be read widely within university circles; Thomas Hobbes spelled out a rival mixture of mechanism and authoritarianism in a series of writings that culminated in the *Leviathan* of 1651. His attempt to find a firm basis for political obligation in natural law, as well as his advocacy of obedience to a single strong ruler and of state control over the church, touched responsive chords among many English. It was thus all the more alarming that he denied the disparity between matter and spirit and, because human reason was too weak to identify any other evident moral principles, suggested there could be no basis for natural law beyond the impulse toward self-preservation. This hardly differed from Epicureanism, the ancient philosophical school most thinkers of the early modern era equated with atheism and libertinism at its most reprehensible. Faced with the alarming proliferation of rival church parties, sects, and philosophies, sensitive young theologians longed to bring the splintered church back together while neutralizing the twin threats of enthusiasm and materialistic Hobbesian atheism.[76]

Even before the revolutionary decades of the 1640s and 1650s, one English clergyman had been led by a distinctive personal odyssey to make strong claims for the capacity of critical reason to ground questions of faith. William Chillingworth (1602–44) had converted to Catholicism as a young Oxford fellow in 1628, aspiring after Christian unity and shaken by the Catholic polemical argument that the Protestants had destroyed this unity at the Reformation. A short stay at a Jesuit seminary on the Continent convinced him that the Roman church was less capacious than he had imagined and no home for those who could not accept transubstantiation. He returned to England, where he gained employment as a tutor in the household of the Viscount Falkland, whose estate at Great Tew, near Oxford, was a regular gathering spot for scholars. The viscount's Catholic wife had engaged Chillingworth in the hope he might draw their children toward Catholicism. He, however, becoming convinced while there that the arguments in favor of the Protestant faith were stronger, returned to the Church of England. The reasoning that led him to this position is explicated in his *The Religion of Protestants a Safe Way to Salvation* of 1637, a point-by-point rebuttal of a contemporary Catholic tract. The core of the work is captured in Chillingworth's statement, "I shall believe nothing which reason will not convince that I ought to believe it." Whereas Catholic polemicists had long seized upon the divisions among Protestants to argue that Scripture lacking the guidance of an authoritative tradition could not be well understood, Chillingworth wanted to demonstrate that the Bible met all critical standards of a reliable historical record and so could rationally be accepted as the word of God. The finer points of dogma that some extracted from Scripture were perhaps impossible to know with certainty, but this was not what was elemental to Christianity. God did not expect fallible humans ever to know the full truth with absolute confidence, but he did expect them to seek it and guaranteed salvation to those who love it. "Though men are unreasonable, God requires not anything but reason," Chillingworth alleged. Hooker's classic of early Anglicanism, the *Laws of Ecclesiastical Polity*, had already asserted the capacity of natural reason to fathom the laws of nature God had inscribed in the universe and thus to serve as a basis for arriving at the proper form of church government. Chillingworth extended the realm of reason to assaying the veracity of the Bible and assenting to those essential truths that defined the core of Christianity.[77]

Amid the upheavals of the civil war and the interregnum, the appeal to the basic verities that reason and natural law could delineate struck a chord among aspiring university theologians. A group of prominent university instructors including Benjamin Whichcote (1609–83), Henry More (1614–87), John Wilkins (1614–72), and Ralph Cudworth (1617–88) began to blend philosophy and theology to articulate a vision of Christianity they hoped would win the assent of all reasonable persons. They in turn trained a generation of students: Simon Patrick (1626–1707), John Tillotson (1630–94), Edward Stillingfleet (1635–99), and Thomas Tenison (1636–1715), thinkers who came to be recognized as forming a distinctive group of "Latitude-men" following the Restoration in 1660.[78] Many of these individuals had been raised in the traditions of a strict predestinarianism but had rebelled against it. Legend had it that More argued so determinedly against the doctrine as a youth that his uncle whipped him for his stubbornness, while Patrick reportedly was terrified as a boy by a sermon on reprobation. These men were drawn to the new philosophy but troubled by what they saw as its atheistic implications, which they devoted many of their early writings to refuting. More and Cudworth earned the label Cambridge Platonists from nineteenth-century scholars for their profession that the knowledge of God was imprinted in the rational soul and that the existence of the spiritual world was the first of certainties. Whichcote was more inclined to ground the existence of God on arguments from design and the natural world. However they arrived at the conclusion, they all tended to see an order inscribed by God in the world or imprinted in the human mind that offered a code of morality largely identical with the divine law and that people could grasp by virtue of their innate rationality.

The admirable design of nature or clear and distinct ideas in the mind may have proved the existence of God, but the divinity's full design for human salvation could not be known without recourse to the Bible. This revealed mysteries beyond rational comprehension, for example, the Trinity. It was nonetheless rational to believe the Bible and to accept the mysteries it revealed since its accounts of the history of God's chosen people and of Christ's life rested on such reliable testimony and was confirmed by prophecies and miracles. As Whichcote put it, "Reason discovers what is natural, and reason receives what is supernatural."[79] What the Bible chiefly taught, these men believed, was a set of moral lessons and sacramental obligations that did not pass far beyond the dictates of natural reason. Morality made up nineteen-twentieths of all religion, according to Whichcote. "All the duties of the Christian religion which respect God are no other but what Natural Light prompts men to, excepting the two sacraments and praying to God in the name and by the mediation of Christ," echoed Tillotson. For Stillingfleet, the conquering of one's passions, the forgiving of injury, the doing of good acts, self-denial, and patience in adversity were the "real expressions of piety." These views were indebted to ancient moral philosophy: Wilkins's handbook for preachers, *Ecclesiastes,* strongly recommended Cicero, Seneca, and Plato. They also had a near kinship with the ideas of the Dutch Remonstrants. Many latitudinarians in fact corresponded with the leading Remonstrants of their day and praised those of the preceding generation, notably Episcopius and Grotius. Grotius's rational vindication of the truth of the Christian religion was so persuasive that his book of that title went through twenty London printings by the end of the seventeenth century. One of the most popular versions was a revised and augmented edition prepared by Patrick.[80]

The writings of Stillingfleet typify the thinking of the latitudinarians. After a Cambridge education, Stillingfleet received ordination in 1657 from an ejected bishop, a sign that he felt a measure of respect for the episcopate swept away by the Long Parliament. Two years later, however, his first book, *Irenicum, A Weapon-Salve for the Churches Wounds,* demonstrated he was no episcopalian irredentist. Adorned on the title page with the passage from Philippians, "Let your moderation be known unto all men," the work reviewed the evidence of the apostolic age, the early church, and the opinions of leading reformers about the diverse institutions of Europe's Protestant churches to show that no clear mandate existed for any particular form of church government. Natural law dictated a few basic points: the worship of God required human association; some had to be placed above others to lead in worship, and they deserved respect; a system of decision making was needed to resolve disputes. Beyond that, whatever institutions were closest to apostolic practice and most suited to advancing the peace of the church were best for a Christian church, and as neither the Bible nor natural spoke explicitly about this, its determination rested in the hands of the secular authorities. Although Stillingfleet expressed a preference for a system mixing episcopal and presbyterian elements, his key point was that all Christians should accept whatever system was decreed by their governors for their national church. As he would likewise remark in two other pamphlets, *The Mischief of Separation* and *The Unreasonableness of Separation,* to rupture the unity of the church over questions of church government was wrong. England's fissures over church government had to be repaired, he argued, because as controversies among Christians had grown, religion itself had come into controversy, and piety had noticeably cooled. The works also rejected the "enthusiastick spirit," implying that genuine prophets were sober, rational people, not those who fell into trances or trembled as they spoke.[81]

Three years after the *Irenicum* tried to call people back into a single national church, *Origines Sacrae, Or a Rational Account of the Grounds of the Christian Faith, as to the Truth and Divine Authority of Scripture* addressed the atheists Stillingfleet believed were becoming more numerous. The work's focal points were the unreliability of ancient texts that hinted the world might be older than Adam and the historical and logical plausibility of the Bible. Simple common sense indicated that the Bible was God's revealed word. It met the criteria for reliable history better than documents that appeared to contradict it. It contained many prophecies that had come true. If certain of the miraculous events it reported defied the laws of nature, these were authenticated by numerous witnesses, whose independent accounts of the central events of the life and work of Jesus agreed quite closely with one another. Its story of the world's creation was more plausible than all rival philosophical accounts of the beginning of the world. In short, the Bible met all normal criteria for judging the trustworthiness of a historical text and the plausibility of the events it reported.[82]

Three years later, still quite young at thirty, Stillingfleet directed his book *A Rational Account of the Grounds of Protestant Religion* to rebutting one of the many Catholic controversialists of the day. This was a fairly conventional piece of anti-Roman argument, covering topics that had long set Protestantism's defenders against Rome's. Yet, because the perennial run-ins between

Protestants and Catholics continued unabated throughout these years, it initiated a large number of replies and counterblasts. One of Stillingfleet's contributions to this fight, *The Doctrine of the Trinity and Transubstantiation Compared as to Scripture, Reason and Tradition,* proposed to prove that although the Trinity was a mystery beyond reason, transubstantiation was positively absurd and self-contradictory.[83]

Not only did Stillingfleet's concerns typify those of the Latitude-Men; his career traced an ascending course typical of many in this group. During the Restoration period, he occupied a series of London pulpits and won such renown for his preaching that Samuel Pepys reported he was deemed "the ablest young man to preach the Gospel of any since the Apostles."[84] He received a bishopric following the Glorious Revolution, as did Patrick and Tenison, while Tillotson became archbishop of Canterbury. The champions of rational theology thus came to occupy leading positions within the church.

By equating faith with the rational acceptance of the Bible's historical reliability, however, Stillingfleet and his associates advanced into what became ever more treacherous terrain as the century advanced. Once Spinoza had denied that the Bible could offer any form of secure knowledge and had questioned the possibility of miracles, once Simon's authoritative works of biblical criticism had accepted that a key proof text for the doctrine of the Trinity, 1 John 5:7, was a late interpolation into the biblical text, and once the historicizing of Holy Writ encouraged readers to think of it not as an inspired whole but rather as a collection of testimonies of unequal validity written at various places and times, it was difficult for many who wanted a rational faith to suppress doubts about basic elements of Protestant orthodoxy. Spinoza's *Theological-Political Treatise* received a partial English translation in 1683 and a full one in 1689. Simon's *Critical History of the Old Testament* was in English by 1683. By 1690, Newton, whose early thought was significantly shaped by Henry More, was privately sharing with John Locke, himself an associate of many latitudinarians, his textual reasons for believing that the doctrine of the Trinity had no biblical foundation.[85]

The view that the doctrine of the Trinity was both irrational and nonbiblical had been heard in England ever since continental anti-Trinitarian works crossed the channel and gained publication during the 1640s; but it was during the decade from 1687 to 1696 that those identifying themselves with the cause of reason began to challenge orthodoxy from all sides. In 1687 a new term, *Unitarian,* made its appearance in Stephen Nye's *A Brief History of the Unitarians, called also Socinians.* The work surveyed the varieties of anti-Trinitarianism from ancient through modern times with a thoroughness that made it a compendium of anti-Trinitarian arguments and ignited a pitched battle over the Trinity that did not subside until 1704. In 1693, a collection of letters and short tracts entitled *The Oracles of Reason* publicized the views of the first self-avowed deist, Charles Blount, whose "Account of the Deist's Religion" proclaimed the sufficiency of a purely natural religion, one with no role for Christ.[86] Two years later John Toland's *Christianity not Mysterious* took up the closely related point that "there is nothing in the Gospel contrary to Reason, nor above it; . . . no Christian Doctrine can be properly called a Mystery."[87] Also in 1695, Locke demonstrated with his *The Reasonableness of Christianity* how dramatically a historicizing approach to Christianity could simplify the fundamentals of the faith. Essaying to answer the classic Protestant question of the nature of saving faith, the work, largely ignoring the New Testament epistles because they were written later, offered a careful historical reconstruction of what Jesus enjoined his followers to believe on the basis of the four Gospels. Locke concluded that Christians simply needed to believe that Jesus was the Messiah and to demonstrate repentance and obedience. Neither pagans nor the ancient Israelites could have known that Jesus was the Messiah; they would be saved if they simply practiced Old Testament righteousness and followed the flame of reason to identify and heed their moral duty. Shortly before publishing the treatise, Locke wrote to a Remonstrant friend in Holland, "When everything in this creed of mine seemed everywhere sound and conformable to the word of God I thought that the theologians . . . ought to be consulted, so that I might see what they thought about the faith. I went to Calvin, Turrettini [a Genevan theologian of the later seventeenth century whom we shall meet shortly] and others, who, I am compelled to admit, have treated that subject in such a way that I can by no means grasp what they say or what they mean; so discordant does everything in them seem to me with the sense and simplicity of the Gospel."[88]

These views naturally alarmed Stillingfleet, and in the last years of his life he directed a series of works against them. His *Discourse in Vindication of the Doctrine of the Trinity* piled up textual evidence in support of the authenticity of the key passages in the Bible supporting the Athanasian understanding of the Trinity and historical evidence that it had not been imposed by force. Although he could accept that the vowel points were not part of the original Hebrew script, he defended Moses' authorship of all of the Pentateuch except a few passages obviously added after his death; in addition, he called attention to the ancient manuscripts that included 1 John 5:7, failing to mention those that omitted them. He took pains to counter the disparagement of "priestcraft" increasingly heard from the likes of Toland and Locke— the claim that the great threat to the simplicity of true religion had always been the clergy's self-serving tendency to bolster its power with invented mysteries, superfluous rituals, and an unnecessary dogmatism.[89] His polemics and those of others who shared his views could not prevent a variety of Unitarians,

Deists, Free-Thinkers, and advocates of Primitive Christianity from gaining toeholds within the Church of England during the upcoming decades; neither had their vision of rational Christianity ever won over that still-greater fraction of the English population that remained loyal to predestinarian principles and a more experiential view of faith. For these Englishmen the latitudinarians were "meer Moral Men, without the Power of Godliness." Nonetheless, the position Stillingfleet and his associates defined would occupy a large portion of the theological center of English Protestantism for more than a century after his death. Strikingly, the chief authority he cited for accepting the authenticity of 1 John 5:7 was none other than Beza, that founding father of Reformed orthodoxy. Even while his silence about the subtleties of predestination, his intellectualist conception of faith, and his more optimistic view of human nature all marked his distance from that orthodoxy, he remained true to certain of its tenets.

From Orthodoxy to Rational Theology in Switzerland

The stress points of theological discussion were different again in Switzerland and its French-speaking borderlands, although here too rational theology gained strength by century's end. As indicated, Cartesian ideas did not reach the academies and universities of this corner of the Reformed world until the 1660s. The theologians of the region were also sensitive to the issues raised by Cappel's biblical criticism because the Buxtorfs of Basel, father and son, were key players in the falling-out with Cappel over the issue of the vowel points. The initial consequence of the arrival of Cartesian and Salmurian currents in the region was to stiffen the resolve of those theologians who had already built strong outworks around orthodoxy in the wake of Arminius and Amyraut. In 1668, Bern's authorities forbade the teaching of Cartesian ideas. In the following year, the Genevan Council of Two Hundred decided to oblige all ministers to sign a strict formulary of orthodoxy. This action, however, revealed that Amyrauldian ideas had penetrated Genevan thought, for two of the city's leading ministers, Louis Tronchin and Philippe Mestrezat, protested they could not sign such a document. After much debate and an initial decision allowing the two to persist in their refusal, the council reversed itself and insisted they sign, which they did "for love of peace."[90]

The divisions revealed within Geneva by this episode so alarmed the theologians of Switzerland's Protestant cantons that they sought a new credal formula. The ministers of Basel and Zurich took the lead. The most outspoken Genevan defender of orthodoxy, François Turrettini, lent his support. They convinced the governing authorities, and in 1674 a diet of the Protestant cantons agreed to have one drafted. The result was the so-called Helvetic Consensus of 1675, composed by Turrettini, Zurich's Johan Heinrich Heidegger, and

Basel's Lukas Gernler. This document was above all an anathematization of the ideas of Amyraut and Cappel. Against Amyraut, it espoused the doctrine of limited atonement. Against Cappel, it insisted upon the literal inspiration of Scripture and the integrity of the Masoretic text, vowels as well as consonants. The great majority of Protestant territories of the region—Zurich, Basel, Bern, Schaffhausen, Biel, Mulhouse, and the Reformed churches of Appenzell, Glarus, and the Grisons—adopted it with little opposition. In Zurich, some ministers protested that it did not go far enough because it did not also condemn Cocceius's teachings. Geneva, however, proved to be divided, open as it was for linguistic reasons to a stronger dose of Salmurian influence. Opposition from the likes of Tronchin and Mestrezat delayed its approval for several years, and only through the efforts of Turrettini was it finally accepted by the Company of Pastors in 1678 and by the Council of Two Hundred in 1679. In Neuchâtel, at the urging of Jean-Rodolphe Ostervald, its subscription was never imposed on the clergy.[91]

The Helvetic Consensus was perhaps the highest statement of high Reformed orthodoxy ever adopted by a major ecclesiastical gathering. Within a generation, it was abandoned by many of the territories that adopted it. In Geneva, the person chiefly responsible for turning the tide was Turrettini's own son, Jean-Alphonse Turrettini (1671–1737). The elder Turrettini had died when the youth was just sixteen, and Jean-Alphonse had thereupon fallen under the spell of Tronchin and the Cartesian Chouet. A grand tour to Leiden, England, and Paris during which he met such luminaries as Newton, Nicolas de Malebranche, and Bernard de Fontenelle completed the younger Turrettini's conversion to the newer modes of thought. Family connections ensured his prompt appointment as rector of the academy in 1701 and professor of theology in 1705. His mature thought showed how the intellectual developments of the century had reinforced the authority of reason within the realm of theology while discouraging excessive exploration of the mysteries of predestination. The preceding century had been one of great progress in philosophy, mathematics, physics, and criticism, he announced to his students in 1703; it was their task to harvest the fruits of this progress. In his theological writings, he employed the tools of biblical criticism, rejected the sort of allegorical readings favored by Cocceius, and insisted that reason was an autonomous source of the knowledge of God, capable of judging the truth of theological doctrine and not just of assisting in the explication of Scripture. His chief work, published in 1735 as the *Treatise of the Christian Religion*, was designed to prove against the deists that the basal doctrines of Reformed Christianity could all meet the test of rational theology, including such points contested by the Tolands and the Newtons of the age as the Trinity and the authenticity of biblical miracles. The doctrines he defined as fundamental nonetheless were not numerous and did not include predestination. In both substance and mode of argumentation, the work was a far cry from the writings of a Beza or a Gomarus.[92]

The ideas that Jean-Alphonse Turrettini taught from Calvin's old lectern in Geneva were just one example of the new rationalism overspreading this region as the seventeenth century gave way to the eighteenth. Slightly older than Turrettini, and a model figure to him, was another scion of a prominent Genevan family, Jean Le Clerc (1657–1736), who ended his life as a literary journalist and professor of ecclesiastical history in the Remonstrant Academy in Amsterdam. Like the younger Turrettini, Le Clerc fell under the spell of Tronchin and Chouet at the Genevan Academy. He completed his studies just as Geneva began to compel all candidates for the ministry to sign the Helvetic Consensus. To postpone having to face the decision about whether or not to sign a document about which he had begun to harbor doubts, he took a position as tutor to a young Huguenot from a prominent robe family, which led him to Saumur and gave him the opportunity to procure more of the books, forbidden in Geneva, for which he was beginning to acquire a taste: those of de Courcelles, Episcopius, and Simon. He started to dabble in biblical exegesis and criticism himself, penning a dissertation on Gomorrah and Lot's wife that intimated that the biblical report of Lot's wife being turned into a pillar of salt was a figure of speech. By 1682, he had been sufficiently indiscreet about his views that reports of his heterodoxy had reached Geneva from prominent Reformed ministers abroad. After returning home briefly to collect his books and property, he fled to Holland for good just prior to the pronouncement of a formal sentence of banishment against him.

Le Clerc's mature writings comprehended a vast range of subjects. His greatest success came from a series of literary periodicals that offered reviews of the latest works of scholarship, notably hard-to-find and censured books. The most important of these, the *Universal and Historical Library,* rivaled Bayle's *News of the Republic of Letters* as an instrument for disseminating knowledge about the most daring publications of the time. His works of biblical criticism expanded the discussion of the authorship of the first five books of the Old Testament begun by Simon and set out naturalistic explanations for many of the miracles reported in the Bible. His pseudonymous *Appendix to Augustine* was an attack on the two pernicious doctrines for which he held that church father chiefly responsible: predestination and *Compelle entrare,* or the justification of the use of force against heretics. His philosophy courses at the Remonstrant Academy in Amsterdam incorporated many of the ideas of Locke and Newton, both correspondents of his. Last of all, he edited the works of Erasmus and a new edition of Grotius's *Truth of the Christian Religion,* to which he added a postscript of his own on how one could know which of the many Christian churches was the best. His answer was that it was the one whose members behaved the best and whose confession of faith did not contain many articles. Genevan booksellers could not keep Le Clerc's works in stock, and when a cousin of Turrettini's visited Amsterdam in 1711, he was asked by a Walloon minister he encountered there if it was true that everybody in Geneva was an Arminian.[93]

Everybody in Geneva was surely not an Arminian, but even those of Turrettini's colleagues in the Genevan pastorate thought to represent the conservative wing of the clergy at the turn of the century—Benedict Pictet (1655–1724), for example—testify in their writings to the changed theological climate. While Pictet upheld the doctrine of predestination, he warned against entering into quarrels over the topic. He rejected the scholastic method and adopted a historicocritical approach to Scripture. His chief pastoral calling was to promote the reform of life rather than the comprehension of doctrine. In this, he displayed many of the same concerns that animated Neuchâtel's leading pastor of the same generation, Jean-Frédéric Ostervald (1663–1747), a champion of liturgical reform and the author of catechetical and practical writings destined to obtain wide circulation throughout the French-speaking Protestant world and beyond. Ostervald's catechism omitted the topic of predestination. It treated moral questions at greater length than the laws of doctrine.[94]

Under the impact of such men, the high orthodoxy of the Helvetic Consensus withered. In 1706, the Genevan authorities repealed the requirement that the territory's ministers sign the document, replacing it with a formulary that mentioned only the church's early confessional documents and the synod of Dort. In 1725, this too was repealed. Basel likewise removed the injunction that its ministers sign the Helvetic Consensus in 1706, while in 1724 the evangelical diet voted as a whole to abrogate it, although Zurich and Bern retained it for use within their possessions.[95]

Along with a new doctrinal atmosphere, new sensibilities about worship were visible in turn-of-the-century Switzerland. In 1690, the psalter of Beza and Clément Marot that had been the cornerstone of Genevan and Huguenot devotion since the Reformation was replaced with a new version whose language incorporated the stylistic changes that had seeped into French over the course of the *grand siècle*. The strict avoidance of the popish observance of times and days that had dominated Geneva since the introduction of the Reformation ended in 1694, when special sermons were introduced on Christmas afternoon. Morning Christmas worship was added as well in 1719, after the pastors saw that the city's population was in any event ceasing to work for the entire day. An Ascension holiday followed two years later. Geneva also brought to an end its insistence that the community absolutely refrain from idolatry. The first breach here stemmed from the changed geopolitical realities of the age of Louis XIV, when the mass began to be celebrated in the residence of the French envoy in 1679; this measure was implemented only after the ministers went door to door to urge inhabitants to remain peaceful. But in 1707 a Lutheran minister was permitted to hold services for the city's German residents, and soon afterward was invited to join the Company of Pastors.[96] After more than a hundred and fifty years of fidelity to the practices forged in the generation of Farel and Calvin, a new era was dawning. It is easy to imagine what John Knox would have said about it.

11

CHANGING POLITICAL
CIRCUMSTANCES ON THE CONTINENT

T he confessional map of continental Europe stabilized during the seventeenth century. Fewer rulers changed their faith, and fewer new Reformed congregations were established than during the dramatic upheavals of the sixteenth century. Still, the situation remained fluid. Rulers occasionally converted. Ruling families died out and were replaced by cousins of a different faith. Wars resulted in the conquest of Protestant territories by Catholic armies and vice versa. Most important, the growth of state power over the course of the seventeenth century led rulers to believe that the toleration religious minorities had wrung from their ancestors might be repealed without the political costs that had forced their ancestors to grant it. Over the same period when the contours of Reformed thought and worship were being transformed from within by the opening rounds of the battle between historicocritical and literal understandings of the Bible, by Puritan practical divinity, and by the rise and fall of high predestinarian orthodoxy, most of Europe's Reformed churches thus also had to confront external political challenges that altered their strength and at times cast their very survival into doubt. On the Continent, only the Swiss had the good fortune to escape the "interesting times" of the proverbial Chinese curse: "May you live in interesting times."

THE POWER OF PRIVILEGE AND PRINCELY FAVOR

An unanticipated consequence of the Reformation was that a number of lands emerged from the upheavals of the sixteenth century with two or more Christian confessions living side by side. Reformed churches were particularly likely to find themselves in just such positions because their theology's emphasis on the need to separate from false worship had so often initiated the formation of breakaway churches. The Reformed churches in this condition were profoundly affected by politics over the course of the late sixteenth and seventeenth centuries. Where they enjoyed favored political status, they gained members. Their protected standing also permitted those within them who believed the initial reformation had fallen short of the goal of truly reforming both the church and the larger society to mount campaigns for further reformation with relatively little fear of the dangers of schism. Where Catholicism remained the royal religion, the Reformed churches declined in size and political influence. Conversion was especially common among the high nobility, avid for preferment and prestige at court. The defection of many aristocrats in turn sapped the overall strength of the church in proportion to the degree of noble protection it had received during its initial growth. In these lands, internal debates in the churches were far less liable to polarize opinion, as the churches knew their footing was too precarious to allow dissension to weaken the larger cause.

Everyday Relations Between the Reformed and Other Faiths

Insofar as the local studies attempted to date enable one to generalize about the relations between the Reformed and their non-Reformed neighbors in those lands where they lived side by side, it appears that once the initial upheavals of the Reformation era gave way to more settled patterns of religious coexistence, these were governed by a mixture of easy everyday contact and enduring mutual suspicion. In France, Reformed and Catholics lived in the same neighborhoods, did business with one another, and socialized with one another. In the small, religiously divided Gascon town of Layrac, local political rivalries cut across the religious divisions rather than following them. Marriage outside the church was far less common. When the Reformed of triconfessional Oppenheim did marry outside the church in the eighteenth century, they were far more likely to do so with Lutherans than with Catholics.[1]

As the high levels of confessional endogamy suggest, the considerable amount of everyday interaction among members of the different faiths did not efface what Etienne François has called the "invisible border" between them. Theologians and historians on the various sides of the religious divi-

354

sions produced an ample literature of controversy dedicated to demonstrating the errors and recalling the crimes of the rival faiths. Catechisms produced in regions of religious pluralism might devote pages to highlighting the errors of the rival faiths. The churches all discouraged attendance at another group's schools or ceremonies. Highly publicized debates between champions of the disparate confessions occurred in many localities in the seventeenth century. These rarely won converts for either side, although when they did these were trumpeted; they had the effect, however, of reinforcing the preexisting convictions of those attending and deepening their awareness of the points of doctrine that separated them from their neighbors.

In an age in which the majority of theologians and political writers of all stripes continued to accept the notion that the state had a responsibility to protect and promote God's law and the true church, zealous churchmen on all sides were quick to denounce violations of the laws governing religious coexistence wherever they perceived them. Clerical assemblies regularly implored the authorities to reduce or eliminate the measures of toleration granted other faiths. Whatever coexistence was achieved between the rival confessions in this era was gained less through an acceptance of religious pluralism as a positive good than through the grudging acceptance of toleration in the strict sense of the word, that is, as acceptance of an evil one would prefer to avoid, and through measures of conflict management designed to minimize the accompanying tensions. In such an atmosphere, it is not surprising that the ordinarily peaceful relations between the members of the divers faiths were irregularly interrupted by violent clashes. Small incidents recurred in every decade in France between 1600 and 1685, as Catholic crowds ransacked Protestant temples or stone-throwing Huguenots tried to drive Catholic missionary religious houses from predominantly Reformed localities. In Poland, where the Catholic population had initially reacted passively to the spread of Protestantism, a new militancy arose after 1570 and continued for several generations. The Reformed temple of Cracow was ransacked in 1574 and the books taken from it burned in a bonfire to the accompaniment of a Te Deum Laudamus. Attacks on the temple and cemetery followed in 1575, 1577, 1587, and 1591, at which point the temple was burned to the ground.

Growth and Campaigns for Further Reformation
in the Netherlands and Transylvania

If the Reformed churches in regions of religious pluralism were largely self-enclosed and self-recruiting communities after the initial period of the faith's expansion, they still gained or lost strength over subsequent generations according to the lay of the political landscape. In those areas in which Reformed princes ruled a multiconfessional state or the Reformed church was the legally

11. Assault on the Reformed Temple of Cracow 1574. This contemporary print depicts the assault on the temple of 1574. Roof tiles are being pried off. Books thrown from the upper story of the church are burned in a bonfire in the lower left. This was one of the first instances of a form of anti-Protestant crowd action that would become increasingly common over the subsequent century and a half. (Jagiellonian Library, Cracow)

privileged church of a republic, the church grew in strength. A vivid illustration of this pattern comes from Brandenburg-Prussia, where Elector John Sigismund faced so resolutely Lutheran a population when he converted early in the seventeenth century that he instituted Reformed services only in the milieu of the court. Initially, just a few noblemen who had previously served the House of Orange or in the Palatinate joined the ruler for services. In time the desire to win the elector's favor drew more. The Great Elector of the later seventeenth century, Frederick Wilhelm (r. 1640–88), was particularly active in appointing court preachers in cities throughout the lands he occasionally visited as a way of spreading Reformed services. By century's end these existed in roughly twenty cities. One preacher proudly contrasted the standing-room-only crowds of 1693 with the experience of the first few preachers, who carried out their jobs in fear for their life and spoke to a mere handful of listeners.[2] The same pattern of consolidation and growth characterized the two largest voluntary churches that benefited from a favorable political situation for most or all of the seventeenth century, the Dutch and the Transylvanian. Similarities in the history of these two churches were additionally reinforced by the educational links that brought many young Hungarian and Transylvanian students to Dutch universities.

Evidence about the numerical growth of the Reformed churches that enjoyed a privileged political status is especially good for the Low Countries. As we have seen, the Reformed church was able to establish itself as the legally privileged church of the seven northern provinces that gained their independence over the course of the revolt against Spain, but only a small fraction of the population initially became full members of the church. Membership in most local churches for which numbers are known at various dates between 1594 and 1704 increased dramatically over these years (table 11.1). Exceptionally good data on 117 rural communities of Friesland around 1744 indicate that at that date Reformed congregants made up 36 percent of the adult population of the region—still a minority of the population, but well up from the figures of 12 to 28 percent in regions of the Low Countries in the first decades of the seventeenth century.[3] Not only did the church increase in size; church elites and secular political elites became increasingly intertwined. The percentage of Leiden city council members who had served as elders of the Reformed church grew from 5 to 55 percent between 1574 and 1640. At any given time in the seventeenth century, between a fifth to a third of consistory members also sat concurrently in the city's Council of Forty. In Utrecht, too, the consistory and the magistracy came to overlap noticeably after 1618.[4]

For Transylvania, there is less hard data about church membership, but the region's emergence as the easternmost citadel of the Reformed tradition is clear enough. For eighty years after 1606, the territory was ruled by a series of

TABLE 11.1

Reformed Church Membership in Nine Localities of the United Provinces,
1594–1704

Friesland			

St. Annaparochie	*Heeg*	*Heerenveen*	*Molkwerum*
1601: 50	1594: 16	1635: 73	1611: 76
1699: 303	1626: 41	1689: 350	1682: 248
	1704: 116		

Bolswaard	*Sneek*	*Sloten*
1603: 216	1613: 524	1602: 40
1661: 1117	1655: 1182	1677: 151

Utrecht	

Utrecht	*Amersfoort*
1620: ca. 2000	1621: 500
1650: ca. 5000	1660: 1300

Sources: Bergsma, *Tussen Gedeonsbende en publieke kerk,* 104–13; Benjamin J. Kaplan, "Confessionalism and Its Limits: Religion in Utrecht, 1600–1650," in *Masters of Light: Dutch Painters in Utrecht during the Golden Age* (San Francisco, 1997), 69; E. P. de Booy, *Kweekhoven der Wijsheid: Basis- en vervolgonderwijs in de steden van de provincie Utrecht van 1580 tot het begin der 19e eeuw* (Zutphen, 1980), 147.

energetic rulers who embraced and favored the Reformed cause. The brief, extraordinary moment of anti-Trinitarian rule under John-Sigismund Zápolyai initially gave way to the domination of the Roman Catholic Báthory family, several of whose members won election to the throne from 1571 to 1608. But Sigismund Báthory (r. 1581–1601 with several interregna) awakened fears for both the safety of the territory and the security of Protestant rights by his espousal of holy war against the Ottomans, his willingness to collaborate with the Habsburgs in this cause, and his appearance of subordination to Jesuit advisors. The turmoil of the Long Turkish War of 1593–1606 was accompanied by bitter internal struggles that ended when a skilled, tough military leader sprung from the lesser gentry, Gábor Bethlen, arranged the assassination of the last Báthory and seized the crown. One of Bethlen's first acts was to confiscate the estates of many of his political opponents and thus to give himself a firm economic foundation on which to govern. Over the next decades he and his successors George I and II Rákóczi built an effective princely state. "As for religion," a Hungarian contributor to the English edition of Giovanni

Botero's *The World* (1630) recorded, "Bethlen himselfe is a zealous Calvinist, seldome going without a Latine testament in his pocket." The Reformed ministers predictably likened both him and his Rákóczi successors to the kings of Old Testament Israel and urged them to take up the mantle of protecting the faith. They did just that, although without abandoning the dictates of political prudence. On several occasions during the Thirty Years War they intervened opportunistically on the Protestant side against the Habsburgs and then withdrew from the conflict when events appeared to become too dangerous, gaining control of seven border counties in eastern Hungary in the process. Bethlen founded an academy at Alba Julia in 1622 and managed to lure to it from war-torn Herborn the theologian and Bible translator Piscator and the great polymath Johann Heinrich Alsted. George I Rákóczi similarly patronized the school of Sárospatak on his family lands.[5] In disputes with other confessions, Bethlen and the Rákóczis backed the Reformed forcefully. In Székelyudvarhely, where the Reformed and the Catholics had shared the church until 1612, the Reformed took it over for their exclusive use and barred Catholic priests from the town in 1614. In 1630 the Catholics regained permission to hold services in the town in a new church they were to build, but after they built it the Reformed took it over and obliged them to use the older one. Elsewhere, in 1619, the superintendent of one church district used his rights of visitation to evict sixty anti-Trinitarians from their benefices. Just how much the number and size of the Reformed churches grew as a result of this support is uncertain, but the number of anti-Trinitarian churches fell from 525 in 1595 to about 200 in the late seventeenth century, and the Reformed must have reaped much of the benefit from these losses.[6]

In the interest of building up the leadership of the Reformed churches, Bethlen and the other aristocratic protectors of the cause in both Transylvania and Hungary sponsored the study at foreign universities of promising young men preparing for clerical careers. In the period 1610–60 alone, upward of a thousand students from these lands completed their education at the most prestigious Reformed universities of western and central Europe. On their return to their homeland, many received appointments as deacons or superintendents. Before 1592, the greatest number of Hungarians studying abroad went to Wittenberg. After a Lutheran formula of orthodoxy was imposed there, Heidelberg and Marburg became the schools of choice. The devastation of the Thirty Years War in turn redirected the paths of most Hungarians toward the universities of the Netherlands, especially Franeker and Utrecht, where Ames and Voetius, respectively, taught. At least one hundred Hungarian and Transylvanian also proceeded to England for part of their education.[7]

For different reasons, pious adherents of the Reformed church in both the

Netherlands and Hungary/Transylvania could easily believe that the initial reformations of their lands had fallen far short of the ideal. The secular authorities in the Netherlands turned a blind eye to the practice of other religions and allowed much of the population to attend Reformed services and yet escape the yoke of church discipline. Churches in much of Hungary had preserved liturgical practices that were eliminated in most Reformed lands and retained a church structure that did not look much like the models endorsed by either Zurich's or Geneva's theologians in the latter part of the sixteenth century. Those who came into contact with the precise piety and strong presbyterial convictions of elements within the English church were likely to find their native churches wanting. In both countries, students returning from England launched movements for the further reformation of these churches in a manner akin to the Puritan campaigns in England.

The early development of what Dutch church historians call the *Nadere Reformatie* (that is, Further Reformation, a phrase in fact taken over from the English) was highly dependent upon Puritan inspiration. No figure was more important in launching this movement than Willem Teelinck (1579–1629), the son of a Zierikzee burghermaster who was completing his preparation for a legal career when he spent eight months in the little Puritan stronghold of Banbury. His later writings would nostalgically recall the wonderful stillness of Banbury's streets on Sundays, when the only noise to be heard was the sound of psalms being sung in family worship. His stay in Banbury convinced him to become a minister. After studying theology at Leiden, where he kept his distance from the battles that were embroiling Arminius and Gomarus, he gained his first parish in 1608 and immediately began an active career as a translator of English practical divinity and a writer of edifying treatises. His brother Eewout also became a celebrated author of edifying literature, as did his parishioner Jacob Cats, the Father Cats whose moralizing verses became one of the staples of seventeenth-century Dutch literature. On taking up his first living, Teelinck became involved in promoting one of the great causes of English precisianism, stricter Sabbath observance. With a fellow member of the Zeeland classis of Schouwen-Duiveland, Gottfried Udemans (also known to have possessed a vast library of English Puritan writers and himself the author of celebrated manuals of spiritual advice), he was able to gain the classis's support for a petition urging the authorities of Zierikzee to prohibit various forms of recreation all day Sunday. Zeeland's clergy brought the question of Sabbath observance before the Synod of Dort. A wider debate about the question ensued over the next decades. During this period only Zeeland's synod accepted Teelinck's English-inspired arguments that the Fourth Commandment was part of the eternal moral law and that all forms of recreation were inappropriate all day Sunday. Relatively untroubled by the Remonstrant controversy and closely tied to England geographically and by seafaring traditions, Zeeland became the great initial center of the Dutch efforts at further reformation.[8]

In 1627, at the low point of Protestant fortunes during the Thirty Years War and a time of suffering and difficulty for the Dutch in their renewed war against Spain, Teelinck published his fullest call for a thorough amendment of Dutch society, his *Necessary Expostulation, Concerning the Present Lamentable State of God's People.*[9] The dozens of sins and forms of inattention to God's word catalogued in this work included many standard components of clerical jeremiads from across the Reformed world: piety had notably cooled since earlier times, heathen feast days continued to be celebrated, attention was lax in church on Sundays. Others, such as the complaint that people came to church only to have their children baptized, reflected the unique compromises of the Dutch religious situation. Still others betokened Puritan influence, for example, the urging of stricter Sunday observance and the call for a national covenant. Teelinck's book was but part of endeavors by churchmen during these dark years to convince secular authorities to take stricter measures to uphold God's law and Christ's true church. Synods and classes multiplied appeals for stricter action against a range of abuses from Sunday mumming and dancing to the toleration given Catholics and Jews.[10] Agitation of this sort occurred several more times in the course of the century. During the 1650s and 1660s, Voetius and his disciples, great admirers of Teelinck and the English practical divines, made Utrecht their base for an active initiative to close the theatres, instill a stricter Sabbath regime, and dedicate *ad pios usus* the rich canonries of the former cathedral chapter that had been preserved as secularized sinecures for the region's leading families. Between 1669 and 1682, especially during the disastrous years that followed the French invasion of 1672, Herman Witsius, Jacobus Koelman, and other clergymen in many of the seven provinces called for a national covenant, attacked such abuses of worship as formulary prayers, and urged a general renewal of morals and piety.[11]

Little is yet known about the reception of these calls for further reformation. According to Ames, Zeeland became renowned in its day as a center of godliness under its practical preachers. In Holland, on the other hand, many opposed too much church oversight of social life; the great poet Joost van den Vondel attacked the "seditious seed" of the Teelincks in several anonymous verses. In Utrecht, Voetius and his allies won a few notable victories by convincing seven members of the chapter to renounce their prebends and by gaining a ban on theatrical performances in the city; but they learned the hard way that the civic authorities were not prepared to tolerate too much criticism of the status quo. Two ministers, one of whom was Teelinck's son

Johannes, lost their posts and were banished from the province for their out-spoken criticism of the usurpation of former church property. Koelman was likewise removed as minister in Sluis in 1675 for rejecting formulary prayers. It appears that in general the regents of the Netherlands proved far more concerned to keep clergymen from stirring up unnecessary controversy than they were to legislate strict Sabbath observance or harsher morals laws.[12] In the end, Dutch promoters of further reformation largely gave up trying to sway the magistrates to act as godly rulers and turned instead to awakening individuals to a stricter regime of piety.[13]

The partisans of further reformation sought other goals in Transylvania and Hungary, but the English connection was again critical. As early as 1610, one Transylvanian known to have studied in England and the Netherlands returned to Nagyvárad to urge the synod to establish lay elders and greater equality among ministers, only to be deprived of his post and banished for his pains. The main campaign of further reformation in the lands under Transylvanian rule came in the middle decades of the century and focused on purging remnants of popish ceremony from the liturgy and replacing the bishop/superintendents with a presbyterial–synodal church government. In 1638 ten Hungarian students in London vowed they would work on their return to restore the full purity of the Christian church and to eliminate all improper hierarchy within it. Word of their oath preceded them home, and the Debrecen synod decided that before ministers could be received, they had to agree to accept the traditional practices of the Hungarian church and to seek change exclusively through recognized church channels. The leader of the London group, János Tolnai Dali, nonetheless enjoyed the support of powerful members of the Rákóczi family. He was appointed to teach at the academy of Sárospatak, where he was soon in hot water for opposing baptisms of sick infants at times other than standard church worship, the elevation of the communion wafer, and the celebration of holidays. His enemies also charged he divided his students into the pious and impious and, in the manner of the Puritan practical divines, urged upon all an unnecessarily strict regime of behavior. He was deprived of his post at Sárospatak, but his patron and protector made him minister of Tokaj and archdeacon of Abaújvár. The clergy of the surrounding area split between supposed Puritans and anti-Puritans, and the issues raised were troublesome enough for the ruling prince to summon the closest thing ever held to a national synod of all of the Hungarian churches. Held in 1646 and attended by 110 delegates from the Transylvanian, Transtibiscan, and Cistibiscan districts, the synod of Szatmár suspended Tolnai Dali from his offices and upheld the church's practices of baptisms of necessity and holidays. It also mandated that students returning from abroad

had to promise not to teach Anabaptism, Socinianism, Puritanism, or Arminianism. A later district synod of Transylvania accepted the appropriateness of
synods and presbyteries in many churches and permitted individual churches
and regions to establish them, but rejected their mandatory founding in light
of "our different political order." The Hungarian debates attracted sufficient
international attention for Samuel Maresius of Groningen to write under a
Transylvanian pseudonym a defense of the existing church order that pointed
to the presence of superintendents and inspectors in many Swiss and German
churches and warned against "English simplicity."

Following Tolnai Dali's suspension, another Transylvanian with experience
of England, Pal Medgyesi, took up the struggle for further reformation. His
Political-Ecclesiastical Dialogue of 1650 urged the establishment of a presbyterian-synodal church order throughout the entire church. He was forced to
leave Transylvania proper but was sheltered by Susanna Lorántffy in the
neighboring counties then under Transylvanian lordship. Medgyesi's proposals to alter the structure of the church were rejected in 1651 by the synod
of the entire Transtibiscan district, but they earned enough support in area
synods in the regions governed by Susanna Lorántffy's favored younger son
for a presbyterial system of church governance to take shape in a few areas.
Agitation over this issue continued for a decade in several of the counties of
Hungary close to Transylvania. Medgyesi also revived the question of liturgical
changes by drafting a new service book with no elevation and prayers adopted
from foreign Reformed liturgies. Coming as it did just after the English civil
war and regicide, the call for such changes seemed to many a dangerous invitation to sectarianism. The Transylvanian diet and George II Rákóczi weighed
in in 1653 with a measure that upheld the power of superintendents to discipline the clergy of their districts and backed their decisions with civil penalties that could include death. Lorántffy riposted by refusing to allow church
visitors on her lands. When the town of Marosvásárhely debated the introduction of a presbyterium, the guilds were polled as to whether or not they supported the idea. The hatters' guild typified the response, saying of the "presbyterial religion," "We do not know what it is, do not understand it, and therefore
do not want to have it brought in."[14] While it lasted, Transylvanian presbyterianism was above all a movement of clergymen exposed to foreign ideas,
protected by some of the highest aristocrats of the land, with little support
among the population at large—just the opposite of the social profile it would
assume in Scotland. Whatever chance it had of producing widespread changes
in the region's churches was probably doomed by the fact that it crested just
when events in England were making Puritanism synonymous with sedition
and regicide.

That the timing of the movement's unfolding and the involvement of Transylvania's political leaders in the internal affairs of the Reformed church condemned the initiative to introduce elements of a presbyterian church order gains further plausibility from the greater success of such actions at the other side of the ancient kingdom of St. Stephen in the Transdanubian church district. Here, where the church synods operated independently of the highest political authorities, a call for lay elders and a consistorial body to aid in church discipline went up in the 1620s. The synod of Pápa accepted this proposal in 1630. In Pápa itself, the board of elders consisted of representatives of elements of the town's power elite: four magistrates, six burghers, and six military men. The board aided the clergy in disciplinary matters, oversaw the schools, and reviewed clerical performance. The leading advocate of this system, János Kanizsai Pálfi, was driven from the region by Catholic nobles in 1634 and fled across the Danube to Komárom, where he spearheaded a drive that ended in the founding of presbyteries throughout the villages of the region that were still functioning twenty years later. In these portions of western Hungary as well as in a few of the regions in which Tolnai Dali and Medgyesi were active, elements of a presbyterial-synodal church thus came to be instituted for at least a while within a national church that otherwise remained under the control of superintendent/bishops.[15] The modest gains of the movement for further reformation in this part of the kingdom hints at the affinity between consistorial and presbyterial-synodal elements of church government and situations where the church had to function without support from ruling princes.

The movement to introduce liturgical changes and a presbyterian-synodal church order in Transylvania finally collapsed amid the political crisis that ended Transylvania's golden age. Eager to support the Protestant cause and dreaming of acceding to the Polish throne, George II Rákóczi intervened in the Swedish-Polish War of 1655 despite warnings from the Porte not to become involved, then suddenly found himself without allies when the Swedes broke off the war just when Ottoman forces moved into Transylvania to punish the vassal state. The principality again became the scene of chaos and battle. In 1660, the Ottomans installed the figurehead Michael I Apafi, whose weak reign, lasting until 1690, would be a time of growing subordination to outside control that culminated in the reestablishment of Habsburg protection over the territory in 1683. Eight years later, amid the string of Habsburg successes that drove the Turks out of Hungary altogether, Transylvania was formally integrated into the Habsburg monarchy. All of the principal figures in the so-called Hungarian Puritan movement died in 1660 or shortly thereafter. As the century drew to a close, the Transylvanian Reformed were thrown on the defensive like their coreligionists in the rest of the Habsburg dominions.

Erosion in Poland, Hungary, and France

While a privileged legal status or the favor of the ruling prince drew members to the Reformed churches of the Netherlands and (for much of the century) Transylvania, the churches of Poland, France, and Habsburg Hungary experienced a contrasting fate. Ruled by Catholic kings who encouraged the conversion of those who sought power at their ever larger and more glittering courts and subjected to ever tighter restrictions on their civil rights and privileges of worship, these churches all suffered an erosion of strength that varied in severity according to the manner in which the faith had spread in each region. At the same time, the churches of France and Poland did not witness internal movements for further reformation, largely because their overriding need to defend their legal privileges and membership against political challenges and would-be converters made them less prone than Europe's other Reformed churches to potentially debilitating internal divisions of any sort.

The ebbing of Reformed strength began earliest and proceeded farthest in Poland, where the movement had always been heavily dependent on aristocratic support. Prominent Protestant noblemen began to return to the Catholic church as early as the 1560s, when, for instance, Nicholas Radziwiłł, son of the founding father of Lithuania's Reformed churches, converted while visiting Italy as a student. Under the Jesuit-influenced King Sigismund III (r. 1587–1632), more tangible considerations swelled the volume of conversions. As foreign observers to the court noted, the king gave preference to Catholics for high office and denied Protestant magnates the "captayneshipps or other offices of proffitt" they needed to maintain the expected style of life at court.[16] The Jesuit order's establishment of some thirty-two prestigious secondary schools also helped win the social elites back for the Roman church, especially as the Protestants appear to have been unable to create schools of equal quality and prestige. In 1578, fully a third of the students in Vilna's large Jesuit academy came from Protestant families. "Their parents sent them to our schools to study good letters and not at all so that they would convert to the Catholic faith. Nonetheless by the grace of God, scarcely one has left without abjuring the errors of their father," the rector boasted a decade later. By the time of Sigismund's death, only five or six senators were Protestant, compared with thirty-six in 1570. A smaller but still substantial percentage of lesser nobles followed the example of the great aristocratic converts.[17]

Because the Warsaw Confederation of 1573 had granted the freedom to establish Protestant churches to noblemen alone, those noblemen who returned to the Catholic church could claim the legal right to end Protestant worship on their lands. Attempts to do so seem rarely to have encountered the effective resistance that might have been expected had more of the population become deeply attached to the new faith. An aggressive Catholic clergy initiated efforts to take back former Catholic churches by either force or petition. In the cities, such actions were reinforced by legal sanctions adopted against Protestant citizens and even, as in Poznań after 1619, by a ban on their settlement in the city. The changing religious climate of Poland's cities is neatly illustrated by successive restorations of Cracow's town hall in 1556 and 1611. After a fire had destroyed the building in the middle of the sixteenth century, the rebuilt edifice was topped by a spire with a gilded ball containing a New Testament and poems praising the Reformation. When the building was renovated in 1611, the ball was refilled with a Catholic Bible, a picture of the future saint Stanislas Kostka, and a splinter from his casket. A law of 1632 forbade the construction of new Protestant or Orthodox churches in royal towns.

By the middle of the seventeenth century, just 40 Reformed churches remained in Little Poland, whereas 265 congregations had gathered around 1570. In Lithuania, the cause retained its strength for a generation longer, even expanding in the first part of the seventeenth century in certain border regions controlled by Reformed magnates. But the devastating Swedish and Russian invasions of the Second Northern War (1655–60) reversed the the footing here and dealt another blow to Protestantism throughout the commonwealth. The Russians so devastated Lithuania that only 45 of the 140 Reformed churches that existed on the eve of the conflict reconstituted themselves after the cataclysm. The Protestants were accused of encouraging and supporting the Swedish incursion that initiated the war—Polish historians still debate the accuracy of this accusation—and new legal restrictions were placed on the various Protestant churches. In 1658, in the midst of the war, anti-Trinitarianism was outlawed, and its adherents were given three years (later reduced to two) to convert or leave the country. This completed the scattering of the leading Polish Socinians that had begun with the closure of the Raków academy twenty years earlier and that facilitated the circulation of their ideas in advanced circles in Holland and England, especially after the publication of the *Library of the Polish Brethren* in Amsterdam between 1665 and 1668.

In the wake of the Second Northern War, laws against Protestantism became still more restrictive. A measure of 1668 forbade new conversions to all brands of Protestantism on pain of banishment and banned Protestant worship in the presence of the court or a diet. By 1700 this was understood as forbidding noblemen from attending Protestant services anywhere other than their home congregation. The 1632 proscription on the building of non–Roman Catholic churches in royal towns was extended to all towns and came to be interpreted as prohibiting the repair of existing churches as well. In

1688, a Reformed minister was tried and convicted for celebrating the Lord's Supper in a place other than a church that existed in 1632, even though the church of the locality had been demolished by a Catholic mob in 1628 and the congregation had subsequently gathered in a nearby manor house. In the face of such measures, what little remained of Polish Protestantism withered. Barely sixty Reformed churches still functioned in Poland, Lithuania, and the cities of Royal Prussia by the middle of the eighteenth century.

In the portion of Hungary that remained under Habsburg control, Rudolf II's ill-fated attempt to impose Catholicism, which resulted in the first legal recognition of Protestant rights of worship by the Treaty of Vienna (1606), proved to be the first sign of an increasingly close association between the Austrian Habsburgs and militant Catholicism. This connection flowered into the distinctive style of *pietas Austraica* over the course of the seventeenth century. In the Habsburg-ruled portions of Hungary, not only did a series of kings make loyalty to Catholicism a key to preferment, as Sigismund III did in Poland; they also pursued on repeated occasions the reduction of Protestant worship and the restriction of Protestant privileges by military means.[18] As in Poland, they were able to win back from the Reformed church many of its greatest aristocratic supporters. In Hungary, however, the spontaneous conversion of both clergymen and entire communities had contributed more to Protestantism's advance than in Poland. The movement was thus able to defend itself with greater vigor and ultimately to suffer less numerical erosion.

Although both Ferdinand II (1619–37) and Ferdinand III (1637–57) were strong champions of Catholicism, the Thirty Years War prevented them from devoting much attention to Hungarian affairs. The task of promoting the Counter-Reformation here thus fell with imperial blessing above all to the vigorous archbishop of Esztergom, Péter Pázmány (1570–1637), a Jesuit-won convert from a Reformed family who worked to introduce the Tridentine decrees, founded three Jesuit seminaries and a new Catholic university, and addressed a series of widely read devotional and controversial works in the vernacular to members of the leading aristocratic families of the region. Reinforcing his able powers of persuasion with promises he would intercede with the emperor to aid those who converted, he won as many as thirty leading nobles back for Rome and encouraged them next to drive Protestant ministers from their lands and close their churches. In spite of the efforts of the Diet to have the rights of the peasants to worship as they chose recognized and reaffirmed, a large number of churches were seized and forced to close— up to three hundred, Protestant spokesmen charged. The Diets of 1646 and 1647 extracted an agreement that ninety churches would be handed back, but this was not done. In many localities, acts were passed excluding Protestants from guilds and forcing them to observe Catholic holidays and contribute to the upkeep of Catholic churches.[19]

During the long reign of Leopold I (1658–1705), the imperial government had its hands freer to pursue the elimination of Protestantism, and it did so at several junctures. The most important came after a conspiracy of magnates was suppressed in 1670. Although involving predominantly Catholic conspirators inspired by discontent over a recent peace treaty with the Ottomans that was seen as having betrayed Hungarian interests, the plot permitted powerful Viennese councillors to argue that the Hungarians, like the Bohemians before them in 1618, had forfeited their privileges by their disloyalty. After the conspiracy was suppressed, the military occupation of Hungary allowed the emperor to try to remake Hungary's constitution and religious makeup with the thoroughness with which Bohemia had been transformed after its ill-fated rebellion was crushed in the first phase of the Thirty Years War. The battle-hardened bishop of Wiener Neustadt, Leopold Kollonich, a veteran of the Order of Malta's campaigns against the Turks, traversed north-central Hungary at the head of a contingent of troops, retaking churches for the Catholics. A special tribunal headed by the archbishop of Esztergom condemned 750 Protestant ministers and teachers on charges of promoting rebellion and praying for Turkish victory. Those who agreed to convert or renounce their stance were set free. Those who resisted were imprisoned and condemned to the galleys. The forced march overland to Naples of the first 40 of these resisters in 1675 and their sufferings on the galley benches until their liberation was negotiated by the Dutch in 1676 were widely reported across Protestant Europe: Hungarian Protestantism was given its most celebrated martyrs.[20]

Always prompt to defend their rights and privileges, the Hungarian nobility rose against this assault on their religious and constitutional liberties. Two thousand men took to the mountains of Slovakia under the leadership of Imre Thököly. Their Transylvanian cousins and the perennially anti-Habsburg French came to their aid, and the fighting escalated into a full-blown religious war. Wherever Thököly passed, he closed Catholic religious houses and seized the churches for the Protestants. Wherever the imperial lieutenant in Hungary, Archbishop György Szelepcsényi, went, he ended Protestant worship. Eighteen Protestant pastors were executed for supporting Thököly, but the rebels eventually carried the day. In 1681, Leopold had to recognize the traditional liberties of the Hungarian nation and the rights of nobles and garrison soldiers to freedom of worship. The agreement also ordered that the status quo as of 1670 be restored, although many of the seized churches were in fact never returned. Finally, the Protestants were granted the right to build one new church per county. But this was not the end of Leopold's attempts to whittle away at Protestant rights of worship. New Habsburg offensives followed the reconquest of the previously Turkish-controlled portions of the kingdom in 1682–86. Other royal decisions between 1691 and 1711 restricted Protestant worship to specified localities and barred it completely in regions reconquered after 1681. Hungary's Protestants retained rights of worship, but far more limited ones than they had had at the beginning of the seventeenth century. Many churches had been closed.

Again, conversions were numerous among the high aristocracy. Whereas all but a handful of the thirty to forty families that sat in the upper house of the Hungarian Diet were Protestant in 1600, no more than six were in 1645. Given the nobles' extensive power over large domains, their conversions could sway thousands of tenants to follow suit, no matter what the Protestants did to secure rights of worship for ordinary congregants. Francis Nádasdy forced nine thousand villagers back into the Catholic church after his conversion early in the century. At the end of the century Pál Esterhazy led thousands of his tenants on a pilgrimage to Mariazell and sponsored the establishment of new religious orders on his lands.[21] Many lesser nobles also converted, but many held firm as well, and most towns remained predominantly Protestant. Studies of the changing strength of the Reformed church in specific localities or regions are lacking, but a rough estimate is that the Reformed retained about fifteen hundred churches and comprised 33 percent of Hungary's population in 1700—significantly less than the 40–45 percent of 1600, but still a far more sizable presence than the retreat of the faith among the high aristocracy might lead one to anticipate.[22] Whereas in Poland a once-numerous set of Reformed churches virtually disappeared by the eighteenth century and would later be marginal in the country's history, in Hungary Reformed believers remained a major component of the population throughout the old regime and played a central role in the appearance of Hungarian nationalism in the nineteenth century.

The fate of France's Reformed churches in the seventeenth century is most easily understood if the periods before and after the revocation of the Edict of Nantes (1685) are considered separately. Under the regime of the Edict of Nantes, the French Reformed suffered fewer vexations than did their Hungarian coreligionists clinging to the terms of the Treaty of Vienna of 1606; yet they too saw their privileges noticeably eroded and their families harried to convert, especially those who desired high office or command. Here, too, the better part of the Protestant high aristocracy returned to the Catholic church, but a populace whose attachment to the cause had been forged in the fire of the Wars of Religion proved far less susceptible to conversion.

The kings of the first half of the century felt a strong commitment to upholding the Edict of Nantes. The state of religion nonetheless remained highly

ENTREE DV ROI DANS LA VILLE DE LA ROCHELLE
LE 1.ᵉʳ NOVEMBRE

LA TRIOMPHANTE ENTREE DV
TRES-CHRESTIEN, CLEMENT, MAGNANIME, ET VICTORIEVX
LOYS xiij. (dit le Iufte) Roy de France & de Nauarre en fa ville de la Rochelle, le 1.Nouemb.1628.

L'entrée du Roi dans la Rochelle.

Ceſte rebellion qui preſumoit d'enfraindre
Tanfiours les ſaincles loix & du Ciel, & du Roy
Maintenant eſt forcée à l'honneur & craindre,
Proſternée à ſes pieds, en piteux deſarroy.

Ceux qu'on croyoit paſſer par le fer, ou la corde,
Pour leurs crimes commis, leurs ſuites & meſfaicts
Reſſentent les doux fruicts de ſa miſericorde,
Sa Clemence les ſauue au lieu d'eſtre defaicts.

Dans la Rochelle il entre en triomphe & en gloire
De Palmes, de Lauriers iuſtement couronné,
Rochelois, benifſez ce tour, & ſa victoire,
Qui vous donne la paix, vous ayant pardonné.

12. King Louis XIII Enters Conquered La Rochelle in 1628. This contemporary engraving shows Louis XIII leading his troops through the gate of La Rochelle on November 1, 1628, after its surrender to the royal forces following a siege of more than a year. The caption praises the "Most Christian, clement, magnanimous, and victorious" ruler for mercifully pardoning the city's rebellious inhabitants despite their presumptuous violation of both divine and human law. The siege cost La Rochelle more than half of its pre-war Protestant population. (Cliché Bibliothèque Nationale de France, Paris)

unstable, for the Catholic Reformation gathered steam in France during the first decades of the seventeenth century, the clergy regularly urging stricter actions against the Reformed, while the Huguenots for their part had taken away from the last phases of the Wars of Religion the disastrous lesson that their place could be preserved only through unrelenting militancy. When the pious young Louis XIII insisted upon the restoration of Catholicism in Béarn and led a military cavalcade across the southwest in 1620 to enforce his will in that territory (see below), he awakened Huguenot fears of a wider plan to undermine the faith across France. Aggressive church members convened an assembly in La Rochelle that revived the system of military circles and aristocratic protectors used to defend the cause during the Wars of Religion. Louis responded by declaring this an act of lèse-majesté and ordering the cause to renounce the actions of the La Rochelle assembly. Many northern Protestants swore oaths disavowing these, but plenty of towns in the south and west refused to do so. Louis unleashed his troops in a series of campaigns between 1621 and 1629 that culminated in the successful four-hundred-day siege of La Rochelle, achieved by blockading much of the harbor of the formerly impregnable city with a mile-long dike. The peace of Alais of 1629 confirmed the clauses of the Edict of Nantes governing Reformed rights of worship but definitively deprived the Huguenots of the military privileges the treaty had accorded them.[23]

After disarming the Reformed, Louis XIII, Richelieu, and later Mazarin limited their attempts to restore religious unity to wooing Huguenot noblemen to convert with promises of pensions and military commands. The strategy bore fruit. Over the course of the seventeenth century, one by one the great aristocratic names of French Protestantism returned to the Catholic fold. In that many small French Reformed churches were *églises de fief* that existed by virtue of the right of noblemen to permit worship on their lands, the conversion of these aristocrats again had wider ramifications. The Protestant-born but Catholic-educated Henry II de Condé became as an adult an ardent persecutor of Huguenots and ended Reformed worship in a number of fiefs he acquired, including the county of Sancerre in 1640. But the case of Sancerre shows the limits as well as the extent of seigneurial influence in determining the larger fate of the French Protestant movement in these years. The town of Sancerre housed a thriving church of about two thousand members when Condé acquired it. He shut the church down in 1641 and shifted 80 percent of the town's tax burden onto its Huguenot inhabitants. During the midcentury revolt of the Fronde, however, the Protestants helped keep the city faithful to Mazarin and Anne of Austria after Condé took up the standard of revolt. The Huguenots were rewarded for their loyalty with a royal brevet that allowed them to reopen a temple. After a decade of interdiction and punitive taxation, the church that resumed worship still had about twelve hundred members.[24] Sancerre illustrates as well why so many Huguenot political thinkers in the seventeenth century became advocates of a strong monarchy, for under the conditions that prevailed in France after the peace of Alais, loyalty to the king appeared for several generations to be the best means of ensuring the preservation and protection of the faith. Theories justifying rights of resistance gave way to renewed emphasis on the duty to obey duly established kings. We have seen how the theologians of Saumur, inspired by Cappel's historical approach to the Bible, developed a justification for the toleration of several faiths when necessary to preserve the public peace.[25]

Louis XIV's assumption of personal rule in 1661 initiated an era of harsher royal treatment of the Huguenots. Commissions were set up to investigate the titles of the kingdom's churches to determine if they met the complicated criteria of the Edict of Nantes governing where churches were permitted to assemble. Instructed to interpret these criteria as restrictively as possible, the commissions ordered the closure of numerous temples. A rising tide of national and local measures limited the access of Protestants to guilds and professions and chipped away at the legal protections granted by the Edict of Nantes. Laws forbade the Reformed churches from accepting converts. To ensure that Protestants who wished to convert to Rome did not suffer economic reprisals from their families for doing so, a special fund was created in 1676 to provide economic assistance to needy converts. The fund was derided by its intended beneficiaries as the *caisse des conversions*. The most bitterly resented rule of all reduced the age of legal majority for making decisions about religious matters to seven. Protestant children above that age who indicated a desire to join the Catholic church were to be taken from their families and raised in Catholic religious houses at their parents' expense. In the same year this measure was enacted, 1681, the eager intendant of Poitou discovered the most effective technique of all for winning converts: royal dragoons were billeted in Protestant households and consumed their hosts' resources until they forswore the faith.

The survival of numerous Reformed baptismal registers for much of the period 1600–85 enables an exceptionally precise tracking of the fate of France's churches.The churches of France (Béarn excepted) had about 930,000 members at the beginning of the seventeenth century. This number declined to roughly 700,000 on the eve of the first *dragonnades* in 1681. Rather than accelerating as persecution increased in the 1660s and 1670s, the decline slowed. Part of the overall drop-off stemmed from the slow movement of conversions to Catholicism, but much of it arose from simple demographic causes, for example, the faith's disproportionate concentration in the kingdom's cities, where rates of reproduction were negative.[26] The precision

with which the fate of these churches may be followed makes their experience clear testimony to the strength of confessional attachment that existed
within this church of converts by choice. Even with the defection of leading
aristocratic champions and the loss of many of their protections and privileges, most of its members remained loyal over three generations. The faith
did, however, undergo a notable change in its social composition as the century passed. The defection of the high aristocracy and the blockage of access
to royal offices and certain liberal professions meant merchants and manufacturers bulked far larger within the leading circles of the faith by 1685 than
they had in 1600, composing, for example, 29 percent of the adult males in
Montpellier's church and 19 percent of those in Rouen's in the 1670s, in comparison with the respective figures for the early part of the century of 11 and 9
percent. This sort of pattern might be seen as evidence of an affinity between
Reformed belief and business success were it not for the fact that a close comparison of wealth accumulation among Catholic and Protestant artisans and
merchants in Montpellier reveals no noticeable difference in the rate at which
members of the two faiths enriched themselves. The pattern derives instead
from the disfavored political standing of the Reformed church and the kinds
of opportunities open to the members of the several faiths.[27]

The Revocation of the Edict of Nantes

After multiplying measures that whittled away at the rights of the Reformed
for more than two decades, Louis XIV decided in October 1685 to revoke the
Edict of Nantes for good. The precise mixture of motives that led him to this
decision will never be known, for the minutes of the relevant council discussions were not preserved. It is nonetheless obvious that his decision stemmed
from a combination of immediate diplomatic calculations and deeper convictions. Louis's honor as most Christian king had recently been tarnished by his
failure to assist in the defense of Vienna against the Ottomans and by battles
with the pope over his rights to nominate bishops in recently acquired territories; he was eager to strike a blow that would demonstrate his solicitude
for Catholicism. An intensified campaign to encourage Protestant conversions
by any means necessary climaxed with new dragonnades across much of the
southwest in the late spring and summer of 1685. As many as three hundred to four hundred thousand Huguenots may have submitted in fear to the
ceremonies of abjuration and conversion. Coming on the heels of exaggerated earlier reports of tens of thousands of conversions, this encouraged Ver-
sailles to harbor the illusion that the RPR (*Religion Prétendue Réformée*) was
on the verge of eradication. With western Europe at peace, Louis was free to
direct his military might to completing this task. Most fundamentally of all,
he shared with the great majority of the political nation the conviction that if

religious uniformity could be obtained without excessive political cost, it remained infinitely preferable to toleration. In light of the ascendant power and military might of the French crown during the seventeenth century, the restoring of that uniformity now seemed to be within his grasp.[28]

"Since the better part of our subjects of the aforesaid RPR . . . embraced the Catholic [faith]," the royal edict revoking the Edict of Nantes declared, all Reformed temples were ordered to be forthwith demolished, the exercise of the Reformed faith was forbidden throughout the kingdom, and pastors were given two weeks to decide if they would abjure the faith and receive a pension or leave the country. The emigration of ordinary church members was prohibited. The revocation was implemented like a carefully organized military operation. Beginning in the regions in which the Huguenots were scarcest, royal troops steadily advanced toward their greatest centers of strength, using the now well-honed techniques of the dragonnades to compel them to come in. Although a few church members fled or, like one wealthy Rouen merchant, regaled the troops billeted in their house with fine meals while steadfastly refusing to set foot in a Catholic church, the great majority of Protestants hastened to abjure as soon as the troops appeared. "The Huguenots can sometimes show such diligence in hastening to convert that a soldier may have to change his lodging several times a day," one triumphant official wrote Condé. Of the 873 men exercising a pastoral charge at the time of the revocation, 681 chose to emigrate, 140 accepted Catholicism permanently, 38 forswore temporarily but then returned to the Reformed faith, and 13 were imprisoned for their stubborn resistance.[29]

The triumph the Catholic authorities felt at the revocation's initial success turned to dismay as it became evident it would prove difficult to make good Catholics out of the new Catholics. Once the converts got over their initial shock and were able to arrange their personal affairs properly, clandestine emigration assumed massive proportions. By following smugglers' paths across the Swiss border or arranging to be picked up by ships at night along isolated stretches of the Atlantic coast, 200,000 Huguenots fled the country, the largest emigration for reasons of conscience since the expulsion of Spain's Moriscos in 1609. The greatest number settled in the Netherlands, England, Switzerland, and the Holy Roman Empire, especially the territories of Brandenburg-Prussia, Hesse-Cassel, and the Palatinate. Smaller numbers found their way to Ireland, North America, and even South Africa, where the arrival of 126 Huguenots in 1688 increased the European population of the fledgling Cape Colony by a fifth.[30]

Liberal historiography long exaggerated the size and economic consequences of the migration, the better to demonstrate the high cost of intolerance. Since the study by Warren Scoville in 1960, it has become accepted

Het weg vlugten der Gereformeerde uyt Vrankryk.

13. "The Flight of the Huguenots from France." This engraving by Jan Luyken initially illustrated the Dutch edition of Elie Benoist's *History of the Edict of Nantes* (1694), one of the many printed works of the later seventeenth century intended to arouse sympathy for the victims of Catholic intolerance and to bolster pan-Protestant solidarity. It combines into a single image many episodes of flight and persecution. Groups of refugees depart by land and sea. Some are questioned by authorities or robbed by highwaymen. The caption informs the viewer that those apprehended were condemned to prison or the galleys. (Rijksmuseum, Amsterdam)

that most of the economic hardships France endured over the next decades must be attributed to the long wars and high taxation of the last years of Louis XIV's reign, not to the economic consequences of the revocation. The Huguenot refugees nonetheless consisted disproportionately of lesser noblemen, professionals, merchants, and urban artisans, many with unusual skills. They played a crucial role in the development of certain luxury trades in the territories in which they settled (for example, the Haarlem and Spitalfields silk industries, stocking and wig making in Brandenburg-Prussia), and in the process not only added to the prosperity of the countries in which they settled but also weakened France's competitive position in the international economy.[31]

By far the most far-reaching consequences of the Huguenot diaspora were ideological, not economic. Prominent writers of the Huguenot refuge included philosophically inclined journalists of the republic of letters like Jean Le Clerc and Pierre Bayle. Bayle's *Historical and Critical Dictionary* provided much of the critical armamentum for the Enlightenment. His *Philosophical Commentary on the Words of Jesus Christ, Compel them to Come In* (1686) stands as one of the century's fullest and most impassioned defenses of religious toleration as a general principle. The refuge also produced outstanding historians. Elie Benoist painstakingly documented the injustices and chicanery that accompanied the erosion of Huguenot rights of worship prior to 1685 in his *History of the Edict of Nantes,* quickly translated into both English and Dutch. Paul Rapin de Thoyras wrote a careful and fluent *History of England* that was the first systematic statement of the Whig vision of English history. These men all contributed in fundamental ways to that critical semantic revolution of the late seventeenth and eighteenth centuries by which toleration came to be construed as a positive virtue. Their work enshrined the revocation of the Edict of Nantes as the great illustration of the evils and folly of religious intolerance. In short, the refugee intellectuals kept alive the memory of the sufferings of their coreligionists, contributed powerfully to the black legend of the tyrannical Louis XIV and the Whig interpretation of English history, and articulated broader theories of religious toleration. All of these actions created precisely the outlook that encouraged the future overstatement of the economic consequences of the revocation.[32]

Most of the newly converted ex-Huguenots who remained in France promptly repented of their abjuration, avoided Catholic services as much as they dared, and drew upon Reformed traditions of family worship to keep alive attachment to the old faith. As early as Christmas 1685, some *nouveaux convertis* were gathering in isolated areas to pray and sing psalms together. In the regions of greatest concentration, itinerant lay preachers began to preside over these gatherings and even administer the sacraments. Royal authorities broke up no fewer than 720 Huguenot assemblies between 1685 and 1687, arresting twelve preachers and sentencing five to death.[33]

More remarkable manifestations of resistance followed. From early 1688 onward, across Dauphiné, the Vivarais, and the Cévennes, young, often illiterate men and women began to sing psalms, preach, and prophesy while in trancelike states, warning of the imminent arrival of the end time and calling upon their neighbors to repent. Royal agents responded vigorously but could not suppress the prophesyings. The anger of those whom they tracked turned to violence when, in the heart of the Protestant Cévennes in 1702 a woolcomber-prophet who claimed to be acting under the Spirit led a party of raiders to free imprisoned resisters held in the house of a leading Catholic missionary, the abbé du Chaila, and murdered the abbot. Other attacks on prominent Catholic personages followed. Royal troops were sent in. For two years, small bands of these Camisards, often led by inspired prophets, waged guerrilla warfare against far larger contingents of soldiers, until the royal military leaders recognized that even a scorched earth policy would not suffice to capture all of the guerrillas and accorded a series of amnesties that ended the fighting.

A few of those permitted to leave the country under the terms of these amnesties created a sensation in London when they resumed prophesying there. But to most Reformed clergymen the inspired preaching of the prophets seemed a dangerous example of that new bugbear of an increasingly rationalist clergy, enthusiasm. In 1713, Antoine Court, a lay preacher who came to reject inspired prophecy after a number of predictions he made under the influence of the spirit failed to come true, set about organizing the scattered assemblies of the resisters along more orthodox lines. In 1715 he convened the first provincial synod of the "desert" in the Cévennes. A decade later the churches of Languedoc established a seminary in Lausanne to give the ministers academic training. Gradually the structures of a presbyterial-synodal Reformed church came to be reinstituted across the kingdom, a church that met in secrecy but with a discipline and practices similar to those of the period prior to 1685. Alternately winked at by the authorities and subjected to periods of renewed repression, this church of the desert functioned until the French Revolution once again brought legal toleration. By that time, the membership of these reconstructed Reformed churches was roughly five hundred thousand. In a country whose population had grown through both natural increase and the annexation of new territory, this was now less than 2 percent of the population. When the two hundred thousand refugees are recalled as well, however, this figure offers further testimony to the remarkable loyalty to their cause of the French Huguenots. Insofar as Louis XIV was never forced by the Camisards to restore formal rights of worship to his Reformed subjects, the revocation of the Edict of Nantes may be said to have represented a display of power that his rivals in Vienna could not match in their Hungarian domains. His might was not such, however, that he could force more than a fraction of France's Huguenots back into full communion with the Roman church. The Protestant minority that survived the revocation underground would be large enough to make the Protestants a noteworthy presence in French political life and in the national political imagination throughout the subsequent centuries.[34]

WHEN THE FAITH OF THE RULER CHANGED

The currents that led ever larger numbers of Europe's aristocrats back to the Catholic church also returned to Catholic rule at least six small territories that had instituted Reformed state reformations. Perhaps the most striking and best-studied such case is that of Béarn, the Pyrenean principality in which Jeanne d'Albret had imposed Reformed worship on all inhabitants by law in 1571.[35] When her son and successor, Henry of Navarre, had to convert to Catholicism in 1593 to make good his claim to the French throne, the papacy insisted that he restore Catholic rights in Béarn as a condition of his absolution. Henry did so in 1599 by the Edict of Fontainebleau, a rough counterpart to the Edict of Nantes that ordered the reestablishment of Catholic worship in a limited number of localities within Béarn. This provoked protests and foot dragging from the estates and the supreme judicial body of the province. It was scarcely less satisfactory to the territory's two formerly exiled Catholic bishops, who were now able to return to their sees of Lescar and Oloron, but who soon also demanded the restoration of all confiscated ecclesiastical property as well as *places de sureté* and *chambres mi-parties* for Béarn's Catholics comparable to those granted the Huguenots in France. Gradually permission was granted for Catholic worship in additional localities, though opposition often made it difficult for the members of the Roman church to benefit from this. When the adolescent Louis XIII threw off his mother's influence in 1617 and asserted his intention to take decisions himself, the leading clerical voices at court easily convinced the pious young king to heed this appeal. Louis ordered the restoration of Catholic worship throughout the province and the return of all former ecclesiastical property. This decree sparked even more vigorous resistance than the initial restoration of Catholicism in 1599. The royal governor was threatened and subjected to insulting demonstrations outside his lodgings. The provincial estates worked together with local Reformed churches to mobilize support from the Huguenot political assemblies of France. Envoys were dispatched to court. The sovereign court of the territory refused to register the edicts on the grounds they violated local privileges. These protests delayed the implementation of the 1617 decree for three years, but Louis XIII refused to budge. After rallying troops to overawe an opposition movement of discontented aristocratic supporters of the Queen Mother, he led those troops to Béarn to ensure the decree's enforcement. The tiny principality dared not offer armed resistance. By 1622 Catholic worship was restored throughout the land.

Most striking about Béarn's experience is that, although the political nation opposed the restoration of Catholicism, the population as a whole evidently welcomed it. By 1630, it may be estimated from the movement of Catholic and Protestant baptisms that roughly three-fifths of Béarn's inhabitants had resumed worshiping within the Catholic church. By 1665–82, provincewide censuses reveal that the Reformed comprised a scant 17–22 percent of the population. The revocation of the Edict of Nantes in 1685 then set off less emigration and resistance in Béarn than in any other region of France in which Reformed churches had been numerous. By the end of the eighteenth century, fewer than five thousand Protestants remained in this region of upward of one hundred thousand inhabitants that had once been entirely Reformed by law. Thirty to fifty years of state-imposed reformation had evidently produced so little genuine attachment to the cause among the bulk of the population that roughly four-fifths of Béarn's inhabitants returned to the Catholic church once toleration was encouraged even before participation in Reformed services was made illegal by the revocation of the Edict of Nantes. The case illustrates the limits of mass adherence to the new faith in such cases of state-sanctioned re-formations. The massive return of the population to the Catholic church also stands as a warning against interpreting elite political resistance to the restoration of Catholicism as evidence of a thorough "protestantization" of the population at large.

An equally thorough re-Catholicization occurred in one nominally Re-formed German territory that passed under Catholic rule during the seventeenth century, the Upper Palatinate, although its population was as much Lutheran as it was Reformed prior to the Catholic takeover. Located on the border of Bavaria far from the Palatine heartland along the Rhine, the Upper Palatinate had been a bastion of Lutheran resistance to the imposition of Reformed worship ever since the resolutely Lutheran Ludwig had served as its statthalter before succeeding to the electoral title from 1576 to 1583. On the eve of the Thirty Years War, the great majority of its nobility remained Lutheran, and a large fraction of incumbent ministers continued to use Lutheran rites. Following Frederick V's disastrous intervention in the Bohemian revolt, Maximilian of Bavaria, the leader of the Catholic League, overran and occupied the region in 1621, an occupation that would become permanent under the terms of the Peace of Westphalia. Maximilian removed all incumbent Protestant clergymen in 1625 and outlawed any faith but the Catholic in 1628, granting the population six months to convert or to leave the territory. Although some parishes quickly made a collective act of conversion, only a handful of people initially attended Catholic services in many others. By quartering troops in the houses of those who would not conform (in what may be the first use of the technique later associated with Louis XIV's dragoons), Maximilian forced the overwhelming majority of the nonnoble population to accept the new order. The petty nobility of the region proved more resistant, and as late as 1651 the majority of the second estate was still loyal to the Lutheran faith. Yet emigration and conversion thinned the ranks of noble Lutherans as well. By 1670 only 112 non-Catholics remained in the territory.[36]

Several other small German Reformed territories came under Catholic or Lutheran control over the course of the seventeenth century without the new faith supplanting the old. Nassau-Siegen is a good example. John VIII of Nassau (1583–1638) received a good Reformed education at Herborn and the noble academy of Kassel, topped off with a grand tour that took him to Geneva and Saumur; but the Arminian controversy awakened doubts in him about aspects of Reformed doctrine, and when he fell in love with the Catholic princess Ernestine Yolande de Ligne, she was able to win him away from the faith of his birth with the aid of a Jesuit to whom she introduced him. In a letter to his father in which he aimed to justify his decision to convert, John cited a series of arguments that he said convinced him of the superiority of the Catholic church: its antiquity; its miracles; the danger to morality posed by the Protestant doctrine of the bondage of the will; and the fact that if the Protestant critique of the Roman church were true, then generations of Christians had had no hope of salvation. His father reduced his inheritance but had the misfortune to die in 1623, just as the first wave of Catholic success in the Thirty Years War crested. The emperor overrode the will and upheld John VIII's claim to the entirety of Nassau-Siegen. On taking power, John introduced toleration for Catholic worship while promising to maintain the Reformed church. In 1626, he outlawed Protestantism. Soon, however, the territory was caught in the maelstrom of the war and alternately conquered by Swedish and imperial forces, each of whom imposed a new religious order. The Peace of Westphalia decreed 1624 as the reference point to which Germany's religious situation would be restored. For Nassau-Siegen that meant a regime of toleration under which the Reformed were in the majority. As the territory rebuilt itself after the war, the Reformed appear to have remained the largest group, although Catholics and Lutherans also lived in it. In 1815 the town of Siegen housed 3,052 Reformed, 542 Catholics, and 30 Lutherans.[37]

The Peace of Westphalia recognized too the force of confessional loyalty by forbidding rulers who subsequently converted to another faith to alter the doctrine and worship of the established church. So when the ruler of Bentheim, Steinfurt, and Tecklenburg took a Catholic wife and converted in 1668 and when the ruling house of Zweibrücken died out and a predominantly Lutheran line of princes began to rule that territory after 1680, the Reformed church remained the settled faith, and the rulers could do no more than decree toleration for their creed.[38] Still, the force of Catholic arms and princely weight could and did win a fraction of the population away from the formerly monopolistic Reformed church. The heartland of the Palatinate along the Rhine and Neckar, which experienced an unusually eventful series of religious changes as the century advanced, illustrates this.

This early German bastion of Reformed sentiment and aggressive pan-Protestant political solidarity suffered for its ruler's role in sparking the Thirty Years War. It too was occupied by Maximilian of Bavaria following the defeat of Frederick V at White Mountain. Here too the population was commanded in 1628 to either take part in Catholic worship or leave. The Swedish conquest and occupation of the region three years later turned the tables in favor of Lutheranism. Catholic forces reconquered the territory once more during the war, but they dared only to establish a regime of toleration this time. A special clause of the Peace of Westphalia then returned this portion of the Palatinate to its original ruling house and restored its religious footing to its pre-1618 state; but the restored Reformed supremacy lasted only for the span of two reigns before the extinction of the ruling line in 1685 caused the territory to pass to a Catholic branch of the family. Swedish diplomatic pressure had already achieved some toleration for Lutheranism after 1648. Now the new Catholic rulers also decreed toleration for Catholicism, sponsored the introduction of Jesuits and Capuchins, and generally labored to advance their faith while respecting the terms of the Peace of Westphalia. The searing French occupation of the territory during the War of the League of Augsburg thereafter heightened religious tensions, as the occupying army consecrated formerly Protestant churches for the use of local Catholics, while the harshness of its scorched-earth policies reinforced Protestant anti-Catholicism. Tensions continued to run high throughout the ensuing decades. Catholic preachers demanded that legal action for slander be taken against Article 80 of the Heidelberg Catechism, which called the mass idolatry. The two faiths battled at law over the control of Heidelberg's main church. In a village in which Catholics and Protestants arranged to share the use of the local church, a Catholic priest became so enraged when his Reformed counterpart allowed services to run overtime while he and his coreligionists waited outside the church, that he pulled out a pistol and shot an unfortunate passerby. At century's end, about two-sevenths of the territory's churches were in Catholic hands and about one-sixth of the population worshiped as Catholics; another fifteen thousand to fifty thousand souls were Lutherans.[39] The Reformed thus

succeeded in retaining their numerical supremacy. At the same time, the upheavals of the seventeenth century increased the number of confessionally
mixed territories within Germany and multiplied opportunities for disputes
to arise over the religious rights of the different faiths, ensuring that confessional rivalries remained at the heart of imperial politics well into the eighteenth century.

In conclusion, if the Reformed were able to benefit from a legally favored
status to enlarge their ranks during the seventeenth century in two parts of
continental Europe, the United Provinces and Transylvania, it was far more
common for members of Reformed churches to face attempts to curtail their
rights. The choices that confronted the Reformed in Nassau-Siegen in 1626,
in the Palatinate in 1628, in Hungary after 1670, and in France after 1685 were
stark indeed: convert, emigrate, or resist. Even when the choices were less
stark, as in Béarn before 1685, where the challenge was simply the lure of restored Cathloc worship, or in Poland, where they faced inducements to convert and the limited curtailment of civil rights, the many instances in which
Catholic rulers altered the Reformed's conditions of existence and worked to
gain their conversion by some combination of threats and promises represent
fascinating test cases of the depth of support of the bulk of Reformed church
members for the cause to which they were bound by either law or choice.

In the final analysis, the fate of the voluntary Reformed churches that suffered infringements of their rights and privileges depended heavily on the
degree to which the churches had been started by either aristocratic fiat or
spontaneous adhesion. Everywhere, in Poland, Hungary, and France, the high
aristocracy proved extremely susceptible to officially sanctioned attempts to
woo converts, although the lesser gentry often was a bastion of fidelity. The
defection of the high aristocracy in turn precipitated the virtual collapse of
the Reformed church in Poland-Lithuania. Because the churches of Hungary
and France had been far less dependent on aristocratic initiative in the beginning, they endured more successfully. In Hungary, the lesser gentry and
towns mounted a tenacious resistance against Habsburg efforts to diminish
their rights, and finally prevented the Habsburgs from revoking the toleration
of Protestantism within the kingdom of St. Stephen. Some two hundred thousand French Huguenots displayed their attachment to their faith in the wake
of Louis XIV's revocation of the Edict of Nantes by fleeing abroad. Still more
defied the commands of Europe's most absolute of monarchs to reconstitute
the forbidden Reformed church in the desert. In both lands, the Reformed
churches preserved the majority of their numerical strength over the seventeenth and eighteenth centuries despite severe persecution. The intellectual
critique Huguenot authors developed of governmental maneuvers to ensure

religious uniformity also contributed much to the eighteenth century's new valorization of religious toleration.

While the French and Hungarian cases demonstrate the depth of attachment to the ancestral faith that could exist in voluntary churches forged in struggle, the case of Béarn, where a large majority of the population returned to Catholicism once the inhabitants of every parish had the opportunity to choose the church in which they would worship, reveals how weak attachment to the Reformed cause could be where a state-sanctioned reformation had enjoyed two generations or less of unchallenged domination during which to inculcate its message. A similar lesson in suggested by the experience of the Upper Palatinate, where attachment to Protestantism, Lutheran as much as Reformed, was somewhat stronger three generations after the initial establishment of a Protestant state church but where a Catholic conqueror with an army at his back was nevertheless able to restore Catholicism to a state of virtually uncontested supremacy over a further two generations. The fate of the Upper Palatinate was unusual within the empire, however. In other Reformed territories that passed under the control of Catholic rulers, the erstwhile monopoly church retained the loyalty of a substantial majority of the population—even in the Palatinate, where Erastus had estimated in the immediate aftermath of the establishment of Reformed worship that only 30 percent of the population knew and confessed the essentials of the faith. This probably testifies at once to the advance of confessional attachment with each passing generation, to its reinforcement by war and conflict, and to the limits that the Peace of Westphalia placed on the erstwhile principle of *cuius regio euis religio.* One wonders as well if differences in either the pre-Reformation religious climate or the process of implementing the Reformation did not also contribute to its quite dissimilar degree of survival in Béarn and the Palatinate. In any event, the fate of the continental Reformed churches amid the political upheavals of the seventeenth century testifies at once to the force and to the limits of princely decision making in shaping the religious allegiance of the bulk of the population as well as to the historical conditions that either promoted or restricted individual attachment to the Reformed cause.

12

BRITISH SCHISMS

In no part of seventeenth-century Europe did changing royal religious policies create greater upheaval than in the British Isles. Scotland and England had emerged from the initial convulsions of the Reformation with two of the most contested and unstable of all Reformed church orders. James VI of Scotland had managed to establish a semblance of order in the Scottish kirk by balancing elements of presbyterial and episcopal church government, but the underlying conflict between these rival ecclesiologies remained. England's mishmash of Reformed theology, unreformed church government, and a partially transformed liturgy produced a still lusher array of conflicts. To the quarrels that divided the church over vestments, elements of the liturgy, and church government during Elizabeth's reign were added new sources of disagreement in the decades just before James VI of Scotland also became James I of England: the rise of the experimental predestinarian tradition, the emergence of proto-Anglican defenses of the church's distinctive liturgy, and the weaving of the native strand of antipredestinarianism that came to be labeled Arminianism once that controversy began to shake the Netherlands. The unification of the crowns added another element of volatility, for once the same person ruled these churches with very different liturgies and traditions, that person was likely to be tempted to impose greater uniformity among them. Even James was not immune to this temptation, but he was enough of an ecclesiastical statesman to avoid disaster. His less flexible son Charles was not. By pursuing uniformity of a stripe that offended much English and even more Scottish opinion, he unleashed a politicoreligious explosion that shattered the structure of the early Stuart churches. The enterprise of creating a new church order to take their place only exacerbated the divisions in both lands. Ultimately, two generations of civil war, regicide, restoration, and further revolution would be required before it was recognized that these had grown so great that the only way to bring peace was to allow several Protestant churches in both kingdoms.

THE CHURCH POLICIES OF THE EARLY STUARTS

At the turn of the seventeenth century, an English church that had divided between advocates of further reformation and defenders of the status quo was giving way to one split between two groups of churchmen that each desired a measure of innovation even while proclaiming itself loyal to the spirit of the early Elizabethan church. Ecclesiology, so divisive in the 1580s, temporarily ceased to provoke contention. Following the crushing of Field's and Cartwright's efforts to establish a presbyterial form of church government, virtually all English churchmen except the handful of ministers who had followed Robert Browne and Henry Barrow into separation were prepared to grant the legitimacy of bishops within the church. Not a single English printed book defended the presbyterian-synodal form of church government between the end of this first presbyterian controversy and 1640. Instead, issues of churchmanship and worship polarized opinion.

On James's accession, those whom their enemies labeled Puritans were still the larger and more aggressive of these two parties. The new king had scarcely reached England before members of this group presented him with the Millenary Petition and won his assent to a conference on church affairs to be held at Hampton Court. The Millenary Petition advocated (1) modest reforms in worship like the elimination of the sign of the cross in baptism; (2) the appointing of a resident preaching minister in every parish; (3) a very limited clerical oath of loyalty to the Thirty-Nine Articles and the royal supremacy in lieu of Whitgift's demand for assent to the Prayer Book and surplice as well; and (4) modifications in the exercise of ecclesiastical discipline that fell short of eliminating existing church courts in favor of a consistorial system.[1] Many members of this wing of the church were also committed to practical divinity and experimental predestinarian theology and bent much of their effort to calling their parishioners to conversion and godly living. Leading figures in this group were the bishops George Abbott, John King, James Montagu, and Lewis Bayly.

A rival group took shape around Richard Neile, Lancelot Andrewes, John

Overall, John Buckridge, John Cosin, and William Laud. Andrewes and Overall were disciples of Baro from Cambridge days. Laud studied at St. John's, Oxford, a Catholic foundation of Queen Mary's reign. Because of their reservations about predestinarian ideas, these men are often called Arminians, but the label is misleading insofar as it suggests that the theology of grace was their central preoccupation and that their ideas derived from the Dutch theologian rather than from native antipredestinarians like Baro. Reverence for the ceremonies and sacraments of the established church and the defending of its property and prerogatives were still more important to them.[2]

In many ways, the priorities of this group represented a reaction against experimental predestinarianism and Puritan piety. Whereas Puritan ministers emphasized the preaching of the word as the critical means of calling people to salvation, they emphasized the importance of prayer and the role of the sacraments as channels of grace. "To prefer preaching before prayer is to magnify the means before the end," one of their number wrote in 1638. Whereas the Puritans shrank from any act of worship that did not appear to have biblical sanction, their rivals wanted to emphasize the sanctity of the church building and ensure respect for the rituals of the church. "The external worship of God in His Church is the great witness to the world that our heart stands right in the service of God," wrote another. Hence they encouraged believers to bow on entering and leaving the church and urged that the communion table be decently covered and railed off, so that it would not be casually used for inappropriate purposes. Whereas Puritan divinity tended to see true Christians as a minority of the elect called to separate themselves from the sinful ways of the world, they identified the Christian community as all those who expressed their belief by obedient participation in church worship. Strict Sabbath rules and the rejection of other holidays, they believed, only alienated people needlessly from devotion. Hence they defended holidays and festive customs that were not manifestly irreverent. Many were also strong defenders of both the economic interests and the dignity of the clerical estate, Jasper Fisher going so far as to state that the "twice-dipt purple of the priesthood" had been sent to earth as heaven's ambassadors. Much of their theological thrust was devoted to fixing the continuity between English church government and ritual and that of the early church. They came to see the English church as standing in a very different relation to the continental Reformed churches than had virtually all English Protestant churchmen of the preceding generations. "Our Church . . . goes upon different Principles from the rest of the Reformed, and so steers her course by another rule than they do," wrote Joseph Mede in 1636. "We look after the Form, Rites and Discipline of Antiquity, and endeavour to bring our own as near we can to that Pattern. We suppose the Reformed Churches have departed farther there-from than

needed." Because of this emphasis on the forms of worship, their Puritan enemies called them Formalists. Laudian is perhaps the least misleading of the
labels proposed by modern scholars.[3]

King James had imbibed from his Scottish upbringing a mainstream Calvinistic belief in predestination, and he would subsequently reaffirm his commitment to it through his support for the Synod of Dort and his silencing of
English critics of its decrees. At the same time, his unpleasant experiences
with Melville and his ilk, together with his commitment to the divine right
of kings, had left him deeply hostile to presbyterianism and determined to
impose his authority over the church. At the Hampton Court conference, he
agreed to such evangelizing practices as strengthening a preaching ministry,
but he made his antipathy to any modification of episcopal powers clear.
When the advocates of disciplinary reform later wished to alter the system of
church courts by parliamentary statute, he angrily prorogued the Parliament
and required all clergymen to subscribe to Whitgift's three articles of 1583, a
move that resulted in some eighty Puritan ministers being deprived of their
posts for refusing to do so.[4]

A partisan of the broader reconciliation of all Protestants, James was a
moderate on questions of worship and came to appreciate the rituals of the
English church. In 1617, complaints that Lancashire authorities were banning Sunday piping and dancing in their war on that region's strong Catholic
survivalism led him to oversee the drafting of the Book of Sports, which defined licit and illicit recreations for a Sunday. Criticizing the views of "puritans
and precise people," the book permitted a broad range of activities after the
hours of worship, including archery, May games, and morris dances. Debate
about the Sabbath question flared up again, costing Bayly a taste of prison (his
bishop's office notwithstanding) for disputing disrespectfully with the king
about the issue. In 1618, James undertook to bring worship in Scotland closer
into line with English practice. The Five Articles of Perth, confirmed by the
General Assembly and the Parliament, commanded communicants to kneel
when receiving the sacrament, permitted private communion and baptism,
instituted the confirmation of children by bishops, and ordered that five holidays be observed. The measure was deeply distasteful to many Scots. In the
region of Saint Andrews and Edinburgh, where vigorous efforts were made to
implement the new articles, a number of laymen were banished and clergymen deprived for their ostentatious rejection of them. Many of the deprived
ministers took refuge in Ulster; others began to organize conventicles to preserve the pure forms of worship in Fife and Edinburgh. In the south and west,
most parish ministers simply ignored the Five Articles.[5]

James's lack of sympathy for precisian sensibilities is evident in such acts,
but he was conciliatory enough to minimize confrontations over such issues.

He did not have his Scottish bishops press enforcement of the Five Articles on every parish. While he expected English ministers to subscribe their approval of the Prayer Book, he instructed his bishops not to discipline too harshly those who omitted details of the rituals, but to try instead to persuade them to conform. His episcopal appointments were divided roughly equally between formalists and evangelizers. Just as he had restored a degree of stability to the Scottish church by balancing elements of presbyterianism and episcopalianism, so he strove to balance the rival factions of the English church.[6]

The permission granted Richard Montagu to publish his antipredestinarian *New Gagg for an Old Goose* in 1624 (see chapter 10) implies that the balance may already have been tipping toward the Laudians by the last years of James's reign, in reaction against Puritan criticism of his failure to intervene in the Thirty Years War and his pursuit of a Spanish marriage. It toppled decisively in that direction under Charles I. A pious man whose aesthetic sensibilities and fear of disorder inclined him toward a church emphasizing spectacle, decorum, and uniformity, Charles unfailingly favored the formalist wing of the church. He increased the tendency visible under James to rely heavily on clergymen as political advisors and administrators, which brought complaints about the growth of "prelacy." Laud quickly became one of his leading advisors. John Spottiswood, archbishop of Saint Andrews, became chancellor of Scotland in 1634. William Juxon, bishop of London, assumed the duties of lord treasurer in 1636.

Historians debate whether Caroline ecclesiastical policies depended upon the king's personal inclinations or were the product of the symbiosis between the king and Laud. Whatever the case, their character was clear. Whereas James had contained debate about predestination by silencing critics of the decrees of Dort, Charles did so by silencing predestinarians. Whereas James had urged moderation in dealing with ministers who omitted elements of the liturgy, Charles ordered his bishops to enforce conformity with zeal. Bishops issued detailed instructions on how to improve church furnishings, erect altar rails, and enforce due reverence for the church building. Keen-eyed visitations were designed to ensure the implementation of these decrees. Laud prosecuted more clergymen for nonconformity and neglect of duty in his first year as bishop of London than his predecessor had done in his entire seven-year tenure. Within a week of his elevation to the archbishopric of Canterbury in 1633, the Book of Sports was reissued, and ministers were ordered to publicize its contents. As necessary, the courts of both Star Chamber and High Commission were used to silence critics.[7]

The "Caroline captivity of the church" transformed the pattern of public opinion about church affairs. Although Laud and his backers viewed their policies as merely restoring the purity of England's original reformation, the

church furnishings on which a few of them insisted encompassed such elements as altar rails nowhere specified in the early Elizabethan canons to
which they appealed. To those now criticized and marginalized as Puritans,
it appeared they were moving England toward popery. Had not Bullinger's *On
the Origin of the Errors* taught as early as 1528 that the corruption of the
medieval church stemmed from the gradual introduction of novel practices
falsely thought to honor God? Was the Church of England not now heading
down the same slippery slope? Other goings-on stoked fear that the English
church was being drawn toward Rome. Lacking his father's taste for theological controversy, Charles did not support anti-Roman preaching and polemic
as James had. His French wife had mass celebrated in her Somerset House
chapel, with growing numbers of courtiers in attendance. Papal envoys were
received at court for the first time since the Reformation, and Charles even
seemed to like one of them. On the Continent, the Thirty Years War was raging, and Catholicism appeared to be advancing. In this context, many of "the
old common moderate sort," in Richard Baxter's phrase, drew closer to the opponents of vestments and the proponents of further reformation. In the more
extreme Puritan circles, the godly debated whether or not it was appropriate
to remain within the communion of the Church of England. Larger and larger
numbers of them decided it was not. Some who left it worked to preserve the
good old cause as wandering apostles within England. More, like John Cotton and his friends, "came to the judgement that by the free preaching of the
word and the actual practice of our church discipline we could offer a much
clearer and fuller witness in another land than in the wretched and loathsome
prisons of London, where there would be no opportunity for books or pens
or friends or conferences." Many first went to the Netherlands, but in 1634
Laud convinced the Dutch authorities to act against the innovations multiplying there. A greater number went to New England, where a new church order
soon took shape.[8]

THE NEW ENGLAND WAY

Although the settlement of New England began in 1618, the great period of
migration came under the darkening shadow of the Laudian ascendancy, between the chartering of the Massachusetts Bay Company in 1628 and the first
year of the civil war in 1643. During this period, twenty-one thousand people
made the transatlantic journey to New England, after which migration there
all but ceased, and its later population growth came almost entirely from natural increase. Many of the migrants simply wanted to catch fish and farm, but
the seventy-six ordained ministers and numerous godly laymen among them
impressed a distinctive character on the new colonies.[9] Given the opportunity
to plant new churches far from the surveillance of an episcopate whose poli-

cies they viewed with growing hostility, they translated the preoccupations and aspirations of Puritan practical divinity into a new set of church practices. The first step in the foundation of most congregations was the drafting and swearing to a covenant, an echo of the Puritan practice of personal covenanting. The tiny earlier groups of English separatists around such figures as Browne and Barrow had already become convinced that every congregation in which the word was taught and the sacraments rightly administered comprised a complete visible church with the power to elect its own officers. Thomas Hooker brought this principle of congregational independence with him to New England from the Netherlands in 1633, and it became a fundamental conviction of most faithful New Englanders. Also apparently in 1633 the church of Boston first amplified experimental predestinarianism's confidence that the elect could discern the signs of grace within themselves into a requirement that candidates for church membership testify about the working of grace in their soul. By 1636, the restriction of church membership to such "visible saints" was the norm among New England churches; it was not universal, however, in that the principle of congregational autonomy allowed individual churches to follow diverse courses. These churches implemented as well the kind of parish-based ecclesiastical discipline the Puritans found so sadly wanting within the Church of England, but because all full members of most churches were deemed to possess saving faith, they all shared in the disciplining and excommunication of church members, rather than leaving this to a consistory of elders and the minister. Worship practices adopted by the New England churches included seated communion, baptism at the front of the church without the sign of the cross, strict Sabbath observance, and the elimination of all other holy days. Even the slightest traces of paganism and superstition in the calendar were regarded with suspicion. For a brief period the General Court of Massachusetts kept dates by calling the months first month, second month, and so on.[10]

The practices of the New England churches were codified in 1648 at a synod convened in Cambridge by the Massachusetts General Court. The church platform established here declared that since the coming of Christ the true visible church was not national, provincial, or classical, but "only congregational." Planks of the platform called for the congregational election of ministers free of any interference from magistrates, bishops, and patrons; a fourfold ministry along the lines set forth in Calvin's *Institutes;* and the admission of "saints by calling" to church membership through a process that recommended but did not require a public declaration of God's manner of working upon the soul. Larger synods were also provided for, the decisions of which were to be received "so farr as consonant to the word of God."[11] This was a structure of church governance unlike any previously seen within the

Reformed tradition. Ministers with wider horizons recognized this and occasionally tried to align the New England churches more closely with practices standard elsewhere, but the laity was quick to defend their methods. The congregation of Woburn insisted in 1642 that it ordain its minister itself rather than allow the ceremony to be performed by clergymen of neighboring communities, lest the laying on of hands by other ministers "be an occasion of introducing a dependency of churches, and so a presbytery."[12]

By restricting church membership to those who could offer testimony of saving faith, the New England way ensured that only a fraction of residents would be full church members. About 80 percent of the early settlers of Milford, Connecticut, 70 percent of Dedham, Massachusetts, taxpayers in 1648, and just under half of Boston's adult population around the same date enjoyed this status. In contrast to the practice of the Dutch Reformed Church, in which, again, only a fraction of adults joined in communion, the infants of those who were not full church members were denied baptism. On the other hand, civil laws required everyone within a town to attend the preaching of the word, whether or not they were church members.[13] In time, the percentage of church members tended to decline, as many of the younger generation raised within the church found it difficult to discern internal evidence of saving faith. By 1678, the percentage was down to 47 percent of adult males in Milford. It thus happened with increasing frequency that babies were born to parents who had themselves been baptized but who had not yet been able to claim the status of saints. Many of them wanted their children received into the covenant of baptism. A synod summoned by the authorities of Massachusetts in 1662 approved such baptism, but individual churches resisted this "half-way covenant" as a dangerous concession to impiety feared to be advancing around them.

The restriction of access to baptism among most New England churches did not mean that the colonies' Puritans had abandoned the ideal of the Christian commonwealth. On the contrary, they advocated the close cooperation of magistrates and ministers, each group, in the purest tradition of Geneva, having authority over its separate but interrelated domain. The Cambridge Platform asserted the duty of magistrates to exercise care in matters of religion, to uphold both tables of the law, and to punish blasphemy, heresy, and schism. The first law code of Massachusetts (1648) drew heavily on biblical authority in decreeing death for a wide range of offenses: severe blasphemy, adultery, male homosexuality, and cursing or striking one's aged parents. It also mandated attendance at church and prohibited defaming of God's ministers. The exact relation between the political and ecclesiastical communities varied from one colony to another. In Massachusetts and New Haven only church members could vote and hold office. In Connecticut all male freeholders possessed these rights. Even if the visible saints admitted to the communion table thus did not monopolize political rights everywhere in New England, they consistently labored to ensure that the secular officials upheld Christian law and promoted the authority of the church and its ministry.[14]

SCOTLAND OVERTURNS EPISCOPACY

While stimulating the great migration to New England, Charles's church policies also stirred massive discontent in Scotland, where he proposed to remake religious life along English lines and did so more thoroughly and less tactfully than his father. His maladroit policies here proved to be his and Laud's undoing in both Scotland and England, for the open rebellion they incited north of the Tweed in turn gave the many Englishmen opposed to them the opportunity to voice their displeasure—an opportunity that had been denied them for the years from 1629 to 1640, when Charles ruled without convoking a Parliament.

Unlike his father, Charles had little direct experience of Scotland and even less good counsel about Scottish affairs. He got his reign off to a bad start by stretching precedent aggressively to reclaim land alienated by his predecessors and thus alienating much of the nobility. With Laud's assistance, he then managed to offend a sizable segment of the remainder of the population with a series of symbolic actions and church policies that flew in the face of the austerity cultivated by the kirk since the Reformation. In 1633 Laud choreographed Charles's Scottish coronation with a great profusion of vestments. Insistence upon the strict enforcement of the Five Articles of Perth compounded the offense. By commissioning all bishops as justices of the peace, bypassing the General Assembly of the church, and promulgating new canons that made no mention of kirk sessions and presbyteries, the two appeared to threaten the Jacobean compromise between presbyterial and episcopal elements of church government. The breaking point came in December 1636 when the crown ordered a new service book to be drawn up and put into general use, then moved slowly to have it drafted and implemented. The details of the book, when it finally appeared in 1637, were bad enough: the number of holidays was increased, baptismal fonts and the sign of the cross were returned to baptism, and provisions were made for the churching of women and graveside prayers. Even worse, the seven months that elapsed before its appearance allowed alarmist rumors to proliferate and gave nobles and clerics troubled by the course of crown policy time to organize against it. When the book—"this vomit of Romisch superstition," as one opponent called it—was introduced in Edinburgh's Saint Giles cathedral on July 23, 1637, "all the common people, especially the women, rose up with such a loud clamour and uproar, so that nothing could be heard; some cried 'Woe, woe!', some cried 'Sorrow, sorrow!

for this doleful day, that they are bringing in Popery among us!' Others did cast their stools against the Dean's face." The demonstration seems to have been planned.[15]

The Edinburgh revolt initiated months of protest meetings and petitions against the prayer book. When the privy council forbade such meetings on pain of treason, the opposition responded with that classic Scottish measure, a band, or covenant. This covenant, however, exceeded all previous ones in scope and ambition, for it was conceived not simply as an agreement among individuals committed to a specific cause, but as an oath to be taken by the entire nation in an act that would bind it collectively before God. Furthermore, the prominence that the metaphor of the covenant had obtained within Reformed theology to describe the conditions governing salvation in the preceding generations made the pact appear still more portentous.[16] Soon known as the National Covenant, the document began by recalling the strongly anti-Roman confession of 1581 and the kingdom's sixteenth-century statutes against papal jurisdiction, idolatry, and interference with the freedom of the church. It then pledged those who accepted it "to labour by all meanes lawful to recover the purity and liberty of the Gospel, as it was stablished and professed" in the first generation after the Reformation. The recent "Novations," it solemnly warned, "do sensibly tend to the re-establishing of the Popish Religion and Tyranny, and to the subversion and ruine of the true Reformed Religion, and of our Liberties, Lawes and Estates." The covenant included a pledge of loyalty to the king and avowed it intended no diminution of the king's authority.[17]

The National Covenant rode a wave of enthusiasm across much of the Lowlands. Ministers painstakingly explained its often convoluted provisions from the pulpit. Some parishes, so its supporters reported, were sensibly transformed at its swearing: the Holy Spirit was felt within the congregation, tears flowed, and the minister prayed over the congregation at length. The precise extent of the partisanship it garnered has yet to be pinpointed, but undoubtedly the majority of the nobility signed. Its partisans did not wait to openly express the specific demands they believed to be implicit in the document, for example, the curtailment of episcopal power and annual convocation of the General Assembly.[18]

Charles was slow to respond: only in May 1638, ten months after the tumult in Saint Giles cathedral, did he name the marquis of Hamilton as special commissioner to deal with the crisis. By the summer of 1638, it was obvious the king had decided to use force if necessary to get the Scots to renounce the covenant. The Covenanters summoned a council to coordinate their activities. Both sides were openly arming.

Before armed conflict began, Charles agreed to call a general assembly, hoping that Hamilton would be able to control it. Just the opposite occurred. Lay opponents of Charles's church policies forced their way into many presbyteries and gained control of the selection of delegates. Bishops and moderate ministers were deterred from attending by threats of violence or were simply excluded. A special committee met before the assembly to mastermind the selection of moderator and decide the business to be presented. When the General Assembly met in Glasgow in November, Hamilton concluded forthwith he could not control the packed gathering and declared it closed. Defying the order, it continued to sit, announcing the independence of the church. Decisions taken condemned the Five Articles of Perth and the prayer book of 1637, abolished episcopacy, and cast eight of the fourteen bishops out of the church. A motion requiring annual meetings of the General Assembly was voted. To underscore the proper Bezan separation of church and state, officers of the church were forbidden to hold any civil office or vote in Parliament.[19]

Charles hoped to undo the decisions of the General Assembly of Glasgow by force of arms, but his actions merely revealed the failure of the efforts he had made during the preceding decade to retool the machinery of government. He first dispatched an army to Edinburgh, calling upon the recently reformed English militia, marshaling feudal service from his nobility, and borrowing heavily against anticipated revenue. The troops and commanders were disappointing, supply problems aggravated their limitations, and when a covenanting force led by veterans of mercenary service in the Thirty Years War stood its ground near the border, the army beat a hasty retreat. Charles then summoned the English Parliament in search of money for a better army but cut short this Short Parliament when it became evident that the assembly would grant nothing unless the kingdom's grievances were redressed. A second mobilization by dint of extraparliamentary means of support proved even more of a fiasco than the first, when the Covenanters crossed the Tweed and defeated the royal troops at Newburn in the second Bishop's War. Their victory announced that the king would have to treat seriously the English Parliament if he hoped to defend his southern kingdom, much less subdue his northern one. In Scotland, meanwhile, effective political authority now rested firmly in the hands of its Parliament and the standing committee it had designated to take decisions between sessions.[20]

The Scottish Revolution of 1637 was not only an uprising in defense of national church traditions threatened by an uncomprehending king and his evil advisors; it was also an internal war between competing tendencies within the Scottish church, for parts of the country were initially hostile to the Covenanters. Aberdeen was the center of such resistance: its university was dominated by theologians who championed episcopacy and crown oversight of the church, and its governor remained loyal to Charles. In 1640, the city was taken by force, and its divinity students were required to sign the covenant. Successive General Assemblies set up commissions to remove ministers who opposed the document. Some ninety-three ministers, about one-tenth of all Scottish clergymen, lost their posts between 1639 and 1643.[21]

Presbyterianism now dominated the ecclesiological theory of the church to the point where the General Assembly of 1642 could proclaim in confident error, "The Reformed kirks do hold, without doubting, their Kirk-Officers and Kirk-Government, by Assemblies higher and lower in their strong and beautiful subordination, to be jure divino and perpetual." But insurrectionaries cannot always allow practice to conform to theory if they wish to remain in control. In practice, the Commission of the Kirk, a central committee appointed by those who controlled the General Assembly, arose as a still more significant element in church governance than the ordinary presbyteries and synods, issuing orders in the name of the entire church and playing the major role in deposing recalcitrant ministers. Under this new regime, the Church of Scotland entered a period of intensified ecclesiastical discipline and renewed the purging of elements of worship deemed to be remnants of popery. Ensuring the nation's fidelity to the covenant it had sworn with God became a guiding light of policy for those who now controlled the church. In many parishes, the power of the kirk session was brought to bear against those who failed to take the covenant.[22]

THE SPLINTERING OF THE CHURCH OF ENGLAND

When Charles called the second of his two Parliaments of 1640 to Westminster in November of that year, the English opponents of his policies at last had a forum in which to pursue their grievances. This Parliament would sit longer than Charles would live. Baxter identified two groups within it that worked together to change the country: the "Good Commonwealth Men," who defended English liberties and the rights of Parliament against "arbitrary government," and "the more Religious Men," troubled by recent innovations in the church. The religious faction wasted no time in certifying their hostility to Laud, formalism, and prelacy. On November 19, the members of Parliament voted to relocate the communion table and take down the altar rails in the parish church of St. Margaret Westminster before celebrating the Lord's Supper. This action triggered others across the capital. Two days later some parishioners of Allhallows Barking sawed off the wooden angels decorating their altar rails and brought them to Westminster to exhibit the outrageous popish innovations lately introduced. Other parish vestries began to reconfigure their churches, often in the face of opposition from those pleased by existing practices. On December 11, an unprecedented throng delivered to Parliament a petition against episcopacy "with all its dependencies roots and

{ Se, heer, Malignants Footerie } { The Sound-Head, Round-Head, Rattle-Head }
{ Retorted on them properly . } { Well plac'd, where best is merited . }

Sound-Head   Rattle-Head   Round-Head

This Foolish World is full of foule mistakes,
Calls Virtue, Vice, & Goodnes Badnes makes
The Orthodox, Sound & Religious Man,
Atheists call Round-Head (late) a Puritan:
Because Hee (roundly) Rattle-Heads, Truths foes,
Plainly depaints, As this next figure showes

See, heer, the Rattle-Heads most Rotten-Heart,
Acting the Atheists or Arminians part;
Under One Cater-cap a Ianus-face,
Rejecting Truth, a Crucifixe t'embrace:
Thus Linsey Wolsie, Priestly-Prelates vile,
With Romish-rubbish did mens Soules beguile

But heer's a Round-Head to the purpose showne,
A Romish-Rounded-Shaving, too well knowne,
A Balld-pate Fryer a Round-Head indeed,
Which doth (almost) Rotunditie exceed:
Since These Round-Heads, with Rattle-Heads, so'gree,
Romish Malignants Round-Heads (right) may be.

14. "The Sound Head, Round Head and Rattle Head". Dating from the spring of 1642, when government control of the press had broken down and England stood on the brink of civil war, this engraving defends the Puritans against the hostile jibes of their antagonists while illustrating their own caricatural view of their Laudian foes. The caption explains that the new party label "Roundhead" does not apply to the "Orthodox, Sound and Religious Man" on the left, though "Atheists" who used to call him a Puritan now call him this. The true Roundhead is the friar with his shaved pate on the right, standing before a chapel decorated with statues and a cross. The two-faced figure in the middle is a "Priestly-Prelate" or Arminian who reveals his true Catholic nature by accepting the crucifix offered by the friar rather than the Bible offered by the Sound Head. (By permission of the British Library)

branches," adorned with fifteen thousand signatures. The petition blamed the bishops not only for discouraging preaching and encouraging superstition and ritual, but also for new levies, the decay of trade, and the recent wars with Scotland. In the same month, the House of Commons set up a committee to receive complaints about "scandalous" ministers who had taught Arminian or popish doctrines or introduced unwonted ceremonies. On December 18, the most scandalous minister of all, Archbishop Laud, was brought under impeachment and arrested along with a dozen of his colleagues. Five years later he would be tried and beheaded for attempting to subvert the fundamental laws of the kingdom and God's true religion by law established.[23]

During the following year, proposals to change the Church of England made relatively little headway in Parliament, largely because of opposition in the House of Lords. But the old church order was beginning to crumble. Church courts ceased to function. The House of Commons encouraged local officials to overlook lay preaching, incidents of iconoclasm, and people absenting themselves from parish services to hear sermons elsewhere.[24] With pulpit and press censorship gone, all of the viewpoints that had gradually built up within the English church now contended to be heard. Existing divisions in the nation's religious life were brought into the open and accentuated, and new ones were discovered. Worship, doctrine, and the sacraments were all hotly argued; no subject, however, attracted more attention than ecclesiology, which now eclipsed both ceremonial issues and the matter of predestination as the bitterest point of division in English religious life.

Although no study has yet mapped all of the contours of the ecclesiological debates of these years, four broad camps may be discerned.[25] One defended episcopacy with a new vigor and historical sophistication. In 1641, the learned archbishop of Armagh, James Ussher, proposed a "Reduction of Episcopacy unto the form of synodical government received in the Ancient Church." The intention was to modify the English church so as to incorporate a hierarchy of synods but preserve bishops as the presiding officers of these gatherings. Although at first appealing to many, this blend of episcopalian and presbyterial-synodal elements faded from view as the rival camps grew polarized and a more strident brand of episcopalianism emerged. Jacobean and Caroline supporters of jure divino episcopacy had already begun to assert that the laying on of hands by a bishop who stood in an unbroken line of succession from the apostolic age was fundamental to the ordination of a proper Christian minister. When their opponents pointed out that such a notion implied that continental Reformed ministers in churches without bishops lacked a legitimate calling, they replied that where political circumstances had created churches without bishops, such churches could still be true churches so long as doctrine was purely taught and the sacraments rightly administered.

In 1642 Jeremy Taylor's *Episcopacy Asserted* took the plunge of insisting that episcopal ordination was a sine qua non of a true church, a principle that would become one of the defining tenets of high Anglicanism. Two years later Ussher brought out a new critical edition of the letters of Ignatius, the first-century martyr whose epistles as reported by Eusebius—if they were not interpolations—provided some of the best evidence that a measure of hierarchy existed among the clergy in the earliest period of the church. Ussher's edition, hailed as a masterpiece of textual criticism, ably defended the genuineness of certain of these contested letters and thus reinforced the claim that bishops and presbyters ceased to be identical offices within the apostolic age of the church.[26]

Congregationalism was a second model of church government. As early as 1635, New England ministers like John Cotton had begun to draft justifications for the distinctive practices that took shape in that part of the world in response to queries and criticisms from colleagues back in England. As censorship collapsed and the pamphlet wars began in England, such works of theirs as *An Apologie of the Churches in New England for Church Government* and *The Churches Resurrection, the True Constitution of a Particular Visible Church* were printed in London. A tiny family of semiseparating congregations within London descended from the assembly founded by Henry Jacob in 1616 had also managed to survive the Laudian persecutions and even to draw new members from those alarmed by the course being taken by the established church. They too preserved the position first articulated by still earlier separatists that each congregation was a complete visible church with the power to elect its own ministers and control access to communion. They now publicly defended that stance in such tracts as Katherine Chidley's *Justification of the Independent Churches of Christ*. Perhaps the most important Puritan theologian during the era of the civil war and interregnum, John Owen, was led in 1645 to embrace the model of self-governing covenanted churches as a result of reading Cotton's *Keys of the Kingdom of Heaven*. He soon established a gathered church alongside his parish flock in Coggeshall— just one of a growing number of such assemblies that took shape in these years.

Not all of these churches followed the New England way. Lay preachers of all stripes proliferated. Some claimed to speak under the direct inspiration of the spirit. Others prophesied the coming of the millennium. Two groups denied the legitimacy of infant baptism and advocated the baptism of adult believers: the Particular Baptists, who shared the Congregationalists' predestinarian theology and conviction that the visible saints could be known; and the General Baptists, who espoused doctrines of general grace and free will they had absorbed in exile from the Dutch Anabaptists. By the 1650s, Quakers,

Ranters, and Fifth Monarchists added to the profusion of radical tongues. The two greatest centers of ferment were London and the encampments of the parliamentary army, newly modeled after 1645, whose chaplains numbered several eloquent preachers freshly returned from New England. Already by 1646, an alarmed Thomas Edwards wrote that England "is become already in many places a chaos, a Babel, another Amsterdam . . . and in the high way to Munster." All those who defended the rights of lay ministers to preach or who gathered churches to follow their own way came to be known as Independents.[27]

Fear that the Church of England would split into a welter of independent congregations and end in anarchy led many to uphold the most obvious Reformed alternative to bishops for maintaining unity of doctrine and worship: a presbyterial-synodal form of church government. Scotland's ever more ardent defenders of this system rushed into the breach created by the disappearance since the 1590s of a native English presbyterian tradition and published strong claims for its biblical foundation. Travers and Cartwright's old *Directory of Church Government* was recovered and published in 1644. The wide band of English opinion that longed for a unified national church without excessive authoritarianism gravitated toward this position, without necessarily accepting all of the Scottish claims for its jure divino basis.[28]

The long tradition of defending the royal supremacy as well as a backlash against the recent strengthening of ecclesiastical prerogatives made what its enemies called Erastianism, the fourth force in England's debates over church government. The Heidelberg doctor was hardly the chief authority for this camp. Its spokesmen also appealed to Bullinger and Gwalther and drew reinforcement from the arguments Grotius had advanced amid the Dutch battles of the 1610s in favor of magisterial control over the church. In fact, Grotius's *Of the Authority of the Highest Powers about Sacred Things, Or, The Right of the State in the Church,* written in 1617, received its first publication in London in 1647 after circulating widely in manuscript. The learned antiquarianism cultivated in the Great Tew circle fortified this current of thought. The lawyer and member of Parliament John Selden was widely considered the head of the Erastians. "His glory is most in the Jewish learning; he avows everywhere that the Jewish State and Church was all one, and so in England it must be that the Parliament is the church," reported one opponent. Clergymen like Thomas Coleman and John Lightfoot likewise defended the Zurich tradition that gave the civil magistrates ultimate authority for the church in a Christian commonwealth by appealing to the example of the church of Israel, "the best Reformed Church that ever was."[29]

Political events determined the outcome of the debate about ecclesiology. As noted, Ussher's proposal for a modified form of episcopacy initially commanded wide support in Parliament, but a rift that ran largely along the fault line of religious sensibility opened about whether Charles I could be trusted to respect the agreements forced upon him. As the gap between Charles I and strenuously anti-Laudian members of the House of Commons widened, the opposition of the bishops in the House of Lords to many proposals for church reform and their loyalty to the king following the outbreak of civil war doomed the episcopate. On September 22, 1642, a month after Charles raised his standard at Nottingham, Parliament suspended the bishops from office. A year later, it passed an ordinance for the "utter demolishing, removing and taking away of all Monuments of Superstition or Idolatry." Altars and the raised chancels on which they might have sat were ordered to be removed from all churches; communion tables were to be moved out of the east end and their rails taken away; tapers, crosses, and crucifixes were to be demolished.[30]

To draft a new church order, an assembly of leading divines was summoned to Westminster. The presbyterian cause dominated the opening debates among the 121 English clergymen and 30 lay delegates at the Westminster Assembly. Most of the small number of supporters of episcopacy named to the gathering refused to attend out of loyalty to the king, and those who did were marginalized—or even imprisoned, as happened to a delegate who dared to write Archbishop Ussher seeking advice. In the beginning, the civil war went poorly for Parliament, forcing it to bid against the king for assistance from Scotland and finally to consent in September 1643 to the Anglo-Scottish Solemn League and Covenant. This pact, made "in the presence of the Almighty God the Searcher of all hearts," pledged the English to bring their church into conformity with "the example of the best Reformed Churches," committed both parties to the nearest possible "conjunction and uniformity in Religion, Confession of Faith, Form of Church-government, [and] Directory for Worship and Catechizing," and urged all who took the covenant to deflect the Lord's wrath from both lands through a sincere reformation of life. In addition, it prompted a group of leading Scottish churchmen to be admitted to the Westminster Assembly in an advisory capacity.

The majority of the delegates who favored a presbyterial-synodal form of church government worked to bring the others around to their position by demonstrating the form's biblical basis point by point; but exegesis proved a time-consuming, contentious business. As the divines puzzled over Scripture, the clash of arms realigned the political situation. The New Model Army proved more successful than the Scottish forces in the warfare against the king and did a better job of claiming credit for joint victories. As the army's power increased, the Independents and Erastians within the assembly grew more assertive and forced the initiation of regular consultations with Parliament, which was less sympathetic to clerical independence. As in the cities of Germany and Switzerland in the first century of the Reformation, the issue of who controlled excommunication became a bone of contention. Repeating the action of Calvin and his fellow pastors in Geneva in 1553, the assembly threatened to resign en masse unless the church's control of an independent system of discipline was recognized. But England in 1645 was not Geneva in 1553, and it was the assembly that backed down this time. The new form of church government for England finally decided upon in conjunction with Parliament and spelled out in measures of August 1645 and March 1646 approximated the presbyterial-synodal churches of Scotland, France, and the Netherlands in its parish-based system of consistorial discipline and four-tiered structure of local, regional, and national synods. But it contained major compromises with Erastian and congregationalist concerns: the decisions of the superior jurisdictions were made advisory rather than binding on individual congregations; government officials conducted the election of parish elders; and sentences of excommunication could be appealed to commissioners chosen by Parliament. These accommodations displeased the Scottish envoys, who castigated the new system as a "lame Erastian presbytery."[31]

With less division, the Westminster Assembly also drew up an order of worship and a confession of faith. The Directory for Public Worship, accepted by the Parliaments of England and Scotland alike in 1645, carved a middle ground between the Presbyterian desire for a fixed liturgy and Independent attachment to extemporary prayer by specifying the order of services but merely suggesting sample prayers. Distilling the practices of the "best Reformed churches" and adding a dash of English Sabbatarianism, it prescribed the discontinuation of all "festival days, vulgarly called Holy Dayes," instituted a simple seated communion, and called for the "Lord's Day" to be given over entirely to such acts of piety, charity, and mercy as singing psalms, repeating sermons in family groups, visiting the sick, and relieving the poor. No ceremonies whatsoever were to accompany funerals, and the pouring or sprinkling of water on the newborn was the sole approved ritual action of baptism, which could be performed only by a minister at a regularly scheduled worship service.[32]

The Westminster Confession of Faith, completed in April 1647, asserted the high Reformed orthodoxy of limited atonement, irresistible grace, and the perseverance of the saints, while avoiding a stand on the finer points of the predestination question debated among supralapsarians, infralapsarians, and Amyrauldians. It also took up the matter of the marks of saving faith that was of such import to the English and struck a middle path between an exclusive reliance upon the evidence of either faith or works. The Scots accepted this confession without modification, and it became one of the basic confessional statements of the Scottish church. The English Parliament approved it in June

1648 with a series of modifications that eliminated its provisions on church censures and synods and made room for a more positive appreciation of liberty of conscience and the power of the civil magistrate over church affairs. The main body of the Church of England would repudiate the confession at the Restoration, but it would remain the basic doctrinal statement of English and New England Congregationalists and be accepted with further revisions on baptism by the Particular Baptists in 1677.[33]

By the time the Westminster Assembly finished meeting regularly in 1647, it was already apparent that the church structure decreed in 1645–46 was having a hard time getting off the ground. Ministers tended to be hostile to the appointment of lay elders. Church members resented elders examining their fitness for communion. Even in London, the greatest center of support for the new order, elders are known to have been elected and presbyteries founded in only 64 of the 108 city parishes, and just 8 of the 12 projected local synods, known as classes, were set up. Elsewhere, classes are known to have been established in only 14 of the kingdom's 40 counties. Attendance at most of them soon fell off to just a handful, and few classes did more than ordain ministers. The projected national synod never met. The majority of English parishes probably never acquired a copy of the new Directory for Public Worship.[34]

Instead of hastening the thorough reformation of England's church for which the godly had long prayed, the civil war destroyed the long-standing consensus that the government ought to impose a single model of religious practice. Oliver Cromwell, now the greatest power in the land, was a devout Puritan who believed so firmly in God's all-controlling providence that he regularly consulted learned ministers to find out what prophecies were coming true. He was sceptical, however, that God could be captured in set forms and shared the Independent belief in liberty for all Protestants of genuinely searching conscience. Many in Parliament and among the London citizenry called for the suppression of lay preachers, the closing of the gathered churches, reconciliation with the king, and the disbanding of an army alarmingly infected by heresy; yet a parliamentary decision to disband the army in the most reckless of manners, without payment of overdue wages, triggered the most fateful acts of the civil war and interregnum: Pride's Purge, the trial and execution of Charles I, and the proclamation of a commonwealth. This chain of events sounded the death knell for all aspirations to create a uniform church order. In 1650, the Rump Parliament repealed the penalties for failing to attend parish worship on Sunday and required instead that citizens simply "resort to some public place where the service and worship of God is exercised, or . . . be present at some other place in the practice of some religious duty, either of prayer, preaching, reading or expounding the scriptures, or conferring upon the same." The action did not institute complete freedom of religious speech or worship. An earlier act of 1650 against "several Atheistical, Blasphemous and Execrable Opinions" condemned the extreme Antinomian views ascribed to the Ranters, while the Cromwellian Instrument of Government of 1653 exempted popery, prelacy, and licentiousness from the broad freedom of religion it otherwise promised. The need for a system of ordaining new ministers and supervising those in place continued to be felt. As early as 1644, a provisional system by which candidates for the ministry were approved by committees of eminent ministers had been created. This was renewed in 1654, as a Committee of Triers composed of nine laymen and twenty-nine ministers. This board was to examine would-be clergymen to determine if they possessed knowledge of the Bible, a blameless life, and saving grace. Oversight of incumbent ministers was vested in lay-dominated county committees of Ejectors, empowered to suspend ministers for popery, violating the Blasphemy Act of 1650, using the Book of Common Prayer, and writing or preaching "any disaffection to the present government." The Triers, who included Congregationalists, Presbyterians, and Baptists in their ranks, approved thirty-five hundred ministerial candidates during the five years they remained in existence; the Ejectors operated in a majority of counties. A degree of government oversight of religion thus continued, but the new system made room within the established parish system for Baptists and Independents, while allowing the members of gathered churches to worship independently of any parish if they so chose.[35]

While gradually relinquishing the quest to create a uniform church order, England's new rulers continued to pursue those other enduring Puritan preoccupations, the creation of an able preaching ministry and the reformation of manners, throughout the civil war and interregnum. Church revenue was reallocated and nationwide collections taken to aid preaching ministers in the north of England, Wales, Ireland, and New England. Early in the First Civil War, a national day of repentance was proclaimed to seek expiation for the country's great sins of bloodshed and idolatry. Later measures called upon the nation to observe all public days of fasting and thanksgiving scrupulously and instituted strict fines for Sunday work and recreation. Theaters were closed, the Book of Sports was ordered to be publicly burned, and harsh new penalties against adultery, cursing, and swearing were inaugurated. On the ground, however, the crusade for the reformation of manners appears to have had uneven success. Warwickshire records indicate no more indictments for Sabbath breach or keeping unlicensed alehouses in the 1650s than in the 1630s. Some of the Cromwellian major-generals employed in 1655 in part to infuse the campaign with new zeal enjoyed some success, but most had to agree with a colleague who ruefully noted, "Wicked magistrates by reason of their number overpower the godly magistrates."[36]

Between the tumult of the period and the inability of the authorities to implement the new laws of the era, a virtually endless range of permutations came to govern religious practice in the localities by the 1650s. Services were supposed to follow the Directory for Public Worship, but many parish ministers still used the Book of Common Prayer or mixed elements from both liturgies. The proliferating number of gathered churches created an ever-increasing variety of alternatives to the parish church. Some of these began to associate among themselves on the basis of clear doctrinal platforms; by 1660 roughly 150 Particular Baptist churches were conjoined in a network of regional associations, while delegates from about 120 Congregational churches met at Savoy Palace in 1658 and agreed upon common principles of church order and the theology of the Westminster Confession. Still more lacked a denominational identity.[37] At the same time, some of the 2,425 clergymen who had lost their parish livings for their loyalty to the king or to liturgical practices now defined as scandalous continued to preach and administer the sacraments where they could, often with the protection of sympathetic gentlemen. Works such as Henry Hammond's *View of the New Directory and a Vindication of the Antient Liturgy of the Church of England* (1645) contributed to the ongoing elaboration of a distinctive Anglican tradition. Several Caroline bishops remained in the country, conferring holy orders on those prospective clergymen who wanted the episcopal laying on of hands that the growing corpus of Anglican apologetics held was the only proper form of ordination.[38] Ministers might thus trace their calling to episcopal or presbyterian ordination, to the approval of the Triers, to congregational election, to the direct inspiration of the Spirit, or to a combination of these. Laymen could worship and take the sacraments in a parish church, a gathered church, or a clandestine Anglican assembly—or in more than one. A law of 1653 made civil marriage possible. An unknown number of couples took advantage of this. People of means began to celebrate family baptisms within the household rather than before any public congregation.[39]

Exhilarating to some, this variety of worship troubled many. The parish ministers in the shires who had to confront this new situation aimed to preserve a degree of unity and collective morale by forming clerical conferences in upward of a dozen counties for the discussion of problems of discipline and doctrine they encountered. The most famous of these groups was Baxter's Worcestershire Association of 1653.[40] More creatively, the splintering of the church gave rise to those currents of rational theology that aimed to reunite believers around a few basic principles of faith and that were taught in the universities during the 1650s by such men as Henry More, John Wilkins, and Benjamin Whichcote. Most of the future party of the latitudemen were students at Cambridge during these years.[41]

In the final analysis, England's civil war and interregnum toppled a church structure that had compelled nearly universal participation prior to the revolution, set off debate about the best form of church to replace it that engendered far greater division over ecclesiological issues than had ever been the case before, and ended with the official abandonment of the quest for a single national church settlement. In the localities, believers could choose among an unprecedented range of separating and semiseparating sects, congregations, and movements. As the publication of Stillingfleet's *Irenicum* in 1660 would demonstrate, however, many English continued to long for a unified national church. The challenge of the Restoration would be to see whether or not such a church could be reassembled.

POLITICAL DIVISION IN THE CHURCH OF SCOTLAND

The civil war and interregnum saw new divisions split the Church of Scotland, too, but here the divisive question was less that of ecclesiology than the political issue: what course of action was dictated by the nation's solemn covenant with God? Discussion of this issue allowed the kingdom's always politically outspoken clergy to become more deeply involved in political affairs than ever before, for who was better qualified than the clergy to expound just what the national commitment to uphold the Gospel entailed? The upshot was one of the most remarkable chapters in the history of the conviction that Beza had stated a century earlier, that the Bible offered a guide to political wisdom surer than the truths of mathematics.

Scotland's intervention in the English civil war was driven by the hope of exporting its presbyterian church order and the fear that this order would never be secure at home so long as Charles I had an army at his command and remained hostile to the National Covenant. The failure of Scottish intervention to produce the hoped-for reformation of the English church along presbyterian lines, however, led many Scots to question allying with an English Parliament that seemed alarmingly indifferent to the spread of sectarianism. Loyalty to the person of the ruler also made up a larger part of Scottish political culture, for the Stuarts were a Scottish dynasty with a tradition of rule stretching back into the mists of time. It was not for nothing that the covenant had proclaimed the duty of obedience to the crown at the same time it committed its signers to uphold the purity of the church. When a defeated Charles surrendered to the Scots rather than to his English enemies in 1646, the first division over what the covenant demanded appeared. One group favored reconciliation with the king. The other opposed any agreement until Charles I committed himself wholeheartedly to the defense of the covenant. The noblemen who dominated the Scottish Parliament inclined toward the first position. After long negotiations, this body approved in December 1647 an Engagement with Charles by which it agreed to support the king—although he would neither sign the covenant himself nor impose its signature on all subjects—in return for his promise to try out the new church order approved by the English Parliament for three years in England and to confirm the Solemn League and Covenant. The churchmen who controlled the Committee of the Kirk objected, claiming that the agreement fell short of the conditions to which the country had committed itself before God and that they had a right to be consulted on decisions about religion.[42]

The signature of the Engagement was followed close on by the renewal of civil war. The Scots marched into England in the king's defense, only to be routed by Cromwell at Preston. The defeat discredited the Engagers and the greater part of the nobility who sided with their cause. Seizing upon the defeat of their enemies, a makeshift band of Covenanters marched from the southwestern hills into Edinburgh in late November 1648 in what became known as the Whiggamore raid. Taking control of the capital, they proclaimed the nation's error to have been to compromise overhastily with "the malignant enemies of truth and godliness." Now, exulted George Gillespie, one of the most powerful figures in the church, "the Lord is about to purge his churches. I have often comforted myself, and still do, with the hopes of the Lord purging this polluted land."[43]

A clerical–populist alliance ruling in the name of the covenant set about this task with determination. A measure of January 1649 drastically trimmed back the number of those eligible for positions of political authority by excluding all who had taken the Engagement from the army or government. The clergy obtained an end to that ancient thorn in the side of ministerial quality and independence, lay patronage. Legislation was written to end inequities in tax collection, to eliminate legal malpractice and perjury, and to reform poor relief in a manner that placed particularly heavy burdens on landlords who dealt harshly with their tenants. Harsh new laws were passed against witches, fornicators, drunks, scolds, and Sunday fishermen. Church committees began a new purge of malignant ministers, while conditions governing access to communion were tightened up in many parishes, and kirk sessions barred from the sacrament those who had not yet signed the covenant.[44]

News that England's Parliament had been purged and the king executed came as a shock to the covenanting regime. Let England's sectaries violate those terms of the Solemn League and Covenant in which the two lands had pledged to preserve the king's person and authority and to bring the English church into line with the example of the best Reformed churches. They would recognize Charles II as king of all Britain if he would accept the covenants. Charles refused their first overtures, hoping his supporters in Ireland and the Highlands might carry him to his thrones without humiliating negotiations. Cromwell's victorious campaign in Ireland and the failure of Montrose's rising in the Highlands crushed these hopes. After much foot dragging and evident ill will, Charles consented to the Scots' terms and entered the country.

Hard on his heels came Cromwell. The key to defending God's cause against the invaders, the leading ministers now preached, was to ensure the purity of its defenders. The example of Gideon, who reduced his army to three hundred righteous men on God's command before defeating the Midianites, offered inspiration. Hundreds of experienced officers and enlisted men whose zeal for the covenants was deemed insufficient were removed. All the men in the English army were "but cyphers making no number to God," the minister Samuel Rutherford reassured Colonel Gilbert Ker just before the showdown. But even though the purges had still left Scotland's army larger than the body of English invaders, Cromwell was able to catch the Scots off guard with a dawn attack at Dunbar and rout them before they could draw up in proper order—in large measure, it appears, because so many midlevel officers had been cashiered. Some three thousand Scots were killed and ten thousand taken prisoner. "Oh, how little of God do we see, and how mysterious is He!" Rutherford exclaimed forlornly soon afterward.[45]

A further split opened in the Covenanter ranks as they groped to understand the reasons for the defeat at Dunbar. For a majority, the outcome proved that the keenness to root out malignancy had been misguided and counterproductive. They accepted repentant Engagers back into the cause and proceeded to Charles II's coronation at Scone. For a minority that included Rutherford, the defeat demonstrated that the country had been unfaithful to the covenants and too lax about accepting into them those who were not committed to them body and soul, beginning with Charles II. They condemned the king's hasty readmission to the National Covenant. To the moderate argument that repentant Engagers had a natural right to fight for their country, Rutherford replied in *The Law and the Prince,* one of the most uncompromising statements of the right of subjects to resist an unjust government, "Light of nature is no rule for a Christian man." The majority of moderate so-called Resolutioners ultimately excluded men like Rutherford from the General Assembly. The purged ministers protested and formed rival General Assemblies in 1651 and 1652. The synod of Glasgow likewise split between Resolutioners and Protesters, and in several regions rival presbyteries filled vacancies with competing ministers.[46]

The rupture did not immediately produce a more widespread or longer-lasting schism within the Church of Scotland for one simple reason. Further

triumphs by Cromwell's army put an end to the country's independence between September 1650 and May 1652 and brought English military rule. In
the ensuing period of Cromwellian domination, some Covenanters, such as
Rutherford, withdrew from political engagement. A few embraced Quakerism
or Congregationalism, which made their appearances in Scotland in this era.
Cromwell tried vainly to mediate the disagreements between Resolutioners
and Protesters, and their rivalry now found its outlet in struggles for control
of the Committee of Triers established for Scotland in 1654.[47] But the Cromwellian church was simply too loose to beget open schism. The divergence between the *pur et dur* and those willing to accept a modicum of compromise
with a fallen world would, however, persist —and resurface.

THE RESTORATION SETTLEMENTS

While it lasted, the Cromwellian church order conferred a uniquely broad, decentralized, and antihierarchical disposition on both England and Scotland.
But it lasted for just the brief period of the regime itself. When the Cromwellian regnancy collapsed soon after the death of its architect and England
went "running unto the King as Israel to bring back David," the system had
few defenders.

The Restoration raised again the question of what sort of church order England and Scotland would have. One group close to the king in exile consisted
of Scottish and English Presbyterians who had opposed army rule. They inclined toward austerity of worship as well as some form of presbyterial church
government and could take hope in the fact that Charles had already accepted
the Solemn League and Covenant. Another group was composed of those who,
while in exile, had actively defended the Book of Common Prayer, the Laudian legacy, and the necessity of episcopal ordination. In substantial agreement with these men but convinced of the need for firm state control over the
church was the man who would become Charles's leading minister, Edward
Hyde, soon Earl of Clarendon. "God preserve us from living in a country where
the church is independent from the State and may subsist by their own acts:
for there all churchmen may be kings," he once declared. Charles II kept his
deepest religious convictions, if he had any, to himself. Those who knew him
best thought him uncertain in his views. He himself said he was an enemy to
all severity in religion, but his experience with the Scots in 1650–51 had left
him with an enduring distrust of presbyterianism, and the royal chapel had
used the Book of Common Prayer in the wake of that debacle.[48]

In the event, the Restoration was a triumph for the formalists and the episcopalians. The initial actions of the crown were publicly conciliatory to all
major factions. A dozen prominent Puritan divines, including Baxter and Edmund Calamy, gained appointment as royal chaplains and were allowed to

preach before the king without reading the liturgy. Baxter and Calamy were also offered bishoprics, which they declined. The partisans of a modified episcopacy such as that proposed earlier by Ussher at first seemed to carry the day in the debate about ecclesiology. A royal declaration of October 1660 promised bishops who would be active preachers and would carry out their administrative tasks the assistance of suffragans and elected presbyters. In the localities, however, some 695 ministers ejected from their livings between 1641 and 1659 returned to their parishes in 1660 and ousted their replacements. After a bill to give the royal declaration of October 1660 force of law was narrowly defeated in the Convention Parliament, the Cavalier Parliament that convened later in 1661 proved strongly revanchist. Although a church conference to consider the liturgy was still in session, it voted immediately to restore the Book of Common Prayer. The hangman was directed publicly to burn the Solemn League and Covenant. Most important, the Cavalier Parliament approved the Act of Uniformity of 1662, which required all ministers to declare before their congregations their unfeigned assent to everything contained in the Book of Common Prayer and instituted fines for administering the sacraments in any other manner. It required all ministers to declare it was unlawful to take up arms against the king and to swear they were in no way bound by the Solemn League and Covenant. It required episcopal ordination for all present and future ministers except aliens serving the refugee churches and obliged preachers to have a license from the bishop or face imprisonment. Finally, it subjected suspensions from communion to episcopal review.[49]

The character of the restored church during the decades that followed is indicated clearly by those who filled key positions. With the demurral of men like Baxter and Calamy, the episcopate came to be dominated by Erastians and exponents of jure divino episcopacy. Several bishops cultivated and revived Laud's legacy, notably Gilbert Sheldon, archbishop of Canterbury from 1663 to 1677, who, after going to great lengths to preserve Laud's papers during the interregnum, now directed the publication of his *Diary, History and Prayers*. John Pearson and John Fell built upon the erudite legacy of Ussher to furnish historical foundation for the thesis that bishops were virtually as old as the church itself and essential to it. Some theologians continued to defend predestination in print from within the established church, but Arminianism dominated theological instruction at Cambridge; at Oxford opinion was divided, but the discussion of controversial topics tended to be shunned. The Restoration purge of the Cambridge colleges cost many young latitudinarians their fellowships, but sympathetic lay patrons helped them find livings in leading London churches, where many of them gained great renown for their preaching. The genre of practical theology continued to be much cultivated, but in reaction to the Puritan emphasis on the workings of grace within the soul of the predestined, such authors as Jeremy Taylor emphasized holy living and moral effort as essential preconditions for the reception of grace. Last but hardly least, the Restoration church committed itself to the cause of monarchy. "The Church of England glories in nothing more than that she is the truest friend to kings and kingly government, of any other church in the world," Robert South declared. It demonstrated this by making the anniversaries of Charles I's execution and Charles II's accession the occasions for sermons throughout the land declaring the absolute sinfulness of armed resistance.[50]

Many, however, were troubled by provisions of the Act of Uniformity. Some ministers in the old Puritan tradition objected to having to assent to everything in the prayer book. Others who had sworn the Solemn League and Covenant balked at renouncing an oath made before God. Still others who had received ordination by the Triers or presbyteries refused to subject themselves to reordination by a bishop. According to Baxter, the subordination of excommunication to episcopal oversight occasioned the greatest resistance of all. Out of one or more of these considerations, by August 24, 1662—ironically enough, Saint Bartholomew's day—more than a thousand clergymen had refused the legislative command to subscribe the Act of Uniformity and lost their livings as a result. Seven hundred ministers had preceded them into unemployment as a result of being displaced by returning incumbents.[51]

The deprived ministers responded in a variety of ways. The gathered churches and sectarian groups that had taken shape prior to the Restoration continued to meet as they could, holding their assemblies in greater secrecy or, in the case of the Quakers, provocatively inviting persecution through public gatherings, sometimes on the ruins of demolished meetinghouses. The dilemmas were greatest for those within the tradition that ran from the moderate Puritanism of the pre-1640 period, with its commitment to church reform from within the national church, through the Presbyterianism of the civil war and interregnum that opposed toleration in the hope of preserving the unity of the church; the heirs to this tradition now faced an established church that insisted upon strict conformity to devotional practices and ecclesiological principles they detested. Some ejected parish ministers in this tradition kept on ministering to their congregations despite their ejection until they were arrested and jailed for doing so, then, like John Quick, began to preach to their fellow prisoners. Others were willing to make at least a temporary peace with the established church. Still others organized secret churches or conventicles they often took care to assemble only at times that did not conflict with parish worship, so that they might create not a schismatic alternative to the established church, but a godly supplement to it. Many deprived ministers became physicians and schoolteachers, certain of the more ambitious of these last dispensing theological instruction. Their schools were the forerunners of the more permanently organized dissenting academies that emerged after 1690.[52]

For the next three decades, the politics of religion would be dominated by the problem of how to respond to all of the gatherings taking place outside the established church. Clarendon initially tried "further and more speedy remedies against the growing and dangerous practices of seditious sectaries . . . who, under pretence of tender consciences, do at their meetings contrive insurrections, as late experience has showed." Attendance at any gathering for religious purposes of more than five people who were not part of the same household became grounds for imprisonment for up to three months. Ejected ministers who would not swear to seek no alteration of religion were banned from coming within five miles of any incorporated town or parliamentary borough, any parish they had ever served, or any place in which they had held conventicles. Nonconformist chronicles began to number the succession of persecutions, although it is evident the local authorities in many areas hesitated to implement the laws to their fullest.[53]

Persecution increased sympathy for the dissidents, and debate intensified as to whether it might not be preferable to grant them greater toleration or try to bring them back into the church through a policy of comprehension. In 1667 a bill introduced into Parliament would have granted ministers some leeway in the observance of ritual forms and allowed those who had received presbyterian ordination to assume church livings without episcopal reordination. It was defeated. After the secret treaty of Dover of 1670 freed Charles II from his dependence on parliamentary supply, he attempted to mitigate the persecution in 1672 by issuing a Declaration of Indulgence that allowed public worship for Protestant dissenters who obtained official licenses for this purpose and private worship for Catholics. The declaration served to reveal just how many people were eager to preach outside the confines of the established church: 1,610 licenses were issued. It also sparked such protest against what Parliament claimed was an illegal use of the royal prerogative that Charles was forced to withdraw it within a year and to enact instead the Test Act, which required the holders of all civil, military, and court offices to take communion within the established church. The indulgence was nonetheless an important moment in the history of the briefly tolerated churches, for it prompted the Presbyterians to resume ordaining ministers of their own and buoyed the spirit of all of the nonconformists by revealing their strength. The Act of Uniformity had evidently failed to bring uniformity. Its legacy instead was to introduce another dichotomy into English religious life, that between the established church and the substantial number of Protestants who worshiped partially or entirely outside it, whose shared experience of persecution forged among them a growing sense of solidarity as Dissenters.[54]

The effective restoration of a unified national church proved equally elusive in Scotland. The points of religious contention were less numerous here than in England, but they were even more uncompromisingly defended. The events of the revolution taught the Stuarts to respect Scottish sensibilities in worship. Charles II never revived the struggles of his predecessors to promote greater liturgical uniformity between the churches of England and Scotland; neither did he insist upon the observance of either the Five Articles of Perth or the canons and prayer book of 1636–37, although a few minor changes such as restoring the Christmas vacation of the Court of Sessions were made. An English nonconformist studying in Glasgow in 1672 at first wondered why there should be any dissenters in Scotland because "the public worship in the churches, though the Archbishop himself preach, is in all respects after the same manner managed as in the Presbyterian congregations in England."[55] The answer, as always in Scotland, lay in the domain of ecclesiology. Charles II was initially prepared to countenance the maintenance of a presbyterial church order, or so he told an emissary of the Resolutioner majority of the church in 1660. But as events made it clear that much of the nobility was fed up with the excesses of clerical assertiveness and political meddling that many associated with presbyterianism, Charles began to see that the Scottish Parliament might be induced to consent to the restoration of bishops and decided to pursue this course to obtain more control over the church. A parliamentary resolution of March 1661 conveyed the government of the church to the care of the king "in such a frame as shall be most agreeable to the word of God, most suteable to monarchical Government, and most complying with the public peace and quyet of the Kingdome," implying a preference for bishops. Five months later Charles announced their restoration. The system that thus came into operation worked essentially like that of the period 1600–38, with kirk sessions, presbyteries, and synods functioning under episcopal authorization and supervision. Three further measures of 1662 completed the contours of the Restoration settlement. One restored lay patronage and required all those who had entered a living since the suppression of patronage in 1649 to obtain presentation from the patron and collation from the bishop. The second declared the covenants of 1638 and 1643 to have been unlawful oaths and annulled "all acts and constitutions ecclesiastick or civill" based upon them. The third outlawed all private religious meetings and conventicles.[56]

The requirement that ministers installed in the past thirteen years obtain presentation and collation proved to be the sticking point that caused many ministers to lose their posts. Some balked at receiving collation from a bishop. Others regarded the very installation of church procedures by secular authorities as an illegitimate Erastian corruption of a properly self-governing church. No fewer than 270 ministers, or roughly a quarter of the total number of pastors active in the country, refused to comply—a higher rate of principled refusals than occurred in England at the same time, despite the narrower range of issues and the fact that not every minister was put to the test. Refusals were most numerous in the southwest, around Glasgow and in Dumfries and Galloway, where more than half of the clergy refused to comply. The next step after deprivation, of course, was the organization of secret assemblies and conventicles in defiance of the law.[57]

The appearance of field conventicles initiated a dynamic of repression and radicalization that escalated into confrontations more fierce than any in England. The first conventicles prompted the institution of heavy fines for failure to attend parish worship. The government soon began to levy these through the use of troops, who were quartered in the houses of violators until they paid. Military expedients exacted a military response. In 1666 a group of Conventiclers, now commonly labeled Whigs after the Whiggamore raid (this is the source of the later English party label), attacked a detachment of soldiers engaged in the collection of fines and rallied upward of a thousand people to march toward Edinburgh in what they vainly hoped would trigger a larger rising. Thirty-six people were executed for their part in this Pentland Rising, and eighty were condemned to be transported to the colonies.[58]

As in England, although with a slightly different chronology, periods of more intense repression alternated with periods of greater indulgence. The Pentland Rising convinced the crown to rely less heavily on troops to enforce church attendance, and confrontations died down. In 1669–73 a pair of declarations of indulgence permitted ejected ministers to return to their parish manses without taking collation, albeit at a reduced level of pay. This lured about eighty of the ejected ministers back into the fold, but, far from putting an end to the conventicles, the slackening of repression allowed them to persist and multiply. In 1674, a number of field preachers were so bold as to assemble in Edinburgh and draw up a system for calling new ministers and setting up their own church courts, thereby laying the groundwork for a schismatic church that was, however, slow to take shape. Faced with the growing scale and organization of the opposition, the authorities set in motion another, still tougher crackdown. A new law required landlords to ensure the conformity of their tenants and servants. When this proved hard to enforce, troops were again employed. To protect themselves from being broken up, field conventicles now swelled to massive proportions and became the occasion for emotional preaching. One assembly on Skeech hill near Dumfries in 1678 was reportedly attended by fourteen thousand people surrounded by armed, mounted guards. In one parish in the heartland of conventicling activity, most of the parish attended field meetings. When the minister remonstrated with one parishioner for doing so, the man called him a "soul murderer" and told him he had obtained more benefit from attending a few conventicles than he had from listening to his sermons for eighteen years.[59] The government met this latter-day hedge preaching by quartering Highland militiamen in the affected parishes, dragonnades before the dragonnades. Arrests brought raids on the prisons to liberate those seized. In May 1679 a raiding party captured the archbishop of Saint Andrews, James Sharp, on a deserted highway and killed him before his daughter's eyes.

The height of conventicling radicalism came in the following year, when a small faction led by the minister Richard Cameron subscribed a covenant dedicated to defending a church free of all state control, with authority exercised "not after a carnal manner by the plurality of votes, or authority of a single person, but according to the word of God." "Seriously considering that the hand of our kings and rulers with them, hath been of a long time against the throne of the Lord, and the Lord upon this account has declared the he will have war with them for ever," they formally renounced their allegiance to Charles II. Cameron soon met the same fate as Archbishop Sharp at the hands of a detachment of royal dragoons, although the Cameronian party survived to print new manifestos and mount new attacks in 1684. The firm use of military power finally succeeded in subduing the Cameronians and bringing the conventicles to a virtual halt by 1686, but not before armed confrontations and summary executions had taken the lives of more than one hundred men and women. A generation later these self-styled defenders of "the true presbyterian kirk and covenanted nation of Scotland" would gain commemoration as martyrs in Robert Wodrow's *Sufferings of the Church of Scotland*.[60]

THE GLORIOUS REVOLUTION AND THE LEGALIZATION OF PROTESTANT PLURALISM

The accession of the Catholic James II in 1685 further destabilized the already shaky Restoration settlements. As the growing power of Louis XIV cast an expanding shadow across Europe, fear of the associated evils of popery and arbitrary government increasingly displaced fear of the twinned evils of sectarianism and sedition among the English political nation. Charles II had managed to secure his brother's accession in part by appointing strong defenders of the dynasty and its rights of succession to key church positions. With all of a convert's conviction and none of his brother's tact, James II managed to squander the church's support within two years by suspending the penalties against nonattendance for Dissenters and Roman Catholics alike, believing that once all disabilities were removed from the exercise of Catholicism, its evident truth would win thousands. Defenders of traditional law of the land grew alarmed by his attempts to alter borough corporations and build

414

up a standing army. When James's queen became pregnant with an heir who threatened to make Catholic kings a permanent feature of British life, William III of Orange, the leader of the anti-French coalition in Europe, decided that his best hope in the conflict he rightly believed to be looming on the horizon was to intervene in England to pry the country from its alliance with France. Invited by a group of collaborators to come and uphold the rights to the throne of his wife, Mary, he launched a successful cross-channel invasion that won a more thorough victory than he could have dared hope for when James II meekly surrendered after the desertion of several of his army units. When the Convention Parliament offered the throne jointly to William and Mary, Britain had a Dutch Reformed king and an Anglican queen.

The man who wore the pants in this marriage had imbibed predestinarian doctrine from his tutor Cornelis Trigland and knew how to work with a church without bishops. His Dutch upbringing had also taught him that the toleration of several churches in one kingdom was not incompatible with political order. His coming raised the expectation that the church settlement would be reviewed again, but he was in no position to dictate it unilaterally. Once in England, he received prominent dissenters cordially and floated a broadening of the church to achieve comprehension on the terms "wherein all the Reformed churches do agree." Such inclusive thinking, however, upset those within the established church who had absorbed the high Anglican claims for the antiquity and superiority of England's distinctive liturgy and the prerogatives of an episcopally governed church marked by a genuine apostolic succession. The archbishop of Canterbury, six bishops, and approximately four hundred clergymen refused to take the oath of allegiance to William and Mary imposed on clerics in April 1689, protesting that by doing so they would break earlier oaths of allegiance to the Stuarts. These nonjurors became the ghostlike conscience of high Anglicanism and the occasion for statements of its newly uncompromising clericalism; their deprivation was illegal, so their proponents claimed, because the church was a separate realm from the state and only ecclesiastical assemblies could remove properly consecrated bishops. William indicated his support for measures brought before the Convention Parliament suspending the Test Act and widening the degree of liturgical latitude allowed ministers within the church, but these encountered strong opposition on the part of the Anglican clergy and its Tory defenders. The king making it clear that he had no intention of being a persecutor, Parliament finally decided that toleration was preferable to a policy of comprehension that most established churchmen believed to threaten the purity and uniformity of Anglican worship. The "Act for exempting their Majesties protestant subjects, dissenting from the Church of England, from the penalties of certain laws," approved by Parliament in May 1689, would be the last major component of the legisla-

TABLE 12.1
Dissenting Congregations in England and Wales, 1715–18

	Number of Congregations	Number of Hearers	Percentage of population
Presbyterians	662	185,430	3.3
Congregationalists	229	67,580	1.1
Particular Baptists	220	44,570	0.7
General Baptists	122	18,800	0.3
Seventh Day Baptists	5	?	—
Quakers	696	39,510	0.7
Total	1934	355,890	6.1

Source: Watts, *Dissenters,* 270, 509–10.

tion that would govern the English church down to the nineteenth century. The act revoked the prohibition of conventicles and removed the penalties for worshiping within them for those willing to swear an oath of loyalty to the ruling monarchs. Ministers of these churches were required to subscribe to the Thirty-Nine Articles but could omit articles about worship and baptism to which the various groups of Dissenters objected. The indulgence did not apply to Catholics and anti-Trinitarians; the Test Act remained in place; and Dissenters still had to pay tithes to the established church. Nothing was said about Dissenting schools.[61]

The legal prohibitions against their assemblies removed, the Dissenters constructed public meetinghouses and began a more settled existence. A calculation of their numbers in 1715–18 based upon a survey ordered by a joint committee set up by the Presbyterians, Congregationalists, and Baptists to protect their political interests found roughly 355,000 "hearers," or about 6 percent of the total population of England and Wales (table 12.1). Scattered widely but unevenly across the country, Dissenters were especially numerous in four kinds of areas: (1) regions of former Puritan strength; (2) districts in which there had been many ejected ministers in 1662; (3) areas in which large, widely separated parishes encouraged a search for alternative places of worship; and (4) textile manufacturing regions.[62] During this period Dissent became increasingly a movement of the humble and the middling sort, people who often attained commercial prosperity and demonstrated growing political confidence and assertiveness. Aristocratic and gentry supporters dropped away or else demonstrated support of the social hierarchy and fitness for public office by taking part in the established church as well as in dissenting congregations. Theologically, the Congregationalists and Particular

Baptists preserved the predestinarian "high Calvinism" articulated by John Owen and Thomas Goodwin well into the eighteenth century. The Presbyterians, who had always cared more about reshaping the established church in a Puritan mold than about the institutional specifics of jure divino presbyterianism, never put in place their own hierarchy of presbyteries and synods after 1689 and experienced something of an identity crisis once it became clear that their great ambition would never be realized. Some of their assemblies evolved in the direction of Congregationalism, others moved toward the liberal theology of Le Clerc, Locke, and early English Unitarianism.[63]

The established church meanwhile experienced difficulty in adjusting to the loss of its official monopoly of worship. The deprivation of the nonjurors allowed William to move the episcopate in a latitudinarian direction. Stillingfleet, Tillotson, Gilbert Burnet, and Tenison all received bishoprics. But the views of bishops of this ilk were out of touch with a parish clergy that had absorbed the high Anglican defense of the church's rituals and doctrines, only to find now that the flock had been given license to wander. The publication of Toland's *Christianity Not Mysterious* and Locke's *Reasonableness of Christianity* reinforced the sense that the basic mysteries of the faith were under attack in a new and godless age. In an ironic twist on the old Reformed tension between the ecclesiological traditions of Zurich and Geneva, Anglicans alarmed by the course in which the church was evolving now pressed two-kingdom views and analogies with England's secular constitution into a cry that clerical convocations were an essential part of the constitution of the English church and needed to be rescued from the obsolescence they had fallen into after the clergy had ceased to vote on its own taxes in 1664. Committed Anglicans were demanding a form of synod and asserting the church's independence from the crown! Their demands were insistent enough that Convocation was revived in 1700. It promptly became the scene of angry confrontations between the bishops in the upper house and the delegates of the rest of the clergy in the lower, who demanded an investigation of alleged heresies in Bishop Burnet's writings, urged the closure of dissenting schools, and denounced occasional conformity (the periodic reception of the sacraments within the established church by people who worshiped primarily in dissenting churches, alleged by its critics as a hypocritical ploy to get around the Test Act). Agitation over church-related issues reached a high point in 1709–10, when the Whig-dominated House of Commons ordered Henry Sacheverell to be brought to trial for preaching an intemperate sermon, subsequently published and widely reprinted, that flayed Whig churchmen, Dissenters, occasional conformity, and unlicensed schools. His trial became the occasion to rally those troubled by the course the church and the nation seemed to be taking. When the jury returned with a mild punishment, joyous crowds coursed through London's streets and sacked several dissenting meeting-houses. It was during this decade that observers began to speak of High and Low Church parties within the Church of England.[64]

In time, the sense of "the church in danger" receded. Convocations were too troublesome and were discontinued again after 1717. Yet the division in sensibility and outlook between High and Low Church Anglicans persisted. The final outcome of England's very long reformation was thus an established Church of England divided between two tendencies, flanked by a number of dissenting sects, each with a somewhat problematic relation to the larger Reformed tradition. The High Church Anglicans valued the beauty of holiness, the distinctive rituals of the English church, and the prerogatives of a clergy consecrated by bishops who stood in an unbroken line of succession from the early church. They tended to see their church as standing apart from the Reformed tradition, possessing its own glorious heritage exemplified in such figures as Baro, Hooker, Laud, and Hammond. The Low Church Anglicans inclined to rational theology and Erastianism and thought moral virtue a higher priority than doctrinal precision. Committed to pan-Protestant solidarity, they envisaged the history of the Reformation as a saga in which the Church of England stood shoulder to shoulder with the continental Protestant churches, took communion with them while abroad, and thus retained kinship with the continental Reformed churches. The Congregationalists and Presbyterians stressed that they were true heirs to "the doctrine of the Church of England . . . as it is contained in the Articles of Religion . . . and declared in the authenticated writings of all of the learned prelates and others for sixty years after the Reformation"—doctrine that was in essential agreement with the larger Reformed tradition. Their distinctive worship practices nonetheless placed them on the margins of continental Reformed practice. When three of the Englishmen sentenced to death for the regicide of Charles I received asylum in Bern and lived out their days in this ur-territory of the Reformed tradition, they attended the established church services regularly and were much remarked upon for their piety, but would not take communion because they felt that access to the communion table was not guarded strictly enough. The thousands of Huguenots who settled in the British Isles after 1685 divided themselves between the established church and Presbyterian assemblies when they could not worship in distinctive refugee churches.[65]

In Scotland, the Glorious Revolution precipitated the final turn of the ecclesiological wheel of fortune that had for so long alternately raised and cast down bishops. Here, the restructuring of the established church was greater than in England for two reasons. First, the Williamite cause was closely linked to the defense of presbyterian principles, for the Claim of Right passed by Scotland's Parliament in April 1689 as the basis for offering William and Mary the throne included among the fundamental principles of the national constitution a condemnation of prelacy. Second, to a man Scotland's bishops refused to swear allegiance to William and Mary. Whether such denial stemmed from personal loyalty to the Stuart dynasty, an ideological commitment to nonresistance, horror at the death of one of their number at the hands of the radical conventiclers, or simply Scotland's greater distance from the plotting and agitation that brought William III to the British Isles, it left William little room to maneuver—though at first he had shown, when visited in London by the bishop of Edinburgh, a willingness to weigh the retention of episcopacy. Given no choice but to ride the wave of Presbyterian sponsorship of his cause, he nonetheless tried to rein in the most emphatic Presbyterian claims for the total autonomy of the church from magisterial oversight and the yearning of many formerly ejected ministers to settle old scores with every Episcopalian rival.[66]

In the conventicling strongholds of the southwest, a Presbyterian *revanche* had begun even before William landed in England, for James VII's and II's acts of toleration had allowed ousted ministers to return to their old parishes and organize services in meetinghouses. Following William's triumph, organized groups of Presbyterians went from parish to parish in the regions of their greatest strength driving out the Episcopalians. Such so-called rabblings continued intermittently into 1691 and in toto displaced 200 ministers in the south and southwest; another 172 were deprived for refusing to pray for William and Mary. Legislation of 1689 and 1690, much of it extracted from an unwilling king by the Presbyterian majority in the Scottish Parliament that threatened to block fiscal legislation at a critical moment of Jacobite threat, defined a new church settlement. All laws that had endorsed episcopal power were repealed. The changes made by the rabblers were given legal sanction, and those Presbyterian ministers ejected from their livings for opposing prelacy who had not already been returned to their parishes were now ordered to be restored to their charges. The Westminster Confession of Faith was ratified, and authority over the church was vested in a revived General Assembly, membership in which was restricted to formerly deprived Presbyterians. Lay patronage rights were repealed and Yule vacations abolished.

The triumph of the Presbyterians proved harder to ensure in the localities than in Parliament. Although the drama of the conventicles has attracted most of the attention of historians of the Restoration Church of Scotland, a growth of commitment to episcopal government also evidently occurred in the generations after 1660. In the wake of the Glorious Revolution many parishes in the north defended their Episcopalian incumbents and refused to allow new and restored ministers to take their place. Many ousted Scottish bishops were able to find shelter under aristocratic wings and to continue to ordain ministers. The restored General Assembly named commissions to purge scandalous and incompetent ministers: in many areas these bodies evolved into instruments of Presbyterian revenge against incumbent Episcopalians. In 1693–94 the Parliament and General Assembly passed laws requiring all ministers to swear an oath declaring that Presbyterianism was the only true form of church government. The acts sparked so much controversy and threatened to instigate so vast an additional purge of incumbents that William intervened to obtain its repeal. To bring the church under control, he cited the crown's authority to convoke and dismiss sittings of the General Assembly, an exercise of secular oversight of church assemblies in line with Dutch traditions; but strict Scottish Presbyterians saw this behavior as unwarranted intervention in the sacred precincts of the temple. A law of 1695 permitted Episcopalian incumbents loyal to William and Mary to retain their positions without having to submit to the oversight of the General Assembly or to state their approval of Presbyterian church government.

The upshot of the Glorious Revolution in Scotland was thus to complete the division into two churches of what had formerly been two schools of thought about church government. In 1707, some 165 Episcopalians still occupied parish manses, primarily in the north and northeast, where the good auspices of their parishioners or the protection of a local aristocrat had protected them against the purges of 1688–95. They gathered in their own synods independent of the main church hierarchy of assemblies. In some parishes with a Presbyterian incumbent, an Episcopalian faction also worshiped in a meeting-house (there were a dozen such in and around Edinburgh by 1700), just as regions of Episcopalian ascendancy might contain Presbyterian minorities worshiping separately. In divided parishes, the death of an incumbent minister could spark armed confrontations between the two parties over the control of the parish church and the naming of a successor. Gradually, however, a modus vivendi evolved. A few towns even brokered arrangements whereby Presbyterian and Episcopalian assemblies shared the parish church.[67]

Having originally separated from the Presbyterians because of their belief in the necessity of episcopal ordination, Scotland's Episcopalians came in this period to differ in liturgy as well. A growing number adopted the Book of Common Prayer. The northward migration of English in the wake of the Union of 1707 and dissemination of Anglican devotional works by the recently founded Society for the Promotion of Christian Knowledge advanced this trend. Early in the eighteenth century, some Scottish Episcopalians revived the prayer book and liturgy of 1636–37. By 1720 most Episcopalian assemblies in Scotland used either this or the Book of Common Prayer.[68]

If loyal Episcopalian incumbents were confirmed in their livings from 1695 onward, the use of prayer books other than the Book of Common Order did

not become legal until 1712. To most Scots, the spread of these books por-
tended a resurrection of popery. Local authorities, in violation of fixed law,
intermittently tried to shut down Episcopalian assemblies that adopted them.
William's death in 1702, however, was followed by the reign of the devoutly
Anglican Queen Anne, while the Union of 1707 meant that the Parliament that
legislated Scottish church affairs was henceforth located in London, not Edinburgh. Even though the Act of Union specified no change in the established
religion in Scotland, an act of Parliament in 1712 formally granted Episcopalians toleration to assemble and worship as they pleased in Scotland. The
Tory-dominated Parliament also delivered a thumb in the eye of Presbyterian
sensibilities by restoring lay patronage and the symbolically charged Christmas vacation of the Court of Sessions. With the toleration act of 1712, Protestant pluralism became legal in Scotland, as it had been in England since
1689.

The Episcopalian cause in Scotland was soon compromised by the enthusiastic participation of many Episcopalians in the Jacobite risings of 1715 and
1745 as well as by the consolidation of Presbyterian control over education
and appointments within the established church. Still, some 130 Episcopalian
clergy were active in 1744; they enjoyed the backing of perhaps half of the
Scottish nobility and many ordinary people in the northeast. Meanwhile, the
restoration of lay patronage in 1712 gave a new cause to those currents within
Scottish Presbyterianism that insisted upon purity from all improper interference. After a number of confrontations pitted candidates for the ministry
chosen by a parish and the local presbytery against candidates chosen by a
disliked lay patron, a breakaway Secession Church split off from the main
body of Scottish Presbyterianism over the issue of patronage in 1733. This
would be the first of several such splits. The established Presbyterian Church
of Scotland was henceforward flanked to one side by an Episcopalian minority
and to the other by breakaway Presbyterian churches that glorified the tradition of the Covenanters and defended the purest principles of church independence. Theologically, all of these churches were slower to be affected
by the rise of rationalism and the retreat from high predestinarian orthodoxy
than their English counterparts, although a number of Scottish theologians
flirted enough with rational theology to inspire such tracts as Thomas Haly-
burton's *Natural Religion Insufficient; and Reveal'd Necessary to Man's Happiness in his Present State* (1714). The most important theological debates
within the established Church of Scotland in the early eighteenth century
pitted proponents of high Calvinism against champions of forms of covenant
theology that downplayed predestination and emphasized Christ's offer of
justifying grace, without going as far as the hypothetical universalism of
Amyraut.[69]

In Scotland, issues of church structure and church–state relations had always been the critical matters of division. In England, worship, ecclesiology, and theology had all entered into the mix. In neither had the old ambition of encompassing the entire nation in a single church been able to survive the bitter divisions that had been created by the events of the seventeenth century.

CONCLUSION TO PART III
Reformed Europe
at the End of the Seventeenth Century

At the end of the seventeenth century, the character and situation of Europe's Reformed churches were significantly changed from a century earlier. In overall numerical terms, the cause had neither grown nor shrunk dramatically; if the Church of England is still accounted Reformed, it probably had grown slightly, thanks to the unusual vigor of the English population during a century of demographic stagnation across most of the Continent. But the geographic distribution of the faithful was strikingly changed. In eastern Europe, the Reformed presence had diminished in Hungary and all but disappeared in Poland-Lithuania. Conversion had eroded the ranks of the French and Béarnais Reformed even before the revocation of legal toleration in 1685 drove as many as two hundred thousand Huguenots abroad and forced many others into the Roman fold, eliminating Reformed Protestantism entirely for a generation as a system of regularly functioning churches, although not as a tradition of faith and loyalty. The incorporation of Transylvania into the Habsburg dominions in 1691 stripped the faith of its status as the most favored religion in what had been its greatest stronghold in east central Europe for most of the century. The wars that raged across the Palatinate, together with the accession of a new Catholic ruling house at century's end, introduced noticeable Catholic and Lutheran minorities into what had been the largest Reformed territory in the Holy Roman Empire. As the seventeenth century gave way to the eighteenth, four areas had emerged as the political and intellectual bastions of the faith: the Protestant portions of Switzerland; the British Isles (although the fellowship between the established Church of England and the rest of Europe's Reformed churches was now contested); the Netherlands, where full members of the Reformed churches were now far more numerous than they had been in 1600; and Brandenburg-Prussia, where the Reformed were a small but increasingly visible and vigorous minority. The numerical evolution of the various national churches over the century's course reveals several larger lessons. Where the faith was a disfavored minority and the Reformed churches had initially been founded by a brief state-sponsored Reformation or by aristocratic fiat, loyalty to it often proved fleeting. Where the initial affiliation had been a matter of individual choice and transmission across the generations had reinforced commitment, it inspired tenacious loyalty. Conversely, where the faith enjoyed a politically privileged status, it drew new members because of its association with power and respectability.

The greatest change during the seventeenth century was that the umbrella of the Reformed tradition came to cover a far wider and more sharply antagonistic range of theological orientations, worship traditions, ecclesiologies, and even splinter churches than it had in 1600. In the domain of theology, several developments fostered the growth of internal conflict. The process of transforming the initial theological insights of the first generations of Reformed theologians into a logically coherent system of theology that could be efficiently transmitted down the generations and defended against the cause's theological adversaries drew attention to issues that the theologians of the first generations had scarcely glimpsed, notably those associated with specifying the character and sequence of the divine decrees of election and predestination. The appearance of neo-scholasticism at the end of the sixteenth century could not entirely displace the tradition's original roots in textual humanism; the internal squabbles between these methods of reading the biblical corpus grew more heated as the advance of biblical scholarship called into question the authenticity of proof texts of important doctrines and heightened the sense of distance between the contemporary world and that of ancient Israel. New philosophies challenged neo-scholasticism's Aristotelian underpinnings. The rise of experimental predestinarianism generated debate about what represented the best testimony that an individual truly possessed saving grace. Whereas the generation of Calvin, Bullinger, and their successors had expressed their differences of opinion over nuances of theology quietly in letters, the world of Reformed theology was riven by open debates between partisans of clearly delineated camps by 1700. On the tangled issue of election and predestination, partisans of high Calvinism argued with Amyrauldian moderates, while latitudinarians pleaded for the entire issue to be dropped.

424

The Arminian views deemed heterodox at Dort, anathematized for several generations by virtually all Reformed churches, and defended only by the outcast Remonstrants, had regained influence among a fraction of both English and francophone Swiss theologians. The churches of the Netherlands and the Lower Rhine were divided between antagonistic parties of Cocceians and Voetians. The Helvetic Consensus still officially upheld high predestinarianism and biblical literalism by law within the Swiss churches, but the advancing tide of theological rationalism was about to win their repeal.

A wide range of liturgical practices already existed within the various Reformed churches in 1600, and certain English and Hungarian reformers aspired to diminish this variation by securing the abolition of rituals far out of the mainstream of Reformed practice. In the end, however, their campaigns failed to carry the day. Instead, the English practical divines' promotion of new private and small group devotional practices increased this diversity. Defenders of the Church of England's liturgy made a positive virtue out of what had initially been defended as a thing indifferent and heightened the polarization between diverse worship sensibilities. While seeking to augment the marks of respect shown to the sacraments, Laud and his successors also insisted on a new self-understanding of their church, one that cast it as the purest descendant of early Christianity, sui generis among the post-Reformation churches and not really part of the Reformed tradition at all. Half a century of intense struggle between the advocates of these two worship sensibilities to impose their preferred pattern throughout the British Isles ended with the recognition that such hegemony was impossible. By the early eighteenth century the population of both countries worshiped in two or more rival churches, some of which used the Book of Common Prayer and others a simplified liturgy close to the Directory for Public Worship.

Ecclesiology, too, already a contested subject in 1600, grew more contested yet. Whereas Scotland's and England's later sixteenth-century struggles between champions of episcopalian and presbyterial-synodal forms of church government had been resolved with an effective compromise between the two systems in Scotland and the suppression of presbyterianism in England, the policies of Charles I and Laud upset the balance in Scotland and allowed presbyterianism to revive and take root far more strongly than before in England. The same fifty-year struggle fought there over liturgical matters also raged over church governance. Amid this struggle, yet another model of church government arose in certain corners of England and America: the congregationalism born of the conjunction of experimental predestinarianism, overseas settlement, and separation. The greatest casualty of the long conflict was the consensus that had prevailed within British churches down to the era of Laud that those who shared doctrines and sacraments were all brothers in

Christ, whatever the details of their liturgy or system of church government. England's nonseparating Puritans now became Dissenters, further subdivided into Presbyterians, Congregationalists, and Baptists. Scotland's rival episcopalian and presbyterian currents of opinion now hardened into warring Episcopalian and Presbyterian parties. By 1700, the British church world was so polarized over questions of ecclesiastical control that those who defended the Zurich and Erastian traditions of royal supremacy were challenged at once by extreme Scottish Presbyterians, who viewed the least degree of lay interference in church appointments as intolerable in a church that should have no king but Christ, and by a High Church party in England that argued that both bishops and Convocation had substantial autonomy by virtue of apostolic succession and the ancient constitution of the church. These debates about ecclesiology were largely confined to Britain, but they were exported to Hungary and Transylvania for the span of a generation, until they faded as the Reformed churches there were thrown on the defensive by the growth of Habsburg power.

Finally, a pan-European sociological phenomenon of the seventeenth century also contributed to a growing sense of separation between the divergent portions of the Reformed world: the decline of academic peregrination. Among the Reformed, this happened in part because certain rulers acted to restrict the movement of students and professors across national borders. The king of France, for instance, refused to allow his subjects to attend the synod of Dort and in 1623 forbade foreigners from taking up ministerial posts within the French Reformed churches, stanching an inflow that had been marked in the preceding generation. It happened in part because many national churches became preoccupied with internal quarrels unique to that church alone, and future ministers saw less benefit in studying abroad than they had before. People and ideas continued to move across national boundaries within the Reformed world. The Hungarian churches especially remained intellectual tributaries of the great Dutch and English universities, while the revocation of the Edict of Nantes cast into exile a generation of leading French pastor-intellectuals who made fundamental contributions to the unfolding international republic of letters of the pre-Enlightenment.[1] It nonetheless is accurate to say that the intellectual distance between the various Reformed churches was greater and the world of Reformed theology more conspicuously divided into distinct geographic networks of discussion and influence in 1700 than it had been a century earlier. The best evidence of this is that whereas at the beginning of the century the acts and decrees of the synod of Dort had been recognized as definitive by virtually all Reformed churches, the most important confessional documents drafted in the middle and late seventeenth century, the Westminster Confession of Faith and the Helvetic Consensus, each remained strictly limited in use and impact to one corner or another of the Reformed world.

Despite the growing lines of division that cut through Europe's Reformed churches, a strong sense of solidarity remained among them, as the financial support and asylum offered the Huguenots by so many Protestant territories after 1685 showed. Something much resembling the "political Calvinism" of the late sixteenth and early seventeenth centuries resurfaced during the wars of the latter part of Louis XIV's reign, as publicists urged pan-Protestant solidarity against the persecuting French, while the prominent refugee Huguenot preacher Pierre Jurieu espied the coming of the millennium and likened William III of Orange to the kings of ancient Israel. Now, however, talk of defending the true faith had to be joined to invocations of European values and the balance of power because the Catholic Austrians were also part of the alliance against Louis XIV.[2] Furthermore, when Reformed refugees and political exiles arrived in their new lands and began to participate in church services there, they were often puzzled by the practices and rivalries they discovered. Occasionally, like the English regicides who ended their days in Bernese territory, they felt they could not in good conscience partake of communion.

As orthodoxy faded before the advance of rationalism, and contemporary commentators came more and more to assess religions in terms of their social utility, the historical experience of Europe's Reformed churches over the course of the seventeenth century gave rise to one final development of note: the faith increasingly came to be associated with armed resistance to unjust rulers and with economic prosperity. Around 1600, Catholic and Reformed polemicists each charged the other with fostering sedition and king killing. Against the backdrop not just of the Dutch revolt and persistent Huguenot resistance, but also of the assassinations of Henry III and Henry IV and the Gunpowder Plot against James I, who was to say who had the stronger case? From the era of the English Revolution onward, the association between rebelliousness and the more zealous brands of Reformed Protestantism grew ever stronger, even though Protestant anti-Catholicism continued to associate popery with tyrannicide and unwarranted interference in the internal affairs of secular polities, and even though a sizable fraction of later seventeenth-century Reformed political theorists vociferously denied the legitimacy of all resistance to the duly constituted political authorities. From the rebellions in Hungary to the resistance of Scotland's Covenanters and Cameronians, from the Glorious Revolution to the uprisings of the Camisards, Reformed Protestants took the lead in virtually all of the most dramatic cases of armed resistance to authority of the second half of the seventeenth century. The old Catholic and Lutheran association of Calvinism and sedition became harder to rebut. Soon the historians of the Huguenot diaspora would recast this association into the positive terms of the evolving Whig saga linking Protestant principles to the cause of liberty.

The shifts that occurred in the Reformed population over the century meant that the faith became concentrated in, and hence associated with, the lands that had prospered most during these difficult times for so much of the Continent, Britain, and the Netherlands. In the economic literature of the turn of the century, the hard times in France after the expulsion of the Huguenots became a parable for the economic costs of intolerance. The link between "Calvinism" and economic success appears to have been drawn for the first time in 1671 by the English economic commentator Slingsby Bethel, who noted the lethargy of the Mediterranean economies and the vigor of the Dutch and English in his lifetime. "There is a kind of natural unaptness to business" in Catholicism, he declared, whereas "amongst the Reformed the greater their zeal, the greater is their inclinations to Trade and Industry, as holding Idleness unlawful." The economic history of Europe down to the end of the nineteenth century would only add to the plausibility of this apparent connection and provoke increasingly sophisticated explanations of why it came about.[3]

An enduring set of associations with the Reformed faith was thus beginning to emerge by the end of the seventeenth century. The questions remain: How thoroughly had the faith in fact remade its adherents? Did it transform their economic and political behavior in a consistent manner?

PART IV

New Calvinist Men and Women?

The *Longman Dictionary of Contemporary English* offers as one definition of *Calvinist,* "Having severe moral standards and tending to disapprove of pleasure."[1] Readers who have come this far will surely be able to identify many of the reasons for this common association of Calvinism with moral rigor. The earliest Swiss reformers absorbed from their youthful Erasmianism a strong concern with individual and collective moral amelioration and strove to make their communities godly Christian commonwealths. The theology of Zwingli, Bullinger, and Calvin all accorded greater attention to personal sanctification than Luther's. Calvin's signal achievement in Geneva was the successful establishment of an autonomous system of ecclesiastical discipline that was in turn adopted by many other Reformed churches. Many Reformed confessions identified discipline as one of the essential marks of a true church. Within the largest national church of a Reformed theological orientation that did not initially adopt a consistorial system of ecclesiastical discipline, the Church of England, practical divines championed a style of personal piety that sought to foster a far more single-minded, systematic pursuit of virtue than any consistory ever dreamed of enforcing. German champions of the Reformed cause also associated it with effective moral discipline. Writing at the end of the sixteenth century, the Herborn theologian Wilhelm Zepper declared that the great accomplishment of the Reformed churches was to have

429

completed Luther's reformation of doctrine with a reformation of life.[2] Wherever and whenever the Reformed cause inspired mass enthusiasm, it awakened high hopes of both individual and collective moral transformation.

Yet the view that would identify Calvinism as the most austere of the major post-Reformation confessional families and the one most focused on promoting disciplined moral behavior no longer commands agreement among Reformation historians. For upward of a generation, historians of Catholicism have emphasized that the devotional practices of the Catholic Reformation encouraged laypeople to pursue a disciplined life of piety whose features shared many elements with those promoted by the English apostles of practical divinity.[3] More recently, prominent German historians have advanced the view that "social disciplining" was an offshoot of the "confessionalization process" and a common concern of all three major post-Reformation confessional families. The splintering of Western Christendom into rival creeds caused territorial rulers to feel compelled to take the care of religion under their wing and to promote both regular participation in church services and faithful attachment to orthodox doctrine, which was specified in ever more detailed confessions of faith. In doing so, they increased the reach of their law-making power and bred dutiful, disciplined subjects.[4] Certain Lutheran territories in Germany, such as Württemberg and Pfalz-Neuburg, instituted parish-based systems of ecclesiastical discipline that were not much different from those characteristic of the Reformed.[5] Even where these were not established, regular ecclesiastical visitations and stricter secular police ordinances encouraged the tighter oversight of moral behavior. Catholicism retained the practice of sacramental confession, another powerful instrument of morals control and individual disciplining, and encouraged more frequent confession. In some areas, too, the Roman church had institutions of moral oversight comparable to the Reformed consistories. In the episcopal city of Liège, two lay *scabini synodales* assisted each of the twenty-four parish priests in reporting parishioners guilty of a wide range of misbehavior to the provost of the cathedral on his annual visits. In Italy and the Iberian lands, the Inquisition brought under its purview some of the forms of personal misbehavior that also preoccupied consistories in Reformed lands, notably blasphemy and the casting of spells.[6]

The recent emphasis on the similarities among the various post-Reformation confessions has been a salutary corrective to the denominational self-absorption and self-congratulation that long marked so much of the historical literature about early modern religion, but it may be wondered if the impulse to see the various confessions as all brothers under the skin has not been carried too far. Those who have championed the new theory of confessionalization have generally been content to indicate the analogous features within the various confessional traditions, rather than comparing their prevalence and impact. Furthermore, much of the theorizing about confessionalization ignores the nuances of the precise belief systems in question and consequently fails to explore the possible implications of these belief systems for the psyches of those raised within them. It is, in any event, now an open question whether or not Reformed reformations engendered a particularly successful reformation of manners, a distinctive work ethic, or indeed any confession-specific sociocultural metamorphoses.

First, however, it must be determined whether or not the Reformation wrought any significant changes at all in the behavior and beliefs of ordinary Christians. In one iconoclastic set of publications, Gerald Strauss touched off a still-ongoing debate about the "success or failure" of the German Reformation by providing copious evidence from parish visitations that the vast effort of post-Reformation Lutheran catechetical instruction left churchmen despairing of its futility because the inhabitants of many villages showed no genuine understanding of Lutheran doctrine for a century or more after 1517. Other historians quickly replied with evidence of places in which the catechism had been mastered.[7] In another iconoclastic article, Strauss questioned perhaps the hoariest of all generalizations about the long-term consequences of the Reformation, namely, that the establishment of Protestantism encouraged Bible reading and thus literacy. Most German church ordinances, he pointed out, devoted substantially more attention to promoting catechetical instruction than direct Bible reading. Furthermore, to date little solid evidence has been found of widespread Bible ownership in Lutheran lands prior to the rise of pietism in the late seventeenth and eighteenth centuries. Perhaps it was not the Reformation but pietism that put the Bible in lay hands.[8] In the wake of these contributions, historians can no longer assume that the doctrines and aspirations of the Reformation were quickly conveyed to and internalized by the majority of the population in the different parts of Europe. On the contrary, the issue of just how thoroughly the alteration of church institutions and theology actually altered practice and understanding at the parish level has also moved to the top of the research agenda.

This final section explores how thoroughly the founding of Reformed churches changed the manners, morals, and beliefs of those raised within them, and how distinctive the Reformed tradition might have been in doing so. For church reformers of all stripes in early modern Europe, the transformation of lay religious life began with the reformation of the parish ministry, the church's agents in every locality. For most of those within the Reformed tradition, a critical element of any reformation of the ministry in turn involved remodeling church offices along the pattern of the apostolic church, making of bishops active parish ministers. Chapter 13 examines the speed and thoroughness of the changes effectively wrought in the education, status, and

job performance of the parish clergy. The survival virtually without modification of the pre-Reformation system of bishops and church courts in England
—in contrast with most other Reformed churches that eliminated bishops,
made parish ministers largely equal, and instituted new systems of collective
self-policing for them—makes it possible as well to use comparisons between
the Church of England and the Reformed churches of the Continent and Scotland to determine if presbyterians were right when they insisted the changing
of the institutional structures of the church was essential to the effective reformation of the parish ministry. Since Calvin's theory of the fourfold ministry
did not restrict the title of minister to those who preached and administered
the sacraments to local congregations, I shall also look here at the teachers,
deacons, and elders of the Reformed churches, paying particular attention to
the elderships that were so important to most Reformed disciplinary systems.

Chapter 14 then examines the functioning of Reformed systems of ecclesiastical discipline where these were established. The considerable recent interest in the practices of social disciplining has combined with the survival of
many good sets of consistorial records to generate a growing body of studies
of how consistorial discipline came to be applied in the divers churches. The
results of these studies will be drawn together to determine how much of a reformation of life this fundamental feature of many Reformed churches in fact
produced and whether or not it was more thorough than that effected by the
Lutheran and Catholic reformations.

The concluding chapter looks at how thoroughly worship and belief
changed among the great mass of Reformed church members, both the ordinary practices of worship in which all members of the churches were expected to partake and the regionally variegated forms of voluntary religion
that took hold among the more pious members of the church community in
parts of Reformed Europe.

For many of these questions, it must be stressed, extensive research is just
beginning. The findings presented in part IV are more tentative and more
likely to be revised by future research than the material contained in the preceding sections. Although the effort has been made to assemble information
about all of Europe's Reformed churches, readers will note that most of the
evidence in this section concerns the larger Reformed churches of western
Europe. Wherever possible, I have attempted to compare the evidence about
Reformed churches or populations with comparable data concerning Lutheranism and Catholicism, so that the transformations wrought by the Reformed
may be assessed in a properly comparative manner. Once again, however, the
state of current scholarship has not always made it possible to do this as consistently as I would have liked. Still, enough is known to permit a preliminary assessment of how thoroughly the great dreams of moral renewal that

accompanied the initial upsurge of enthusiasm for the Reformed cause came to be actualized, and what it meant to live and worship as a member of a Reformed church during the sixteenth and seventeenth centuries. Once this information has been drawn together, it will also be possible to assess the classic theories that assign Calvinism a distinctive place in the making of the modern world.

13

THE REFORMATION OF THE MINISTRY

T he Protestant Reformation wrought few transformations more thorough than that which restructured what had previously been called the first estate. Wherever the Reformation triumphed, it scaled back the size of the clergy, reduced clerical privileges, and eliminated regular orders, sacramental ordination, and the requirement of priestly celibacy. In place of the dignity conferred by the reenacting of the sacrifice of the mass and the physical handling of God's body and blood, it proposed to rest ministerial authority on the capacity truthfully to expound the Bible. The waning centuries of the Middle Ages had already witnessed the emergence of two linked aspirations: that parish clergymen be able to preach, read homilies, or otherwise convey points of doctrine to their parishioners in addition to performing the rites of the church; and that they receive a university education to prepare them for this. The Reformation's redefinition of Sunday worship services as *die Predigt* or *la prêche* rather than the mass completed the conversion of the parish clergy from mediating priesthood to pastoral ministry and revised the accompanying expectations that governed its education and behavior. In the case of the Reformed tradition, the redefinition of ministerial roles and status was particularly complex because the most influential theologian within that tradition placed four kinds of church officers within the category of minister, including part time, unpaid elders and deacons. Com-

435

mon modern usage, of course, tends to reserve the term for full-time clergymen exercising the cure of souls. In order to be true to both actors' and observers' categories, the ministry in both senses of the term will be examined
here.

THE REFORMED PASTORATE

The Reformation transformed the full-time clergy from a privileged estate to
a learned profession: if that is an overstatement, it is but a modest one. The
change was more rapid and more thorough in the continental Reformed
churches than in the Church of England. Divines of the era who argued that a
thorough renovation of church institutions was necessary to create an effective preaching ministry were not misguided.

As we have seen, the Reformation was in many ways a revolution against
the clergy. The initial mobilization that drew people into the Reformed camp
and fostered the establishment of Reformed churches drew much of its
strength by galvanizing hostility toward the Catholic clerical order. Satires
depicted the pope and his monks as self-serving frauds who sought to keep
lay folk ignorant of the Bible so they could line their purses. Crowd actions
targeted monastic houses for attack. The assertion of the right of the secular authorities, not theologians, to adjudge disputes about Christian doctrine
undergirded every magisterial Reformation. Not only were the regular orders
dissolved wherever a Reformed church came to be founded; many Reformed
churches also abolished all or most formal distinctions of status and duties
among those whom they believed could be indifferently labeled bishops, pastors, or presbyters, and reduced the enormous disparities in remuneration
that formerly set the lifestyles of aristocratic bishops dramatically apart from
those of poor country vicars. So many branches were lopped off the clerical tree that the full-time ministry became a mere fraction of its former size.
The pre-Reformation bishopric of Utrecht, which encompassed most of the
territory that became the independent Dutch Republic, housed an estimated
18,000 clergymen in 1500. In the seventeenth century the number of parish
ministers there was 1,524.[1]

The status and legal privileges of the clergy were reduced too. Theologian-
jurists in the Reformed tradition rejected the medieval conception of the
three orders in which "those who pray" occupied the first rank. Instead, they
tended to locate the ministry among the educated professionals and state servants. Hesse's Hermann Fabronius distinguished four social orders in his *Political Duties of Christian Authorities and Subjects* (1623): officeholders of all
sorts, the knighthood, those who worked the land, and those who herded ani-
mals. Ministers belonged to the first of these categories alongside royal and local officials.[2] Vestiges of pre-Reformation clerical privileges survived in many

areas. Ministers in Hesse-Kassel continued to enjoy tax exemptions for their glebe lands and the right to brew beer without paying excises. Clergymen continued to sit in the Hessian Estates, as they did in Scotland's Parliament in those periods when the office of bishop existed, this latter despite the fact that Beza advised the Scots that clerical political representation was an inappropriate mingling of the spiritual and temporal spheres. Gábor Bethlen bestowed generous privileges on the Reformed clergy in Transylvania, according them noble status as well as special tax exemptions. The pastors of the French Reformed churches enjoyed the same exemption from the chief land tax, the *taille,* as their Catholic counterparts. These instances notwithstanding, the Reformed clergy lost many aspects of the distinctive legal status that Catholic prelates had enjoyed prior to the Reformation. Clerical representation ended in the only two provincial estates of the United Provinces to which clergymen had been admitted before 1572, the states of Zeeland and Utrecht. Dutch and Hessian ministers paid many taxes. We have seen how Switzerland's ministers fought and died alongside their fellow citizens at Kappel.[3]

Although anticlerical sentiments gave impetus to the Reformation and although the triumph of Protestantism meant a sharp reduction in the size and legal privileges of the clergy, the Reformation emphatically did not deny the ministry all special functions and power. The doctrine of the priesthood of all believers threatened briefly to eliminate all distinctions between laypeople and clergy, but this soon became one of the "lost doctrines of the Reformation."[4] As soon as the upheavals of the Peasants' War showed the dangers of asserting it too blithely, the leading Reformed theologians started to insist that only trained theologians could be authoritative interpreters of the Bible. Zwingli's short tract *The Ministry,* written in the tumultuous year 1525, said that teaching Scripture was a job for ministers only, even if laypeople could discern true preaching from false. This reinstated the distinctive function and dignity of the ministry while preserving the view that the civic magistrates could make decrees on religious matters. The French confession of faith explicitly anathematized "all visionaries who would like, so far as lies in their power, to destroy the ministry."[5] Numerous treatises exalted the special calling of ministers as interpreters and expositors of the divine word, to the point of eroding the principle that laypeople could judge issues of doctrine. An anonymous late seventeenth-century Huguenot sermon distinguished ministers and believers as follows: "To be one of the faithful is to be among God's people, but it is to stay at the foot of the mountain. To be a minister is to be separated from that people, to go up Mount Sinai, and to converse with God. To be one of the faithful is to listen submissively to the orders of one's sovereign. To be a minister is to be set apart to announce the divine Gospel."[6] Robert Some called ministers "the lord's ambassadors, the salt of the earth, the light of the world, the dispensers of God's mysteries, the builders of God's church and the chariot and horsemen . . . of a Christian kingdom." To the Hartford minister Samuel Stone they were "a speaking aristocracy in face of a silent democracy."[7] The devaluation of the laity's theological judgment was made explicit by a decision of the French national synod of 1571 that excluded elders from voting on questions of doctrine when these came before church synods, at least at the level of colloquial assemblies; only ministers and professors of theology could vote.[8]

Some lay capacity to judge the truth of ministerial professions continued to be recognized. A frequently reprinted French Reformed devotional work of the late seventeenth century told believers that while in church they should focus their full attention on the pastor and listen carefully to what he told them; once home, however, they should imitate the example of the Bereans and search Scripture to make sure that what the minister had said was so.[9] Separatist groups and gathered churches frequently went farther and denied any special authority to the ministry. In general, however, it may be said that while wresting doctrinal decision making away from the Roman hierarchy by appealing to the capacity of the secular authorities to judge disputes about doctrine, Reformed theologians reinforced the prophetic authority of the ministry as a group through their insistence that the distinctive forms of expertise possessed by learned ministers enabled them to converse with God in ways denied to laymen. Indeed, if the Reformation was in certain ways a revolution against the clergy, it was a very curious sort of anticlerical revolution, incited by clergymen and legitimating itself through appeal to a complex sacred text originally written in a variety of ancient languages. The result was to confer great power on those who could convincingly position themselves as authoritative interpreters of that text, as the influence wielded by leading Reformed theologians would demonstrate time and again, from the Zurich of the 1520s to the Utrecht of the 1650s.

Properly exercising this redefined calling required extensive education. To become a minister "one must be steeped in Scripture, know many languages, [and] be cognizant of philosophy and civil and ecclesiastical history," declared Pierre Du Moulin in one ordination sermon.[10] Hence the great emphasis on founding institutions to promote the education of present and future clergymen, beginning with the establishment of the Prophezei by Zwingli in 1525 and its imitation in many other churches and proceeding through the creation of at least thirty new universities, academies, *gymnasia,* and other institutions of higher learning in the Reformed world. The urgency with which the Reformed desired such institutions is well illustrated by the actions of the French and Dutch churches. Within a few years of the establishment of the first churches under the cross, some larger urban churches in both countries

set up seminarlike "propositions" to give candidates for the ministry an adequate grounding in Scripture. Almost as soon as the Huguenots seized power
in parts of France in 1561–62, they attached theological instruction to existing schools in Orléans and Nîmes. In the Netherlands, the creation of the university of Leiden followed the Sea Beggars' conquest of Holland by just three
years, and Reformed theological instruction was dispensed in Ghent during its
brief period as a stronghold of the faith. Where the Reformed took over existing universities, both curricular reforms to encourage instruction in Greek
and Hebrew and institutional foundations destined to support those training
for the ministry often followed. At Heidelberg, Frederick II founded in 1563 a
residential college for poor scholars training for the ministry, the Collegium
Sapientiae, with a portion of the revenue from confiscated church property.
Emmanuel College, Cambridge, was founded by noble benefactors in 1584
with the explicit aim of "rendering as many persons as possible fit for the
sacred ministry of the Word and the Sacraments." Its statutes encouraged students to proceed as quickly as possible to their degrees and then to resign
their fellowships to take up parish livings.[11] As in the Lutheran and Catholic worlds as well, a flood of university reforms and new foundations thus followed the Reformation. Formal training in an institution of higher learning
became expected of future ministers.

A worthy Reformed minister had to be more than just learned. The numerous sermons and treatises of the late sixteenth and seventeenth centuries that
spelled out the obligations of the pastor's calling cited exemplary behavior,
forthrightness in reprimanding vice, polished speech, and the ability to console troubled souls as other required attributes. English writers in the tradition of experimental predestinarianism added that ministers ought to possess
evidence of inward sanctification. Huguenot authors, as befitted an embattled
minority, stressed they should be skilled controversialists. The Catholics were
becoming steadily cleverer debaters, Du Moulin noted; they could no longer
be defeated with the jawbone of an ass.[12]

Reformed church orders and synodal decrees translated these expectations
into regulations. Geneva's church rules decreed that ministers should be suspended immediately if they were found guilty of any one of a series of offenses:
gambling, dancing, blasphemy, serious brawling, perjury, whoring, theft,
drunkenness, usury, heresy, and "rebellion against the ecclesiastical order."
Fraternal correction was to be applied to those who handled Scripture
strangely, were negligent in study, scolded their parishioners inappropriately,
or seemed dissolute in dress or gesture. Virtually identical regulations found
their way into the Béarn discipline of 1563 and the decisions of the Wesel
Convent of 1568.[13] Several decades later, the General Assembly of the Scottish church drew up a copious list of actions deserving of censure that defined

15. "The Portraicture of the Learned and Religious Mr Dr Sutton." Reformed ministers were a frequent subject for engraved portraits during the seventeenth century. The
text accompanying this portrait of the London lecturer Thomas Sutton, taken from the
larger engraved broadsheet of 1624 "The Christians Jewel" (see below, illustration 18),
adds a succinct panegyric that highlights the essential attributes of a worthy minister:
learning, uncorrupted doctrine, and a godly life. Inventories of household possessions
reveal that Reformed families occasionally hung such portraits of prominent ministers
in their homes. (Copyright the Society of Antiquaries of London)

an even more precise model of the good pastor. The parish minister was to
shun such behavioral faults as gambling, dancing, swearing, brawling, quarreling, and light and wanton behavior. He was not to engage in unseemly occupations like innkeeping, trade, or nonpastoral service in noble households. A
disinclination to study and to acquire books, excessively obscure or scholastic
preaching, negligence in visiting the sick, and the failure to reprimand public
sins, especially on the part of the great, were all decreed to merit a reprimand.
Ministers were not to bring lawsuits without the advice of the presbytery, and
they were to take special care to practice family devotions and to act in a
spiritual manner in all company.[14] Hungarian synods defined a similarly detailed code of behavior and added that ministers should not wear fur coats or
golden collars, should not keep weapons, hawks, or hunting dogs, and should
leave all social gatherings immediately if music and dancing began. Zurich
synodal statutes warned rural ministers against mixing socially with the peasantry or adopting their customs.[15] The code of ministerial conduct thus combined many aspects of the behavior expected of pre-Reformation priests with
an increased emphasis on the minister's role as biblical student, preacher, and
moral tribune.

This code was then enforced through the collective censure of bad behavior that was a regular feature of classical or presbyterial gatherings in most
Reformed churches as well as through parish visitations in many. Little is
known about how the system of clerical censure worked in practice in most

churches. In the Pays de Vaud it took the form of having the ministers gathered at the colloquy assemblies leave the room in turn while their peers discussed their behavior and performance, then return to receive the judgments of the group. The rules governing these sessions specified they were to be *censures et non morsures* (censures, not bites). Instances of misbehavior that were not common knowledge were not to be mentioned to the group until the colleague who had observed the behavior privately admonished the erring pastor and saw no amelioration. Penalties for relatively minor transgressions varied from reprimands through fines and forced apologies on bended knees before the group. Cases of public scandal and gross negligence of duty were referred to secular authorities.[16]

In many parishes, church visitations checked up on various aspects of ministerial behavior and performance. Visitations in the synod of Aberdeen in 1675 inquired the following of the elders and heads of household:

1. If there be preaching on the Lord's day and how often;
2. If the minister preaches to their edification, and be carefull in reproveing sinne, both privatlie and publicklie . . . ;
3. If he keep at home, not stirring abroad unnecessarilie;
4. If his conversatione be without lightnes or vanitie, grave and exemplarie in pietie;
5. If he doe, without necessitie resort to taverns;
6. If he administrat the sacrament of the Lord's Supper, and how often in the yeir;
7. If he be carefull to debarr from it all such as are scandalous;
8. If discipline be diligentlie and impartiallie exercised;
9. If he be carefull to visit the sick when he is informed, and called therto;
10. If he be a good example to the people in ordering his owne familie;
11. If he visite the townes and families in his parochine, and excite them to pietie . . . ;
12. If he be diligent in catechiseing, especiallie in taking paines to prepare young persones befor they partake of the Lord's Supper;
13. If he be carefull to maintaine and promote peace and love among all people.[17]

Equally comprehensive protocols governed church visitations in many provinces of the Netherlands. Here, the visits in practice were often less searching than the regulations demanded. In one classis of South Holland, visitors inspected up to eleven a parishes a day, so they could hardly have grilled the residents at length.[18] Through their annual regularity and threat of more intensive investigation if things were found to be amiss, even such hasty visitations nonetheless represented a powerful instrument for enforcing standards

441

of pastoral performance. Indeed, through these procedures of visitation and collective censure, the Reformed ministers conformed remarkably to the ideal type of a profession, that is, a self-policing occupational group requiring specialized knowledge and educational credentials for entry and continued adhesion after admission to a formalized code of ethics. One of the shortcomings of the English church those concerned about the reformation of the ministry felt most acutely was the absence of systems of clerical discipline enforced by presbyterial-synodal gatherings. England's bishops were expected to tour the parishes of their dioceses once every three years, but there was great variety in the assiduousness with which they carried out this obligation.[19]

While insisting upon dedicated service and proper behavior by parish ministers, churchmen wanting to create a worthy pastorate battled to offer even those who served the smallest and poorest rural parishes a sound financial footing. From the first generation of the Reformation to the era of orthodoxy, Reformed theologians defended the economic interests of the clergy by stating that once property had been given to the church it became permanently dedicated to spiritual ends. "The acquisition and use of ecclesiastical property is a matter of divine right," intoned that monument of seventeenth-century instruction, Johannes Wollebius's *Compendium of Christian Theology*.[20] The amount of erstwhile church property that found its way into lay hands or was used by the secular authorities for such purposes as repaying war debts has yet to be computed with any accuracy for most territories that established a Reformed state church. In all of the provinces of the Low Countries except Utrecht, glebe lands continued to support the parish minister, while municipal or provincial agencies took over most monastic and episcopal property and used the revenue to supplement pastoral livings, fund schools and charitable organizations, and grant pensions for ministers' widows. In Utrecht, however, the vast possessions of that cathedral city's five chapters continued —to the enduring dismay of the Reformed clergy, who repeatedly sought to reclaim this property for pious uses—to maintain lucrative capitular positions now bestowed on lay members of the leading families of the city and surrounding province. Among the German territories that instituted Reformed state churches, the Palatinate stands out as a region whose rulers were unusually scrupulous about ensuring that former church property was used for religious, charitable, and educational ends, while the rulers of Hesse were exceptionally unrestrained in laying their hands on church lands. Here, at least 40 percent of the wealth of the pre-Reformation church was diverted to the princes' own purposes.[21]

The ideal of the Reformed churches may have been a learned, pastorally committed, morally exemplary, and financially secure ministry, but in their initial years the churches often had to scramble to fill ministerial positions

442

and could not be too exigent about whom they admitted. They also had trouble paying their new ministers. As congregations sprang up by the hundreds in France in 1561–62, pastors were ordained and placed in charge of fledgling churches after having received as little as two months' irregular training in Paris and some experience as an elder. *Duitse klerken,* former schoolmasters or artisans whose only preparation for the ministry may have come from attendance at the prophesyings of refugee churches, were an important segment of the early Dutch ministers. One detailed study of the classis of Delft found evidence of university education in only four of the twenty-six pastors appointed prior to 1580 who were not former Catholic clergymen; another in only fifteen of seventy-nine ministers appointed in the classis of Dordrecht between 1572 and 1599.[22] Despite the willingness to press hastily trained men into ministerial service, many parishes were left at first without pastors deemed capable of preaching or administering the sacraments at all. The extreme case was Scotland, where scarcely a quarter of roughly one thousand parishes had ordained ministers in 1567. The others made do with readers, who, as their name would suggest, read passages from Scripture, or "exhorters," who could also comfort parishioners and administer baptisms and marriages. In the churches of France and the Netherlands, the earliest Reformed ministers faced great dangers and found themselves obliged to flee from one land to another more than once. Even where matters were more stable, ministerial incomes had often been eroded by the combination of inflation, the usurpation of some church land, and the cessation of incidental forms of income like fees for the performance of anniversary masses.[23]

Compounding the problems of the first generation in the eyes of many was the fact that a significant number of the earliest Reformed ministers were holdovers from the Catholic church, although the percentage of such ministers was higher in areas in which the Reformation was implemented in the 1520s and 1530s than in those in which the break came in the 1560s—a sign of how Catholicism and Protestantism increasingly came to be perceived as incompatible alternatives as the decades advanced and confessional lines became more sharply demarcated. In both Zurich and Bernese territories, nearly three-quarters of the rural curés retained their livings at the Reformation. By contrast, only about a third of Béarn's incumbents and 18–25 percent of the parish priests of Scotland stayed on to serve the new regime. Only 5–10 percent of parish priests in the Netherlands kept their livings through the upheavals of the late sixteenth century there, although the presence of many other ex-religious in the ranks of the new Reformed ministers meant that former Catholic clerics made up 17 percent overall of the north Netherlands pastors appointed before 1600.[24] Many leading figures in the new churches, beginning with Calvin himself, were wary of ex-monks and priests who sought to become ministers and advised that they be examined particularly carefully before being admitted to the pastorate. The need was such that many were nonetheless accepted.

Unsurprisingly, a sizable proportion of those initially pressed into service thus proved inadequate for the task. In both the Palatinate and the French Midi, 10 percent of all pastors received between 1560 and 1600 were discharged from office, most often for recurrent drunkenness and other forms of notorious misconduct, for "bad doctrine," or for practicing medicine, which violated the rules of the French church. Others who might have deserved dismissal undoubtedly remained in office because rural parishioners were more inclined to complain about ministers who were excessively censorious than about those who had a few drinks at the tavern or tended the sick. The consistory of Nîmes's church had to deal with pastors whose families coiffed their hair with excessive finery and hired musicians to play at an engagement party as well as with a pastor who impregnated a serving woman.[25]

Despite these initial difficulties in filling the ministry with capable candidates, the churches appear over the long run to have succeeded well in supplying their congregations with learned ministers whose behavior conformed to the standards defined by the churches' rules. This took longer than elsewhere in the British Isles, especially in England. The very large gaps that needed to be plugged in Scotland's post-Reformation parish ministry and England's combination of a limited recasting of ecclesiastical structures, unsteady royal and episcopal commitment to the ideal of a preaching ministry, and the disruptive consequences of the civil war and interregnum both slowed the transformation.

Step one was filling the holes in the parish ministry. In both the Pays de Vaud and Holland, all parishes appear to have been provided with ministers by the 1580s. The turmoil of the Wars of Religion meant that the French Reformed church could not address this problem systematically until peace returned in 1598, but the small shortfall of ministers that existed in 1598 was made good within less than two decades. Scotland still had the yawning chasm of "above foure hundredth parock kirks destitute of the ministrie of the word" in 1596, but this shortfall was remedied by approximately 1620, and by 1638, some 150 young expectants waited impatiently for benefices.[26]

Step two was ensuring that those who filled parish benefices were trained in the university. Once the first generation of ministers died off, graduates made up the overwhelming majority of newly ordained pastors in those continental churches that have been studied to date. In 1619, 94 percent of clergymen in the Palatinate could boast of formal university instruction in theology. Less than 5 percent of all ministers ordained after 1604 in the Netherlands lacked a university education, and from 1630 onward this figure fell below

TABLE 13.1

Percentage of Graduates among the Clergy of Four English Regions

	ca. 1525	ca. 1560	ca. 1580	ca. 1600	ca. 1620	ca. 1640	ca. 1650	ca. 1660	ca. 1670
Surrey	34	23	30						
Diocese of Worcester		19	23		52	84			
Diocese of Oxford	38	50		80	96				
Leicestershire			31	58		90	70	80	95

Sources: Rosemary O'Day, *The English Clergy: The Emergence and Consolidation of a Profession 1558–1642* (Leicester, 1979), 233; R. Peters, "The Training of the 'Unlearned' Clergy in England during the 1580s: A Regional Study" in *Miscellanea Historiae Ecclesiasticae III* (Lovain, 1970), 184–85; John Pruett, *The Parish Clergy under the Later Stuarts: The Leicestershire Experience* (Urbana, 1978), 14, 23, 42–43.

1 percent. Change came a bit more slowly in Scotland. Nearly a quarter of all ministers lacked university degrees in five Scottish presbyteries around 1600; in the remote Orkney Islands, the degreeless were in the majority. A generation later a university degree was the rule even in the Orkneys.[27] England lagged still more (table 13.1). The religious oscillations of the years between 1535 and 1562 discouraged many from entering the clergy, so pre-Reformation levels of ministerial education were not reattained until the 1580s. The percentage of graduates then increased impressively until 1640, but the turmoil of the civil war and interregnum again reversed the trend. Educational levels comparable to those of most continental Reformed churches in the early seventeenth century were not obtained until well into the Restoration. Only around 1700, it appears, did the peculiarly English post-Reformation ecclesiastical practice of requiring parish incumbents to obtain a special license to preach finally fall into abeyance, the surest sign that the ideal of an educated pastor in every parish had finally been obtained.[28] In spite of the boast of the Restoration divine who claimed that "in the long reign of Queen Elizabeth and King James the Clergy of the Reformed Church of England grew the most learned of the world,"[29] the slowness of the English church in achieving the ideal of an educated ministry stands out in comparative perspective.

Once university training became the norm for ministers, the apprenticeship for the task became an extended one. The autobiography of John Bell offers a vivid picture of how one earnest, precocious Scottish lad prepared himself at the end of the seventeenth century. Bell's pious mother oriented him toward a pastoral career from early in life, achieving such success that one of his childhood games was to preach to his playmates. The son of a Glasgow merchant, he began grammar school at ten. Within a year he was reading books of practical divinity, and a year later he had joined a group of youths who met regularly for prayer. During summers, he prepared condensations of treatises on logic and metaphysics. Such application enabled him to master Latin, Greek, and philosophy and to receive his master of arts degree by sixteen. Passing on to university, he supplemented the regular study of theology with extra activities designed to assist him as a pastor. He studied each chapter of the Westminster Catechism for two weeks, accumulating extracts from the best theologians relevant to it. He collected "the most material doubts I could find in the whole Bible" and assembled them in a book with their answers and a good index. He sought out "the soul troubles of such exercised persons as I found in the whole town" to improve his understanding of difficult cases of conscience. A group of students to which he belonged attended sermons in the different churches of Glasgow each Sunday and then assembled to hear reports on each one. At the tender age of twenty, his professors suggested to him that he was ready for a minister's post, and after entering into trials for a position in the presbytery of Lanark by preaching in the vacant parishes, he quickly gained a living.[30]

Bell's precocity and application enabled him to begin his career at an unusually young age for the late seventeenth century. There being a surplus of candidates in most churches by this time, future ministers often had to fill a schoolmaster's post or find other employment for several years before obtaining a parish living. Ministers in Hesse-Kassel took up their first pastorate at approximately age twenty-eight in the years 1650–79 and at thirty-one between 1680 and 1709.[31]

Bell was unusually single-minded in preparing for his calling. Other future ministers allowed themselves more worldly distractions along the way. The distinguished Metz pastor Paul Ferry wrote poetry as a student and included lessons in music and portraiture in the education of his son he hoped would follow him in the ministry. The authorities of Saumur's academy worried in the 1640s that theology students wore wigs, attended balls, and dueled. Still, expectations about the level of assiduousness that might be expected from students remained very high, to judge by the following dismayed report the Genevan pastor Benedict Pictet sent Nicholas Bernouilli of Basel about his son who was lodging with him: "*Monsieur,* your son is a mediocre student; I have never been able to get more than thirteen hours of work a day from him; his example is unfortunately followed by others; young people do not want to understand that to become a useful *savant* their lamp must go on before the artisan's."[32]

Once appointed, ministers were generally considered to be attached to the church that they served or that had initially sponsored their education. Many remained in the same parish for much of their career. A clear hierarchy of remuneration and status nonetheless existed in virtually every country, with the largest urban churches typically paying more than others. The careers of the most eminent pastors of the French and Dutch Reformed churches took them up a ladder of positions to ever larger and more prestigious congregations. The path to an episcopate or deanery in England and Scotland, however, rarely passed through an ordinary parish living.

The remuneration afforded most parish ministers became substantial in time. Between 1590 and 1640, parliamentary commissions in Scotland raised ministerial stipends and equalized parish revenues; by 1640 most ministers probably enjoyed a larger income than the majority of landed proprietors. In Zweibrücken, where clerical incomes in 1550 compared poorly to those in 1520, efforts to redress this problem brought ministers' salaries by 1600 to almost two-thirds the level of the duchy's judges, although they did not eliminate the disparities in endowment between parishes. The minimum salary paid to parish ministers in the Netherlands was regularly raised. Once again, the Church of England was the great exception. Its pre-Reformation rectories, vicarages, and perpetual curacies of widely varying values remained unchanged until Queen Anne's Bounty of 1704 instituted a modest effort to tax the comfortable livings to increase the endowment of the very poorest ones. Although increased agricultural production and rising land values fueled a hefty increase in income for the better endowed livings, the gulf between the richest and poorest livings widened, and many of the poorest remained too meager to support a clergyman in an appropriate style. The result was that pluralism never disappeared from the English church as it did from all of the more thoroughly reorganized Reformed churches. On the contrary, it made a comeback in the seventeenth century, when the percentage of Leicestershire livings held in plurality rose from 13 percent in 1603 to 40 percent in 1714. Where the Reformed churches were voluntary associations of believers, the economic difficulties of the parish ministry remained hard to fix, as pastors had to depend for their salaries upon congregational assessments, accumulated bequests, and noble largesse. It appears that in such churches as France's the large congregations and those located in major cities offered their ministers comfortable salaries in the seventeenth century, but many small churches could not do the same and regularly fell into arrears with their payments.[33]

Some exceptions notwithstanding, most Reformed ministers thus received at least a comfortable minimum salary by the seventeenth century. Their wealth and marriage connections by this time also placed them as solidly in the ranks of the learned professions. By origin, many came from slightly more modest backgrounds. Most Scottish ministers were the offspring of small to middling merchants, craftsmen, and small landed proprietors. Dutch pastors typically came from the ranks of urban merchants, artisans, and such rural professionals as scribes, judges, and surgeons. With the passing of the generations, a goodly fraction also came to be ministers' sons. In the Netherlands, pastors who were children of pastors rose from 18 percent of new ministers in the first quarter of the seventeenth century to 29 percent in the last quarter. Many studies have found comparable figures.[34] But the minister's calling was prestigious, and young ministers often married above their family of origin— in the Netherlands, for instance, into the ranks of silk and cloth merchants, doctors, booksellers, army officers, Latin school regents, and city officials.[35] In those places where large fortunes were rare, ministers could appear positively rich. The average size of New England's ministers' estates placed them in the top 15 percent of the citizenry, while the median fortunes revealed by Scottish ministers' wills at midcentury ranked above those of all other major groups in the population except leading merchants and landholders.[36] Elsewhere most were at least comfortable. Increasingly, at least in France and England, they were also genteel as well. The average Leicestershire minister in 1714 inhabited a comfortable parsonage of eight or more rooms and paid taxes that placed him in the top 20 percent of shire taxpayers. Cushioned chairs in the parlor and a subscription to the *Monthly Mercury* announced his refinement to all who paid call.[37] In the self-sufficient French Reformed church, ministerial fortunes were more varied. One pastor of the large urban congregation of Metz can be seen from his inventory after death to have owned a house in town, a country house with garden, and land in six villages, while another possessed gold, silver, and diamond jewelry worth well over four times his annual salary. Both were owed many small, often old debts, suggesting they frequently lent money to needy congregants. But in the synod of Haut-Languedoc-Haute-Guyenne, a region with many small churches of the sort that often had a hard time paying their ministers, a survey in 1669 found thirteen of the eighty ministers to be rich, thirty-nine "middling accommodated," and twenty-eight frankly poor.[38]

Writing at the beginning of the seventeenth century, an erstwhile Huguenot who had returned to the Catholic church identified three kinds of Reformed pastors: wise and kindly ones who lived peaceably with their flocks; austere reformers of morals; and learned ministers occupied by their studies. Michel de Bourgaut, the pastor of Roquecourbe from 1584 to 1611, seems to have exemplified the first type. When he died, the church scribe noted he had been "gifted with excellent good graces in theology, medicine, and music which he exercised in this church and was much regretted by the entire church. Two *consuls* and four elders carried his body to its burial." The decision of the national synod in 1571 ordering the dismissal of ministers who simultaneously practiced medicine clearly had not cost him either his position or the respect and affection of his parishioners. Isaac Sylvius, the pastor of Layrac in the first decades of the seventeenth century, was more the austere reformer of morals. The church's consistorial registers are thick with disciplinary cases during his tenure, as he sought repeatedly to force the petty d'Artagnans of his small Gascon town to cease hiring dancing teachers and to leave off their masked balls. After he ventured sharp criticism of the local governor and his wife in 1618, the colloquy thought it wisest to shift him temporarily to nearby Vic-Fézensac to let tempers cool. Of a different stripe again was the minister of Blain in Brittany for nearly three decades prior to the revocation of the Edict of Nantes, Philippe Le Noir de Crevain. Although he was evidently conscientious about preparing his sermons, visiting the sick, and attending to his prayers, the rather limited demands of his small church left him with lots of spare time for "honest diversions." Being, he confessed, disinclined to company and lacking "the talents necessary for conversation," he retired to his study. Over the course of his lifetime, he wrote a Latin treatise on civil and ecclesiastical rhetoric, a heroic poem based upon the four Gospels, a reworking of Marot and Beza's translation of the Psalms, a treatise on arithmetic using counting stones, and an ecclesiastical history of the province's Reformed churches, most of which he never published. He devoted in addition many hours simply to filling up two large folio notebooks with his notes and observations on his reading matter, from Jean Crespin's *History of the Martyrs* to the Koran to Descartes' *Discourse on Method.*[39]

Le Noir de Crevain was undoubtedly more of a bookworm than most Reformed ministers, but the range and depth of his literary interests were not extraordinary, to judge by the surviving evidence of pastors' libraries. A balance sheet of the cultural capital of another Huguenot pastor is recorded in the exceptionally detailed surviving inventory of the library of Abraham de La Cloche, who died in Metz in 1656, leaving behind 838 books, of which 765 can be identified on the basis of this document. As might be expected, 60 percent of de La Cloche's books were religious or theological in character, and many were tools for the practical demands of his position. Owning no fewer than eighteen full or partial editions of the Bible, including versions in Greek, Hebrew, and Syriac, plus numerous concordances, commentaries, and language dictionaries, de La Cloche was admirably equipped for the study of Scripture. He was abreast of the latest controversies about the antiquity of the various Hebrew editions of the Old Testament, for he owned both Cappel and Buxtorf on the subject of the vowel points. His books on theology suggest a wide acquaintance with the full Reformed tradition, with Calvin (22 editions) and Pierre Du Moulin (15 volumes) appearing on his shelves in the greatest frequency, other French and Genevan theologians following close behind, but German, Swiss, English, and to a lesser extent Scottish and Dutch Reformed authors all also appearing. A copy of Bayly's *Practice of Piety,* several English and German prayer books, and a small number of Huguenot devotional writings offer hints about the character of his devotional life. Alongside this vast theological library was a scarcely less impressive collection of literary, historical, and scientific books. De La Cloche had access to both a great range of ancient authors and such moderns as Erasmus, Montaigne, Ariosto, and d'Aubigné. He owned several volumes of plays and a copy of Castiglione's *Courtier,* although none of the more recent French treatises on the art of behaving as an *honnête homme.* Some 86 books on history and geography offered a strongly Protestant version of the events and discoveries of the past several centuries, notably the deeds and misdeeds of the papacy as reported by authors like John Bale, the events of the French Wars of Religion as memorialized by the leading Huguenot historians, and the recent fate of Protestant arms in Germany and the Low Countries. Finally, de La Cloche had the opportunity to supplement his many school texts in philosophy with further reading on aspects of mathematics, medicine, and natural philosophy, including the works of Giordano Bruno and Girolamo Cardano.[40]

De La Cloche had a larger and more varied library than most Reformed clergymen of his generation, but not dramatically so. The most systematic study of the contents of Reformed ministerial libraries has been carried for the duchy of Zweibrücken in 1609. Although drawing upon a set of visitation records that are incomplete because they do not always list the nonreligious books owned by the pastors in question, this study turns up an average of 111 books per manse library, 20 percent of them on secular subjects. On the peripheries of the British world, Scottish ministers in the first third of the seventeenth century and New England clergymen over the full course of the century typically had libraries of about 100 books. Library inventories of two seventeenth-century French and Hessian clergymen of no enduring note both list more than 500 volumes, while leading Reformed theologians numbered their books in the thousands.[41] A valuable point of comparison here comes from a study of book-ownership among the Catholic curates of two Italian dioceses, Novara and Rimini, in the early seventeenth century. These parish priests owned roughly 25 books on average. In lieu of the biblical commentaries and works of dogmatic theology found in abundance in the studies of the Reformed ministers, their libraries were dominated by cases of conscience, guides to the administration of confession, and collections of postils.[42] The Reformed ministry without doubt had greater biblical knowledge and theological training than its post-Tridentine Catholic counterpart. Its members also shared more of the general learned culture of the age than did the Catholic parish clergy.

In sum, the establishment of Reformed churches not only transformed the size, status, and self-definition of the clergy. In time, the churches were generally able to put in place the sort of learned, morally respectable, and economically comfortable preaching ministry that had become their ideal. If the creation of such a ministry was indeed the key to effecting a broader metamorphosis of religious life, as so many reformers believed it was, then the west European Reformed churches must all be adjudged to have realized at least this portion of their ambitions with a fair measure of success by some point in the seventeenth century. Of course, the realizing of this goal meant that the pastors of rural communities now inhabited a cultural world vastly unlike that of their parishioners and were part of a professional group whose distinctive values and esprit de corps were reinforced by the sociability that accompanied classical gatherings and clerical conferences. The gulf between clergyman and community may have widened as a result.

That the English church took longer than the others to achieve a university-educated preaching ministry also deserves to be underscored. This suggests that that country's unreformed church structures indeed impeded the accomplishment of certain modifications sought by church reformers. It is also another reason godly English clergymen felt a need to develop new styles of evangelization.

The transformation of the parish clergy was hardly unique to the Reformed churches. The Lutheran world witnessed similar changes, and the Catholic Reformation worked through its seminaries to create a new model of the parish priest, even as it retained the idea of a mediating priesthood, clerical celibacy, and more distinctions of legal status for the clergy than did the Protestant churches. The parish clergy changed greatly throughout Europe as a result of the Reformation, but the emphasis on biblical learning and preaching was particularly strong in the Protestant churches.

DOCTORS, ELDERS, AND DEACONS

The establishment of a learned, economically comfortable parish ministry widened the gulf between pastors and most of their parishioners everywhere in Protestant Europe, but one feature of many Reformed churches may have cut in the opposite direction in a way that had no parallel in Lutheran churches: the role played by lay elders and deacons in church administration. According to many modern exegetes, Calvin's doctrine of the fourfold ministry effected uniquely participatory and even protodemocratic church institutions. If Calvin himself, as we have noted (see chapter 3), regarded his church order as aristocratic rather than democratic, a Lasco believed that elders should be elected by the entire congregation. Calvin allowed for the election of the initial group of elders, and one can imagine that the system both of them advocated of involving lay parishioners in the exercise of church discipline might have prevented the emergence of the sort of anticlericalism that often arose where the pastor alone was the central agent of ecclesiastical discipline. The rules elaborated by the first churches to adopt a full presby-terial-synodal church order also gave lay elders an equal role with ministers in the larger assemblies of the church. The role of consistories and classes in vetting prospective pastors in many Reformed churches gave them a say in the selection of the clergy. On the other hand, as has just been seen, the original Reformation impetus to promote the priesthood of all believers was quickly challenged by reasserted claims for greater clerical competence in determining dogma. Many sixteenth- and seventeenth-century opponents of presbyterianism depicted it as a powerful new form of clericalism and re-jected the argument that lay elders served as an effective check on ministerial authority. The replacing of episcopal government with presbyterial, Thomas Aston warned amid the English debates of the early 1640s, meant replacing 26 bishops with 9,324 parish popes, whose authority would scarcely be re-strained by elders serving terms of six months to a year because their tem-porary status weakened them in comparison with "hee that is *perpetuus Dic-tator,* Chancellour, Arbiter for life in his petty popedome."[43] The issues of how widely the various ancillary ministries came to be established, who filled them, and how much power they retained are thus vital not simply in under-standing the refashioning of the ministry within the Reformed tradition, but also the broader questions of how the Reformed churches stood in relation to the larger communities of which they were a part and what the social conse-quences of their founding might have been. The character of the elders de-serves particular attention because they were the central agents in the exer-cise of church discipline.

Of the three additional ministerial offices highlighted by Calvin, that of doctor assumed the least sharply defined status within the various Reformed churches. Because many medieval schools were church-run and because medieval ecclesiastical authorities often tried to assume oversight of schools, according teachers a form of clerical status was no novelty. Before Calvin, Zwingli had suggested in his *Defense of the Sixty-Seven Articles* (1523) that teachers had a place among the clergy, just as did those who cared for the poor.[44] The chapter of the Genevan ecclesiastical ordinances of 1541 devoted to doctors contained telling ambiguities. It sketched a plan for the reform of the city's schools that called for the installation of two lecturers in theology, a secondary school with a regent and two lecturers, and a teacher for little children. While all seem to have been looked upon as doctors or teachers and subject to the same collective discipline as other ministers, the lecturers in theology were said to be "the degree nearest to the ministry and most closely joined to the government of the church." The French, Belgic, Scottish, and Second Helvetic confessions all omitted any mention of this order of minister. Walter Travers' *Full and plaine declaration of Ecclesiasticall Discipline* included doctors, but Thomas Cartwright's *Directory of Church Government* did not. Scotland's First Book of Discipline made provisions for readers and exhorters to read the common prayers and Scriptures in parishes lacking a fully qualified minister, but only the Second Book of Discipline defined the office of doctor, which it did in terms very similar to those used for the readers in the First Book of Discipline, adding that the faculty of colleges and universities were to be viewed as doctors, too. It also specified that doctors had a share in the government and assemblies of the church. In the Netherlands, the Wesel Convent of 1568 spoke of doctors and outlined the related office of prophet, which involved explaining Scripture in church meetings, examining prospective students in theology, and taking part in ecclesiastical discipline. These measures, however, were only provisional and were not mentioned or ratified at later national synods.[45]

In practice, the offices of reader and exhorter gradually disappeared from the Scottish church. They likewise disappeared from England, where readers, or lectors, were appointed to serve in a number of parishes in the aftermath of Elizabeth's succession when properly ordained Protestant ministers could not be found for every parish. A parochial office of teacher who expounded doctrine either in the absence of a minister or as a pastoral assistant also made a short-lived appearance in the first years of the Massachusetts Bay Colony and found its way from there into the equally short-lived form of church government created by the Westminster Assembly. A comparable office of catechists who assisted ministers in some parishes, served in their absence in others, and were allowed to attend church synods may be discerned in the early years of the church in Poland. It may have survived longer here than elsewhere.[46]

The definition of university professors as church doctors with rights of participation in church assemblies survived more widely, especially in the case of the professors of divinity whom Calvin had called the degree closest to the ministry. In Geneva, France, the Low Countries, and to a lesser degree Scotland, professorships of divinity and Hebrew were generally bestowed upon ordained ministers who continued to exercise a pastoral charge at the same time, but professors of these disciplines who did not concurrently fill a pastorate also frequently gained admittance to consistories and synods. Schoolmasters and teachers in lower schools do not appear to have retained an identification as church doctors or to have participated ex officio in the governing assemblies of the church.[47]

If ordinary schoolteachers rarely formed part of church bodies, the churches still aspired to regulate public instruction in order to make it an instrument of orthodox religious indoctrination. Scotland's presbyteries battled to advance their power to examine and license prospective schoolmasters. In the Netherlands, where the details of church–state relations varied from city to city and province to province, some towns, such as Haarlem, permitted independent primary schools of all confessions and (over the protest of church synods) allowed Catholics to teach in the municipally funded Latin schools. Others in which church–state ties were tighter, such as Dordrecht and Arnhem, required schoolmasters to be vetted by the classes before appointment and to sign the Dutch confession of faith. In rural schools, the church typically had a voice in approving appointments and setting the curriculum. Village schoolmasters helped out in worship in modest ways, as for instance by reading passages from Scripture prior to the Sunday sermon. In some southern French towns under Huguenot political control prior to 1629, the consistory likewise appointed and oversaw the schoolmaster.[48]

While many Reformed confessions and church orders omitted mention of the doctor's office, the office of deacon appeared with far greater regularity. Its functions, however, varied widely. In some churches, deacons largely replicated the role played by teachers or readers in the British churches. In others, they oversaw poor relief. Often, they soon disappeared. The ambiguity about their duties derived from the biblical texts that offered the chief source for subsequent discussions of the *diakonia*, Acts 6:1–6, which suggest that deacons may assist in charitable distributions or aid the *episkopos* more broadly, especially with his liturgical tasks. Bucer depicted the deacons as doing some of both, and the Bernese church included deacons who were a sort of assistant pastor who ministered in the pastor's absence. Calvin focused exclusively on the charitable function. The two sorts of deacons he distinguished in the Genevan ecclesiastical ordinances of 1541, those who administered the property and collected the funds used for the poor and those who distributed the alms, replicated separate offices that had already been created at the moment of the initial Genevan Reformation in 1535, when the various hospices and charitable institutions that had previously existed in the city were amalgamated into a single *hôpital-général*. The two kinds of hospital offices were simply allowed to function as before, and the officeholders were chosen like other secular officials at the annual civic elections, with no consultation with the pastors.[49]

In their earliest years, some French churches followed the Bucerian and Bernese tradition and assigned deacons the tasks of supervising catechization and reading Scripture as well as collecting and disbursing alms for the poor and sick. Although the possibility that deacons might assist in public worship was dropped from the French discipline in 1571, the practice survived in some churches, for example, Layrac's, where deacons still taught the catechism and read from the Bible to open services in the early seventeenth century. A broader tendency also developed in the French church for the consistories to take over the administration of poor relief. By the seventeenth century, Layrac's church was somewhat unusual in having deacons at all.[50] Surprisingly, the Scots and Dutch followed the Genevan model more closely than the French did. The chief function of deacons in both of these churches was the collection and distribution of alms for the church's poor. Scotland had few formal mechanisms for poor relief before the Reformation, but when a series of statutes between 1574 and 1592 produced a parish-based system for the relief of poverty modeled after the English poor law of 1572, the responsibility for levying and disbursing the funds came to reside not with the still-embryonic justices of the peace but with the kirk sessions. The church and its deacons thus came to control the national system of poor relief as it developed here. Poor relief institutions were already much more mature prior to the Reformation in the Netherlands, and here great variety once again became the rule in the way in which the civic and the ecclesiastical fit together. Certain cities, such as Leiden, preserved preexisting welfare systems controlled by the city fathers and allowed the church no role in poor relief. Others, such as Haarlem and Amsterdam, permitted church-run welfare systems administered by deacons alongside the civic system. Still others, such as Dordrecht and Groningen, in the Scottish manner placed poor relief entirely under the purview of the church's deacons. In Scotland and the Netherlands, the deacons also took seats in the kirk sessions, or *kerkeraads,* of some but not all parishes.[51]

The distinction Calvin made between two kinds of deacons, those who collected alms and those who distributed them, rarely survived in the larger Reformed churches. Only a very few churches likewise actualized the possibility that he mentioned in his theological writings that women might fill this ministry. For Lambert Daneau in the late sixteenth century, the disappearance of deaconesses since the time of the primitive church was a fortunate development that demonstrated how features of the early church might wisely be discarded. The seventeenth-century Parisian pastor Jean Daillé was more willing to imply that this might have been a laudable institution. Neither, however, betrayed any awareness of Reformed churches in their lifetimes that actually had deaconesses. In fact, the churches of Amsterdam, Wesel, and perhaps several other cities of the Rhineland did institute such a post to attend to the needs of poor widows and single women, but they were exceptional in doing so.[52]

Because of the importance accorded by so many Reformed churches to independent systems of discipline, the eldership was the most consistently widespread and powerful of the ancillary ministries of the Reformed churches.

Elders appeared in all churches with consistorial systems of discipline. They not only had the task of supervising the behavior of church members. In most churches, they also participated in larger ecclesiastical assemblies and oversaw the appointment and behavior of ministers. In France, they also ran the church's economic affairs and usually displaced the deacons and assumed control of poor relief.[53]

The rules for selecting elders varied considerably and depended upon the broader pattern of church–state relations. Where the ties were close, some elderships might be reserved for members of the city or village council, as they were in Geneva, Hesse, the Palatinate, Groningen, and some Scottish burghs. The regular congregational election of elders persisted for only a decade or two in a few places where a Lasco's influence was strong, for example, the refugee churches of Frankfurt and Wesel and some smaller Dutch churches. England's presbyterian experiment of 1645 also specified the congregational election of elders, but the system, of course, proved abortive. Some churches, like those in the region of Delft and the short-lived one in Sluis in West Flanders, combined election and co-optation by having the entire congregation vote upon a slate of candidates prepared for it by the consistory. Most commonly, however, after an initial election the consistory itself then chose its new members and presented them to the congregation for approval. The stamp of approval of the ruling authorities was also required in Hesse and the Palatinate, where princely authority remained strong even though the ruling house allowed a system of consistorial discipline to be set up. The length of the term for which elders served varied even more widely, from one year to life, churches in the same territory often adopting highly divergent practices. Most elders held office much longer than the six-month to one-year terms pessimistically foreseen by Thomas Aston.[54]

Elders tended to be drawn from the more substantial members of the church community, but a degree of diversity also seems to have been desired in order to ensure good relations with different elements of the local population. Given the great sociological variety among localities across Europe, generalizations about the status of parish elders are less valuable than studies of individual cases. In the Scottish rural parish of Stow, about one-tenth of the mid-seventeenth-century elders were village craftsmen, another tenth millers, while the great majority of the body was composed of working farmers, some of them tenants and others small proprietors. In Liberton in the barony of Craigmillar, the elders were all tenants of the laird of Craigmillar, but neither he nor any of the lesser lairds of the parish ever joined the kirk session. In the urban parish of Canongate, most elders were merchants or master craftsmen. We have seen how the church officers of the Dutch Reformed Church overlapped more and more with the civic power elites as the generations passed (see chapter 11). By the second quarter of the seventeenth century, Leiden's elders were predominantly merchants and textile manufacturers whose tax payments placed them in the upper third of urban taxpayers, although a few paid only modest sums. As the century advanced, members of the learned professions began to nudge merchants aside in keeping with the broader evolution of the city's social structure. French lists of elders reveal still more minor royal officers or members of the learned professions, not to mention a sprinkling of noblemen, reflecting France's different social order. Still, it was hardly uncommon for such men to sit alongside locksmiths and cobblers. In cities like Nîmes with large Huguenot majorities, many members of the consistory went on to become city council members, just as in late seventeenth-century Netherlands. The Chorrichters of the Bernese countryside, although not strictly speaking ministers according to Zwinglian ecclesiology, also tended to be the more weighty members of the village community and not infrequently were future village *ammanns* as well.[55]

In exercising their charge, elders might occasionally fray the bonds of neighborhood. When John VI of Nassau-Dillenburg introduced consistorial discipline there in 1582, he had a hard time at first finding suitable elders in many rural communities because the system was widely perceived as intrusive and unnecessary. A majority of villages inspected in 1590 could not meet the quota of one presbyter for each twenty to thirty households: many people refused the office when offered it, and those who accepted repeatedly fell short of the desired moral character. Many did not attend communion, one had fathered an illegitimate child, and another was known for urinating under the table when he drank. Those who tried to carry out their charge complained that their neighbors criticized them as traitors. Unlike the Swiss cities, in which public rhetoric insisted upon the need for communal moral purity even before the Reformation, these villages saw church discipline as a betrayal of community traditions rather than an extension of them. The office of elder suffered as a result.[56] Nassau-Dillenburg probably was an extreme case. In Delft and the surrounding Delfland, church records fail to indicate a single case of refusal of an appointment to the elder's office between 1572 and 1621, although eight men attempted to get out of being deacons. Elsewhere in the Netherlands, a small minority of those chosen as elders begged off, but they usually cited the demands of their occupation, never the fear of being seen as traitors by their neighbors.[57] In most Reformed churches, discipline was at least accepted as an integral part of church life from the start, even if it was not always eagerly embraced by all, and the eldership appeared to be an essential church function. Just as the elders were drawn from the better sort of people in any given locality but hardly from a narrow coterie, so their activities largely served to maintain the bonds between church and community, even if it sometimes led to their being deemed traitors to the community.

To what extent did lay elders conserve the decision-making power within larger church assemblies that the presbyterial-synodal system initially afforded them? The answer varied from one country and province to another. In France, the Rhineland, and the Dutch church provinces of North Holland, Zeeland, and Friesland, equal numbers of pastors and elders were supposed to represent each church or classis at synodal gatherings. In practice, absenteeism tended to be somewhat higher among the elders, leaving the pastors in a majority in most gatherings; in Friesland from 1583 to 1618, they made up 57 percent of the identifiable synodal attendees. Minutes of these gatherings fail to specify who dominated discussions or introduced key measures. Still, here lay participation remained significant, although not preponderant. Other provinces of the Netherlands scaled lay participation sharply back. In South Holland, each classis was allowed to depute three ministers and only one elder to every synod. Overijssel and Gelderland had shifted to this pattern as well by 1610. In Groningen fully 87 percent of the synod attendees were ministers between 1597 and 1620. The exclusion of elders from synods was most pronounced in Scotland. Elders rarely attended presbyterial and synodal meetings in the period 1585–1637, and their presence there ultimately came to be regarded as entirely unsuitable. At the Restoration they were explicitly excluded from presbytery meetings.[58] Here, presbyterianism indeed appears to have been an ideology that promoted clerical power, and it is no wonder that so many of those who warned at the time that presbyterianism equaled clericalism were Scottish or English. A milder reclericalization of the church occurred in France, the Netherlands, and the Rhineland, but here laymen retained considerable power in the highest councils of the church.

Despite the trend toward the reclericalization of church synods and the determination of dogma, Reformed elders—and often deacons as well—continued to play a central role in the day-to-day administration of many aspects of parish-level church life and in the larger regional and national assemblies of certain territorial churches. In the exercise of church discipline, ministers could count on the assistance of elders of high community standing. Most Reformed churches were communities of charity, with their own system for collecting and distributing alms. Many not only dispensed catechetical instruction within the framework of weekly services but oversaw one or more primary schools. The churches were rarely truly democratic by any understanding of that term. They were more aristocratic, were subject to varying degrees of princely oversight, and were increasingly reclericalized. Rather than being the straightforward implementation of a program outlined in the writings of Calvin or any other Reformed theologian, the ancillary ministries of the Reformed churches reveal how much the institutional development of these churches involved the partial and selective implementation of these programs, shaped by institutional needs and local power contexts as much as by the concern to revive the institutions of the early church. Nonetheless, a measure of lay participation in the administration of the church and considerable lay involvement in the exercise of discipline did continue to characterize many Reformed churches throughout the sixteenth and seventeenth centuries. In this way, they differed from Lutheran churches and may have been well suited institutionally to attempt a reformation of manners and the inculcation of new habits of worship and belief among their members. Of course, altering long-established patterns of behavior and belief was no easy matter.

14

THE EXERCISE OF DISCIPLINE

Nothing is more beautiful or truly Christian among men than good order," reads a Greek inscription in the copy of the *Treatise on the Discipline of the Church* once owned by the pastors of Neuchâtel. "Discipline is the sinews of the church," echoes a Latin tag on the first page of a Nîmes consistorial register.[1] These assertions of the importance of proper church discipline express the same values that led godly visitors to Calvin's Geneva to rhapsodize about the exemplary moral order established there. There, as we have seen (see chapter 3), an exceptionally active church consistory backed by the power of the civic authorities summoned one adult resident in eight to appear before it each year in the decade after 1555 for a wide range of moral shortcomings from adultery to disrespect for one's elders. One adult in twenty-five was suspended from communion each year. Noblemen of the stature of Jacques Spifame, sieur de Passy, the former bishop of Nevers, found that the penalty for adultery compounded by an attempt to defraud the consistory was death. The austerity of the moral order imposed is testified to alike by the grudgingly admiring comments of Jesuit visitors and the extraordinarily low rates of illegitimate births and prenuptial conceptions revealed by the parish registers. The consistory was the essential agency for effecting the communal moral regeneration that appeared so attractive to so many amid the initial excitement of the Reformation.

The registers of many consistories, kirk sessions, chorgerichte, and other local and regional Reformed discipline courts survive as fat yet manageable record sets in many European archives. As interest has grown in recent years in the history of parish-level religious practice, popular culture, and the "disciplining of society," many studies have explored the implementation of Reformed church discipline both in major cities and rural villages, often relying heavily on quantitative analyses of the frequency of kinds of cases.[2] The quality of the evidence imposes limits on these studies. First, the cases recorded in consistory registers represent just part of the full array of disciplinary actions undertaken by a Reformed church, for the theory governing discipline dictated that, except in cases of serious public sin, people were to be called before the consistory only after a variety of less formal attempts at fraternal correction had been made. A rare set of papers preserved by one Utrecht elder of the early seventeenth century shows that only half of the problems he encountered while visiting church members in their homes were passed up the ladder to the consistory. Second, some churches drew a veil over cases that reached the consistory in order to protect the reputation of the individuals in question; or else they struck from the records offenses for which proper amends were made. The same elder's papers suggest that the Utrecht consistory actually discussed more than three times as many cases as its surviving records would suggest.[3] Third, the work of the consistory cannot be equated with the entire moralizing offensive of the church, for ministers are known to have flayed specific vices through their sermons and during house visits, even during periods when the consistory records contain no cases of reprimands for the vice in question.[4] Fourth, quantitative breakdowns of offenses computed from the archives of repression always contain a fundamental ambiguity. Do the levels of the offenses revealed testify to the actual frequency of the behavior in question? or to the degree to which it troubled those doing the repressing? When a long-term study finds a tenfold decline in the number of cases of fornication taken up by a church's consistory, is one to conclude that the church members became ten times more chaste? that the church's elders grew ten times less vigilant about watching for this offense? or that the scribe of the consistory became ten times more solicitous of his neighbors' reputations? This ambiguity is compounded for the period under discussion by the enormous tangle of rival courts and institutions that claimed jurisdiction over the regulation of behavior during the early modern era and by the very uneven survival of their records. Wherever Reformed churches enjoyed the support of political authorities, they sought tough secular laws against many forms of misbehavior and may have divided the enforcement of behavioral norms in ways that left certain kinds of offenses to the secular courts. The absence of certain kinds of offenses in consistorial records thus may imply not the rarity of the offense in the community in question, but that another jurisdiction handled such cases. Although criminal court records could show how strictly the secular authorities enforced morals laws, where they survive at all from this period they tend to be far more cumbersome and difficult to analyze than consistorial records. They have consequently been far less studied, and almost never in tandem with consistorial records.

Notwithstanding the shortcomings in the evidence, all of which need to be kept in mind in evaluating the findings of the recent studies of Reformed discipline in action, these studies have provided a far clearer picture of the operation of Reformed disciplinary institutions than is yet available for the comparable institutions of either Lutheran or Catholic territories. From them, one can learn whether Geneva was typical or atypical of Reformed communities, how energetically various Reformed churches worked to realize the dreams of moral regeneration that commonly accompanied their establishment, and—at least to a certain measure—how much headway they made toward attaining those aspirations.

GOALS AND PROCEDURES

Faced with the tendency of certain historians to lump the actions of Reformed consistories indiscriminately alongside secular courts as instruments of "social control," one leading social historian of church discipline has argued that the history of sin and the history of crime must not be confounded. "Penitential church discipline," so the argument runs, should be distinguished from "punitive secular discipline." The church was concerned with restoring sinners to a good relationship with God and their neighbors and with preserving the sacral-transcendental unity of the eucharistic community. The magistrates protected civil order and promoted the common welfare.[5]

Although this argument has the merit of emphasizing that the goals and methods of ecclesiastical discipline and secular law enforcement were not identical, it implies a neater distinction between them than often existed in either theory or practice. Calvin assigned church discipline a range of ends. In addition to preserving the purity of the eucharistic community, he argued that it was needed to keep the good from being corrupted by the company of the wicked and to bring sinners to shame and repentance—ends that state justice could serve as well. The Scottish confession simply assigned discipline the task of repressing vice and encouraging virtue, without mentioning the theme of the purity of the eucharistic community.[6] Further, the history of sin and the history of crime resist easy differentiation for the simple reason that much sin had long been criminalized and more tended to be as church reformers of all confessional orientations won a measure of support for their call to reinvigorate the law by resting it more firmly on Christian principles. And the line between secular and ecclesiastical responsibility for either the oversight of morality or the admission of church members to communion was never similarly drawn where Reformed churches were established. At the same time, while church discipline reached farther than state discipline, it did not extend to the full sweep of human sinfulness. William Ames thought it inappropriate for those infirmities that are common to most believers. Voetius asserted that the church could not judge hidden things.[7] Last of all, a consistent distinction cannot be made between church discipline and secular jurisdiction in terms of the sorts of punishments they administered. With rare exceptions that were promptly reprimanded by regional synods, the Dutch and French Reformed churches used only spiritual sanctions, for example, penances and exclusion from communion, but the Scottish church drew heavily on shaming punishments and fines, while the consistory of Valangin in the principality of Neuchâtel variously meted out censures, excommunications, fines, prison terms, the pillory, and banishment.[8] In view of the eagerness with which Calvin enlisted Geneva's secular authorities to back up ecclesiastical punishments with penalties of their own, it is difficult to see the use of monetary fines or corporal punishment in these latter churches as a corruption of the original character of church discipline. The distinction between penitential and punitive discipline is most useful if these are seen as ideal types. The actual purposes and methods of discipline in the Reformed churches fell at a range of points between these ideal types, and it is probable that nearly every church felt some degree of tension between the various ends of discipline identified by theologians like Calvin.

One of the most important issues in assessing the character of consistorial discipline and how heavy its weight lay on church members is that of knowing how cases came before the various Reformed disciplinary boards. Did church members turn willingly to the consistory for the resolution of their disputes and actively report wayward brethren to the body out of an interest in their amelioration and the preservation of church and community? or was discipline generally something imposed by clerical and lay elites on an unwilling church population, as it appears to have been in Nassau-Dillenberg? Just how tight was consistorial surveillance?

The elders were the central agents of the consistory's work. As we have seen, most elders tended to come from the substantial segment of the church community. To that extent, church discipline was exercised by local elites dispersed geographically throughout the community. The elders' explicit charge was to watch over the portion of the community assigned to their charge and to report any misdeeds to the consistory. At each weekly consistory meeting of Le Mans' church, each elder, minister, and deacon reported in turn on the scandals he had observed. The body as a whole then decided if the matter was to be taken up before the entire body, assigned to one of the elders, who would speak to the individual in question in private, or simply dropped. In many churches, elders and ministers visited the houses of all members on a regular schedule at least once per year, and these visits occasionally gave rise to matters taken up by the consistory. In parts of Scotland, the Palatinate, and the French Midi, elders patrolled the streets during the hours of worship, looking for church members skipping the service to work or play. Some churches extended the reach of their disciplinary effort by appointing secret agents to watch for misdeeds, a procedure also used by the state-run morals tribunal of Lutheran Württemberg. In Aberdeen the task of listening for bad language was assigned to secret "censurers and captors" who had the power to fine on the spot those whom they overheard swearing or blaspheming; if the guilty person had no money, he or she received a stroke on the hand. Last of all, elders might use discreet inquiries of their own or stakeouts to verify reports received. The consistory of Ganges in southern France deputized one elder to inquire of neighbors if it was true, as they had heard, that one church member still had a crucifix or statues of the saints in her house. On another occasion, a group of elders from the same church climbed a hill so they could peer over a garden wall to observe an encounter between a man and a woman whom they suspected of carrying on an affair.[9]

In their duty to oversee the behavior of the faithful, consistories drew upon voluntary community support, too. Amsterdam's church had a bag in which church members could drop reports of blameworthy incidents; its rules specified that only signed reports would be investigated. One Montauban case of a servant woman who had given birth to an illegitimate child in a nearby village began when an unknown informant left an unsigned note reporting the event on a counter in that city's temple one Sunday. People were not reluctant to report neighbors and friends. One member of the English church of Amsterdam informed on another woman because she "kept good meat till it stank and threw it in the burgwal and went dancing abroad." A refugee in London found himself before the consistory after a friend to whom he had confided that he had gotten a woman pregnant passed the confidence along to the body. Certain events could even provoke enthusiastic neighborhood spying. No fewer than eight witnesses stood ready to confirm to Geneva's elders in 1611 that "the wife of Jehan Comparet and a foreign soldier were seen kissing in the corner of a window, and she took off her neckband and uncovered her breasts, which he kissed, then picked her up by the waist, after which nothing more could be seen."[10]

In the densely packed urban neighborhoods and intimate village communities of early modern Europe, little could have escaped the eyes or ears of the consistory if such active community cooperation had been regularly forth-

coming. It clearly was not. In late seventeenth-century Stirlingshire, fornication was a chief concern of the kirk sessions. Nearly all cases taken up involved a pregnancy and came to the attention of the session only once the
pregnancy could no longer be concealed. On investigation, the kirk session
usually found that neighbors had known for some time what had been going
on between the couples implicated.[11] Many church members resented the in-
trusion of the consistory and were reluctant to betray friends and neighbors
to it. Some of those informed upon—between 4 and 20 percent in different
churches of Scotland and southern France in the later sixteenth century—
simply did not respond to consistorial summonses. Certain of those who did
turned angrily on the consistory or on those whose reports landed them before it. "We're being kept in a Spanish Inquisition," one inhabitant of the Pays
de Vaud complained late in the seventeenth century, even though by then the
system of discipline was well over a century old.[12]

Once a matter came to the attention of the consistory, the elders and ministers had a number of steps at their disposal. Cases of serious violations of the
law might be referred to the secular authorities. In many instances of interpersonal or family quarrels, the consistory's first aim was to broker a reconciliation. If such could be arranged, the parties were brought together for a
handshake and a pledge to respect one another as honorable and trustworthy.
If members of the same family, they were admonished to love and obey one
another according to their prescribed role within the family. If no such reconciliation could be arranged or if the nature of the case did not lend itself
to that solution, the alleged infraction was duly investigated. If the accusation
was found to be true, the consistory then applied a scale of penalties that augmented in severity in proportion to the seriousness of the offense, its degree
of public notoriety, and the willingness of the accused to express contrition
for their behavior and to promise future amendment. The church of Nîmes
appears to have been typical of many in having six purely spiritual penalties
of ascending severity: (1) censure by an individual elder; (2) censure before
the consistory as a whole; (3) a formal apology and penance before the consistory (4) a similar reparation before the entire church on a Sunday prior
to communion; (5) suspension from communion; and (6) full excommunication. Public expressions of repentance before the entire church tended to be
reserved for actions that gave offense to the entire community. In the French
churches, Geneva, and the refugee churches of England, this was most commonly required of those who had "polluted themselves in idolatry" by partak-
ing of Catholic sacraments. Full excommunication was a harsh penality, for it
typically meant cutting the individual off from all social contacts with church
members. As a result, it was sparingly applied: in ten churches of Languedoc
and Aquitaine for which records survive from the later sixteenth century, only

22 full excommunications were pronounced, as opposed to 509 suspensions from communion.[13] In churches such as Scotland's that relied more heavily on fines and shaming punishments, the scale of penalties ran from rebukes through escalating fines or a specified number of Sabbath-day appearances on the "stool of repentance" to excommunication, which here was supposed to encompass not only the severing of social relations but also, after 1579, confiscation of the excommunicated person's property if no reconciliation occurred within forty days. Because of the severity of this sanction, it was sparingly applied, and other penalties like the stocks were preferred for those who displayed no contrition, could not pay their fines, or were guilty of shameless behavior.[14] Within the Zurich tradition, in which exclusion from communion was not an option, the Bernese chorgericht imposed fines, imprisonment for short periods, and the ritual of *Herdfall,* which obliged the sinner to kiss the ground and ask God for forgiveness. The Herdfall came to appear archaic and fell out of use in the seventeenth century.[15]

Public apologies and shaming penalties stung in an age that valued honor strongly, and those ordered to recognize their faults before the congregation frequently refused to do so for months or tried to negotiate less humiliating terms. In some instances, however, the system could serve as a means for wayward church members to obtain relief from guilt and to reconcile themselves with the community in the manner that penance ideally functioned within the Catholic church. When Jehane Saloe confessed her adultery before the French church of London in 1560, many in the church broke into tears at her evident regret for her behavior, accepting her back into the communion of the faithful. A study of Nîmes suggests that people often felt remorse over the rows that set them against their neighbors and could be brought to make peace with relatively little arm-twisting.[16]

In the numerous times and places in the history of the Reformed churches in which disputes broke out over whether or not the territorial church should have an autonomous system of church discipline (for example, Geneva in the 1540s and 1550s, the Palatinate in the 1560s, Utrecht in the 1580s), as well as in regions such as the Grisons, where such systems developed gradually in the absence of legislation by the secular authorities, the most important partisans of such systems were generally ministers and church synods or colloquies. This lends support to the view that consistorial discipline was an instrument of Protestant neoclericalism. As noted, lay members of the consistory were typically prominent members of the community. To the extent this was the case, these bodies were instruments of elite control. In such regions as Geneva, many German Reformed territories, Scotland, Béarn, and parts of France before 1629, they were also linked to the secular authorities. When seeking vigorously to eliminate behavior that much of the population thought unexceptionable, they could encounter a great deal of passive resistance and appear to many an inquisitorial "new popery." Yet aspirations for a regeneration of community morality regularly found expression within and helped to fuel the popular appeal of the Reformation cause in its first phase of growth. In all battles over consistorial discipline, the cause was always able to rally pious laymen, while certain ministers opposed it.[17] The ordinary exercise of consistorial discipline relied upon a measure of community support and co-operation. During periods of natural disaster or national crisis, when maintaining the purity of the eucharistic community and eliminating widespread sins came to seem urgent, support for the activities of the consistory could become intense, as it could when charismatic ministers convinced their auditors of the need for congregational renewal. The exercise of consistorial discipline thus always operated within a complex field of local power negotiations, poised between being an instrument of elite control and a system of community self-regulation. Much depended upon the tact and ambitions of the consistory members themselves. Much likewise depended upon the larger political context in which they worked.

PATTERNS OF CONSISTORIAL ACTIVITY

In spite of the ambiguity of statistics derived from the archives of repression, two key findings emerge from the many recent quantitative studies of consistorial discipline. First, the intensity of consistorial surveillance in Geneva in the decades following Calvin's defeat of the "libertines" was anything but typical of Reformed church discipline as a whole. Unless their records are drastically less complete than Utrecht's appear to have been, local church disciplinary boards in most times and places examined many fewer cases per capita than did Calvin and his Genevan colleagues between 1555 and 1564. Only when locally powerful ministers temporarily spearheaded moralizing offensives were Genevan levels of consistorial vigor and severity approached or exceeded. Second, above and beyond the often dramatic short-term fluctuations tied to the efforts of individual ministers or brief moral panics, the exercise of discipline varied among the Reformed churches. In some, it also changed over time. The political context in which the elders were operating and the degree of community support they enjoyed for the goal of moral reformation largely account for these differences.

The most straightforward way to measure the vigilance and severity of consistorial oversight is to calculate the percentage of communicating church members called to appear before the consistory each year and the frequency of exclusions from communion. Unfortunately, many quantitative studies fail

TABLE 14.1

Two Measures of Consistorial Vigilance

A. Convocation Rates Per Annum

Geneva, 1564–69: 1 communicant in 8

Montifieth (Scotland), 1579–81: 1 communicant in 61

Saint Andrews, 1570–79: 1 communicant in 56

1580–89: 1 communicant in 30

1590–99: 1 communicant in 26

Valangin (principality of Neuchâtel), 1590–1667: 1 adult in 40

B. Frequency of Suspension from Communion Per Annum

Geneva, 1564–69: 1 adult in 25

Meyrueis (France), 1589–92: 1 communicant in 130

Montauban, 1596–97: 1 communicant in 150

Anduze, 1660–63: 1 communicant in 250

St. Annaparochie (Friesland), 1601–32: 1 communicant in 150

1633–63: 0

Sources: Monter, "Consistory of Geneva," 484; Graham, *Uses of Reform,* 97, 129, 219; Jeffrey R. Watt, "The Reception of the Reformation in Valangin, Switzerland, 1547–1588," *Sixteenth-Century Journal* 20 (1989): 94; Mentzer, "Marking the Taboo," 125–26; Archives Communales d'Anduze, GG 45; Benedict, *Huguenot Population,* 149; Wiebe Bergsma, "Een Dorp op het Bildt: Gereformeerden in St. Annaparochie in de zeventiende eeuw," in M. Bruggeman et al., eds., *Mensen van de Nieuwe Tijd* (Amsterdam, 1996), 151–52.

to compute these simple statistics or do so without indicating if the frequency rates have been calculated with reference to the entire Reformed population or only to communicating adult members. Fairly precise rates of convocation and suspension from communion are available for seven other communities besides Geneva (table 14.1). In most of these localities, the consistory handled less than a fifth of the business relative to the size of the congregation that the Genevan consistory did around the time of Calvin's death. Only one case listed in table 14.1 comes close to approaching Genevan levels of strictness: Saint Andrews in the 1580s and 1590s, the era of Andrew Melville's ministry there. Less complete statistics also reveal spikes in consistorial activity under the influence of other fiery ministers, as in Utrecht during Voetius's time, where the number of people excluded from the sacraments suddenly jumped from roughly 3 per year to 78 in 1658 and 167 in 1659, or in Sluis, where at the height of the activity of another partisan of further reformation, Jacobus Koelman, no fewer than 100 of 1,200 church members were excluded from communion.[18] Charismatic partisans of strict discipline could thus occasionally inspire brief moments of rigor comparable to that of Calvin's Geneva. Such cases, however, stand out as exceptions to the far less vigorous deployment of consistorial authority that was evidently the norm. Even in Geneva, the strictness of the 1560s may not have been maintained for long, for it is known that where 1 out of every 3 Genevans called before the consistory was suspended from communion in 1559, the suspension rate fell to 1 in 7 in 1605 and 1 in 13 in 1721.[19]

The fact that zealous ministers and brief moralizing crusades could affect the pattern of consistorial activity in individual congregations argues for the importance of building larger generalizations about regional or chronological patterns of consistorial activity from studies covering several communities or long periods of time. Fortunately, a number of studies of sufficient scale exist to enable this to be done. Scotland offers one well-studied case. In this traditionally loosely governed land, despite the apparent ferocity of a system built upon shaming punishments and fines, the degree of intervention into aspects of church members' lives was relatively limited.[20]

Kirk sessions and presbyteries shared the administration of discipline in Scotland. As the first formal institutions for the enforcement of impersonal norms of behavior to be set up throughout the country, and as the product of a revolutionary reformation supported by only a fraction of the political nation, they moved carefully at first. Combined data from eight kirk sessions and four presbyteries reveal that between 1560 and 1610, fully 55 percent of kirk session cases and 48 percent of those heard by the presbyteries were about sexual misconduct, the great majority involving the most serious and publicly known offenses of adultery, unmarried cohabitation, and fornication resulting in pregnancy. The other large categories of offenses examined by the kirk sessions were Sabbath breach (11 percent), slander (5 percent), absence from worship (4 percent) and disapproved religious practices (4 percent, consisting primarily of persisting Yuletide festivities). The presbyteries, whose members tended to be of higher status than those who staffed the kirk sessions, and which commanded more authority by virtue of representing a cluster of parishes and ministers, also worked to bring under control the feuds that were so common among the unruly Scottish nobility. The focal point of 5 percent of their cases was the repression of violence. They also tackled many cases of disapproved religious practices (15 percent), Sabbath breach (5 percent), and disobedience of church decrees (5 percent). That so much of these bodies' deliberations were directed at a few categories of offenses suggests that many other forms of sin were overlooked. Only a Melville in a university town dared to tackle during these years the kinds of everyday offenses such as drunkenness, cursing, and swearing that were the standard fare of consistories in other lands and times. The timidity of the kirk sessions and presbyteries in wielding their authority is understandable in light of the evident contempt that often greeted their opening assays at action. As many as half of the people summoned before them simply refused to appear in the 1560s and 1570s. With the passing decades, however, instances of recalcitrance declined markedly, indicating a growing acceptance of the system.[21]

Throughout the seventeenth century, Scottish church discipline continued to be preoccupied above all with sexual misconduct, although the scope of offenses examined widened slightly. Between 1605 and 1635, three well-studied kirk sessions heard more cases about people who worked or engaged in unlawful pastimes during the time of Sunday services (50 percent) than about sexual misconduct (28 percent), with absence from worship (11 percent) and slander (5 percent) again showing as other major sticking points. Sexual misconduct still made up 53 percent of the work of three presbyteries during the same time, with absence from worship (26 percent), Sabbath breach (18 percent), and assault (4 percent) again occupying most of the rest of their attention.[22] A large study of the records of eleven kirk sessions from Stirlingshire between 1637 and 1747 finds sex still troubling the church elders more than anything else: the 57 percent of cases revolving around sexual matters that they examined now included couples who began to have intercourse prior to marriage as well as unwed mothers and notorious adulterers. The kirk sessions of this period heard in addition a broader panoply of other kinds of cases: not simply Sabbath breach (11 percent), slander (6 percent), and absence from worship (2 percent), but also drunkenness (7 percent), disobedience (6 percent), and cursing and swearing (5 percent). Over the years 1637–1747, times of intensified surveillance alternated with periods of relaxation. The covenanting years from 1640 to 1652, the first years following the Restoration, and the years from 1695 to 1705 were the periods of most vigorous kirk session activity.[23]

Unlike the Scottish, the French churches initially labored toward a wide-ranging reformation of manners in the Genevan mode. The dream of moral renewal bulked large in the movement's initial expansion here, and in the Midi many churches rode the first wave of growth into a position of local political dominance. Even during the dangerous year 1561 when the faith had not yet won legal toleration, Le Mans's elders reprimanded new church members for gaming, making liturgical items for Catholic churches, and scandalizing their papist neighbors by boasting of having eaten meat during Lent.[24] A statistical analysis of thousands of cases heard by Nîmes's consistory between 1561 and 1614 displays a far lengthier agenda of consistorial topics than Scottish records from the same period. Breaking the cases down according to the nature of the accusation, one arrives at the following distribution of activity:

470

	Percentages
conflicts and quarrels	25
dogmatic discipline or absence from services	16
magic, popish practices	15
dancing	13
sexual misconduct	9
betrothal disputes or irregularities	6
plays, carnival, charivaris	6
family problems	5
gambling	4
drunkenness, gluttony, luxury	3[25]

Because the Reformed controlled Nîmes politically for most of this period, the consistory also helped the secular magistrates mount crackdowns against prostitution, dueling, and dancing. Indeed, the bastions of Protestant strength across southern France incited one another to greater rigor throughout the turbulent decades of the late sixteenth century. In 1589 the Nîmes church began to admonish apothecaries for selling rouge after receiving a letter from Orange complaining about excessively made up Nîmoises who had visited that city. Montauban's church suspended several prominent noblewomen from communion for their excessively elaborate coiffures around the same time.[26]

Such vigorous consistorial exercises in remaking the behavior of the Huguenot faithful became rarer after the Edict of Nantes and virtually disappeared after the Peace of Alais (1629) revoked the political and military privileges that the 1598 edict had granted the Protestants. The number of disciplinary cases handled by Nîmes's consistory fell more than sixfold over a century—from 240 per year in 1578–1604 to 75 per year in 1615–54 to just 39 per year in 1655–84—even though the church's membership declined by less than 20 percent during these years.[27] The decline may have been greater yet in those regions in which the Huguenots made up just a small minority of the population. By the second half of the seventeenth century, the surviving consistorial registers of several northern French churches scarcely contain any entries other than those pertaining to church finances, administration, and poor relief. One suspects that a measure of unrecorded formal and informal admonition continued in these churches, but foreign visitors, even Scottish ones, remarked on the decay of discipline. The reason for the decay is encapsulated in the defiant words of one church member to an elder of Ganges in 1600: "If you do not want to give me Communion, I'll go drink white wine with the Papists." Once Catholic worship was everywhere restored and the Huguenots had lost their political control of certain regions, the consistories feared driving members out of the church by acting too strictly against lesser

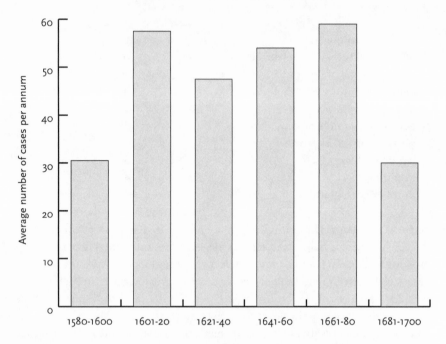

Graph 14.1. Volume of Discipline Cases before the Amsterdam Kerkeraad, 1580–1700

transgressions. Even in Anduze, in the heart of overwhelmingly Protestant Cévennes, most sexual misconduct cases noted in the consistory registers in the 1660s were notorious public scandals. The zeal that the French churches had once displayed for the reformation of manners had given way, by the late seventeenth century, to censuring of only particularly serious, public sins, even where the movement was strongest.[28]

The records of Amsterdam's *kerkeraad* reveal still another pattern. Amsterdam was one of seventeenth-century Europe's urban giants, having one hundred thousand inhabitants early in the century and more than two hundred thousand by 1680. Even though less than a quarter of Amsterdammers were full Reformed church members, the church was larger than Nîmes's, with its roughly ten thousand members. Nonetheless, the number of cases heard by Amsterdam's kerkeraad peaked in the decade 1611–20 at just sixty-seven per year, scarcely a quarter of the volume of business of Nîmes's consistory in the period 1578–1604 (graph 14.1). As in Nîmes, although less dramatically, a slackening of zeal may also have occurred over time, for while the volume of consistorial activity oscillated within relatively stable limits between 1578 and 1700, the city's population doubled, and a modestly growing percentage of the population joined the church. Although the Amster-

472

TABLE 14.2
The Nature of Discipline Cases before the Amsterdam Kerkeraad,
1578–1700 (%)

Nature of offense	1578–1620	1621–60	1661–1700
Sexual misconduct	22	32	49
Quarrels and violence	14	8	4
Insults	13	8	2
Drunkenness	12	10	9
Dogmatic discipline	11	15	10
Family problems	10	10	14
Bankruptcy	6	8	13
Dancing	4	—	—
Other	8	8	2

Statistics computed from Roodenburg, *Onder censuur,* passim.

dam consistory never tried anything like the sustained campaign to remodel
church members' behavior mounted by the French churches in their early
years, it was not as limited in its activities as many Scottish kirk sessions.
During its first four decades of existence the kerkeraad divided its attention
among a whole array of problems: adultery, fornication, violent quarrels, insults, drunkenness, doctrinal deviance, bankruptcy, domestic problems, and
dancing (table 14.2). In time, it gave up summoning people for dancing and
addressed many fewer disputes over violence and insults, while acting with
increased strictness against adultery and other sexual sins—a strictness revealed not simply by a fivefold increase in the number of adultery cases heard,
but also by the harsher punishments handed down for like offenses. The
tighter regulation of sexual behavior by church and state alike has been discerned over this period in Arnemuiden and Rotterdam, too. After 1670, Rotterdam's consistory began to investigate couples suspected of having premari-
tal sex, while its secular courts penalized more and more people for illicit
sexual relations of brief duration and little notoriety. The amount of attention
the elders and ministers devoted to cases of bankruptcy in all periods is another striking feature of consistorial activity in this commercial metropolis.
Although a distinction was made between bankruptcies that resulted from the
individual merchant's fraud or waste and defaults due to circumstances beyond the individual's control, the failure to maintain one's credit was a fundamental offense against the community of merchants; and those who could not
meet their obligations were suspended from communion while the consistory
investigated the nature of the failing and watched to see that a fair settlement
was reached. Amsterdam's kerkeraad appears to have been less an instrument

for the wholesale remaking of social morality than a body that upheld and reinforced the values by which most respectable burghers desired to live.[29]

Extensive studies of two other congregations, Emden and Stettlen, the second a rural parish close to Bern, have found that their disciplinary boards grew more, not less, active with time. The number of cases heard by Emden's presbyterium went from 575 in 1558–62 to 792 in 1695–99, albeit after a decline in two intervening five-year samples. Stettlen's chorgericht handled an average of 18 offenses per annum between 1595 and 1623 and 30 per year during the last third of the seventeenth century.[30] Both tribunals, like their counterparts in France and the Netherlands, took under consideration the full gamut of moral lapses and family disputes (table 14.3). The study of Stettlen has the added interest of showing a purely secular disciplinary tribunal in the Zurich tradition in action. Staffed by six laymen, with the village pastor attending its meetings but acting only as an advisor and scribe, this chorgericht worked with a vigor that would have done many a consistory proud. It recurrently chastised or fined villagers for such offenses as drunkenness, slander, blasphemy, dancing, excessive luxury, and idleness. The body's competence extended to a number of police matters, for example, theft and lodging of unauthorized strangers, not typically handled by consistories. Over the course of the seventeenth century, the chorgericht seemingly became more fully accepted by the villagers of Stettlen and inculcated greater reverence for God and his church, for it tackled fewer cases of resistance to church authority and more of blasphemy and misdemeanor in church. The number of cases of dancing and theft declined, while those of gambling increased. Emden's presbyterium, by contrast, at first had to face a great deal of doctrinal deviance and even outright defection from the church—hardly surprising in this port of refuge for so many kinds of dissenters from the Netherlands—but these kinds of cases rapidly declined, to be replaced by more intervention in family quarrels. In both communities, the amount of attention devoted to the most important categories of offenses displayed no clear pattern of change over time.

For all of the divergences across time and space that characterized the activity of Reformed disciplinary tribunals, a common set of affairs animated the great majority of them. Both tables of the Ten Commandments, the one citing duties to God and the other duties to one's kindred human beings, required upholding. From the vantage point of Reformed sensibilities, the first-table duties to God meant above all avoiding idolatry and false worship. A prime goal of consistories and chorgerichte became eliminating Catholic vestiges from the private devotional practices of church members and forbidding attendance at the ceremonies of competing churches in the vicinity. Scotland's kirk sessions fought Yule celebrations. Huguenot consistories warned church

TABLE 14.3

The Nature of Discipline Cases before the Emden Presbyterium
and Stettlen Chorgericht, 1558–1699 (%)

Emden Nature of offense	1558–62	1596–1600	1645–49	1695–99
Sexual misconduct	10	10	14	21
Quarrels and violence	10	29	21	10
Slander	6	3	6	2
Drunkenness	8	16	9	12
Dogmatic discipline	34	16	14	9
Family problems	9	14	23	35
Economy and occupation	15	6	11	8
Defection from congregation	6	3	1	1
Other	2	3	1	2
	n = 575	n = 110	n = 361	n = 792

Stettlen Nature of offense	1595–1632	1633–66	1667–99
Sexual misconduct	5	5	4
Quarrels, violence, slander	10	9	13
Drunkenness, gluttony, wastefulness	14	9	15
Family problems	10	6	9
Nonattendance, misdemeanor in church	10	24	19
Swearing and blasphemy	11	15	15
Resistance to church authorities	11	4	7
Theft	7	2	3
Gambling	4	9	8
Dancing	7	9	2
Other	11	8	5
	n = 696	n = 816	n = 982

Statistics computed from Schilling, "Calvinism and the Making," 44; Schmidt, *Dorf und Religion,* computerized appendix.

members against sending their children to Jesuit schools, forbade them from acting as godparents to Catholics, and deemed the offense of leaving the church temporarily to marry outside the faith deserving of public reparation before the congregation. In the conditions of extreme religious pluriformity found in the Netherlands, the Amsterdam kerkeraad had to warn church members to avoid the fellowship of Catholics, Anabaptists, Lutherans, Remonstrants, Brownists, Quakers, Labadists, and Collegiants. It also toiled to prevent church members from becoming servants in Jewish households. In the Palatinate, ping-ponged back and forth between Lutheranism and Reformed Protestantism four times in twenty-five years, the consistories of several villages deployed much of their energy in the years after the final establishment of Reformed worship in 1584 to persuading inhabitants attached to Lutheran ways to join in the simpler communion services restored in that year. These efforts defined and reinforced the boundaries of the church community. Consistorial action thereby contributed to the process of confessional identity formation that was one of the essential trends of the long Reformation era.

Beyond warning church members against retaining popish practices and taking part in the rites of other churches, Reformed disciplinary bodies were led by their worry over first-table offenses to promote the church's own worship practices, to reprove the casting of spells, to reprimand blasphemy, and occasionally even to warn believers about indirectly abetting idolatry. Few consistories imagined they could ensure that church members mastered Reformed doctrine with quite the vigor that Geneva's displayed when it told some of those who had failed to master the catechism to hire tutors. Saint Andrews's kirk session nonetheless decreed in the 1590s that all those who wished to marry had to be able to repeat the Lord's Prayer, Apostle's Creed, and Ten Commandments, and fined several people for their inability to do so. In the 1670s, Nîmes's consistory undertook a campaign to encourage regular family devotions and Bible reading. Many churches waged battle on inappropriate behavior during Sunday hours of worship; Scottish kirk sessions were fixated on this issue and fined individuals at various times for fishing, playing golf, and walking together in the fields on the Sabbath.[31] Magical practices attracted steady consistorial attention, and swearing and blasphemy still more. Some churches not only investigated reports that congregation members had preserved instruments of idolatry like crucifixes and religious statues in their homes, but also admonished painters, goldsmiths, and other artisans for making objects that might be "misused for idolatry by all who come to the church." The Amsterdam consistory castigated the sculptor Hendrik de Keyser when it got wind he was carving a statue of Saint John the Evangelist for a church in 's-Hertogenbosch.[32]

476

Consistorial action against second-table offenses tended to be concentrated in a number of areas. As we have seen, illicit sex preoccupied many disciplinary bodies. By far the greatest number of cases heard in this domain had to do with adulterous relationships, notorious concubinage, and heterosexual unions that led to the pregnancy of unmarried women. Prostitution was also a serious issue, and some churches were vigilant in censuring betrothed couples who began to have sex before marriage, as subsequently divulged by a birth too soon after their wedding. By contrast, very few cases of homosexuality, bestiality, incest, rape, infanticide, and abortion appear in the consistorial registers, probably because they would have been considered so serious as to require direct referral to the secular courts. Masturbation, that great eighteenth- and nineteenth-century fixation, also rarely or never preoccupied church elders. It is impossible to know if such indifference is because it was in fact rare, because it was rarely detected, or because it was not regarded as a serious offense.

Drinking, gambling, dancing, and other aspects of festive culture such as youth groups, charivaris, and carnival or other holiday celebrations were another major preoccupation of most consistories, for all of these practices were believed to abet sexual temptation, conflict, and neglect of one's family. The regional variations that occur in the extent of concern with these issues often conform strikingly to the era's stereotypes about national character. Amsterdam's kerkeraad summoned before it a steady procession of drunks who had to be carted home in barrows, were observed sleeping in the streets, or had imbibed excessively while making their rounds in the night watch. In Emden and Stettlen as well, cases of drunkenness appeared frequently on the presbyterium's and chorgericht's dockets (see table 14.3). The consistories of the French Midi, by contrast, far more regularly did battle with families that held balls in carnival time, men who dressed as women on Mardi Gras, and youth groups that staged charivaris. As late as the 1660s, the consistory of Anduze, in the heart of the Huguenot Cévennes, was still waging an apparently losing fight against a set of overactive and aggressive youth groups whose members disturbed the sleep of the inhabitants at night with their loud swearing and on one occasion even broke into several houses to steal musical instruments, which they then used to serenade young women reputed to be of easy virtue before carrying them off "to do ill with them."[33] Although the consistories may simply have been responding to the prevailing stereotypes about local vices, these contrasts may indicate that the practices in question were more widespread in some parts of Europe than others.

The relative absence of consistorial activity in some domains seems as crucial as its frequency in others. Economic ethics is one such area. The leading student of Calvin's economic and social ideas has laid bare an impressive legacy of pronouncements about economic matters, including even an approving citation of the ancient Hebrew custom of periodically redistributing property to aid the poor. The medieval scholastics condemned loans at interest as usurious, although in time a growing number of them deemed licit certain of the subterfuges, including "triple contracts" and silent partnerships, Europe's merchants developed to avoid the legal condemnation of money lending. Luther, Zwingli, Bullinger, and Viret echoed the long-standing Christian condemnation of usury, but Calvin parted company with them. Valuing commerce equally with agriculture rather than inferior to it, he rethought the issue in terms of the distinction between consumption and production. Moderate rates of interest were acceptable when loans were made for commercial purposes, he judged. His attitude here may have been shaped by his having lived with the rich merchant Etienne de la Farge while a student in Paris and his observations in mercantile Geneva during his mature years. He still condemned profiting from a neighbor's distress or charging interest on loans to the poor. Above all, he stressed that people should deal fairly with one another in all economic transactions.[34]

The early disciplines of the various Reformed churches displayed as much variety on the question of usury as the early Reformed theologians. In Béarn, where Viret's influence was strong, the church forbade any "profit on money lent." The Heidelberg Catechism was equally severe. The French synod of 1562 adopted a policy closer to Calvin's, allowing "some mediocre profit" on loans within bounds defined by the king's ordinances and the principles of charity. The French also decreed that pirates and others who obtained goods unjustly should be excluded from communion. As the slave trade grew in the seventeenth century, synods warned against the selling of slaves to cruel or negligent masters who would not care for their spiritual education, but they did not condemn the trade. The Dutch banned *lombardiers* (small moneylenders) from communion but allowed some interest to be taken on commercial loans. Reformed theological opinion continued to be divided over the question of the appropriateness of loans at interest throughout the seventeenth century, with a gradual trend toward greater leniency.[35]

This corpus of theological and synodal pronouncements notwithstanding, the consistories of Geneva, Amsterdam, and Emden are the only ones studied to date that paid enough attention to overseeing the economic behavior of church members for such cases to make an appearance among the statistically significant preoccupations of a church disciplinary body. The Genevan consistory, which devoted about 5 percent of its activity between 1542 and 1564 to such cases, was shocked to discover people making short-term loans at annual rates that worked out to more than 100 percent. It also investigated and broke up the brotherhood of the Griffarins, which journeymen printers had created to defend their work interests. In addition to investigating bank-ruptcies to ensure there was no improper behavior, Amsterdam's consistory censured an individual who did not pay his rent, another who failed to repay a loan, a third who used false weights and measures, and a number of church members guilty of sloth. It likewise backed the city's drapers in their program of enforcing guild work rules against the journeymen shearers, who appear to have been well organized in the defense of their interests. In the first gen-eration in Geneva and in commercial cities like Amsterdam and Emden, the church thus actively upheld some of its strictures against excessive rates of interest and exploitative business practices, while condemning as disorderly the attempts of journeymen to organize in defense of their interests. But this appears to be the extent of consistorial interest in economic inequalities and abuses. In light of the general absence of consciousness about economic issues in most localities, the thrust of consistorial discipline in the domain of eco-nomic behavior probably must be located in the broader program to combat drunkenness, gaming, and other forms of "dishonest recreation."[36]

Except in Scotland, where the maintenance of the eucharistic community never appears to have been identified as a goal of ecclesiastical discipline, the endeavor to build a loving fellowship around the communion table prompted consistories to spend much of their time reconciling quarrels. French church regulations stipulated that parties in lawsuits ought to be exhorted to work out their disagreements without having recourse to court. The agreements bro-kered in response to this injunction often specified detailed terms of settle-ment. Such reconciliations did not always last, however. More than one out of three couples summoned before the consistory of Bacharach for marital dis-cord appeared before the body more than once. Brokering this sort of infra-judicial resolution of family and neighborhood quarrels was nonetheless an invaluable social function in an age when recourse to the law was costly, un-certain, and, as always, as likely to exacerbate conflicts as to solve them.[37]

Having been initially created to replace the ecclesiastical courts of the Ro-man Catholic church, Reformed consistories and *Ehegerichte* also adjudi-cated disputed marriage engagements, separations, and petitions for divorce. The Protestant Reformation is often presented as a crossroads in the history of divorce in that every territory except England that broke with Rome altered the law to permit divorce in cases of adultery. In certain territories, notably the Reformed portions of Switzerland, divorce was also permitted in cases of willful desertion and grave incompatibility. In practice, however, Reformed consistories granted very few divorces during the sixteenth and seventeenth centuries—never more than one per thousand marriages, and often scarcely one per hundred thousand. Wherever couples had begun to live apart, the church bodies labored unfailingly to force them back under the same roof, even when aware of a long history of violence between them. An excellent study of the principality of Neuchâtel shows that it was only in the eighteenth century, when attitudes toward family relations had changed noticeably, that the Reformation's transformation of the law of divorce began to have widespread practical consequences. Prior to 1700, disputes about engagements occupied far more consistorial attention than divorce suits. The church tribunals defended the authority of parents to have a say in the marriage decisions of their children, but they left the last word to the children. In Neuchâtel, those who defied their parents' advice were reprimanded for disobedience, but their marriage promises remained binding if they were of age and had freely made a pact before witnesses; furthermore, their parents had to provide dowries for such marriages. Even if the parties reconsidered and testified they no longer wished to be married, a pact before witnesses was considered binding and could not be broken. The principles that the tribunal upheld above all were responsibility for one's actions and the sanctity of contract. Affection was not assumed to be an essential precondition for marriage, as it would be in the eighteenth century, when the consistory began to grant divorces on grounds of cruelty and incompatibility, and the number of petitions for divorce increased.[38]

Consistorial intervention in family and marital affairs was governed by the hierarchical assumptions about gender roles that prevailed at the time. It is anachronistic to depict Calvin or the Reformed churches of this era as protofeminist, as a few exegetes have done. Calvin's commentaries restated prevailing explanations of why men were universally superior to women "by privilege of nature." Reformed disciplinary institutions viewed husbands as the head of the household and urged them to treat their weaker helpmeets with loving consideration. When Montauban's consistory addressed a couple it had managed to reconcile, it instructed the woman to heed her husband while admonishing him to take better care of the "exceedingly weak vessel" placed under his dominion.[39]

Within the context of such assumptions, the consistories nonetheless often treated women with more evenhandedness and acted more aggressively to defend their interests in the household than most other institutions of the age. One consequence of their hierarchical view of marital relations was that men received the lion's share of the blame for disorderly households. Because they were also more likely than women to be found engaging in most forms of disorderly public behavior, they invariably made up the majority of those summoned before church disciplinary bodies—between 62 and 67 percent in three cases studied so far.[40] The sex ratio of those summoned before the chorgericht in the Bernese countryside for marital conflicts was so heavily weighted toward men that the historian of this institution speaks of its alliance with women to uphold responsible masculine behavior within the family. A resident of the Genevan countryside complained shortly after 1600 that the consistory had created a "paradise for women" through its excessively zealous oversight of family relations.[41] Aggregating all forms of offenses, women appear to have been suspended from communion at roughly the same rates as men in both Calvin's Geneva and the French Midi in the late sixteenth century. In cases of sexual misdemeanors, penalties handed down to both sexes were similar for comparable offenses in Neuchâtel and Stirlingshire— a pattern that contrasts strikingly with the secular courts of both Lutheran and Catholic territories in Germany, where a double standard led to harsher penalties for women in cases of adultery and fornication. The total number of those accused of sexual misbehavior before Reformed disciplinary bodies likewise split close to fifty-fifty, although the sex ratio shifted from a slight majority of men to a slight majority of women between the sixteenth and seventeenth centuries.[42]

Most Reformed churches also embraced the principle that rank should carry no privileges in the domain of church discipline, but this principle was difficult to implement in the strongly hierarchical early modern world. A good example of both the practical concessions individual churches might be willing to make to locally powerful figures of high birth and the disapproval of such concessions by larger church bodies is the church of Ganges's treatment of the baron of that locality after it learned he had been dancing. Rather than summon him before the consistory, as it would have an ordinary offender, the consistory dispatched one of its members to his residence to beg permission to censure him in the privacy of his domicile. He graciously consented but soon repeated the offense, prompting a visit to his residence from the entire consistory. For this special treatment, the church was reprimanded by the provincial synod.[43] There are many instances of consistories rebuking the powerful and prominent—even the prince of Condé was barred from communion in La Rochelle in 1578 after he authorized acts of piracy—yet such actions could provoke strong reactions. When a group of Scottish ministers tried to excommunicate several leading noblemen in the council of James VI and I, he was led to splutter, "A Scottish presbytery . . . agreeth as well with monarchy as God and the Devil! Then Jack and Tom and Will and Dick shall meet and censure me and my council." A statistical analysis reveals that the highborn in Scotland were less likely than commoners to be pursued by the kirk sessions for behavioral misdeeds, that they more frequently avoided appearances or judgments when pursued, and that they received less harsh penalties for comparable actions when censured, even if they did not escape scot-free. Church visitations in the Hungarian county of Zemplén found that blasphemy and swearing went unpunished among those living in noble households, even though measures against these offenses were otherwise enforced. The nobility of the Pays de Vaud enjoyed exemption from consistorial discipline and strove to gain the same for its servants.[44]

CHURCH DISCIPLINE AND STATE DISCIPLINE

A full, properly comparative assessment of the disciplinary effects of the Reformed churches would look not only at the actions of the church's own disciplinary bodies, but also at those of the state courts in those areas where a Reformed church became the established church of the land. As earlier chapters have shown, the triumph of a Reformed reformation was followed time and again by harsher civil laws against certain violations of the divine commandments. Once in place, Reformed consistories and synods often appealed to the secular authorities for further measures against vices that they perceived to be on the increase, worked in tandem with the magistrates in certain instances to suppress such vices, and referred certain kinds of crimes to the secular authorities for punishment rather than handling them inside the church. But the Lutheran and Catholic Reformations were also often accompanied by harsher legislation against different forms of sin, notably sexual misbehavior, blasphemy, the size and lavishness of wedding celebrations, and gambling. Furthermore, within certain other confessional traditions, most notably the Lutheran, state campaigns to punish vice more severely constituted the core of the process of "social disciplining" in the wake of the Reformation. Both the relative extent of the intensification of penalties against various sorts of misdeeds in Catholic, Lutheran, and Reformed countries, and the relative thoroughness of the laws' enforcement, are thus relevant for assessing Reformed reformations comparatively.

Unfortunately, there have been few comparisons of the severity of the relevant laws across territories of divergent confessional affiliations. Likewise, few studies have tackled the criminal court records—so forbidding in their mass and murky in their jurisdictional boundaries—to see how laws on such matters were actually enforced. Until more research has been carried out, discussion of this topic must remain highly speculative. But consider a working hypothesis: prior to the Reformation preoccupation with ensuring community purity through legislation against adultery, blasphemy, and luxury was more intense in some regions of Europe than others, Switzerland and south Germany being among the centers of such focus. With the Reformation, the issue intensified and spread across the Continent in areas affiliated with all three major confessions, but this trend was most marked in Reformed territories.

The legal penalties decreed for adultery seem to support these hypotheses. This was a crime about which the Old Testament offered clear guidance, for according to Leviticus 21:10 adultery merits death. A broader campaign against sexuality outside of marriage was already under way in parts of Europe as the fifteenth century gave way to the sixteenth, as is illustrated by the closing of public brothels across much of Germany and France. Within this context, the Carolina, Charles V's new law code of 1532 intended as a model for the individual territories of the empire, included tougher penalties for many sexual offenses, including the death penalty for adultery. Local law revisions that followed in Catholic and Lutheran as well as Reformed portions of the empire repeated this last provision, demonstrating that the institution of the death penalty for adultery was hardly confession-specific. But the roll call of Reformed territories in which the death penalty was instituted for adultery in the wake of the Reformation was especially long and widely dispersed. At a minimum, it encompassed (to proceed in the chronological order in which the territories enacted such laws) Basel, Scotland, Geneva, Béarn, the Palatinate, Friesland (from 1586 to 1602 only), Zweibrücken, Bern, Virginia, Transylvania, Massachusetts, and England (from 1650 to 1660 only); the legislation to this effect in England came at the high-water mark of Puritan political influence during the interregnum. The only territories with an established church of a Reformed stripe in which it appears clear that death never was the penalty for adultery during this period were Holland and Zeeland, in keeping with the general reluctance of Dutch political authorities wholeheartedly to embrace the principles championed by the Reformed church. Leading Reformed ministers argued strongly for such a policy, and its institution in most areas was linked to the cause's ascendancy.[45]

Because the execution of an adulterer was sufficiently unusual to be noted by contemporaries, researchers have some idea of whether or not the laws were applied. In the Geneva of the period 1555–75 they certainly were. Several residents were in fact put to death for adultery in the early 1560s even before the death penalty was formally instituted for the crime, and when the Small Council displayed an inclination to mitigate the law's severity in 1581, the Company of Pastors called it a great treasure and urged its vigorous enforcement. Beza noted with some pride that a prominent couple met death for the crime in Orléans when that city was under Huguenot domination in 1563, while in the Palatinate in 1571 a man was decapitated for impregnating his serving woman. But these instances appear to testify primarily to the exceptional climate that prevailed in these places in these years, for death sentences appear never to have been handed down for adultery in either Basel or Massachusetts. Search of many of the surviving English court records from the decade when the death penalty was in effect there has turned up only four capital sentences. In Scotland, the most common penalty for adultery appears to have been the repeated Sunday appearances in the stool of repentance in the front of the church decreed by the kirk sessions. There was often a gap between the letter of the law and the reality of judicial practice. And not only Reformed territories put convicted adulterers to death. Capital sentences are known to have been carried out for this crime in Catholic Münster, Lutheran Memmingen and Nuremberg, and biconfessional Augsburg.[46]

Another indication that in an era when laws were being stiffened across Europe they were made even stiffer in Reformed territories comes from a comparative study of the police measures enacted by the local communities of the religiously divided Grisons during the sixteenth century. Here, local measures against dancing, drunkenness, and sexual offenses multiplied in Catholic as well as Reformed communities in the generations after 1520. Nevertheless, the volume and scope of legislation on economic and sexual behavior enacted in the Reformed communities exceeded that in the Catholic communities.[47]

For most Western readers at the dawn of the twenty-first century, of course, what stands out most is the harshness of the moral code informing the law in territories of all three confessions, rather than any nuances of variation between them. The limited information currently available still suggests that the Reformed may have earned their reputation for severe moral standards and hostility to pleasure, even if there was a gap between the letter of the laws passed and the manner in which they were enforced.

HOW GREAT THE IMPACT?

Great hopes of moral renewal accompanied the spread of the Reformed cause, and consistorial systems of discipline were the essential agencies of attempted renewal wherever they were established, but the ultimate question is, Were the Reformed truly reformed in any meaningful way?

The trends in the number of cases of sorts revealed by the quantitative studies of consistorial activity are by themselves of only limited utility in exploring this question. Emden's presbyterium and Amsterdam's kerkeraad dealt with growing numbers of instances of sexual misconduct and drunkenness between the late sixteenth century and the end of the seventeenth, while cases of quarrels and violence remained steady in the former, dropped off in the latter, and increased before Stettlen's chorgericht. But the numbers alone cannot reveal whether the changes reflected changes in the actual incidence of the forms of behavior practiced or simply shifts in the focus of attention of the disciplinary tribunals. The most illuminating studies of church discipline have been those that have supplemented the statistical investigation of the activity of the church boards with close reading of the details of the cases they handled or with complementary evidence from other sources. In these instances, it becomes possible to interpret the meaning of the statistical trends.

In Emden, the endless crusade against drunkenness waged by the city's presbyterium seemingly cannot be credited with any significant long-term impact on alcohol use because not only did such cases remain numerous, but the details of the cases of inebriation changed little over time and contemporary observers at the end of the period still saw drunkenness as the "tribal vice" of the East Frisians. On the other hand, a new sensitivity toward violence does appear to have developed by the end of the seventeenth century: a number of those convoked before the presbyterium in the 1690s admitted their actions had violated principles of "Christian gentleness," whereas no spontaneous mention of such principles appears in the evidence from the earlier time periods studied. In Amsterdam, too, the details of the cases of insults and brawling that came before the kerkeraad imply that less crudely violent forms of behavior came to characterize the city's residents as the seventeenth century advanced. Likewise in Scotland a student of aristocratic life has demonstrated the decline of the blood feud in the years between 1570 and 1625. The new church presbyteries cannot claim all the credit for this transformation, for the clergy preached strenuously against taking an eye for an eye, and the crown used its legal and patronage powers to combat the practice. Still, the domain of interpersonal violence and impulse control does appear to have been one in which the pressure of the church tribunals made a difference.[48]

Sexual behavior appears to have been another such area. The numerical frequency of cases of sexual misconduct rarely declined over time, but it will be recalled that in the Netherlands people began to be regularly summoned and reprimanded for casual instances of fornication in the later seventeenth century; previously such cases were exceptional. Stirlingshire's kirk session records reveal a number of voluntary confessions of fornication at the end of the seventeenth century, whereas earlier the elders always had to take the initiative in convoking those guilty of this offense. A broad study of Scottish illegitimacy rates finds a fall from a national average of 5.3 percent in the 1660s to 3 percent in the 1720s. The evidence does not permit the calculation of trustworthy rates before that time, but other forms of data suggest that standards of sexual propriety were laxer yet in early sixteenth-century Scotland, children born out of wedlock being accepted with relatively little stigma. In the wake of the Reformation, Scottish aristocrats reduced the frequency of their sexual adventures outside marriage or at least carried them on more discreetly. Not only does the surveillance of sexual misconduct appear to have intensified; it also appears to have gradually inculcated among the populace at large a more explicit recognition of the church's ethical norms, even among those who violated them.[49] Several studies also credit the consistories and chorgerichte with reinforcing the importance of the nuclear family and encouraging a new tenor of marital relations.[50]

Thanks to the existence of an entire academic discipline devoted to studying the production and consumption of works of art, how fully church members obeyed the churches' injunctions against making and possessing objects associated with Catholic idolatry can be assessed particularly well. Although Dutch art historians have recently highlighted the case of Jan Victors, a full member of the Reformed church whose oeuvre hints that he endeavored to conform to the strictest Reformed iconographic principles, many other seventeenth-century Reformed artists are known to have accepted commissions to paint Catholic altarpieces or to have produced paintings and sculptures that glorified the pope, expressed Roman doctrine, and included content that their church would have seen as conducive to idolatry. Jacob Jordaens, the Flemish master whose lavish baroque would appear to typify the art of the Counter-Reformation, was in fact a member of the tiny Reformed congregation that continued to assemble in Antwerp after the city was retaken by the Spanish. It appears the great majority of Reformed artists were willing to defy the disciplinary code of their church rather than to pass up lucrative commissions.[51] On the other hand, the artistic objects displayed in Reformed homes differed strikingly from those owned by their Catholic neighbors in religiously divided Metz in the middle of the seventeenth century. The Huguenots scrupulously avoided crucifixes and paintings of crucifixion scenes. Only a few owned the sorts of paintings of the Virgin, the saints, and the Magdalen found by the dozens in the city's Catholic households.[52] If this was more broadly typical, virtually all church members had internalized their confession's abhorrence of owning potentially idolatrous images, even if most artists and artisans in their ranks refused to accept the economic and professional sacrifice entailed in ceasing to produce such objects for Catholic use.

Assessing Reformed discipline comparatively is an even more delicate matter. The Reformed churches did not possess the era's strictest systems of ecclesiastical discipline. That distinction went to certain smaller churches, notably the Czech Brethren and the Anabaptists. Comparing the Reformed to the other two major post-Reformation church families, however, it would appear that the Reformed churches had the most vigorous disciplinary systems, even when the disciplinary mechanisms that existed within the other confessional traditions are duly recognized. Reformed consistories or Ehegerichte existed in many more regions than did the comparable systems found in some Catholic or Lutheran territories. They exercised a more continuous oversight of church members' behavior than did the visitation systems of most Lutheran and Catholic churches—or the church courts of England, for that matter. (In Lutheran Oldenburg, ecclesiastical inspectors visited the average parish barely once every ten years.)[53] If much still remains to be learned about the operations of the various forms of church and state discipline in Lutheran and Catholic territories, the conclusion is likely to be that they were generally a less continuous presence in community life than the Reformed consistories or Ehegerichte. They also did not play the role in reconciling private disputes and intervening in family disputes that these institutions did.

Cross-confessional comparisons of the behavior of people of similar status who lived close to one another in religiously divided areas are in their infancy, but those undertaken so far have yielded suggestive results. The comparison of rates of illegitimacy and prenuptial conceptions between Huguenots and Catholics living in the same regions of France during the seventeenth century indicates consistently lower rates of both among Huguenots.[54] Of course, it is difficult to know in this case if this disparity can be ascribed to the dissimilar doctrinal coloration of the two churches or to the pressures that exist in many minority communities to demonstrate exemplary behavior. By contrast, a comparative examination of the style of life and level of expenditure at Germany's Reformed and Lutheran princely courts found little to distinguish them. Similarly, differences cannot be detected in the consumption patterns or distribution of household expenditures between private consumption, savings, and investment in business affairs among samples of Catholic and Reformed artisans in seventeenth-century Amiens.[55] The taint of sexual immorality appears to have been rarer within the minority community of French Huguenots than among France's Catholic majority, but it does not seem that the Reformed could be distinguished from their Catholic and Lutheran neighbors by their austerity of dress or propensity to save or invest.

The belief that the reforming of the church would effect a dramatic moral transformation of the wider community regularly accompanied the initial surge of the Protestant cause across Europe; the dream of a reformation of manners continued to fire the imagination of church members throughout subsequent generations; but the realities of the behavioral changes attempted and achieved through the creation of new systems of church discipline fell far short of the highest hopes. A few documents of the movement's springtime such as the Beggar's Summons in Scotland hinted at a new set of relations between rich and poor, but the transformations yearned for by the most energetic and successful prophets of the cause were above all personal ones: chastity, sobriety, peaceful and charitable relations with one's neighbors, the dutiful and supportive exercise of a set of family roles assumed to be hierarchical and patriarchal, one's word as bond once given. Briefly, in certain times and places, a Calvin, a Melville, a Voetius, or even a more anonymous local reformer of morals like an Isaac Sylvius of Layrac might inspire a vigorous plan to promote these habits by identifying and summoning before the consistory a large number of those who strayed. These instances, however, were more the exception than the norm. Most church disciplinary bodies contented themselves with dealing with the most notorious sinners or a more restricted range of sins. In the early years of France's Reformed churches, its consistories went on a relatively wide-ranging moralizing offensive, but once the fear of losing members to the Catholic majority became overriding and the minority status and political vulnerability of the church became inescapable, its disciplinary ambitions shriveled. In Scotland, the new church courts had to tread cautiously from the start, and while they grew more confident and more assertive in time, they rarely extended their reforming to the full orbit of sins that their counterparts in other countries endeavored to attack. Only in such regions as Emden and canton Bern do the church tribunals appear to have been able to exercise steady pressure across the generations to effect a broad moral transfiguration among the population at large. Even there, they often made little headway in eradicating customs deeply rooted in local folkways and everyday patterns of sociability. Hearty drinking bouts remained the despair of church elders throughout Germanic lands. The consistory of Anduze fought a long, losing battle against raucous youth groups. That people's proclivity to drink and dance might survive sustained endeavors to eliminate them should hardly have surprised adherents of a faith that so emphasized humankind's ineradicable sinfulness. It nonetheless was repeatedly discouraging for ministers faced with the unhappy recognition of this truth among their parishioners. Within scarcely a decade of the establishment of Reformed churches in some areas, church leaders were writing despairingly of their failure to effect any amendment of life among the populace.

Still, the ample capacity of human beings to resist efforts to reform them is not the whole story, and ministerial proclamations of failure should not be taken at face value. Church discipline did not transform all church members into paragons of virtue or even make much progress at all in eliminating drinking and dancing. Painters could rarely be induced to forego the profits and prestige that came from fulfilling commissions for the Catholic church. Reformed patterns of spending and consumption do not look different from Catholic and Lutheran ones. Yet the disciplinary actions of the various Reformed churches did effect detectable changes in many areas of behavior, above all where they were abetted by such contemporaneous developments as the strengthening of the state's control over the exercise of permissible violence. Feuding, interpersonal violence, and sexual misconduct apparently declined. The importance of the nuclear family may have been strengthened and a new tenor of marital relations encouraged. The evidence of church members in the late seventeenth century expressing sorrow for their un-Christian anger or spontaneously confessing sexual misconduct to the consistory testifies that the pressure of church discipline helped to inculcate a new moral sensibility. Furthermore, even when campaigns to bring about forms of moral amendment failed to achieve their stated goals, the campaigns themselves preserved the dream of amelioration and passed it along to later generations. Above all else, the presence of consistories and chorgerichte in so many Reformed churches would have made the experience of belonging to one of these churches that of living under a constant measure of surveillance by the church's elders. In those areas in which the ideals animating these institutions remained alive and were successfully conveyed to the congregation, they would have made the experience one of participating in a community of believers who felt a measure of responsibility for each other's behavior. In these ways, discipline truly was the sinews of the church.

15

THE PRACTICE OF PIETY

In spite of the tendency of many contemporaries to see concern with the reformation of life as the most characteristic feature of the Reformed churches, the changes first noticed and most strenuously protested by the formerly Lutheran inhabitants of the German territories that experienced second reformations were such liturgical transformations as the fractio panis and the elimination of the formula of exorcism from baptism. This was so because the rituals of church life shaped the everyday experience of faith as no other aspect of religion in early modern Europe did. The calendar of observances ordered the passing of time. The structure of the liturgy gave tangible expression to the abstractions of doctrine and bestowed form and meaning on the central rites of passage in people's lives. In contrast with either the Catholic or the Lutheran church, Reformed worship was characterized by a particularly single-minded focus on the sacred text of the Bible as preached, read, and sung and by a zeal to eliminate all unscriptural elements from the liturgy. Sociological observers from Max Weber onward have spoken of the Reformed tradition as promoting a thorough rationalization of time and a "disenchantment of the world."

The Reformed churches not only altered the structure of formal worship. Reformed churchmen, like their Lutheran and Catholic counterparts, sought to inculcate knowledge of the basic tenets of the faith in their congregations, so that its members might grasp the truths that would lead them to salvation—and recognize the errors of the rival confessions that tried to lure them away. Like their Lutheran and Catholic counterparts, they encouraged a regimen of household prayer and meditation in order to reinforce the practices and values of organized church worship. With perhaps greater single-mindedness than their Lutheran counterparts and certainly more zeal than the Catholics, they labored to make lay Bible reading a central component of family worship. The most enthusiastic promoters of this cause aimed at nothing less than a complete recasting of believers' thoughts. "It is necessary, if possible," Pierre Jurieu wrote in 1675, "to habituate our heart to conceive its thoughts and form its meditations exclusively in the terms of the Holy Spirit."[1]

If Bible reading and family devotions were promoted within all Reformed churches, the English apostles of practical divinity championed an even more elaborate regimen of personal and small group piety. An intense schedule of daily prayer and meditation, the regular review of one's behavior at the end of the day, journal keeping to monitor one's behavior and growth in grace, personal and group covenants pledging virtuous behavior, and participation in conventicles and Bible study groups with like-minded souls were just some of the habits of "daily walking" these churchmen advocated. Initially at least, all of these activities were framed within the experimental predestinarian theology characteristic of this circle of English divines, so that believers who took part in this activity organized much of their effort to discerning within themselves the marks of their election and to keeping alive their confidence that they possessed saving grace. From England, many of these practices and much of this style of piety spread to other Reformed churches, but it did not everywhere come to characterize Reformed piety. Where embraced, these practices shaped the outlook and psychological experience of believers with a force revealed through hundreds of diaries and autobiographies.

Just how thorough and widespread were the transformations of lived religious culture effected by the Reformed churches?

PATTERNS OF COLLECTIVE WORSHIP

A remarkably vivid picture of the liturgical changes introduced by the Reformed and how contemporary Catholics perceived these is provided by a satire published in France in 1556, just as its first Reformed churches were taking shape: *The Parisian Passwind Answering the Roman Pasquino, On the Life of Those who Have Moved to Geneva, and Claim to Live According to the Reformation of the Gospel.* Beza created the figure of Passwind, a messenger recently returned from Geneva, in an anti-Catholic polemic of 1553. The anonymously published *Parisian Passwind* replies by having the character retail all of the most slanderous gossip available about the leaders of the

Genevan and Lausanne churches and the women he identifies as their whores and mistresses, while interspersing details of the unedifying worship and customs of these "Lutherans." Although hostile, the details about Reformed worship clearly draw on firsthand observation of the church practices of the region. Because certain details suggest those of the Pays de Vaud rather than Geneva, the dialogue is generally attributed to Anthoine Cathelan, a French Franciscan known to have spent seven months in Lausanne.[2]

"Pray tell me about the state of their churches, and how they govern themselves within them," Pasquino asks. Passwind gladly complies:

> It is just like being inside a school. There are benches everywhere, and a pulpit in the middle for the preacher. Before it are low benches for women and small children; and around them are higher ones to seat the men, with no difference of status. The stained glass windows are just about all knocked out, and the plaster dust is up to the ankles.

Do they pray there, Pasquino asks. If so, how?

> As soon as they enter the church, each one takes care to choose a spot to sit as in a school, and they wait for the preacher to come into the pulpit. As soon as the preacher appears, they all get on their knees except for him, who stands while he prays, his head uncovered and his hands joined, and he makes up a prayer from his imagination, which he ends with the Lord's Prayer and without the *Ave Maria,* all in French, and the people reply softly: So be it. And twice a week (only in the cities) before the sermon they sing a psalm or a part of one all together, men, women, maidens and children, all seated. And if any one makes a prayer on entering the church, he is pointed to and scoffed at, and held to be a Papist and idolator. Likewise if he is accused of owning a book of hours or a rosary, or has images in his house, or rests on holidays, he is immediately called before the consistory for punishment.[3]

Further along in the work, Passwind offers an account of their communion services:

> Three or four times a year, according to the will of the authorities, two tables are set up in the church, each covered with a tablecloth, and a lot of hosts are set on the left, and three or four cups or glasses on the right, with lots of pots full of either white or red wine below the table. And after the sermon the preacher comes down from the pulpit and goes to the end of the table on the side where the hosts are, and with his head uncovered and standing places a piece in each person's hand, saying "Remember that Jesus Christ died for you." Each person eats his piece while walking to

the other end of the table, where he takes something to drink from one of the Lords, or another person deputized for this task, without saying anything, while sergeants with their heads uncovered pour the wine and provide additional hosts if they run out. Throughout all of this, somebody else reads from the pulpit in the vernacular with his head uncovered the gospel of Saint John, from the beginning of the thirteenth chapter, until everyone has taken their piece, both men and women, each one at their different table . . . and after this collation is done they all go dine.

Pasquino: Since you say they take this collation and then go dine, . . . I'd like to know if they fast out of any reverence for the event.

Passwind: You are much more scrupulous and imaginative than they are! Once I asked one if such a *cène* was done while fasting, and he told me rudely that Jesus Christ had done his *cène* with his apostles after supping."[4]

Passwind also describes baptisms, marriages, and funerals. The simplicity of baptisms amazed him:

After the sermon, the preacher or deacon . . . recites four or five prayers written by Calvin or others. . . . And even though there may be several children, they only say "I baptize you" once, and then throw water with their bare hands onto the face of the children, whom they have taken from the hands of the midwife. They only have one godfather or godmother in their baptisms who carries the infant at the front of the line, and then comes the midwife carrying a basin of water and a towel so that the preacher or deacon can dry his hands. Then the men and women follow behind, one of each for each child, side by side, as if only one man or one woman could be a godparent, which shows clearly their foolishness and ignorance concerning this institution. And what is worse, they don't care if their infants die without being baptized, which declares quite simply how they stand with regard to the foundation of our entire Christian Religion. . . . The Lutherans call their children and daughters after the names of the holy personages who lived before Jesus Christ, in order to destroy by any means the memory of the saints canonized after our lord Jesus Christ whom the holy mother Church commemorates. Some they call Abraham or David or Jacob or Daniel or Isaiah; the others Samuel, Nepthalim, Judith, or Esther or Rebecca or some other name.[5]

His description of their marriages offers keen details about regional wedding rituals:

Those who want to do the will of Calvin, the great Satrap of Geneva, do as follows. The groom and his party, all carrying bouquets or rosemary branches, go to find the bride and her party who are waiting at her lodging. She is dressed as they do there, that is to say with her head covered if she is a widow and with her hair down if she is a maiden, and is wearing a hat of flowers whether she is a widow or a maiden, while the women in her party each have a bouquet in their hand or on their breast. Then they all go to the sermon, the men in front two by two, then the groom leading his bride by the hand for fear of losing her, then the women behind two by two, and in this formation they go as far as the door of the church (which they call the temple), and there they all take their places and wait for the preacher to start. After the sermon, the groom takes the bride by her hand again and they proceed to the door of the choir or the steps where the high altar used to be, and there the deacon or the minister in his absence joins them by a ceremony as long or longer than ours, his head uncovered and facing the people, emphasizing that he only does so to ratify in the presence of the church the promise they had already among themselves. Then they all return to the groom's house in the same order, and after dinner everyone retires so that the married couple can chat about their private matters. . . . Those who don't care too much for Calvin and his fellows do the same and also go to and return from the church with a Swiss tambourine or another instrument, and after dinner they dance or play in their chambers in great secrecy on pain of being called before the Consistory.[6]

Most dismaying of all in Passwind's eyes were the funerals:

Now you are asking me about the most pitiable behavior in all human nature, for as soon as the man or woman dies, those of the household dress the body if they wish, then notify their relatives and neighbors to accompany them, and those who have the job of ringing the church bells (which are only rung for sermons) and digging graves and carrying the dead, two of them carry the dead person on their shoulder as we carry reliquaries in processions, the bodies covered with cloth or linen, then the men follow two by two, and then the women likewise, some laughing, some crying, and thus they go to throw the body into the grave without saying anything or making any more ceremony than for a dog or a horse.[7]

Every Reformed church would not have followed exactly these rituals, nor would most theologians have insisted upon strict uniformity of practice among all truly reformed churches, even if the persistence of an unusually large number of pre-Reformation rituals in England and Hungary stoked in reaction some in those lands to carry the generalized Reformed horror of idolatry to such a fever pitch that the separatist John Canne could describe the sign of the cross made over an infant during baptism as "the mark of the beast,

a juggler's gesture, a magical instrument, a rite and badge of the devil, a har-
lot which stirreth up to popish lust."[8] In 1571, Beza received a letter from an
unknown location with three questions: (1) During communion did the bread
have to be taken from the pastor by hand, or could the minister place it directly into the communicant's mouth? (2) Should baptism involve aspersion
or immersion of the infant? and (3) Is the breaking of the communion bread
necessary? He replied that breaking the bread, placing it in the communicant's hand, and immersing children in the baptismal water were the original
and preferred practices, but that none of these were matters over which to
destroy fraternity.[9] Whether the churches purged worship of extrabiblical elements as exhaustively as the Genevans and Scots or whether they retained
such features as kneeling for communion, the use of altars for the eucharistic
ritual, and funereal prayers, as the English and Hungarians initially did, the
establishment of Reformed worship marked a striking break from prior practice.

One of the ways in which the Reformed churches broke the pattern of late
medieval worship most profoundly was in the calendar of worship. Before the
Reformation, the forty to sixty holy days observed by the church made each
year a cycle of remembrance of the life and passion of Christ, the Virgin,
and the saints. The recurring alternation of times of feast and times of fast
was one of the most basic rhythms of life. Most Reformed churches rejected
the observance of all special days for worship other than Sundays, or else retained only the most central Christian holidays. Geneva and Scotland had no
holidays at all. Zurich, Bern, the Palatinate, the Netherlands, and the French
Reformed churches observed Christmas, Easter, Ascension, and Pentecost.
The Netherlands and the Palatinate added New Year's Day. As noted, here the
English church's retention of many pre-Reformation customs—it preserved
no fewer than twenty-seven holy days—sparked exceptional rigorism among
those who came to oppose such liberality. That rigorism bred the strict English sabbatarian opposition to all holidays other than Sundays that spread to
the Netherlands in the early seventeenth century. Battles over the observation
of such holidays as Christmas recurred intermittently in the Dutch church.
When Christmas observance was suspended for a while in various communities like Utrecht, libels denounced "the Jewish church" that would drive out
Christ and his birthday. Whether a Reformed church recognized a few holy
days or none at all, the shift to a far more regular rhythm of days of work
and days of devotion amounted to a dramatic regularization of the weekly and
yearly cycle. In many areas, people remained deeply attached to Christmas
rituals. Popular pressure in Geneva even prompted recurrent initiatives during the seventeenth century by its Small Council to revive the celebration of
Christmas; these finally overrode the opposition of the Company of Pastors

and restored the holiday in 1694. The elimination of most holidays, however, prompted little apparent resistance.[10]

The suspension of dietary rules prohibiting the consumption of meat during Lent and on certain days of the week in every Reformed church but Scotland's transformed another basic rhythm of life. The removal of calendrical dietary restrictions did not entirely do away with fasting in the Reformed churches, however. Fasting was central to the exceptional days of prayer and worship held when extraordinary calamities betokened the need to implore God to divert his wrath. These extraordinary occasions, together with the regular communions and the time of preparation that preceded them became the great moments of intensified devotion within a church calendar that otherwise followed a steady rhythm.[11]

The regular exercises of Reformed worship revolved around the Sunday service, which was built around the exposition of the word. The service described by Passwind was typical of most Reformed churches. The singing of hymns other than the psalms set to music was practiced in some of the churches of Germanophone Switzerland in the first generation of the Reformation, but Calvin saw the psalms as the supremely appropriate expression of faith. Once the metrical translation of Marot and Beza was translated into German by Ambrosius Lobwasser of Koenigsberg in 1573, they also became the exclusive church songs of the Germanophone Reformed, as they were of virtually every other Reformed church. Only in Hungary did hymns other than the psalms comprise a regular part of Sunday worship prior, until many churches reintroduced original hymns early in the early eighteenth century.[12] But the sermon was the undoubted focus of each Sunday's assembly. Ministers typically proceeded systematically through a book of the Bible of their choice, although the sequence might be interrupted for special occasions. Even though French ministers regularly turned over an hourglass as they began to remind themselves to keep their sermons to a reasonable length, one student of French preaching has estimated that the average sermon lasted for an hour and twenty minutes. It would be rash to assert that the behavior of every Reformed congregation conformed to Daniel Defoe's report from Scotland in 1707 that "in a whole church full of people, not one shall be seen without a Bible . . . [and] if you shut your eyes when the minister names any text of Scripture, you shall hear a little rustling noise over the whole place, made by turning the leaves of the Bible." Dutch paintings of sermons in progress typically show only a few listeners with Bibles open before them. But it was not only in circles of the English godly that the most pious members of the congregation knew they would have to review and discuss the sermon at home afterward; as a boy, the minister's son Jacques Merlin had to give his parents an explanation of the sermons he heard in Paris and Geneva in the 1560s and

1570s.[13] It was not for nothing that French Protestants spoke of going to the *prêche* on Sundays.

Passwind described the worshipers he had observed as arranging themselves on benches amid plaster dust "with no difference of status" as if in a school. Where the Reformed faith became the established religion and was able to take over the existing churches, they indeed not only stripped them of their images and altars and removed most stained glass but reorganized the interior space. In the larger former cathedrals and churches, benches were clustered around the pulpit in the nave, while the former choir was used for baptisms, marriages, and the Eucharist. New churches were designed like lecture halls or auditoria; experiments were made with Greek cross, square, octagonal, and round shapes to permit as many people as possible to sit within earshot of the pulpit, and balconies were often added to pack in still more. In place of the altarpieces and statues that ornamented Catholic churches in profusion, painted boards with the Ten Commandments and other biblical passages were the only decoration allowed in most Reformed temples, although funerary monuments to leading church members or great champions of the cause found their way back in to some churches as well, despite criticism from rigorist preachers.[14] This introduction of monuments to leading church members was just one sign of the deference to figures of prominence that crept into many churches. Even though church bodies fought to defend the principle that there should be no distinctions among brothers in faith about where they might sit in church, the best pews soon began to be reserved for groups within the congregation or put up for sale to the highest bidder in a number of areas, including Geneva, the Pays de Vaud, and many French and English churches. Status-driven conflicts soon followed. In Nîmes, the theology students who opened the services with readings from the Bible went on strike after the reservation of special benches for noblemen, lawyers, doctors, and bourgeois left them too far from the pulpit.[15] Once again, the church's aspiration to be a space of equality in a hierarchical society had to accommodate itself to the prevailing power relations. A desire for seemliness made the separation of the sexes a standard part of seating patterns from early on. This may be observed in Geneva, many French churches, and, to judge by paintings of Dutch church interiors during service time, the Netherlands.[16]

Evidence about the assiduousness of attendance at Sunday services is spotty. Wherever the Reformed faith was the state church and even in some situations of religious pluralism, attendance might be required by law. The requirement of weekly attendance at lengthy sermons at first met resistance in many places. Absenteeism was a major problem in both the county of Neuchâtel and the Palatinate in the second half of the sixteenth century. In the Palatinate, pastors complained that those who did turn up for the sermon

16. The Nieuwe Zijds Chapel of Amsterdam during Services. This painting of ca. 1660 attributed to Johannes Coesermans shows how the Reformed rearranged formerly Catholic church buildings to accommodate their services. Prior to the Reformation the Nieuwe Zijds Chapel was a celebrated pilgrimage chapel built on the spot of the great eucharistic miracle of 1345, when a consecrated host came through a fire unscathed. "Purified" in 1578 when Amsterdam cast its lot with the revolt against Spain, the chapel was put to a variety of uses before being turned over in 1620 to the Reformed congregation established for the many German immigrants in the rapidly growing city. The minister preaches from the pulpit on the right. Two church wardens sit in the pew of honor at the base of the central pillar, their Bibles open before them. An open Bible also rests on the ledge at the bottom of the painting. (Rijksmuseum Het Catharijneconvent, Utrecht)

17. Interior View of the Reformed Temple at Charenton. Located two leagues outside Paris, the temple of Charenton served the important Huguenot community that grew up during the early seventeenth century in the capital. This 1648 watercolor by an unknown artist shows the interior of the second church building, designed by Salomon de Brosse after a Catholic crowd burned the previous temple to the ground in 1621. The rectangular arrangement is one of the most common ones for newly constructed Reformed churches. The elevated pulpit stands toward one end of the building. Two balconies run around all four sides of the building. High above the pulpit is a board with the Ten Commandments. (Det Kongelige Bibliotek, Copenhagen, Thott 434, 8o, p. 133.)

too often read *Till Eulenspiegel*, laughed, or munched on nuts and tossed the shells from the balcony onto those sitting below. Visitations hint that the crowds at the main Sunday services grew larger and more respectful with time. In Zweibrücken in 1608–09, attendance at the main Sunday services was judged to be good in sixty-five parishes, acceptable in nine, and inadequate in fourteen. By the late seventeenth century, high rates of attendance seem to have been the norm in Scotland, and kirk sessions strove for perfect attendance. Records of the searches for absentees made by the elders of one parish show the already small number of forty-four truants in the 1690s, but four decades later the number was just five, and a growing number of these cases mention that neighbors were "given offense" by those who worked on Sunday.[17]

For the voluntary churches, church attendance can be gauged only on the basis of private diaries that note the diarist's daily activities. David Beck, a schoolmaster in The Hague, faithfully attended both the regular Sunday morning sermon and the afternoon sermon on the Heidelberg Catechism for most of 1624 until child care obligations cut into his attendance during the last four months of the year. He also attended 26 sermons on 19 midweek days, including 3 on Christmas. In all, he heard a total of 112 sermons that year. Marguerite Mercier made the trip from Paris to Charenton approximately three Sundays each month and often attended the Thursday *prêche* and special sermons of preparation for communion as well. By contrast, Paul de Vendée, sieur de Vendée and Bois-Chapeleau, recorded that he attended services 17 times in 1617 and 20 in 1618.[18]

In addition to the main Sunday morning worship service, most churches had an afternoon sermon or catechism class and one or more weekday sermons. Despite ordinances in Geneva in 1546 and Neuchâtel in 1554 that demanded at least one member of every family attend these weekday sermons, attendance fell far below Sunday levels, as the diaries of Beck and Mercier intimate. As a result, midweek services tended to become less frequent over time. In Bernese territory, the original Reformation mandate of 1528 called for three weekly sermons. A law of 1587 ordered two. In 1748 an ordinance mandated just one.[19]

Communion practices varied. The service Zwingli created in Zurich instructed communicants to sit in groups around the communion table and alternated the reading of the relevant biblical texts with antiphonal prayers and the recitation of the Apostle's Creed, prior to the distribution of the bread and wine. This became the model for the rest of Allemanic Switzerland as well, although communion was received standing by congregants who filed past the communion table in Bern. Passwind's description offers a fair description of the ritual Calvin developed in Geneva, which largely displaced the Zwinglian ritual in the Pays de Vaud, although he failed to note that the distribution of the elements was preceded by a brief prayer and an admonition to communicants to examine themselves carefully to ensure they partake worthily. This form of service also became the rule in the French Reformed churches and heavily influenced the Palatine communion service, which in turn was the model for most other Reformed territories in Germany. In East Friesland, John a Lasco instituted still another form of simple communion service, performed seated around a table, that became the model for the service in Scotland, the Netherlands, and some nearby German churches. The Polish general synod of 1578 specified that churches could have communicants receive the elements either standing or kneeling but prohibited seated communions despite their prevalence in other Reformed churches, as these were associated with the anti-Trinitarians and were said to offend the simple. Then there were the half-reformed liturgies of the Thirty-Nine Articles and the Hungarian churches. The articles retained kneeling reception and special vestments; the Hungarians, altars and the elevation of the host. The separation of men and women, whether at two tables or by having the women take communion after the men, was enforced in France, too, but it is unclear if it was the norm.[20]

Only professing believers could be admitted to communion. In practice, this meant that young people were not admitted until they could either show mastery of the catechism, which was required in Geneva and the Pays de Vaud, or recite such basic texts as the Apostle's Creed, the Lord's Prayer, and the Ten Commandments, the practice in Scotland and certain French churches. Of course, those under sentence of suspension from communion were excluded, and Paul's exhortation in I Corinthians 11 that believers examine themselves to ensure they are worthy of participating lest they profane the body and blood of the Lord was integrated into many churches' services of preparation for communion. In the Palatinate and the Pays de Vaud, weddings were forbidden in the weeks just before or around each quarterly communion, these being understood as solemn periods of preparation and self-examination. The genre of manuals of preparation for communion often included increasingly detailed schemas of the self-examination required. The need for intensive self-examination, careful preparation for communion, and even on occasion some form of confession was nonetheless far more strongly emphasized in Lutheran liturgies than in the average Reformed one. As Beza admitted to a Silesian correspondent in 1573, nothing could be done about hypocrites who presented themselves even though unworthy.[21] The Congregationalists took a long step beyond all previous Reformed churches when they began to require evidence of saving faith for admission to communion.

Although Calvin had hoped to institute weekly communion, this was too dramatic a departure from the prevailing late medieval custom of a single annual communion, and the Genevan Council authorized quarterly communions. Communion three or four times a year became the norm in most other continental Reformed churches as well, although the sacrament was celebrated monthly in Basel, Nassau-Dillenberg, and among English and New England Congregationalists, and six times yearly in Hungary and certain Dutch cities. At the other extreme, most Scottish parishes celebrated the Eucharist only once or twice a year, and ministers could postpone the ceremony if they judged their parish unworthy, so that it was not uncommon for five or ten years to elapse between communions—this notwithstanding the provisions of the First Book of Discipline, reiterated by a law of 1616, that called for quarterly communions in the burghs and biannual services in rural areas. Practice varied within the Church of England, as some cities and market towns had monthly communion in the late seventeenth century, the largest number of churches celebrated the Lord's Supper three or four times a year, and another sizable minority held only one or two communion services each year.[22]

Scattered data for France, the Netherlands, and the Pays de Vaud suggest that nearly all eligible believers attended the Lord's Supper each time it was celebrated in these churches. Participation in the single annual celebration of the Lord's Supper in the Angus village of Monifieth between 1576 and 1584 likewise seems to have been nearly universal. By contrast, a sizable minority of the population avoided communion altogether in villages of the Palatinate in the late sixteenth century, and many more people partook only once or twice each year. Movement toward more frequent communion between 1555 and 1618 was slow. In about ten English parishes for which evidence is available from different points between 1570 and the late seventeenth century, the percentage of those who did their Easter duty ranged from 38 to nearly 100 percent of those old enough to be eligible, but only a small minority took communion on every occasion it was offered. In Trelech, Wales, 150 people turned out for communion on Easter, but scarcely 30 at Christmas and Whitsun.[23] In those regions in which attendance was less than universal, women were always more numerous at the communion table than men. The sociological breakdown of those reprimanded in the Bernese countryside for failure to take communion offers no clues that the absentees were concentrated among specific wealth or status groups. The reasons offered the church authorities for missing communion ranged from the theologically acceptable ones that the absentee felt unworthy or was at odds with another member of the congregation and thus could not commune in genuine fellowship, to less appreciated excuses like they "forgot the time," were in "want of cloathes," or did not believe that communion had ever made anybody better. For the pious who attended the Lord's Supper faithfully, the ritual often became another high point of the devotional year approached in intensity only by the irregular fast days.[24]

Perhaps in part because of their infrequency, Scotland's eucharistic celebrations became charged with special emotion at times when the church was felt to be in peril in the seventeenth century. Following the introduction of the Perth articles in 1618, many of those troubled by the new rituals began to travel long distances "to seek the Communion where it was ministered in puritie." In the southwest of Scotland and in the Scottish settlements in Ulster, the communion assemblies grew into three-day gatherings marked by fiery warnings of damnation for sinners who communicated unworthily and urgent calls to experience a new birth in Christ. Robert Glendinning's sermons so moved the population around Antrim that one eyewitness reported many were "stricken, and swoon with the Word—yea, a dozen in one day carried out of doors as dead, so marvellous was the power of God smiting their hearts for sin, condemning and killing." Such "extasies and enthusiasms" prompted official disapproval, but neither episcopal condemnations nor the decision of the General Assembly in 1645 that no more than three parishes could join for a single communion and only one sermon of preparation could precede the Lord's Supper stopped these communion fairs. They were especially numerous and enthusiastic among the extreme Covenanters in the 1650s. Kept under control after the Restoration, they burst forth again after the Presbyterian triumph of 1689 on a surge of nostalgia for the fervent emotion of the earlier gatherings and became a regular, if still controversial, part of Scottish worship. Critics deplored them in terms strikingly similar to the earlier literature of condemnation of pilgrimages as opportunities for the all too profane pleasures that resulted when young men and women went off on journeys together, and as occasions for a "flash of devotion" and contrition that impeded rather than promoted lasting sanctification. They nonetheless became a highly emotional focus of devotional experience for many; Scottish spiritual diaries of the years 1680–1720 abound in recollections of the bliss of these communions. Recent historians have convincingly identified these Scottish communion fairs as the direct ancestor of later evangelical revivalism.[25]

One of the features of Reformed belief that most shocked Passwind was its rejection of the idea that baptism was essential for salvation, a point of view that indeed sharply challenged widespread pre-Reformation practices and beliefs. In much of the Continent before the Reformation, Catholic teaching on this point generated such dread about unbaptized infants being condemned to hell or limbo that parents typically sought to have their newborns baptized within forty-eight hours of birth and expected midwives to baptize babies who appeared to be in imminent danger of death, as the church authorized them to do. Cults formed around saints believed to have the power to revive stillborn babies long enough for them to receive a valid baptism. Most Reformed baptismal rituals conformed to the simple ceremony described by Passwind "in the face of the congregation," although both the Bernese church and the English Book of Common Prayer preserved the use of baptismal fonts; the latter had the further feature of instructing the pastor to make the sign of the cross on the baby's forehead while proclaiming his or her reception into the church, which aroused the hackles of such partisans of a purer church as John Canne. While the great majority of Reformed theologians insisted on restricting baptisms to the hours of worship to emphasize that anxiety about infants dying without the sacrament was misplaced and to indicate that the ritual was above all a sign of incorporation into the church and a seal of Christ's promise of salvation, certain Reformed churches were willing to countenance special baptisms of necessity at other times when the newborn was dangerously ill.[26] In the churches where this was forbidden, ministers were occasionally cursed for their refusal to perform such baptisms in the first generation after the Reformation, while consistories had to administer a number of reprimands to church members who had had midwives or Catholic clergymen baptize their dying babies. In one Scottish case, the father of an illegitimate child whose mother had died begged that baptism be performed at once, as no woman would nurse an unbaptized child. While some believers of subsequent generations continued to worry about their children dying without baptism—early in the twentieth century some inhabitants of remote areas of the Scottish Lowlands still believed that unbaptized children would return to haunt their parents, folklorists have reported—most church members, after several generations, seem to have accepted the Reformed understanding of baptism without great qualms. Parish registers show that the average time parents were willing to wait before having their infants baptized lengthened over the generations following the Reformation, while a growing percentage of babies were allowed to die unbaptized.[27] As noted, the elimination of the formula of exorcism from baptism seems only to have generated debate and resistance in late sixteenth-century Germany (see chapter 7).

Geneva's law specifying the kinds of names that could be bestowed on children appears to have had no counterpart in statute elsewhere in Reformed Europe, but other churches and churchmen spoke on the question. The discipline of the French churches led parents to choose names for their offspring from the Bible and forbade pagan names and those like Ange and Baptiste that indicated a status beyond the condition of ordinary mortals. Some English and Dutch churchmen, too, opposed unbiblical and "vaine or idle names." A few English parish ministers even repeated the action that had caused such controversy in Geneva during Calvin's lifetime, refusing to heed the requests

TABLE 15.1
Naming Patterns in France and the Swiss Borderlands, 1500–1700

		Old Testament Names (%)	Saints' Names (%)
Geneva	pre-Reformation	2	32
	1560–70	33	2
	1607–17	21	14
	1650	18	
	1700	16	
Neuchâtel	1590–1600	33	14
Lausanne	1572–80	21	20
Avenches	1570–85	13	34
Commugny	1573–85	5	22
Rouen	1565	50	0
	1576–85	36	0
La Rochelle	1563–65	36	0
	1579–80	20	1
Orléanais-Berry	1591–1620	39	
	1621–50	39	
	1651–82	30	
Saumur	1593–1620	22	
	1651–84	16	

Sources: Willy Richard, *Untersuchungen zur Genesis der reformierten Kirchenterminologie der Westschweiz und Frankreichs* (Bern, 1959), 202, 205, 217–26; Laplanche, *L'Ecriture, le sacré et l'historie,* 709–10; Benedict, *Rouen,* 105–6, 149–50; Gueneau, "Protestants du Centre," 275; Philippe Chareyre, "Les protestants de Saumur au XVIIe siècle, religion et société," in *Saumur, capitale européenne du protestantisme au XVIIe siècle* (Fontévraud, 1991), 38–39.

of parents or godparents who sought to bestow nonbiblical names on their children.[28]

The degree to which members of the Reformed churches departed from the preexisting repertoire of names hallowed by family and community tradition in order to follow these prescriptions offers an interesting measure of their willingness to adopt a new Reformed identity. Fully a third of families in Geneva in the 1560s and in Neuchâtel in the 1590s gave their children Old Testament names with scant prior currency in the region. The percentage of parents who did so declined steadily in the Pays de Vaud as one moved from the chief town of Lausanne to the smaller one of Avenches and finally to the village of Commugny, a sign of the less enthusiastic embrace of the movement in the countryside than in the city (table 15.1). A still higher percentage of the

voluntary members of the French churches announced their break with tradition by choosing Old Testament names in the first years of those churches'
existence. Here, as in Geneva, however, the percentage of such names declined over time, indicating a reversion to tradition—and perhaps too in
France an unwillingness to impose so high a profile and dangerous an identity on their children. A highly distinctive pattern of names expressing thanks
for divine gifts or exhorting the namesake to virtue (for example, Increase
Mather, Praise-God Barbon) emerged between 1580 and 1600 among those
linked to the presbyterian movement in Northamptonshire and East Sussex,
from whence it migrated to New England, where it flourished.[29] In adopting
such distinctive names, the godly were announcing their separation from the
mass of carnal Christians around them.

One aspect of the regularization of time promoted by the Reformed
churches was the elimination of the prohibition of weddings during Lent and
Advent, although here once again the English church was a case apart: the
closed periods for marriages were never formally suppressed except from 1645
to 1660. In Geneva, France, the Netherlands, and New England, the Reformed
quickly abandoned the old church-determined patterns of marriage seasonality with little evidence of any lingering attachment that would suggest it was
a deeply rooted custom. Strikingly, the Huguenots in southern France soon
began instead to avoid marrying in May, as did their Catholic neighbors in
the same period, while in the Netherlands marriages clustered in the same
month. In southern France, May marriages were believed to produce barren
families; in the Netherlands they were seen as lucky. The Reformed elimination of Catholic calendrical prohibitions apparently did not promote a consistent scepticism about beliefs concerning propitious and unpropitious times.
In Scotland, the one Reformed region in which Lent survived the Reformation
as a season to abstain from meat, marriage remained rare during Lent until
1640, after which respect for the old prohibition largely disappeared.[30]

In addition to the lack of worry about whether or not sickly infants were
baptized before they died, the feature of Reformed worship that most troubled
Passwind was the absence of graveside ceremony and prayers from the dead.
The breathtaking restraint exercised in this domain was among the most radical of all breaks with pre-Reformation religious practice, for it meant an end
to the economy of prayer for remembered relatives and spiritual kin and to
the community between the living and the dead that were among the most
prominent features of the late medieval spiritual landscape. As the wording of
the section on funerals in Scotland's First Book of Discipline specifies, it was
precisely the rejection of the theological principles underlying prayers for the
dead and the concern to eliminate any purchase for lingering respect for the
value of prayers for the dead that dictated the simplicity of Reformed funerals:

For avoiding of all inconveniences we judge it best, that neither singing nor reading be at buriall. For albeit things sung and read may admonish some of the living to prepare themselves for death, yet shall some superstitious think that singing and reading of the living may profite the dead. And therefore we think it most expedient that the dead be conveyed to the place of buriall with some honest company of the kirk, without either singing or reading; yea without all kind of ceremony heretofore used, other than that the dead be committed to the grave, with such gravity and sobriety, as those that be present may seeme to feare the judgements of God, and to hate sinne which is the cause of death.[31]

Reformed manuals on how to prepare for death replaced the pre-Reformation emphasis on the deathbed struggle that the dying person had to fight against despair and the devil's temptations, largely through sacramental means, with an emphasis on consoling both the dying person and those gathered around the deathbed by remarking how those with faith would vanquish death. Attention was thus diverted from the moment of death toward the individual's earlier pilgrimage to faith. Believers were reassured that even if they uttered some horrible blasphemy in a final moment of pain or delirium, those who had lived their lives according to God's word would reach heaven. Edifying accounts of the dying hours of prominent ministers depicted these models of piety voicing their assurance that they were being draped with Christ's glory and swept up to paradise, thereby offering a final consolation to those gathered around the deathbed that was also an ultimate act of service to and glorification of God.[32]

So sharp a break with previous practices was not always easy to implement, for if the Reformed did not demand the full panoply of Catholic ceremonies, it was difficult to forego all ceremony and commemoration of the deceased. In lieu of a graveside prayer or church sermon, some Huguenot pastors offered "remonstrances" outside the house of the deceased as the body was being transported to the cemetery. Synods permitted this custom to continue. Synods and consistories were more disapproving of the ringing of church bells during a funeral cortege, of large retinues or paid mourners accompanying the funeral procession, and of ornate tombstones to commemorate the deceased. The censure of these practices, however, reveals continuing attachment to them as well. Strikingly, a persisting desire to commission masses for souls in purgatory has been detected in only one upland corner of a region in which resistance to a state-imposed Reformed reformation was quite strong, the Aspe valley of Béarn. Precisely because the value of prayers and masses for the dead ranked among the most fundamental theological issues in dispute in the Reformation—and perhaps also because the Catholic church's

507

sale of such prayers was often resented—their abandonment seems to have troubled Reformed church members less than it did Catholic observers like Passwind.[33] Rejecting prayers for souls in purgatory was a central part of what the Reformation was about.

If practice thus occasionally lagged behind prescription, and if regional variations affected both the extent of Reformed liturgical transformation and the extent to which they were accepted by the population at large, in the final analysis it is difficult to avoid the impression that the bulk of the truly dramatic changes in organized worship decreed by the Reformed churches were ultimately accepted by virtually all church members with surprisingly little fuss. To be sure, most members of the English and German state churches continued to content themselves with a single annual communion. Some popular pre-Reformation practices endured. New rituals such as the French funeral exhortations occasionally moved into the voids of the new liturgical order. It remained impossible to turn out more than a fraction of the population for midweek sermons. The number of truly ardent early converts was greater in the cities than in the countryside and in the voluntary churches than in those established by act of state. Still, the recalcitrance that initially greeted certain new rituals dissipated with time. More striking yet is the near-complete absence of resistance to many of the changes that struck most directly at key devotional practices of the pre-Reformation church. Near universal participation in the Lord's Supper each time it was celebrated became the norm among full members of the French, Dutch, and Swiss Reformed churches. In Scotland a distinctive, highly emotional style of occasional, strongly revivalistic communions took shape; this would exercise great influence in the later history of Protestant religiosity. If it be objected that the enthusiasm for certain distinctive marks of Reformed identity declined with time and that what is being observed here is simply the triumph of conformism, it may be replied that conformity provides much of the shape of most people's religious lives. Even for those who simply conformed, membership in a Reformed church brought a dramatic shift in the experience of the collective rituals of worship. A sober concentration on psalm singing and the preaching of the word replaced the ornate rituals of the Mass and the elaborate panoply of paraliturgical rituals characteristic of late medieval Catholicism. A radically simplified calendar of worship (except in Scotland) flattened and regularized the shape of time, making communion times and irregular fast days in moments of peril stand out as the new high points of pious concentration. That the regularization of the calendar of worship did not breed consistent scepticism about all beliefs concerning fortunate and unfortunate times underscores that religious experience remained just one compartment of behavior and that the changes wrought by the Reformation did not bring about a consistent remolding of every facet of consciousness.

FAMILY DEVOTIONS, BIBLE READING, AND CATECHISM

If Sunday and midweek worship services were occasions for Reformed church members to hear biblical wisdom imparted by their pastors and to express their faith in the sober rituals of their churches, churchmen saw Sunday worship as just one part of of the devotional life of the conscientious Christian. The household should be a second place of worship, and the family a little church, devotional writers repeated time and again. They consequently advocated the regular reading of the Bible and devotional books in the home, for, as Samuel Ward wrote in 1621, while sermons are "as showers of rain that water for the instant, books are as snow that lies longer on the earth."[34]

Mastery of the principal prayers, knowledge of the catechism, and a basic ability to read were the fundamental preconditions for family worship. Admission to communion, we have seen, came to be tied to the ability to make a simple profession of faith that consisted of demonstrating an adequate knowledge of either the catechism or certain prayers and texts of the church. The establishment of Reformed churches was quickly followed by catechetical education, both in church and in primary schools, and elementary instruction in reading and writing. Leo Jud's first Zurich catechism of 1534 initiated a long line of Reformed catechisms, among which those of Calvin and the Heidelberg Catechism attained particularly widespread adoption. In many churches, Sunday afternoon services were given over to catechetical instruction. In seventeenth-century France, many congregations had not only a "particular catechism" for children each Sunday afternoon, but also a "large catechism" that was held quarterly before each communion service; all adults were expected to attend and to be prepared to answer questions to determine if they still knew their catechism. The synod of Dort went further and decreed three forms of catechizing in the Low Countries: at home, at school, and in church. More than admission to communion could depend upon demonstrating an adequate mastery of the basic points of religion. Congregations in France and Scotland made this a requirement for receiving alms. In Hesse, the Palatinate, many Swiss churches, and certain Scottish congregations, those wishing to marry first had to appear before the minister to show their command of the catechism. A Palatine measure of 1593 prohibited people from settling in any locality without adequate knowledge of the basic points of religion.[35]

Emphasis on mastery of the catechism also promoted the provision of elementary education. In Poland in 1578, the General Synod of Piotrków called upon all church patrons to set aside at least one zloty per peasant to found common schools for their instruction, an injunction repeated in 1583 with the added threat of disciplinary action against those who failed to do so. In 1628, the States of Drenthe ordered every parish to hire a schoolmaster whose qualifications were approved by the local classis to offer instruction by the end of the year. Those that failed to comply would be specially taxed for this purpose. The Scottish Parliament passed acts ordering the creation of schools in every parish in 1616, 1633, 1646, and 1696. The repetition of these measures insinuates that they did not bear immediate or universal fruit. Still, many villages ultimately came to have schools that did not have them before the Reformation. Good evidence about several regions of lowland Scotland reveals that schools existed in 29 to 57 percent of all parishes in the first third of the seventeenth century and had been created in 79 percent by 1696.[36]

When the authorities visited three primary schools run by Huguenot women in their homes in Lyon in 1679, they found the boys and girls being taught from the New Testament, the psalter of Marot, and the *Alphabet and Catechism of Geneva*. These works, the alphabet, the Bible, and the catechism, formed the ABC of Reformed education. Whereas the school ordinances of Lutheran Germany rarely ordered classroom Bible reading, preferring instead the memorization of doctrinally safe catechisms, the authorities of the Reformed parts of Hesse mandated the use of the Bible. Full editions of the Bible aimed specifically at young people were also distinctive to Reformed regions of Germany. Ample lists of the books used in church-related primary schools in the province of Utrecht have permitted one researcher to determine that the curriculum was devoted to subjects in the following proportions:

	Index value
reading	100
catechism	100
spelling	66
Bible knowledge	49
writing	10
arithmetic	5
history	4

Writing was typically taught after reading, so only those students able to spend several years in elementary schools learned this skill.[37]

Inclusion of the Bible in primary instruction was just part of a larger enterprise of boosting private Bible reading that is amply attested to in the records of the Reformed churches from their earliest years onward. Some of the first entries in Geneva's consistory registers admonished church members to buy a Bible. A Scottish law of 1579 ordered all gentlemen with an annual income of three hundred pounds and all "substantious yeomen or burgesses" worth five hundred pounds to acquire a Bible and psalmbook. Several kirk sessions and presbyteries went further and ordered all men and women who could read to acquire them. In printer-poor Poland, the provincial synod of Ozarow in 1596 simply ordered each church to obtain a Bible "where it can be had." It was expecting a good deal to require all churchgoers to possess a Bible: as late as the eighteenth century in the region of Zurich a full copy of the sacred text still cost nearly three full days' salary for a master carpenter and five for an unskilled worker. To overcome the economic barrier to widespread Bible ownership, charitable individuals and groups distributed Bibles to those too poor to afford them. In 1634, the London draper Charles Parrett made provision in his will to purchase a Bible for "every old poore cottager dwelling in the Parish of Boebrickhill in the Countrye of Buckingham . . . for their better Instruction."[38] Strauss's argument that the Reformation may not have promoted Bible reading as energetically as once thought cannot be extended from the Lutheran territories of Germany to the Reformed churches.

Alongside the promotion of Bible ownership went initiatives in many Reformed churches to foster family worship and devotion. One of the earliest decisions of the Le Mans consistory was an admonition to all heads of households to make sure prayers were said in their house morning, evening, and before and after meals. The Wesel Convent in 1568 decreed that elders should regularly visit all houses in their neighborhood to see if church members were carrying out family devotions. A similar decree in Nassau-Dillenberg added that the visitations should note whether the Bible was being read as well as prayers being said. A number of Scottish churches passed out books of "Family Exercises" to members in the 1630s and 1640s, while Geneva's pastors drew up a set of "Instructions for the people in faith and piety" around 1670 that prompted family Bible reading, psalm singing, and regular exercises of piety morning, evening, and before and after meals. Such exertions were neither universal nor consistent. Nîmes's unusually complete and well-studied run of consistory records uncovers no evidence of the furtherance of family devotions until the 1670s, when it suddenly appears. The endeavor to turn the family into a little church was nonetheless widespread.[39]

Studies have just begun to explore in a reliable statistical manner the extent to which these measures were implemented. In the generations immediately after the Reformation, the authorities were often convinced that the duty of spreading catechetical education was ignored. The Palatine law of 1593 prohibiting people from settling or marrying unless they showed mastery of five basic points of religion came after a citywide examination revealed that barely a third of Heidelberg's inhabitants could recite five points of the faith:

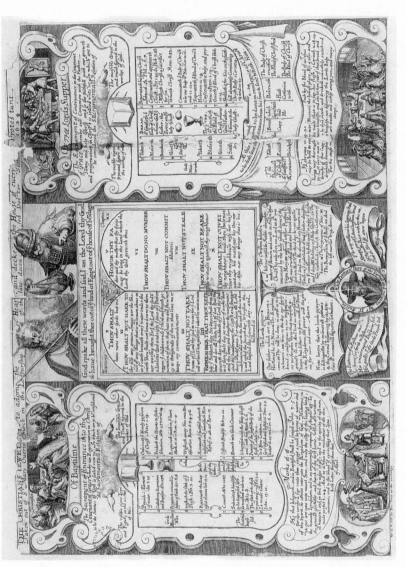

18. "The Christians Jewel to Adorne the Heart and Decke the House of Every Protestant." This 1624 English sheet for posting in the home includes the text of the Ten Commandments, the Lord's Prayer, and the Credo, as well as short explanations of the sacraments of baptism and communion. The illustrations in the bottom corners depict the sacraments being celebrated. In the top corners are the Jewish ceremonies that prefigure them, circumcision and Passover. At the center bottom is the portrait of the London lecturer Thomas Sutton with verses lauding him, reproduced as Illustration 14. (Copyright the Society of Antiquaries of London.)

TABLE 15.2

Knowledge of the Catechism in Eighty-six
Zweibrücken Villages, 1560–1609

	Percentage of Parishes in which Ecclesiastical Visitors Judge Responses		
	Good	Adequate	Inadequate
1560	24	33	43
1609	44	36	20

Source: Vogler, "Vie religieuse en pays rhenan," 799.

the Ten Commandments, the Apostle's Creed, the Lord's Prayer, and brief explanations of the meaning of the sacraments of baptism and communion. Such a poor performance amounted to "a horrible, culpable, and pagan blindness" in the eyes of the city's ministers. Church visitations in the duchy of Zweibrücken rated parishes on whether the children examined in them displayed a good, an adequate, or an inadequate knowledge of the catechism. Less than a quarter of all parishes earned a good mark in 1560, while the responses were judged inadequate in 43 percent (table 15.2). Over the ensuing fifty years, the visitors were able to detect some improvement, but even in 1609 results were less than splendid: 44 percent of all parishes earned a good rating, and 20 percent were still judged inadequate. At the end of the seventeenth century, mastery of the catechism was still decidedly spotty. In the small town of Oppenheim, 34 percent of the youths presenting themselves for communion for the first time between 1693 and 1713 had learned the entire catechism well, 54 percent had learned parts of it, and 12 percent could not answer a single question put to them about it. Girls generally seem to have learned the document better than boys. According to the notes of a Frisian minister based on his visits to the houses of his thirty-six full church members in good standing in this same period, just seven of the members had a good understanding of the catechism, nineteen had some knowledge of the faith, 5 members were "ignorant," and five simply refused to learn the catechism. Even so all were admitted to communion.[40] The requirement that church members master the catechism in order to be admitted to the Lord's Supper thus seems to have been enforced with charity, and even in 1700 thorough mastery of the catechism was the exception rather than the rule in small-town and rural congregations. The percentage of those who had mastered the catechism well was nonetheless higher than it had been in the first generation after the Reformation.

TABLE 15.3

Literacy in Canton Zurich, 1625–1749

| | Percentage of the Population Judged Able to . . . | | | |
| | . . . Read | | . . . Write | |
	Men	Women	Men	Women
1625–49	44	13		
1675–99	62	31	26	2
1725–49	72	60	33	7

Source: Marie-Louise von Wartburg-Ambühl, *Alphabetisierung und Lektüre. Untersuchung am Beispiel einer ländlichen Region im 17. und 18. Jahrhundert* (Bern, 1981), 85–86, 94.

If many villagers had only a partial grasp of the contents of the catechism, this was probably not because they were incapable of reading, but instead because the sort of rote learning demanded by catechetical instruction was not to their taste. The evidence of growing literacy and a wider diffusion of religious books among Reformed populations as the period advanced is considerable. Particularly good evidence about literacy skills comes from the rural sections of canton Zurich, where parish ministers often recorded the ability of their parishioners to read and write. This information shows an increase in both skills between the second quarter of the seventeenth century and the second quarter of the eighteenth (table 15.3). Even at this later date, a sizable minority of men and women alike could not read, and only a small number possessed the ability to write. The percentage of those who could read was yet strikingly higher than the percentages of those being given good marks for their knowledge of the catechism in the documents just cited. Furthermore, in rural households where reading aloud in groups was common, it was not necessary for every family member to be able to read for all to have access to written texts.

In other areas, historians have had to make do with that rough proxy of literacy skills, the ability to sign one's name. For Scotland, a geographically ambitious study of signature rates has shown a large change over time. In 1597, lowland parishes could still be found where the entire corps of church elders could not produce a single member able to sign a document. In the middle of the seventeenth century, roughly a quarter of the adult male population of the Lowlands could sign. By the middle of the eighteenth century this figure had risen to 65 percent.[41] Studies of signature rates in the seventeenth century in a variety of other Reformed congregations likewise disclose rising and fairly high, although varying, signature rates. Those studies that have compared the

TABLE 15.4
Signature Rates among the Reformed in Six Localities, 1600–1702 (%)

	Reformed			Catholics of same locale where known		
	Men	Women	Combined	Men	Women	Combined
Montpellier 1675	62	30		60	25	
Lubéron 1633–34			51			47
Ganges 1670–85	51	16				
Marsillargues 1668–83	42	10				
Geneva 1600–30	70	23				
1698–1702	90	45				
Amsterdam 1630	57	32				
1680	70	44				

Sources: M.-M. Compère, "Ecole et alphabétisation en Languedoc aux XVIIe et XVIIIe siècles" in F. Furet and J. Ozouf eds., *Lire et écrire. L'alphabétisation des français de Calvin à Jules Ferry,* 2 vols. (Paris, 1977), 2: 88–89; G. Audisio, "Se marier en Lubéron: Catholiques et Protestants vers 1630" in *Histoire sociale, sensibilités collectives et mentalités. Mélanges Robert Mandrou* (Paris, 1985), 128; Monter, "Women in Calvinist Geneva." 205; A. M. van der Woude, "De alfabetisering" in *Algemene Geschiedenis der Nederlanden,* 7: 262.

signature rates of Protestants and Catholics of comparable status in similar communities have found either that these were virtually identical or that the Protestants enjoyed only a slight superiority.[42]

Before concluding too rapidly that the Reformed emphasis on the word did not promote elementary education with any greater force than the contemporary Catholic program to spread primary education for catechetical purposes, it must be noted that studies of early modern literacy have recurrently shown that the ability to read but not to write was extremely widespread where devotional reading was prized. Two remarkable volumes recording the spiritual experiences of those Scots born again at the Cambuslang revival of 1743 reveal that all seventy-four of the relatively humble women whose conversion is recounted could read; only eight of them could write.[43] The Reformed stress on affording believers direct access to the text of Scripture likely produced an unusually high percentage of people who learned to read but not to write. Writing skills, on the other hand, were far more the product of economic imperatives than confessional affiliation. By the late seventeenth century, a hefty majority of Reformed believers in most areas would have been able either to read the Bible themselves or have it read to them by somebody in their family. One comparative point is meanwhile certain. The impulse to the founding of

TABLE 15.5

Book Ownership in Canton Zurich, 1625–1749

Percentage of households with	0 books	1 book	2+ books
1625–49	52	24	24
1675–99	34	11	55
1725–49	8	1	91

Source: Calculated from von Wartburg-Ambühl, *Alphabetisierung und Lektüre*, 108–14.

schools and the promotion of literacy was no greater in Reformed territories than in Lutheran ones. Certain German Lutheran territories had schools in virtually every village by 1609. Sweden achieved nearly universal adult literacy by the mid–eighteenth century.[44]

The same sources that indicate the diffusion of reading and writing skills in the Zurich countryside also show that by the last quarter of the seventeenth century, roughly two-thirds of rural households contained at least one book, usually a Bible, a psalter, a prayer book, or a popular devotional classic such as Johann Arndt's *True Christianity* or Bayly's *Practice of Piety* (table 15.5). By the middle of the eighteenth century, virtually every rural household contained at least one book; the pastor of Wiesendangen recorded that "during my visit, I found only two houses without any book; their inhabitants excused themselves by telling me they knew their prayers by heart and recited the prayers printed in the psalter. . . . Everywhere I was assured that all these useful books were read assiduously; on several occasions during my visits, parishioners even asked my advice about passages of the Bible or psalter that were unclear to them." Once again, this source is nearly unique, although an investigation made in the middle of the seventeenth century by one Scottish kirk session claimed to find no families in the parish lacking Bibles, and several English authors of the early eighteenth century reported that Bible ownership was virtually universal in Scotland—perhaps with some exaggeration, the better to shame their English compatriots into greater zeal for reading Scripture.[45] Even taking into account the fact that postmortem inventories frequently fail to record items of modest worth and thus underestimate the actual extent of book ownership, these documents suggest a somewhat different picture. They identify books—nearly always including a Bible—in roughly 70 percent of Reformed households in mid-seventeenth-century Metz, in 40 to 60 percent of households in several Massachusetts counties in the seventeenth century, in 44 to 49 percent of inventories from three Kentish cities in the 1630s, in 45 percent of inventories from Geneva around 1700, and in 34 percent of the inventories of Amiens merchants and weavers in the seventeenth century.[46] Still, these levels of book ownership exceed by far those found in Catholic populations at the same time. Whereas more than two-thirds of the inventories concerning Metz's Reformed inhabitants reveal books, books appear in just 21 to 25 percent of the inventories of the city's Catholic households. This disparity reinforces the hypothesis that a higher percentage of the Reformed were able to read but not write than was the case for the Catholics.

Anecdotal glimpses of everyday life found in court and notarial records from the seventeenth-century Netherlands flesh out the picture of widespread book ownership. These reveal lackeys taking a break from work to read the New Testament, a guildsman reviewing chapters of the Bible over breakfast, and the wife of a drunkard reading him passages from Scripture to get him to mend his ways. English diaries and spiritual autobiographies, although drawn from the ranks of the godly and thus not representative of the population as a whole, also disclose books being carefully read and circulated among people of humble status. Thomas Chubb, a chandler's assistant, was part of a group of journeymen in and around Salisbury who, armed with notes they had written on relevant scriptural passages, met regularly in the first decade of the eighteenth century to debate theological issues. Richard Baxter's autobiography tells of his upbringing in a pious freeholder's household in which the Bible was regularly read, and a poor day laborer once lent the family his battered copy of Edmund Bunny's *Book of Christian Exercise.* An index of the impregnation of life by biblical culture comes from the upland regions of the Pays de Vaud, where the facades of chalets constructed in the seventeenth century were commonly engraved with prayers and pious verses from the psalter, the Bible, and religious poetry.[47] Testimony of a deeper interiorization comes from a Poitou schoolmaster's recollections of his pious wife: "She lived in the fear and love of God, and the study of his sacred word was her greatest delectation from her childhood on. She was also well versed in the history of the martyrs, and she avidly read all of the works designed to help fortify her against death. She also gave a great deal of her time and attention to our psalms, and these were so deeply engraved in her heart, that it was not uncommon at night to hear her sing bits of them in her sleep."[48]

Some diaries offer evidence as well of regular private prayer and family devotions. The scholar Jacques Spon claimed to give over an hour each morning and evening to prayer and meditation. Sir Archibald Johnston, whose wife often read the Bible or Johann Gerhard's *Meditations* in bed, noted their regular prayers together. But these practices were in all likelihood not general. As a young man, the future Presbyterian minister George Trosse was apprenticed as a merchant and sent abroad for that purpose to France, where he lodged briefly with a pastor. "We had no *Family-Prayer* in this *Minister's* House," he recalled, "(tho' I do not know but the *Family* might pray together in their *own Chamber*)." Only once, on a Sunday, did the minister's son read a chapter of the Bible, a psalm "and some part of their *Common-Prayer*."[49] If this was the situation in a minister's household, one must assume it was common in the houses of ordinary church members.

The strong emphasis on catechesis and family Bible reading within the Reformed churches thus produced only mixed results insofar as mastery of the catechism was involved. While the marks handed out by ecclesiastical visitors rose as the generations passed, many rural church members still had a shaky knowledge of these texts at the end of the seventeenth century. Literacy skills and especially the ability to read, however, had become quite widespread by this period in most Reformed communities, and a large segment of the population would have owned a Bible or other devotional book. It's impossible to know whether in any particular family this would have served as the basis for regular family devotions, for irregular reading and prayer in church, or simply as a talisman used to protect the family against harm, as folklorists have shown the Bible to have been used across the German-speaking world in the eighteenth century.[50] Many humble church members nonetheless did acquire acquaintance with Scripture, and that the Reformed reformation promoted a new relation with the printed word characterized by the intensive reading and rereading of the Bible and devotional classics is plausible. In this domain, the Reformed differed from their Catholic neighbors, even if they were not more likely to have attained writing skills useful for their occupations. Full comparisons with Lutheranism are as yet impossible, for no good studies of book ownership in Lutheran territories have been carried out for the period before the eighteenth century, when pietistic initiatives introduced a new element into the equation.[51] It does seem clear the Reformed promoted Bible reading among the young more consistently than did the Lutherans before the rise of pietism. Reformed Protestantism was indeed a religion of the book, and one that brought religious books into many humble households by the end of the seventeenth century.

THE PURITAN MANNER OF GODLINESS

While all of the Reformed churches encouraged a devotional life of regular prayer, family exercises, and Bible reading, the English practical divines of the generation of Greenham, Rogers, and Perkins evolved a style of piety that urged upon pious believers a far more complete blueprint for daily walking. Trosse's dismay at the absence of family devotions in the household of the French minister with whom he lodged reflects the contrast between these norms and the expectations of pious behavior that prevailed elsewhere in the Reformed world. Furthermore, because the English practical divines inspired laymen who came under their auspices to keep journals and prepare testimonies of their growth in grace, exceptional documentation exists not only about the ways in which such people were supposed to live, but about their personal spiritual experiences as well. Over three hundred private journals and more than a hundred autobiographies from Puritan and Dissenting milieus survive for seventeenth-century England and New England. One pious Londoner alone, the turner Nehemiah Wallington, produced between 1618 and 1658 more than fifty volumes of private notebooks relating to his interior life.[52] The extraordinary combination of an abundant prescriptive literature and numerous surviving private diaries has in turn permitted historians of Puritan devotion to paint a vivid picture of the spiritual experiences of those whose religious lives were shaped by this style of piety.[53]

Most of the godly, no matter how inclined they were in their autobiographies to depict their early lives as ones of sin, appear to have grown up in families that were themselves accounted pious and that gave them sober, churchgoing upbringings. Their first awakening to a more serious consideration of spiritual matters often came when either a book they read or a sermon they heard convinced them that living an upright life was insufficient for salvation unless they could find clear evidences of saving faith within themselves. The traditions of preaching to conversion and promulgating lists of marks of saving faith heightened lay sensitivity to the issue of assurance. Once awakened to the need to make their election sure, many began to worry deeply they could not find in their lives the marks of election listed by the devotional treatises—hardly surprisingly in that the lists were long and often contradictory. So convinced as a young man that "God had forsaken me, and that I should never be saved" Wallington attempted suicide several times and was held back on other occasions only by the pain it would have caused his family and the discredit it would have brought to the godly community. He was hardly alone in experiencing such despair. Many diaries reveal comparable anguish. The Buckinghamshire physician Richard Napier treated no fewer than ninety-one melancholy patients who confided to him they were "doubtful of salvation."[54]

With time and dedication in the exercises of piety, most ardent professors came to attain a measure of conviction that they possessed saving faith. Frequently, they were even vouchsafed moments of rapture, such as the one Wallington experienced in 1643: "The Lord (like a tender Father or Mother) comes Softly on me, withdraws the curtain, looks on me: when I least think on Him, He wakes me and takes me to Himself in such heavenly meditations that I did see things unutterable, which broke my rocky heart that mine eyes gushed out tears to think that ever such a holy, all glorious God should any way regard such an unholy, polluted creature." These could alternate with

519

periods of renewed doubt, as devotions grew cold and old doubts crept in. At such times, another pious Londoner, John Crook, "could not perceive any amendment in my self, but the same youthful vanities drew away my mind when opportunities offered. . . . I durst not leave off my duties, for then I thought the Devil will prevail over me."[55] The desire to reinforce the stirrings of the spirit that betokened divine grace and to serve the God who granted such moments of assurance and rapture led Wallington not only to make his extraordinary array of journals, but also to rise each morning between 2 and 5 A.M. for a period of prayer before getting down to work at 6 A.M. and to attend up to nineteen sermons in a single week. It was difficult to keep from nodding off when listening to so many sermons, so Wallington took along peppercorns or cloves to bite when his head began to fog. Lady Margaret Hoby preferred another technique to make herself more attentive, always attending sermons on an empty stomach.[56] Communion and fast days stood out as high points amid the routine of Sunday and midweek worship, moments when one renewed one's covenant with God after a period of prayer and preparation; many of the godly sought communion repeatedly. Meanwhile, in order to effect an amendment of his life, Wallington wrought a set of articles to live by that he extended irregularly from 1619 to 1631 until it contained seventy-seven entries he tried to review each week, levying small fines on himself for every infraction.[57] The godly life as shaped by the English literature of practical divinity thus came to be, in the most familiar of Puritan metaphors, an arduous pilgrimage toward the heavenly city. Pious believers spiraled between doubt and reassurance toward an ever-closer relationship with God, feeling themselves led to serve him faithfully and to seek his presence through prayer and communion.[58]

"Putting a difference between men and men . . . has been the chief work of the godly ministers in England in this last age," Thomas Goodwin wrote in 1639. In calling would-be saints to the narrow way and setting them off on a lengthy pilgrimage, the practical asked them to turn away from many of the customs of the world around them. As a modern historian has written, "The effect on society of the religion of protestants and its moral values was to polarize communities between those who gadded to sermons and those who gadded to dances, sports, and other pastimes; those whose speech was seasoned with godly salt and those who used the traditional oaths."[59] The ratio of those who gadded to sermons to those who gadded to dances cannot be known with precision, but the estimate of one member of the former group, made in 1617, that only one Englishman in twenty was truly Christian may offer some order of magnitude for old England. New England was another matter entirely: an Essex vicar who emigrated to Massachusetts wrote back enthusiastically that in the bay colony "the better part" were also "the greater part."[60] A number of historians have suggested that the godly came preponderantly from the wealthier inhabitants of England's increasingly stratified rural communities, who saw in Puritan piety a justification of their prosperity and a discipline for controlling the poorer part of the community. Detailed local studies have generally failed to substantiate this. One such study that cleverly compared the wills and estates of those families in Sussex that chose names like Praise-God and Deliverance for their children with those that chose more conventional names in order to identify the godly fraction of the population found no meaningful wealth differences between the two groups; the most visible disparity was that the godly tended to ask that the money for their daughters' marriage portions be invested at "meet" rates of interest, while their less zealous neighbors specified this be done at "most profit." This is just one of the many bits of evidence implying that, for all of the intensity and regularity of their practice of piety, the godly were not necessarily assiduous or successful in accumulating wealth. Wallington filled eleven volumes with accounts of God's mercies and his "returns of prayer," four noting his sins and the remedies for them offered by Scripture, two recording notorious judgments of God, three noting covenants and engagements, four on the benefits he had obtained from the Lord's Supper and fast days, and one examining the marks that proved he was a child of God. The one kind of book he did not keep was business records, and his livelihood was always precarious.[61]

Because Puritan devotion offers such exceptional sources and has been so well studied, the pious praxis of the English godly has often been presumed to be generally typical of Reformed devotion. In fact this was not the case. Initially a peculiarity of the English, the devotional patterns stimulated by the literature of practical divinity did spread to other portions of the Reformed world but hardly to all—at least not prior to 1700. Although some continental ministers, for example, Teelinck and Voetius, were smitten by this style of piety, others sharply criticized it. The story of the larger European reception of English practical divinity has to date been little explored, but it is one of the central themes of the history of Reformed piety in this era. It appears the spiritual preoccupations and devotional patterns associated with English practical divinity were most rapidly and eagerly received north of the border in Scotland. With more of a time lag, they also took strong root in the Netherlands. By contrast, they awakened relatively little following in the French-speaking churches. The Germanophone Reformed territories were situated somewhere between these extremes.

That the English literature of practical divinity found its way quickly into Scotland hardly surprises, given the absence of a linguistic border between the two realms and the fact that sixteenth- and seventeenth-century Scottish printers and booksellers produced relatively few works of their own, importing most of their stock from London.⁶² The prompt reception of English practical divinity is hinted at by the evidence of both devotional works by Scots authors and by the diaries kept by pious Scots. William Cowper, a devotional writer who was ten years Perkins's junior, echoed much of the elder man's language, speaking of the "Golden Chaine of Salvation" and the obligation of each Christian to find infallible tokens of effectual calling. Works by Rogers, Bayly, Perkins, Downame, and other English practical divines are mentioned in the diary of Archibald Johnston of Wariston for the years 1632–39. His journal is a combination of a memorial of God's mercies, a catalogue of his sins, and a record of his prayers, meditations, and sermons attended, set in the larger context of an intense interest in discerning the marks of election. The very fact he and numerous other Scots kept spiritual journals and diaries of conscience of this sort bespeaks the influence of the English traditions of practical divinity. These documents also disclose many of the same practices, preoccupations, and anxieties as those found among the English godly.⁶³ The practice of drawing up personal covenants gained especially wide prevalence in Scotland because it fit so well with broader Scottish practices of bonding and covenanting. Scottish diaries are not uncommonly little more than records of repeated personal covenants and their repeated violation, often because of strong drink.⁶⁴ If the piety of Scots Calvinism developed distinctive accents with an especially strong emphasis on covenanting and its protorevivalistic communion fairs, much of its vocabulary and grammar was nevertheless drawn from the tradition of English practical divinity.

Translation, too, carried the writings of practical Englishmen to the Continent, but the works of the two greatest expositors of currents within this tradition met decidedly different fates. Bayly's *Practice of Piety,* the vast compilation of prayers, meditations, and reflections for all moments in life that was England's most frequently reprinted devotional work in the seventeenth century, swept across all Reformed regions of the Continent. The work went through at least forty-nine Dutch printings, twenty-eight German editions, twenty French printings, and was also translated into Hungarian, Czech, Polish, Romansch, Swedish, and the "Massachusetts Indian language." When it appeared in Hungarian, the minister at Debrecen, where it was printed, was bombarded with requests for copies from other ministers and even from his archdeacon. A petition from churchmen in Hanau and Herborn circulated in 1633 to the churches of Great Britain urged them to prepare a full compendium of practical divinity because the recent translation of *The Practice of Piety* "hath taken so much with many godly souls, that we find thereby wrought in them a very great growth of that religious disposition, which doth consist in a pure and modest profession of heavenly truth." "Books composed by the English about the way to practice piety are running from hand to hand,"

Moyse Amyraut wrote about France in 1660.[65] Because the work advocated such practices as regular family prayer, the daily review of one's behavior, and strict observance of the full Christian Sabbath, its popularity would have served as a vehicle to further these practices throughout the continental Reformed churches.

In contrast with this *summa* of the methodical aspects of English practical divinity, the writings of the greatest early exponent of its tradition of experimental predestinarianism, Perkins, met a decidedly more uneven reception. While enormously popular in the Netherlands, where ninety-three editions of one or another of his works were published, he found little favor in France, winning just five French-language editions. His work also made its way into German (thirty-five editions), Hungarian (seven), Welsh (four), and Czech (four).[66]

The eager reception of both Perkins and Bayly in the Netherlands formed just part of a wider enthusiasm for the work of England's practical divines in that country. Leading Dutch churchmen from Teelinck through Voetius filled their shelves with English devotional writings and contributed personally to the task of translating them. Between 1598 and 1622, no fewer than 60 English books of piety were translated; the 114 editions of these works represented more than half of all the devotional works published in the United Provinces in these years.[67] As noted in chapter 11, precisians of the ilk of Teelinck and Voetius were inspired by the example of such Puritan towns as Banbury and incorporated the ideas and goals of English sabbatarianism into their attempts to convince the authorities to impose godly order on Dutch society. Late in the century, Cocceians as well as Voetians would embrace many of the practices and ideas advocated by the English authors.

An important shift also occurred in the focus of those Dutch churchmen who sought further reformation over the course of the century. As the governing regents revealed themselves to be steadfastly unreceptive to appeals for stricter government action against sin, ministers shifted their focus to calling individual believers to conversion. As this occurred, both the self-segregating devotional practices characteristic of the English godly and the tradition of experimental predestinarianism came to the fore. Conventicles of pious church members who gathered on Sunday afternoons to discuss the morning sermon were present in Dordrecht by 1646. A church member in Utrecht protested in the 1650s about the "new theology" of precisian pastors that made excessive demands of church members and awakened in them unnecessary doubts about their salvation. After Jacobus Koelman was removed from his ministry at Sluis in 1675 for his outspoken opposition to formulary prayers and Christmas church services, he became an itinerant preacher who organized and defended conventicles, even while spurring those who joined these gatherings to remain in the communion of the established Reformed church as well. Such popular pious writers of the second half of the century as Wilhelmus à Brakel (1635–1711) and Herman Witsius (1636–1708) repeatedly trumpeted the experimental predestinarian theme of the need for believers to make their election sure and offered their readers lists of the marks of grace they could employ to determine if they were among the minority of formal church members who indeed possessed saving faith. Indicative of the shifting currents is the publication in 1680 in Amsterdam of *God's Wondrous Work for and in the Born Again,* which recounts the coming to assurance of faith of an individual troubled by his election in the manner of the conversion narratives of the English gathered churches.[68]

By the later part of the century, the *fijnen* who set themselves apart from the rest of the congregation by their austere lifestyle, Bible-laced speech, and attendance at conventicles had become a butt of satire, just like England's Puritans a century earlier. Aside from their propensity to gather in small groups for prayer and theological discussion, their pious praxis does not emerge from obscurity until the eighteenth century, when appreciable numbers of diaries and journals of conscience begin to carry through from this milieu. These divulge an absorption with personal conversion and rebirth, an anxious searching for the signs of inward grace, and an acute searching for the indicia of divine providence in everyday life, all of which seem very familiar to those acquainted with the British and North American religious landscape.[69] Dutch Calvinism has subsequently had a revivalistic, born-again wing very similar to British and North American evangelicalism.

Such currents received a far cooler reception among the French and Genevan Reformed in the seventeenth century. Amyraut, the most influential figure of the mid-seventeenth-century French church, criticized works like Bayly's as offering entirely too mechanical an approach to piety, as if their authors were trying to teach a trade. Huguenot memoirs and family account books survive in some abundance from the seventeenth century, but they betray neither the attention to making one's election sure nor the personal covenanting characteristic of British and later Dutch diaries. Huguenot ministers, under constant pressure to defend their flock against Catholic controversialists seeking converts, inclined toward a more intellectualist and less experiential understanding of the nature of saving faith, one in which recognizing the truth of justification by faith alone was more critical than sensing the presence of grace in the heart. As we have seen, rates of communion taking were high among the Huguenots, but their piety seems to have been built far more around the scrupulous participation in the ordinary forms of worship than around an intense regimen of private devotions and sober Sunday afternoons. When Trosse recalled his sojourn in Brittany in the home of a Protestant minister, it was not only the absence of regular family prayers that surprised him. The pastor even permitted his daughter to attend dances on Sunday afternoons! When this man of God died one Sunday after falling from a tower he was repairing, Trosse's sympathy could not prevent his thinking the death an example of God's wondrous judgments against Sabbath breakers.[70]

France and the Netherlands are the two extremes with regard to the continental reception of English practical divinity. To judge by the evidence of devotional literature and its circulation, Reformed piety in the Germanic-speaking world was characterized by an only partly confession-specific set of concerns and practices that was open to an unusually broad range of influences. English practical divinity played a growing role but obtained the kind of force it did in the Netherlands in but a few regions close to the Dutch border. In addition to the works of Perkins and Bayly, those of Baxter, Bunyan, and Daniel Dyke achieved a measure of popularity. English devotional authors were usually first printed in such Reformed cities as Basel, Hanau, Herborn, and Oppenheim. Once translated, they often transcended the confessional barrier and were reprinted in Lutheran cities as well. Their rate of publication and republication became quite important between 1660 and 1720, the early years of the development of German pietism. Such classics of Lutheran devotion as Arndt's *Garden of Paradise* likewise circulated widely in Reformed areas. It does not appear German Protestants kept spiritual journals and diaries of conscience before the eighteenth century. On the other hand, agitation for a greater concentration on practical piety did spill over from the Netherlands into neighboring regions in the 1660s and 1670s. Theodore Undereyck, a fiery preacher of conversion who had spent time in England, organized private assemblies for Bible reading first in Mülheim a/d Ruhr in the 1660s and then in Bremen after 1670. Local synods in Cleves and Mark funded translations of leading Dutch pious authors. The synod of Mark required all clergymen in 1674 to pledge themselves to the study of piety as well as orthodox doctrine. Conventicles of pious women who withdrew from the ordinary amusements of society and began to meet for prayer and religious discussion also appeared in Bern in the 1690s.[71]

Mature Reformed piety was thus characterized by a variety of styles as the seventeenth century drew to a close. Because of the extraordinary documentation associated with it, the patterns of behavior associated with English practical divinity and especially its experimental predestinarian stream are well known. Nothing shows better than the personal records kept by those in this tradition how profoundly the outlook and experiences of devout believers could be molded by the content of their faith. To equate Calvinist devotion too narrowly with the intense preoccupation with making one's election sure and the methodical pursuit of moral improvement characteristic of English practical divinity, however, is to simplify a complex picture. This style of piety took hold in just a fraction of the membership of certain Reformed churches. Its varied reception highlights once again that this style of piety cannot be seen as simply a logical outgrowth of the Reformed tradition's theological preoccupation with predestination, but had its own flowering, one shaped by the situation in which the first clerical exponents of the tradition found themselves in England's half-Reformed church, by the intensity of their links to theologians in other parts of the Reformed world, and by the status of the other Reformed churches. Once again, content and context worked together in shaping the Reformed tradition.

HOW GREAT THE IMPACT?

After returning to Geneva from the synod of Nîmes in May 1572, Beza wrote to several correspondents that in the churches he visited along the route, people hated the pope and there were few superstitions, but there were also many of no religion and few who were truly pious. The number of church members was growing, but few put their faith into practice.[72] Beyond illustrating that the reformers' reach often exceeded their grasp, his remarks remind one that religious commitment can be measured in various ways: according to the extent to which people identified themselves strongly with membership in a given church, according to the regularity and intensity of their performance of certain ritual practices, according to the extent to which values and ideas endorsed by the church shaped their total mental universe, or according to the extent to which their church's ethics shaped their moral behavior. In assessing the consequences for lay belief and religious practice of the exertions of Europe's Reformed churches to cast worship in new molds, it is also important to distinguish between the state churches, where the faith was imposed on all by law, and the voluntary churches, which comprised only a small segment of the population tied to the church by a combination of personal choice and family tradition.

In the first years of the Reformation in those regions in which the Reformed church established itself in defiance of the authorities, part of the population ardently embraced the central elements of the Reformed message, often at high risk to its safety and prosperity. In some countries, most notably France and Poland, another part rallied to the defense of the rituals the new converts mocked. In the Netherlands, the numerous executions in the name of the old faith had so eroded attachment to it that few came to its defense, opening the way to the remarkable dissociation of church membership from citizenship during the Dutch Revolt that allowed many in seventeenth-century Netherlands to live outside full membership in any church. Joining the new Reformed churches in these countries during their first generation meant taking on a powerful new identity. Up to half of all new converts were willing to proclaim this by choosing Old Testament names for their children that had no precedents in their family tradition. Conversion also entailed the defiant rejection of many of the practices most characteristic of Catholic devotion. The new church members refused all masses and prayers for the dead and married during Lent without hesitation, although occasionally consistories had to deal with the lingering attachment to magical practices or dancing at a Catholic festival.[73] No studies have been undertaken to illuminate how thoroughly these new converts mastered the details of Reformed doctrine. Beza's reports that the Huguenots he encountered in southern France hated the pope and superstition more than they led truly pious lives may be revealing here, but they should be weighed against the brave, often detailed defenses of key points of Reformed doctrine left by ordinary men and women arrested and tried for heresy.

With the passage of the generations, those who remained attached to what now became the faith of their ancestors grew less assertive about underscoring their confessional identity. The percentage of Old Testament names declined. The Huguenots of some parts of northern France began to avoid marrying during Lent lest they offend their Catholic neighbors. Consistories dealt with more cases of people attending Catholic festivals, acting as godparents for Catholic children, or even sending their children to Jesuit schools between 1590 and 1640 than during the first generation. Yet the members of these voluntary churches retained a clear sense of their separateness and showed themselves to be quite scrupulous about keeping devotional imagery associated with Catholicism out of their houses. They partook regularly in the quarterly celebrations of the Lord's Supper and often owned Bibles and works of piety. The clearest indications of their continuing commitment are the willingness of some two hundred thousand of them to choose the dangers and uncertainties of flight and exile after the revocation of the Edict of Nantes and the attachment displayed to the reconstituted church of the desert by so many of those who remained in France. How thorough was the mastery of doctrine among those who remained loyal? The case of Pierre Lézan, who lived through the revocation of the Edict of Nantes in the little Cévenol town of Saint-Hippolyte-du-Fort, is enlightening. As an erstwhile *consul* and the secretary of the consistory, he was a man of local importance. When one of his sons abandoned the Reformed faith in Paris in 1682, he recorded in his *livre de raison* that he and his wife were so pained they almost died. When the crown ordered the demolition of the town's temple in 1678, he viewed the incident as God's just punishment for the community's sins. In 1700, he drew up a "faithful abridgment" of his beliefs for the benefit of his children, so that they might remember the religion into which they were baptized and remain true to it. This document is striking for its concision. The essence of the Reformed faith as he presented it lay in three divergences from Catholicism: (1) we address our prayers to God and Christ alone, while Catholics also pray to the saints; (2) we say our prayers in a language understood by all, while the Roman church, in order to keep people ignorant, uses a language they cannot understand; (3) we celebrated the Eucharist in accordance with the Bible and the practice of the church up until the Council of Constance, while the Roman church took the cup away from the people after Constance. Emotionally attached to the Reformed church and eager to transmit this attachment to subsequent generations, he at the same time had a fairly limited conception of the church's doctrine that avoided abstract points and highlighted basic features of worship. These he defined largely in terms of how they differed from Catholic practice, although with the aid of some rather striking historical knowledge.[74]

Wherever the Reformation was imposed from above by an act of state, many more new church members were initially apathetic or hostile, and a far smaller percentage of church members eagerly embraced their new identity, especially in agricultural villages. Erastus estimated that in the Palatinate barely 30 percent of the population knew and confessed the basics of the faith after it was introduced there in the 1560s. In the rural Pays de Vaud, only 5 percent of church members chose Old Testament names for their children. Consistories had to battle to get people to learn their catechism and to uproot continued attachment to Catholic practices. Yule celebrations proved tenacious, as did the belief that newborns should not be allowed to die unbaptized. People generally displayed less attachment to masses and prayers for the dead, although these could survive in some isolated or linguistically distinct regions. In the Aspe valley of Béarn, a stronghold of Catholic resistance to that territory's state reformation, 83 percent of wills from the period 1571–99 included bequests for funeral masses; just 2 percent did elsewhere in Béarn.[75]

In these territories, the creation of a new Reformed identity and new patterns of religious life required a longer process of indoctrination and acculturation. Movement in this direction was generally visible within a generation, but it was decidedly uneven. All that can be observed in the domain of catechetical mastery is a modest increase in the percentage of those accounted to have learned the catechism well and a corresponding decline in the percentage of those judged to have learned it poorly. On the other hand, when allowance is made for reading aloud in family groups, a sizable fraction of the rural population of many areas would have gained access to the Bible and books of piety by the late seventeenth century, and some villagers undoubtedly began to make the singing of psalms and the reading of Scripture part of their regular domestic routine. Numbers of communicants remained highly variable: in the Pays de Vaud, most church members participated each time the ritual was celebrated, but in the Palatinate and England, many declined to do so except at Easter. The difficulties rulers increasingly began to encounter around 1600 when they sought to change the established church order show that confessional identity had taken strong root by then; but of course the greatest defenders of the old order tended to be the political and social elites. In Béarn, the political nation stoutly resisted the restoration of Catholicism, but once ordinary people had a choice about the church in which they preferred to worship, Protestantism shrank to a minority faith. The most rapid and consistent change seems to have been the eradication of Catholic survivals and the enforcement of conformity to the new ritual and liturgical order. Church members grew more comfortable with waiting to baptize their children and began to marry during Lent, whereas they had previously hesitated to do so. The celebration of abolished holy days withered. This change appears to have been completed in most areas between 1600 and 1650.

In a world in which many simply conformed to the established church, the ultimately accepted transformation of the ordinary practices of worship must be accounted one of the major religious changes wrought by the establishment of the Reformed churches. The narrative of events showed time and again that both those strongly committed to the cause of the Reformation and those deeply attached to Catholic practices were activist minorities; but this does not mean the mere conformism of the remaining majority lacked personal meaning to those who simply accepted whatever rituals the authorities decreed. Even for mere conformists, the words of the established liturgy became the phrases that were remembered in times of trial to comfort, inspire, or make sense of events. The patterns of the fixed rituals shaped the patterns of people's lives. Familiarity eventually bred attachment, as the groundswell of petitioning for the Book of Common Prayer in England in 1641–42 and its continued use after it was supposed to be replaced with the Directory for Public Worship in 1645 demonstrates.[76] It also bred the visceral reaction against the many forms of Catholic devotion now branded as superstitious, together with the sense of personal superiority to such benighted stupidity, that, as journals and travel accounts testify, many Reformed Protestants felt when they observed Catholic rituals. Even if some of the practices of Reformed devotion, notably fast days, can be made to fit an anthropological definition of magic, the claim that Reformed Reformations promoted a certain disenchantment of the world is difficult to deny. A Reformed pattern of worship also gave time a more regular shape. It ended an economy of salvation that linked the living and the dead in communities of prayer and remembrance. It downplayed the final deathbed struggle to die a good death and emphasized instead the obligation of living a life of faith. These important changes followed from mere conformity.

Many churchmen, of course, strove for far more than just outward conformity to the rituals of the church. The English apostles of practical divinity and those ministers in other parts of the Reformed world who drew inspiration from them urged believers to take up the pilgrim's staff and follow the narrow path. They were to separate themselves from many activities of the world, observe a strict regimen of daily devotions, ensure they could find within themselves evidence of an effectual calling, and use that conviction to fuel an ongoing process of sanctification. For those who heard their call—godly English Puritans and Dissenters, Scottish Covenanters, the Dutch *fijnen*—the pilgrimage typically began with some anxious searching for reassurance about their election, a search they often had to renew many times. It then drew them into a new fellowship built around attendance at sermons, Bible study groups, and earnest discussions of their returns of prayer. Above all, it opened the door to an intense inner life and a no-less-systematic effort of self-amelioration, both of which required careful ongoing monitoring. The self-identified "better part" who followed this path became the "greater part" only in a few colonies of settlement for the span of a generation, after which the percentage of full church members began to decline. Otherwise these people were never more than a small minority.

As historians of the new devotion of the seventeenth century have stressed, certain practices of this minority, for example, the regular examination of one's behavior at the end of each day, were part of a larger stock of Christian devotional practices they shared with the era's most devout Catholics and Lutherans. At the same time, comparison of the mainstays of devotional literature and of practices of piety across the three confessions suggests important disparities. The classics of Lutheran piety display an affective, mystical piety built around the visualization of Christ's life and sacrifice. Catholic devotion retained fierce practices of physical mortification, and Catholic devotional authors often appealed to the senses in ways that seem rare among the Reformed, recommending that men fight the temptations of lust by imagining beneath the pretty face that arouses them the skull that will rot in the grave and prodding blasphemers to punish the tongues that offended God by licking the earth of a churchyard. For all its incorporation of practices that transcended the confessional divide, the pattern of Reformed practical piety at its most intense had a distinctive style and psychology.[77]

Pierre Jurieu hoped that one day the faithful would form all of their thoughts in the language of the psalms. So complete a remolding of the culture and consciousness of individual believers was almost never achieved in practice, no matter how hard the most pious might try. The goal certainly was never attained on a community level, even in the greatest strongholds of the voluntary churches. An enduring image of the Huguenot Cévennes, repeated by historians of great prominence, holds that in that bastion of French Prot-estantism folk culture was so thoroughly remade that folklorists could find no lullabies when they looked for them in the nineteenth century because women rocked their children to sleep by the sound of the psalms. While it is true that snatches of the liturgy or portions of works of piety were often set to music and sung by the faithful in this region as they went about their daily business, it has also been seen that aggressive youth groups survived in this region despite consistorial efforts to bring them to heel, and that when the be-lief that May was an unlucky time to marry spread throughout the region, the Huguenots, like their Catholic neighbors, avoided marrying in this month.[78] Even in its greatest citadels of fidelity, Reformed belief was never a total cul-ture. Values and practices deriving from sources other than the Bible always coexisted and interacted with the word.

Just as the extent to which religion shaped people's cultural universe in this era should not be exaggerated, so too the clear evidence of secular attitudes or a degree of religious indifference should not lead to it being unduly mini-mized either. Once again, a well-illuminated individual case illustrates this point well. In the first decades of the seventeenth century, a Frisian farmer in Het Bildt, Dirck Jansz. kept a diary dedicated primarily to noting the weather and the state of his crops that also sheds some light on his religious outlook. For much of his life, until he finally joined the congregation at the communion table in 1624, he was one of those *liefhebbers* who attended Reformed services when he chose but did not formally profess the faith. Well before 1624, how-ever, he recorded in the diary prayers for God's mercy that show he shared some of the beliefs and practices of the full church members. When his first wife lay on her deathbed in 1618, a vision came to her: an angel appeared and told her she had been delivered from all of her afflictions. Jansz. prayed that her joy would not be turned to grief, and after she died content, he prayed he might be reunited with her in everlasting joy after his death. He copied rhymes into the diary, including the following:

> If property is lost, nothing is lost.
> If courage is lost, much is lost.
> If honor is lost, more is lost.
> If the soul is lost, all is lost.

This unchurched *liefhebber* did not doubt the existence of angels and thought it worth recording that nothing was more important than saving one's immor-tal soul.[79]

Generalizations about religious practice must always take into account that the intensity and character of individual religiosity vary widely in any complex society. The range of variation was particularly large across Europe's Reformed churches, for they accepted a measure of liturgical variety as legitimate, included both minority communities composed of voluntary adherents and state churches in which the participation of the entire population was mandatory, and proved unequally receptive to the new currents of piety that formed within some of them as the period advanced. The initial changes of belief and worship were naturally greater when people embraced the cause by personal choice rather than government fiat. Even in the former areas, Beza appears to have perceived matters correctly when he noted that people's voluntary espousal involved a transformation of personal identity, the hatred of the pope, and a rejection of Roman ritual more often than it did a thoroughgoing change of private practices of devotion. In places where the religion was imposed by law and a component of the population initially preserved some attachment to features of the old religious order, change came with time; but change was more in the outward forms of worship and in the gradual absorption of the psalter and the Bible into personal and family devotion than in the mastery of the abstractions of doctrine taught in the catechism. Where the collective metamorphoses appeared inadequate to a portion of the most pious under the stimulus of the ambitious models and techniques of personal transformation proposed by the English practical divines, these individuals set themselves apart from the rest by a set of activities that aimed to mold all of their thoughts in the language of the psalms. As they learned to their anguish, even they could rarely banish all worldly thoughts and remake themselves as completely as the apostles of practical divinity would have wished. Most Reformed believers did not make as thorough an effort. Still, even occasional sermon attenders in the Netherlands who were not full church members understood the world and the individual's place within it in simple Christian terms. The transformations of practice effected by every Reformed church created a new set of sensibilities over the long run. For all its internal variations, Reformed Europe possessed a distinctive religious culture that set it apart from Europe's other confessions and imparted a characteristic sensibility and range of experiences to those raised within it.

CONCLUSION TO PART IV
Final Reflections on Calvinism
and the Making of the Modern World

As I indicated in the introduction, one goal of this book has been to explore the issues raised by the historical and sociological theories that accord the Reformed tradition a distinctive role in the making of the modern world. Throughout the preceding chapters, readers will have noted some details that appear to lend support to the claim that Calvinism was fertile soil for the growth of capitalism and resistance to autocratic rule and others that modify or argue against such claims. Now is the moment to draw these threads together.

The argument that Calvinism served to beget or encourage the emergence of modern liberal democracy typically rests on two assertions: that the Reformed tradition frequently emboldened resistance to unjust authority and that the congregational, consistorial, and presbyterial-synodal forms of church government found within the Reformed tradition offered lay participants in these systems a useful apprenticeship in self-government. The first of these associations retained a great deal of plausibility for a long stretch of European history, from perhaps 1650 to 1950. We have seen that rebellion and resistance theories came to seem peculiarly characteristic of the Reformed during the later seventeenth and early eighteenth centuries, when so many uprisings, from the Hungarian plains to the hills of the Cévennes and from the Whiggamore raiders to the Glorious Revolution, were staged by Reformed

Protestants. In the wake of these events, Whig historians turned what had previously been a staple of Catholic anti-Calvinism, the charge that the faith was
seditious by nature, into a positive point of pride. After Rome turned resolutely against the principles of modern liberalism in reaction to the French
Revolution, its theologians' earlier advocacy of such theories tended to be
forgotten. Protestant polemicists ceased to charge, as they had in the seventeenth century, that the Catholics were the true advocates of king killing.

As the early chapters of this book show, however, the theoretical justification of resistance to rulers believed unjustly to prevent the proper worship
of God was neither an invention nor a monopoly of the Reformed tradition.
Lawyers and scholastic theologians articulated political theories that rooted
government in the consent of the governed and justified resistance to rulers
who violated divine law even before the Middle Ages drew to a close. Although
Luther initially refused to countenance any form of armed resistance to imperial authority, he was convinced at Torgau in 1530 to amend his views to
allow the princes of the empire to resist imperial commands by force. Amid
the interim crisis a number of Lutheran theologians went further and justified
resistance to the attempted restoration of a Catholic church order with the
argument that subordinate magistrates had a responsibility to defy orders by
their superiors that violated divine or natural law. Catholic theologians also
legitimated armed resistance to ungodly rulers in a number of instances in
the sixteenth century and even justified the killing by ordinary citizens of a
tyrant-king during the crisis of the Catholic League in France. Calvin, for his
part, wrote the first edition of his *Institutes* to demonstrate to Francis I that
the evangelical movement was not subversive of political order as its enemies
charged, and he always warned his followers not to take direct action in defiance of the legally constituted political authorities. At the same time, he incorporated the argument that subordinate magistrates might possess the authority to resist unjust commands into the *Institutes,* criticized ruling French
kings in bitter terms from the pulpit, and was even briefly drawn into conspiring against the crown when he believed that such activity had the legal
justification provided by the expected leadership of the first prince of the
blood, Anthony of Navarre. Just as Calvin was internally divided between his
concern for order and his belief in the necessity of obeying God's commands
rather than those of man, so successive generations of Reformed theologians
split over the issue of whether and when armed resistance to rulers' demands
was justified. In France, to cite just the best-known instance, theories legitimizing resistance to unjust rule gained considerable support among the Reformed in the wake of the Saint Bartholomew's Massacre in 1572, receded in
favor of a strict doctrine of unqualified obedience to rulers during the years
of the seventeenth century when royal edicts represented the faith's chief

protection against its enemies, then arose again among some political theorists in exile after the revocation of the Edict of Nantes in 1685. Catholic
and Lutheran theologians and political writers displayed similar divisions and
changes of opinion over the course of the early modern period.

Although the justification of armed resistance to rulers who failed to protect and uphold the true faith was not the monopoly of any post-Reformation
confession, the various confessions did not all embrace and act upon such
theories with equal frequency. Heinz Schilling's case study from 1981 of Lutheran Lemgo's spirited resistance to the count of Lippe's attempt to impose a
new Reformed church order on it in 1609 was a milestone in historical thinking about the late Reformation era. It underscored that Lutheranism was not
always the politically passive faith of long-standing legend and suggested that
whatever connections happened to develop in any given time and place between a given confession and a proclivity toward either promoting or resisting
princely absolutism were the product of contingent historical circumstances.[1]
This instance notwithstanding, it remains the case that at certain critical moments Lutheran church leaders held back from establishing churches under
the cross or from defending such churches by force when the Reformed
plunged ahead and did so—most notably in the Low Countries in 1566, where
the Lutheran refusal to oppose the duly constituted authorities contributed
to the Reformed church's assumption of leadership in the movement of resistance to Habsburg rule. Having gained legal protection for their confession in
the Peace of Augsburg of 1555, Germany's Lutherans subsequently associated
their cause with the defense of the imperial constitution and the established
order, worked to cast Calvinism as seditious, and were more reluctant than
the Reformed to advocate resistance. The Catholics, holding their belief in a
divinely ordained papal monarchy, were hardly so reticent in theory. The association of Catholicism with resistance and rebellion remained plausible so
long as the Catholic League, the Gunpowder Plot, and the writings of such
Jesuit advocates of a contractual theory of government as Juan de Mariana
and Francisco Suárez remained fresh in people's minds. In practice, there
were simply fewer occasions after the wind turned in Catholicism's favor after
1600 in which Catholic populations found themselves in a situation in which
resistance to a Protestant ruler seemed justified and viable. Surveying the entire period 1517–1700, one cannot avoid concluding the Reformed embraced
and acted upon such views more than any other confessional group. This is
not because of any enduringly distinctive features of Reformed thinking about
political obligation. It stems instead from two other foundation stones of Reformed theology: its profound hostility to idolatrous forms of worship and
its conviction that certain kinds of church institutions derived from scriptural authority. The former drove Reformed believers to separate themselves

from the church of Rome in situations in which other evangelicals were prone to compromise, and thus to find themselves especially often on a footing of threatened minority impelled to fight for its ability to worship as it pleased. The latter sparked movements of resistance to perceived threats to the purity of the proper church order. In such situations, the common stock of European resistance theories justified the group's refusal to submit.

The second claim—namely, that the self-governing structures of many Reformed churches fostered democracy by offering laymen practical experience in church government—is more difficult to assess. Wherever the doctrine of the fourfold ministry influenced church structures, it guaranteed laymen a role in the administration of discipline, the oversight of poor relief, and, in the non-state-supported churches, the day-to-day economic administration of the church. Laymen also were members of the provincial and national synods of most Reformed churches, although in some their participation waned with time. Elders and deacons tended to be drawn from the better-off and more upstanding families of the locality, but they were a spiritual aristocracy drawn from a range of occupations that was by no means identical with the temporal aristocracy or the most highly privileged groups. In numerous Dutch towns, service as an elder or deacon was often the first step toward becoming associated with municipal government. The difficulty lies in knowing whether the experience in church government that laymen acquired in these roles contributed in any meaningful way to the long-term growth and success of representative government or democracy—or whether it was qualitatively different from the kind of experience Catholics or Lutherans might acquire as churchwardens or other parish-level officers.

It is clearly anachronistic to consider Calvin's theory of church government democratic. He himself labeled it aristocratic—properly so, if we understand the word in the sense of "government by the best." Other systems of church government, for example, that of John a Lasco, incorporated more broadly democratic elements such as the congregational election of ministers, but these did not attain wide and enduring acceptance. As the more sophisticated expositors of a link between Calvinism and democracy have argued, truly democratic forms of church government underwent their most important development within the Reformed tradition when the self-governing congregations of the New England way and the English Independents and Baptists took shape.[2] Here indeed the larger body of full church members assumed most of the decision-making and disciplinary powers exercised by the consistories of those Reformed churches organized on Genevan lines. The question remains: Can it be demonstrated that the members of these churches played an essential role in the unfolding of modern democracy?

Here one comes to perhaps the most important point with regard to the assessment of the claim of a link between Calvinism and democracy. Both the world itself and the historiography of the European state have changed enough in the past half century that this link now seems less self-evident or compelling than it did to Alexis de Tocqueville in the first half of the nineteenth century and still did to John T. McNeill in 1954.[3] The post–World War II extension of democratic regimes across Europe has meant that successful, stable parliamentary democracies are no longer so exceptional or so disproportionately found in predominantly Protestant, especially Reformed, countries as they formerly were. Over the same period, under the impact of the experience of Nazism and Communism, the Catholic church has abandoned the opposition to liberal theories of religious freedom and the rights of man that characterized it from the French Revolution until well into the twentieth century, thereby removing the inclination of historians to project the church's modern conservatism back into the past. Finally, in what is both a cause and a consequence of the first development, historians of the early modern era have increasingly highlighted the vitality of representative institutions and the success of movements in their defense in regions from Catalonia to Mecklenburg to Sweden that stand outside the standard narrative of Whig historiography that for so long drew the road to modern democracy down a path centered in England and its overseas colonies. The most persuasive macrohistorical or macrosociological accounts of the origins of dictatorship and democracy in the West now tend to root the origins of representative government and of institutionalized checks on government power in the common European experience of a feudal, decentralized, corporative Middle Ages. They explain either the survival or dismantling of these institutions over the early modern period by geopolitical and economic circumstances that shaped how the military–fiscal Leviathan grew in each country. Religion plays no causal role in these accounts.[4] However much the roots of liberal democracy might appear to be part of a common European heritage, of course, the history of the twentieth century stands as a reminder that its current apparent triumph was anything but inevitable or easy and that Great Britain and its erstwhile overseas colonies were crucial to its survival and defense in the dark years of the middle of that century. It is also the case, however, that historians of both Britain and America have found the tracing of clear and consistent connections between Puritanism or sectarian Protestantism and those countries' modern political arrangements more and more problematic. In short, the connections historians once saw as evidence of an affinity between Calvinism and representative or limited government now appear to be either the product of contingent historical circumstances or simply unnecessary to account for the evolution of the basic features of modern political arrangements in the West.

The view that Calvinism contributed something essential to the distinctive course of European economic growth is even more complicated to assess, for this argument has taken at least three forms. The oldest may be dated back at least to Slingsby Bethel's *The Present Interest of England Stated* (1671), with its disparaging remarks about Catholics' "natural unaptness to business" (see p. 428). Both confessional rivalries and mercantilist commonplaces shaped Bethel's views. His tract was a plea for the toleration of Dissent on grounds of economic utility, so his claim that papists lacked aptitude for business served to justify why the same toleration need not be granted them. He attributed the poor economic performance of Catholic countries to the "multitude of lazie Priests and Jesuits" found within them, while the true religion of the Reformed was "an argument of their wit"; he approvingly cited a German state official to the effect that the superior "understandings" of the Reformed made them "abler merchants."[5] In other words, Protestants were smarter than Catholics, whose economies were further dragged down by a glut of lazy clerics. If the former assertion was an obvious expression of confessional bias, the latter claim was a stock theme of mercantilist writers in both Catholic and Protestant lands and was often accompanied by the statement that the enforced leisure of the many Catholic feast days depressed productivity even more. So widely accepted were these views that certain Catholic rulers reduced the number of holy days in order to bolster productivity.[6]

These last views retain a measure of commonsense plausibility, especially since Dutch pay records of the seventeenth century reveal individuals working more than three hundred days per year in the wake of the suppression of Catholic feast days there.[7] The leading historian of the early modern economy, Jan de Vries, has recently suggested even that an "industrious revolution" preceded the industrial revolution. By this he means that Europeans came to work increasingly long hours over the early modern centuries, as the highly seasonal work rhythms, chronic underemployment, and preference for leisure characteristic of many corners of the preindustrial economy receded before more labor-intensive agricultural techniques, the spread of by-employment and rural industry, and the growing tax demands of the state.[8] This recognition of the importance of changing work rhythms for economic growth might be thought to make historians receptive either to the argument that the longer work year and lighter religious establishment of Protestant lands gave them an economic advantage over Catholic countries, or to the Weberian diagnosis of a new work discipline encouraged by religious stimuli. In his definitive history of the early modern Dutch economy, however, de Vries explores the question of whether or not Calvinism played a causal role in the country's economic success, only to conclude that it probably did not. Many factors can plausibly be cited to explain the competitive success of the Dutch and English relative to the Spanish or Italians in the seventeenth century

without invoking religion: the greater productivity of their agricultural economies, their more efficient shipping and energy technologies, England's lower
wages, the Dutch abundance of capital. Insofar as de Vries has invoked socio-
psychological factors to account for early modern industriousness, he has
stressed the pull of new consumer goods and appetites, not the push of church
discipline.[9] Further doubt is cast upon the importance of the confessional factor by the fact that extensive statistical evidence from Montpellier, a city divided nearly equally between Catholics and Huguenots, fails to reveal that the
Reformed accumulated wealth more rapidly than their Catholic neighbors of
similar status over the years 1600–70, as would be expected if their ability
to work more days indeed offered them an economic advantage.[10] There is
simply no evidence that Protestants outworked Catholics when they lived side
by side and that this enabled them to enrich themselves more rapidly.

The sorts of economic advantages that mercantilist authors associated with
Protestantism are not those emphasized by twentieth-century advocates of
the view that Calvinism and capitalism were linked. For much of the century,
research and debate about this topic focused on the possibility that Reformed
churchmen adopted a more supple view of loans at interest and thus championed forms of capitalism the medieval church discouraged. On this issue, a
difference of moral sensibilities may well have separated the Reformed world
from the Catholic in the wake of the Reformation. Just as Calvin was rethinking the legitimacy of loans at interest outside the framework defined by the
medieval scholastics, a prominent French lawyer who ultimately remained
within the Catholic church, Charles Du Moulin, did the same in a very similar manner. His book, however, was placed on the Index, and no Catholic author followed in his footsteps without his orthodoxy being challenged until
the eighteenth century. Debate between laxists and rigorists within the Roman church centered around the legitimacy of the various contractual and
accounting subterfuges merchants used to evade the usury prohibition. Pious
merchants wrestled with their conscience about them, and at least some, such
as the famous Simon Ruiz, refused to get involved in operations their less
scrupulous colleagues undertook.[11] Within the Reformed world, the moral
sticking point appears simply to have been what level of interest was appropriate. As Owen Chadwick has written, "Reformed divinity, being less chained
to precedent, adjusted itself a little more rapidly to the new economy." Still,
although laws that began to allow lending within fixed limits may have been
more widely or more rapidly adopted in Reformed lands during the sixteenth
and seventeenth centuries, Catholic as well as Protestant territories promulgated such laws. Liège's church courts displayed the same diminishing severity in their treatment of accused usurers as Holland's consistories.[12] If a
variation of moral sensibilities separated Catholic theologians from some of

the Reformed on the matter of usury, it has yet to be demonstrated this made any practical difference in the relative efficiency of credit markets.

The most sophisticated diagnosis of a possible link between Calvinism and capitalism remains Weber's, which argued not that a distinctive Calvinist economic ethic existed, but rather that the doctrine of predestination gave a distinctive psychological intensity to Calvinists' pursuit of a common Christian economic ethic. That is, it forced believers to confront at every moment the question of whether or not they were among the elect and to quiet their doubts through virtuous behavior. As we have seen, predestination did indeed come to assume a central place within Reformed theology in the late sixteenth and early seventeenth centuries, and as it did so a number of highly influential English theologians began to stress the need for individual believers to make their election sure and to develop a highly rationalized literature of practical piety containing systematic techniques of self-monitoring and moral improvement. This tradition was not simply a logical outgrowth of the increased emphasis on predestination, however; it was also a response to the distinctive pastoral situation that faced godly English clergymen in a half-Reformed land lacking a full preaching ministry and a settled system of parochial discipline. While this literature ultimately obtained a wider diffusion, it received a cool reception in important parts of the Reformed world, notably its French-speaking corners, and it always represented just one strand of Reformed piety. The authors in this tradition disagreed among themselves about whether upright living or interior experiences of grace represented the best proof of election. The emphasis on right living increased as the seventeenth century advanced, but this happened just as predestinarian theology retreated. The English godly unquestionably set themselves apart from their neighbors through aspects of their lifestyle and religious behavior, but the most attentive studies of their economic behavior have ended by rejecting the notion that scrupulous piety fostered economic success. Nehemiah Wallington, that paragon of Puritan piety introduced in chapter 15, struggled to make a living, and the godly as a group do not appear to have been more economically successful than their less pious neighbors.[13]

If the practices advanced by the English practical divines were never generally characteristic of the Reformed tradition as a whole, the Reformed churches did create a more widely established and active system of church discipline than either the Lutheran or Catholic churches, even if parallel structures may be observed in certain Lutheran and Catholic territories as well. Contemporary observers who credited the Reformed with a successful reformation of manners saw discipline as the key to their success in this domain. We have seen, however, that outside commercial cities most Reformed disciplinary boards devoted the lion's share of their efforts to restraining illicit sexual behavior, reconciling quarreling spouses and neighbors, and reproving dancing and drunkenness, not to monitoring economic behavior. The campaigns against drink and dancing seem to have made scant headway against these ancestral vices. The few studies that have compared the lifestyles and spending patterns of members of the different confessions of similar status do not reveal major discrepancies between the Reformed and either the Catholics or the Lutherans, although the Anabaptists did have a solid reputation in the Netherlands for their simplicity of life.

In the final analysis, the assessment of Weber's account of the psychology of European Calvinism must be that, even while capturing certain substantive features of the psychology of Reformed doctrine and practice, his ideas exaggerate the extent to which they characterized the faith as a whole and attribute them too simply to a single cause. More important, nearly a century of research has yet to uncover compelling evidence that these attitudes and practices consistently had what might be called spillover effects, that is, consequences outside the domain of purely religious behavior. True to his formation in the German school of historical economics, Weber believed that modern capitalism comprehended a distinctive pattern of rational economic calculation. He searched for the origins of that mentality in extra-economic sources, religion above all, because it seemed the most powerful shaper of people's behavior. But the history of accounting can suggest another scenario, one in which capitalism generated its own rationality, as techniques like double-entry bookkeeping, which allowed merchants to calculate the return on their investments with new precision, arose within Mediterranean merchant communities in the later Middle Ages and then gradually spread across Europe independently of religious considerations. Contemporary Weberians who tout the force of religion in accounting for economic growth today similarly highlight spillover effects, claiming, for instance, that the spread of evangelical Protestantism in contemporary Latin America is likely to stimulate economic growth there because the practices of literacy and thrift it promotes are "perfectly suited" to nurturing economic success in the stage of primitive accumulation.[14] What early modern evidence indicates is that the doctrines and traditions of Calvinism profoundly molded its more committed adherents' religious psychology and sensibility; but its effects in furthering reading skills to give believers access to the Bible did not generate more widespread writing skills of the sort that were of commercial utility than was the case among neighboring Catholic populations; its effects in shaping aspects of people's moral behavior did not have demonstrable consequences for their habits of getting and spending. In the same way that the leading current accounts of the origins of democracy and dictatorship in the West tend to leave religion out of that story, economic historians of premodern Europe no longer see compelling reasons to grant religious factors a dominant role in the long-term growth of the European economy. Their refusal to do so seems well founded.

If the claims once made so confidently about Calvinism's importance in shaping modern political and economic attitudes thus no longer appear warranted—indeed, if they now look more and more like products of a bygone age of confessional rivalry—should one conclude that the tale told in this book is one of sound and fury, signifying nothing? Certainly not. First of all, the story has encompassed the birth pangs of essential features of contemporary Protestant Christianity, both amid the initial upheavals of the Reformation and as a result of the no-less-important developments of the century following. Until the Reformed tradition loses all meaning and coherence, all those who belong to one of the many Protestant churches that can be linked either genetically or intellectually to it will continue to feel a connection to its beginning centuries. After the dramatic changes of the past half century, the nature of this connection may, for many denominations, no longer be what it was a generation or two earlier. To the members of those mainline Reformed denominations whose traditions have been most dramatically altered by theological rationalism, ecumenical outreach, and therapeutic optimism, the ideas and practices whose history has been recounted here may appear scarcely less alien than they do to the growing numbers of university students today to whom the entire world of organized Christianity is terra incognita. They still comprise an important part of such churchgoers' denominational identity and self-understanding—the lost faith of their parents and grandparents. Even within these churches, furthermore, it is not unknown for advocates of change to build support for contemporary causes by pointing where possible to the words and deeds of the original reformers. In the more traditionalist Reformed churches as well as in some evangelical churches of recent vintage, the sense of direct connection to the ideas and practices examined here remains stronger yet. The history of the earliest church practices and the ideas of the leading sixteenth- and seventeenth-century theologians on such issues as grace and assurance remain charged with inspiration and authority, as much of the historical writing devoted to these subjects continues to show.

For those who are not members of these churches but simply seek to understand the Reformed tradition because of its fundamental importance both to European history and to our contemporary world—a task that I would argue becomes increasingly urgent as higher education and the mass media grow steadily more secular, yet evangelical religion exerts an enduring hold over much of the population—Calvinism still merits a prominent role in certain metanarratives of Western modernization. As we have seen, it effected a more thorough routinization of time than the other major post-Reformation confessions, even if its adherents did not abandon all beliefs about holy and propitious days and seasons. It effected a more thorough, if again incomplete, disenchantment of the world. It certainly was not the only post-Reformation confession vigorously to promote elementary schooling and stricter codes of individual conduct, as has been rightly stressed by those historians who insist upon the parallel consequences of the Catholic and Protestant Reformations. In its strenuous effort to inspire a life lived according to the strict dictates of God's word, it nonetheless contributed powerfully to the spread of mass literacy and reinforcement of the individual conscience, those fundamental developments of the early modern centuries.

Yet the essential historical importance of the story told here does not lie in its connections to metanarratives of modernization; it lies in its centrality for understanding that now-bygone era when confessional principles and attachments became structural elements of European society. The stance of those recent historians who have approached the subject with a sense of anthropological otherness unquestionably appears more appropriate than that of those who continue to insist on its links to that quicksilver concept *modernity*. The particular variant of the broader Reformation call for evangelical renewal that insisted on purging from worship all rites without explicit biblical sanction and on eliminating from eucharistic doctrine all possible confusion between created matter and a God who is spirit first gained official sanction within a small, distinctive corner of the Continent nestled on the periphery of its largest states. From there, the polysemous message of its early prophets was able to go forth and crystallize dissatisfaction with the Roman church across much of the Continent, in some areas by virtue of its capacity to offer ordinary Christians motivation and models for forming alternatives to the established church, in others by virtue of its ability to convince rulers and their key theological advisors of its fidelity to Holy Writ. The consequences shook many states to their foundations. The establishment of Reformed churches in defiance of the authorities, the resistance of Reformed believers to state-sponsored ecclesiastical innovations they viewed as infringements against the purity of God's ordinances, and the fear of a Catholic plot to roll back the advances of the Reformation: each precipitated some of the bitterest conflicts of the late sixteenth and seventeenth centuries. Even when the religious transformations associated with the movement's spread did not occasion full-scale civil war, the alteration of the traditional form of worship—occasionally as many as three or four times within a few decades—placed the local clergy before a series of difficult decisions of conscience that led many to resign their posts. For ordinary believers in virtually every generation, the decision of whether or not to join a Reformed church, to embrace a specific contested point of Reformed doctrine, or to refuse to abandon one when ordered by the authorities to do so could be a literally life-changing decision, casting individuals upon the paths of exile or assuring them of access to positions of power and respectability. The story of the establishment and defense of Europe's various Reformed churches is fundamental to the history of the late sixteenth and seventeenth centuries.

If the fatal flaw of theories crediting Calvinism with distinctive consequences for economic behavior or political development is that they exaggerate the spillover effects of religious doctrine outside the religious domain, the great shortcoming of the recent emphasis on the parallel consequences of the Lutheran, Reformed, and Catholic Reformations is that it downplays each faith's distinctiveness *within* the domain of culture and religious life. For all of the undoubted similarities between the various confessions and for all of the porosity of confessional boundaries to the motifs and practices of the new devotion of the late sixteenth and seventeenth centuries, it made a difference in people's life experience whether they were raised as Lutherans, Reformed, or Catholics. It made a difference as well where and when within each tradition they were raised, for none were monolithic or static. Each confession had its own set of styles of devotion. Each had its own doctrinal and psychological points of friction.

Even for those church members who did little more than observe the basic obligations of their faith, the confession they professed molded elements of their sensibility, subjected them to specific forms of ecclesiastical and communal oversight, and became a vital component of their social identity. Ordinary Reformed believers experienced a very different relation to the Bible and to other complex written texts than did their Catholic counterparts. They came to hold a deeply rooted antipathy to the use of images in worship and to certain forms of relations to holy places and holy objects that bred a visceral reaction against these practices when they saw them among Catholics. They were inclined to believe they were uniquely liberated from superstition and hence especially enlightened. Reformed reformations meant a dramatic reduction in the size, variety, and privileges of the clerical estate and forced a protracted renegotiation of the relation between church and state that was resolved in almost as many ways as there were Reformed churches. They also made it possible for clergymen who were persuasive biblical expositors to exercise extraordinary influence at key moments of change.

For the most thoroughly committed and pious Reformed believers, the fact of belonging to the tradition shaped their religious experience, psychology, and pattern of social relations more profoundly yet. Where the Puritan way of godliness prevailed, life became a troubling quest for assurance of election. Melancholy and depression came in the form of an unshakeable conviction of inescapable reprobation. Religious ecstasy came in the form of transports of joy during private prayer or, in Scotland, amidst the emotion of a several-day-long communion fair. Where Puritan practical divinity did not take root and the Reformed were a minority of the population, an exemplary fidelity to the public ordinances of worship, a tradition of loyalty sealed by the blood of pious ancestors, and a firm intellectual and emotional conviction of the truth of fundamental doctrines defined the narrow path to salvation.

The history of the establishment, spread, and further alterations of Europe's Reformed churches thus offers a panorama of the power—and limits—of a religious tradition's ability to transform the world and the behavior of individual believers. It also suggests some insights into the nature of the form of religious tradition that was the post-Reformation Christian confession. The various confessions of this period took shape amid the rapidly changing events of the early Reformation through a process of theological discussion, debate, and boundary definition that was profoundly entangled with relations of political and religious power. Decisions by those outside a given group about whom they would not recognize in fellowship could be as important to boundary definition as the convictions of the group's leading theological authorities. Once codified, confessions of faith set limits to the range of beliefs acceptable within the churches that accepted them, for new ministers were required to subscribe to their principles, and catechisms expounded these to the ordinary believers, but they did not fix doctrine once and for all. The pressure for doctrinal systematization and elaboration that resulted from the churches' institutional maturation, changes in their external political circumstances, and transformations in other domains of organized knowledge all raised new issues for debate and called inherited certitudes into question. The international movement of books, students, and exiles transplanted knowledge of practices characteristic of certain regions into others where they challenged established usage. The deepest imperative incumbent on believers remained to profess Christ's teachings purely, not to obey the text of any human document, so pressure to make adherents conform to a confession of faith could always be, and often was, countered by paraphrasing Paul to the effect that one was not of Zwingli or of Calvin or of Arminius but of Christ. On the one hand, the appearance of new debates and disagreements begat further, still more detailed confessions of faith that drew the bounds of orthodoxy tighter and created more of the anathematized positions that served as negative poles against which orthodoxy defined itself: Arminianism and antinomianism in addition to Anabaptism, anti-Trinitarianism, ubiquitarianism and popery. On the other hand, these anathematized positions continued to have their defenders, whose arguments convinced some people attached to the main body of the Reformed churches as the intellectual landscape changed, forcing the abandonment of the narrowest of the confessions in many circles by the early eighteenth century. A confessional tradition was thus not a fixed set of dogmatic positions so much as an enduring and expanding range of doctrinal possibilities. Local traditions and historical circumstance determined which ones were predominant at any given time and place, but the others retained the potential to be discovered or rediscovered as historical circumstances changed.

With the passage of the generations, a confessional tradition became more than a set of abstract beliefs: it became an element of personal and family identity, a group one cleaved to or rebelled against because one's ancestors had belonged to it and because it marked one off from the adherents of other rival groups. In the case of the Reformed, the confession did not initially dictate any particular institutional structure for the visible church, deeming this a thing indifferent. The structures of the many national and regional Reformed churches were shaped by the interaction between the upbringing and convictions of the most influential local reformers, the force of the larger international models of the best form of a Reformed church at the time when the church in question first took shape, the preexisting ecclesiopolitical traditions of the localities in which these were established, and the historical and political circumstances under which they were born. As battles over ecclesiology arose and intensified, certain groups elevated principles of church polity into fundamental doctrines. Others continued to resist this. If the Reformed tradition was an invisible but powerful legacy shaping the experience and outlook of those raised within it, it was thus also one that was richly variegated, internally divided, and above all gradually yet ceaselessly changing. The historical circumstances of its birth profoundly and enduringly shaped it, yet it never remained constant, as both internal processes of change and altered external circumstances sparked new ramifications.

NOTES

The notes for each chapter are preceded by a bibliographical note.

INTRODUCTION

1. John a Lasco, *Toute la forme & maniere du Ministere Ecclesiastique en l'Eglise des estrangers, dressée a Londres* ([Emden], 1556), "Au lecteur."
2. *New York Times,* October 10, 1998, "Hillary Clinton Heading to East Europe."
3. A subsequent volume edited by Menna Prestwich, *International Calvinism, 1541–1715* (Cambridge, 1985), currently is the best introduction to the subject. As a collection of essays by leading scholars surveying the faith's history in different regions of Europe and America, however, this work lacks the unity of vision and interpretation that a single author can provide.
4. I explore the reasons for the neglect of these themes by most historians of Calvinism in "The Historiography of Continental Calvinism," in Hartmut Lehmann and Guenther Roth, eds., *Weber's Protestant Ethic: Origins, Evidence, Contexts* (Cambridge, 1993), 305–26.
5. Steve Bruce, *Religion in the Modern World: From Cathedrals to Cults* (Oxford, 1996), 20: "A measured evaluation of the Weber thesis would be that it is plausible and fits what we know"; Peter Berger, "The Desecularization of the World: A Global Overview," in Berger, ed., *The Desecularization of the World: Resurgent Religion and World Politics* (Grand Rapids, 1999), 16.
6. Amy L. Sherman, *The Soul of Development: Biblical Christianity and Eco-*

nomic Transformation in Guatemala (Oxford, 1997); David Landes, *The Wealth and Poverty of Nations: Why Some Are So Rich and Some So Poor* (New York, 1998), 174–79; and, for a positive evaluation of the Weber thesis by a leading Reformation historian, Robert M. Kingdon, "L''etica del capitalismo' tra religione e politica," in Valerio Castronovo, ed., *Storia dell'economia mondiale,* 5 vols. (Rome, 1996–99), 2:375–88.

7. Silvana Seidel Menchi, "Italy," in Bob Scribner et al., eds., *The Reformation in National Context* (Cambridge, 1994), 182–83.

8. Michael Mann, *The Sources of Social Power,* vol. 1 of *A History of Power from the Beginning to* A.D. *1760* (Cambridge, 1986), 2.

9. Uwe Plath, "Zur entstehungsgeschichte des Wortes 'Calvinist'," *Archiv für Reformationsgeschichte* 66 (1975): 213–23.

CHAPTER 1. ZURICH CONTRA WITTENBERG

Bibliographical Note   The standard edition of Zwingli's works and correspondence, still slightly incomplete, is E. Egli et al., eds., *Huldreich Zwinglis sämtliche Werke,* which has been published in various locations since 1905 as part of the Corpus Reformatorum, vols. 88–101. Only a fraction of Zwingli's writings have ever been translated into English; the fullest selection is to be found in three volumes originally edited by Samuel Macauley Jackson and recently reprinted by Labyrinth Press: *Commentary on True and False Religion* (Durham, N.C., 1981); *On Providence and Other Essays* (Durham, N.C., 1983); and *Early Writings* (Durham, N.C., 1987). Key documents of the Zurich Reformation are printed in E. Egli, ed., *Aktensammlung zur Geschichte der Zürcher Reformation in den Jahren 1519–1533* (Zurich, 1879). Comparable volumes exist for Basel and Bern: Emil Dürr and Paul Roth, eds., *Aktensammlung zur Geschichte der Basler Reformation in den Jahren 1519 bis Angang 1534,* 6 vols. (Basel, 1921–50), and Rudolf Steck and Gustav Tobler, eds., *Aktensammlung zur Geschichte der Berner Reformation,* 2 vols. (Bern, 1923).

   Zwingli has been far less extensively studied than Luther. The best short introduction to the man and his work in light of recent scholarship is Ulrich Gäbler, *Huldrych Zwingli: His Life and Work* (Philadelphia, 1986). G. R. Potter, *Zwingli* (Cambridge, 1976), is authoritative for the detailed narrative of his career, while W. P. Stephens, *The Theology of Huldrych Zwingli* (Oxford, 1986), offers the best introduction to his thought. R. W. Walton, *Zwingli's Theocracy* (Toronto, 1967), is fundamental both for understanding the course of the Zurich Reformation and Zwingli's views on the relation between church and state. Much light is also shed on the course of the Zurich Reformation by such studies of early Anabaptism as Harold S. Bender, *Conrad Grebel, 1498–1526: The Founder of the Swiss Brethren* (Goshen, Ind., 1950); John H. Yoder, "The Turning Point of the Zwinglian Reformation," *Mennonite Quarterly Review* 32 (1958): 128–40; Martin Haas, "Der Weg der Täufer in die Absonderung. Zur Interdependenz von Theologie und sozialem Verhalten," in Hans-Jürgen Goertz, ed., *Umstrittenes Täufertum 1525–1975. Neue Forschungen* (Göttingen, 1975), 50–78; James M. Stayer, *Ana-*

baptists and the Sword, 2d ed. (Lawrence, Kan., 1976), chaps. 3, 5, 6; and id., "Wilhelm Reublin: A Picaresque Journey Through Early Anabaptism," in Goertz, ed., *Profiles of Radical Reformers* (Scottdale, Pa., 1982), 107–17. Highly illuminating studies of individual aspects of Zwingli's life, work, and thought include Stayer, "Zwingli and the 'Viri Multi et Excellentes': The Christian Renaissance's Repudiation of *Neoterici* and the Beginnings of Reformed Protestantism," in E. J. Furcha and H. W. Pipkin, eds., *Prophet, Pastor, Protestant: The Work of Huldrych Zwingli after Five Hundred Years* (Allison Park, Pa., 1984); A. E. McGrath, "Humanist Elements in the Early Reformed Doctrine of Justification," *Archiv für Reformationsgeschichte* 73 (1982): 5–19; and Charles Garside, Jr., *Zwingli and the Arts* (New Haven, 1966).

Despite a slight tendency to claim too much for his subject, Gottfried W. Locher, *Die Zwinglische Reformation im Rahmen der europäischen Kirchengeschichte* (Göttingen, 1979), offers the fullest overview of the Zwinglian Reformation on a European scale. Bruce Gordon, "Switzerland," in Andrew Pettegree, ed., *The Early Reformation in Europe* (Cambridge, 1992), and Kaspar von Greyerz, "Switzerland," in Bob Scribner et al., eds., *The Reformation in National Context* (Cambridge, 1994), are excellent brief English-language accounts of the course of the Reformation in Switzerland. A fuller survey may be found in Rudolf Pfister, *Kirchengeschichte der Schweiz,* vol. 2, *Von der Reformation bis zum Zweiten Villmerger Krieg* (Zurich, 1974). Gordon Rupp, *Patterns of Reformation* (Philadelphia, 1969), is excellent on both several lesser Swiss reformers and Karlstadt. Carlos Eire, *War Against the Idols: The Reformation of Worship from Erasmus to Calvin* (Cambridge, 1986), masterfully combines the history of theology and the history of urban agitation for the Reformation in Switzerland and is fundamental to understanding the entire history of the Reformed tradition in its first three generations. Walther Köhler, *Zürcher Ehegericht und Genfer Konsistorium,* 2 vols. (Leipzig, 1932–42), is extremely important for the institutional history of the early Reformed churches in Switzerland and nearby south Germany. Other important works on the early Reformation in Switzerland include Kurt Guggisberg, *Bernische Kirchengeschichte* (Bern, 1958); Hans Rudolf Lavater, "Zwingli und Bern," in *450 Jahre Berner Reformation* (Bern, 1980), 60–103; Hans R. Guggisberg, *Basel in the Sixteenth Century: Aspects of the City Republic before, during, and after the Reformation* (St. Louis, 1982); and id., "The Problem of 'Failure' in the Swiss Reformation: Some Preliminary Reflections," in E. I. Kouri and Tom Scott, eds., *Politics and Society in Reformation Europe* (London, 1987), 188–209.

If one widens the lens still further, James S. Preus, *Carlstadt's Ordinaciones and Luther's Liberty: A Study of the Wittenberg Movement 1521–22* (Cambridge, Mass., 1974), Martin Brecht, *Martin Luther: Shaping and Defining the Reformation 1521–1532* (Minneapolis, 1990), and Mark U. Edwards, *Luther and the False Brethren* (Stanford, 1975), are fundamental for understanding Luther's role in the process that ultimately split magisterial Protestantism into two camps, the Lutheran and the Reformed. A seminal work that sought to account for that division was Bernd Moeller, *Reichsstadt und Reformation* Schriften des Vereins für Reformationsgeschichte 180 (Gütersloh, 1962), subsequently expanded for its French and English translations, *Villes d'Empire et réformation* (Geneva, 1966), and *Imperial Cities and the Reformation* (Philadelphia 1972), then republished once again in Germany with an extensive afterword by the author reevaluating his key arguments in the light of subsequent research, *Reichsstadt und Reformation: Bearbeitete Neuausgabe* (Berlin, 1987). Peter Blickle, *Communal Reformation: The Quest for Salvation in Sixteenth-Century Germany* (Atlantic Highlands, N.J., 1992), is another, more recent interpretation of relevance. Important local studies that contribute to understanding the relations between the Swiss and south German Reformations and the Lutheran–Zwinglian rivalry within the Holy Roman Empire during Zwingli's lifetime include Friedrich Roth, *Augsburgs Reformationsgeschichte,* 4 vols. (Munich, 1901–11); Hermann Buck, *Die Anfänge der Konstanzer Reformationsprozesse. Österreich, Eidgenossenschaft und Schmalkaldischer Bund 1510/22–1531* (Tübingen, 1964); Hans-Christoph Rublack, *Die Einführung der Reformation in Konstanz von dem Anfängen bis zum Abschluss 1531* (Gütersloh, 1971); Wolfgang Dobras, *Ratsregiment, Sittenpolizei und Kirchenzucht in der Reichsstadt Konstanz 1531–1548: Ein Beitrag zur Geschichte der oberdeutsche-schweizerischen Reformation* (Gütersloh, 1993); Miriam Usher Chrisman, *Strasbourg and the Reform: A Study in the Process of Change* (New Haven, 1967); Thomas A. Brady, Jr., *Protestant Politics: Jacob Sturm (1489–1553) and the German Reformation* (Atlantic Highlands, N.J., 1995); and Ernst Koch, "'Zwinglianer' zwischen Ostsee und Harz in den Anfangsjahren der Reformation (1525–1532)," *Zwingliana* 16 (1985): 517–45.

1. Denis Crouzet, *Jean Calvin: Vies parallèles* (Paris, 2000), 24; Guillaume Farel, *Du vray usage de la croix de Jesus-Christ* (Neuchâtel, 1865), 146–48; Eire, *War Against the Idols,* chap. 1, esp. 8–9. The literature on late medieval religiosity, the cult of images and of the eucharist, and the relation between these and the Reformation is vast. Key titles in addition to Eire include Bernd Moeller, "Religious Life in Germany on the Eve of the Reformation," in Gerald Strauss, ed., *Pre-Reformation Germany* (New York, 1972), 13–42; Francis Rapp, *L'Eglise et la vie religieuse en Occident à la fin du Moyen Age* (Paris, 1971); Richard Trexler, "Sacred Images in Florentine Religion," *Studies in the Renaissance* 19 (1972): 7–41; Miri Rubin, *Corpus Christi: The Eucharist in Late Medieval Culture* (Cambridge, 1991); Eamon Duffy, *The Stripping of the Altars: Traditional Religion in England 1400–1580* (New Haven, 1992).
2. Heiko A. Oberman, ed., *Forerunners of the Reformation: The Shape of Late Medieval Thought Illustrated by Key Documents* (New York, 1966); Barry Collett, *Italian Benedictine Scholars and the Reformation: The Congregation of Santa Giustina of Padua* (Oxford, 1985).
3. *Histoire ecclésiastique des églises réformées au royaume de France,* eds. G. Baum, E. Cunitz, and R. Reuss (Paris, 1883–9), 1:1–8; Jean Crespin, *Histoire des martyrs persecutez et mis a mort pour la verité de l'evangile, depuis le*

temps des apostres jusques a present, ed. Daniel Benoit (Toulouse, 1885–89), 1:xlvii–xlviii; Theodore Beza, *Les vrais pourtraits des hommes illustres en piete et doctrine, du travail desquels Dieu s'est servi en ces derniers temps, pour remettre sus la vraye Religion en divers pays de la Chrestienté* (Geneva, 1581).

4. Jacques Rossiaud, "Prostitution, jeunesse et société dans les villes du Sud-Est au XVe siècle," *Annales: Economies, Sociétés, Civilisations* 31 (1976): 291; Louis Binz, *Vie religieuse et réforme ecclesiastique dans le diocèse de Genève pendant le Grand Schisme et la crise conciliaire (1378-1450)* (Geneva, 1973); Nicole Lemaitre, *Le Rouergue flamboyant: Le clergé et les fidèles du diocèse de Rodez 1417-1563* (Paris, 1988), parts 1–2; Peter Heath, *The English Parish Clergy on the Eve of the Reformation* (London, 1969); Jan Buntinx, "Geschil tussen de stad en de pastoors van Diksmuide over de kosten van begrafenissen en toedienen van sacramenten (1563)," *Bulletin de la Commission royale d'histoire* 154 (1988): 227–38; Potter, *Zwingli,* 79; Francis Rapp, *Réformes et Reformation à Strasbourg: Eglise et société dans le diocèse de Strasbourg (1450–1525)* (Paris, 1974), esp. 246, 261.

5. Michel Veissière, *L'éveque Guillaume Briçonnet (1470-1534): Contribution à la connaissance de la Réforme catholique à la veille du Concile de Trente;* Lemaitre, *Rouergue flamboyant,* chaps. 8–10; Paul Broutin, *L'évêque dans la tradition pastorale du XVIe siècle* (Bruges, 1953); Jennifer Britnell, *Jean Bouchet* (Edinburgh, 1986), 192–93; Jean-Pierre Dedieu, "'Christianisation' en Nouvelle Castille: Catéchisme, communion, messe et confirmation dans l'archevêché de Tolède, 1540–1650," *Mélanges de la Case de Velazquez* 15 (1979): 261–94; Sara T. Nalle, *God in La Mancha: Religious Reform and the People of Cuenca, 1500-1650* (Baltimore, 1992), 8–26, 106–11.

6. These statistics are calculated on the basis of the information in Hans-Joachim Köhler, "Erste Schritte zu einem Meinungsprofil der frühen Reformationszeit," in Volker Press and Dieter Stievermann, eds., *Martin Luther: Probleme seiner Zeit* (Stuttgart, 1986), 244–81.

7. Bernd Moeller, "Was wurde in der Frühzeit der Reformation in den deutschen Städten gepredigt?" *Archiv für Reformationsgeschichte* 75 (1984): 176–93; Hans-Jürgen Goertz, *Pfaffenhass und gross Geschrei: Die Reformatorischen Bewegungen in Deutschland 1517-1529* (Munich, 1987); Steven Ozment, *The Reformation in the Cities: The Appeal of Protestantism to Sixteenth-Century Germany and Switzerland* (New Haven, 1975); Mark U. Edwards, Jr., *Printing, Propaganda, and Martin Luther* (Berkeley, 1994); Miriam Usher Chrisman, "Lay Response to the Protestant Reformation in Germany, 1520–1528," in Peter N. Brooks, ed., *Reformation Principle and Practise: Essays in Honour of Arthur Geoffrey Dickens* (London, 1980), 35–52; id., *Conflicting Visions of Reform: German Lay Propaganda Pamphlets, 1519-1530* (Atlantic Highlands, N.J., 1996), esp. chaps. 6–8; Paul A. Russell, *Lay Theology in the Reformation: Popular Pamphleteers in Southwest Germany 1521-1525* (Cambridge, 1986); Martin Haas, "The Path of the Anabaptists into Separation: The Interdependence of Theology and Social Behavior," in James M. Stayer and Werner O. Packull, *The Anabap-*

tists and Thomas Müntzer (Dubuque, 1980), 80: "Wherever in Switzerland the common people intervened directly before 1525, they . . . could be mobilized most easily for iconoclasm, breaking fast restrictions, tithe refusal, and insulting priests and monks of the old faith"; Claire Cross, *Church and People 1450–1660* (London, 1976), 76: "The populace at large, when attracted to Protestantism at all, seems to have been much more attracted by its anti-authoritarian, anti-sacramental and iconoclastic aspects."

8. For the successive editions of this work, which did more than any other to spark research into the mass appeal of the Reformation and the politics of its establishment in the cities of Germany and Switzerland, see the bibliographic note to this chapter, above.

9. Moeller, *Reichsstadt und Reformation: Bearbeitete Neuausgabe,* 71, 90–93.

10. E.g., Philip Melanchthon and Johannes Brenz. Still lacking is a careful study of a large sample of evangelical preachers across Germany that seeks to determine whether or not any factors in their background or education consistently correlate with how they aligned themselves on the issues that divided Zwinglians from Lutherans.

11. For this and the following paragraphs, I have relied primarily upon Preus, *Carlstadt's Ordinaciones and Luther's Liberty;* Brecht, *Luther: Shaping and Defining the Reformation 1521–1532,* 25–66; and Rupp, *Patterns of Reformation,* 79–110. Key texts are usefully collected in Ronald J. Sider, ed., *Karlstadt's Battle with Luther: Documents in a Liberal-Radical Debate* (Philadelphia, 1978).

12. Margarete Stirm, *Die Bilderfrage in der Reformation* (Gütersloh, 1977), part 1; Emil Sehling et al., eds., *Die evangelische Kirchenordnung des XVI Jahrhunderts* (Leipzig and Tübingen, 1902–), 3:87, 4:370, 8:49, 15:75–76.

13. Edwards, *Luther and the False Brethren,* chaps. 1, 2, esp. 52.

14. Leonhard von Muralt, "Renaissance und Reformation," in *Handbuch der Schweizer Geschichte* (Zurich, 1980), 1:391–430; Markus Mattmüller, *Bevölkerungsgeschichte der Schweiz,* part I (Basel, 1987), 198–202; Kurt Messmer and Peter Hoppe, *Luzerner Patriziat* (Munich, 1976); F. L. Taylor, *The Art of War in Italy 1494–1529* (Cambridge, 1921), chap. 6; Bert S. Hall, *Weapons and Warfare in Renaissance Europe: Gunpowder, Technology, and Tactics* (Baltimore, 1997), 164–76. Mattmüller offers the following estimates of the size of Switzerland's most important cities: Basel, 9,500 inhabitants in 1501; Zurich, 5,080 inhabitants in 1529; Saint-Gall, 4,500 inhabitants in 1527; Fribourg, 4,400 inhabitants in 1477; Bern, 3,245 inhabitants in 1499; Lucerne, 2,800 inhabitants in 1487; Schaffhausen, 2,500 inhabitants in 1529; Solothurn, 1,900 inhabitants in 1416.

15. Walton, *Zwingli's Theocracy,* chap. 1; Moeller, *Reichstadt und Reformation: Bearbeitete Neuausgabe,* 72.

16. Stayer, "Zwingli and the 'Viri Multi et Excellentes'," esp. 146.

17. Rudolf Dellsperger, "Zehn Jahre bernischer Reformationsgeschichte: Eine Einführung," in *450 Jahre Berner Reformation* (Bern, 1980), 33.

18. Zwingli, *Sämtliche Werke,* 7:245.

19. Walton, *Zwingli's Theocracy,* 169.

20. Zwingli, *Sämtliche Werke*, 7:35–36; Gäbler, *Zwingli*, 39–40, 43; Potter, *Zwingli*, 25–27, 39–46.

21. Gäbler, *Zwingli*, 46–50; Stayer, "Zwingli and the 'Viri Multi et Excellentes'," esp. 143.

22. Eire, *War Against the Idols*, 77–78; Walton, *Zwingli's Theocracy*, chap. 2.

23. Potter, *Zwingli*, 28–39.

24. Ibid., 71, 76–81; Gäbler, *Zwingli*, 52–54.

25. Zwingli, *Commentary on True and False Religion*, esp. 92–93, 321. See further Stephens, *Theology of Zwingli*, passim.

26. Zwingli, *On Providence*, 166; id., *Commentary on True and False Religion*, 341. Cf. Martin Luther, "The Bondage of the Will," in *Works* (St. Louis, 1955–86), vol. 33, esp. 261–63.

27. Zwingli, *On Providence*, 128–234, esp. 138, 180, 186; Stephens, *Theology of Zwingli*, 97–107, esp. 97.

28. Gäbler, *Zwingli*, 52–55; Walton, *Zwingli's Theocracy*, 58–75; Bernd Moeller, "Zwingli's Disputationen: Studien zu den Anfängen der Kirchenbildung und des Synodalwesens im Protestantismus," *Zeitschrift der Savigny-Stiftung für Rechtsgeschichte* 56 (1970): 275–323; Heiko Oberman, *Masters of the Reformation: The Emergence of a New Intellectual Climate in Europe* (Cambridge, 1981), 190–239.

29. Gäbler, *Zwingli*, 56–58; Walton, *Zwingli's Theocracy*, 88–93.

30. Gäbler, *Zwingli*, 63–71; Walton, *Zwingli's Theocracy*, 133–38; Potter, *Zwingli*, 97–104; Moeller, "Zwingli's Disputationen"; Oberman, *Masters*, 190–239.

31. Eire, *War Against the Idols*, 79–81; Garside, *Zwingli and the Arts*, 104–28.

32. Gäbler, *Zwingli*, 76–81; Potter, *Zwingli*, 131–3; Garside, *Zwingli and the Arts*, 129–45.

33. Gäbler, *Zwingli*, 50–51, 93–94; Stayer, "Reublin," 108–10; Stayer, *Anabaptists and the Sword*, 97.

34. Walton, *Zwingli's Theocracy*, 157–75.

35. Bender, *Grebel;* Yoder, "Turning Point"; Potter, *Zwingli*, 160–97; Stayer, *Anabaptists and the Sword*, chap. 5.

36. Garside, *Zwingli and the Arts*, 156–60.

37. Lee Palmer Wandel, *Always Among Us: Images of the Poor in Zwingli's Zurich* (Cambridge, 1990), 145–62.

38. Yngve Brilioth, *Eucharistic Faith and Practice: Evangelical and Catholic* (London, 1930), 157–62; Zwingli, "A Short and Clear Exposition of the Christian Faith," in *On Providence and Other Essays*, 287–91.

39. Potter, *Zwingli*, 220–23; Gottfried Locher, "In Spirit and in Truth: How Worship in Zurich Changed at the Reformation" in *Zwingli's Thought: New Perspectives* (Leiden, 1981), 28–29; Robert C. Walton, "Heinrich Bullinger," in Jill Raitt, ed., *Shapers of Religious Tradition in Germany, Switzerland, and Poland 1560–1600* (New Haven, 1981), 70–71; Martin Brecht, "Die Reform des Wittenberger Horengottesdienstes und die Entstehung der Zürcher Prophezei," in H. A. Oberman, E. Saxer, A. Schindler, and H. Stucki, eds., *Reformiertes Erbe: Festschrift für Gottfried W. Locher zu seinem 80. Geburtstag* (Zurich, 1992), 49–62;

Andrew Pettegree, *Foreign Protestant Communities in Sixteenth-Century London* (Oxford, 1986); G. D. Henderson, "The Exercise," in *The Burning Bush: Studies in Scottish Church History* (Edinburgh, 1957), 42–60; Patrick Collinson, *The Elizabethan Puritan Movement* (London, 1967), 168–76.

40. Köhler, *Zürcher Ehegericht*, 1:28–230; Johannes Plomp, *De Kerkelijke Tucht bij Calvin* (Kampen, 1969), 24–26.

41. Egli, ed., *Aktensammlung zur Geschichte der Zürcher Reformation*, 453–54; Anton Lagiardèr, "Das reformierte Zürich und die Fest- und Heiligentage," *Zwingliana* 9 (1953): 497–525.

42. Bruce Gordon, *Clerical Discipline and the Rural Reformation: The Synod in Zurich, 1532–1580* (Bern, 1992).

43. Egli, ed., *Aktensammlung zur Geschichte der Zürcher Reformation*, 533, 598, 651–52; Potter, *Zwingli*, 202–03.

44. Oberman, *Forerunners of the Reformation*, 252–53.

45. Cornelisz Hoen, "A Most Christian Letter," in Oberman, ed., *Forerunners of the Reformation*, 275.

46. Martin Luther, "The Adoration of the Sacrament" in *Works* 36:269–306, esp. 279; Brecht, *Luther: Shaping and Defining the Reformation 1521–1532*, 75–76.

47. Potter, *Zwingli*, 287–93; Gäbler, *Zwingli*, 132; J. Wayne Baker, *Heinrich Bullinger and the Covenant: The Other Reformed Tradition* (Athens, Ohio, 1980), xv.

48. The standard account of the sacramentarian debate is Walther Köhler, *Zwingli und Luther: Ihr Streit über das Abendmahl nach seinen politischen und religiösen Beziehungen* (Leipzig and Gütersloh, 1924–53). See also Potter, *Zwingli*, 287–93; Gäbler, *Zwingli*, 131–38; Rupp, *Patterns of Reformation*, 23–27; Edwards, *Luther and the False Brethren*, 82–111; Brecht, *Luther: Shaping and Defining the Reformation 1521–1532*, 293–334; R. Emmet McLaughlin, *Caspar Schwenkfeld, Reluctant Radical: His Life to 1540* (New Haven, 1986), 61–76.

49. Edwards, *Luther and the False Brethren*, 88, 103.

50. Rublack, *Einführung der Reformation in Konstanz*, 16; Emil Egli, *Schweizerische Reformationsgeschichte* (Zurich, 1910), 196–200; Lavater, "Zwingli und Bern," 64–66; Guggisberg, *Bernische Kirchengeschichte*, 55–75.

51. Blickle, *Communal Reformation*, 14–20; Gordon, "Switzerland," 77.

52. Irena Backus, *The Disputations of Baden, 1526 and Berne, 1528: Neutralizing the Early Church* (Princeton, 1993), 1–78; Potter, *Zwingli*, 225–40; Gäbler, *Zwingli*, 112–13; Rupp, *Patterns of Reformation*, 28–30.

53. Rupp, *Patterns of Reformation*, 372; Locher, *Zwinglische Reformation*, 366; Potter, *Zwingli*, 271–75.

54. Backus, *Disputations of Baden and Berne*, 79–122; Guggisberg, *Bernische Kirchengeschichte*, 101–31; Locher, *Zwinglische Reformation*, 276–82; Eire, *War Against the Idols*, 110–12.

55. Locher, *Zwinglische Reformation*, 364–408.

56. Potter, *Zwingli*, 262–63; Köhler, *Zürcher Ehegericht*, 1:231–356; Plomp, *Kerkelijke Tucht*, 31–35.

57. Garside, *Zwingli and the Arts*, 130.

58. Locher, *Zwinglische Reformation*, 418–41; Guggisberg, "The Problem of 'Failure' in the Swiss Reformation"; Potter, *Zwingli*, 267; Egli, *Schweizerische Reformationsgeschichte*, 198–200, 218; Messmer and Hoppe, *Luzerner Patriziat*, passim. In thinking about the reasons for resistance to the Reformation in Switzerland, I have also profited from Kaspar von Greyerz's unpublished "Möglichkeiten und Grenzen der schweizerischen Reformation."

59. Stayer, *Anabaptists and the Sword*, chap. 3; Potter, *Zwingli*, 347–55; Locher, *Zwinglische Reformation*, 189–91, 350–54; Brady, *Protestant Politics*, 65.

60. Chrisman, *Strasbourg and the Reform*, 144–51; René Bornert, *La Réforme protestante du culte à Strasbourg au XVIe siècle (1523–1598)* (Leiden, 1981), 487–91.

61. Hermann Buck, *Die Anfänge der Konstanzer Reformationsprozesse, Österreich: Eidgenossenschaft und Schmalkaldischer Bund 1510/22–1531* (Tübingen, 1964); Rublack, *Einführung der Reformation in Konstanz*, esp. 82–92; Dobras, *Ratsregiment*, esp. 183, 375; Marcia Kay Lewis, "Ambrosius Blaurer and the Reformation in Constance" (Ph.D. diss., University of Iowa, 1974); Köhler, *Zürcher Ehegericht*, 2:89–121.

62. Lewis, "Blaurer," 188.

63. Philip Schaff, *The Creeds of Christendom* (New York, 1877), 3:3–73; "An Account of the Faith of Huldreich Zwingli, Submitted to the German Emperor Charles V, at the Diet of Augsburg," in *On Providence and Other Essays*, 33–62; Arthur C. Cochrane, ed., *Reformed Confessions of the Sixteenth Century* (Philadelphia, 1966), 51–88.

64. Roth, *Augsburgs Reformationsgeschichte*, 1:197–217, 2:7–22; Köhler, *Zürcher Ehegericht*, 2:305; Moeller, *Imperial Cities*, 93–94; Katharina Sieh-Burens, *Oligarchie, Konfession und Politik im 16. Jahrhundert: Zur sozialen Verflechtung der Augsburger Bürgermeister und Stadtpflege 1518–1618* (Munich, 1986), esp. 135–43; Philip Broadhead, "Popular Pressure for Reform in Augsburg 1524–1534," in Wolfgang Mommsen et al., eds, *Stadtbürgertum und Adel in der Reformation* (Stuttgart, 1979), 80–87.

65. Moeller, *Imperial Cities*, 93–95; Wilfried Enderle, "Ulm und die evangelischen Reichsstädte im Südwesten," in Anton Schindling and Walter Ziegler, eds., *Die Territorien des Reichs im Zeitalter der Reformation und Konfessionalisierung* (Münster, 1988–93), 5:201; Sigrid Jahns, *Frankfurt, Reformation und Schmalkaldischer Bund: Die Reformations-, Reichs- und Bündnispolitik der Reichsstadt Frankfurt am Main 1525–1536* (Frankfurt, 1976), esp. 149–51.

66. Hardheaded scepticism about transubstantiation surfaced so recurrently in late medieval heretical movements that one suspects doubt about the doctrine always warred with belief. Rubin, *Corpus Christi*, 113, 320–34.

67. Koch, "'Zwinglianer' zwischen Ostsee und Harz"; Heinz Schilling, "Alternatives

to the Lutheran Reformation and the Rise of Lutheran Identity," in Andrew C. Fix and Susan C. Karant-Nunn, eds., *Germania Illustrata: Essays on Early Modern Germany Presented to Gerald Strauss* (Kirksville, Mo., 1992), 99–120; McLaughlin, *Schwenkfeld,* esp. 91–93, 110–15.

68. Potter, *Zwingli,* 378–82; Brady, *Protestant Politics,* 56 ff.

69. See below, 65–67; Heinrich Richard Schmidt, "Der Schmalkaldische Bund und die oberdeutschen Städte bis 1536: Ein Beitrag zur politischen Konfessionalisierung im Protestantismus, *Zwingliana* 18 (1989): 36–61.

70. W. D. J. Cargill Thompson, "Luther and the Right of Resistance to the Emperor," in Derek Baker, ed., *Church, Society and Politics* (Oxford, 1975), 12:159–202.

71. For this and the subsequent paragraphs, Potter, *Zwingli,* 343–419; Gäbler, *Zwingli,* 141–52.

CHAPTER 2. SWITZERLAND AND GERMANY

Bibliographical Note   The figures discussed in this chapter were overshadowed for so long by Calvin that modern critical editions of their papers and writings are still frequently incomplete or lacking. The Institute for Swiss Reformation History in Zurich has been publishing *Heinrich Bullinger Werke* slowly since 1972. To date the series covers his correspondence through 1538 and his theological writings through 1527. His diary is available in an edition by Emil Egli, *Diarium (Annales vitae) der Jahre 1504–1574* (Basel, 1904), while his most important work, *The Decades,* may be consulted in a nineteenth-century edition by Thomas Harding (4 vols, Cambridge, 1849–52). Vermigli's works are appearing far more rapidly in English translation in *The Peter Martyr Library,* 7 vols. to date (Kirksville, Mo., 1994–), usefully complemented by J. C. McLelland and G. E. Duffield, eds., *The Life, Early Letters and Eucharistic Theology of Peter Martyr* (Appleford, 1989). For Musculus, one must make do with the original published editions of his works, although Reinhard Bodenmann, *Wolfgang Musculus (1497–1563), Destin d'un autodidacte lorrain au siècle des Réformes: Etude basée sur la biographie établie par son fils, la correspondance personnelle et de nombreux autres documents d'époque* (Geneva, 2000), is a critical edition of the earliest biography of his life and many other helpful elements toward a future biography. As the corpus of a Lasco's letters and publications is by far the smallest, he has been best served, thanks to A. Kuyper, ed., *Joannis a Lasco, Opera tam edita quam inedita* (Amsterdam, 1866), and W. F. Dankbaar's edition of Marten Micron, *De Christlicke Ordinancien der Nederlantscher Ghemeinten te Londen (1554)* (The Hague, 1956).

Still also lacking are outstanding full biographies of any of these men. Bullinger's early life has been the subject of an excellent study by Fritz Blanke, *Der junge Bullinger* (Zurich, 1942), reprinted as part of the less satisfactory Blanke and Immanuel Leuschner, *Heinrich Bullinger, Vater der reformierten Kirche* (Zurich, 1990). Robert C. Walton, "Heinrich Bullinger" in Jill Raitt, ed., *Shapers of Religious Tradition in Germany, Switzerland, and Poland 1560–1600* (New Haven, 1981), 69–87, offers a quick overview in English. Topical studies of value include Walther Hollweg, *Heinrich Bullingers Hausbuch: Eine Untersuchung über die Anfänge der reformierten Predigtliteratur* (Giessen, 1956); J. Wayne Baker, *Heinrich Bullinger and the Covenant: The Other Reformed Tradition* (Athens, Ohio, 1980); and Hans Ulrich Bächtold, *Heinrich Bullinger vor dem Rat: Zur Gestaltung und Verwaltung des Zürcher Staatswesens in den Jahren 1531 bis 1575* (Bern, 1982). Vermigli's life within the Catholic church has been far better served by Peter McNair, *Peter Martyr in Italy: An Anatomy of Apostasy* (Oxford, 1967) than has his work in exile by Marvin W. Anderson, *Peter Martyr: A Reformer in Exile (1542-1562)* (Nieuwkoop, 1975). On his thought, see especially John Patrick Donnelly, *Calvinism and Scholasticism in Vermigli's Doctrine of Man and Grace* (Leiden, 1976); and Frank A. James III, *Peter Martyr Vermigli and Predestination: The Augustinian Inheritance of an Italian Reformer* (Oxford, 1998). For Musculus the key starting points are Bodenmann, *Musculus,* and Rudolf Dellsperger et al, eds., *Wolfgang Musculus (1497-1563) und die oberdeutsche Reformation* (Berlin, 1997). For a Lasco: Hermann Dalton, *John a Lasco: His Earlier Life and Labours* (London, 1886); Oskar Bartel, *Jan Laski* (Berlin, 1981); and Basil Hall, "John a Lasco: The Humanist Turned Protestant, 1499-1560," in *Humanists and Protestants 1500-1900* (Edinburgh, 1990), 171-206. Important books on wider themes explored in this chapter are also rare, but Philippe Denis, *Les Eglises d'étrangers en pays rhénans (1538-1564)* (Paris, 1984), and Andrew Pettegree, *Emden and the Dutch Revolt: Exile and the Development of Reformed Protestantism* (Oxford, 1992) are noteworthy exceptions to this generalization.

1. Büsser, "Bullinger, Nicht Calvin," *Neue Zürcher Zeitung* 6/7 no. 261 (Nov. 1976), 59.
2. Walton, "Bullinger," 85.
3. Richard A. Muller, *Post-Reformation Reformed Dogmatics,* vol. 1, *Prolegomena to Theology* (Grand Rapids, 1987), 69.
4. Patrick Collinson, "England 1558-1640," in Prestwich, ed., *International Calvinism,* 214-15.
5. My account of Bullinger's career down to the time he was called to Zurich rests primarily upon Blanke, *Der junge Bullinger;* Emil Egli, *Diarium.*
6. Bullinger, *Diarium,* 5-6.
7. J. Wayne Baker, "Church, State, and Dissent: The Crisis of the Swiss Reformation, 1531-1536," *Church History* 57 (1988): 135-52; id., "In Defense of Magisterial Discipline: Bullinger's 'Tractatus de Excommunicatione' of 1568," in U. Gäbler and E. Herkenrath, eds., *Heinrich Bullinger 1504-1575: Gesammelte Aufsätze zum 400. Todestag* (Zurich, 1975), 1:141-59; Plomp, *Kerkelijke Tucht,* 26.
8. Baker, "Church, State, and Dissent," 136; Pamela Biel, *Doorkeepers at the House of Righteousness: Heinrich Bullinger and the Zurich Clergy 1535-1575* (Bern, 1991), 59-63; Heinrich Bullinger, *The Decades,* ed. Thomas Harding (Cambridge, 1849-52), 2:44, 3:343; Bächtold, *Bullinger vor dem Rat.*
9. This and the following paragraphs rest primarily upon Hastings Eells, *Martin*

Bucer (New Haven, 1931), chaps. 14–16, 20–22; Martin Brecht, *Martin Luther: The Preservation of the Church 1532–1546* (Minneapolis, 1993), 39–59, 323–52; Gordon, "Switzerland," 87; Guggisberg, *Bernische Kirchengeschichte,* 198–212; André Bouvier, *Henri Bullinger réformateur et conseiller oecuménique le successeur de Zwingli, d'après sa correspondance avec les réformés et les humanistes de langue française* (Neuchâtel, 1940), 117–49; Jules Bonnet, ed., *Letters of John Calvin* (Philadelphia, 1855–58), 1:65–449, esp. 437.

10. *Registres de la Compagnie des Pasteurs de Genève* (Geneva, 1962–), 1:64–72; Jean-François Gilmont, *Jean Calvin et le livre imprimé* (Geneva, 1997), 21–25; Paul Rorem, *Calvin and Bullinger on the Lord's Supper* (Bramcote, England, 1989).

11. Walter Hildebrandt and Rudolf Zimmermann, *Bedeutung und Geschichte des zweiten helvetischen Bekenntnisses* (Zurich, 1938); Jacques Courvoisier, ed., *La Confession Helvétique Postérieure* (Neuchâtel, 1944).

12. Bullinger's career as an author may be followed through Joachim Staedtke, *Heinrich Bullinger Bibliographie, Werke,* part 1, vol. 1 (Zurich, 1972).

13. Eire, *War Against the Idols,* 86–88.

14. Henry Bullinger, *The Decades,* 1:292; Eire, *War Against the Idols,* 236–37; Carlo Ginzburg, *Il Nicodemismo* (Turin, 1970), 113–14; Büsser, "Bullinger, nicht Calvin"; id., "Bullinger et Calvin," *Etudes Théologiques et Religieuses* 63 (1988): 35.

15. Hollweg, *Bullingers Hausbuch,* passim, esp. 69–70, 75.

16. Georg Finsler, *Zwingli-Bibliographie* (Zurich 1897; repr. Nieuwkoop, 1968); Staedtke, *Heinrich Bullinger Bibliographie.*

17. Hollweg, *Bullingers Hausbuch,* 102–03; Büsser, "Bullinger et Calvin," 35.

18. Bullinger, *Decades;* Walton, "Bullinger"; Rorem, *Calvin and Bullinger on the Lord's Supper;* Baker, *Bullinger and the Covenant;* Cornelis P. Venema, "Heinrich Bullinger's Correspondence on Calvin's Doctrine of Predestination, 1551–1553," *Sixteenth Century Journal* 17 (1986): 435–50; Baker, "Heinrich Bullinger, the Covenant, and the Reformed Tradition," *Sixteenth Century Journal* 29 (1998): 359–76.

19. Karin Maag, *Seminary or University? The Genevan Academy and Reformed Higher Education, 1560–1620* (Aldershot, 1995), 131–37; Christoph Zürcher, *Konrad Pellikans Wirken in Zürich 1526–1556* (Zurich, 1975); E. Egli, "Biblianders Leben und Schriften," in Egli, *Analecta Reformatoria* (Zurich, 1901), 2:1–144; *Oxford Encyclopedia of the Reformation,* s.v. "Theodore Bibliander," "Rudolf Gwalther."

20. For this and the next paragraph: J. C. McLelland and G. E. Duffield, eds., *The Life, Early Letters and Eucharistic Theology of Peter Martyr* (Appleford, 1989); McNair, *Peter Martyr in Italy;* Anderson, *Peter Martyr: A Reformer in Exile;* Salvatore Corda, *Veritas Sacramenti: A Study in Vermigli's Doctrine of the Lord's Supper* (Zurich, 1975); James, *Peter Martyr Vermigli and Predestination,* esp. 5; Joachim Staedtke, "Der Zürcher Prädestinationsstreit von 1560," *Zwingliana* 9 (1953): 536–46; Baker, *Bullinger and the Covenant,* 39–42; John Patrick Don-

nelly, *A Bibliography of the Works of Peter Martyr Vermigli* (Kirksville, Mo., 1990), 98–127.

21. Maag, *Seminary or University?* 136; Micron, *De Christlicke Ordinacien,* ed. Dankbaar, 3, 18.

22. For Musculus's biography: Bodenmann, *Musculus.* For his theology and influence: Helmut Kressner, *Schweizer Ursprünge des anglikanischen Staatskirchentums* (Gütersloh, 1953), esp. chap. 2; Dellsperger et al., eds., *Musculus und die oberdeutsche Reformation,* esp. 299–310, 325–27, 401–04; and James Thomas Ford, "Wolfgang Musculus on the Office of the Christian Magistrate," *Archiv für Reformationsgeschichte* 91 (2000): 149–67.

23. Wolfgang Musculus, *Common Places of the Christian Religion* (London, 1578), esp. 413, 1298–1314; Kressner, *Schweizer Ursprünge;* Ford, "Musculus on the Christian Magistrate."

24. Musculus, *Common Places,* 515–17, 746; Bodenmann, *Musculus,* 200–05, 335, 503–38.

25. W. Nijenhuis, *Calvinus Oecumenicus: Calvijn en de eenheid der Kerk in het licht van zijn Briefwisseling* (The Hague, 1959), 10–11.

26. Bullinger, *Werke,* part 1, vol. 1, "Vorwort"; Hollweg, *Bullingers Hausbuch,* 13; Blanke and Leuschner, *Bullinger,* Abbildungen 2 Teil, figure 2.

27. Traugott Schiess, ed., *Bullingers Korrespondenz mit den Graubündnern,* 3 vols. (Basel, 1904–06, repr. Nieuwkoop 1968); id., "Ein Jahr aus Bullingers Brief-wechsel," *Zwingliana* 6 (1934): 16–17; Werner Graf, "Evangelische Kirchen-ordnung im Freistaat Gemeiner Drei Bünde," *Zwingliana* 11 (1963): 635; Delio Cantimori, *Eretici Italiani del Cinquecento: Richerche storiche,* 3d ed. (Florence, 1978), 72–80, 88–107, esp. 89; George Huntston Williams, *The Radical Reformation,* 3d ed. (Kirksville, Mo., 1992), 837–49.

28. Much of the correspondence between Zurich and England or English corre-spondents is published in *Original Letters Relative to the English Reformation, Written during the Reigns of King Henry VIII, King Edward VI, and Queen Mary: Chiefly from the Archives of Zurich,* ed. Hastings Robinson, 2 vols. (Cambridge, 1846–47); *The Zurich Letters, Comprising the Correspondence of Several En-glish Bishops and Others, with some of the Helvetian Reformers during the Early Part of the Reign of Queen Elizabeth,* ed. Hastings Robinson, 2 vols. (Cam-bridge, 1842–45). See also Diarmaid MacCulloch, *Thomas Cranmer: A Life* (New Haven, 1996), 176ff.

29. Bullinger, *Epistola ad ecclesias hungaricas earumque pastores scripta MDLI/Sendschreiben an die ungarischen Kirchen und Pastoren 1551,* ed. Barnabas Nagy (Budapest, 1968); István Schlégl, "Die Beziehungen Heinrich Bullingers zu Ungarn," *Zwingliana* 12 (1960): 330–70.

30. Theodor Wotschke, ed., *Die Briefwechsel der Schweizer mit den Polen* (Leipzig, 1908); Staedtke, *Bullinger Bibliographie,* 178, 200.

31. Roth, *Augsburgs Reformationsgeschichte,* 2:51–52; Jahns, *Frankfurt,* 221–24; Brecht, *Luther: Shaping and Defining the Reformation,* 450; id., *Luther: The*

Preservation of the Church, 34, 39; id., "Luthertum als politische und soziale Kraft in den Städten," in F. Petri, ed., *Kirche und gesellschaftlicher Wandel in Deutschen und Niederländischen Städten der werdenden Neuzeit* (Cologne, 1980), 15ff.

32. Roth, *Augsburgs Reformationsgeschichte*, vol. 2, chaps. 8–9; Brecht, *Martin Luther: The Preservation of the Church*, 39–59; Hermann Ehmer, "Württemberg," in Schindling and Ziegler, eds., *Territorien des Reichs im Zeitalter der Reformation*, 5:174–75; Günter Vogler, "The Anabaptist Kingdom of Münster in the Tension Between Anabaptism and Imperial Policy," and James M. Stayer, "Christianity in One City: Anabaptist Münster, 1534–35," in Hans J. Hillerbrand, ed., *Radical Tendencies in the Reformation: Divergent Perspectives* (Kirksville, Mo., 1988), 99–134; Rudolfine Freiin von Oer, "Münster," in Anton Schindling and Walter Ziegler, eds., *Die Territorien des Reichs im Zeitalter der Reformation und Konfessionalisierung* (Münster, 1989–1997), 3:113–20; Jahns, *Frankfurt*, esp. 400–01.

33. Roth, *Augsburgs Reformationsgeschichte*, vol. 2, chaps. 10–11; Gottfried Seebass, "Die Augsburger Kirchenordnung von 1537 in ihrem historischen und theologischen Zusammenhang," in Reinhard Schwarz, ed., *Die Augsburger Kirchenordnung von 1537 und ihr Umfeld* (Gütersloh, 1988), 33–58; Gunther Gottlieb et al., *Geschichte der Stadt Augsburg* (Stuttgart, 1984), 400; James Thomas Ford, "Unter dem Schein der concorden und confession: Wolfgang Musculus and the Confessional Identity of Augsburg, 1531–1548," in Rudolf Dellsperger et al., eds., *Musculus*, 23–36; Locher, *Zwinglische Reformation*, 470, 499; Enderle, "Ulm," 402; Ehmer, "Württemberg," 176; Anton Schindling and Georg Schmidt, "Frankfurt am Main, Friedberg, Wetzlar," in Schindling and Ziegler, eds., *Territorien des Reichs im Zeitalter der Reformation*, 4:46; Brady, *Protestant Politics*, 115–16.

34. Moeller, *Imperial Cities and the Reformation*, 110–11; Bornert, *Réforme protestante du culte à Strasbourg*, 218–31; J. C. McLelland and G. E. Duffield, eds., *Life and Letters of Peter Martyr*, 68–70; James M. Kittelson, "Marbach v. Zanchi: The Resolution of Controversy in Late Reformation Strasbourg," *Sixteenth Century Journal* 8 (1977): 31–44; Ford, "Unter dem Schein," 128; *Geschichte der Stadt Augsburg*, 403–4.

35. Locher, *Zwinglische Reformation*, 636; Koch, "'Zwinglianer' zwischen Ostsee und Harz," 519; McLaughlin, *Schwenkfeld*, 115.

36. Jan R. Weerda, "Entstehung und Entwicklung der Gottesdienstordnungen der reformierten Gemeinde zu Emden," in *Nach Gottes Wort reformierte Kirche* (Munich, 1964), 23; Menno Smid, *Ostfriesische Kirchengeschichte* (*Ostfriesland im Schutze des Deiches*, vol. 6) (Pewsum, The Netherlands, 1974), 135–60; Heinz Schilling, "Calvinism and Urban Republicanism: The Emden Experience," in *Civic Calvinism in Northwestern Germany and The Netherlands, Sixteenth to Nineteenth Centuries* (Kirksville, Mo., 1991), 18–21. These works variously date a Lasco's appointment as superintendent to late 1542 or 1543.

37. For this and the subsequent paragraphs I have relied on Dalton, *John a Lasco;*

Bartel, *Jan Laski;* Ambroise Jobert, *De Luther à Mohila: La Pologne dans la crise de la Chrétienté 1517–1648* (Paris, 1974), 97–104; and Hall, "John a Lasco."

38. Wim Janse, *Albert Hardenberg als Theologe: Profil eines Bucer-Schülers* (Leiden, 1994).

39. In addition to the works cited in the preceding note, see Smid, *Ostfriesische Kirchengeschichte,* 165–71; Heinz Schilling, ed., *Die Kirchenratsprotokolle der Reformierten Gemeinde Emden 1557–1620* (Cologne, 1989–92), 1:xi–xvii.

40. For the complex problems associated with the textual history of this work, see Micron, *De Christlicke Ordinancien,* ed. Dankbaar.

41. Since Jacques Couvoisier first drew attention to Bucer's importance as a theorist of the church and the key source of Calvin's ideas on this subject, a series of excellent studies have examined this subject: Courvoisier, *La notion d'église chez Bucer dans son développement historique* (Paris, 1933); Willem van 't Spijker, *De ambten bij Martin Bucer* (Kampen, 1970), Eng. tr. *The Ecclesiastical Offices in the Thought of Martin Bucer* (Leiden, 1996); Gottfried Hammann, *Entre la secte et la cité: Le projet d'Eglise du Réformateur Martin Bucer (1491–1551)* (Geneva, 1981); Amy Nelson Burnett, *The Yoke of Christ: Martin Bucer and Christian Discipline* (Kirksville, Mo., 1994).

42. A Lasco, *Opera,* 2:49, 57–59, 101–05, 132.

43. Heinz Schilling, "Calvinism and Urban Republicanism: The Emden Experience," in *Civic Calvinism in Northwestern Germany and The Netherlands* (Kirksville, Mo., 1991), 15.

44. A Lasco, *Toute la forme & maniere du Ministere Ecclesiastique en l'Eglise des estrangers, dressée a Londres* ([Emden], 1556), 69, 80, 288, "Au lecteur."

45. Pettegree, *Emden,* esp. chaps. 3, appendix; Heinz Schilling, *Niederländische Exulanten im 16. Jahrhundert: Ihre Stellung im Sozialgefüge und im religiösen Leben deutscher und englischer Städte* (Gütersloh, 1972), 177, 179.

46. Denis, *Eglises d'étrangers en pays rhénans;* Andrew Pettegree, *Foreign Protestant Communities in Sixteenth-Century London* (Oxford, 1986); id., *Emden;* Schilling, *Niederländische Exulanten.*

47. Clyde L. Manschreck, *Melanchthon: The Quiet Reformer* (New York, 1958), is the standard English-language biography and includes a good discussion of Melanchthon's changing eucharistic ideas and his relations with Luther. For the popularity of Melanchthon's *Commonplaces:* Ralph Keen, *A Checklist of Melanchthon Imprints through 1560* (St. Louis, 1988).

48. Andrew Pettegree, "The London Exile Community and the Second Sacramentarian Controversy, 1533–1560," *Archiv für Reformationsgeschichte* 78 (1987): 223–52.

CHAPTER 3. CALVIN AND GENEVA

Bibliographical Note   The standard edition of Calvin's writings and correspondence, *Joannis Calvini Opera quae supersunt omnia,* eds. W. Baum, E. Cunitz, and E. Reuss, 59 vols. (Brunswick, 1863–80) also includes many documents about events in Geneva during his lifetime. Other key sources for the history of Geneva and its church are *The Lawes and Statutes of Geneva, as well con-cerning ecclesiastical Discipline, as civill regiment* (London, 1562); *Registres de la Compagnie des Pasteurs de Genève,* ed. J-F. Bergier et al., 13 vols. to date (Geneva, 1964–); *Registres du Consistoire de Genève au temps de Calvin,* ed. Thomas A. Lambert et al., 1 vol. to date (Geneva, 1996–); *Correspondance de Théodore de Bèze* 23 vols. to date (Geneva, 1960–); and Michel Roset, *Les chro-niques de Genève* (Geneva, 1894). The standard English edition of Calvin's *Insti-tutes* was prepared by J. T. McNeill, *Institutes of the Christian Religion* Library of Christian Classics, 20–21, 2 vols. (Philadelphia, 1960), while Ford Lewis Battles prepared a good translation of the first edition of 1536 (Grand Rapids, 1986).

The best single introduction to Calvin's life and thought remains the ven-erable François Wendel, *Calvin: The Origins and Development of His Reli-gious Thought* (London, 1963). Among the numerous biographies devoted to him William J. Bouwsma, *John Calvin: A Sixteenth Century Portrait* (Oxford, 1988), Denis Crouzet, *Jean Calvin: Vies parallèles* (Paris, 2000), and Alister E. McGrath, *A Life of John Calvin* (Oxford, 1990) stand out as especially stimu-lating, while the old Williston Walker, *John Calvin: The Organiser of Reformed Protestantism (1509–1564)* (New York, 1906) remains the most workmanlike account of all of the major episodes of his life. Alexandre Ganoczy, *The Young Calvin* (Philadelphia, 1987), is a brilliant reconstruction of his early intellec-tual development and break with Rome. Jean-François Gilmont, *Jean Calvin et le livre imprimé* (Geneva, 1997) offers a fascinating introduction to his work as an author, while Richard A. Muller, *The Unaccommodated Calvin: Studies in the Foundation of a Theological Tradition* (Oxford, 2000), facilitates read-ing him historically. Particularly important studies of aspects of his mature theology include André Biéler, *La pensée économique et sociale de Calvin* (Geneva, 1959), B. A. Gerrish, *Grace and Gratitude: The Eucharistic Theology of John Calvin* (Minneapolis, 1993), and, richest of all in its implications, Harro Höpfl, *The Christian Polity of John Calvin* (Cambridge, 1982). For his work in Geneva and the politics of the Genevan Reformation, the valuable recent study of William G. Naphy, *Calvin and the Consolidation of the Genevan Reformation* (Manchester, 1996) does not fully supersede the massive and still extremely illu-minating older studies of Amédée Roget, *Histoire du peuple de Genève depuis la Réforme jusqu'à l'Escalade* 7 vols. (Geneva, 1870–1883), a classic of liberal historiography, and Emile Doumergue, *Jean Calvin, les hommes et les choses de son temps* 7 vols. (Lausanne-Paris, 1899–1927), deeply apologetic but also deeply researched. Henri Naef, *Les origines de la Réforme à Genève* 2 vols. (Geneva, 1936–68) and E. William Monter *Calvin's Geneva* (New York, 1967) are also very helpful. Searching light is cast on aspects of Calvin's work and in-fluence in Geneva by the latter author's "The Consistory of Geneva, 1559–1569," *Bibliothèque d'Humanisme et Renaissance* 38 (1976): 467–484, "Historical Demography and Religious History in Sixteenth-Century Geneva," *Journal of Interdisciplinary History* 9 (1979): 399–427, and "Women in Calvinist Geneva (1550–1800), *Signs* 6 (1980): 189–209, as well as by Robert M. Kingdon, *Adul-*

tery and Divorce in Calvin's Geneva (Cambridge, Mass., 1995). For Calvin's work in promoting the spread of Protestantism beyond Geneva, see especially W. Nijenhuis, *Calvinus Oecumenicus: Calvijn en de eenheid der Kerk in het licht van zijn Briefwisseling* (The Hague, 1959) and Robert M. Kingdon, *Geneva and the Coming of the Wars of Religion in France, 1555-1563* (Geneva, 1956). Some stimulating reflections on the reasons for his distinctive success in Geneva may be found in William J. Bouwsma, "The Peculiarity of the Reformation in Geneva" in Steven Ozment, ed., *Religion and Culture in the Renaissance and Reformation* (Kirksville, Mo., 1989), 65-77, while Heiko Oberman's short *De erfenis van Calvijn: grootheid en grenzen* (Kampen, 1988) contains the insights of a master of Reformation studies whose larger study of Calvin was cut short by his recent death.

For Calvin's key French-speaking collaborators and associates, who all need further study, one may consult *Guillaume Farel 1489-1565. Biographie nouvelle écrite d'après les documents originaux par un groupe d'historiens, professeurs et pasteurs de Suisse, de France et d'Italie* (Neuchâtel, 1930); Jean Barnaud, *Pierre Viret, sa vie et son oeuvre 1511-1571* (Saint Amans, 1911, repr. Nieuwkoop, 1973); Paul-F. Giesendorf, *Théodore de Bèze* (Geneva, 1949); and Tadataka Maruyama, *The Ecclesiology of Theodore Beza* (Geneva, 1978).

1. On this see especially *Guillaume Farel,* esp. 171-284, 338-47, 362-418; Henri Vuilleumier, *Histoire de l'Eglise réformée du pays de Vaud sous le régime bernois* 4 vols. (Lausanne, 1927-33), 1:25-266; Eire, *War against the Idols,* 119-21.
2. Naef, *Origines de la Réforme à Genève,* esp. 2:17; Monter, *Calvin's Geneva,* 1-63.
3. This and the following paragraphs rest on Anthoine Fromment, *Les actes et gestes merveilleux de la cité de Genève* (Geneva, 1854), esp. 13; Roset, *Chroniques de Genève,* 161-238, esp. 210-11, 214-15, 233; Doumergue, *Calvin,* 2:110-49; Naef, *Origines de la Réforme à Genève,* 2:315-66; Monter, *Calvin's Geneva,* 49-56; *Guillaume Farel,* 298-337; Eire, *War against the Idols,* 122-51; Biéler, *Pensée économique et sociale de Calvin,* 61; Roget, *Histoire du peuple de Genève,* 1:1-10; Robert M. Kingdon, "The Control of Morals in Calvin's Geneva" in Lawrence P. Buck and Jonathan W. Zophy, eds., *The Social History of the Reformation* (Columbus, 1972), 5-6.
4. Calvin, preface to *Commentary on the Book of Psalms* (1557). I have used the translation of G. R. Potter and Mark Greengrass, *John Calvin* (London, 1983), 45-6.
5. *Calvini Opera,* 9:891.
6. Ganoczy, *Young Calvin,* argues particularly persuasively against the thesis of direct influence on Calvin from his teachers at Paris. For the most recent arguments in favor of this view, see Oberman, *Erfenis van Calvijn,* 26; McGrath, *Life of Calvin,* chap. 2.
7. Calvin's teacher, L'Estoile, particularly emphasized the reconciliation of different

passages, in which enterprise he was less inclined to interpret individual passages as products of the immediate historical milieu that had produced them than were more humanistic contemporary legal scholars such as Ulrich Zasius. Calvin, too, was more inclined to use the Old Testament to illuminate the New than were such historicizing contemporaries as Erasmus and Servetus. I owe these observations to Prof. Michael Monheit, to whom I am deeply grateful. See also on the influence of Calvin's legal education on his thought and career the valuable article of Basil Hall, "John Calvin, the Jurisconsults and the *Ius Civile*" in G. J. Cuming ed., *Studies in Church History* (Leiden, 1966), 202–17. Robert Kingdon has emphasized the ways in which Calvin's legal training made him attractive to his future employers in Geneva.

8. Quirinus Breen, *John Calvin: A Study in French Humanism* (Grand Rapids, 1931).
9. On the evolution of Calvin's reforming vocation, I have relied particularly heavily on Ganoczy, *Young Calvin.*
10. Doumergue, *Calvin,* 4:1–11; Wendel, *Calvin,* 111–22; McGrath, *Life of Calvin,* 136–40; Gilmont, *Calvin et le livre,* 69.
11. Gerrish, *Grace and Gratitude,* esp. 9; Höpfl, *Christian Polity,* passim.
12. Wendel, *Calvin,* 122–44; Ganoczy, *Young Calvin,* 133–81.
13. In citing from the *Institutes of the Christian Religion,* I have relied upon the edition and translation of John T. McNeill and Ford Lewis Battles (Philadelphia, 1960), as well as Battles' translation of the 1536 edition. The passages quoted in this paragraph are from *Institutes,* I.16.i, III.7.i; *Institutes* (1536 ed.), 177.
14. *Institutes* (1536 ed.), 3, 4, 113, 115, 179, 183.
15. *Calvini Opera,* 5:233–312, 6:537–614; Eire, *War against the Idols,* 195–275, esp. 220.
16. *Institutes* (1536 ed.), 102–22; *Institutes,* IV.17; *Petit traité de la sainte Cène* in *Calvini Opera,* 5:429–60; Gerrish, *Grace and Gratitude,* passim.
17. *Institutes* (1536 ed.), 61; *Institutes,* IV.12.i-vii; Höpfl, *Christian Polity,* 63–4, 100–02, 115–21; van 't Spijker, *Ecclesiastical Offices in the Thought of Martin Bucer,* esp. 219–28; James Martin Estes, *Christian Magistrate and State Church: The Reforming Career of Johannes Brenz* (Toronto, 1982), 82–94; Plomp, *Kerkelijk Tucht bij Calvijn;* Hamann, *Entre le secte et la cité;* A. Demura, "Calvin's and Oecolampadius's Concept of Church Discipline" in W. H. Neuser, ed., *Calvinus ecclesiae Genevensis custos* (Frankfurt, 1982), 187–9; Burnett, *Yoke of Christ.*
18. van 't Spijker, *Ecclesiastical Offices,* 173, 177.
19. *Institutes,* IV.3.iv-ix.
20. *Institutes* (1536 ed.), 188.
21. Höpfl, *Christian Polity,* 97.
22. *Institutes* (1536 ed.), 224, 225, 215.
23. *Institutes* III.19.xv; IV.20.ii-vi.
24. *Institutes* IV.4.xii; IV.20.viii; Höpfl, *Christian Polity,* 124, 153–5.
25. Max Engammare, "Calvin monarchomaque? Du soupçon à l'argument," *Archiv*

für Reformationsgeschichte 89 (1998): 212ff; James D. Tracy, *Erasmus of the Low Countries* (Berkeley, 1996).

26. *Institutes,* III.21–24, esp. 21.i; V.23.xii, 924n; Höpfl, *Christian Polity,* 227–40, esp. 228; Wendel, *Calvin,* 263–84.

27. Bibliothèque de la Société de l'Histoire du Protestantisme Français (Paris), MS 388, fo. 104; *Ceremonies et coutumes religieuses de tous les peuples du monde* (Amsterdam, 1783), III, 115; McGrath, *Life of Calvin,* 135, 139–40, 297; Jacques Pannier, *Calvin écrivain* (Paris, 1930), 35.

28. Rodolphe Peter and Jean-François Gilmont, *Bibliotheca Calviniana. Les oeuvres de Jean Calvin publiées au XVIe siècle* (Geneva, 1993–2000).

29. Gilmont, *Calvin et le livre,* passim, esp. 19, 49–52, 71–92; *Bibliotheca calviniana,* 2:622.

30. Robert W. Richgels, "The Pattern of Controversy in a Counter-Reformation Classic: The *Controversies* of Robert Bellarmine," *Sixteenth Century Journal,* 11 (1980): 3–15.

31. Ganoczy, *Young Calvin,* 108–11; *Calvini Opera,* 21:39–40, 42, 107–08, 117–18.

32. *Calvini Opera,* 21:71.

33. *Calvini Opera,* 10:5–14.

34. Roget, *Histoire du peuple de Genève,* 1:35–111; Doumergue, *Calvin,* 2:269–90; Gabrielle Berthoud, *Antoine Marcourt, réformateur et pamphlétaire. Du "Livre des Marchans" aux Placards de 1534* (Geneva, 1973), 34–35.

35. Denis, *Eglises d'étrangers en pays rhénans,* 496–501, 513–18. The precise date of the establishment of the French church's independent system of discipline and poor relief cannot be determined with precision, but it seems probable that this occurred during Calvin's time in Strasbourg.

36. *Calvini Opera,* 11:218, 293; Roget, *Histoire du peuple de Genève,* 1:113–315; Doumergue, *Calvin,* 2:653–710; Walker, *Calvin,* 245–64; Monter, *Calvin's Geneva,* 64–71; Berthoud, *Marcourt,* 34–84; Bruce Gordon, "Calvin and the Swiss Reformed Churches" in Andrew Pettegree et al., eds., *Calvinism in Europe 1540–1620* (Cambridge, 1994), 68–69.

37. "Quon luy interdise la communion de la cene et quon le denonce au magistrat". The ecclesiastical ordinances of 1541 have been edited many times. For some convenient editions, see *Calvini Opera,* 10:15–30, esp. col. 29; *Registres de la Compagnie des Pasteurs,* 1:1–13, esp. 12. Plomp, *Kerkelijke Tucht,* 177–89 is particularly good on the successive revisions of the ordinances and their interpretation. See also *Lawes and Statutes of Geneva.*

38. Plomp, *Kerkelijke Tucht,* 189.

39. *Institutes,* IV.12.ii–v.

40. This and the following paragraph are based on *Registres du consistoire;* Robert M. Kingdon, "The Geneva Consistory in the time of Calvin" in Pettegree et al., eds., *Calvinism in Europe,* 21–34; Jeffrey M. Watt, "Women and the Consistory in Calvin's Geneva," *Sixteenth Century Journal* 24 (1993): 429–430; Naphy, *Calvin and the Consolidation of the Genevan Reformation,* 109–10,

whose statistical breakdown of the consistory's activity in 1542, 1546, and 1550 I have slightly reworked to obtain the figures presented here.

41. Doumergue, *Calvin*, 5:200.

42. *Calvini Opera*, 21:342-3; Roget, *Histoire du peuple de Genève*, 2:233-34; *Registres de la Compagnie des Pasteurs*, 1:29; Emile Rivoire and Victor van Berchem, eds., *Les sources du droit du canton de Genève* (Aarau, 1927-1935), vols. 2, 3; Marie-Lucile de Gallatin, "Les ordonnances sumptuaires à Genève au XVIe siècle," *Mémoires et Documents publiés par la Société d'Histoire et d'Archéologie de Genève*, 36 (1938): 193-275; Kingdon, *Adultery and Divorce in Calvin's Geneva*, 116-18.

43. Gillian Lewis, "Calvinism in Geneva in the Time of Calvin and of Beza (1541-1605)" in Prestwich, ed., *International Calvinism*, 46; Naphy, *Calvin and the Consolidation*, 58-59; idem "The Renovation of the Ministry in Calvin's Geneva" in Andrew Pettegree, ed., *The Reformation of the Parishes: The Ministry and the Reformation in Town and Country* (Manchester, 1993), 127; *Calvini Opera*, 11:no. 389; Doumergue, *Calvin*, 6:5-23.

44. Roset, *Chroniques*, 297; Paul-F. Geisendorf, ed., *Livre des habitants de Genève* Vol. 1 *1549-1560* (Geneva, 1957); Monter, *Calvin's Geneva*, chap. 7; Alfred Perrenoud, *La population de Genève du XVIe au début du XIXe siècle: étude démographique* (Geneva, 1979); Naphy, *Calvin and the Consolidation*, chap. 4.

45. Naphy, *Calvin and the Consolidation*, 102, 146-50; Roset, *Chroniques*, 342; Roget, *Histoire du peuple de Genève*, 2:247-48, 264, 290, 3:43.

46. Roget, *Histoire du peuple de Genève*, 3:44-45, 61-62, 145-48, 4:133-95, esp. 177; Doumergue, *Calvin*, 7:4-5, 26; R. Peter, "Genève dans la prédication de Calvin" in Neuser, ed., *Calvinus ecclesiae Genevensis custos*, 37. Just as Berthelier had originally been a defender of Calvin's, the leader of the party opposed to Calvin, Ami Perrin, had been one of the leading iconoclasts in 1535. Oberman, *Erfenis van Calvijn*, 30.

47. Roget, *Histoire du peuple de Genève*, 4:197-336; Doumergue, *Calvin*, 7:26-66; Monter, *Calvin's Geneva*, 85-88; Robert M. Kingdon, "Social Control and Political Control in Calvin's Geneva," *Archiv für Reformationsgeschichte*, Special Issue 1993, 529-30.

48. *Calvini Opera*, 15:nos. 2306, 2309, 2329; Roget, *Histoire du peuple de Genève*, 4:321-24; Doumergue, *Calvin*, 7:72-73.

49. Roget, *Histoire du peuple de Genève*, 5:5-97; Doumergue, *Calvin*, 7:92-105.

50. *Calvini Opera*, 21:79.

51. Monter, "Consistory of Geneva, 1559-1569."

52. Roset, *Chroniques*, 377; Monter, "Historical Demography and Religious History," 415; Willy Richard, *Untersuchungen zur Genesis der reformierten Kirchenterminologie der Westschweiz und Frankreichs mit besonderer Berücksichtigung der Namengebung* (Bern, 1959), 191-217; A. Lynn Martin, *The Jesuit Mind: The Mentality of an Elite in Early Modern France* (Ithaca, N.Y., 1988), 88.

53. *Calvini Opera*, 21:21, 367, 370-77; Roget, *Histoire du peuple de Genève*, 2:207-23; Doumergue, *Calvin*, 6:83-90; Walker, *Calvin*, 295-97.

54. *Calvini Opera,* 8:93-138; 14:334-37, 371-85; *Registres de la Compagnie des Pasteurs,* 1:80-131; Roset, *Chroniques,* 346-48; Roget, *Histoire du peuple de Genève,* 3:157-206, 235-48, esp. 237; Doumergue, *Calvin,* 6:146-56, 162-69; Walker, *Calvin,* 315-21; Peter and Gilmont, *Bibliotheca Calviniana,* 1:445-48; Vuilleumier, *Histoire de l'Eglise réformée du pays de Vaud,* 1:647ff.

55. *Calvini Opera,* 8:453-872; Roget, *Histoire du peuple de Genève,* 4:1-131; Doumergue, *Calvin,* 6:187-442; Joseph Lecler, *Histoire de la tolérance au siècle de la Réforme* (Paris, 1955), 1:312ff.

56. *Calvini Opera,* 9:321-40; Henri Fazy, ed., "Procès de Valentin Gentilis et de Nicolas Gallo (1558)," *Mémoires de l'Institut National Genevois* 14 (1878-79): 1-102, esp. 5, 8, 17; Roget, *Histoire du peuple de Genève,* 5:145-70; Doumergue, *Calvin,* 6:451-99; Benedictus Aretius, *A Short History of Valentinus Gentilis the Tritheist* (London, 1696); *Dizionario Biographico degli Italiani* (Rome, 1960-97), s.v. "Giorgio Biandrata," "Valentino Gentile"; Delio Cantimori, *Eretici Italiani del Cinquecento* (Florence, 1977), chaps. 15-22; Williams, *Radical Reformation,* 943-78.

57. Monter, *Calvin's Geneva,* 162.

58. *Lawes and Statutes of Geneva,* iii; Monter, *Calvin's Geneva,* 88, 173-76, 178-80; Heidi-Lucie Schlaepfer, "Laurent de Normandie," in *Aspects de la propagande religieuse* (Geneva, 1957), 176-230.

59. Pierre de Ronsard, *Discours des Misères de ce Temps,* ed. Jean Baillou (Paris, 1949), 84-85; Alain Dufour, "Le mythe de Genève au temps de Calvin," in *Histoire politique et psychologie historique* (Geneva, 1966), 85-130; Francis M. Higman, *Censorship and the Sorbonne: A Bibliographical Study of Books in French Censured by the Faculty of Theology of the University of Paris, 1520-1551* (Geneva, 1979), 64; William Monter, "French *Parlements* and the Myths of Geneva, 1548-1555," in Wolfgang Kaiser et al., eds., *Eidgenössische 'Grenzfälle': Mülhausen und Genf* (Basel, 2001), 221-34.

60. Rivoire and van Berchem, *Sources du droit du canton de Genève,* passim, esp. 3:24.

61. Denis, *Eglises d'étrangers en pays rhénans,* 242.

62. Bouwsma, "Peculiarity of the Reformation in Geneva."

63. Vuilleumier, *Histoire de l'Eglise réformée du pays de Vaud,* vol. 1, chap. 7; *Guillaume Farel,* part 3.

64. Denis, *Eglises d'étrangers en pays rhénans,* 344, 451, 593-618; id., "Calvin et les églises d'étrangers: Comment un ministre intervient dans une église autre que la sienne" in Neuser, ed., *Calvinus Ecclesiae Genevensis Custos,* 69-92.

65. Doumergue, *Calvin,* 6:539-68; Nijenhuis, *Calvinus Oecumenicus,* 11-18, 141-73.

66. E. W. Zeeden, "Calvins Einwirken auf die Reformation in Polen-Litauen: Eine Studie über den Reformator Calvin im Spiegel seiner polnischen Korrespondenzen," in *Konfessionsbildung: Studien zur Reformation, Gegenreformation und Katholischen Reform* (Stuttgart, 1985); Nijenhuis, *Calvinus Oecumenicus.*

67. Bouvier, *Bullinger,* 150-51; Plath, "Zur Entstehungsgeschichte des Wortes 'Cal-

vinist'," 215; Pettegree, "London Exile Community and the Second Sacramentarian Controversy," 249–51.

68. *Calvini Opera,* 18:no. 3485; 9:892; Bouvier, *Bullinger,* 167; Nijenhuis, *Calvinus Oecumenicus,* 43–44.

69. *Calvini Opera,* 18:nos. 3422, 3456.

70. Roget, *Histoire du peuple de Genève,* 5:225–48; Doumergue, *Calvin,* 7:124–54; S. Stelling-Michaud, *Le livre du recteur de l'Académie de Genève (1559–1878),* 6 vols. (Geneva, 1959–80); Gillian Lewis, "The Geneva Academy," in Pettegree et al., eds, *Calvinism in Europe,* 35–63, esp. 50; Maag, *Seminary or University?.*

CONCLUSION TO PART I

1. Graf, "Evangelische Kirchenordnung im Freistaat Gemeiner Drei Bünde," 624–48; Ulrich Pfister, "Reformierte Sittenzucht zwischen kommunaler und territorialer Organisation: Graubünden, 16.-18. Jahrhundert," *Archiv für Reformationsgeschichte* 87 (1996): 293–307.

2. Vuilleumier, *Histoire de l'Eglise réformée du pays de Vaud,* 1:255, 280ff.

3. Pettegree, *Foreign Protestant Communities,* 72; Bouvier, *Bullinger,* 107–09; Baker, "In Defense of Magisterial Discipline."

4. Cochrane, ed., *Reformed Confessions of the 16th Century,* 220–301.

5. *Calvini Opera,* 15:1977, 2005, 2028, 2189. See also Euan Cameron, *The Reformation of the Heretics: The Waldenses of the Alps, 1480–1580* (Oxford, 1984), 157–62; Monter, *Calvin's Geneva,* 134–35; Kingdon, *Geneva and the Coming of the Wars of Religion,* passim, esp. 2.

6. See above, 65–66; Guido Marnef, *Antwerp in the Age of the Reformation: Underground Protestantism in a Commercial Metropolis, 1550–1577* (Baltimore, 1996), 80; Alastair Duke, *Reformation and Revolt in the Low Countries* (London, 1990), 114.

CHAPTER 4. FRANCE: CONSTRUCTION OF A MINORITY CHURCH

Bibliographical Note   The historical literature about each national Reformed church has been shaped in distinctive ways by the outcome of the Reformation in the country in question and by the later experience of the various Protestant churches there. What has molded the literature about French Protestantism above all is the fact that the cause was a minority movement that was accused by its enemies of being seditious from the moment of its emergence, that experienced two great blows with the Saint Bartholomew's Massacre of 1572 and the revocation of the Edict of Nantes in 1685, and that still in the nineteenth and early twentieth centuries had to defend itself against the accusation that it was an alien element in a Catholic country. This has produced a historiography that emphasizes the political history of the movement and the story of its struggle for legal recognition while largely neglecting its institutional and theological development. The country's rich archives and the fact that the Protestants constituted a clearly identifiable fraction of the population have also given rise to many studies of the faith's social composition.

Key published sources include Jean Crespin, *Histoire des martyrs,* ed. D. Benoît, 3 vols. (Toulouse, 1884–87); *Histoire ecclésiastique des églises réformées au royaume de France,* eds. G. Baum, E. Cunitz, and R. Reuss, 3 vols. (Paris, 1883–89); A. L. Herminjard, ed., *Correspondance des réformateurs dans les pays de langue française,* 9 vols. (Geneva, 1886–87); and the correspondence of Calvin and Beza cited in the bibliographical note for chapter 3, above. There are two imperfect editions of the decisions of the national synods: John Quick, *Synodicon in Gallia Reformata,* 2 vols. (London, 1692), and Jean Aymon, *Actes ecclésiastiques et civils de tous les synodes nationaux des Eglises Réformées de France,* 2 vols. (The Hague, 1710). For the early growth of the movement, Pierre Imbart de la Tour, *Les origines de la Réforme,* 4 vols. (Paris, 1905–35) remains unsurpassed. Mark Greengrass, *The French Reformation* (Oxford, 1987), is an alert short treatment in English; Denis Crouzet, *La genèse de la Réforme française 1520–1562* (Paris, 1996), is a fuller recent French account; and Henry Heller, *The Conquest of Poverty: The Calvinist Revolt in Sixteenth Century France* (Leiden, 1986) is a materialist interpretation with vivid chapters on several local circles of early Protestants. Other essential studies are the essays and articles of Francis Higman now collected in his *Lire et découvrir: La circulation des idées au temps de la Réforme* (Geneva, 1998); Raymond Mentzer, *Heresy Proceedings in Languedoc, 1500–1560* Transactions of the American Philosophical Society 74 (Philadelphia, 1984); and William Monter, *Judging the French Reformation: Heresy Trials by Sixteenth-Century Parliaments* (Cambridge, Mass., 1999). David Nicholls "The Theatre of Martyrdom in the French Reformation," *Past & Present* 121 (1988): 49–73, provides a striking picture of the rituals accompanying heresy executions.

For the relation between Geneva and the "planting" of Reformed churches across France, the two studies of Robert M. Kingdon, *Geneva and the Coming of the Wars of Religion in France, 1555–1563* (Geneva, 1956), and *Geneva and the Consolidation of the French Protestant Movement, 1564–1572: A Contribution to the History of Congregationalism, Presbyterianism, and Calvinist Resistance Theory* (Geneva, 1967) remain fundamental. Scott M. Manetsch, *Theodore Beza and the Quest for Peace in France, 1572–1598* (Leiden, 2000), now ably covers the later period. An older literature, essential for the narrative of events, wrote the story of the crucial period from the establishment of Reformed churches through the violence of the civil wars with primary reference to events at the center and the rivalries of the high aristocracy. Particularly important here are Lucien Romier, *Les origines politiques des guerres de religion,* 2 vols. (Paris, 1913–14); id., *Le royaume de Cathérine de Médicis,* 2 vols. (Paris, 1922); id., *La conjuration d'Amboise* (Paris, 1923); id., *Catholiques et Huguenots à la cour de Charles IX* (Paris, 1924); Henri Naef, *La conjuration d'Amboise et Genève* (Geneva, 1922); and, for the broader picture, Jean H. Mariéjol, *La Réforme et la Ligue: L'Edit de Nantes (1559–1598),* vol. 6, part 1 of Ernest Lavisse, *Histoire de France* (Paris, 1904), and James Westfall Thompson, *The Wars of Religion in France 1559–1576: The Huguenots, Catherine de Medici and Philip II* (Chicago, 1909). A large number of more recent works have taken the form of local or regional studies, tend to put more emphasis on the symbolic conflicts between the two faiths, and see the civil wars as welling up from below. Two seminal articles by Natalie Zemon Davis, "Strikes and Salvation at Lyon" and "The Rites of Violence," both available in her *Society and Culture in Early Modern France* (Stanford, 1975), inspired this trend. Local studies that are especially informative about the history of the Reformed churches include Louise Guiraud, *La Réforme à Montpellier* (Montpellier, 1918); Joan Davies, "Persecution and Protestantism: Toulouse, 1562–1572," *The Historical Journal* 22 (1979): 31–51; Philip Benedict, *Rouen during the Wars of Religion* (Cambridge, 1981); Barbara B. Diefendorf, *Beneath the Cross: Catholics and Huguenots in Sixteenth-Century Paris* (Oxford, 1991); the more broadly conceived Marc Venard, *Réforme protestante, Réforme catholique dans la province d'Avignon-XVIe siècle* (Paris, 1993); Michel Cassan, *Le temps des guerres de religion: Le cas du Limousin (vers 1530–vers 1630)* (Paris, 1996); and Penny Roberts, *A City in Conflict: Troyes during the French Wars of Religion* (Manchester, 1996). Denis Crouzet, *Les guerriers de Dieu: La violence au temps des troubles de religion vers 1525–vers 1610,* 2 vols. (Seyssel, 1990), presents a striking cultural interpretation of the dialectic that he believes drove the descent into confessional violence and civil war, while Olivier Christin, *Une révolution symbolique: L'iconoclasme huguenot et la reconstruction catholique* (Paris, 1991), is an excellent study of a central aspect of Huguenot crowd actions. Also important are N. M. Sutherland, *The Huguenot Struggle for Recognition* (New Haven, 1980), and Philip Benedict et al., eds., *Reformation, Revolt and Civil War in France and the Netherlands 1555–1585* (Amsterdam, 1999).

Although the institutional and theological aspects of the sixteenth-century French Reformed churches remain far less well studied, recourse may still be had to Jacques Pannier, *Les origines de la Confession de foi et la Discipline des Eglises réformées de France: Etude historique* (Paris, 1936); the very important Janine Garrisson-Estèbe, *Protestants du Midi 1559–1598* (Toulouse, 1980); Glenn S. Sunshine, "From French Protestantism to the French Reformed Churches: The Development of Huguenot Ecclesiastical Institutions, 1559–1598" (Ph.D. diss., University of Wisconsin-Madison, 1992); and Philippe Denis and Jean Rott, *Jean Morély (ca 1524–ca 1594) et l'utopie d'une démocratie dans l'église* (Geneva, 1993).

1. Herminjard, *Correspondance des Reformateurs* 1:62–63; Imbart de la Tour, *Origines de la Réforme,* vol. 3, esp. 170; W. G. Moore, *La Réforme allemande et la littérature française: Recherches sur la notoriété de Luther en France* (Strasbourg, 1930); Guy Bédouelle, *Lefèvre d'Etaples et l'intelligence des Ecritures* (Geneva, 1976); Michel Veissière, *L'évêque Guillaume Briçonnet (1470–1534): Contribution à la connaissance de la Réforme catholique à la veille du Concile de Trente* (Provins, 1986).
2. Imbart de la Tour, *Origines* 3:205; R. J. Knecht, *Francis I* (Cambridge, 1982), 141–45, 202–25; Bédouelle, *Lefèvre d'Etaples,* 90–135.

3. Imbart de la Tour, *Origines* 3:368–415; Mentzer, *Heresy Proceedings in Langue-doc;* Monter, *Judging the French Reformation,* chaps. 3–4; Roget, *Histoire du peuple de Genève* 3:134.

4. R. J. Knecht, "Francis I: 'Defender of the Faith'?," in E. W. Ives, R. J. Knecht, and J. J. Scarisbrick, eds., *Wealth and Power in Tudor England: Essays Presented to S. T. Bindoff* (London, 1978), 106–27; Francis M. Higman, *Censorship and the Sorbonne: A Bibliographical Study of Books in French Censured by the Faculty of Theology of the University of Paris, 1520–1551* (Geneva, 1979), 56–64; James K. Farge, *Orthodoxy and Reform in Early Reformation France: The Faculty of Theology of Paris, 1500–1543* (Leiden, 1985), 208–13.

5. Moore, *Réforme allemande et la littérature française,* 446–55; Francis M. Higman, "Les traductions françaises de Luther, 1524–1550," in Jean-François Gilmont, *Palaestra Typographica. Aspects de la production du livre humaniste et religieux au XVIe siècle* (Aubel, Belgium, 1984); id., "Le levain de l'évangile," in Henri-Jean Martin and Roger Chartier, eds., *Histoire de l'édition française* (Paris, 1982), 1:305–25 (both now reprinted in *Lire et découvrir,* 201–32, 15–52); Bernd Moeller, "Luther in Europe: His Works in Translation 1517–46," in E. I. Kouri and Tom Scott, eds., *Politics and Society in Reformation Europe: Essays for Sir Geoffrey Elton on his Sixty-Fifth Birthday* (New York, 1987), 235–65.

6. Imbart de la Tour, *Origines* 3:435–54; Higman, *Censorship and the Sorbonne,* 52–53, 107–16; id., "Levain de l'évangile," 312–17; J. M. De Bujanda, Francis M. Higman, and James K. Farge, eds., *Index de l'Université de Paris, 1544, 1545, 1547, 1549, 1551, 1556* (Sherbrooke, Québec, 1985), 84–86.

7. *Histoire ecclésiastique* 1:67.

8. Natalie Zemon Davis, "The Protestant Printing Workers of Lyons in 1551," in *Aspects de la propagande religieuse* (Geneva, 1957), 247–57; "Une chronique de l'établissement de la Réforme à Saint-Seurin d'Uzet en Saintonge: Le registre de baptêmes de Jean Frèrejean (1541–1564)," *Bulletin de la Société de l'Histoire du Protestantisme Français* 50 (1901): 141–42.

9. Mentzer, *Heresy Proceedings in Languedoc,* esp. 101, 112–22; William Monter, "Les executés pour hérésie par arrêt du Parlement de Paris (1523–1560)," *Bulletin de la Société de l'Histoire du Protestantisme Français* 142 (1996): 197, 216–17; Imbart de la Tour, *Origines* 4:251–52, 327–42.

10. This was the number of churches reported to have sent delegates to the first national synod in May of that year. Philippe de Félice, "Le Synode national de 1559," *Bulletin de la Société de l'Histoire du Protestantisme Français* 105 (1959): 6. For the foundation and early growth of the first churches, see especially the *Histoire ecclésiastique* 1:117–29.

11. *Relation des troubles excités par les calvinistes dans la ville de Rouen depuis l'an 1537 jusqu'en l'an 1582* (Rouen, 1837), 12.

12. On the scale of the propaganda efforts of this period: Francis M. Higman, "Le domaine français 1520–1562," in Jean-François Gilmont, ed., *La Réforme et le livre: L'Europe de l'imprimé (1517–v. 1570)* (Paris, 1990), 127; Kingdon, *Geneva and the Coming,* chap. 9. On the demands for new pastors and dramatic growth:

Calvini Opera 18:3386, 19:3552, 3553, 3590, 3703; "Une mission à la Foire de Guibray: Lettre d'un ministre normand à Calvin," *Bulletin de la Société de l'Histoire du Protestantisme Français* 28 (1879): 455–64. Quantitative substantiation of these reports of rapid growth is provided by several surviving baptismal registers of new churches from this period: Benedict, *Rouen,* 235, 254.

13. Garrisson-Estèbe, *Protestants du Midi,* 83. The same author offers a slightly more generous estimate on 64.

14. Peter Wilcox, "L'envoi de pasteurs aux Eglises de France: Trois listes établies par Colladon (1561–1562)," *Bulletin de la Société de l'Histoire du Protestantisme Français* 139 (1993): 347–74; *Guillaume Farel,* 688–707; Vuilleumier, *Histoire de l'Eglise réformée du pays de Vaud* 1:687; Geisendorf, *Bèze,* chaps. 4–7.

15. Brilioth, *Eucharistic Faith and Practice,* 179; Pannier, *Origines de la Confession de foi;* H. Jahr, *Studien zur Uberlieferungsgeschichte der Confession de foi von 1559* (Neukirchen, 1964); *Confessions et catéchismes de la foi réformée* (Geneva, 1986), 111–27; Bernard Roussel, "Le texte et les usages de la Confession de foi des Eglises réformées de France d'après les Actes des Synodes nationaux, 1559–1659," in M.-M. Fragonard and M. Peronnet, eds., *Catéchismes et confessions de foi* (Montpellier, 1995), 31–60; Sunshine, "From French Protestantism to the French Reformed Churches," esp. 140–42.

16. Sunshine, "From French Protestantism to the French Reformed Churches," esp. 158–74; Aymon, *Tous les Synodes Nationales,* esp. 1–5, 111, 114; Pierre Dez, "Les Articles Polytiques de 1557 et les origines du régime synodal," *Bulletin de la Société de l'Histoire du Protestantisme Français* 103 (1957): 1–9; Bernard Roussel, "La *Discipline* des Eglises réformées de France en 1559: Un royaume sans clergé?" in M. Magdelaine et al., eds., *De l'Humanisme aux Lumières, Bayle et le protestantisme* (Oxford, 1996), 169–91; esp. 186–87, 191; Yves Gueneau, "Protestants du Centre 1598–1685 (Ancienne province synodale d'Orléanais-Berry): Approche d'une minorité" (Thèse de 3e cycle, Université François Rabelais de Tours, 1982), 341.

17. Denis and Rott, *Morély;* Kingdon, *Geneva and the Consolidation,* 62–137, esp. 63.

18. Monluc, *Commentaires,* ed. Paul Courteault (Paris, 1964), 481; the estimate of 1.5 to 2 million church members around 1562 is my own, based upon estimates of the total number of churches and the surviving demographic evidence about this and later periods in the church's history. A comparable estimate may be found in Greengrass, *French Reformation,* 43.

19. Davis, *Society and Culture,* 6–7; Benedict, *Rouen,* chap. 3; Emmanuel Le Roy Ladurie, *Les paysans de Languedoc* (Paris, 1966), 341–44; Edmond Belle, "La Réforme à Dijon des origines à la fin de la lieutenance générale de Gaspard de Saulx-Tavanes (1530–1570)," *Revue Bourguignonne* 21 (1911): 44; James R. Farr, "Popular Religious Solidarity in Sixteenth-Century Dijon," *French Historical Studies* 14 (1985): 192–214; Mack P. Holt, "Wine, Community and Reformation in Sixteenth-Century Burgundy," *Past & Present* 138 (1993): 58–93; Roberts, *City in Conflict,* 81–82.

20. Benedict, *Rouen,* 86; Barbara B. Diefendorf, "Les divisions religieuses dans les

familles parisiennes avant la Saint-Barthélémy," *Histoire, économie et société* 7 (1988): 63–66.

21. Jean-Marie Constant, "The Protestant Nobility in France during the Wars of Religion: A Leaven of Innovation in a Traditional World," in Benedict et al., eds., *Reformation, Revolt, and Civil War,* 70.

22. Nicolas Pithou de Chamgobert, *Chronique de Troyes et de la Champagne durant les guerres de Religion (1524–1594),* ed. Pierre-Eugène Leroy (Reims, 1998), 182–84; *Satyres Chrestiennes de la cuisine Papale* (Geneva, 1560; repr. Geneva, 1857); *Mémoires de Condé* (London, 1740); Anatole de Montaiglon and James de Rothschild, eds., *Recueil des poésies françoises des XVe et XVIe siècles,* 15 vols. (Paris, 1855–78), vol. 7; P. Tarbé, ed., *Recueil des poésies calvinistes (1550–1566)* (Geneva, 1968); Vittorio de Caprariis, *Propaganda e pensiero politico in Francia durante le guerre di religione I (1559–1572)* (Naples, 1959), chaps. 1–2; Geneviève Guilleminot, "Religion et politique à la veille des guerres civiles: Recherches sur les impressions françaises de l'année 1561" (Thèse de l'Ecole des Chartes, 1977); Philip Benedict, "The Dynamics of Protestant Militancy: France, 1555–1563," in Benedict et al., eds., *Reformation, Revolt, and Civil War,* 38–39; Benedict, "Of Marmites and Martyrs: Images and Polemics in the Wars of Religion," in *The French Renaissance in Prints from the Bibliothèque National de France,* exhibition catalogue (Los Angeles, 1994), 108–13, 117–20; A. N. Galpern, *The Religions of the People in Sixteenth-Century Champagne* (Cambridge, 1976), 109–35; Daniel Toussaint, *The Exercise of the faithfull soule* (London, 1583), dedication; "Chanson spirituelle," in *Epistre au Roy, pour l'Eglise de Lion* (Lyon, 1562).

23. Beza, *Correspondance* 1:150. For the larger political narrative of this period: Romier, *Conjuration d'Amboise.*

24. W. Nijenhuis, "The Limits of Civil Disobedience in Calvin's Last-known Sermons: Development of His Ideas on the Right of Civil Resistance," in *Ecclesia Reformata: Studies on the Reformation* (Leiden, 1994), 2:73–97; Engammare, "Calvin monarchomaque?" *Archiv für Reformationsgeschichte* 89 (1998): 207–26; Naef, *Conjuration d'Amboise et Genève;* Romier, *Conjuration d'Amboise;* Kingdon, *Geneva and the Coming,* chap. 7; Jacques Poujol, "De la Confession de Foi de 1559 à la Conjuration d'Amboise," *Bulletin de la Société de l'Histoire du Protestantisme Français* 119 (1973): 158–77; Beza, *Correspondance* 3:63–64; Alain Dufour, "L'affaire de Maligny (Lyon, 4–5 septembre 1560) vue à travers la correspondance de Calvin et de Bèze," *Cahiers d'Histoire* 8 (1963): 269–80.

25. Romier, *Conjuration d'Amboise,* 68–70; Crouzet, *Genèse de la Réforme française,* 570–90; Christin, *Révolution symbolique,* 69–71; Philip Benedict, "The Dynamics of Protestant Militancy: France, 1555–1563," in Benedict et al., eds., *Reformation, Revolt, and Civil War,* 40–48; Kingdon, *Geneva and the Coming,* 68–76; Robert D. Linder, *The Political Ideas of Pierre Viret* (Geneva, 1964), 136; A. H. Guggenheim, "Beza, Viret, and the Church of Nîmes: National Leadership and Local Initiative in the Outbreak of the Religious Wars," *Bibliothèque d'Humanisme et Renaissance* 37 (1975): 40.

26. Sutherland, *Huguenot Struggle for Recognition,* 119–36; Mario Turchetti, *Con-*

cordia o tolleranza? François Bauduin (1520–1573) e i "moyenneurs" (Geneva, 1984).

27. Beza, *Correspondance* 4:254–55, 87; Guggenheim, "Beza, Viret, and the Church of Nîmes," 33–36, 44–47; Romier, *Catholiques et Huguenots à la cour de Charles IX,* book 6.

28. We are very poorly informed about what happened in those cities that were controlled by the Protestants in 1562–63, in part because many documents pertaining to this period were destroyed. For some evidence about the dynamics of radicalization in the Huguenot cities, see Bernard de Lacombe, *Les débuts des guerres de religion (Orléans 1559–1564): Catherine de Médicis entre Guise et Condé* (Paris, 1899), 170ff.; Benedict, *Rouen,* 97–99; Guiraud, *Réforme à Montpellier,* 243–85; Léon Ménard, *Histoire civile, ecclesiastique et litteraire de la ville de Nismes* (Paris, 1750–58), 4:343–77.

29. Important overviews of the Wars of Religion include Mariéjol, *Réforme et la Ligue;* Thompson, *The Wars of Religion in France;* Benedict, *Rouen;* R. J. Knecht, *The French Wars of Religion 1559–1598* (London, 1989); Mack P. Holt, *The French Wars of Religion 1562–1629* (Cambridge, 1995); Arlette Jouanna, *La France du XVIe siècle 1483–1598* (Paris, 1996), chaps. 21–40. These form the basis for this and subsequent paragraphs.

30. Quentin Skinner, *The Foundations of Modern Political Thought,* 2 vols. (Cambridge, 1978), 2:302–48; Robert M. Kingdon, "Calvinism and Resistance Theory, 1550–1580," in J. H. Burns, ed., *The Cambridge History of Political thought 1450–1700* (Cambridge, 1991), 200–14.

31. Garrisson-Estèbe, *Protestants du Midi,* 83; Philip Benedict, *The Huguenot Population of France, 1600–1685: The Demographic Fate and Customs of a Religious Minority,* Transactions of the American Philosophical Society 81 (Philadelphia, 1991), 75–76.

32. Michel Reulos, "Les débuts des Communautés réformées dans l'actuel département de la Manche (Cotentin et Avranchin)," *Revue du département de la Manche* 24 (1982): numéro spécial, "Réforme et Contre-Réforme en Normandie," 43; Katherine L. M. Faust, "A Beleaguered Society: Protestant Families in La Rochelle, 1628–1685" (Ph.D. diss., Northwestern University, 1980), 7; Philippe Joutard et al., *Les Cévennes: De la montagne à l'homme* (Toulouse, 1979), 115; Raymond A. Mentzer, "Ecclesiastical Discipline and Communal Reorganization among the Protestants of Southern France," *European History Quarterly* 21 (1991): 167–70; Aymon, *Synodes* 1:74, 159, 2:23.

33. Nicolas de Bordenave, *Histoire du Béarn et Navarre,* ed. Paul Raymond (Paris, 1873), is the official contemporary history of the Béarnais reformation by a Protestant minister and historiographer to the crown. Valuable modern accounts include C. Dartigue-Peyrou, *Jeanne d'Albret et le Béarn* (Mont-de-Marsan, 1934); Marc Forissier, *Histoire de la Réforme en Béarn,* 2 vols. (Tarbes, 1951–53); and Mark Greengrass, "The Calvinist Experiment in Béarn," in Pettegree, Duke, and Lewis, eds., *Calvinism in Europe.* These works form the basis for this and following paragraphs.

34. Charles Frossard, *La discipline ecclésiastique du pays de Béarn* (Paris, 1877).
35. The chief clauses of the 1571 edict may be found in Dartigue-Peyrou, *Jeanne d'Albret et le Béarn,* 145–64.

CHAPTER 5. SCOTLAND: A REVOLUTIONARY REFORMATION

Bibliographical Note   The many battles and schisms over ecclesiological issues in Scotland since the Reformation have bred a historiography that is attentive to the early institutional development of the Scottish church, driven by the question of whether or not its original institutions appear to be episcopalian or presbyterian. The leading historian who inclines in the direction of the former interpretation is Gordon Donaldson. His *The Scottish Reformation* (Cambridge, 1960) remains the best single volume treatment of the subject, while his *Scotland: James V to James VII* (New York, 1966) is the best overall narrative history of the country during the sixteenth and seventeenth centuries. The leading historian who inclines toward the latter view is James Kirk. Many of his important articles are now collected in his *Patterns of Reform: Continuity and Change in the Reformation Kirk* (Edinburgh, 1989). He has been particularly active as an editor of key church documents with ample introduction and commentary, notably *The Second Book of Discipline* (Edinburgh, 1980), *Visitation of the Diocese of Dunblane and Other Churches 1586–1589* (Edinburgh, 1984), and *The Records of the Synod of Lothian and Tweeddale, 1589–1596, 1640–1649* (Edinburgh, 1977). Other important published sources for the history of the Scottish Reformation are John Knox, *History of the Reformation in Scotland,* ed. William C. Dickinson, 2 vols. (London, 1949); John Knox, *On Rebellion,* ed. Roger A. Mason (Cambridge, 1994); William D. Maxwell, ed., *John Knox's Genevan Service Book 1556* (Edinburgh, 1931); James K. Cameron, ed., *The First Book of Discipline* (Edinburgh, 1972); *Acts and Proceedings of the General Assemblies of the Kirk of Scotland [The Booke of the Universall Kirk of Scotland],* 4 vols. (Edinburgh, 1839–45); and *Acts of the Parliament of Scotland,* 11 vols. (Edinburgh, 1814–44).

More recent histories have attempted to follow the development of the movement in the localities in the manner of so many histories of the larger European Reformation, although the paucity of sources for Scotland makes this difficult. Ian B. Cowan, *The Scottish Reformation: Church and Society in Sixteenth Century Scotland* (London, 1982), is an attempt at synthesis from this point of view, while important local studies include Michael Lynch, *Edinburgh and the Reformation* (Edinburgh, 1981); Allen White, "The Impact of the Reformation on a Burgh Community: The Case of Aberdeen," in Lynch, ed., *The Early Modern Town in Scotland* (London, 1987), 81–101; and Frank D. Bardgett, *Scotland Reformed: The Reformation in Angus and the Mearns* (Edinburgh, 1989). Lynch's "Calvinism in Scotland, 1559–1638," in Menna Prestwich, ed., *International Calvinism* (Oxford, 1985), 225–55, in a good short synthesis. On the key figures in the events that shaped the Scottish Reformation, I have found Jenny Wormald, *Mary Queen of Scots: A Study in Failure* (London, 1988), and Jasper Ridley,

John Knox (Oxford, 1968), especially illuminating. Particularly important studies of specific aspects of the new Scottish Reformed church in the first generations of its existence include W. I. P. Hazlett, "The Scots Confession 1560: Context, Complexion and Critique," *Archiv für Reformationsgeschichte* 78 (1987): 287–320; David Mullan, *Episcopacy in Scotland: The History of an Idea, 1560–1638* (Edinburgh, 1968); Duncan Shaw, *The General Assemblies of the Church of Scotland, 1560–1600* (Edinburgh, 1964); and Walter Roland Foster, *The Church Before the Covenants: The Church of Scotland, 1596–1638* (Edinburgh, 1975).

1. Lynch, *Edinburgh and the Reformation,* 2; Mullan, *Episcopacy,* 28–29; Ridley, *Knox,* 1. For good introductions to Scottish society and history in this period: T. C. Smout, *A History of the Scottish People 1560–1830* (London, 1965); Jenny Wormald, *Court, Kirk, and Community: Scotland 1470–1625* (London, 1981); R. A. Houston and I. D. White, eds., *Scottish Society 1500–1800* (Cambridge, 1989).

2. Cowan, *Scottish Reformation,* 90–94; James Kirk, "The 'Privy Kirks' and their Antecedents: The Hidden Face of Scottish Protestantism," in W. J. Sheils and Diana Wood, eds., *Voluntary Religion* (Oxford, 1986), 155–70; Jane E. A. Dawson, "The Scottish Reformation and the Theatre of Martyrdom," in Diana Wood, ed., *Martyrs and Martyrologies* (Oxford, 1993), 260.

3. The best guides through Scotland's tangled political history in this period are Donaldson, *James V to James VII,* and Wormald, *Mary.* Unless otherwise noted, these provide the foundations for all assertions about Scottish political history throughout this chapter. On Knox's preaching and the geography of Protestant strength in these years, see also Cowan, *Scottish Reformation,* 89–114; Ridley, *Knox,* 27–64.

4. H. Robinson, ed., *Original Letters Relative to the English Reformation,* 2 vols. (London, 1846–47), 1:434; Wormald, *Mary,* 53–75, esp. 82; Cowan, *Scottish Reformation,* 89–114; Ridley, *Knox,* 101.

5. Gottfried Locher, "Zwingli's Influence in England and Scotland," in *Zwingli's Thought: New Perspectives* (Leiden, 1981), 372–73; James Kirk, "The Religion of Early Scottish Protestants," in Kirk, ed., *Humanism and Reform: The Church in Europe, England, and Scotland, 1400–1643: Essays in Honour of James K. Cameron* (Oxford, 1991), 361–411.

6. Ridley, *Knox,* 84–129, 189–240; Hazlett, "Scots Confession," 300–01; Kirkwood Hewat, *Makers of the Scottish Church at the Reformation* (Edinburgh, 1920), 144.

7. Knox, *History of the Reformation,* 1:118, 136–38, 148.

8. Cowan, *Scottish Reformation,* 112–14; Donaldson, *James V to James VII,* 51; Kirk, *Patterns of Reform,* 12–15.

9. Ridley, *Knox,* 305.

10. Knox, *On Rebellion,* passim, esp. xv–xvii; Jane E. A. Dawson, "The Two John Knoxes: England, Scotland and the 1558 Tracts," *Journal of Ecclesiastical History* 42 (1991): 555–76, esp. 559. See also J. H. Burns, "The Political Ideas of

the Scottish Reformation," *Aberdeen University Review* 36 (1955–56): 251–68; Jane E. A. Dawson, "Revolutionary Conclusions: The Case of the Marian Exiles," *History of Political Thought* 11 (1990): 257–72.

11. Knox, *The Copy of a Letter Delivered to the Lady Mary, Regent of Scotland; The Appellation of John Knox . . . to the nobility, estates and commonalty;* and *A Letter Addressed to the Commonalty of Scotland,* in Knox, *On Rebellion,* 72–129, esp. 99, 109,

12. The text may be found in Knox, *History of the Reformation* 2:255–56. I am unaware of any good study of the document's dissemination and posting.

13. Ridley, *Knox,* 317–34, 396; Knox, *History of the Reformation* 1:162–63.

14. Ridley, *Knox,* 335–60.

15. Jacques Poujol, "Un épisode international à la veille des guerres de religion: La fuite du Comte d'Arran," *Revue d'Histoire Moderne et Contemporaine* 8 (1961): 199–210.

16. Knox, *History of the Reformation* 1:250, reprinted in Knox, *On Rebellion,* 170.

17. Knox, *History of the Reformation,* 351; Wormald, *Mary,* 102–05.

18. Cameron, ed., *First Book of Discipline,* esp. 3–14, 95n; William McMillan, *The Worship of the Scottish Reformed Church, 1550–1638* (London, 1931), 42–43; Wormald, *Mary,* 93.

19. *Dictionary of Scottish Church History and Theology* (Edinburgh, 1993), s.v. "John Douglas," "John Row," "John Spottiswoode," "John Winram"; Shaw, *General Assemblies,* 158; Lynch, "Calvinism in Scotland," 229–30.

20. The text of the Scottish confession of faith may be found in Arthur C. Cochrane, ed., *Reformed Confessions of the Sixteenth Century* (Philadelphia, 1966), 159–84. Hazlett, "Scots Confession," offers a detailed theological analysis.

21. Maxwell, ed., *John Knox's Genevan Service Book;* James Kirk, "The Influence of Calvinism on the Scottish Reformation," in *Records of the Scottish Church History Society* 18 (1974): 161; Cameron, ed., *First Book of Discipline,* 183–84; *Acts of the Parliaments of Scotland* 3:353, 453; McMillan, *Worship,* 324–25; Benedict, *Huguenot Population,* 81.

22. Cameron, ed., *First Book of Discipline* is an excellent modern critical edition of the Book with commentary. See also Gordon Donaldson, "'The Example of Denmark' in the Scottish Reformation," *Scottish Historical Review* 27 (1948): 57–64; id., *Scottish Reformation,* 77–79, 115; James K. Cameron, "The Cologne Reformation and the Church of Scotland," *Journal of Ecclesiastical History* 30 (1979): 39–64.

23. Cameron, ed., *First Book of Discipline,* 96–107, 174–79, 184–87.

24. Lynch, *Edinburgh,* 97, 190; White, "Aberdeen," 94–96; Bardgett, *Scotland Reformed,* 148–58.

25. Cowan, *Scottish Reformation,* 134–36; Jenny Wormald, "'Princes' and the Regions in the Scottish Reformation," in Norman Macdougall, ed., *Church, Politics and Society: Scotland 1408–1929* (Edinburgh, 1983), 65–84; Wormald, *Mary,* 105.

26. Mullan, *Episcopacy,* 27–29; Donaldson, *Scottish Reformation,* 121–28; Bardgett, *Scotland Reformed,* chap. 5.

27. *Acts and Proceedings of the General Assemblies;* Shaw, *General Assemblies,* xi–xii, 166–71; Kirk, ed., *Second Book of Discipline,* 13, 115–18.

28. *Acts and Proceedings of the General Assemblies* 1:207–14; Gordon Donaldson, ed., "Lord Chancellor Glamis and Theodore Beza," *Miscellany of the Scottish History Society* 9:89–113; Kirk, ed., *Second Book of Discipline,* 23–45, esp. 44.

29. Donaldson, ed., "Glamis and Beza," 102–05; Maruyama, *Ecclesiology of Beza,* 175–78; Bruce Gordon, "Zurich and the Scottish Reformation: Rudolf Gwalther's *Homilies on Galatians* of 1576," in Kirk, ed., *Humanism and Reform,* 207–20.

30. Kirk, ed., *Second Book of Discipline,* is the fullest account of the drafting and implementation of the book as well as its text. See also Kirk, "'The Polities of the Best Reformed Kirks': Scottish Achievements and English Aspirations in Church Government after the Reformation," *Scottish Historical Review* 59 (1980): 22–53; Mullan, *Episcopacy,* 43–44, which I have found more convincing than Donaldson, *Scottish Reformation,* 203–06.

31. Kirk, ed., *Second Book of Discipline,* 130–37; George R. Hewitt, *Scotland under Morton 1572–1580* (Edinburgh, 1982), 110–16; Michael F. Graham, *The Uses of Reform: 'Godly Discipline' and Popular Behavior in Scotland and Beyond, 1560–1610* (Leiden, 1996), 130–36.

32. Kirk, ed., *Second Book of Discipline,* 136–45; Donaldson, *James V to James VII,* 178–81; Mullan, *Episcopacy,* 54–60; Alan R. Macdonald, "The Subscription Crisis and Church-State Relations 1584–1586," *Records of the Scottish Church History Society* 25 (1994): 222–55.

33. Mullan, *Episcopacy,* 75–76; Foster, *The Church Before the Covenants,* 7–31, 85.

34. Cowan, *Scottish Reformation,* chap. 8; Lynch, *Edinburgh,* 190; G. D. Henderson, *Religious Life in Seventeenth-Century Scotland* (Cambridge, 1937), 34; Lynch "Calvinism in Scotland," 250.

35. James Kirk, "The Kirk and the Highlands at the Reformation," *Northern Scotland* 7 (1986): 1–22; Jane Dawson, "Calvinism and the Gaidhealtachd in Scotland," in Pettegree, Duke, and Lewis, eds., *Calvinism in Europe,* 231–53.

36. *Acts and Proceedings of the General Assemblies* 2: 716, and, more generally, 716–24; Kirk, ed., *Visitation of the Diocese of Dunblane,* xxiv–xxv, xxxvi. Local studies revealing similar patterns are White, "Aberdeen," 87; Mary Black Verschuur, "Enforcing the Discipline of the Kirk: Mr. Patrick Galloway's Early Years as Minister at Perth," in W. Fred Graham, ed., *Later Calvinism: International Perspectives* (Kirksville, Mo., 1994), 226–27.

37. Margaret H. B. Sanderson, "Catholic Recusancy in Scotland in the Sixteenth Century," *The Innes Review* 21 (1970): 87–107; Allan I. Macinnes, "Catholic Recusancy and the Penal Laws, 1603–1707," *Records of the Scottish Church History Society* 24 (1992): 27–63, esp. 35. For the very different situation in the United Provinces, see below, 195.

38. For this and the subsequent paragraph: *Acts of the Parliament of Scotland,* vols. 2, 3 passim, esp. 2:539, 3:25, 138–39, 212–13; Wormald, "'Princes' and the Regions"; Bruce Lenman, "The Limits of Godly Discipline in the Early Modern Period with Particular Reference to England and Scotland," in Kaspar von

Greyerz, ed., *Religion and Society in Early Modern Europe 1500–1800* (London, 1984), 134–37; G. D. Henderson, *The Scottish Ruling Elder* (London, 1935), 101–34; Michael Graham, "The Civil Sword and the Scottish Kirk, 1560–1600," in Graham, ed., *Later Calvinism,* 237–48; Smout, *History of Scottish People,* chap. 3.

CHAPTER 6. THE NETHERLANDS:
ANOTHER REVOLUTIONARY REVOLUTION

Bibliographical Note   A fruitful division of labor between secular and church historians has produced an ample literature tracing both the course of the Reformation's development in different portions of the Netherlands and the early institutional and theological development of the Dutch Reformed churches. The long-standing debate within the Netherlands over the place of the Reformed church within the national community has particularly drawn the attention of historians to how the Reformed churches came to establish their legally privileged situation in the north and how church–state relations were organized in the wake of Dutch independence. Important collections of documents include C. Hooijer, ed., *Oude Kerkordeningen der Nederlandsche Hervormde Gemeenten (1563–1638)* (Zaltbommel, 1865), F. L. Rutgers, ed., *Acta van de Nederlandsche Synoden der zestiende eeuw* (The Hague, 1899; repr. Dordrecht, 1980); J. F. Gerhard Goeters, ed., *Die Akten der Synode der Niederländischen Kirchen zu Emden vom 4.-13. Oktober 1571* (Neukirchen, 1971); and J. Reitsma and S. D. van Veen, eds., *Acta der Provinciale en particuliere synoden, gehouden in de Noordelijke Nederlanden gedurende de jaren 1572–1620,* 8 vols. (Groningen, 1892). Gerard Brandt, *The History of the Reformation and Other Ecclesiastical Transactions in and about the Low Countries,* 2 vols. (London, 1720–23), is an early history that is still valuable. The studies of Alastair Duke now collected in *Reformation and Revolt in the Low Countries* (London, 1990) have done more to renew the historiography of the entire course of the long Dutch Reformation than any other works. For the early growth of the Reformation, key regional studies include Gérard Moreau, *Histoire du Protestantisme à Tournai jusqu'à la veille de la Révolution des Pays-Bas* (Paris, 1962); Johan Decavele, *De dageraad van de Reformatie in Vlaanderen (1520–1565),* 2 vols. (Brussels, 1975), and Clasina Rooze-Stouthammer, *Hervorming in Zeeland* (Goes, 1996). J. J. Woltjers, *Friesland in Hervormingstijd* (Leiden, 1962), is an extremely important study of the entire century, while Guido Marnef, *Antwerp in the Age of the Reformation: Underground Protestantism in a Commercial Metropolis, 1550–1577* (Baltimore, 1996), focuses on the central years from the foundation of a Reformed church through the Pacification of Ghent. The subsequent period of the "Calvinist Republics" in the south is well studied in André Despretz, "De instauratie der Gentse Calvinistische Republiek (1577–1579)," *Handelingen der Maatschappij voor Geschiedenis en Oudheidkunde te Gent* n. s. 18 (1963): 119–229; Johan Decavele, *Het Eind van een rebelse droom: Opstellen over het Calvinistich bewind te Gent (1577–1584)* (Ghent, 1984); and Guido Marnef,

Het Calvinistich bewind te Mechelen 1580–1585 (Kortrijk, 1987). C. C. Hibben, *Gouda in Revolt: Particularism and Pacifism in the Revolt of the Netherlands 1572–1588* (Utrecht, 1983); Joke Spaans, *Haarlem na de Reformatie: Stedelijke cultuur et kerkelijk leven, 1577–1620* (The Hague, 1989); John Paul Elliott, "Protestantization in the Northern Netherlands, A Case Study: The Classis of Dordrecht 1572–1640" (Ph.D. diss., Columbia University, 1990), P. H. A. M. Abels and A. P. F. Wouters, *Nieuw en ongezien: Kerk en samenleving in de classis Delft en Delfland 1572–1621* (Delft, 1994); and Benjamin J. Kaplan, *Calvinists and Libertines: Confession and Community in Utrecht, 1578–1620* (Oxford, 1995), are all rich studies of the Reformed church's conquest of privileged status in the north and the subsequent negotiations with the political authorities to define the precise relation between church and community.

Geographically broader studies of key episodes include Phyllis Mack Crew, *Calvinist Preaching and Iconoclasm in the Netherlands 1544–1569* (Cambridge, 1978); Solange Deyon and Alain Lottin, *Les casseurs de l'été 1566: L'iconoclasme dans le Nord de la France* (Paris, 1981); Andrew Pettegree, *Emden and the Dutch Revolt: Exile and the Development of Reformed Protestantism* (Oxford, 1992); H. A. Enno van Gelder, *Revolutionnaire Reformatie: De vestiging van de Gereformeerde Kerk in de Nederlandse gewesten, gedurende de eerste jaren van de Opstand tegen Filips II, 1575–1585* (Amsterdam, 1943). For theology and institutions, L. A. van Langeraad, *Guido de Bray: Zijn leven en werken* (Zierikzee, 1884); W. Nijenhuis, "Variants within Dutch Calvinism in the Sixteenth Century," *Acta Historiae Neerlandicae* 12 (1979): 48–64; D. Nauta, ed., *De synode van Emden. Oktober 1571* (Kampen, 1971); id., *De nationale synode van Dordrecht 1578. Gereformeerden uit de Noordelijke et Zuidelijke Nederlanden bijeen* (Amsterdam, 1978); and id., *De nationale synode te Middelburg in 1581: Calvinisme in opbouw in de Noordelijke et Zuidelijke Nederlanden* (Middelburg, 1981) are especially helpful.

1. A. F. Mellink, "Prereformatie en vroege reformatie," in *Algemene Geschiedenis der Nederlanden,* 15 vols. (Haarlem, 1977–82), 6:148; Duke, *Reformation and Revolt,* chap. 2; for the comparison with France: Higman, "Les traductions françaises de Luther," which, however, fails to provide the precise date of publication of many of the translations in question.

2. Mellink, "Prereformatie en vroege reformatie," 146–54; Decavele, *Dageraad,* 1:235–321, esp. 248, 284; Duke, *Reformation and Revolt,* chaps. 2–5.

3. For the sources for this paragraph, see the works cited in table 6.1. For the national total and international comparisons: Duke, *Reformation and Revolt,* 71; William Monter, "Heresy Executions in Reformation Europe, 1520–1565," in O. P. Grell and B. Scribner, eds., *Tolerance and Intolerance in the European Reformation* (Cambridge, 1996), 48–64; Henk van Nierop, "The Nobility and the Revolt of the Netherlands," in Benedict et al., eds., *Reformation, Revolt and Civil War,* 89–90.

4. Duke, *Reformation and Revolt,* 18–19, 101.

5. Decavele, *Dageraad* 1:239, 598–606; Duke, *Reformation and Revolt,* 44–45; Moreau, *Tournai,* 386–90.

6. Pettegree, *Emden,* 252–311; Nijenhuis, *Calvinus oecumenicus,* 38–39; Phyllis Mack Crew, *Calvinist Preaching and Iconoclasm in the Netherlands 1544–1569* (Cambridge, 1978), 58.

7. Moreau, *Tournai,* 90–116; Pettegree, *Emden,* 18–108, 231; Denis, *Eglises d'étrangers en pays rhénans,* 161ff.; Decavele, *Dageraad* 1:330–32, 373–81.

8. G. Verhoeven, *Devotie en negotie: Delft als bedevaartplaats in de late middeleeuwen* (Amsterdam, 1992), esp. 162–65; Marnef, *Antwerp,* 52–54; Woltjer, *Friesland,* 98; Duke, *Reformation and Revolt,* 9. Cf. Philip Benedict, "The Catholic Response to Protestantism: Church Activity and Popular Piety in Rouen, 1560–1600," in James Obelkevich, ed., *Religion and the People, 800–1700* (Chapel Hill, 1979), 187.

9. The organized churches under the cross known to have existed prior to 1566 are listed in Johan Decavele, *Het eind van een rebelse droom* (Ghent, 1984), 21; Rooze-Stouthammer, *Hervorming in Zeeland,* 154–59.

10. Johan Decavele, "Reformatie en begin katholieke restauratie 1555–1568," in *Algemene Geschiedenis der Nederlanden* 6:168–70; Cochrane, ed., *Reformed Confessions of the Sixteenth Century,* 185–219; L. A. van Langeraad, *Guido de Bray: Zijn leven en werken* (Zierikzee, 1884); E. M. Braekman, "Les sources de la *Confessio Belgica," Bulletin de la Commission de l'histoire des Eglises Wallonnes,* ser. 2, 7 (1961): 3–24.

11. Van Langeraad, *Guido de Bray,* 123; F. R. J. Knetsch, "Church Ordinances and Regulations of the Dutch Synods 'Under the Cross' (1563–1566) Compared with the French (1559–1563)," in Kirk, ed., *Humanism and Reform,* 187–205.

12. Duke, "Dissident Propaganda and Political Organization at the Outbreak of the Revolt of the Netherlands," in Benedict et al., eds., *Reformation, Revolt and Civil War,* 119–32; Henk van Nierop, "A 'Beggars' Banquet': The Compromise of the Nobility and the Politics of Inversion," *European History Quarterly* 21 (1991): 419–43; Geoffrey Parker, *The Dutch Revolt* (London, 1977), 64–71.

13. Beza, *Correspondance* 7:127; Crew, *Calvinist Preaching,* 7–8; Marcus van Vaernewijck, *Van de beroerlicke tijden in die Nederlanden en voornamelijk in Ghendt, 1566–1568,* excerpted and translated in Alastair Duke, Gillian Lewis, and Andrew Pettegree, eds., *Calvinism in Europe 1540–1640* (Manchester, 1992), 145–47; Guido Marnef, "Het Protestantisme te Brussel, ca. 1567–1585," *Tijdschrift voor Brusselse Geschiedenis* 1 (1984): 59; cf. Duke, *Reformation and Revolt,* 118–25.

14. Much has recently been written about the events of 1566 in the Low Countries. For good accounts, see Parker, *Dutch Revolt,* 74–80, esp. 79; Duke, *Reformation and Revolt,* chap. 6; David Freedberg, *Iconoclasm and Painting in the Revolt of the Netherlands* (New York, 1988); Deyon and Lottin, *Les casseurs de l'été 1566;* Andrew Pettegree, "The Exile Churches during the *Wonderjaar,"* in J. van den Berg and P. Hoftijzer, eds., *Church, Change and Revolution* (Leiden, 1991), 80–99; J. G. C. Venner, *Beeldenstorm in Hasselt 1567* (Leeuwarden, 1989); R. van

Roosbroeck, *Het Wonderjaar te Antwerpen (1566–1567)* (Antwerp, 1930); Robert du Plessis. *Lille and the Dutch Revolt: Urban Stability in an Era of Revolution 1500–1582* (Cambridge, 1991), 203–32.

15. Parker, *Dutch Revolt*, 81–82; van Roosbroeck, *Wonderjaar te Antwerpen*, 172–76; Woltjers, *Friesland*, 148–88; W. J. Formsma et al., *Historie van Groningen: Stad en land* (Groningen, 1981), 218–19.

16. J. W. Pont, *Geschiedenis van het Lutheranisme in de Nederlanden tot 1618* (Haarlem, 1911), 60–92, 139–92.

17. Pettegree, *Emden*, 239.

18. Pont, *Geschiedenis van het Lutheranisme*, 62ff.

19. Marcel Backhouse, "Peiling naar de social status van de Kortrijkse Hervormden (1566–1585)," *Tijdschrift voor Geschiedenis* 89 (1976): 394–412; *Algemene Geschiedenis der Nederlanden* 6:180; Venner, *Beeldenstorm in Hasselt*, 194–213; Marnef, *Antwerp*, 92–100, 171–84; Duke, *Reformation and Revolt*, 127; van Nierop "Nobility and the Revolt," 88–91.

20. Parker, *Dutch Revolt*, 93; A. A. van Schelven, "Het Verzoekschrift der Drie Millioen Goudguldens (October 1566)," *Bijdragen voor Vaderlandsche Geschiedenis en Oudheidkunde* 9 (1930): 1–41; van Roosbroeck, *Wonderjaar te Antwerpen*, 214ff.

21. Martin van Gelderen, *The Political Thought of the Dutch Revolt 1555–1590* (Cambridge, 1992), 74–88, esp. 88; van Roosbroeck, *Wonderjaar te Antwerpen*, 214–15; Jozef Scheerder, "Eenige nieuwe bijzonderheden betreffende het 3.000.000 goudguldens rekwest (1566)," in *Miscellanea historica in honorem Leonis van der Essen* (Brussels, 1947), 563.

22. Van Gelderen, *Political Thought of the Dutch Revolt*, 88; van Roosbroeck, *Wonderjaar te Antwerpen*, 183–88, 335.

23. Parker, *Dutch Revolt*, 94–99; Crew, *Calvinist Preaching*, 18–20; van Langeraad, *Guido de Bray*, 68–87, xliv; Marcel F. Backhouse, "Guerrilla War and Banditry in the Sixteenth Century: The Wood Beggars in the Westkwartier of Flanders (1567–1568)," *Archiv für Reformationsgeschichte* 74 (1983): 232–56.

24. On the actions of the duke of Alva: Parker, *Dutch Revolt*, 105–17; on the history and decisions of the Wesel Convent and Emden synod: Rutgers, ed., *Acta van de Nederlandsche Synoden der zestiende eeuw*, 1–119; Goeters, ed., *Akten der Synode der Niederländischen Kirchen zu Emden;* Nauta, ed., *Synode van Emden,* especially the article by J. J. Woltjers, "De politieke betekenis van de Synode van Emden"; for the count of the Netherlandish churches in exile and under the cross at this time: Benjamin J. Kaplan, "Calvinists and Libertines: The Reformation in Utrecht, 1578–1618" (Ph. D. diss., Harvard University, 1989), 11.

25. This and the following paragraphs are based on Enno van Gelder, *Revolutionnaire Reformatie,* esp. 17–32; Duke, *Reformation and Revolt,* chap. 9; Henk van Nierop, *Het Verraad van het Noorderkwartier: Oorlog, terreur en recht in de Nederlandse Opstand* (Amsterdam, 1999).

26. Rutgers, ed., *Acta van de Nederlandsche Synoden der zestiende eeuw,* 133–75.

27. *Nieuw Nederlandsch Biografisch Woordenboek* (Leiden, 1911), s.v. "Coolhaes";

J. P. van Dooren, "Caspar Coolhaes: Het een en ander uit zijn leven vóór en na de synode van Middelburg," in *De Nationale Synode te Middelburg in 1581: Calvinisme in opbouw in de Noordelijke en Zuidelijke Nederlanden* (Middelburg, 1981), 174–83; Olivier Fatio, *Nihil Pulchrius Ordine: Contribution à l'étude de l'établissement de la discipline ecclésiastique aux Pays-Bas, ou Lambert Daneau aux Pays-Bas (1581–1583)* (Leiden, 1971), 36–40; Hibben, *Gouda in Revolt,* 123–29.

28. C. Hooijer, *Oude Kerkordeningen der Nederlandsch Hervormde Gemeenten (1563–1638)* (Zaltbommel, 1865); Brandt, *History of the Reformation* 1:313–24, 407–21, 438, 2:66; H. A. Enno van Gelder, *Getemperde Vrijheid* (Groningen, 1972), 10–13, 19–38; Nijenhuis, "De publieke kerk," in *Algemene Geschiedenis der Nederlanden* 6:337; G. D. J. Schotel, *De Openbare Eeredienst der Nederl. Hervormde Kerk in de Zestiende, Zeventiende et Achttiende Eeuw* (Haarlem, 1870), 321–24.

29. The distinctive relation between the Reformed church and Dutch civil society is clearly explained in Duke, *Reformation and Revolt,* 290–93; and Heinz Schilling, "Religion and Society in the Northern Netherlands," in *Religion, Political Culture and the Emergence of Early Modern Society: Essays in German and Dutch History* (Leiden, 1992), 353–412. For the decision of the Dordrecht synod of 1578: Rutgers, ed., *Acta van de Nederlandsche Synoden der zestiende eeuw,* 270. For the relative strength of *liefhebbers* and full church members in Leiden: Parker, *Dutch Revolt,* 154. See also below, 199–200.

30. L. J. Rogier, *Geschiedenis van het katholicisme in Noord-Nederland in de zestiende en zeventiende eeuw,* 3 vols. (Amsterdam, 1945–47); James D. Tracy, "With and Without the Counter-Reformation: The Catholic Church in the Spanish Netherlands and the Dutch Republic, 1580–1650," *Catholic Historical Review* 71 (1985): 547–75; Pont, *Geschiedenis van het Lutheranisme,* part 2; Israel, *Dutch Republic,* chap. 16; Hans Knippenberg, *De Religieuze Kaart van Nederland: Omvang en geografische spreiding van de godsdienstige gezindten vanaf de Reformatie tot heden* (Assen, 1992).

31. Parker, *Dutch Revolt,* 156–78; Hibben, *Gouda in Revolt,* 52–93; van Nierop, *Verraad van het Noorderkwartier,* chaps. 5, 8, esp. 86, 159; E. H. Kossmann and A. F. Mellink, *Texts Concerning the Revolt of the Netherlands* (Cambridge, 1974), 128.

32. Brandt, *History of the Reformation* 1:330–8; Despretz, "Instauratie der Gentse Calvinistische Republiek"; Decavele, *Eind van een rebelse droom,* chap. 3; Marnef, "Protestantisme te Brussel," 63–78; Parker, *Dutch Revolt,* 189–90.

33. Decavele, *Eind van een rebelse droom,* 53–60, 105–12; Parker, *Dutch Revolt,* 190–216.

34. Woltjer, *Friesland,* chaps. 13–16, esp. 267–69, 282, 308–11; L. H. Wagenaar, *Het Leven van Graf Willem Lodewijk* (Amsterdam, n. d.), esp. 271–73; van Gelder, *Revolutionnaire Reformatie,* 132–58; Formsma et al., *Historie van Groningen,* 227, 362–63.

35. Hooijer, ed., *Oude Kerkordeningen,* 362–74; *Geschiedenis van Gelderland*

(Zutphen, 1975), 2:347–52; J. Lindeboom, "Die Groninger Kerkorden," in *Ecclesia* (The Hague, 1959), 1:138–49; *Historie van Groningen: Stad en Land* (Groningen, 1981), 362–67; Heinz Schilling, *Civic Calvinism,* 105–14; Wiebe Bergsma, *Tussen Gedeonsbende en publieke kerk: Een studie over het gereformeerd protestantisme in Friesland, 1580–1650* (Hilversum, 1999), 133–38.

36. Brandt, *History of the Reformation* 1:346–49, 370–71, 378–80, 404, 433, 446; Kaplan, *Calvinists and Libertines,* chaps. 1–5.

37. Enno van Gelder, *Getemperde vrijheid,* 27; Duke, *Reformation and Revolt,* chaps. 9–10, esp. 228–29; Bergsma, *Tussen Gedeonsbende en publieke kerk,* 250; C. A. Tukker, *De classis Dordrecht van 1573 tot 1609* (Leiden, 1965); Elliott, "Protestantization," 164; H. ten Boom, *De Reformatie in Rotterdam, 1530–1585* (Rotterdam, 1987), 154–55.

38. Abels and Wouters, *Nieuw en ongezien* 1:230–39; Spaans, *Haarlem,* 89; Bergsma, *Tussen Gedeonsbende en publieke kerk,* 113.

39. J. Briels, "De Zuidnederlandse immigratie 1572–1630," *Tijdschrift voor Geschiedenis* 100 (1987): 331–55; id., *Zuid-Nederlanders in de republiek 1572–1630: Een demografische en cultuurhistorische studie* (Sint-Niklaas, 1985); Abels and Wouters, *Nieuw en ongezien* 1:233–34, 150–55; Bergsma, *Tussen Gedeonsbende en publieke kerk,* 111–13; Spaans, *Haarlem,* 89; Elliott, "Protestantization," 148, 167.

40. Wiebe Bergsma, "Calvinismus in Friesland um 1600 am Beispiel der Stadt Sneek," *Archiv für Reformationsgeschichte* 80 (1989): 258.

41. Abels and Wouters, *Nieuw en ongezien* 1:294–306, 408; Elliott, "Protestantization," 157. See also Heinz Schilling, "Das Calvinistische Presbyterium in der Stadt Groningen während der frühen Neuzeit und im ersten Viertel des 19 Jahrhunderts: Verfassung und Sozialprofil," in Schilling and H. Diederiks, eds., *Bürgerliche Eliten in den Niederlanden und Nordwestdeutschland* (Cologne, 1985), 194–204, 246; id., "Calvinistische Presbyterien in Städten der Frühneuzeit— Eine kirchliche Alternativform zur bürgerlichen Repräsentation (mit einer quantifizierenden Untersuchung zur holländischen Stadt Leiden)," in Wilfried Ehbrecht, ed., *Städtische Führungsgruppe und Gemeinde in der Werdenden Neuzeit* (Cologne, 1980), 429–35.

42. Abels and Wouters, *Nieuw en ongezien* 1:261; A. T. van Deursen, *Bavianen en Slijkgeuzen: Kerk en kerkvolk ten tijde van Maurits en Oldenbarnevelt* (Assen, 1974), 132–35; Bergsma, "Calvinismus in Friesland," 271.

43. G. Groenhuis, *De Predikanten: De social positie van de gereformeerde predikanten in de Republiek der Verenigde Nederlanden voor 1700* (Groningen, 1977), chap. 3; Schilling, "Religion and Society in the Northern Netherlands"; Simon Schama, *The Embarrassment of Riches: An Interpretation of Dutch Culture in the Golden Age* (New York, 1987), 93–125; Reitsma and van Veen, eds., *Acta der Provinciale en particuliere synoden* 5:47, 56–57, 148–49; Elliott, "Protestantization," 157; Abels and Wouters, *Nieuw en ongezein,* part 6;

P. Scherft, "De generale synode van Middelburg en de Zeeuwse Statenordonnaties van 8 februari 1583," in *De Nationale Synode te Middelburg,* 140–43.

44. J. F. van Beeck Calkoen, *Onderzoek naar den Rechtstoestand der Geestelijke et Kerkelijke Goederen in Holland na de Reformatie* (Amsterdam, 1910); Elliott, "Protestantization," chap. 8; Abels and Wouters, *Nieuw en ongezein,* parts 7–8; Spaans, *Haarlem,* chaps. 5–7; van Gelder, *Getemperde vrijheid; Groot Placaet-Boeck Inhoudende de Placaten en Ordonnantien vande Hoogh Mog. Heeren Staten Generael der Vereenighde Nederlanden, ende vande Ed. Groot Mog. Heeren Staten van Hollandt ende West-Vrieslandt, Mitgaders vande Ed. Mog. Heeren Staten van Zeelandt,* 9 vols. (The Hague, 1658–1770), 1:351.

CHAPTER 7. THE EMPIRE: REFORMATION BY PRINCELY FIAT

Bibliographical Note The later Reformation era has never had the appeal for historians of the German Reformation of the period prior to 1555. The best overviews of the development of the Reformed churches and of German Protestantism more generally in this period are still to be found in such older works as Heinrich Heppe, *Geschichte des deutschen Protestantismus in den Jahren 1555–1581,* 4 vols. (Marburg, 1852–59), and James I. Good, *The Origin of the Reformed Church in Germany* (Reading, Pa., 1887). Important edited collections of sources include Emil Sehling, ed., *Die evangelischen Kirchenordnungen des XVI. Jahrhunderts,* 8 vols. to date (Leipzig and Tubingen, 1902–); August Kluckhohn, ed., *Briefe Friedrich des Frommen, Kurfürsten von der Pfalz,* 2 vols. (Brunswick, 1868–72); and the many volumes of Lower Rhenish synodal and consistorial acts published by the Verein für Rheinische Kirchengeschichte. Recent work has largely been shaped by Heinz Schilling's *Konfessionskonflikt und Staatsbildung: Eine Fallstudie über das Verhältnis von religiösem und sozialem Wandel in der Frühneuzeit am Beispiel der Grafschaft Lippe* (Gutersloh, 1981), with its provocative argument linking the second reformations to territorial state building and its challenge to the dichotomy long enshrined in German historiography between a Calvinism thought to be antiauthoritarian and protodemocratic and a Lutheranism cast as politically passive and protoabsolutist. Two valuable collections of case studies explore the issues raised by Schilling's work: Schilling, ed., *Die reformierte Konfessionalisierung in Deutschland-Das Problem der "Zweiten Reformation"* (Gütersloh, 1986), and Meinrad Schaab, ed., *Territorialstaat und Calvinismus* (Stuttgart, 1993). Bodo Nischan, *Prince, People, and Confession: The Second Reformation in Brandenburg* (Philadelphia, 1994), narrates events in that territory. The work of the preceding generation displayed more interest in the theological and biographical considerations shaping the establishment of Reformed churches in this era. Particularly valuable are Ruth Wesel-Roth, *Thomas Erastus: Ein Beitrag zur Geschichte der reformierten Kirche und zur Lehre von der Staatssouveränität* (Lahr, 1954); Jürgen Moltmann, *Christoph Pezel (1539–1604) und der Calvinismus in Bremen* (Bremen, 1958); Thomas Klein, *Der Kampf um die Zweite Reformation in Kursachsen 1586–1591* (Cologne,

1962); Walter Hollweg, *Der Augsburger Reichstag von 1566 und seine Bedeutung für die Entstehung der Reformierten Kirche und ihres Bekenntnisses* (Neukirchen, 1964); Volker Press, *Calvinismus und Territorialstaat: Regierung und Zentralbehörden der Kurpfalz 1559–1619* (Stuttgart, 1970); and Rolf Glawischnig, *Niederlande, Kalvinismus und Reichsgrafenstand 1559–1584: Nassau-Dillenburg unter Graf Johann VI* (Marburg, 1973).

Aside from the books of Good and Nischan, the English-language literature on Germany's second reformations is decidedly limited, but Henry J. Cohn, "The Territorial Princes in Germany's Second Reformation, 1599–1622," in Prestwich, ed., *International Calvinism*, 135–66, and R. Po-Chia Hsia, *Social Discipline in the Reformation: Central Europe 1550–1750* (London, 1989), chap. 2, are good brief accounts of the subject. Schilling's chapter, "Between the Territorial State and Urban Liberty: Lutheranism and Calvinism in the County of Lippe," in R. Po-Chia Hsia, ed., *The German People and the Reformation* (Ithaca, 1988), conveniently summarizes his *Konfessionskonflikt und Staatsbildung*. Several essays in his *Civic Calvinism in Northwestern Germany and the Netherlands, Sixteenth to Nineteenth Centuries* Sixteenth Century Essays and Studies 17 (Kirksville, Mo., 1991), explore Emden's history in this period. See also Kaspar von Greyerz, *The Late City Reformation: The Case of Colmar, 1522–1628* (Wiesbaden, 1980); and Owen Chadwick, "The Making of a Reforming Prince: Frederick III, Elector Palatine," in R. B. Knox, ed., *Reformation, Conformity and Dissent: Essays in Honour of Geoffrey Nuttall* (London, 1977), 44–69.

1. Ernst Koch, "Der kursächsische Philippismus und seine Krise in den 1560er und 1570er Jahren," in Schilling, ed., *Reformierte Konfessionalisierung,* 60–73.
2. Schaff, *Creeds of Christendom* 1:258–339, 3:93–180; Heppe, *Geschichte des deutschen Protestantismus,* vol. 3; Good, *Origin of the Reformed Church in Germany,* 241–44.
3. *Registres de la Compagnie des Pasteurs* 4:23–24; Beza, *Correspondance* 7:82–83, 250–52, 8:83–85; Moltmann, *Pezel,* 61–66; August Kluckhohn, "Der Sturz der Kryptocalvinisten in Sachsen," *Historische Zeitschrift* 18 (1867): 77–127.
4. Nischan, *Prince, People, and Confession,* 161.
5. For this and the subsequent paragraph: Bodo Nischan, "The 'Fractio Panis': A Reformed Communion Practice in Late Reformation Germany," *Church History* 53 (1984): 17–29; id., "The Second Reformation in Brandenburg: Aims and Goals," *Sixteenth Century Journal* 14 (1983): 177ff.; Paul Münch, "Kirchenzucht und Nachbarschaft," 237; Harry Oelke, *Die Konfessionsbildung des 16. Jahrhunderts im Spiegel illustrierter Flugblätter* (Berlin, 1992), 358–71; Alois Schröer, *Die Reformation in Westfalen: Der Glaubenskampf einer Landschaft* (Munster, 1979), 1:468; Jill Raitt, *The Colloquy of Montbéliard: Religion and Politics in the Sixteenth Century* (Oxford, 1993), esp. chaps. 3–5.
6. Beza, *Correspondance* 7:250; Hollweg, *Augsburger Reichstag,* 121–22.
7. See Bernard Vogler, *Vie religieuse en pays rhénan dans la seconde moitié du XVIe siècle (1556–1619)* (Lille, 1974), 1170–72; Karl Wolf, "Zur Einführung des

reformierten Bekenntnisses in Nassau-Dillenburg," *Nassauische Annalen: Jahr-buch des Vereins für Nassauische Altertumskunde und Geschichtsforschung* 66 (1955): 182; Gerhard Menk, "Absolutistiches Wollen und verfremdte Wirklichkeit-Der calvinistische Sonderweg Hessen-Kassels" in Schaab, ed., *Territorialstaat und Calvinismus,* 208-09.

8. Lorna Jane Abray, *The People's Reformation: Magistrates, Clergy, and Commons in Strasbourg, 1500-1598* (Ithaca, 1985), 135-37, 142-51; von Greyerz, *Late City Reformation,* esp. 124-62; Hans-Georg Aschoff, "Bremen," in Schindling and Ziegler, eds., *Territorien des Reichs* 3:50-51; Rudloff Ortwin, "Bremen," in *Theologische Realenzyklopädie* (Berlin, 1977-), 7:156-59; Moltmann, *Pezel,* 16-38, 106-65; Smid, *Ostfriesische Kirchengeschichte,* 175-268, 309; Heinz Schilling, "Calvinism and Urban Republicanism: The Emden Experience," in *Civic Calvinism,* 11-39.

9. Although there is as yet no comprehensive study and accounting of the devel-opment of Reformed churches in this region, synodal and other administrative records permit one to obtain a rough estimate of the number and strength of these churches. See Eduard Simons, ed., *Synodalbuch: Die Akten der Synoden und Quartierskonsistorien in Jülich, Cleve und Berg 1570-1610* (Neuwied, 1909), esp. 654; Johann Arnold von Recklinghausen, *Reformations-Geschichte der Länder Jülich, Berg, Cleve, Meurs, Mark, Westfalen und der Städte Aachen, Cöln und Dortmund* (Elberfeld, 1818; repr. Osnabrück, 1977), 83; Johann Victor Bredt, *Die Verfassung der reformierten Kirche in Cleve-Jülich-Berg-Mark* (Ansbach, 1938), 54, 56. For the larger story of the development of the churches in this region, see also Heinz Schilling, *Exulanten;* id., "Innovation through Migration: The Settlements of Calvinistic Netherlanders in Sixteenth- and Seventeenth-Century Central and Western Europe," *Histoire sociale-Social History* 16 (1983): 7-34; Schroer, *Reformation in Westfalen* 1:477; Herbert Smolinsky, "Jülich-Kleve-Berg," in Schindling and Ziegler, eds., *Territorien des Reichs* 3:87-103; Rutgers, ed., *Acta van de Nederlandsche Synoden,* 118-19.

10. Joachim Whaley, *Religious Toleration and Social Change in Hamburg, 1529-1819* (Cambridge, 1985), 120-21.

11. The importance of geographical patterns of bureaucratic recruitment in in-fluencing the confessional destiny of the different German territories, and especially the Palatinate, is stressed by Volker Press, "Stadt und territoriale Konfessionsbildung," in Franz Petri, ed., *Kirche und gesellschaftlicher Wandel in deutschen und niederländischen Städten der werdenden Neuzeit* (Cologne, 1980), 251-96.

12. August Kluckhohn, "Wie ist Kurfürst Friedrich III von der Pfalz Calvinist geworden?" *Münchner Historisches Jahrbuch* (1866): 421-520; Chadwick, "Making of a Reforming Prince."

13. Emil Sehling, ed., *Die evangelischen Kirchenordnungen des XVI. Jahrhun-derts,* vol. 14 *Kurpfalz* (Tübingen, 1969), 264-427; Rutgers, ed., *Acta Neder-landsche Synoden,* 57-58, 134; Lothar Coenen, ed., *Handbuch zum Heidel-berger Katechismus* (Neukirchen, 1963); Fred H. Klooster, *The Heidelberg*

Catechism: Origin and History (Grand Rapids, 1981); I. John Hesselink, "The Dramatic Story of the Heidelberg Catechism," in Graham, ed., *Later Calvinism*, 273–88; Lyle D. Bierma, "Vester Grundt and the Origins of the Heidelberg Catechism," in ibid., 289–310; *Theologische Realenzyklopädie*, s.v. "Heidelberger Katechismus."

14. Hollweg, *Augsburger Reichstag von 1566*.
15. Ibid., 137–212; Beza, *Correspondance* 6:219–25, 7:20–21, 45–46, 64, 154–56, 172–74, 286–87; Locher, *Zwinglische Reformation*, 605; Claus-Peter Clasen, *The Palatinate in European History 1555–1618* (Oxford, 1963), 8–11.
16. Sehling, ed., *Kirchenordnungen* 14:409–24.
17. Wesel-Roth, *Erastus*; Press, *Calvinismus und Territorialstaat*, 121–23, 247–50.
18. Theodore Beza, *Tractatus pius et moderatus de vera Excommunicatione & christiano Presbyterio* (London, 1590); Beza, *Correspondance* 11:149–54, 157–62, 253–57; Brandt, *History of the Reformation* 1:288; Wesel-Roth, *Erastus*, 103–12; J. Wayne Baker, "In Defense of Magisterial Discipline: Bullinger's 'Tractatus de Excommunicatione' of 1568," in Ulrich Gäbler and Erland Herkenrath, eds., *Heinrich Bullinger 1504–1575: Gesammelte Aufsätze zum 400. Todestag* (Zurich, 1975), 141–59; Maruyama, *Ecclesiology of Theodore Beza*, 112–22.
19. Sehling, ed., *Kirchenordnungen* 14:436–41, 448–51; Wesel-Roth, *Erastus*, 64–65; Press, *Calvinismus und Territorialstaat*, 247–50.
20. Press, *Calvinismus und Territorialstaat*, 267–379; Meinrad Schaab, "Obrigkeitlicher Calvinismus und Genfer Gemeindemodell: Die Kurpfalz als frühestes reformiertes Territorium im Reich und ihre Einwirkung auf Pfalz-Zweibrücken," in Schaab, ed., *Territorialstaat und Calvinismus*, 36–39, 62–63; Clasen, *Palatinate*, 37; Bernard Vogler, *Le clergé protestant rhénan au siècle de la Réforme (1555–1619)* (Paris, 1976), 312–13.
21. Gustav Bauer, *Die Reformation in der Grafschaft Wittgenstein und ihre Durchführung bis zum Tode Graf Ludwig des Älteren* (Laasphe, 1954), 25–99; Schroer, *Reformation in Westfalen*, 216–18, 451–54; Georg Schmidt, "Die zweite Reformation in den Reichsgrafschaften: Konfessionswechsel aus Glaubensüberzeugung und aus politischem Kalkül?" in Schaab, ed., *Territorialstaat und Calvinismus*, 97–136.
22. Glawischnig, *Niederlande, Kalvinismus und Reichsgrafenstand*, 57–125; W. H. Neuser, "Die Einführung der presbyterial-synodalen Kirchenordnung in den Grafschaften Nassau-Dillenburg, Wittgenstein, Solms und Wied im Jahre 1586," *Jahrbuch für Westfälische Kirchengeschichte* 71 (1978): 47.
23. Schaff, *Creeds of Christendom* 1:564; Neuser, "Einführung," 48–58; Wolf, "Einführung des reformierten Bekenntnisses in Nassau-Dillenburg," 160–90.
24. Glawischnig, *Niederlande, Kalvinismus, und Reichsgrafenstand*, 142–79; Schmidt, "Zweite Reformation in den Reichsgrafschaften," 113–16.
25. Gerhard Menk, *Die Hohe Schule Herborn in ihrer Frühzeit (1584–1660)* (Wiesbaden, 1981).
26. *Die Selbstbiographie des Heidelberger Theologen und Hofpredigers Abraham Scultetus (1566–1624)*, ed. G. A. Benrath (Karlsruhe, 1966), 30–31, quoted

by Cohn, "Territorial Princes," 134. For the developments in Saxony under Christian I, see Klein, *Kampf um die Zweite Reformation;* Karlheinz Blaschke, "Religion und Politik in Kursachsen 1586–1591," in Schilling, ed., *Reformierte Konfessionalisierung,* 79–97.

27. Janssen, *History of the German People* (London, 1906), 9:226–28; Moritz Ritter, *Deutsche Geschichte im Zeitalter der Gegenreformation und des Dreissigjährigen Krieges (1555–1648)* (Stuttgart, 1895; repr. Darmstadt, 1974), 2:60.

28. Sehling, ed., *Evangelische Kirchenordnungen* 2:528–40; Good, *Origin of the Reformed Church in Germany,* 346; H. Wäschke, *Geschichte Anhalts im Zeitalter der Reformation* (Köthen, 1913), 2:470–76; H. Duncker, *Anhalts Bekenntnisstand während der Vereinigung der Fürstentümer unter Joachim Ernst und Johann Georg (1570–1606)* (Dessau, 1892).

29. Heinrich Heppe, *Kirchengeschichte beider Hessen* (Marburg, 1876), part 4; Karl E. Demandt, *Geschichte des Landes Hessen* (Cassel, 1972), 238–48; Manfred Rudersdorf, "Hessen," in Schindling and Ziegler, eds., *Territorien des Reichs* 3:275–83.

30. Schroer, *Reformation in Westfalen* 1:456–65; Israel, *Dutch Republic,* 386.

31. Werner-Ulrich Deetjen, "Der Konfessionswechsel im Herzogtum Zweibrücken," in Schilling, ed., *Reformierte Konfessionalisierung,* 98–103; Meinrad Schaab, "Obrigkeitlicher Calvinismus und Genfer Gemeindemodell: Die Kurpfalz als frühestes reformiertes Territorium im Reich und ihre Einwirkung auf Pfalz-Zweibrücken," in Schaab, ed., *Territorialstaat und Calvinismus,* 35–51.

32. Schilling, *Konfessionskonflikt und Staatsbildung,* 159–77; Schroer, *Reformation in Westfalen* 1:466–67.

33. Karl Czok, "Der 'Calvinistensturm' 1592/93 in Leipzig-seine Hintergründe und bildliche Darstellung," *Jahrbuch zur Geschichte der Stadt Leipzig* (1977): 123–44; Good, *Origin of the Reformed Church in Germany,* 338–44; Klein, *Kampf um die Zweite Reformation,* 162–67; Siegfried Hoyer, "Stände und calvinistische Landespolitik unter Christian I (1587–1591) in Kursachsen," in Schaab, ed., *Territorialstaat und Calvinismus,* 137–48.

34. Good, *Origin of the Reformed Church in Germany,* 358; Menk, "Absolutisches Wollen," 201–09.

35. Schilling, *Konfessionskonflikt und Staatsbildung,* 225–59.

36. For this and the subsequent paragraph: Nischan, *Prince, People, and Confession,* passim, esp. 187, 210; Rudolf von Thadden, "Die Fortsetzung des 'Reformationswerks' in Brandenburg-Preussen," in Schilling, ed., *Reformierte Konfessionalisierung,* 233–50.

37. Modest second reformations were also initiated between 1609 and 1616 in several of the largely autonomous duchies within Silesia. Their rulers were often linked by ties of marriage to the ruling houses of Anhalt and Brandenburg. These did not spread much beyond the circles of court and *gymnasium.* Good, *Origin of the Reformed Church in Germany,* 383–85; Franz Machilek, "Schlesien," in Schindling and Ziegler, eds., *Territorien des Reichs,* 2:129.

38. Available population estimates for individual territories ca. 1600 include: the

Rhine Palatinate: 3–400,000; Zweibrücken: 60,000 (Vogler, *Clergé,* 14); Hesse-
Cassel: 200,000; Hanau: 48,000 in 1754 (Demandt, *Geschichte des Landes
Hessen,* 244, 299); Nassau-Dillenburg: 50,000 (Glawischnig, *Niederlande,
Kalvinismus und Reichsgrafenstand,* 9); Lippe excluding Lemgo: 35,000 (Schilling, *Konfessionskonflikt und Staatsbildung,* 58–59); Bremen: 21,000; Emden:
15,000; Mulhouse: 8,000; Wesel: 6,000 (all from Paul Bairoch, Jean Batou, and
Pierre Chèvre, *La population des villes européennes de 800 à 1850* [Geneva,
1988], 4–5, 9, 25, 28); Colmar: 5,000 Reformed (Peter G. Wallace, *Communities and Conflict in Early Modern Colmar: 1575–1730* [Atlantic Highlands, N.J.,
1994], 57, 79). The other Wetterau counties can be roughly estimated to have had
50,000 inhabitants, Bentheim-Steinfurt-Tecklenburg 30,000; and the Reformed
sections of East Friesland 40,000.

39. This estimate is derived by extrapolation from the figures provided for nineteen
of the empire's twenty-six universities by Franz Eulenburg, *Die Frequenz der
deutschen Universitäten von ihrer Gründung bis zur Gegenwart,* Abhand-
lungen der Philologisch-Historischen Klasse der Königliche Sächsischen Gesellschaft der Wissenschaften 24 (Leipzig, 1904), 100–01. Enrollments in Herborn
fell considerably below those in the other three universities, so eliminating it
from these calculations would not substantially alter the results.

40. Moltmann, *Pezel,* 147, 163ff.; Otto Veeck, *Geschichte der Reformierten Kirche
Bremens* (Bremen, 1909), 57–65.

41. *Index Aureliensis,* passim; Vogler, *Vie religieuse en pays rhénan,* 345–53.

42. Brandt, *History of the Reformation* 3:6–7, 87, 215–18, 232, 238, 256, 266–67;
Nischan, *Prince, People, and Confession,* 237–41.

43. Schilling, "Between the Territorial State and Urban Liberty," 276–77; Hsia, *So-
cial Discipline,* 3, 28; Schmidt, "Zweite Reformation in den Reichsgrafschaften."
For a more nuanced judgment: Meinrad Schaab, "Schlusswort," in Schaab, ed.,
Territorialstaat und Calvinismus, 271–72.

44. Ole P. Grell, ed., *The Scandinavian Reformation* (Cambridge, 1995), esp. 5,
9–10; id., "Huguenot and Walloon Contributions to Sweden's Emergence as a
European Power, 1560–1648," *Proceedings of the Huguenot Society of London*
24 (1992): 371–84; Michael Roberts, *The Early Vasas: A History of Sweden
1523–1611* (Cambridge, 1968), 274–76, 289, 412–26.

CHAPTER 8. ENGLAND: THE UNSTABLE SETTLEMENT OF A CHURCH

Bibliographical Note   The historiography of English religion over the full two
centuries examined in this book is characterized by a series of important debates,
each born from the attempt to revise a central element in the previously standard
account of the country's religious history. Each of these debates has generated
a great deal of research into the questions it serves to highlight, but the debates
rarely connect to one another, and the concentration on the questions they highlight has also led to a neglect of many others. Working through the literature on
English religious history is rather akin to picking one's way through intensely

worked minefields, then traversing important stretches of largely undisturbed ground in search of a few good guideposts.

Key published sources for the history of the English Reformation through the reign of Elizabeth I include two important collections edited by Hastings Robinson: *Original Letters Relative to the English Reformation,* 2 vols. (Cambridge, 1846–47), and *The Zurich Letters, or the Correspondence of Several English Bishops and Others, with Some of the Helvetian Reformers during the Reign of Queen Elizabeth,* 2 vols. (Cambridge, 1842–45); Gerald Bray, ed., *Documents of the English Reformation* (Minneapolis, 1994); Joseph Ketley, ed., *The Two Liturgies,* A.D. *1549, and* A.D. *1552* (Cambridge, 1844); James C. Spalding, ed., *The Reformation of the Ecclesiastical Laws of England, 1552* (Kirksville, Mo., 1992); John Foxe, *Acts and Monuments,* 8 vols. (London, 1837–41); John Jewel, *Works,* 4 vols. (Cambridge, 1845–50); William Whitgift, *Works,* 3 vols. (Cambridge, 1851); id., *An admonition to the Parliament* ([London] 1572); Thomas Cartwright, *A Replye to an answere made of M. Doctor Whitgift Agaynste the Admonition to the Parliament* ([London] 1573); id., *A full and plaine declaration of Ecclesiasticall Discipline* ([Heidelberg] 1574); Roland G. Usher, ed., *The Presbyterian Movement in the Reign of Queen Elizabeth as Illustrated by the Minute Book of the Dedham Classis 1582–1589* (London, 1905); and Richard Hooker, *Of the Laws of Ecclesiastical Polity,* ed. George Edelen, 4 vols. (Cambridge, Mass., 1977–81).

The debate spurred by the revisionist historians of the early Reformation has focused above all on the speed with which Protestant ideas took root in the country and has examined this issue primarily through the medium of local studies. The revisionist view has given rise to an admirable work of synthesis: Christopher Haigh, *English Reformations: Religion, Politics, and Society under the Tudors* (Oxford, 1993), now the best general history of the English Reformation. The erstwhile standard work and chief target of the revisionists' criticism, A. G. Dickens, *The English Reformation* (London, 1964; rev. ed., 1989), retains a great deal of value. Other helpful recent overviews include Richard Rex, *Henry VIII and the English Reformation* (New York, 1993); Diarmaid MacCulloch, *The Later Reformation in England 1547–1603* (New York, 1990); and Susan Doran and Christopher Durston, *Princes, Pastors and People: The Church and Religion in England 1529–1689* (London, 1991). Some of the best revisionist work, notably J. J. Scarisbrick, *The Reformation and the English People* (Oxford, 1984) and Eamon Duffy, *The Stripping of the Altars: Traditional Religion in England 1400–1580* (New Haven, 1992), has been concerned to demonstrate the vitality and persistence of late medieval Catholicism. For all its accomplishment, it must be said that this work neglects to consider that strong commitment to the various forms of late medieval Christianity might have been exactly what bred enthusiasm for the Reformation through a process of disenchantment with and anger against the cults to which people had previously been attached in the wake of the emergence of the evangelical critique. Margaret Aston, *England's Iconoclasts,* vol. 1, *Laws Against Images* (Oxford, 1988), is an important study of what in many areas was the great expression of precisely this process, although with the emphasis primarily on laws and theology rather than crowd action in this first volume. Among the many local studies of the course of the Reformation and the growth of Protestant sentiment in different localities, A. G. Dickens, *Lollards and Protestants in the Diocese of York 1509–1558* (Oxford, 1959); Christopher Haigh, *Reformation and Resistance in Tudor Lancashire* (Cambridge, 1975); and Susan Brigden, *London and the Reformation* (Oxford, 1989) are highly important. A. G. Dickens, "The Early Expansion of Protestantism in England 1520–1558," *Archiv für Reformationsgeschichte* 78 (1987): 187–222, summarizes much additional work on that question.

With so much attention having recently been devoted to the pace and extent of changes in belief and practice among the population at large, less work has been devoted to such important questions for the story here as the character and content of early Reformation propaganda, the relation between the English reformers and continental developments, and the religious beliefs and decision making of the leading policy makers. Much illumination about these questions may nonetheless be found in William A. Clebsch, *England's Earliest Protestants 1520–1535* (New Haven, 1964); John N. King, *English Reformation Literature: The Tudor Origins of the Protestant Tradition* (Princeton, 1982); Diarmaid MacCulloch, *Thomas Cranmer: A Life* (New Haven, 1996); id., *Tudor Church Militant: Edward VI and the Protestant Reformation* (London, 1999); Peter Newman Brooks, *Thomas Cranmer's Doctrine of the Eucharist: An Essay in Historical Development,* 2d ed. (London, 1992); and Christina H. Garrett, *The Marian Exiles: A Study in the Origins of Elizabethan Puritanism* (Cambridge, 1938).

For the Elizabethan period, Patrick Collinson's work has been important in reshaping understanding of the character of the church and the nature of Puritanism. Three essential books of his cut through the period from very different angles of approach: *The Elizabethan Puritan Movement* (London, 1967); *Archbishop Grindal 1519–1583: The Struggle for a Reformed Church* (Berkeley, 1979); and *The Religion of Protestants: The Church in English Society 1559–1625* (Oxford, 1982). *Godly People: Essays in English Puritanism and Protestantism* (London, 1983), collects many important essays. Other valuable studies of the nature of the Elizabethan settlement, the campaigns to modify it, the emerging Anglican defense of it, and the character of English theology more broadly in this era are Norman L. Jones, *Faith by Statute: Parliament and the Settlement of Religion 1559* (London, 1982); Peter Lake, *Moderate Puritans and the Elizabethan Church* (Cambridge, 1982); id., *Anglicans and Puritans? Presbyterianism and English Conformist Thought from Whitgift to Hooker* (London, 1988); A. F. S. Pearson, *Thomas Cartwright and Elizabethan Puritanism 1535–1603* (Cambridge, 1925); B. R. White, *The English Separatist Tradition from the Marian Martyrs to the Pilgrim Fathers* (Oxford, 1971); H. C. Porter, *Reformation and Reaction in Tudor Cambridge* (Cambridge, 1958); and C. M. Dent, *Protestant Reformers in Elizabethan Oxford* (Oxford, 1983).

1. E.g., MacCulloch, *Cranmer,* the most deeply researched recent account of ecclesiastical policy making at the highest levels under Henry VIII and Edward VI. See esp. 520–35, 610–24.

2. Scarisbrick, *Reformation and English People;* Haigh, ed., *The English Reformation Revised* (Cambridge, 1987); Haigh, *English Reformations;* Duffy, *Stripping of the Altars.*

3. Collinson's gradual rethinking of the main contours of Elizabethan and Jacobean church history may be followed through his *Elizabethan Puritan Movement, The Religion of Protestants,* and the essays collected in *Godly People.* Nicholas Tyacke's early article, "Puritanism, Arminianism and Counter-Revolution," in Conrad Russell, ed., *The Origins of the English Civil War* (London, 1973), 119–43, was critical to the reinterpretation of this period of English church history, while important aspects of this reinterpretation are worked out in Lake, *Moderate Puritans* and *Anglicans and Puritans?.*

4. See above, 174, and also William A. Clebsch, "The Earliest Translation of Luther into English," *Harvard Theological Review* 56 (1963): 75–86; Clebsch, *England's Earliest Protestants,* passim, esp. 241–42; David M. Loades, "Le livre et la Réforme anglaise avant 1558," in Gilmont, ed., *La Réforme et le livre,* 271–76; Aston, *England's Iconoclasts,* 211–12. For the chronology of executions, cf. Philip Hughes, *The Reformation in England* (London, 1950–54), 1:126; Foxe, *Acts and Monuments,* vol. 4 passim; Haigh, *English Reformations,* 67.

5. Maria Dowling, "Anne Boleyn and Reform," *Journal of Ecclesiastical History* 35 (1984): 30–46; E. W. Ives, *Anne Boleyn* (Oxford, 1986), chap. 14, esp. 303; Joseph S. Block, *Factional Politics and the English Reformation 1520–1540* (Woodbridge, Suffolk, 1993), esp. 38–40; Clebsch, *England's Earliest Protestants,* 253–57.

6. Quoted in Basil Hall, "The Early Rise and Gradual Decline of Lutheranism in England (1520–1600)," in *Humanists and Protestants,* 216.

7. MacCulloch, *Cranmer,* chaps. 8–11, esp. 359, 525; C. H. Smyth, *Cranmer and the Reformation under Edward VI* (Cambridge, 1926), esp. 271, 293.

8. King, *English Reformation Literature,* 26–29, 88; Haigh, *English Reformations,* 168–69; Loades, "Le livre et la Réforme anglaise," 281–84.

9. Clebsch, *England's Earliest Protestants,* 1–3, 127, 137–53; Hall, "Early Rise and Gradual Decline of Lutheranism," 213–36; Aston, *England's Iconoclasts,* 435; MacCulloch, *The Later Reformation in England,* 67; MacCulloch, *Cranmer,* 60–67, 173–85; *Original Letters* 1:13, 37–38; Claire Cross, "Continental Students and the Protestant Reformation in England in the Sixteenth Century," in Baker, ed., *Reform and Reformation,* 35–57.

10. Dalton, *A Lasco,* 364–78; James Martin Estes, *Christian Magistrate and State Church: The Reforming Career of Johannes Brenz* (Toronto, 1982), 14–15; Manschrek, *Melanchthon,* 282; Martin Greschat, *Martin Bucer: Ein Reformator und seine Zeit* (Munich, 1990), 228–34.

11. Smyth, *Cranmer and the Reformation,* chaps. 3–6; Constantin Hopf, *Martin Bucer and the English Reformation* (Oxford, 1946); Basil Hall, "Bucer et

l'Angleterre," in *Strasbourg au coeur religieux du XVIe siècle* (Strasbourg, 1977), 401–29; Donnelly, *Humanism and Scholasticism*, 174–81; Collinson, *Godly People*, chaps. 2, 8, 9.

12. Brooks, *Cranmer's Doctrine of the Eucharist;* MacCulloch, *Cranmer*, 354–57, 380–83, 390–92, 615.

13. For this and the subsequent paragraph: *The Two Liturgies*, A.D. *1549, and* A.D. *1552;* Edward C. Ratcliff, *The Booke of Common Prayer of the Churche of England: Its Making and Revisions 1549–1661* (London, 1949); G. J. Cuming, *A History of Anglican Liturgy* (London, 1982), 39–86; *Original Letters* 1:79, 87; Smyth, *Cranmer and the Reformation*, 202–19; MacCulloch, *Cranmer*, chaps. 10, 11; Ridley, *Knox*, 88; Porter, *Reformation and Reaction*, 64; Donnelly, *Humanism and Scholasticism*, 173.

14. Bray, ed., *Documents of the English Reformation*, 284–311; Donnelly, *Humanism and Scholasticism*, 176.

15. *The Statutes of the Realm* (London, 1810–28), IV, 2 & 3 Edw. VI, c. 19; 5 & 6 Edw. VI, c. 3; *A Dictionary of English Church History* (London, 1912), 351; David Cressy, *Bonfires and Bells: National Memory and the Protestant Calendar in Elizabethan and Stuart England* (Berkeley, 1989), 6–7; J. Wickham Legg, *English Church Life from the Restoration to the Tractarian Movement* (London, 1914), 260–61; Keith Thomas, *Religion and the Decline of Magic* (New York, 1971), 620–21; David Cressy, "The Seasonality of Marriage in Old and New England," *Journal of Interdisciplinary History* 16 (1985): 14–15; E. A. Wrigley and R. S. Schofield, *The Population History of England 1541–1871* (Cambridge, Mass., 1981), 298–300; Smyth, *Cranmer and the Reformation*, 257.

16. The text of the proposed changes has now been edited by James C. Spalding, *The Reformation of the Ecclesiastical Laws of England, 1552* (Kirksville, Mo., 1992). On the reasons for their failure, see 41–42; MacCulloch, *Cranmer*, 532–35.

17. The origins and history of this system do not appear to be well studied, but see H. Leith Spencer, *English Preaching in the Late Middle Ages* (Oxford, 1993), 163–67, 179–81.

18. Haigh, *English Reformations*, 203–34; Brigden, *London*, 575.

19. Claire Cross, *Church and People 1450–1660* (London, 1976), 112–13; Cross, "Parochial Structure and the Dissemination of Protestantism in Sixteenth-Century England: A Tale of Two Cities," in Derek Baker, ed., *The Church in Town and Countryside*, Studies in Church History 16 (Oxford, 1979), 269–78; Dickens, "Early Expansion of Protestantism," 197–213; Haigh, *English Reformations*, 189–96.

20. White, *English Separatist Tradition*, 11.

21. Garrett, *Marian Exiles;* Edward J. Baskerville, *A Chronological Bibliography of Propaganda and Polemic Published in English between 1553 and 1558* (Philadelphia, 1976). It is noteworthy that a census of works of Catholic religious propaganda published on the Continent between 1564 and 1568 finds the smaller number of forty-six books. A. F. Allison and D. M. Rogers, "A Catalogue

of Catholic Books in English, 1558–1640," *Recusant History* 3 (1956): 1–185, esp. 176.

22. G. J. Mayhew, "The Progress of the Reformation in East Sussex 1530–1559: The Evidence from Wills," *Southern History* 5 (1983): 38–67, esp. 46, 52; R. Whiting, "'For the Health of My Soul': Prayers for the Dead in the Tudor South-West," *Southern History* 5 (1983): 68–94; David Palliser, *Tudor York* (Oxford, 1979), 250–51; W. J. Sheils, *The Puritans in the Diocese of Peterborough 1558–1610* (Northampton, 1979), 16–17, 22; Caroline Litzenberger, *The English Reformation and the Laity: Gloucestershire, 1540–1580* (Cambridge, 1997), passim, esp. 168–87.

23. There also was little enthusiasm for reviving confraternities. Ronald Hutton, "The Local Impact of the Tudor Reformations," in Haigh, ed., *English Reformation Revised,* 131.

24. Jones, *Faith by Statute,* 9; Claire Cross, *The Royal Supremacy in the Elizabethan Church* (London, 1969), 71; Collinson, *Elizabethan Puritan Movement,* 191; Haigh, *English Reformations,* 237–38; W. T. MacCaffrey, "Elizabethan Politics: The First Decade, 1558–1568," *Past & Present* 24 (1965): 26–27; MacCulloch, *Tudor Church Militant,* 185–94.

25. Jones, *Faith by Statute,* passim; Haigh, *English Reformations,* 240–42; Cross, *Royal Supremacy,* 75; Bray, ed., *Documents,* 284–311.

26. N. M. Sutherland, "The Marian Exiles and the Establishment of the Elizabethan Regime," *Archiv für Reformationsgeschichte* 78 (1987): 253–84; Ralph Houlbrooke, "The Protestant Episcopate 1547–1603: The Pastoral Contribution," in Felicity Heal and Rosemary O'Day, eds., *Church and Society in England: Henry VIII to James I* (London, 1977), 83; V. J. K. Brook, *A Life of Archbishop Parker* (Oxford, 1962); Patrick Collinson, *Archbishop Grindal 1519–1583: The Struggle for a Reformed Church* (Berkeley, 1979); W. M. Southgate, *John Jewel and the Problem of Doctrinal Authority* (Cambridge, Mass., 1962), 9, 17–23; V. Norskov Olsen, *John Foxe and the Elizabethan Church* (Berkeley, 1973); Dent, *Oxford,* 88; *Zurich Letters,* passim; Bernard Vogler, "Europe as Seen Through the Correspondence of Theodore Beza," in Kouri and Scott, eds., *Politics and Society in Reformation Europe,* 254.

27. *Zurich Letters* 1:231; Dent, *Oxford,* 4, 8–11, 238; Charles David Cremeans, *The Reception of Calvinistic Thought in England* (Urbana, 1949), 65; Andrew Pettegree, "The Reception of Calvinism in Britain," in Wilhelm Neuser and Brian Armstrong, eds., *Calvinus Sincerioris Religionis Vindex* (Kirksville, Mo., 1997), 276–79; M. St. Clare Byrne and Gladys Scott Thomson, "'My Lord's Books': The Library of Francis, Second Earl of Bedford, in 1584," *Review of English Studies* 7 (1931): 396–405; Susan Foister, "Paintings and Other Works of Art in Sixteenth-Century English Inventories," *Burlington Magazine* 123 (1981): 278.

28. Cross, *Royal Supremacy,* 59, 60, 75; Collinson, *Elizabethan Puritan Movement,* 45, 50–53; MacCaffrey, "Elizabethan Politics," 26–27.

29. Collinson, "Towards a Broader Understanding of the Early Dissenting Tradition," in *Godly People,* 527–62; id., *Elizabethan Puritan Movement,* 22–28; Hall, "Puri-

tanism: The Problem of Definition," in *Humanists and Protestants*, 237–54; Lake, *Moderate Puritans;* John Spurr, *English Puritanism, 1603–1689* (New York, 1998), 17–27.

30. *Zurich Letters* 2:355; Beza, *Correspondance* 6:197, 7:154ff, 340ff., 8:98, 117; Knox, *History of the Reformation in Scotland* 2:198–201; Collinson, *Elizabethan Puritan Movement*, 55–97, 367; G. J. R. Perry, *A Protestant Vision: William Harrison and the Reformation of Elizabethan England* (Cambridge, 1987), 149; Pearson, *Cartwright*, 17; Porter, *Reformation and Reaction*, 121–31.

31. Spalding, ed., *Reformation of the Ecclesiastical Laws of England*, 50–52; MacCulloch, *Cranmer*, 610–11, 624; Collinson, *Elizabethan Puritan Movement*, 116–17.

32. An admonition to the Parliament, Bii, Biii and passim. For the context: Patrick Collinson, "John Field and Elizabethan Puritanism," in *Godly People*, 337–49; id., *Elizabethan Puritan Movement*, 101–21.

33. *The Victoria History of the County of Northampton*, 4 vols. (London, 1906), 2:44–45, prints the full text of the Northampton order, which also included requirements concerning church attendance, house-to-house visits prior to each communion to examine the state of parishioners' lives, and a regular ministerial exercise. See also W. J. Sheils, *The Puritans in the Diocese of Peterborough, 1558–1610* (Northampton, 1979), 24–28; Collinson, *Elizabethan Puritan Movement*, 141ff.

34. For this and the following paragraphs: Collinson, *Elizabethan Puritan Movement*, part 3; Pearson, *Cartwright*, passim, esp. 46–54; Maruyama, *Ecclesiology of Beza*, 174–94.

35. Cartwright, *Replye;* id., *Full and plaine declaration of Ecclesiasticall Discipline;* Pearson, *Cartwright*, 46–54, 86–101, 137; Maruyama, *Ecclesiology of Beza*, 125–28. Not one of the treatises of the 1570s actually uses the word *presbyterianism* or anything similar. According to the *Oxford English Dictionary, presbyterial* appeared for the first time in 1592, *presbyterianism* in 1644.

36. Usher, ed., *Minute Book of the Dedham Classis;* White, *English Separatist Tradition*, 47–49; Pearson, *Cartwright*, 211–22; Collinson, *Elizabethan Puritan Movement*, part 4; id., *Grindal*, part 4.

37. Whitgift, *Works*, 3:170–71, 295, 313; Lake, *Anglican and Puritans?* 49–64; Kressner, *Schweizer Ursprünge des anglikanischen Staatskirchentums.*

38. Collinson, *Godly People*, 348–55; id., *Elizabethan Puritan Movement*, 222–90.

39. *A Directory of Church Government* (London, 1644); Collinson, *Elizabethan Puritan Movement*, part 6; Collinson, *Godly People*, 363–67; Pearson, *Cartwright*, 233, 252–56.

40. Collinson, *Elizabethan Puritan Movement*, parts 7–8.

41. Richard Hooker, *Of the Laws of Ecclesiastical Polity* (selections), ed. Arthur Stephen McGrade (Cambridge, 1989), xix; Hooker, *Of the Laws of Ecclesiastical Polity* (a full critical edition), ed. George Edelen, 4 vols. (Cambridge, Mass., 1977–81), 34; Lake, *Puritans and Anglicans?* passim, esp. 50–51, 91, 159, 167; Norman Sykes, *Old Priest and New Presbyter* (Cambridge, 1957), esp. 60–66; Willem

Nijenhuis, *Adrianus Saravia (c. 1532-1613): Dutch Calvinist, First Reformed Defender of the English Episcopal Church Order on the Basis of Ius Divinum* (Leiden, 1980).

42. Anthony Milton, *Catholic and Reformed: The Roman and Protestant Churches in English Protestant Thought 1600-1640* (Cambridge, 1995), part 2.

CHAPTER 9. EASTERN EUROPE: LOCAL REFORMATIONS

Bibliographical Note Primary source materials are considerably more abundant for Protestantism's early history in Poland than in Hungary. Poland also boasts a long and distinguished tradition of historical scholarship that during the Communist era produced studies marked by unusually supple and imaginative varieties of historical materialism. Finally, the German historian Gottfried Schramm wrote a great deal about the Polish Reformation during the 1960s that was in close touch with contemporary German work on the social history of the Reformation. For all of these reasons, the literature on the Polish Reformation answers far more of the questions the student of the wider European Reformation brings to the subject than is the case for Hungary. The strong orientation of most of the scholarship on Poland toward the social context of the Reformation does mean, however, that the institutional and religious history of the Reformed churches has been relatively neglected. In Hungary, by contrast, the survival to the present of a significant Reformed community has produced a literature written largely by historians attached to divinity faculties that is aimed above all else at diagnosing the theological outlook of the region's various early Protestant apostles.

The early synods of the Polish Reformed churches have been published by Maria Sipallyo, ed., *Akta Synodów Róznowierczych w Polsce,* 3 vols. (Warsaw, 1966-83). Stanislas Lubieniecki, *History of the Polish Reformation and Nine Related Documents,* ed. George Huntston Williams (Minneapolis, 1995), is a valuable early history with extensive annotation. The old histories of Valerian Krasinski, *Historical Sketch of the Rise, Progress, and Decline of the Reformation in Poland,* 2 vols. (London, 1838-40), and Paul Fox, *The Reformation in Poland: Some Social and Economic Aspects* (Baltimore, 1924), retain much utility, but by far the best general account of the subject is Ambroise Jobert, *De Luther à Mohila: La Pologne dans la crise de la Chrétienté 1517-1648* (Paris, 1974). Because of anti-Trinitarianism's importance in the region, George Huntston Williams, *The Radical Reformation,* 3d ed. (Kirksville, Mo., 1992), also is indispensable for both Poland and Hungary. Specialized studies of importance include Janusz Tazbir, *A State Without Stakes: Polish Religious Toleration in the Sixteenth and Seventeenth Centuries* (Wydawniczy, 1973); Gottfried Schramm, *Der polnische Adel und die Reformation 1548-1607* (Wiesbaden, 1965); id., "Lemberg und die Reformation," *Jahrbücher für Geschichte Osteuropas,* n.s. 11 (1963): 343-50; id., "Protestantismus und städtische Gesellschaft in Wilna (16.-17. Jahrhundert)," *Jahrbücher für Geschichte Osteuropas,* n.s. 17 (1969): 187-214; id., "Nationale und soziale Aspekte des wiederstarkenden Katholizismus in Posen (1564-1617)," in *Festschrift Percy Ernst Schramm,* 2 vols. (Wiesbaden, 1964), 2:61–71; id., "Lublin und das Scheitern der städtischen Reformation in Polen," *Kirche im Osten* 12 (1969): 33–57; id., "Reformation und Gegenreformation in Krakau: Die Zuspitzung des konfessionellen Kampfes in der polnischen Hauptstadt," *Zeitschrift für Ostforschung* 19 (1970): 1–41; Michael G. Müller, *Zweite Reformation und städtische Autonomie im königlichen Preussen. Danzig, Elbing und Thorn in der Epoche der Konfessionalisierung (1557–1660)* (Berlin, 1997), conveniently summarized in English in "Late Reformation and Protestant Confessionalization in the Major Towns of Royal Prussia," in Karin Maag, ed., *The Reformation in Eastern and Central Europe* (Aldershot, 1997), 192–210, a valuable collection of essays. Even those who cannot read Polish will find much of value in the journals *Reformacja w Polsce* and its successor, *Ordodzenie I Reformacja w Polsce,* thanks to the French and English summaries.

The decisions of the Hungarian church synods of the sixteenth century have been edited and published by Áron Kiss, *A XVI. században tartott magyar református zsinatok végzései* (Budapest, 1881). Sadly, there is little secondary work in west European languages about the Hungarian Reformation that can be strongly recommended. The most authoritative and comprehensive overviews are the two works of Mihaly Bucsay, *Geschichte des Protestantismus in Ungarn* (Stuttgart, 1959), and *Die Protestantismus in Ungarn 1521–1978: Ungarns Reformationskirchen in Geschichte und Gegenwart* (Vienna, 1977). For English-language readers, the best starting points are the essays on the region in Prestwich, ed., *International Calvinism;* Maag, ed., *Reformation in Eastern and Central Europe;* and such collective histories as Thomas Brady, Heiko Oberman, and James Tracy, eds., *Handbook of European History 1400–1600,* 2 vols. (Leiden, 1994–95); Bob Scribner, Roy Porter, and Mikulás Teich, eds., *The Reformation in National Context* (Cambridge, 1994); and Andrew Pettegree, ed., *The Reformation World* (London, 2000). F. Szakály, "Türkenherrschaft und Reformation in Ungarn um die Mitte des 16. Jahrhunderts," *Etudes historiques hongroises* (1985): 437–58; and Earl Morse Wilbur, *A History of Unitarianism in Transylvania, England, and America* (Cambridge, Mass., 1952) are important monographic studies.

1. For essential background on the Polish-Lithuanian Commonwealth, see Norman Davies, *God's Playground: A History of Poland,* 2 vols. (Oxford, 1981), vol. 1; Jobert, *Luther à Mohila;* Jerzy Kloczowski et al., *Histoire religieuse de la Pologne* (Paris, 1987); J. K. Fedorowicz, M. Bogucka, and H. Samsonowicz, eds., *A Republic of Nobles: Studies in Polish History to 1864* (Cambridge, 1982).
2. Jan de Vries, *European Urbanization 1500–1800* (Cambridge, Mass., 1984), 19, 39.
3. Tazbir, *State Without Stakes,* chaps. 1–2, esp. 30.
4. Maria Bogucka, "Towns in Poland and the Reformation. Analogies and Differences with Other Countries," *Acta Poloniae Historica* 40 (1979): 56; Fox, *Reformation in Poland,* 21–32.
5. Gottfried Schramm, "Danzig, Elbing und Thorn als Beispiele städtischer Refor-

mation (1517–1558)," in H. Fenske, W. Reinhard and E. Schulin, eds., *Historia Integra: Festschrift für Erich Hassinger* (Berlin, 1977), 125–54; Zofia Kratochwil, "Reformacja i kontrreformacja w Chojnicach w latach 1518–1772," *Rocznik Gdanski* 52 (1992): 67–88, summarized in *Acta Poloniae Historica* 70 (1994): 203–04.

6. Lubieniecki, *History of the Polish Reformation,* 103–04, 133–34, 138–40, 436–40, 484; Theodor Wotschke, *Die Briefwechsel der Schweizer mit den Polen* (Leipzig, 1908), 3–17; above 65, 112.

7. Lubieniecki, *History of the Polish Reformation,* 107–08, 395, 483, 485, 766; Jobert, *Luther à Mohila,* 110ff.; Schramm, "Reformation und Gegenreformation in Krakau," 19–21; Williams, *Radical Reformation,* 992; Fox, *Reformation in Poland,* 43.

8. Lubieniecki, *History of the Polish Reformation,* 105, 126, 138–40, 452–53, 475; Jobert, *Luther à Mohila,* 68.

9. Lubieniecki, *History of the Polish Reformation,* 104–06; Tazbir, *State without Stakes,* 61–65; Fox, *Reformation in Poland,* 44–46.

10. Tazbir, *State without Stakes,* 65–67; Fox, *Reformation in Poland,* 47.

11. Tazbir, *State without Stakes,* 69–71, 80–81; Schramm, "Protestantismus und städtische Gesellschaft in Wilna," 201.

12. Tazbir, *State without Stakes,* 91–101.

13. Fox, *Reformation in Poland,* 47; Lubieniecki, *History of the Polish Reformation,* 105; Tazbir, *State without Stakes,* 46–47, 59.

14. Lubieniecki, *History of the Polish Reformation,* 116–17, 144–45, 154–55; Williams, *Radical Reformation,* 1004, 1009–11, 1019; Jobert, *Luther à Mohila,* 107–11.

15. The fullest account of a Lasco's activities following his return to Poland is Halina Kowalska, *Dziatalnosc Reformatorska Jana Laskiego w Polsce 1556–1560* (Wroclaw, 1969) (with French resumé). See also Jobert, *Luther à Mohila;* Williams, *Radical Reformation,* 1013–20, 1026–27; id., "The Polish-Lithuanian Calvin during the Superintendency of John Laski, 1555–60," in Brian Gerrish, ed., *Reformation Perennis: Essays on Calvin and the Reformation in Honor of Ford Lewis Battles* (Pittsburgh, 1981), 129–58; Naunin, "Die Kirchenordnungen des Johannes Laski," *Deutsche Zeitschrift für Kirchenrecht* 19 (1909): 24–40, 196–236, 348–75.

16. Earl Morse Wilbur, *A History of Unitarianism: Socinianism and Its Antecedents* (Cambridge, Mass., 1945), chaps. 20–30; Lubieniecki, *History of the Polish Reformation,* esp. 176, 267; Williams, *Radical Reformation,* 1009, 1020, 1042–50; Fox, *Reformation in Poland,* 28; Jobert, *Luther à Mohila,* 121–33.

17. Tazbir, *State without Stakes,* 86.

18. Jerzy Kloczowski, "Catholic Reform in the Polish-Lithuanian Commonwealth," in John W. O'Malley, ed., *Catholicism in Early Modern History 1500–1700: A Guide to Research* (St. Louis, 1987), 83–91; Lubieniecki, *History of the Polish Reformation,* 223, and, for further incidents, 225–26, 602; Tazbir, *State without Stakes,* 104–07; Jobert, *Luther à Mohila,* 241–70.

19. Tazbir, *State without Stakes,* 86–88; *The New Schaff-Herzog Encyclopedia of Religious Knowledge,* 13 vols. (New York, 1908–14), s.v. "Consensus of Sendomir"; Schramm, "Protestantismus und städtische Gesellschaft in Wilna," 199. On the situation in the Czech lands, see S. Harrison Thomson, *Czechoslovakia in European History,* 2d ed. (Princeton, 1953), 100–01; Locher, *Zwinglische Reformation,* 654–66; R. J. W. Evans, "Calvinism in East Central Europe: Hungary and Her Neighbours, 1540–1700," in Prestwich, ed., *International Calvinism,* 169–71, 173–74; Jiri Pesek, "Protestant Literature in Bohemian Private Libraries c. 1600," and Joachim Bahlcke, "Calvinism and Estate Liberation Movements in Bohemia and Hungary (1570–1620)," in Maag, ed., *Reformation in Eastern and Central Europe,* 36–49, 75–76.

20. Beza, *Correspondance* 2:319ff, 10:194–97; Wotschke, *Briefweschel der Schweizer mit Polen,* passim; Vogler, "Europe as Seen Through the Correspondence of Beza," 259; Jobert, *Luther à Mohila,* 134ff.; *Theologische Realenzyklopädie,* s.v. "Confessio Helvetica Posterior"; Staedtke, *Bullinger Bibliographie,* 237–38.

21. The most useful work here is the early nineteenth-century account of the Protestant historian Krasinski, *Historical Sketch of the Rise, Progress, and Decline of the Reformation in Poland,* esp. 2:74–75, 80, 294–95.

22. Schramm, "Protestantismus und städtische Gesellschaft in Wilna," 198. Tazbir, *State without Stakes,* 128, asserts that in the seventeenth century Reformed worship in Poland included many Catholic elements, including the use of railed altars, and that the cult of the Virgin survived in Protestant circles.

23. These statistics are based on Henryk Merczyng, *Zbory I Senatorowie Protestanccy w Dawnej Rzeczypospolitej* (Warsaw, 1904), supplemented by Waclaw Urban and conveniently summarized in Janusz Tazbir, "La géographie du protestantisme polonais aux XVIe–XVIIe siècles," in *Miscellanea Historiae Ecclesiasticae V* (Louvain, 1974), 156; Jobert, *Luther à Mohila,* 142–44; Schramm, *Polnische Adel und die Reformation,* 107–08.

24. Müller, *Zweite Reformation und städtische Autonomie im königlichen Preussen;* Jan Baszanowski, "Statistics of Religious Denominations and Ethnic Problems in Gdansk in XVII–XVIII Centuries," *Studia Maritima* 7 (1988): 54–55. Between 1631 and 1650, the first years for which such evidence is available, the Reformed accounted for 7.5 percent of all baptisms in Danzig, as opposed to 86.1 percent for the Lutherans and 6.4 percent for the Catholics.

25. Schramm, *Polnische Adel und die Reformation,* 91, 107–08; Lubieniecki, *History of the Polish Reformation,* 223, 225–26, 602, 722; Roman Zelewski, "Zaburzenia wyznaniowe w Krakowie: Okres przewagi roznowiercow 1551–1573," *Odrodzenie i Reformacja w Polsce* 6 (1961): 91–111 (with French summary); Schramm, "Reformation und Gegenreformation in Krakau," 20; id., "Lemberg"; id. "Lublin"; Jobert, *Luther à Mohila,* 145, 203.

26. Vera Zimányi, *Economy and Society in Sixteenth and Seventeenth Century Hungary (1526–1650)* (Budapest, 1987), offers an excellent introduction to the economic and social history of the region. For patterns of university attendance,

see Bucsay, *Geschichte des Protestantismus,* 163; Géza Szabo, *Geschichte des ungarischen Coetus an der Universität Wittenberg, 1555-1613* (Halle, 1941).

27. The two works of Bucsay, *Geschichte des Protestantismus in Ungarn* and *Die Protestantismus in Ungarn* provide the most authoritative account of the Hungarian Reformation in a west European language and will serve as the basis for the remainder of this section, except as otherwise noted. See also on this early period Béla K. Király, "The Sublime Porte, Vienna, Transylvania and the Dissemination of the Protestant Reformation in Royal Hungary," in Király, ed., *Tolerance and Movements of Religious Dissent in Eastern Europe* (Boulder, Colo., 1975), 199-204; and for Mary's religious views, Paula Sutter Fichtner, *Ferdinand I of Austria: The Politics of Dynasticism in the Age of the Reformation* (New York, 1982), 74-75.

28. C. R. Betts, "The Reformation in Difficulties: Poland, Bohemia, and Hungary," in G. R. Elton, ed., *The New Cambridge Modern History,* vol. 2, *The Reformation 1520-1559* (Cambridge, 1958), 196. Other authorities place the number of bishops slain at six.

29. Szakály, "Türkenherrschaft und Reformation in Ungarn," 439-46.

30. Szakály, "Türkenherrschaft und Reformation in Ungarn," 454-57; Graeme Murdock, "Death, Prophecy and Judgement in Transylvania," in Bruce Gordon and Peter Marshall, eds., *The Place of the Dead: Death and Remembrance in Late Medieval and Early Modern Europe* (Cambridge, 2000), 217.

31. Szakály, "Türkenherrschaft und Reformation in Ungarn," 446-54, esp. 451; Bucsay, *Geschichte des Protestantismus in Ungarn,* 48-86, esp. 58; Gedeon Borsa, "Le livre et les débuts de la Réforme en Hongrie," in Gilmont, ed., *La Réforme et le livre,* 375-92.

32. Katalin Péter, "Tolerance and Intolerance in Sixteenth-Century Hungary," in Scribner and Grell, eds., *Tolerance and Intolerance,* 250-55; Pierre Costil, *André Dudith humaniste hongrois 1533-1589* (Paris, 1935), esp. 141, 173-74, 193, 339-50; R. J. W. Evans, *Rudolf II and His World: A Study in Intellectual History 1576-1612* (Oxford, 1973), 105-10; Betts, "Reformation in Difficulties," 199.

33. Evans, "Calvinism in East Central Europe," 176; Ö. Miklós, *A magyar protestáns egyházalkotmány kialakulása a reformáció századában* (Pápa, 1942).

34. David P. Daniel, "Hungary," in Andrew Pettegree, ed., *The Early Reformation in Europe* (Cambridge, 1992), 59-68; Borsa, "Livre et Réforme en Hongrie," 382; J. G. Bauhofer, *History of the Protestant Church in Hungary* (Boston, 1854), 87-88; Locher, *Zwinglische Reformation,* 657-58; E. de Koulifay, "L'influence du Calvinisme sur la Réforme hongroise," *Bulletin de la Société de l'Histoire du Protestantisme Français* 84 (1935): 91-103; István Schlégl, "Die Beziehungen Heinrich Bullingers zu Ungarn," *Zwingliana* 12 (1960): 330-70; Bullinger, *Epistola ad ecclesias hungaricas,* ed. Nagy.

35. Lubieniecki, *History of the Polish Reformation,* 270-78; Williams, *Radical Reformation,* 1109-18; Earl Morse Wilbur, *A History of Unitarianism in Transylvania, England, and America* (Cambridge, Mass., 1952), chaps. 3-4.

36. Lubieniecki, *History of the Polish Reformation,* 674, 678; Peter F. Sugar, *South-eastern Europe under Ottoman Rule, 1354–1804* (Seattle, 1977), 153.

37. Evans, *Rudolf II and His World,* 68–70; Mihály Bucsay, "A reformáció százada (1520–1608)," in Sándor Bíró et al., *A magyar református egyház történeti* (Budapest, 1949; repr. Budapest, 1994), 89–90.

38. The latest estimate of Protestant strength, reducing earlier estimates, is offered by Katalin Péter, *Papok és nemesek: Magyar művelődéstörténeti tanulmányok a reformációval kezdödö másfél éusszázadból* (Budapest, 1995). I am grateful to Graeme Murdock for calling this to my attention and for his independent confirmation of these estimates, based upon the listing of Reformed churches in S. Ladányi, ed., *Magyarországi református egyháztörteneti lexikon. Histoire des revolutions de Hongrie . . . avec les Mémoires du Prince François Rakoczy sur la guerre de Hongrie et ceux du comte Betlem Niklos sur les Affaires de Transilvanie* (The Hague, 1739), 205; Bucsay, *Geschichte des Protestantismus in Ungarn,* 64; Jean Bérenger, *Histoire de l'Empire des Habsbourg 1273–1918* (Paris, 1990), 204.

39. Bucsay, *Geschichte des Protestantismus in Ungarn,* 120–23.

40. Bucer, *De Regno Christi,* in Wilhelm Pauck, ed., *Melanchthon and Bucer,* Library of Christian Classics (Philadelphia, 1969), 213; E. Illyés, *Egyházfegyelem a magyar református egyházban* (Debrecen, 1941), chap. 3; Graeme Murdock, "Church Building and Discipline in Early Seventeenth-Century Hungary and Transylvania," in Maag, ed., *Reformation in Eastern and Central Europe,* 136–54.

CONCLUSION TO PART II

1. This description of the working of the various church bodies in France, Scotland, and the Netherlands is based primarily on the reading of the surviving records from each level of assembly. Minutes of a large number of French provincial synods and *colloques* may be found in the Auzière papers of the Bibliothèque de la Société de l'Histoire du Protestantisme Français and in the Bibliothèque de l'Arsenal, MS 6554. For the Netherlands, I have used J. P. van Dooren, ed., *Classicale Acta, 1573–1620: Particuliere synode Zuid-Holland I: Classis Dordrecht 1573–1600* (The Hague, 1980), and Reitsma and van Veen, eds., *Acta der Provinciale en particuliere synoden gehouden in de Noordelijke Nederlanden;* and for Scotland James Kirk, ed., *The Records of the Synod of Lothian and Tweeddale 1589–1596, 1640–1649* (Edinburgh, 1977). See also Gueneau, "Protestants du Centre," 38; C. A. Tukker, *De classis Dordrecht van 1573 tot 1609* (Leiden, 1965); Abels and Wouters, *Nieuw en ongezien,* part 1; van Deursen, *Bavianen en Slijkgeuzen,* 5–12; Wiebe Bergsma, "Gereformeerden en doopsgezinden: Van concurrentie tot gedwongen acceptatie," *Doopsgezinde Bijdragen,* n.s. 20 (1994): 141–56; W. F. Dankbaar, "De kerkvisitatie in de Nederlandse gereformeerde kerk in de 16de en 17de eeuw," *Nederlands Archief voor Kerkgeschiedenis* 38 (1952): 38–55; Foster, *Church before the Covenants,* chaps. 4–6.

2. Foster, *Church before the Covenants,* 117–32; Shaw, *General Assemblies,* 20, 97.

3. Sipallyo, ed., *Akta Synodów Róznowierczych w Polsce,* esp. 3:8; Kiss, *A XVI. Században tartott magyar református zsinatok végzései.* Personal communications from Graeme Murdock also provided invaluable clarification of the administrative practices of the Hungarian churches.
4. *First Book of Discipline,* 122–23; Foster, *Church Before the Covenants,* 39–65.
5. Münch, *Zucht und Ordnung;* Luise Schorn-Schütte, *Evangelische Geistlichkeit in der Frühneuzeit* (Gütersloh, 1996), 57–67. The Hessian church structure included irregular general synods, yearly diocesan synods, and, after 1610, regular classical assemblies.
6. Quoted in Patrick Collinson, "England and International Calvinism 1558–1640," in Prestwich, ed., *International Calvinism,* 213.
7. Martin H. Körner, *Solidarités financières suisses au 16e siècle* (Lausanne, 1980), 260, 263, 390–91; Bucsay, *Geschichte des Protestantismus in Ungarn,* 144; Roger Stauffenegger, *Eglise et société: Genève au XVIIe siècle* (Geneva, 1983), 189; Kirk, ed., *Records of Synod of Lothian,* xxviii; Foster, *Church Before the Covenants,* 107; Vuilleumier, *Histoire de l'Eglise réformée du pays de Vaud* 2:188; *Acts and Proceedings of the General Assemblies of the Kirk of Scotland,* 5 vols. (Edinburgh, 1839–45), 3:854.
8. Jean Taffin, *Des marques des enfans de Dieu, et des consolations en leurs afflications* (Saumur, 1606); S. van der Linde, *Jean Taffin: Hofprediger en Raadsheer van Willem van Oranje* (Amsterdam, 1982), part 1.
9. Janine Garrisson, *Les Protestants au XVIe siècle* (Paris, 1988), 134; Israel, *Dutch Republic,* 572.
10. Rutgers, *Nederlandsche synoden,* 56; Aymon, *Tous les synodes* 1:157; Sunshine, "From French Protestantism to the French Reformed Churches," 103.
11. Aymon, *Tous les synodes* 1:257–58; *Registres de la Compagnie des Pasteurs* 9:230, 7:292; G. J. Hoenderdaal, "The Debate about Arminius Outside the Netherlands," in T. H. Lunsingh Scheurleer and G. H. M. Posthumus Meyjes, eds., *Leiden University in the Seventeenth Century: An Exchange of Learning* (Leiden, 1975), 144; Münch, *Zucht und Ordnung,* 127; Stauffenegger, *Eglise et société,* 246.
12. *An Harmony of the Confessions of the Faith of the Christian and Reformed churches, which purelie professe the holy doctrine of the Gospell in all the chiefe Kingdomes, Nations, and Provinces of Europe* (Cambridge, 1586); *Registres de la Compagnie des Pasteurs* 4:99–100, 362–71, 386–92, 395–99; Good, *Origin of the Reformed Church in Germany,* 243ff.; Sunshine, "From French Protestantism to the French Reformed Churches," 101–04; Vuilleumier, *Histoire de l'Eglise réformée du pays de Vaud* 2:178–79; Moltmann, *Pezel,* 112, 148.
13. Beza, *Correspondance* 10:250–53, 11:168–85, 12:8; Aymon, *Tous les synodes* 2:501; Brandt, *History of the Reformation* 2:180; *Registres de la Compagnie des Pasteurs* 9:230.
14. Good studies of the thought world of these figures are much needed. Béatrice Nicollier de Weck, *Hubert Languet (1518–1581): Un réseau politique international de Mélanchthon à Guillaume d'Orange* (Geneva, 1995), offers an excellent

examination of one important individual in this political tradition whose religious views turn out on examination to be more Philippist than Calvinist.

15. On international Protestant solidarity, its importance, and its limits, see Kervyn de Lettenhove, *Les Huguenots et les Gueux,* 6 vols. (Bruges, 1883–85); Bernard Vogler, "Le rôle des Electeurs palatins dans les guerres de religion en France (1559–1592)," *Cahiers d'histoire* 10 (1965): 51–85; Clasen, *Palatinate in European History;* Charles Wilson, *Queen Elizabeth and the Revolt of the Netherlands* (Berkeley, 1970); F. G. Oosterhoff, *Leicester and the Netherlands 1586–1587* (Utrecht, 1988); W. B. Patterson, *King James VI and I and the Reunion of Christendom* (Cambridge, 1997).

INTRODUCTION TO PART III

1. T. Brienen et al., *De Nadere Reformatie: Beschrijving van haar voornaamste vertegenwoordigers* (The Hague, 1986), 5, 351.

CHAPTER 10. THEOLOGICAL DISPUTES IN
THE AGE OF ORTHODOXY

Bibliographical Note   The literature on the subjects discussed in this chapter is extremely uneven. On subject after subject the more recent literature has struggled to work itself free of broad and often anachronistic theological categories used by earlier generations of theologian-historians, whose work nonetheless remains useful, if only because of its sweep. Heinrich Heppe, *Reformed Dogmatics,* rev. ed. (London, 1950) gives a good taste of this work. Richard A. Muller is the best recent guide to early Reformed orthodoxy in such books as *Christ and the Decree: Christology and Predestination in Reformed Theology from Calvin to Perkins* (Durham, N.C., 1986); *Post-Reformation Reformed Dogmatics,* vol. A, *Prolegomena to Theology* (Grand Rapids, 1987); and *God, Creation, and Providence in the Thought of Jacob Arminius: Sources and Directions of Scholastic Protestantism in the Era of Early Orthodoxy* (Grand Rapids, 1991). On the Arminian controversy in the Netherlands, A. T. van Deursen, *Bavianen en Slijkgeuzen kerk en kerkvolk ten tijde van Mavrits en Oldenbarnevelt* (Assen, 1974) is a masterful study from the point of view of the social history of religion; the details of the theological and ecclesiological quarrels must be pieced together from specialized studies. The history of English "Arminianism" is currently a minefield. Nicholas Tyacke, *Anti-Calvinists: The Rise of English Arminianism c. 1590–1640* (Oxford, 1987), and Peter White, *Predestination, Policy and Polemic: Conflict and Consensus in the English Church from the Reformation to the Civil War* (Cambridge, 1992), offer dramatically different assessments of the course and significance of the theological debates. See also White, "The Rise of Arminianism Reconsidered," *Past & Present* 101 (1983): 34–54; Peter Lake, "Calvinism and the English Chrch 1570–1635," *Past & Present* 114 (1987): 32–76; Tyacke and White, "Debate: The Rise of Arminianism Reconsidered," *Past & Present* 115 (1987): 201–29; and Peter Lake, "Predestinarian Propositions," *Journal of Ecclesiastical History* 46 (1995): 110–23. I have found Tyacke more convincing than White. In many ways, the older and often neglected study of Dewey A. Wallace, *Puritans and Predestination: Grace in English Protestant Theology 1525–1695* (Chapel Hill, 1982), is still the best guide to the theological issues; the work also has the great merit of covering the entire century. Also excellent is H. C. Porter, *Reformation and Reaction in Tudor Cambridge* (Cambridge, 1958), which includes several fine chapters on Puritan practical divinity. On this latter topic, other valuable works that approach the subject from the point of view of the history of theology and spirituality are William Haller, *The Rise of Puritanism* (New York, 1938); Perry Miller, *The New England Mind: The Seventeenth Century* (New York, 1939); Edmund S. Morgan, *Visible Saints: The History of a Puritan Idea* (New York, 1963); Ian Breward, ed., *The Works of William Perkins* (Appleford, Berks., 1970); Lynn B. Tipson, "The Development of a Puritan Understanding of Conversion" (Ph.D. diss., Yale University, 1972); R. T. Kendall, *Calvin and English Calvinism to 1649* (Oxford, 1979); and Patrick Collinson, *Godly People: Essays in English Protestantism and Puritanism* (London, 1983).

For both French Reformed theology and the history of biblical scholarship, François Laplanche, *L'Ecriture, le sacré et l'histoire: Erudits et politiques protestants devant la Bible en France au XVIIe siècle* (Amsterdam, 1986), is a masterpiece. The same author's *Orthodoxie et prédication: L'oeuvre d'Amyraut et la querelle de la grâce universelle* (Paris, 1965), is the best introduction to that important theologian. On Cartesianism's implications for Reformed theology, Thomas A. McGahagan, "Cartesianism in the Netherlands, 1639–1676: The New Science and the Calvinist Counter-Reformation" (Ph.D. diss., University of Pennsylvania, 1976); Paul Dibon, "Scepticisme et orthodoxie réformée dans la Hollande du Siècle d'Or," in R. H. Popkin and C. B. Schmitt, eds., *Scepticism from the Renaissance to the Enlightenment* (Wolfenbüttel, 1987); and Michael Heyd, *Between Orthodoxy and the Enlightenment: Jean-Robert Chouet and the Introduction of Cartesian Science in the Academy of Geneva* (The Hague, 1982), are particularly helpful. A. C. Duker, *Gisbertus Voetius*, 4 vols. (Leiden, 1897–1915), is a massive treatment of that central figure of seventeenth-century Reformed theology. Central works on the sea change in Reformed thought in the last part of the century include W. P. C. Knuttel, *Balthazar Bekker, de Bestrijder van het Bijgeloof* (The Hague, 1906); Annie Barnes, *Jean Le Clerc (1657–1736) et la république des lettres* (Paris, 1938); Elisabeth Labrousse, *Pierre Bayle*, 2 vols. (The Hague, 1963–64); Maria-Cristina Pitassi, *De l'orthodoxie aux lumières: Genève 1670–1737* (Geneva, 1992); Frederick C. Beiser, *The Sovereignty of Reason: The Defense of Rationality in the Early Enlightenment* (Princeton, 1996); Barbara J. Shapiro, *John Wilkins, 1614–1672: An Intellectual Biography* (Berkeley, 1969); Isabel Rivers, *Reason, Grace, and Sentiment: A Study in the Language of Religion and Ethics in England, 1660–1780*, vol. 1, *Whichcote to Wesley* (Cambridge, 1991); John Marshall, *John Locke: Resistance, Religion and Responsibility* (Cambridge, 1994); and Robert E. Sullivan, *John Toland and the Deist Controversy: A Study in Adaptations* (Cambridge, Mass., 1982). I received Jonathan I. Israel,

Radical Enlightenment: Philosophy and the Making of Modernity 1650–1750
(Oxford, 2001) too late to absorb all of its riches.

1. Marcus Friedrich Wendelin (1584–1652) was rector of the gymnasium in Zerbst (Anhalt) and the author of *Christianae theologiae systema maius* (1656). David Pareus (1548–1622), a professor at Heidelberg and former student of Ursinus, edited the most faithful and frequently reprinted version of Ursinus's extremely popular explicatory lectures on the Heidelberg Catechism (published 1591). The *Synopsis Papismi* (1594) of the Cambridge-educated Andrew Willet (1562–1621) was one of the most frequently reprinted responses to Cardinal Bellarmine's *Disputations against the Heretics of Our Time*. John Sharp (1572–1648) was educated at Saint Andrews and taught in France and Scotland. His *Cursus Theologicus* was published in Geneva in 1618. The quotation is from Walter Roland Foster, *Bishop and Presbytery: The Church of Scotland, 1661–1688* (London, 1958), 156–57.
2. Donnelly, *Calvinism and Scholasticism in Vermigli*, esp. 28.
3. Ibid., 195–96; Muller, *Post-Reformation Reformed Dogmatics*, 28–40, 76.
4. Beza, *Correspondance* 4:9 and no. 282; Donnelly, *Calvinism and Scholasticism in Vermigli*, 187–91; Jill Raitt, *The Eucharistic Theology of Theodore Beza: Development of the Reformed Doctrine* (Chambersburg, Pa., 1972), 71–73; John S. Bray, *Theodore Beza's Doctrine of Predestination* (Nieuwkoop, 1975).
5. For an excellent brief assessment of Ramus's place in the history of philosophy, see Charles B. Schmitt and Quentin Skinner, eds., *The Cambridge History of Renaissance Philosophy* (Cambridge, 1988), 184–86. For his influence on Reformed theology: Miller, *New England Mind*, chap. 5; Keith L. Sprunger, "Ames, Ramus, and the Method of Puritan Theology," *Harvard Theological Review* 59 (1966): 133–51; Donald K. McKim, "The Function of Ramism in Perkins' Theology," *Sixteenth Century Journal* 16 (1985): 503–18.
6. Heyd, *Between Orthodoxy and the Enlightenment*, 13–15; Vuilleumier, *Histoire de l'Eglise réformée du Pays de Vaud* 2:108–09.
7. Muller, *Post-Reformation Reformed Dogmatics*, esp. 83–87. For a classic statement of the contrary view, see Basil Hall, "Calvin Against the Calvinists," in G. E. Duffield, ed., *John Calvin* (Appleford, Berks., 1966), 19–37.
8. Richard A. Muller, "The Debate over the Vowel Points and the Crisis in Orthodox Hermeneutics," *Journal of Medieval and Renaissance Studies* 10 (1980): 53–72; Laplanche, *L'Ecriture, le sacré et l'histoire*, 77–81.
9. Hall, "Calvin against the Calvinists," 27–28; Tipson, "The Development of a Puritan Understanding of Conversion," 91–127; Muller, *Christ and the Decree*, 79–96; David A. Weir, *The Origins of the Federal Theology in Sixteenth-Century Reformed Thought* (Oxford, 1990), 69–74. See also John S. Bray, *Theodore Beza's Doctrine of Predestination* (Nieuwkoop, 1975).
10. See above, 68, 103–04, 205, and also Kittelson, "Marbach vs. Zanchi," 37; Roget, *Histoire du peuple de Genève* 3:343–44; For other examples of the anxieties that might be provoked by predestination, see Ridley, *Knox*, 133; Michael Macdonald,

Mystical Bedlam: Madness, Anxiety, and Healing in Seventeenth-Century En-gland (Cambridge, 1981), 224; Wallace, *Puritans and Predestination,* 75; Robert Ergang, *The Potsdam Führer: Frederick William I, Father of Prussian Militarism* (New York, 1941), 33–34. For the reassurance it offered amid tribulations: Crew, *Calvinist Preaching and Iconoclasm,* 73; Jacques Fontaine, *Mémoires d'une famille huguenote* (Toulouse, 1887), 143.

11. White, *Predestination, Policy, and Polemic,* 96–97, 99–100; Wallace, *Puritans and Predestination,* 67; Milton, *Catholic and Reformed,* 427.

12. Jill Raitt, *The Colloquy of Montbéliard: Religion and Politics in the Sixteenth Century* (Oxford, 1993); Vuilleumier, *Histoire de l'Eglise réformée du Pays de Vaud* 2:131–33; James I. Good, *History of the Swiss Reformed Church since the Reformation* (Philadelphia, 1913), 46–55.

13. Tyacke, "Rise of Arminianism Reconsidered," *Past & Present* 115 (1987): 206; Porter, *Reformation and Reaction in Tudor Cambridge,* chaps. 13–18; Wallace, *Puritans and Predestination,* 65–73; Bray, ed., *Documents of the English Reformation,* 399–400; White, *Predestination, Policy, and Polemic,* 96–123.

14. The standard biography of Arminius in English is Carl Bangs, *Arminius: A Study in the Dutch Reformation* (Nashville, 1971). It should be read in conjunction with Muller, *God, Creation, and Providence in the Thought of Arminius.* On the first stages in the controversy, see also Abels and Wouters, *Nieuwe en ongezien,* 149.

15. *The Works of James Arminius,* tran. Nichols and Bagnall, 3 vols. (Auburn, N.Y., 1853), 3:279–525; Muller, *God, Creation, and Providence in the Thought of Arminius,* 162, 250–52.

16. Bangs, *Arminius,* 263, 269–70.

17. Hugo Grotius, *Ordinum Hollandiae ac Westfrisiae pietas,* ed. Edwin Rabbie (Leiden, 1995), 15–16, 133; Douglas Nobbs, *Theocracy and Toleration: A Study of the Disputes in Dutch Calvinism from 1600 to 1650* (Cambridge, 1938), 27–49.

18. W. van 't Spijker et al., *De synode van Dordrecht in 1618 et 1619* (Houten, 1987), 22.

19. Jan den Tex, *Oldenbarnevelt* (Cambridge, 1973), 511–19.

20. Brandt, *History of the Reformation* 2:74–76, 93–95.

21. Good accounts of this central period in the Arminian controversy may be found in ibid., vol. 2; van Deursen, *Bavianen,* chap. 12, esp. 241; Abels and Wouters, *Nieuwe en ongezien,* 149–82; Israel, *Dutch Republic,* 421–49, esp. 439; and L. Wüllschleger, *Scheurmakers en Nieuwlichters: Over Remonstranten en Contra-Remonstranten te 's-Gravenhage (1612–1618)* (Leiden, 1989).

22. Van Deursen, *Bavianen,* chap. 15, esp. 315–16.

23. Those summoned to defend the Remonstrant cause at the Synod of Dort in 1618 were on average nine years younger than the ministerial deputies to the synod. Van 't Spijker et al., *Synode van Dordrecht,* 184. Similarly, a comparison of the original signers of the 1610 Remonstrance listed in Uytenbogaert, *Kerckeliike Historie* (Rotterdam, 1647), 529 and ten leading Contra-Remonstrants listed in ibid., 534, and van 't Spijker et al., *Synode van Dordrecht,* drawing upon the biographical information in *Nieuw Nederlandsch Biografisch Woordenboek,*

607

10 vols. (Leiden, 1911–37), and *Biografisch Lexicon voor de Geschiedenis van het Nederlandse Protestantisme* (Kampen, 1977–88), also suggests the relative youth of the Remonstrants and the prominence of non-Hollanders among the Contra-Remonstrants.

24. [Henricus Slatius], *De Gepredestineerden Dief* (n.p., 1619); Grotius, *Ordinum Hollandiae ac Westfrisiae Pietas,* 236–39; "Jacob spraak tot Amasa: Vrede met u my Broeder," single-sheet placard, ca. 1617 (Andover Harvard Divinity School Library, broadsides, box 1); Brandt, *History of the Reformation* 2:194; van Deursen, *Bavianen,* 279–97, 336–37.

25. Cited in Pieter Geyl, *The Netherlands in the Seventeenth Century,* part 1, 1609–48, 2d ed. (London, 1961), 62. This work provides a clear brief discussion of these events, as does Herbert H. Rowen, *The Princes of Orange: The Stadholders in the Dutch Republic* (Cambridge, 1988), 46–51.

26. There is no fully adequate modern history of the synod. H. Kaajan, *De Groote Synode van Dordrecht in 1618–1619* (Amsterdam, n.d.) and van 't Spijker et al., *Synode van Dordrecht,* are the fullest recent accounts but elide many points of controversy, while A. H. W. Harrison, *Beginnings of Arminianism to the Synod of Dort* (London, 1926), chaps. 9–10, is necessarily briefer. K. Dijk, *De strijd over Infra- en Supralapsarisme in de Gereformeerde Kerken van Nederland* (Kampen, 1912); Tyacke, *Anti-Calvinists;* and White, *Predestination, Polity, and Polemic,* are helpful on the theological debates. To gain a fuller sense of the issues and maneuverings, recourse must be had to such older works as Brandt, *History of the Reformation,* vol. 3; and the eyewitness letters in John Hales, *The Golden Remains of the Ever-Memorable Mr John Hales of Eton College* (London, 1659).

27. Convenient editions of the canons of the synod of Dort include Schaff, *Creeds of Christendom,* 550–97; Bray, ed., *Documents of the English Reformation,* 453–78.

28. Israel, *Dutch Republic,* 462–63.

29. *The Confession or Declaration of the Ministers or Pastors Which in the United Provinces are called Remonstrants, Concerning the Chief Points of Christian Religion* (London, 1676); Joannes Tideman, *De Stichting der Remonstrantsche Broederschap, 1619–1634* (Amsterdam, 1871–72); id., *De Remonstrantsche Broederschap: Biographische Naamlijst van hare Professoren, Predikanten et Proponenten* (Haarlem, 1847), 29–39. The history of the Remonstrant Brotherhood is surprisingly little studied. The short G. J. Hoenderdaal and P. M. Luca, eds., *Staat in de vrijheid: De Geschiedenis van de Remonstranten* (Zutphen, 1982), offers the best recent introduction, while much valuable infomation is also to be found in Israel, *Dutch Republic.*

30. Israel, *Dutch Republic,* 464–65, 478–513.

31. Ibid., 641, 654–55; Tideman, *Remonstrantsche Broederschap,* passim; id., *De Remonstranten te Haarlem* (Haarlem, 1887), 41, 44. The estimates of the size of individual Remonstrant congregations are derived by extrapolation from the number of baptisms celebrated in the Remonstrant churches and include children as well as adults.

32. G. J. Hoenderdaal, "The Debate about Arminius Outside the Netherlands," in T. H. Lunsingh Scheurleer and G. H. M. Posthumus Meyjes, eds., *Leiden University in the Seventeenth Century: An Exchange of Learning* (Leiden, 1975), 137–59; Aymon, *Synodes* 2:145, 184, 298–323; Yves Gueneau, "Protestants du Centre 1598–1685 (Ancienne province synodale d'Orléanais-Berry): Approche d'une minorité" (thèse de troisième cycle, Université François Rabelais Tours, 1982), 373; *La France Protestante,* s.v. "Etienne de Courcelles" and "Daniel Tilenius"; Maria-Cristina Pitassi, *De l'orthodoxie aux lumières,* 15–16; David G. Mullan, "Theology in the Church of Scotland 1618–c.1640: A Calvinist Consensus?" *Sixteenth Century Journal* 26 (1995): 595–617, esp. 598.

33. On the English debates, the fundamental works are Tyacke, *Anti-Calvinists,* and White, *Predestination, Polity, and Polemic.* On ecclesiastical policy and its broader context, one must also consult H. R. Trevor-Roper, *Archbishop Laud, 1573–1645* (Oxford, 1940); id., *Catholics, Anglicans and Puritans: Seventeenth Century Essays* (Chicago, 1987), 51–60; Kenneth Fincham, ed., *The Early Stuart Church, 1603–1642* (Stanford, 1993); Andrew Foster, "Church Policies of the 1630s," in Richard Cust and Ann Hughes, eds., *Conflict in Early Stuart England: Studies in Religion and Politics 1603–1642* (London, 1989), 193–223; Foster, *The Church of England 1570–1640* (London, 1994); Julian Davis, *The Caroline Captivity of the Church: Charles I and the Remoulding of Anglicanism, 1625–1641* (Oxford, 1992). A preliminary investigation of the influence of Arminius on the theology of English "Arminians" in the 1620s suggests that "for all their conversance with parallel developments in the Low Countries, they never reproduced anything like the full scholastic panoply of Arminius's reformed system building." Lake, "Predestinarian Propositions," 121.

34. Tyacke, *Anti-Calvinists,* 36, 89, 106; Kenneth Fincham and Peter Lake, "The Ecclesiastical Policies of James I and Charles I," in Fincham, ed., *Early Stuart Church.*

35. On the content of Montagu's work: Wallace, *Puritans and Predestination,* 84; White, *Predestination, Policy and Polemic,* 218–22; on James's support for its publication: Tyacke, *Anti-Calvinists,* 103–05; Sheila Lambert, "Richard Montagu, Arminianism and Censorship," *Past & Present* 124 (1989): 47–50; on Montagu and Arminius: Trevor-Roper, *Catholics, Anglicans, and Puritans,* 63.

36. Wallace, *Puritans and Predestination,* 84–90; White, *Predestination, Policy and Polemic,* 232.

37. My assessment here agrees with Wallace, *Puritans and Predestination,* 101, passim; Lake, "Predestinarian Propositions," 121.

38. Laplanche, *Orthodoxie et prédication,* 87–107.

39. Ibid., 109–67, esp. 118–27; Laplanche, *L'Ecriture, le sacré et l'histoire,* 1–3; Brian Armstrong, *Calvinism and the Amyraut Heresy: Protestant Scholasticism and Humanism in Seventeenth Century France* (Madison, 1969), esp. 88–95; R. P. van Stam, *The Controversy over the Theology of Saumur, 1635–1650: Disrupting Debates among the Huguenots in Complicated Circumstances* (Amsterdam, 1988), 29–141.

40. Laplanche, *Orthodoxie et prédication,* 179–267; Armstrong, *Calvinism and the Amyraut Heresy,* 97–119; van Stam, *Controversy over the Theology of Saumur,* 183–411.

41. Laplanche, *Orthodoxie et prédication,* 308–13; Wallace, *Puritans and Predestination,* 133; N. H. Keeble, *Richard Baxter, Puritan Man of Letters* (Oxford, 1982), 27, 42, 71–72; Vuilleumier, *Histoire de l'Eglise réformée du Pays de Vaud* 2:472–74; Gerrit Keizer, *François Turrettini: Sa vie et ses oeuvres et le Consensus* (Kampen, 1900), 170–71.

42. Collinson, *Godly People,* 539. David Zaret develops a similar interpretation: *The Heavenly Contract: Ideology and Organization in Pre-Revolutionary Puritanism* (Chicago, 1985), esp. chaps. 4, 5.

43. Richard Rogers, *Seven Treatises containing such direction as is gathered out of the Holie Scriptures, leading and guiding to true happines, both in this life, and in the life to come; and may be called the practise of Chritianitie* (London, 1603), preface. See also Sprunger, *The Learned Doctor William Ames: Dutch Backgrounds of English and American Puritanism* (Urbana, 1972), 158–59; Alexandra Walsham, "'Domme Preachers'? Post-Reformation English Catholicism and the Culture of Print," *Past & Present* 168 (2000): 102–08.

44. Haller, *Rise of Puritanism,* chaps. 1–4; Porter, *Reformation and Reaction,* chap. 10; Kenneth L. Parker and Eric J. Carlson, *"'Practical Divinity': The Works and Life of Rev'd Richard Greenham* (Aldershot, 1998); Gijsbert Voetius, "Concerning Practical Theology," in John W. Beardslee III, ed., *Reformed Dogmatics: J. Wollebius, G. Voetius, F. Turretin* (New York, 1965), 274; Breward, ed., *Works of Perkins,* appendix 1.

45. H. S. Bennett, *English Books and Readers 1603 to 1640* (Cambridge, 1970), 93; Zaret, *Heavenly Contract,* 148; Sprunger, *Ames,* 155; below, 522; C. J. Sommerville, *Popular Religion in Restoration England* (Gainesville, 1977).

46. Hartmut Lehmann, *Das Zeitalter des Absolutismus: Gottesgnadentum und Kriegsnot* (Stuttgart, 1980), 114–23.

47. Quoted in Tipson, "Puritan Understanding of Conversion," 292. Similar sentiments in Perkins, *Works,* 361; William Bradshaw, *A Preparation to the Receiving of the Sacrament,* quoted in Edmund S. Morgan, *Visible Saints: The History of a Puritan Idea* (New York, 1963), 76; Thomas Doolittle, *Treatise concerning the Lords supper* (London, 1667), sig. A 3; Richard A. Kendall, *Calvin and English Calvinism to 1649* (Oxford, 1979), 80.

48. Dent, *Plain Man's Pathway,* 233–34; Downame, *The Please of the Poore,* quoted in A. L. Beier, "The Social Problems of an Elizabethan Country Town: Warwick, 1580–90," in Peter Clark, ed., *Country Towns in Pre-industrial England* (New York, 1981), 72; Wallace, *Puritans and Predestination,* 113–20; David D. Hall, ed., *The Antinomian Controversy, 1636–1638: A Documentary History,* 2d ed. (Durham, 1990); Emery Battis, *Saints and Sectaries: Anne Hutchinson and the Antinomian Controversy in the Massachusetts Bay Colony* (Chapel Hill, 1962).

49. Wallace, *Puritans and Predestination,* 120–57; C. F. Allison, *The Rise of Moralism: The Proclamation of the Gospel from Hooker to Baxter* (New York, 1966);

Peter Toon, *The Emergence of Hyper-Calvinism in English Nonconformity 1689–1765* (London, 1967).

50. Morgan, *Visible Saints,* esp. 87–106; Michael Watt, *The Dissenters,* vol. 1, *From the Reformation to the French Revolution* (Oxford, 1978), 170–72.

51. Watt, *Dissenters,* 65–66.

52. *A Garden of Spirituall Flowers,* sigs. G 3–6; Haller, *Rise of Puritanism,* 119; Collinson, *Religion of Protestants,* 242–44.

53. On the Puritan doctrine of the Sabbath, John H. Primus, *Holy Time: Moderate Puritanism and the Sabbath* (Macon, 1989), offers a valuable corrective to the somewhat undiscriminating revisionism of Kenneth L. Parker, *The English Sabbath: A Study of Doctrine and Discipline from the Reformation to the Civil War* (Cambridge, 1988). See also Winton U. Solberg, *Redeem the Time: The Puritan Sabbath in Early America* (Cambridge, Mass., 1977), part 1. The political debates over this issue are treated below.

54. *Garden of Spirituall Flowers,* sigs. B 4, F 7–9; Bayly, *Practice of Piety* (London, 1654), chap. 6, 151; E. Brooks Holifield, *The Covenant Sealed: The Development of Puritan Sacramental Theology in Old and New England, 1570–1720* (New Haven, 1974), 194–96; Hall, *Occasional Meditations,* quoted in Frank Livingstone Huntley, *Bishop Joseph Hall and Protestant Meditation in Seventeenth-Century England* (Binghamton, N.Y., 1981), 34–35; Charles E. Hambrick-Stowe, *The Practice of Piety: Puritan Devotional Disciplines in Seventeenth-Century New England* (Chapel Hill, 1982), 143–86, esp. 163–64; Mather, *Diary,* quoted in Keith Thomas, *Man and the Natural World: A History of the Modern Sensibility* (New York, 1987), 38.

55. Rogers, *Seven Treatises,* 589; *Garden of Spiritual Flowers,* 61; Bayly, *Practice of Piety;* Baxter, *Christian Directory* (London, 1673).

56. John Bradford, *Writings* 1:35; M. M. Knappen, ed., *Two Elizabethan Puritan Diaries* (Chicago, 1933); Perkins, *Works,* ed. Breward, 406, 408; John Beadle, *A Journall or Diary of a Thankfull Christian,* ed. Germaine Fry Murray (New York, 1996), xxxii; Haller, *Rise of Puritanism,* 97–98; Owen C. Watkins, *The Puritan Experience: Studies in Spiritual Autobiography,* 18–24; Marguerite Bourcier, *Les journaux privés en Angleterre de 1600 à 1660* (Paris, 1976), 69, 323–60; Kaspar von Greyerz, *Vorsehungsglaube und Kosmologie: Studien zu englischen Selbstzeugnissen des 17. Jahrhunderts* (Göttingen, 1990), 24–25; Tom Webster, "Writing to Redundancy: Approaches to Spiritual Journals and Early Modern Spirituality," *Historical Journal* 39 (1996): 37–38.

57. Rogers, *Seven Treatises,* 477–92, esp. 477, 489–90.

58. The extent to which laymen in different parts of the Reformed world embraced this style of piety and its various components will be examined in chap. 15.

59. Allison, *Rise of Moralism;* J. Sears McGee, *The Godly Man in Stuart England: Anglicans, Puritans, and the Two Tables 1620–1670* (New Haven, 1976); Sommerville, *Popular Religion in Restoration England,* esp. 89.

60. The best account of the controversies provoked by the spread of Cartesianism in the Low Countries is McGahagan, "Cartesianism in the Netherlands."

In this and the successive paragraphs, I have also drawn upon René Descartes and Martin Schoock, *La Querelle d'Utrecht,* ed. Theo Verbeeck (Paris, 1988); Jacques Basnage de Beauval, *Annales des Provinces-Unies* (The Hague, 1726), 1:453–54; Josef Bohatec, *Die cartesianische Scholastik in der Philosophie und reformierten Dogmatik des 17. Jahrhunderts* (Leipzig, 1912; repr. Hildesheim, 1966); Ernst Bizer, "Reformed Orthodoxy and Cartesianism," *Journal for Theology and the Church* 11 (1965): 20–82; Richard H. Popkin, "Cartesianism and Biblical Criticism," in Thomas M. Lennon, John M. Nicholas, and John W. Davis, eds., *Problems of Cartesianism* (Montreal, 1982); Dibon, "Scepticisme et orthodoxie réformée"; Dibon, "Deux théologiens wallons face à Descartes et à sa philosophie: André Rivet (1572–1651) et Samuel Desmarets (1599–1673)," in Dibon, *Regards sur la Hollande du siècle d'or* (Naples, 1990), 343–57; Theo Verbeek, *Descartes and the Dutch: Early Reactions to Cartesian Philosophy, 1637–1650* (Carbondale, Ill., 1992); Israel, *Dutch Republic,* 889–99.

61. Duker, *Voetius,* vol. 1. This massive work provides the essential biographical details about Voetius, but good contextualized studies of his thought and accomplishments as a minister and professor remain much needed.

62. Ibid., vols. 2–3, passim; Geyl, *Netherlands in the Seventeenth Century* 2:109–13; F. A. van Lieburg, *De Nadere Reformatie in Utrecht ten tijde van Voetius: Sporen in de gereformeerde kerkeraadsacta* (Rotterdam, 1989).

63. John E. Platt, *Reformed Thought and Scholasticism: The Arguments for the Existence of God in Dutch Theology, 1575–1650* (Leiden, 1982).

64. Descartes and Schoock, *Querelle d'Utrecht,* 29–33, 160; Duker, *Voetius* 2:161–72.

65. On the spread of Cartesianism: Mordechai Feingold, "Mathematical Sciences and New Philosophies," in Nicolas Tyacke, ed., *Seventeenth-Century Oxford* (Oxford, 1997), 405ff.; Heyd, *Between Orthodoxy and the Enlightenment,* 55–86, 116–44.

66. John E. Platt, "Sixtinus Amama (1593–1629): Franeker Professor and Citizen of the Republic of Letters," in G. T. Jensma et al., *Universiteit te Franeker 1585–1811* (Leeuwarden, 1985), 236–48; Peter T. van Rooden, *Theology, Biblical Scholarship and Rabbinical Studies in the Seventeenth Century: Constantijn L'empereur (1591–1648) Professor of Hebrew and Theology at Leiden* (Leiden, 1989), 66–73; Laplanche, *L'Ecriture, le sacré et l'histoire,* 39–41.

67. Cappel's achievements and importance form the subject of part 2 of Laplanche, *L'Ecriture, le sacré et l'histoire.* See also Muller, "Debate over the Vowel Points"; Hans-Joachim Kraus, *Geschichte der historisch-kritischen Erforschung des Alten Testaments,* 3d ed. (Neukirchen, 1982), 47–50.

68. Beza, *Correspondance* 6:15–21.

69. Laplanche, *L'Ecriture, le sacré et l'histoire,* 716–18.

70. The best study of Cocceius's life and thought is Gottlob Schrenk, *Gottesreich und Bund im älteren Protestantismus vornemlich bei Johannes Cocceius* (Gütersloh, 1923; repr. Giessen, 1985). Heiner Faulenbach, *Weg und Ziel der Erkenntnis Christi: Eine Untersuchung zur Theologie des Johannes Coccejus* (Neukirchen, 1973); and Charles S. McCoy, "The Covenant Theology of Johannes Cocceius" (Ph.D. diss., Yale University, 1956), are other modern studies. [Pierre

de Joncourt], *Entretiens sur les differentes methodes d'expliquer l'Ecriture et de precher, De ceux qu'on appelle Cocceiens et Voetiens dans les Provinces Unies* (Amsterdam, 1707); and Basnage de Beauval, *Annales des Provinces-Unies* 1:456, 2:769–79 help clarify the contemporary reception of his thought. See also A. Ypey and I. J. Dermout, *Geschiedenis der Nederlandsche Hervormde Kerk* (Breda, 1822), 2:456–72; S. D. van Veen, *Zondagsrust en Zondagsheiliging in de zeventiende eeuw* (Nijkerk, n.d.); Duker, *Voetius* 2:204ff.; Evenhuis, *Ook dat was Amsterdam* 3:117–39; Gerstner, *Thousand Year Covenant*, 71–73; Leszek Kolakowski, *Chrétiens sans Eglise: La conscience religieuse et le lien confessionnel au XVIIe siècle* (Paris, 1969), chap. 5.

71. [Joncourt], *Entretiens sur les différentes methodes,* 80.

72. Ernestine van der Wall, "Cartesianism and Cocceianism: A Natural Alliance?" in Michelle Magdelaine et al., eds., *De l'Humanisme aux Lumières, Bayle et le Protestantisme: Mélanges en l'honneur d'Elisabeth Labrousse* (Oxford, 1996), 445–55.

73. Van Veen, *Zondagsrust,* 123–28.

74. Knuttel, *Bekker,* 133; R. B. Evenhuis, *Ook dat was Amsterdam,* 5 vols. (Amsterdam, 1965–78) 3:122; Israel, *Dutch Republic,* 663–64, 1030.

75. [Joncourt], *Entretiens sur les différentes méthodes;* Israel, *Dutch Republic,* 663–69; Bucsay, *Geschichte des Protestantismus in Ungarn,* 114.

76. The era of the English Civil War and Interregnum is treated in more detail below. On Hobbes's thought and the alarm it evoked among contemporaries, Richard Tuck, *Hobbes* (Oxford, 1989); A. P. Martinich, *Hobbes: A Biography* (Cambridge, 1999); Samuel I. Mintz, *The Hunting of Leviathan: Seventeenth-Century Reactions to the Materialism and Moral Philosophy of Thomas Hobbes* (Cambridge, 1962); and Jon Parkin, *Science, Religion and Politics in Restoration England: Richard Cumberland's De Legibus Naturae* (Bury St Edmunds, 1999), 66–72, 141–54, are very useful.

77. William Chillingworth, *The Religion of Protestants: A Safeway to Salvation,* 4th ed. (London, 1674); Robert R. Orr, *Reason and Authority: The Thought of William Chillingworth* (Oxford, 1967), esp. 160; Beiser, *Sovereignty of Reason,* esp. 10–12, 125.

78. Much has been written about the latitudinarians. Rivers, *Reason, Grace, and Sentiment,* 25–88, offers perhaps the best introduction to the group and its thought. Also helpful are Gilbert Burnet, *History of His Own Time* (London, 1724), 1:186–89; Basil Willey, *The Seventeenth-Century Background* (London, 1934), chap. 8; Shapiro, *Wilkins;* Parkin, *Science, Religion and Politics in Restoration England;* and Sullivan, *Toland.*

79. Quoted in James O'Higgins, *Anthony Collins: The Man and His Works* (The Hague, 1970), 45.

80. Ibid., 45; Edward Stillingfleet, *Origines Sacrae: Or a Rational Account of the Grounds of Christian Faith,* 5th ed. (London, 1680), epistle dedicatory; Norman Sykes, *From Sheldon to Secker: Aspects of English Church History 1660–1768* (Cambridge, 1959), 143, 151; Rivers, *Reason, Grace, and Sentiment,* 35; Jacob

Termeulen and P. J. J Diermanse, *Bibliographie des écrits imprimés de Hugo Grotius* (The Hague, 1950), 467–535. This last work shows that, although Grotius's *Truth of the Christian Religion* was translated into many languages, it attained considerably wider distribution in England than anywhere else in Europe in this period.

81. Stillingfleet, *Irenicum* (London, 1662); John Marshall, "The Ecclesiology of the Latitude-men 1660–1689: Stillingfleet, Tillotson and 'Hobbism'," *Journal of Ecclesiastical History* 36 (1985): 407–27.

82. Stillingfleet, *Origines sacrae* (London, 1662).

83. Stillingfleet, *A Rational Account of the Grounds of Protestant Religion* (London, 1665); id., *A Discourse Concerning the Idolatry Practiced in the Church of Rome* (London, 1671); id., *Vindication of the Protestant Grounds of Religion* (London, 1673); id., *The Jesuits Loyalty* (London, 1677); id., *The Doctrines and Practices of the Church of Rome Truly Represented; In answer to a Book Intituled A Papist Misrepresented* (London, 1686); id., *The Doctrine of the Trinity and Transubstantiation Compared as to Scripture, Reason and Tradition* (London, 1687).

84. *DNB*, s.v. "Stillingfleet, Edward."

85. Gerard Reedy, "Spinoza, Stillingfleet, Prophecy, and 'Enlightenment'" in J. L. Lemay, ed., *Deism, Masonry and the Enlightenment* (Newark, Del., 1987), 51–53; John Marshall, *John Locke: Resistance, Religion and Responsibility* (Cambridge, 1994), 329ff.; Isaac Newton, *Correspondence* 3:1688–94, ed. H. W. Turnbull (Cambridge, 1961), 83–129.

86. H. John McLachlan, *Socinianism in Seventeenth-Century England* (Oxford, 1951); Wilbur, *Unitarianism in Transylvania, England, and America,* chaps. 10–12; Roger L. Emerson, "Latitudinarianism and the English Deists," in Lemay, ed., *Deism, Masonry and the Enlightenment,* 19–48; *The Oracles of Reason* (London, 1693).

87. Toland, *Christianity not Mysterious,* ed. P. McGuinness, A. Harrison, and R. Kearney (Dublin, 1997).

88. Locke, *The Reasonableness of Christianity,* ed. John C. Higgins-Biddle (Oxford, 1999); Marshall, *Locke,* part 3, esp. 412.

89. Stillingfleet, *Discourse in Vindication of the Doctrine of the Trinity* (London, 1697).

90. Laplanche, *L'Ecriture, le sacré et l'histoire,* 245–47, 299–313, 578–82; Rudolf Pfister, *Kirchengeschichte der Schweiz,* vol. 2, *Von der Reformation bis zum Zweiten Villmerger Krieg* (Zurich, 1974), 486–90; Barnes, *Le Clerc,* 25; Pitassi, *De l'orthodoxie aux lumières,* 15–16.

91. Schaff, *Creeds of Christendom* 1:477ff.; Good, *History of the Swiss Reformed Church,* 149, 165–68; Pfister, *Kirchengeschichte der Schweiz,* 490–98; Gerrit Keizer, *François Turrettini: Sa vie et ses oeuvres et le Consensus* (Kampen, 1900); Vuilleumier, *Eglise réformée du Pays de Vaud* 2:503–31; Pitassi, *De l'orthodoxie aux lumières,* 16–20. The text of the Consensus may be found in

E. F. Karl Müller, *Die Bekenntnisschriften der reformierten Kirche* (Leipzig, 1903; repr. Zurich, 1987), 861-70.

92. Jean-Alphonse Turrettini, *Traité de la verité de la religion chretienne* (Geneva, 1740-44); Laplanche, *L'Ecriture, le sacré et l'histoire*, 623-31; Heyd, *Between Orthodoxy and the Enlightenment*, 198-202; Maria-Cristina Pitassi, "L'apologétique raisonnable de Jean-Alphonse Turrettini," in Pitassi, ed., *Apologétique 1680-1740: Sauvetage ou naufrage de la théologie?* (Geneva, 1991), 99-118; id., "De l'exemplarité au soupçon: L'église genevoise entre la fin du XVIIe et le début du XVIIIe siècle," in Kaiser et al., eds., *Eidgenössische 'Grenzfälle,'* 280-82.

93. Barnes, *Le Clerc,* passim; Pitassi, *De l'orthodoxie aux lumières,* 52.

94. Laplanche, *L'Ecriture, le sacré et l'histoire*, 618-22, 632-39; R. Grétillat, *Jean-Frédéric Ostervald 1663-1747* (Neuchâtel, 1904).

95. Pitassi, *De l'orthodoxie aux lumières,* 51-55; id., "De l'exemplarité au soupçon," 284-91; Good, *History of the Swiss Reformed Church,* 169-97.

96. Pitassi, *De l'orthodoxie aux lumières,* 35, 55-61; Jean Gaberel, *Histoire de l'Eglise de Genève depuis le commencement de la Réformation jusqu'à nos jours,* 3 vols. (Geneva, 1858-62), 3:47.

CHAPTER 11. CHANGING POLITICAL CIRCUMSTANCES
ON THE CONTINENT

Bibliographical Note Good work on many of the topics surveyed in this chapter remains scarce. The French Huguenots are the best studied of the minority Reformed churches of the seventeenth century. Elisabeth Labrousse, *Une foi, une loi, un roi? La Révocation de l'Edit de Nantes* (Geneva, 1985), and Daniel Ligou, *Le Protestantisme en France de 1598 à 1715* (Paris, 1968), offer the best overviews. The essays now collected in Philip Benedict, *The Faith and Fortunes of France's Huguenots, 1600-1685* (Aldershot, 2001), attempt to renew the social and religious history of the group. Yves Gueneau, "Protestants du Centre 1598-1685" (thèse de troisième cycle, Université François Rabelais de Tours, 1982), is an excellent regional study. Gregory Hanlon, *Confession and Community in Seventeenth-Century France: Catholic and Protestant Coexistence in Aquitaine* (Philadelphia, 1993), looks at the social dynamics of a single religiously divided small town. Bernard Dompnier, *Le vénin de l'hérésie: Image du protestantisme et combat catholique au XVIIe siècle* (Paris, 1985), surveys Catholic missionary enterprises. Amid the abundant and uneven literature on the aftermath of 1685, Pierre Chaunu, "La décision royale (?): Un système de la Révocation," in Roger Zuber and Laurent Theis, eds., *La Révocation de l'Edit de Nantes et le protestantisme français en 1685* (Paris, 1986), 13-28; Philippe Joutard, "The Revocation of the Edict of Nantes: End or Renewal of French Protestantism?" in Prestwich, ed., *International Calvinism*, 339-58; Joutard, ed., *Les Camisards* (Paris, 1976); and Warren C. Scoville, *The Persecution of the Huguenots and French Economic Development 1680-1720* (Berkeley, 1960), are helpful and important. The seventeenth-century situation of the Reformed churches of Hungary and Transylvania is the subject of an excellent Oxford Ph.D thesis (1996) by Graeme Murdock, now published under the title *Calvinism on the Frontier, 1600–1660: International Calvinism and the Reformed Church in Hungary and Transylvania* (Oxford, 2000). For Poland, see Janusz Tazbir, "The Fate of Polish Protestantism in the Seventeenth Century," in J. K. Fedorowicz, M. Bogucka, and H. Samsonowicz, eds., *A Republic of Nobles: Studies in Polish History to 1864* (Cambridge, 1982), 201–27, as well as the relevant sections of the works by Jobert, Tazbir, and Schramm mentioned in the biographical note for chapter 9. The kinds of outstanding local studies that have recently renewed our understanding of the Dutch Reformation rarely advance very far into the seventeenth century, but two exceptions are Wiebe Bergsma, *Tussen Gedeonsbende en publieke kerk: Een studie over het gereformeerd protestantisme in Friesland, 1580–1650* (Hilversum, 1999), and Charles de Mooij, *Geloof kan Bergen verzetten: Reformatie en katholieke herleving te Bergen op Zoom 1577–1795* (Hilversum, 1998); Bergen op Zoom's location in States Brabant makes it difficult, however, to generalize its experience beyond the purely local context. An enthusiastic band of Dutch historians has recently devoted a great deal of energy to studying the so-called *Nadere Reformatie,* but the value of their pioneering work has been limited by a steep measure of historiographic insularity and a failure to distinguish among the disparate strands of a movement that may have been less unified than they suggest. Much of the research of this group is presented in the journal *Documentatieblad Nadere Reformatie.* The collective works *De Nadere Reformatie: Beschrijving van haar voornaamste vertegenwoordigers* (The Hague, 1986), and *Het eigene van de Nederlandse Nadere Reformatie* (Houten, 1992), provide an overview of the topic and a good introduction to the work of this group, as does the collective article "Nadere Reformatie: Opnieuw een poging tot begripsbepaling," *Documentatieblad Nadere Reformatie* 19 (1995): 107–84. Much more could be done with all of these subjects, and still more yet with the history of Germany's Reformed communities, for which Josef Krisinger, "Religionspolitik des Kurfürsten Johann Wilhelm von der Pfalz," *Düsseldorfer Jahrbuch* 47 (1955): 42–125, and Peter Zschunke, *Konfession und Alltag in Oppenheim* (Wiesbaden, 1984), suggest promising lines of investigation.

1. This and the subsequent paragraphs are primarily based upon Hanlon, *Confession and Community;* Dompnier, *Vénin de l'hérésie;* Benedict, *Faith and Fortunes,* chaps. 9, 10; Etienne François, *Protestants et catholiques en Allemagne, Identités et pluralisme: Augsbourg, 1648–1806* (Paris, 1993); Zschunke, *Konfession und Alltag in Oppenheim;* Tazbir, *State without Stakes.*
2. Rudolf von Thadden, *Die Brandenburgisch-preussischen Hofprediger im 17. und 18. Jahrhundert* (Berlin, 1959), esp. 60, 68–69.
3. Figure calculated from Bergsma, *Tussen Gedeonsbende en publieke kerk,* 120–26. For the early seventeenth century figures, see above, 199.
4. Heinz Schilling, "Calvinistische Presbyterien in Städten der Frühneuzeit-

eine kirchliche Alternativform zur bürgerlichen Repräsentation (mit einer quantifizierenden Untersuchung zur holländischen Stadt Leiden)," in Wilfried Ehbrecht, ed., *Städtische Führungsgruppen und Gemeinde in der Werdenden Neuzeit* (Cologne, 1980), passim, esp. 434; Benjamin J. Kaplan, "Confessionalism and Its Limits: Religion in Utrecht, 1600–1650," in *Masters of Light: Dutch Painters in Utrecht during the Golden Age,* exhibition catalogue (San Francisco, 1997), 401.

5. The clearest guide through Transylvanian history in this period is Sugar, *Southeastern Europe under Ottoman Rule,* 155–63. For the religious history, see Murdock, "International Calvinism and the Reformed Church of Hungary and Transylvania"; id., "Death, Prophecy and Judgement in Transylvania," in Bruce Gordon and Peter Marshall, eds., *The Place of the Dead: Death and Remembrance in Late Medieval and Early Modern Europe* (Cambridge, 2000), esp. 208.

6. Murdock, "International Calvinism and the Reformed Church of Hungary and Transylvania," 22, 112ff.; Wilbur, *History of Unitarianism in Transylvania, England, and America,* 126.

7. Murdock, "International Calvinism and the Reformed Church of Hungary and Transylvania," chap. 2.

8. W. J. M. Engelberts, *Willem Teelinck* (Amsterdam, 1898); K. Exalto, "Willem Teelinck (1579–1629)." in Brienen et al., *De Nadere Reformatie,* 17–47; W. J. op 't Hof, "De Nadere Reformatie in Zeeland: Een eerste schets," in A. Wiggers et al., *Rond de kerk in Zeeland* (Delft, 1991), 43; id., *Voorbereiding en bestrijding: De oudste gereformeerde pietistische voorbereidingspreken tot het Avondmaal en de eerste bestrijding van de Nadere Reformatie in druk* (Kampen, 1991), part 2; P. J. Meertens, "Godefridus Cornelisz Udemans," *Nederlands Archief voor Kerkgeschiedenis,* n.s. 18 (1936): 65–106; Hugo B. Visser, *De Geschiedenis van den Sabbatsstrijd onder de Gereformeerden in de Zeventiende Eeuw* (Utrecht, 1939), 50–114.

9. Willem Teelinck, *Nootwendigh Vertoogh, Aengaende den tegenwoordigen bedroefden staet van God's volck* (Amsterdam, 1627).

10. Israel, *Dutch Republic,* 474–77.

11. Duker, *Voetius,* vol. 2, chaps. 4, 5; Herman Witsius, *Twist des Heeren met sijn wijngaert* (Leeuwarden, 1669); Christophilus Eubulus [Jacobus Koelman], *De Pointen van nodige Reformatie* (Flushing, 1678); *Concept van Nader Reformatie, in de Leer, Ordre, en Zeden Opgestelt door Gedeputeerden des Classis van Zuyd-Beverlant* (Utrecht, 1682); L. F. Groenendijk, "Jacobus Koelman's actieplan voor de nadere reformatie," *Documentatieblad Nadere Reformatie* 2 (1978): 121–26. See also the general works on the Nadere Reformatie cited in this chapter's notes for further reading; Wilhelm Goeters, *Die Vorbereitung des Pietismus in der Reformierten Kirche der Niederlände bis zur Labadistischen Krisis 1670* (Leipzig, 1911).

12. William Ames, *Of Conscience* (London, 1643), dedication; Israel, *Dutch Republic,* 477, 692–94; Duker, *Voetius* 3:148–75; Fred A. van Lieburg, *De Nadere*

Reformatie in Utrecht ten tijde van Voetius: Sporen in de gereformeerde kerkeraadsacta (Rotterdam, 1989); Llewellyn Bogaers, "Een kwestie van macht? De relatie tussen het wetgeving op het openbaar gedrag en de ontwikkeling van de Utrechtse stadssamenleving in de zestiende en zeventiende eeuw," *Volkskundig Bulletin* 11 (1985): 102–26, esp. 116; T. Brienen, "Johannes Teellinck (ca. 1623–1674)" in T. Brienen et al., *Figuren en thema's van de Nadere Reformatie,* 3 vols. (Kampen, 1987–93), 2:47–48.

13. See below, 523–24.

14. Murdock, "International Calvinism and the Reformed Church of Hungary and Transylvania," chaps. 5–6, esp. 223.

15. Murdock, "International Calvinism and the Reformed Church of Hungary and Transylvania," 37–38; Bucsay, *Geschichte des Protestantismus in Ungarn,* 109.

16. George Carew, "A Relation of the State of Polonia and the United Provinces of that Crowne Anno 1598" excerpted in Lubieniecki, *History of the Polish Reformation,* ed. Williams, 395; Schramm, *Polnische Adel und die Reformation,* 146, 206; Kazmierz Tyszkowski, "Przejscie Lwa Sapiephy na Katolicyzm w 1586 v.," *Reformacja w Polsce* 2 (1922): 198–203, with French summary. Some insights into the broader phenomenon of aristocratic conversion to Catholicism are offered by Susan Rosa, "'Il était possible aussi que cette conversion fût sincère': Turenne's Conversion in Context," *French Historical Studies* 18 (1994): 632–66; Günter Christ, "Fürst, Dynastie, Territorium und Konfession: Beobachtungen zu Fürstenkonversionen des ausgehenden 17. und beginnenden 18. Jahrhunderts," *Saeculum* 24 (1973): 367–87.

17. For this and the following paragraphs: Schramm, *Polnische Adel und die Reformation,* passim, esp. 59, 107, 135–38, 205–06, 258; id., "Protestantismus und städtische Gesellschaft in Wilna," 212; id., "Lublin" 50–57; id., "Nationale und soziale Aspekte des wiedererstarkenden Katholizismus in Posen," 67–71; Tazbir, "Fate of Polish Protestantism"; id., *State without Stakes,* chaps. 11–12, esp. 166, 170, 194, 200; Marceli Kosman, "Programme of the Reformation in the Grand Duchy of Lithuania and How It Was Carried Through (ca. 1550-ca. 1650)," *Acta Poloniae Historia* 35 (1977): 41; Michael G. Müller, "Toleration in Eastern Europe: The Dissident Question in Eighteenth-Century Poland-Lithuania," in O. P. Grell and R. Porter, eds., *Toleration in Enlightenment Europe* (Cambridge, 2000), 218–20; Jan Baszanowski, "Statistics of Religious Denominations and Ethnic Problems in Gdansk," 55, which reveals baptisms in the Reformed church constituting 7.5 percent of all baptisms in Danzig in 1631–50 and 4 percent in 1701–25.

18. R. J. W. Evans, *The Making of the Habsburg Monarchy, 1550–1700* (Oxford, 1979); Jean Bérenger, *Histoire de l'empire des Habsbourg, 1273–1918* (Paris, 1990); and Charles Ingrao, *The Habsburg Monarchy 1618–1815* (Cambridge, 1994), offer the best general accounts of the Habsburgs and their policies in Hungary in this period.

19. Murdock, "International Calvinism and the Reformed Church of Hungary and Transylvania," 19–20; *Historical Dictionary of Hungary* (Lanham, Md., 1997), s.v. "Pázmány"; Endre Tóth, "Az ellenreformáció győzelme," in Sándor Bíró et al.,

A magyar református egyház történeti, 90; István György Tóth, ed., *Relationes missionariorum de Hungaria et Transilvania (1627-1707)* (Rome, 1994), 74-77; Bérenger, *Histoire de l'empire des Habsbourg,* 295-97, 334-48.

20. For this and the subsequent paragraph: *A short Memorial of the most grievous sufferings of the Ministers of the Protestant Churches in Hungary* (London, 1676), excerpted in C. A. Macartney, ed., *The Habsburg and Hohenzollern Dynasties in the Seventeenth and Eighteenth Centuries* (New York, 1970); Franz von Krones, "Zur Geschichte Ungarns (1671-1683): Mit besonderer Rücksicht auf der Thätigkeit und die Geschichte des Jesuitenordens," *Archiv für Österreichische Geschichte* 80 (1893): 353-457; Jean Bérenger, "La contre-réforme en Hongrie au XVIIe siècle," *Bulletin de la Société de l'Histoire du Protestantisme Français* 120 (1974): 1-32; Kalman Benda, "La Réforme en Hongrie," *Bulletin de la Société de l'Histoire du Protestantisme Français* 122 (1976): 30-53; Miklos Dezsö, "L'histoire des galériens Hongrois," *Bulletin de la Société de l'Histoire du Protestantisme Français* 122 (1976): 54-65; Evans, *Making of the Habsburg Monarchy,* 237-38, 248-49; John P. Spielman, *Leopold I of Austria* (London, 1977), 61-72, 83-92, 131-41.

21. Evans, *Making of the Habsburg Monarchy,* 240, 247-49; Zimányi, *Economy and Society in Sixteenth and Seventeenth Century Hungary,* 103; Bérenger, "Contre-réforme en Hongrie," 14.

22. Benda, "Réforme en Hongrie," 49; personal communication from Graeme Murdock.

23. This and the subsequent paragraph are based above all on Elie Benoist, *Histoire de l'Edit de Nantes,* 5 vols. (Delft, 1693-95); Holt, *The French Wars of Religion,* chap. 7; Janine Garrisson, *L'Edit de Nantes et sa révocation: Histoire d'une intolérance* (Paris, 1985); Ligou, *Le Protestantisme en France de 1598 à 1715;* David Parker, *La Rochelle and the French Monarchy: Conflict and Order in Seventeenth-Century France* (London, 1980), esp. 115-16; *Edits déclarations et arrests concernans la réligion réformée 1662-1751* (Paris, 1885); Paul Gachon, *Quelques préliminaires de la Révocation de l'Edit de Nantes en Languedoc (1661-1685)* (Toulouse, 1899); A. T. van Deursen, *Professions et métiers interdits: Un aspect de l'histoire de la Révocation de l'Edit de Nantes* (Groningen, 1960).

24. Gueneau, "Protestants du Centre," 415-16; Benedict, *Huguenot Population,* 45, 127.

25. See above, 337; Laplanche, *L'Ecriture, le sacré, et l'histoire,* 379-411; Hartmut Kretzer, *Calvinismus und französische Monarchie im 17. Jahrhundert* (Berlin, 1975).

26. Benedict, *Huguenot Population,* part 1, esp. 10, 71-72, 76-77.

27. Ligou, *Le Protestantisme en France de 1598 à 1715,* chap. 11; Benedict, *Faith and Fortunes,* chaps. 1, 3.

28. Jean Orcibal, *Louis XIV et les Protestants* (Paris, 1951); Labrousse, *Une foi, une loi un roi?* 188-95; Chaunu, "La décision royale (?)."

29. E. and E. Haag, eds., *La France protestante,* 10 vols. (Paris, 1846-1859), 10:389-

92; Joutard, "The Revocation of the Edict of Nantes: End or Renewal?" 339–58, esp. 342, 344; Samuel Mours, "Les pasteurs à la Révocation de l'Edit de Nantes," *Bulletin de la Société de l'Histoire du Protestantisme Français* 114 (1968): 67–105, 292–316.

30. Myriam Yardeni, *Le refuge protestant* (Paris, 1985), part 2; Michelle Magdelaine and Rudolf von Thadden, eds., *Le refuge huguenot* (Paris, 1985); S. P. Engelbrecht, *Geschiedenis van die Nederduitsch Hervormde Kerk van Afrika,* 3d ed. (Pretoria, 1953), 20. Valuable studies of the Huguenots in various lands in which they settled include Jon Butler, *The Huguenots in America* (Cambridge, Mass., 1982); Robin Gwynn, *Huguenot Heritage: The History and Contribution of the Huguenots in Britain* (London, 1985); Bernard Cottret, *The Huguenots in England: Immigration and Settlement c. 1550–1700* (Cambridge, 1991).

31. Scoville, *The Persecution of the Huguenots and French Economic Development;* Natalie Rothstein, "Huguenots in the English Silk Industry in the Eighteenth Century," in Irene Scouloudi, ed., *The Huguenots in Britain and Their French Background 1550–1800* (Totowa, N.J., 1987), 125–42; E. Boning, P. Overbeek, and J. Verveer, "De huisgenoten des geloofs: De immigratie van de Huguenoten 1680–1720," *Tijdschrift voor Geschiedenis* 100 (1987): 364–66; S. Jersch Wenzel, *Juden und "Franzosen" in der Wirtschaft des Räumes Berlin-Brandenburg* (Berlin, 1978).

32. H. R. Trevor-Roper, "A Huguenot Historian: Paul Rapin," in Scouloudi, ed., *Huguenots in Britain,* 3–19; Labrousse, *Pierre Bayle;* and more generally Erich Haase, *Einführung in die Literatur des Refuge* (Berlin, 1959); Geoffrey Adams, *The Huguenots and French Opinion 1685–1787: The Enlightenment Debate on Toleration* (Waterloo, Ont., 1991); and Myriam Yardeni, *Repenser l'histoire: Aspects de l'historiographie huguenote des guerres de religion à la Révolution française* (Paris, 2000), 120–35, 163–206. On the semantic shifts of the eighteenth century and the history of the idea of toleration, Labrousse, *Une foi, une loi, un roi?* 95, and Edward Peters, *Inquisition* (Berkeley, 1989), 156–77, are highly insightful.

33. For this and the next paragraph: Charles Bost, *Les prédicants protestants des Cévennes et du Bas-Languedoc 1684–1700* (Paris, 1912); Joutard, ed., *Les Camisards;* id., "The Revocation of the Edict of Nantes: End or Renewal?" 358–66.

34. Daniel Ligou and Philippe Joutard, "Les déserts (1685–1800)," in Robert Mandrou et al., *Histoire des Protestants en France* (Toulouse, 1977), 211–53; Yves Krumenacker, *Les Protestants du Poitou au XVIIIe siècle (1681–1789)* (Paris, 1998); id., "L'élaboration d'un modèle protestant: Les synodes du Désert," *Revue d'Histoire Moderne et Contemporaine* 42 (1995): 46–70.

35. See above, 149–51. The following discussion of events in Béarn draws primarily upon Christian Desplat, "Edit de Fontainebleau du 15 avril 1599 en faveur des Catholiques du Béarn," in *Réformes et Révocation en Béarn XVIIe–XXe siècles* (Pau, 1986), 223–46; E. Puyol, *Louis XIII et le Béarn* (Paris, 1872); A. Lloyd

Moote, *Louis XIII, the Just* (Berkeley, 1989), 120–24; Greengrass, "Calvinist Experiment in Béarn," in Pettegree et al., eds., *Calvinism in Europe,* 139–42; Benedict, *Huguenot Population,* 71–73.

36. Robert Dollinger, *Das Evangelium in der Oberpfalz* (Neuendettelsau, 1952), esp. 68; Josef Hanauer, *Die bayerischen Kurfürsten Maximilian I und Ferdinand Maria und die katholische Restauration in der Oberpfalz* (Regensburg, 1993), esp. 5, 76–77, 83–85, 111, 128.

37. Alois Schroër, *Die Kirche in Westfalen in Zeiten der Erneuerung* (Munster, 1987), 414–31.

38. Schroër, *Kirche in Westfalen,* 439–51; Frank Konersmann, "Presbyteriale Kirchenzucht unter landesherrlichem Regiment: Pfalz-Zweibrücken im 17. und 18. Jahrhundert," in S. Brakensiek et al., eds., *Kultur und Staat in der Provinz: Perspektiven und Erträge der Regionalgeschichte* (Bielefeld, 1992), 328, 330.

39. Krisinger, "Religionspolitik Johann Wilhelm von der Pfalz," esp. 71, 99; Dieter Stievermann, "Politik und Konfession im 18. Jahrhundert," *Zeitschrift für Historische Forschung* 18 (1991): 177–99, esp. 181–83.

CHAPTER 12. BRITISH SCHISMS

Bibliographical Note The literature on seventeenth-century English church history is vast and characterized by little continuity between the interpretive debates that engage those who work on the first half of the century and those who work on the era from the Restoration onward. For the fascinating period of the Civil War and interregnum, the highly visible activities of dissenters of all sorts has tended to draw the attention of scholars away from the study of how religion changed in law and among the bulk of people in the localities. For many topics it is most useful to go back to the original sources. Important collections include John P. Kenyon, *The Stuart Constitution* (Cambridge, 1966); Alden T. Vaughan, ed., *The Puritan Tradition in America 1620–1730* (Columbia, S.C., 1972); Williston Walker, ed., *The Creeds and Platforms of Congregationalism* (New York, 1893; repr. Boston, 1960); C. H. Firth and R. S. Rait, eds., *Acts and Ordinances of the Interregnum, 1642–1660* (London, 1911); *Documents relating to the Settlement of the Church of England by Act of Uniformity of 1662* (London, 1862); and William Croft Dickinson and Gordon Donaldson, eds., *A Source Book of Scottish History,* 2d ed. (London, 1961).

The central interpretive debate that has recently galvanized scholars working on the period leading up to the English Revolution revolves around the nature of English "Arminianism" and the extent to which it upset a previously dominant "Calvinist" theological consensus within the church. The works of Tyacke and White signaled in the bibliographical note for chapter 10 are central here and cover a range of issues beyond the narrowly theological. Still more comprehensive yet for church policy and worship are the essays collected in Kenneth Fincham, ed., *The Early Stuart Church, 1603–1643* (Stanford, 1993), which usefully summarize much recent research. Anthony Milton, *Catholic and Re-*

formed: The Roman and Protestant Churches in English Protestant Thought 1600–1640 (Cambridge, 1995), is an extremely illuminating study of the church's self-understanding and relationship to the continental Reformed churches.

In the copious literature on the activities of the hotter sort of Protestants just prior to and during the English Revolution, and on the evolution from Puritanism to Dissent, the following are useful: John Spurr, *English Puritanism, 1603–1689* (New York, 1998); Murray Tolmie, *The Triumph of the Saints: The Separatist Churches of London, 1616–1649* (Cambridge, 1977); C. G. Bolam et al., *The English Presbyterians: From Elizabethan Puritanism to Modern Unitarianism* (London, 1968); Michael Watts, *The Dissenters,* vol. 1, *From the Reformation to the French Revolution* (Oxford, 1978); Christopher Hill, *The World Turned Upside Down: Radical Ideas During the English Revolution* (New York, 1972); and J. F. McGregor and Barry Reay, eds., *Radical Religion in the English Revolution* (Oxford, 1984). How religious life actually changed in both law and the localities during the period 1640–60 remains understudied, but the essays now collected in John Morrill, *The Nature of the English Revolution* (Harlow, Essex, 1993), present the results of the most important recent exploration of this issue. The old John Stoughton, *Ecclesiastical History of England from the Opening of the Long Parliament to the Death of Oliver Cromwell* (London, 1867), also remains useful for this period, while John W. Packer, *The Transformation of Anglicanism 1643–1660, with special reference to Henry Hammond* (Manchester, 1969), and Robert S. Paul, *The Assembly of the Lord: Politics and Religion in the Westminster Assembly and the 'Grand Debate'* (Edinburgh, 1985), are noteworthy studies of specific subjects. John Spurr, *The Restoration Church of England 1646–1689* (New Haven, 1991), renews the understanding of that period. There is no comparable synthesis for the years after 1688, but the following are most helpful: G. V. Bennett, "William III and the Episcopate," in Bennett and J. D. Walsh, eds., *Essays in Modern English Church History in Memory of Norman Sykes* (Oxford, 1966); id., "Conflict in the Church," in Geoffrey Holmes, ed., *Britain after the Glorious Revolution 1689–1714* (London, 1969); id., *The Tory Crisis in Church and State 1688–1730: The Career of Francis Atterbury Bishop of Rochester* (Oxford, 1975); Mark Goldie, "The Nonjurors, Episcopacy, and the Origins of the Convocation Controversy," in Eveline Cruickshanks, ed., *Ideology and Conspiracy: Aspects of Jacobitism 1689–1759* (Edinburgh, 1982), 15–35; and Julian Hoppitt, *A Land of Liberty? England 1689–1727* (Oxford, 2000), chap. 7.

For Scotland, Maurice Lee, Jr., *The Road to Revolution: Scotland under Charles I, 1625–1637* (Urbana, 1985); David Stevenson, *The Scottish Revolution 1637–1644: The Triumph of the Covenanters* (New York, 1973); id., *Revolution and Counter-Revolution in Scotland, 1644–1651* (London, 1977); Ian Cowan, *The Scottish Covenanters, 1660–1688* (London, 1976); A. Ian Dunlop, *William Carstares and the Kirk by Law Established* (Edinburgh, 1967); and T. N. Clarke, "The Scottish Episcopalians 1688–1720" (Ph.D. diss., University of Edinburgh, 1987) offer the most useful guides through the course of events over the century.

John Coffey, *Politics, Religion and the British Revolutions: The Mind of Samuel Rutherford* (Cambridge, 1997), is a rich and illuminating study of a central figure in the upheavals of the 1640s, while Walter Roland Foster, *Bishop and Presbytery: The Church of Scotland, 1661-1688* (London, 1958), sheds light on the day-to-day functioning of the church after the Restoration.

1. This document is printed in John P. Kenyon, *The Stuart Constitution* (Cambridge, 1966), 132ff. For Whitgift's articles of subscription and the opposition they provoked, see above, 251-52.
2. On this group, see especially Tyacke, *Anti-Calvinists;* Trevor-Roper, *Catholics, Anglicans and Puritans,* 44-47; Stanley Greenslade, "The Authority of the Tradition of the Early Church in Early Anglican Thought," in *Tradition im Luthertum und Anglikanismus,* Oecumenica 1971-72 (Gütersloh, 1972), 23-27; Tyacke, "Archbishop Laud," and Peter Lake, "The Laudian Style: Order, Uniformity and the Pursuit of the Beauty of Holiness in the 1630s," in Fincham, ed., *The Early Stuart Church,* 51-70, 161-85; Charles Carleton, *Archbishop William Laud* (London, 1987); Milton, *Catholic and Reformed.* These works form the basis for the discussion to follow.
3. Lake, "Laudian Style," 169; Greenslade, "Authority of Tradition," 27; Milton, *Catholic and Reformed,* 501; Baxter, *Autobiography,* ed. N. H. Keeble (London, 1974), 36.
4. Mark H. Curtis, "Hampton Court Conference and its Aftermath," *History* 46 (1961): 1-16; Fincham and Lake, "The Ecclesiastical Policies of James I and Charles I," in Fincham, ed., *The Early Stuart Church,* 24-32; Kenyon, *Stuart Constitution,* 126-27.
5. Solberg, *Redeem the Time,* 71-74; Mullan, *Episcopacy in Scotland,* 151-62; P. H. R. Mackay, "The Reception Given to the Five Articles of Perth," *Records of the Scottish Church History Society* 19 (1977): 185-201.
6. Fincham, ed., *The Early Stuart Church,* 24-33, 71-78, 93-103.
7. Michael B. Young, *Charles I* (New York, 1997), 108ff.; Fincham, ed., *The Early Stuart Church,* 36-49, 51-70, 78-91, 103-13; Carleton, *Laud,* esp. 71, 77ff.
8. Peter Lake, "Anti-Popery: The Structure of a Prejudice," in Richard Cust and Ann Hughes, eds., *Conflict in Early Stuart England: Studies in Religion and Politics 1603-1642* (London, 1989), 72-106; Caroline Hibbard, *Charles I and the Popish Plot* (Chapel Hill, 1983); Fincham, ed., *The Early Stuart Church,* 15; Tom Webster, *Godly Clergy in Early Stuart England: The Caroline Puritan Movement c. 1620-1643* (Cambridge, 1997), part 3; Francis J. Bremer, *Congregational Communion: Clerical Friendship in the Anglo-American Puritan Community, 1610-1692* (Boston, 1993), chaps. 4-5; Stephen Foster, *The Long Argument: English Puritanism and the Shaping of New England Culture, 1570-1700* (Chapel Hill, 1991), chaps. 3-4.
9. David Cressy, *Coming Over: Migration and Communication between England and New England in the Seventeenth Century* (Cambridge, 1987), esp. 50, 75-

77, 87; W. A. Speck and L. Billington, "Calvinism in Colonial North America, 1630–1715," in Prestwich, ed., *International Calvinism,* 267.

10. Vaughan, ed., *Puritan Tradition in America,* 74–78; Morgan, *Visible Saints,* chap. 3; David D. Hall, *The Faithful Shepherd: A History of the New England Ministry in the Seventeenth Century* (Chapel Hill, 1972), chaps. 4–7; Emil Oberholzer Jr., *Delinquent Saints: Disciplinary Action in the Early Congregational Churches of Massachusetts* (New York, 1956), esp. 33.

11. Vaughan, ed., *Puritan Tradition in America,* 98–115; Williston Walker, ed., *The Creeds and Platforms of Congregationalism* (New York, 1983; repr. Boston, 1960), 156–237.

12. Foster, *Long Argument,* 171.

13. Gerald F. Moran, "Religious Renewal, Puritan Tribalism, and the Family in Seventeenth-Century Milford, Connecticut," *William and Mary Quarterly,* 3d ser., 36 (1979): 239–40, 246; Hall, *Faithful Shepherd,* 100; Morgan, *Visible Saints,* 123.

14. Walker, ed., *Creeds and Platforms,* 234–37; Vaughan, ed., *Puritan Tradition,* 161–72.

15. Allan I. Macinnes, *Charles I and the Making of the Covenanting Movement 1625–1641* (Edinburgh, 1991); Lee, *Road to Revolution,* esp. 209; Gordon Donaldson, *The Making of the Scottish Prayer Book of 1637* (Edinburgh, 1954); Stevenson, *Scottish Revolution,* 16, 35–47, 58–63; Coffey, *Rutherford,* 42–45; Mullan, *Episcopacy in Scotland,* 174–77.

16. John Morrill, ed., *The Scottish National Covenant in its British Context 1638–1651* (Edinburgh, 1990), 11, 37–50.

17. Dickinson and Donaldson, eds., *Source Book of Scottish History* 3:95–104.

18. Stevenson, *Scottish Revolution,* 86–87; Morrill, ed., *Scottish National Covenant,* 14–15, 31.

19. Gordon Donaldson, ed., *Scottish Historical Documents* (Edinburgh, 1970), 194–201; id., *James V to James VII,* 320–22; David Stevenson, "The Radical Party in the Kirk, 1637–45," *Journal of Ecclesiastical History* 25 (1974): 135–65; Mullan, *Episcopacy in Scotland,* 178ff.

20. Mark Charles Fissel, *The Bishops' Wars: Charles I's Campaigns against Scotland, 1638–1640* (Cambridge, 1994); Conrad Russell, *The Fall of the British Monarchies 1637–1642* (Oxford, 1991), chaps. 3–4.

21. Stevenson, *Scottish Revolution,* 101–02; id., "Deposition of Ministers in the Church of Scotland under the Covenanters, 1638–1651," *Church History* 44 (1975): 321–35; Julia Buckroyd, *Church and State in Scotland 1660–1681* (Edinburgh, 1980), 12.

22. Stevenson, *Scottish Revolution,* 250–52; id., "The General Assembly and the Commission of the Kirk, 1638–1651," *Records of the Scottish Church History Society* 19 (1975): 67–76; Paul, *Assembly of the Lord,* 67; George I. Murray, ed., *Records of Falkirk Parish: A Review of the Kirk Session Records of Falkirk, from 1617 to 1689* (Falkirk, 1887); T. C. Smout, *A History of the Scottish People, 1560–1830,* 84–85.

NOTES TO PAGES 397-402

23. Baxter, *Autobiography*, 53; Anthony Fletcher, *The Outbreak of the English Civil War* (London, 1981), 92, 109ff.; Keith Lindley, *Popular Politics and Religion in Civil War London* (Aldershot, 1997), 37-45.

24. Morrill, *Nature of the English Revolution*, 45–90, esp. 56–58, 73.

25. The introductions to the first two volumes of *Complete Prose Works of John Milton*, 8 vols. (New Haven, 1953–82), 1:1–210, 2:1–216, provide the fullest, but still not entirely satisfactory, survey of the pamphlet debates of these years.

26. *Complete Prose Works of Milton* 1:115–8; Bolam et al., *English Presbyterians*, 36, 65; Spurr, *Restoration Church*, 137ff.; Packer, *Transformation of Anglicanism*, 105ff.; G. V. Bennett, "Patristic Tradition in Anglican Thought, 1660–1900," in *Tradition im Luthertum und Anglikanismus*, Oecumenica 1971–72 (Gütersloh, 1972), 64–66.

27. *Complete Prose Works of Milton* 1:140–42; Watts, *Dissenters*, 94–111, esp. 111; Tolmie, *The Triumph of the Saints*, 1–119; Bremer, *Congregational Communion*, 117ff.; Stephen Foster, "English Puritanism and the Progress of New England Institutions, 1630–1660," in David D. Hall, John M. Murrin, and Thad W. Tate, eds., *Saints and Revolutionaries: Essays on Early American History* (New York, 1984), 26; Peter Toon, *God's Statesman: The Life and Work of John Owen* (Exeter, 1971), 18–27; Hill, *World Turned Upside Down;* J. F. McGregor, "The Baptists: Fount of All Heresy," in McGregor and Reay, eds., *Radical Religion in the English Revolution*, 23–64; Ian Gentles, *The New Model Army in England, Ireland and Scotland 1645–1653* (Oxford, 1992), chap. 4.

28. *Complete Prose Works of Milton* 2:92–107; Watts, *Dissenters*, 89–92; Bolam et al., *English Presbyterians*, 29–42.

29. John Selden, *Table-Talk* (London, 1696), 56–57, 158; Thomas Coleman, *A Brotherly Examination Re-examined* (London, 1646), esp. 16–17; John Lightfoot, *Works*, 2 vols. (London, 1684), iv; *Complete Prose Works of Milton* 2:125; Hugo Grotius, *The Magistrates Authority in Matters of Religion Asserted, Or the Right of the State in the Church* (London, 1655); J. N. Figgis, "Erastus and Erastianism," *Journal of Theological Studies* 2 (1900): 66–101, esp. 78–79; Paul, *Assembly of the Lord*, 127–32.

30. Baxter, *Autobiography*, 29–32; Lindley, *Popular Politics and Religion*, 256–58; Firth and Rait, eds., *Acts and Ordinances of the Interregnum* 1:265–66.

31. Firth and Rait, eds., *Acts and Ordinances of the Interregnum* 1:749–57, 833–38; Paul, *Assembly of the Lord*, esp. 382–87; Cross, *Church and People*, 202; Stevenson, *Revolution and Counter-Revolution*, 63; Coffey, *Rutherford*, 210–11.

32. Firth and Rait, eds., *Acts and Ordinances of the Interregnum* 1:582–607; Horton Davies, *Worship and Theology in England*, vol.2, *From Andrewes to Baxter and Fox, 1603–1690* (Princeton, 1975), 405ff.

33. Firth and Rait, eds., *Acts and Ordinances of the Interregnum* 1:582–607; Bray, ed., *Documents of the English Reformation*, 486–512; Benjamin B. Warfield, *The Westminster Assembly and Its Work* (Oxford, 1931), 55ff.

34. Charles E. Surman, ed., *The Register-Booke of the Fourth Classis in the Province of London*, Harleian Society Publications 82–83 (London, 1953); Lindley, *Popu-*

lar Politics, 276; Watts, *Dissenters*, 117; Bolam et al., *English Presbyterians*, 44; John Morrill, "The Church in England, 1642–9," in Morrill, ed., *Reactions to the English Civil War 1642–1649* (New York, 1983), 97, 104; Paul, *Assembly of the Lord*, 392.

35. Firth and Rait, eds., *Acts and Ordinances of the Interregnum* 1:521–26, 2:409–12, 423–25, 855–58, 968–90; J. C. Davis, "Cromwell's Religion," in John Morrill, ed., *Oliver Cromwell and the English Revolution* (London, 1990), 181–208; Blair Worden, "Toleration and the Cromwellian Protectorate," in W. J. Sheils, ed., *Persecution and Toleration*, Studies in Church History 21 (Oxford, 1984), 199–233; Paul, *Assembly of the Lord*, 466; Toon, *God's Statesman*, 36; Ivan Roots, *Commonwealth and Protectorate: The English Civil War and Its Aftermath* (New York, 1966), 176–78; Jeffrey R. Collins, "The Church Settlement of Oliver Cromwell," *History* 87 (2002), 27–30.

36. Firth and Rait, eds., *Acts and Ordinances of the Interregnum* 1:22, 26, 80–82, 420–22, 669–71, 905, 1070–72, 2:197–200, 342–48, 383–87, 409–12, 1000, 1162; Roots, *Commonwealth and Protectorate*, 180; Christopher Durston, "Puritan Rule and the Failure of Cultural Revolution, 1645–1660," in Durston and Jacqueline Eales, eds., *The Culture of English Puritanism, 1560–1700* (New York, 1996).

37. Morrill, "The Church in England, 1642–9," 104ff.; Lindley, *Popular Politics*, 282–87; B. R. White, "The Organisation of the Particular Baptists, 1644–1660," *Journal of Ecclesiastical History* 17 (1966): 209–26; Watt, *Dissenters*, 151–68; Bremer, *Congregational Communion*, 190–200.

38. Packer, *Transformation of Anglicanism;* Norman Sykes, *From Sheldon to Secker: Aspects of English Church History 1660–1768* (Cambridge, 1959), 7–8; Spurr, *Restoration Church*, 14–20. Those clergymen who followed the king into exile also contributed importantly to the development of Anglicanism in this period. R. S. Bosher, *The Making of the Restoration Settlement* (Westminster, 1951) 5, 9–48, is a good introduction to their efforts and importance.

39. David Cressy, *Birth, Marriage and Death: Ritual, Religion, and the Life-Cycle in Tudor and Stuart England* (Oxford, 1997), 178–80.

40. Baxter, *Autobiography*, 77–78, 84; Geoffrey Nuttall, "The Worcestershire Association: Its Membership," *Journal of Ecclesiastical History* 1 (1950): 197–206; Frederick J. Powicke, *A Life of the Reverend Richard Baxter 1615–1691* (London, 1924), 165–66; William A. Shaw, *A History of the English Church during the Civil Wars and under the Commonwealth*, 2 vols. (London, 1900), 2:152–74.

41. See above, 343–44.

42. Stevenson, *Revolution and Counter-Revolution*, 1–15, 99–105; Donaldson, *James V to James VII*, 329–40.

43. Coffey, *Rutherford*, 219.

44. Stevenson, *Revolution and Counter-Revolution*, 133–45; Coffey, *Rutherford*, 55; G. D. Henderson, *The Scottish Ruling Elder* (London, 1935), 131.

45. Stevenson, *Revolution and Counter-Revolution*, 154–79; Coffey, *Rutherford*, 249.

46. Stevenson, *Revolution and Counter-Revolution,* 180–205; Coffey, *Rutherford,* 54–55, 146–87, 250–52; Cowan, *Covenanters,* 32; Gordon Donaldson, "The Emergence of Schism in Seventeenth-Century Scotland," in Donaldson, *Scottish Church History* (Edinburgh, 1985), 214–15.

47. Donaldson, *James V to James VII,* 343–57; Coffey, *Rutherford,* 56–60, 250–52; Donaldson, "Emergence of Schism," 213–18; Toon, *God's Statesman,* 98; Julia Buckroyd, *Church and State in Scotland 1660–1681* (Edinburgh, 1980), 7–11.

48. C. E. Whiting, *Studies in English Puritanism from the Restoration to the Revolution, 1660–1688* (New York, 1931), 3–4; Cowan, *Covenanters,* 44; Bosher, *Making of Restoration Settlement,* chap. 3; G. R. Abernathy, *The English Presbyterians and the Stuart Restoration,* Transactions of the American Philosophical Society, vol. 55, part 2 (Philadelphia, 1965), 17–18; Spurr, *Restoration Church,* 29–32.

49. *Documents relating to the Settlement of the Church of England by the Act of Uniformity of 1662* (London, 1867), 386–404; Bosher, *Making of Restoration Settlement,* chaps. 4–5; Spurr, *Restoration Church,* 32–40; Sykes, *Sheldon to Secker,* 3–6; Abernathy, *The Presbyterians and the Restoration,* 66–93.

50. Spurr, *Restoration Church,* 47–50, 279–330; Sykes, *Sheldon to Secker,* 7–8; Bennett, "Patristic Tradition in Anglican Thought," 74–76; Marshall, *Locke,* 35–41; id., "Ecclesiology of the Latitude-men"; Burnet, *History of His Own Time* 1:189; Wallace, *Puritans and Predestination,* 159–60, 166–68; Nicholas Tyacke, "Arminianism and the Theology of the Restoration Church," in S. Groenveld and M. Wintle, eds., *The Exchange of Ideas: Religion, Scholarship and Art in Anglo-Dutch Relations in the Seventeenth Century,* Britain and the Netherlands 11 (Zutphen, 1994), 68–83; Allison, *Rise of Moralism;* McGee, *Godly Man,* 143–52; Bennett, "Conflict in the Church," 155.

51. The latest estimate places the total number of clergymen of all sorts ejected in England and Wales between 1660 and 1662 at 2,029. Watts, *Dissenters,* 219. For the varied grounds of their refusal, see Whiting, *Studies,* 1; Bolam et al., *English Presbyterians,* 81–82; Gerald R. Cragg, *Puritanism in the Period of the Great Persecution 1660–1688* (Cambridge, 1957), 225.

52. Watt, *Dissenters,* 227–37; Whiting, *Studies,* esp. 26–39; Bolam et al., *English Presbyterians,* 79–88; Olive M. Griffiths, *Religion and Learning: A Study in English Presbyterian Thought from the Bartholomew Ejections (1662) to the Foundation of the Unitarian Movement* (Cambridge, 1935), esp. 28; Irene Parker, *Dissenting Academies in England* (Cambridge, 1914; repr. New York, 1969), 46–49.

53. *Documents relating to the Settlement of the Church of England,* 478.

54. Kenyon, *Stuart Constitution,* 382–86; Bolam et al., *English Presbyterians,* 89–90; Sykes, *Sheldon to Secker,* 68–83; Watts, *Dissenters,* 244–49; John Spurr, "From Puritanism to Dissent, 1660–1700," in Durston and Eales, eds., *Culture of English Puritanism,* 247–52.

55. Quoted in Foster, *Bishop and Presbytery,* 127.

56. This and the subsequent paragraphs rest primarily upon Buckroyd, *Church and*

State, chaps. 3–5; Donaldson, *James V to James VII,* 358–65; Cowan, *Covenanters,* chap. 2; Foster, *Bishop and Presbytery.* For key extracts from the legislation, see Dickinson and Donaldson, *Source Book of Scottish History* 3:159.

57. Cowan, *Covenanters,* chap. 3; Donaldson, *James V to James VII,* 365–6.

58. Cowan, *Covenanters,* chap. 4; Donaldson, *James V to James VII,* 367; Buckroyd, *Church and State,* 65–67.

59. Cowan, *Covenanters,* chaps. 5–6; Dickinson and Donaldson, *Source Book of Scottish History,* 3:165–74; Buckroyd, *Church and State,* 84–85, 100–01; D. E. Easson, "A Scottish Parish in Covenanting Times," *Records of the Scottish Church History Society* 10 (1948): 111–24, esp. 119.

60. Robert Wodrow, *The History of the Sufferings of the Church of Scotland, the Restauration to the Revolution,* 2 vols. (Edinburgh, 1721–22); Cowan, *Covenanters,* chaps. 7–8; Dickinson and Donaldson, *Source Book of Scottish History,* 3:170–84; Buckroyd, *Church and State,* 130–35; Hector Macpherson, "The Wigtown Martyrs," *Records of the Scottish Church History Society* 9 (1947): 166–84.

61. E. Neville Williams, *The Eighteenth-Century Constitution 1688–1815* (Cambridge, 1960), 42–46; Goldie, "Nonjurors"; Bennett, "William III and the Episcopate," 106–16; Nicholas Tyacke, "The 'Rise of Puritanism' and the Legalizing of Dissent, 1571–1719," and Jonathan I. Israel, "William III and Toleration," in Ole P. Grell, Israel and Tyacke, eds., *From Persecution to Toleration: The Glorious Revolution and Religion in England* (Oxford, 1991), 39–44, 129–55.

62. Watts, *Dissenters,* 270–71.

63. Ibid., 290–91; Bolam et al, *English Presbyterians,* 21–27, 113–235.

64. Goldie, "Nonjurors, Episcopacy, and the Origins of the Convocation Controversy"; Bennett, "Conflict in the Church," 166–75; Geoffrey Holmes, *The Trial of Doctor Sacheverell* (London, 1973).

65. Sykes, *Old Priest and New Presbyter,* 143; Vuilleumier, *Eglise réformée du Pays de Vaud* 3:56; Gwynn, *Huguenot Heritage,* 101; Fontaine, *Mémoires d'une famille huguenote,* 262.

66. John Cunningham, *The Church History of Scotland* (Edinburgh, 1859), vol. 2, chap. 7, remains a useful account of this period. Also helpful on aspects of Scottish church history in the wake of the Glorious Revolution are William Ferguson, *Scotland: 1689 to the Present* (Edinburgh, 1968), chaps. 1, 4; Cowan, *Covenanters,* chaps. 9, 10; Dunlop, *Carstares;* Ian B. Cowan and Spencer Earle, *The Scottish Episcopal Church* (Ambler, Pa., 1966); Clarke, "Scottish Episcopalians"; and Craig Rose, *England in the 1690s: Revolution, Religion and War* (Oxford, 1999), chap. 7. These are the chief sources for this and the following paragraphs.

67. National Library of Scotland, Wodrow MS 4o 82, fos. 30ff; Cunningham, *Church History of Scotland* 2:311–12; Clarke, "Scottish Episcopalians," 263–64; Rose, *England in the 1690s,* 216.

68. Clarke, "Scottish Episcopalians," 186, 353–63.

69. John Macleod, *Scottish Theology in Relation to Church History since the Reformation* (Edinburgh, 1943), chap. 4; Thomas Torrance, *Scottish Theology: From John Knox to John McLeod Campbell* (Edinburgh, 1996), 224–29.

CONCLUSION TO PART III

1. Hilde de Ridder-Symoens, "Mobility," in *A History of the University in Europe,* vol. 2, *Universities in Early Modern Europe (1500–1800)* (Cambridge, 1996), 416–48; Wansink, *Politieke Wetenschappen,* 7–9; G. T. Jensma, F. R. H. Smit, and F. Westra, eds., *Universiteit te Franeker 1585–1811* (Leeuwarden, 1985), 57ff.; Janine Garrisson, *Les Protestants au XVIe siècle* (Paris, 1988), 134–35.

2. Walter Rex, "Bayle's Article on David," in *Essays on Pierre Bayle and Religious Controversy* (The Hague, 1965), 213–25, 248–50; Elisabeth Labrousse, "Le Refuge hollandais: Bayle et Jurieu," *XVIIe Siècle* 76–77 (1967): 90–92; H. D. Schmidt, "The Establishment of 'Europe' as a Political Expression," *Historical Journal* 9 (1966): 172–78.

3. Slingsby Bethel, *The Present Interest of England Stated* (London, 1671), 21; Paul Münch, "The Thesis before Weber: An Archeology," in Lehmann and Roth, eds., *Weber's Protestant Ethic,* 51–71.

INTRODUCTION TO PART IV

1. *Longman Dictionary of Contemporary English,* 3d ed. (London, 1995), s.v. "Calvinism."

2. Zepper, *Von der Christlichen Disziplin/oder Kirchenzucht,* quoted in Paul Münch, "Reformation of Life: Calvinism and Popular Culture in Germany around 1600: The Paradigm of Nassau-Dillenburg," in L. Laeyendecker, L. G. Jansma, and C. H. A. Verhaar, eds., *Experiences and Explanations: Historical and Sociological Essays in Religion in Everyday Life* (Leeuwarden, 1990), 42–43.

3. H. Outram Evennett, *The Spirit of the Counter-Reformation* (Cambridge, 1968); Louis Châtellier, *L'Europe des dévots* (Paris, 1987).

4. E. W. Zeeden, *Die Entstehung der Konfessionen: Grundlagen und Formen der Konfessionsbildung im Zeitalter der Glaubenskämpfe* (Munich, 1965); Heinz Schilling, "Die Konfessionalisierung im Reich-religiöser und gesellschaftlicher Wandel in Deutschland zwischen 1555 und 1620," *Historische Zeitschrift* 246 (1988): 1–25; id., "Confessional Europe," in Thomas A. Brady Jr., Heiko Oberman, and James D. Tracy, eds., *Handbook of European History 1400–1600: Late Middle Ages, Renaissance and Reformation* (Leiden, 1994–95), vol. 2, chap. 21; Wolfgang Reinhard, "Konfession und Konfessionalisierung in Europa," in Reinhard, ed., *Bekenntnis und Geschichte: Die Confessio Augustana im historischen Zusammenhang* (Munich, 1981), 165–89; id., "Zwang zur Konfessionalisierung? Prolegomena zu einer Theorie des konfessionellen Zeitalters," *Zeitschrift für historische Forschung* 10 (1983): 257–77; Hsia, *Social Discipline in the Reformation;* Susan Karant-Nunn, *The Reformation of Ritual: An Interpretation of Early Modern Germany* (London, 1997). Heinrich Richard Schmidt, "Sozialdisziplinierung? Ein Plädoyer für das Ende des Etatismus in der Konfessionalisierungsforschung," *Historische Zeitschrift* 265 (1997): 639–82, has an important critical review of the entire literature on confessionalization.

5. Helga Schnabel-Schüle, "Calvinistische Kirchenzucht in Württemberg? Zur Theorie und Praxis der württembergischen Kirchenkonvente," *Zeitschrift für*

Württembergische Landesgeschichte 49 (1990): 169–223; id., "Der grosse Unterschied und seine kleinen Folgen. Zum Problem der Kirchenzucht als Unterscheidungskriterium zwischen lutherischer und reformierter Konfession," in Monika Hagenmaier and Sabine Holtz, eds., *Krisenbewusstsein und Krisenbewältigung in der Frühen Neuzeit* (Frankfurt, 1992), 197–214.

6. Adriano Prosperi, *Tribunali della coscienza Inquisitori, confessori, missionari* (Turin, 1996); Leon-E. Halkin, "Réforme catholique et police ecclésiastique dans la principauté de Liège au XVIe siècle," *Revue de l'Histoire de l'Eglise de France* 75 (1989): 21–33; Jean-Pierre Dedieu, "Les causes de foi de l'Inquisition de Tolède (1483–1820)," *Mélanges de la Casa de Velazquez* 14 (1978): 148, 155–58; E. W. Monter and John Tedeschi, "Toward a Statistical Profile of the Italian Inquisitions, Sixteenth to Eighteenth Centuries," in Gustav Henningsen and John Tedeschi, eds., *The Inquisition in Early Modern Europe: Studies on Sources and Methods* (DeKalb, Ill., 1986), 133–35.

7. The major statements in this debate are Gerald Strauss, "Success and Failure in the German Reformation," *Past and Present* 67 (1975): 30–63; James M. Kittelson, "Successes and Failures in the German Reformation: The Report from Strasbourg," *Archiv für Reformationsgeschichte* 73 (1982): 153–75; Geoffrey Parker, "Success and Failure during the First Century of the Reformation," *Past and Present* 136 (1992): 43–82. Heinrich Richard Schmidt, *Dorf und Religion: Reformierte Sittenzucht in Berner Landgemeinden der Frühen Neuzeit* (Stuttgart, 1995), 96–99, offers the fullest recent bibliography and overview of the contributions to this ongoing discussion.

8. Richard Gawthrop and Gerald Strauss, "Protestantism and Literacy in Early Modern Germany," *Past and Present* 104 (1984): 31–55.

CHAPTER 13. THE REFORMATION OF THE MINISTRY

Bibliographical Note The minutes of the classical and synodal gatherings of the different Reformed churches organized along presbyterial-synodal lines offer a fundamental source for determining the actual workings of the churches in question and the ideals and reality of the various ministerial offices. Good published sets of such records include J. P. van Dooren, ed., *Classicale Acta, 1573–1620: Particuliere synode Zuid-Holland I: Classis Dordrecht 1573–1600* (The Hague, 1980); J. Reitsma and S. D. van Veen, eds., *Acta der Provinciale en particuliere synoden gehouden in de Noordelijke Nederlanden gedurende de jaren 1572–1620*, 8 vols. (Groningen, 1892); W. P. C. Knuttel, ed., *Acta der Particuliere Synoden van Zuid-Holland 1621–1700*, 6 vols. (The Hague, 1908–16); James Kirk, ed., *The Records of the Synod of Lothian and Tweeddale 1589–1596, 1640–1649* (Edinburgh, 1977); the numerous volumes of synodal, presbyterial, and classical acts for the churches of the Rhineland published by the Verein für Rheinische Kirchengeschicte, including Hermann Kelm, ed., *Protokolle der reformierten Synoden des Herzogtums Jülich 1677 bis 1700* (Cologne, 1986); Albert Rosenkranz, ed., *Generalsynodalbuch: Die Akten der Generalsynoden von Jülich, Kleve, Berg und Mark 1610–1755*, 2 vols. (Dusseldorf, 1966); and the volumes edited by Sipallyo and Kiss cited in the bibliographical note for chapter 9.

Walter Roland Foster's two exemplary studies, *Bishop and Presbytery: The Church of Scotland, 1661–1688* (London, 1958), and *The Church before the Covenants: The Church of Scotland, 1596–1638* (Edinburgh, 1975), explore the workings of all the major institutions of the Scottish church in two periods of its existence. Work on the social history of the ministry gathered steam in the later 1970s with the appearance of Bernard Vogler, *Le clergé protestant rhénan au siècle de la Réforme* (Paris, 1976); G. Groenhuis, *De Predikanten: De sociale positie van de gereformeerde predikanten in de Republiek der Verenigde Nederlanden voor ± 1700* (Groningen, 1977); John Pruett, *The Parish Clergy under the Later Stuarts: The Leicestershire Experience* (Urbana, 1978); Rosemary O'Day, *The English Clergy: The Emergence and Consolidation of a Profession 1558–1642* (Leicester, 1979); and, subsequently, Luise Schorn-Schütte, *Evangelische Geistlichkeit in der Frühneuzeit* (Gütersloh, 1996). Some older institutional-theological histories also remain very useful, notably Robert W. Henderson, *The Teaching Office in the Reformed Tradition: A History of the Doctoral Ministry* (Philadelphia, 1962); A. van Ginkel, *De Ouderling* (Amsterdam, 1975); and G. D. Henderson, *The Scottish Ruling Elder* (London, 1935). Outstanding social studies of the eldership are Solange Bertheau, "Le consistoire dans les Églises réformées du Moyen-Poitou au XVIIe siècle," *Bulletin de la Société de l'Histoire du Protestantisme Français* 116 (1970): 332–59, 513–49; W. H. Makey, "The Elders of Stow, Liberton, Canongate and St. Cuthberts in the Mid-Seventeenth Century," *Records of the Scottish Church History Society* 17 (1970): 155–67; Heinz Schilling, "Calvinistische Presbyterien in Städten der Frühneuzeit-eine kirchliche Alternativform zur bürgerlichen Repräsentation (mit einer quantifizierenden Untersuchung zur holländischen Stadt Leiden)," in W. Ehbrecht, ed., *Städtische Führungsgruppen und Gemeinde in der Werdenden Neuzeit* (Cologne, 1980), 385–444; and id., "Das Calvinistische Presbyterium in der Stadt Groningen während der frühen Neuzeit und im ersten Viertel des 19 Jahrhunderts: Verfassung und Sozialprofil," in H. Schilling and H. Diederiks, eds., *Burgerliche Eliten in den Niederlanden und Nordwestdeutschland* (Cologne, 1985), 195–273.

1. Fred van Lieburg, *Profeten en hun vaderland: De geografische herkomst van de gereformeerde predikanten in Nederland van 1572 to 1816* (Zoetermeer, 1996), 61, 99; Bergsma, *Tussen Gedeonsbende en publieke kerk,* 24.
2. Schorn-Schütte, *Evangelische Geistlichkeit,* 414.
3. Robert S. Rait, *The Parliaments of Scotland* (Glasgow, 1924), 167–68; Roland Mousnier, *L'Assassinat d'Henri IV* (Paris, 1964), 327; Schorn-Schütte, *Evangelische Geistlichkeit,* 253; personal communication from Henk van Nierop; Murdock, "International Calvinism and Hungary," 22.
4. Bob Scribner, "Politics and the Institutionalisation of Reform in Germany," in *New Cambridge Modern History,* vol. 2, *The Reformation,* 2d ed. (Cambridge, 1990), 181–82.

5. Bruce Gordon, "Preaching and the Reform of the Clergy in the Swiss Reformation," in Pettegree, ed., *Reformation of the Parishes,* 66; Cochrane, ed., *Reformed Confessions of the Sixteenth Century,* 153.

6. Françoise Chevalier, *Prêcher sous l'Edit de Nantes: La prédication réformée au XVIIe siècle en France* (Geneva, 1994), 36.

7. Peter Lake, "Richard Kilby: A Study in Personal and Professional Failure," in W. J. Sheils and Diana Wood, eds., *The Ministry: Clerical and Lay* (Oxford, 1989), 221; David D. Hall, *Worlds of Wonder, Days of Judgment: Popular Religious Belief in Early New England* (Cambridge, Mass., 1989), 12–13. See also James L. Ainslie, *The Doctrines of the Ministerial Order in the Reformed Churches of the 16th and 17th Centuries* (Edinburgh, 1940), 9–11.

8. Quick, *Synodicon in Gallia Reformata* 1:95–6.

9. Jean de Focquembergues, *Le Voyage de Beth-el, ou sont representez les devoirs de l'Ame Fidele en allant au Temple, et en retournant* (Paris, 1665), 25, 44.

10. Pierre Du Moulin, *Sixieme Decade de Sermons* (Geneva, 1647), 165.

11. Maag, *Seminary or University?* 158–59; Webster, *Godly Clergy,* 15–18. For a partial list of new Reformed institutions of higher learning created during these years, see Mark Greengrass, *Longman Companion to the European Reformation c. 1500–1618* (London, 1998), 268, which may be usefully supplemented with Lubor Jilek, ed., *Historical Compendium of European Universities* (Geneva, 1984).

12. Maag, *Seminary or University?* 106–10; Patrick Collinson, "Shepherds, Sheepdogs, and Hirelings: The Pastoral Ministry in Post-Reformation England," in Sheils and Wood, eds., *Ministry,* 189–95; Richard Baxter, *The Reformed Pastor,* ed. William Brown (Edinburgh, 1974), esp. chap. 1; Pierre Du Moulin, *Cinquième Décade de Sermons* (Geneva, 1645), sermon 8, *Sixieme Decade,* 165.

13. Fills, *Lawes and Statutes of Geneva,* 5–6; Frossard, *Discipline ecclésiastique du Béarn,* 29; Rutgers, *Acta van de Nederlandsche Synoden der Zestiende Eeuw,* 33–34. Cf. Glenn S. Sunshine, "French Protestantism on the Eve of St-Bartholomew: The Ecclesiastical Discipline of the French Reformed Churches, 1571–1572," *French History* 4 (1990): 358.

14. *Acts and Proceedings of the General Assemblies of the Kirk of Scotland* 3:865.

15. Murdock, "Church Building and Discipline," 152–53; Gordon, *Clerical Discipline,* 101–05.

16. Vuilleumier, *Histoire de l'Eglise réformée du Pays de Vaud* 2:83.

17. Foster, *Bishop and Presbytery,* 103–04.

18. Dankbaar, "Kerkvisitaties," 46–51; Wiebe Bergsma, "Gereformeerden en doopsgezinden. Van concurrentie tot gedwongen acceptatie," *Doopsgezinde Bijdragen* 20 (1994): 142–43, 150–56.

19. Pruett, *Parish Clergy,* 7; Felicity Heal, *Of Prelates and Princes: A Study of the Economic and Social Position of the Tudor Episcopate* (Cambridge, 1980), 238; Collinson, *Religion of Protestants,* 66–67.

20. John. W. Beardslee III, ed., *Reformed Dogmatics: J. Wollebius, G. Voetius, F. Turretin* (Oxford, 1965), 143–44.

21. Van Beeck Calkoen, *Rechtstoestand der Geestelijke en Kerkelijke Goederen in Holland;* L. J. van Apeldoorn, *De Kerkelijke Goederen in Friesland: Beschrijving van de Ontwikkeling van her Recht omtrent de Kerkelijke Goederen in Friesland tot 1795* (Leeuwarden, 1915); Jan de Vries, "Searching for a Role: The Economy of Utrecht in the Golden Age of the Dutch Republic," in *Masters of Light,* 53; Duker, *Voetius* 2:294-334; Henry J. Cohn, "Church Property in the German Protestant Principalities," in Kouri and Scott, eds., *Politics and Society in Reformation Europe,* 158-87, esp. 168, 171.

22. Philippe Le Noir de Crevain, *Histoire ecclesiastique de la Bretagne,* ed. B. Vaurigaud (Paris, 1851), 65; Abels and Wouters, *Nieuw en ongezien* 1:433; Elliott, "Protestantization," 178; Garrisson-Estèbe, *Protestants du Midi,* 134-35. Van Lieburg, *Profeten,* 58, indicates that 78 percent of Dutch ministers appointed prior to 1600 had some higher education, but he may be relying on a sample skewed toward the more permanent and better-known ministers.

23. See above, 170, 287-88; *First Book of Discipline,* 106, 111; Vuilleumier, *Histoire de l'Eglise réformée du Pays de Vaud* 1:267-68; Greengrass, "Calvinist Experiment in Béarn," 134; Garrisson-Estèbe, *Protestants du Midi,* 138-41; Penny Roberts, "The Demands and Dangers of the Reformed Ministry in Troyes, 1552-72," in Pettegree, ed., *Reformation of the Parishes,* 153-74; Vogler, *Clergé protestant rhénan,* 86, 149-57.

24. Gordon, "Preaching," 68; Vuilleumier, *Histoire de l'Eglise réformée du Pays de Vaud* 1:226; Vogler, *Clergé protestant rhénan,* 99; Forissier, *Histoire de la Réforme en Béarn* 1:273-74; Donaldson, *Scottish Reformation,* 85; C. H. Haws, *Scottish Parish Clergy at the Reformation 1540-1574* (Edinburgh, 1972), viii; Groenhuis, *Predikanten,* 163; van Lieburg, *Profeten,* 58-61.

25. Garrisson-Estèbe, *Protestants du Midi,* 146-47; Vogler, *Clergé protestant rhénan,* 103-04; Philippe Chareyre, "Le Consistoire de Nîmes 1561-1685" (Thèse de doctorat d'état, Université Paul Valéry, 1987), 617.

26. Vuilleumier, *Histoire de l'Eglise réformée du Pays de Vaud* 1:269-70; Abels and Wouters, *Nieuw en ongezien* 1:58; Jean-Paul Pittion, "Les académies réformées de l'Edit de Nantes à la Révocation," in R. Zuber and L. Theis, eds., *La Révocation de l'Edit de Nantes et le protestantisme français en 1685* (Paris, 1986), 191; Gueneau, "Protestants du Centre," 366; Foster, *Church before the Covenants,* 137, 153.

27. Vogler, *Clergé protestant rhénan,* 75; van Lieburg, *Profeten,* 58; Abels and Wouters, *Nieuw en ongezien* 1:433; Foster, *Church before the Covenants,* 133.

28. Bishop Wake of Lincoln told his clergy in 1707 that he had a "better Opinion, both of your Learning and Discretion, than to supose that any among you, who has been admitted to a Cure of Souls, should not be fit to preach to the People to whom it has pleased God to call him." Pruett, *Parish Clergy,* 45.

29. John Hacket, quoted in Collinson, *Religion of Protestants,* 95.

30. "The Most Memorable Passages of the life and times of Mr. J. B. written by himself 1706," National Library of Scotland, Wodrow MS 4to LXXXII, fos. 26-28.

31. Schorn-Schütte, *Evangelische Geistlichkeit,* 310-13, 519; also Pruett, *Parish*

Clergy, 54; Walter Makey, *The Church of the Covenant, 1637–1651: Revolution and Social Change in Scotland* (Edinburgh, 1979), 102.

32. Roger Mazauric, *Le pasteur Paul Ferry* (Metz, 1964), 24, 29–30, 58; D. de Chavigny, *L'Eglise et l'Académie protestantes de Saumur* (Saumur, 1914), 102; Martin J. Klauber, "Reformed Orthodoxy in Transition: Bénédict Pictet (1655–1724) and Enlightened Orthodoxy in Post-Reformation Geneva," in Graham, ed., *Later Calvinism,* 95n.

33. Foster, *Church before the Covenants,* 167; Makey, *Church of the Covenant,* 115–22; Vogler, *Clergé protestant rhénan,* 157–60; Groenhuis, *Predikanten,* 134–47; Pruett, *Parish Clergy,* 52, 82–110; Hanlon, *Confession and Community,* 128; Labrousse, *Une foi, une loi, un roi?"* 49; Paul de Félice, *Les Protestants d'autrefois,* 3 vols. (Paris, 1897–9), 2:209–18.

34. Van Lieburg, *Profeten,* passim, esp. 139, 158, 170, 173; Schorn-Schutte, *Evangelische Geistlichkeit,* 86, 489–92 (pastors' sons 29 percent of new pastors in Hesse-Cassel 1586–1630, 31 percent 1631–85); Makey, *Church of the Covenant,* 97 (pastors' sons 17 percent of new pastors 1616–38, 27 percent 1648); Gueneau, "Protestants du Centre," 367–68 (pastors' sons 16 percent of new pastors 1598–1695).

35. Groenhuis, *Predikanten,* 162; Hall, *Faithful Shepherd,* 183. The pastoral marriages I have come across in my research in the parish registers of French Reformed churches suggest this pattern as well.

36. Hall, *Faithful Shepherd,* 183; Foster, *Church before the Covenants,* 167–68; Makey, *Church of the Covenant,* 115.

37. O'Day, *English Clergy,* 172–89; Pruett, *Parish Clergy,* 107, 136–51, 161.

38. Archives Départementales de la Moselle (Metz), B 3354–55 (inventories after death of Abraham de la Cloche and Theophile Le Coullen); Robert Garrisson, *Essai sur l'histoire du Protestantisme dans la Généralité de Montauban sous l'intendance de N.-J. Foucault 1674–1684* (Mialet, 1935), 247–60.

39. Garrisson-Estèbe, *Protestants du Midi,* 145–52; Archives Départementales du Tarn (Albi), E 5363, entry of January 20, 1611; Gregory Hanlon, *L'Univers des gens de bien. Culture et comportements des élites urbaines en Agenais-Condomois au XVIIe siècle* (Bordeaux, 1989), 215–16; Hanlon, *Confession and Community,* passim; Benedict, *Faith and Fortunes,* chap. 8.

40. Archives Départementales de la Moselle, B 3357, inventory of April 13, 1656. Benedict, *Faith and Fortunes,* 181–83, offers a slightly more extended analysis.

41. Vogler, *Clergé protestant rhénan,* 237; Hall, *Worlds of Wonder,* 44; R. A. Houston, *Scottish Literacy and the Scottish Identity: Illiteracy and Society in Scotland and Northern England, 1600–1800* (Cambridge, 1985), appendix 2; W. R. Foster, "Ecclesiastical Administration in Scotland, 1600–1638" (Ph.D. diss., Edinburgh University, 1963), appendix F (the evidence in these last two works about the value of Scottish clerical libraries has been turned into an estimate of their size on the evidence from Robert H. Macdonald, ed., *The Library of Drummond of Hawthornden* [Edinburgh, 1971], 38, that the average book in early seventeenth-

century Scotland cost ten shillings, and on the further assumption that it cost
as much again to bind a book); Puyroche, "La Bibliothèque d'un pasteur à la fin
du XVIe siècle," *Bulletin de la Société de l'Histoire du Protestantisme Français*
7 (1872): 327–37 (662 books in the library of Jean de Brunes 1604); Schorn-
Schütte, *Evangelische Geistlichkeit,* 224 (622 books in the library of Johan
Heinrich Caul 1704); Mazauric, *Ferry,* 124 (2,596 books in the library of Paul
Ferry); W. J. van Asselt, "Voetius en Coccejus over de rechtvaardiging" in J. van
Oort et al., eds., *De onbekende Voetius* (Kampen, 1989), 35 (4,777 books in the
library of Voetius 1677).

42. Angelo Turchini, *Clero e fedeli a Rimini in età post-Tridentina* (Rome, 1978),
91–95; Thomas Deutscher, "Seminaries and the Education of Novarese Parish
Priests, 1593–1627," *Journal of Ecclesiastical History* 32 (1981): 314.

43. Judith Maltby, *Prayer Book and People in Elizabethan and Early Stuart England*
(Cambridge, 1998), 166.

44. "[The clergy are those] who teach in the church; who proclaim God's Word; who
translate the Greek and Hebrew language; who distribute help and alms to the
poor." Quoted in Walton, *Zwingli's Theocracy,* 173.

45. *Calvini Opera* 10:21–22; Travers, *Full and plaine declaration,* 139–41, 147, 155,
158–59; *Directory of Church Government; First Book of Discipline,* 106, 111;
Second Book of Discipline, 176, 187–90; Rutgers, *Acta van de Nederlandsche
Synoden,* passim, esp. 16–17; Henderson, *Teaching Office.*

46. Kirk, ed., *Second Book of Discipline,* 84–88; Foster, *Church before the Covenants,* 107–08; O'Day, *English Clergy,* 130; Henderson, *Teaching Office,* chaps.
6–8; Hall, *Faithful Shepherd,* 95–96; Sipallyo, *Akta Synodów Róznowierczych w
Polsce,* vol. 3, passim, esp. 73, 86.

47. Quick, *Synodicon* 1:96; Henderson, *Teaching Office,* 67–70, 115.

48. Spaans, *Haarlem na de Reformatie,* chap. 5; Abels and Wouters, *Nieuw en
ongezien,* part 8; Elliott, "Protestantization," 425ff.; H. A. Enno van Gelder, *Vrijheid en Onvrijheid in de Republiek* (Haarlem, 1947), 143; Hanlon, *Univers des
gens de bien,* 215.

49. Sunshine, "From French Protestantism to the French Reformed Churches,"
154–89; Robert M. Kingdon, "The Deacons of the Reformed Church in Calvin's
Geneva," in *Mélanges d'histoire du XVIe siècle offerts à Henri Meylan* (Geneva,
1970), 81–90.

50. Sunshine, "From French Protestantism to the French Reformed Churches," 160–
216; Anjubault and H. Chardon, eds., *Recueil de pièces inédites pour servir
à l'histoire de la Réforme et de la Ligue dans le Maine* (Le Mans, 1867), 18;
Garrisson-Estèbe, *Protestants du Midi,* 90–91; Hanlon, *Univers de gens de bien,*
215.

51. *First Book of Discipline,* 178–79; Kirk, ed., *Second Book of Discipline,* 98–99,
207–08; Rosalind Mitchison, "North and South: The Development of the Gulf in
Poor Law Practice," in Houston and Whyte, eds., *Scottish Society,* 200–07; Elliott,
"Protestantization," 366–78; Spaans, *Haarlem,* chap. 6; Abels and Wouters,

Nieuw en Ongezien, part 7; Charles H. Parker, Jr., *The Reformation of Community: Social Welfare and Calvinist Charity in Holland, 1572–1620* (Cambridge, 1998); van Deursen, *Bavianen en Slijkgeuzen,* chap. 6.

52. McKee, *Calvin on the Diaconate,* 218–21; Doumergue, *Calvin* 5:305–06; Parker, *Reformation of Community,* 120; Groenhuis, *Predikanten,* 22, 40.

53. The fullest histories of the elder's office and duties in Reformed churches are A. van Ginkel, *De Ouderling* (Amsterdam, 1975); Henderson, *The Scottish Ruling Elder.*

54. Fills, *Lawes and Statutes of Geneva,* 8vo; Aymon, *Tous les synodes* 1:111; Isaac d'Huisseau, *La Discipline des Eglises Reformées de France* (Geneva, 1666), 30; Abels and Wouters, *Nieuw en ongezien* 1:371–76; Denis, *Eglises d'étrangers,* 491; van Deursen, *Bavianen en Slijkgeuzen,* 83–92; Brandt, *History of the Reformation in and about the Low Countries* 2:66; Foster, *Church before the Covenants,* 68–71; Münch, *Zucht und Ordnung,* 125; Schorn-Schutte, *Evangelische Geistlichkeit,* 60–61; Morrill, "Church in England," 155–58; A. Bauwens and D. van der Bauwhede, eds., *Acta van de Kerkeraad van de Nederduits Gereformeerde Gemeente te Sluis 1578–1587* (Torhout, 1986), 19–20.

55. W. H. Makey, "The Elders of Stow, Liberton, Canongate and St. Cuthberts in the Mid-Seventeenth Century," *Records of the Scottish Church History Society* 17 (1970): 155–67; Schilling, "Calvinistiche Presbyterien im Städten der Frühneuzeit," 423, 429–32; Archives Communales de Lunel, GG 34 (list of the elders of Lunel that reveals one nobleman, a notary, a merchant, a receiver of the *grenier à sel,* two men of unidentified status claiming the honorific "sieur," and four master artisans); Garrisson-Estèbe, *Protestants du Midi,* 92–102; Bertheau, "Consistoire dans les Eglises réformées du Moyen-Poitou," 350–59; "A Montpellier au XVIe siècle d'après les registres d'état civil huguenot," *Bulletin de la Société de l'Histoire du Protestantisme Français* 48 (1899): 86; Chareyre, "Consistoire de Nîmes," 161; Schmitt, *Dorf und Religion,* 55–58; also Abels and Wouters, *Nieuw en ongezien* 1:381–84; Schilling, "Calvinistische Presbyterium Groningen," 224; id., "Reformierte Kirchenzucht als Sozialdisziplinierung? Die Tätigkeit des Emder Presbyteriums in den Jahren 1557–1562," in Schilling and W. Ehbrecht, eds., *Niederlande und Nordwestdeutschland: Studien zur Regional- und Stadtgeschichte Nordwestkontinentaleuropas im Mittelalter und in der Neuzeit* (Cologne, 1983), 270.

56. Paul Münch, "Kirchenzucht und Nachbarschaft: Zur sozialen Problematik des calvinistischen Seniorats um 1600," in E. W. Zeeden and P. T. Lang, eds., *Kirch und Visitation: Beitrage zur Erforschung des frühneuzeitlichen Visitationswesens in Europa* (Stuttgart, 1984), 236–41.

57. Abels and Wouters, *Nieuw en ongezien,* 1:358–60; Herman Roodenburg, *Onder Censuur: De kerkelijke tucht in de gereformeerde gemeente van Amsterdam, 1578–1700* (Hilversum, 1990), 110.

58. The patterns of representation in the continental churches discussed in this paragraph have been determined from Reitsma and van Veen, *Acta der Provinciale et Particuliere Synoden 1576–1620;* Knuttel, *Acta der Particuliere*

Synoden van Zuid-Holland 1621–1700; Bibliothèque de la Société de l'Histoire du Protestantisme Français, MS Auzière 579 (1); Pierre Bolle, *Le Protestant dauphinois et la république des synodes à la veille de la Révocation* (Lyon, 1985), 13; Wolfgang Petri, ed., *Die reformierten klevischen Synoden im 17. Jahrhundert,* 3 vols. (Dusseldorf, 1973–78), vols. 2, 3 passim; Kelm, ed., *Protokolle der reformierten Synoden des Herzogtums Jülich,* 5 and passim; Rosenkranz, ed., *Generalsynodalbuch,* vol. 1, passim. On Scotland: Michael F. Graham, *The Uses of Reform: Godly Discipline and Popular Behavior in Scotland and Beyond, 1560–1610* (Leiden, 1996), 142–43; Foster, *Church before the Covenants,* 88–89; Makey, *Church of the Covenants,* 133–35; Foster, *Bishop and Presbytery,* 72; Henderson, *Scottish Ruling Elder,* 166.

CHAPTER 14. THE EXERCISE OF DISCIPLINE

Bibliographical Note   Published consistory records offer the best view of church discipline in action. Good editions include, in addition to the Genevan records noted in the bibliographical note for chapter 3: Heinz Schilling and Klaus-Dieter Schreiber, eds., *Die Kirchenratsprotokolle der Reformierten Gemeinde Emden 1557–1620,* 2 vols. (Cologne, 1989–92); *Actes du consistoire de l'église française de Threadneedle Street, Londres,* Publications of the Huguenot Society of London 38 and 48 (Frome, 1937, London, 1969); "Papier et registre du consistoire de l'église du Mans réformée selon l'évangile," in Anjubault and H. Chardon, eds., *Recueil de pièces inédites pour servir à l'histoire de la Réforme et de la Ligue dans le Maine* (Le Mans, 1867); A. Bauwens and D. van der Bauwhede, eds., *Acta van de Kerkeraad van de Nederduits Gereformeerde Gemeente te Sluis 1578–1587* (Torhout, 1986); Henry Paton, ed., *Dundonald Parish Records: The Session Book of Dundonald 1602–1731* (Edinburgh, 1936); James Kirk, ed., *Stirling Presbytery Records, 1581–1587* (Edinburgh, 1981); "Registre des advis du Consistoire de l'Eglize Réformée de Blois," in Paul de Félice, ed., *La Réforme en Blaisois: Documents inédits* (Orléans, 1885; repr. Marseille, 1979).

    Two important articles pioneered the quantitative study of consistory registers to examine church discipline in action: J. Estèbe and B. Vogler, "Le genèse d'une société protestante: Etude comparée de quelques registres consistoriaux languedociens et palatins vers 1600," *Annales: E.S.C.* 31 (1976): 362–88; and E. William Monter, "The Consistory of Geneva, 1559–1569," *Bibliothèque d'Humanisme et Renaissance* 38 (1976): 467–84. The most important studies that have followed in their wake include Heinz Schilling, "Reformierte Kirchenzucht als Sozialdisziplinierung? Die Tätigkeit des Emder Presbyteriums in den Jahren 1557–1562," in Schilling and W. Ehbrecht, eds., *Niederlande und Nordwestdeutschland: Studien zur Regional- und Stadtgeschichte Nordwestkontinentaleuropas im Mittelalter und in der Neuzeit* (Cologne, 1983), 261–327; id., "Calvinism and the Making of the Modern Mind: Ecclesiastical Discipline of Public and Private Sin from the Sixteenth to the Nineteenth Century," in his *Civic Calvinism in Northwestern Germany and the Netherlands* (Kirksville, Mo., 1991), 41–68; Stephen J. Davies, "Law and Order in Stirlingshire 1637–

1747" (Ph.D. diss., University of St Andrews, 1984); Mathieu Gerardus Spiertz, "Die Ausübung der Zucht in der Ijsselstadt Deventer in den Jahren 1592–1619 im Vergleich zu den Untersuchungen im Languedoc und in der Kurpfalz," *Rheinische Vierteljahrsblätter* 19 (1985): 139–72; Raymond A. Mentzer, *"Disciplina nervus ecclesiae:* The Calvinist Reform of Morals at Nîmes," *Sixteenth Century Journal* 18 (1987): 89–115; Philippe Chareyre, "Le Consistoire de Nîmes 1561–1685" (Thèse de doctorat d'état, Université Paul Valéry, 1987); Martin Ingram, *Church Courts, Sex and Marriage in England, 1570–1640* (Cambridge, 1987); Geoffrey Parker, "The 'Kirk by Law Established' and the Origins of 'The Taming of Scotland': St Andrews 1559–1600," in Leah Leneman, ed., *Perspectives in Scottish Social History* (Aberdeen, 1988), 1–32; Herman Roodenburg, *Onder censuur: De kerkelijke tucht in de gereformeerde gemeente van Amsterdam, 1578–1700* (Hilversum, 1990); Heinrich Richard Schmidt, *Dorf und Religion: Reformierte Sittenzucht in Berner Landgemeinden der Frühen Neuzeit* (Stuttgart, 1995); Michael F. Graham, *The Uses of Reform: Godly Discipline and Popular Behavior in Scotland and Beyond, 1560–1610* (Leiden, 1996). There is an excellent bibliography and overview of the relevant literature in Heinz Schilling, ed., *Kirchenzucht und Sozialdisziplinierung im frühneuzeitlichen Europa,* Zeitschrift für Historische Forschung Beiheft 16 (Berlin, 1994), together with a number of good shorter essays. Another excellent collection of essays is Raymond Mentzer, ed., *Sin and the Calvinists: Morals Control and the Consistory in the Reformed Tradition* (Kirksville, Mo., 1994). All of this work must be interpreted in the light of the crucial discoveries reported in Judith Pollmann, "Off the Record: Problems in the Quantification of Calvinist Church Discipline, *Sixteenth Century Journal,* forthcoming. In a more thematic vein, Rosalind Mitchison and Leah Leneman, *Sexuality and Social Control: Scotland 1660–1780* (Oxford, 1989), and Jeffrey R. Watt, *The Making of Modern Marriage: Matrimonial Control and the Rise of Sentiment in Neuchâtel, 1550–1800* (Ithaca, 1992), stand out.

1. *Guillaume Farel,* 713n; Mentzer, *"Disciplina,"* 89n.
2. The most important of these studies are listed above in this chapter's bibliographical overview. These form the chief basis of this chapter, although I have also relied upon numerous other studies and direct examination of some consistory records.
3. Pollmann, "Off the Record," 5, 17; Aymon, *Tous les synodes* 1:141; Bertheau, "Consistoire dans les Eglises de Moyen-Poitou," 527; Roodenburg, *Onder Censuur,* 22.
4. During the second half of the seventeenth century Amsterdam's preachers preached vigorously against the sin of dancing, added admonitions against it to the catechism, and urged believers during house visits not to send their children to dancing classes. Nevertheless, the records of the Reformed *kerkeraad* do not contain a single case of a church member being admonished by the body for dancing. Roodenburg, *Onder Censuur,* 322. Similarly, the elders and deacons of

Saint Andrews had the power to fine blasphemers on the spot, but no records of any such fines are known to have survived, and the town's kirk session records contain almost no cases of blasphemy. It is unclear if this is because the elders did nothing about the offense or did not record their fines in the kirk session records. Parker, "'Kirk by Law Established'," 16–17.

5. Heinz Schilling, "'History of Crime' or 'History of Sin'?—Some Reflections on the Social History of Early Modern Church Discipline," in Kouri and Scott, eds., *Politics and Society in Reformation Europe,* 289–310. Schilling draws here on remarks by Elton in his "Introduction: Crime and the Historian," in J. S. Cockburn, ed., *Crime in England 1550–1800* (London, 1977), 2–6.

6. Moltmann, *Pezel,* 157; Calvin, *Institutes,* IV.12.v; Cochrane, ed., *Reformed Confessions,* 177.

7. William Ames, *Conscience, with the Power and Cases thereof, divided into Five Bookes* (London, 1643), book 4, chap. 29, 86; Roodenburg, *Onder Censuur,* 139.

8. Roodenburg, *Onder Censuur,* 125–26; Watt, *Making of Modern Marriage,* 52.

9. Anjubault and Chardon, *Recueil de pièces inédites,* 18–19; Fills, *Lawes and Statutes of Geneva,* 8, 16–17; Beza, *Correspondance* 14:268; Roodenburg, *Onder Censuur,* 109, 118; Henderson, *Scottish Ruling Elder,* 109; M. Oudot de Dainville, "Le consistoire de Ganges à la fin du XVIe siècle," *Revue d'histoire de l'Eglise de France* 18 (1932): 466; Helga Schnable-Schüle, "Calvinistische Kirchenzucht in Württemberg? Zur Theorie und Praxis der württembergischen Kirchenkonvente," *Zeitschrift für Württembergische Landesgeschichte* 49 (1990): 181.

10. Herman Roodenburg, "Predestinatie en groepscharisma: Een sociologische verkenning van de conflicten tussen Calvinisten en andere gelovigen in de Republiek c.1580–c.1650," *Amsterdams Sociologisch Tijdschrift* 8 (1981–82): 267; Raymond A. Mentzer, "Morals and Moral Regulation in Protestant France," *Journal of Interdisciplinary History* 31 (2000): 1; Alice C. Carter, *The English Reformed Church in Amsterdam in the Seventeenth Century* (Amsterdam, 1964), 159; Pettegree, *Foreign Protestant Communities,* 188; Stauffenegger, *Eglise et société* 2:865.

11. Davies, "Law and Order in Stirlingshire," 83–86.

12. Graham, *Uses of Reform,* 211, 229, 254, 326, 329, 333; Pettegree, *Foreign Protestant Communities,* 188; Vuilleumier, *Histoire de l'Eglise réformée du Pays de Vaud* 2:728.

13. Chareyre, "Consistoire de Nîmes," 372–80; Mentzer, "Marking the Taboo: Excommunication in French Reformed Churches," in Mentzer, ed., *Sin and the Calvinists,* 102; *Registres du consistoire de Genève* 1:xxiii; Beardslee, ed., *Reformed Dogmatics,* 146.

14. Parker, "'Kirk by Law Established'," 12–13; Graham, *Uses of Reform,* 44–48 and passim.

15. Schmidt, *Dorf und Religion,* 49–50.

16. Estèbe and Vogler, "Genèse d'une société protestante," 365; Abels and Wouters, *Nieuw en ongezien,* 2:124; *Actes du consistoire de l'Eglise française de Threadneedle Street* 1:12–13, 77; Chareyre, "'The Great Difficulties One Must Bear to

Follow Jesus Christ': Morality at Sixteenth Century Nîmes," in Mentzer, ed., *Sin and the Calvinists,* 79–80.

17. See above, 168–69, 215; Pfister, "Reformierte Sittenzucht"; Pettegree, *Foreign Protestant Communities,* 164–81, esp. 174; Kaplan, *Calvinists and Libertines,* esp. chaps. 3, 4.

18. Van Lieburg, *Nadere Reformatie in Utrecht,* 76; Roodenburg, *Onder Censuur,* 139. The connection between Melville's work in Saint Andrews and the spike in consistorial activity in the 1590s is shown by Parker, "'Kirk by Law Established'," 15–16.

19. Stauffenegger, *Eglise et société* 2:861.

20. This and the following paragraphs summarize the findings of Graham, *Uses of Reform;* Foster, *Church before the Covenants,* chaps. 4–5; Davies, "Law and Order in Stirlingshire"; Parker, "'Kirk by Law Established'"; Smout, *History of the Scottish People,* 74–93; John Di Folco, "Discipline and Welfare in the Mid-Seventeenth Century Scots Parish," *Records of the Scottish Church History Society* 19 (1975): 169–83; Bruce Lenman, "The Limits of Godly Discipline in the Early Modern Period with Particular Reference to England and Scotland," in Kaspar von Greyerz, ed., *Religion and Society in Early Modern Europe 1500–1800* (London, 1984), 124–45.

21. Graham, *Uses of Reform,* esp. 267, 276, 198–99.

22. Foster, *Church before the Covenants,* 75–76, 98–99.

23. Davies, "Law and Order in Stirlingshire," chap. 3, esp. 104–20, 131–34.

24. Anjubault and Chardon, *Recueil de pièces inédites,* passim.

25. These figures are calculated from the numbers provided in Chareyre, "Great Difficulties," passim.

26. Chareyre, "Consistoire de Nîmes," 86–87, 483, 509; Garrisson-Estèbe, *Protestants du Midi,* part 3; Graham, *Uses of Reform,* chap. 9; Oudot de Dainville, "Consistoire de Ganges"; Mentzer, *"Disciplina."*

27. Figures calculated from Chareyre, "Great Difficulties," 64. For the city's population, Benedict, *Huguenot Population,* 147.

28. Graham, *Uses of Reform,* chap. 9, esp. 341; Jean Plattard, "Un étudiant écossais en France en 1665–1666: Journal de voyage de Sir John Lauder," *Mémoires de la Société des Antiquaires de l'Ouest,* 3d ser., 12 (1935): 72; Bertheau, "Consistoire dans les Eglises de Moyen-Poitou," 527ff.; Gueneau, "Protestants du Centre," 347; Alfred Leroux, "L'Eglise réformée de Bordeaux de 1660 à 1670 (d'après le cinquième registre du Consistoire)," *Bulletin de la Société de l'Histoire du Protestantisme Français* 69 (1920): 177–208, esp. 190–91; Elisabeth Labrousse-Goguel, "L'Eglise réformée du Carla en 1672–1673 d'après le registre des déliberations de son Consistoire," *Bulletin de la Société de l'Histoire du Protestantisme Français* 106 (1960): 22–53, 191–231; 107 (1961): 223–72; de Félice, ed., *Réforme en Blaisois;* Archives Communales d'Anduze (at Archives Départementales du Gard), GG 45 (consistory register of Anduze, 1659–73).

29. The bulk of this paragraph rests on Roodenburg's exemplary *Onder censuur,* esp. 281, 286, 321–23, 377–81. For the evidence about other Dutch localities:

Manon van der Heijden, "Secular and Ecclesiastical Marriage Control: Rotterdam, 1550–1700," in A. Schuurman and P. Spierenburg, eds., *Private Domain, Public Inquiry: Families and Life-Styles in the Netherlands and Europe, 1550 to the Present* (Hilversum, 1996), 45, 53; Marijke Gijswijt-Hofstra, "Toverij voor Zeeuwse Magistraten en Kerkeraden, Zestiende tot Twintigste Eeuw," in Gijswijt-Hofstra and W. Frijhoff, eds., *Nederland Betoverd: Toverij en Hekserij van de Veertiende tot in de Twintigste Eeuw* (Amsterdam, 1987), 104.

30. Schilling, "Calvinism and the Making," 44; figures for Stettlen computed from the computerized statistical appendix to Schmidt, *Dorf und Religion.* Stettlen's total population stood at roughly 250 around 1600 and 300 around 1680. Unfortunately, Schmidt tabulated his data according to the number of distinct offenses noted in the records, not to the number of individuals called before the body, making comparison between its convocation rates and those of the consistories listed in table 14.1 difficult.

31. Parker, "Success and Failure," 78n; Chareyre, "Consistoire de Nîmes," 725ff; Henderson, *Scottish Ruling Elder,* 132; Davies, "Law and Order in Stirlingshire," 94.

32. Volker Manuth, "Denomination and Iconography: The Choice of Subject Matter in the Biblical Paintings of the Rembrandt Circle," *Simiolus* 22 (1993–94), 242. For similar cases: Foster, *Church before the Covenants,* 98; Anjubault and Chardin, *Recueil,* 7; Chareyre, "Consistoire de Nîmes," 571–72.

33. Estèbe and Vogler, "Genèse," 379–83, 384–85; Watt, "Reception," 94; Roodenburg, *Onder censuur,* 338–44; A. C. Anduze GG 45, fos. 52, 79–80, 98, 108, 123, 142; Alfred Soman and Elisabeth Labrousse, "Le registre consistoriale de Coutras, 1582–1584," *Bulletin de la Société de l'Histoire du Protestantisme Français* 126 (1980): 220; Chareyre, "Consistoire de Nîmes," 509–19.

34. André Biéler, *La pensée économique et sociale de Calvin* (Geneva, 1959); id., *L'humanisme social de Calvin* (Geneva, 1961), esp. 53. In the vast literature on Calvin's economic ideas and their place in the larger history of Christian teachings on this subject, R. H. Tawney, *Religion and the Rise of Capitalism* (New York, 1926); Henri Hauser, "Les idées économiques de Calvin," in *La modernité du XVIe siècle* (Paris, 1963), 105–33; John T. Noonan, Jr., *The Scholastic Analysis of Usury* (Cambridge, Mass., 1957); and Jacob Viner, "Religious Thought and Economic Society: Four Chapters of an Unfinished Work," *History of Political Economy* 10 (1978): 1–192, are also particularly useful. For the views of Bullinger and Viret, see Bullinger, *Decades* 2:40–44; Linder, *Viret,* 100.

35. Garrisson-Estèbe, *Protestants du Midi,* 304; Vogler, "Vie religieuse en pays rhénan," 1030–31; Aymon, *Tous les synodes* 1:10–11, 26, 75, 2:565; S. Cuperus, *Kerkelijk Leven der Hervormden in Friesland tijdens de Republiek,* 2 vols. (Leeuwarden, 1916–20), 2:81; R. B. Evenhuis, *Ook dat was Amsterdam,* 5 vols. (Amsterdam, 1965–78), 2:156; Ernst Beins, "Die Wirtschaftsethik der Calvinistischen Kirche der Niederlande 1565–1650," *Archief voor Kerkgeschiedenis* 24 (1931): 82–156; H. M. Robertson, *Aspects of the Rise of Economic Individualism: A Criticism of Max Weber and His School* (Cambridge, 1933),

chap. 4; Tawney, *Religion and the Rise of Capitalism,* chap. 4. Godefridus Udemans, *'t Geestelyck Roer van 't Coopmans Schip* (Dordrecht, 1640), 182–83, warned against selling slaves to Spanish or Portuguese masters and urged that slaves be emancipated once they became good Christians.

36. Mark Valeri, "Religion, Discipline, and the Economy in Calvin's Geneva," *Sixteenth Century Journal* 28 (1997): 128–30; Davis, "Strikes and Salvation"; Evenhuis, *Ook dat was Amsterdam* 2:145–56; Smout, *History of Scottish People,* 84–85.

37. Aymon, *Tous les synodes* 1:38; Chareyre, "'Great Difficulties'," 83; Soman and Labrousse, "Registre consistorial de Coutras," 194–200.

38. This paragraph is based primarily on Watt, *Making of Modern Marriage.* See also Steven Ozment, *When Fathers Ruled: Family Life in Reformation Europe* (Cambridge, Mass., 1983), 80–99; Roderick Phillips, *Untying the Knot: A Short History of Divorce* (Cambridge, 1991), chap. 1; Kingdon, *Adultery and Divorce,* passim; Joel Harrington, *Reordering Marriage and Society in Reformation Germany* (Cambridge, 1995), esp. 87–91, 167–69, 197–203, 270.

39. Harrington, *Reordering Marriage,* 72; Mentzer, "Marking the Taboo," 124–25; John Lee Thompson, *John Calvin and the Daughters of Sarah: Women in Regular and Exceptional Roles in the Exegesis of Calvin, His Predecessors, and His Contemporaries* (Geneva, 1992). Cf. André Biéler, *L'Homme et la femme dans la morale Calviniste* (Geneva, 1963); Jane Dempsey Douglass, *Women, Freedom, and Calvin* (Philadelphia, 1985).

40. Naphy, *Calvin and the Consolidation,* table 13; Schilling, "Calvinism and the Making," 48; Mentzer, *"Disciplina,"* 109–10.

41. Schmidt, *Dorf und Religion,* 241–89, esp. 247–50, 284–85; E. William Monter, "Women in Calvinist Geneva (1550–1800)," *Signs* 6 (1980): 191. Similar findings in Harrington, *Reordering Marriage and Society,* 263.

42. Monter, "Consistory of Geneva," 479–80, where the percentage of women excommunicates matches almost exactly the percentage of women summoned before the consistory as revealed by Naphy, *Calvin and the Consolidation,* table 13; Mentzer, "Marking the Taboo," 124–25; Watt, *Making of Modern Marriage,* 100; Davies, "Law and Order in Stirlingshire," 122; Isabel V. Hull, *Sexuality, State, and Civil Society in Germany, 1700–1815* (Ithaca, 1996), 83; Harrington, *Reordering Marriage and Society,* 226–27, 230; Monter, "Women in Calvinist Geneva"; Schilling, "Calvinism and the Making," 48; Graham, *Uses of Reform,* 286.

43. Oudot de Dainville, "Consistoire de Ganges," 470.

44. Kevin C. Robbins, *City on the Ocean Sea: La Rochelle, 1530–1650* (Leiden, 1997), 221; Graham, *Uses of Reform,* chap. 7; Davies, "Law and Order in Stirlingshire," 126–27; Vuilleumier, *Histoire de l'Eglise réformée du Pays de Vaud* 2:732; Murdock, "International Calvinism and the Reformed Churches of Hungary," 249–50.

45. Hull, *Sexuality, State, and Civil Society,* 78n; *Acts of the Parliament of Scotland* 3:212; Kingdon, *Adultery and Divorce,* 116–17; Garrisson-Estèbe, *Protestants du Midi,* 297; Sehling, ed., *Evangelische Kirchenordnungen* 14:487;

G. F. Baron thoe Schwartzenberg en Hohenlansberg, ed., *Groot Placaat en Charter-Boek van Vriesland,* 5 vols. (Leeuwarden, 1768–93) 4:580; Frank Konersmann, "Disziplinierung und Verchristlichung von Sexualität und Ehe in Pfalz-Zweibrücken im 16. und 17. Jahrhundert," *Blatter für pfälzische Kirchengeschichte und religiöse Volkskunde* 58 (1991): 30; Schmidt, *Dorf und Religion,* 192; G. L. Haskins, *Law and Authority in Early Massachusetts* (New York, 1960), 80; Keith Thomas, "The Puritans and Adultery: The Act of 1650 Reconsidered," in D. Pennington and K. Thomas, eds., *Puritans and Revolutionaries: Essays in Seventeenth-Century History Presented to Christopher Hill* (Oxford, 1978), 257, 271; Murdock, "International Calvinism and the Reformed Church of Hungary," 283; *Groot Placaet-Boeck* 1:334–35, 351, 592–93, 596, 3:507.

46. Kingdon, *Adultery and Divorce,* 117–19, 179; Eugène Choisy, *L'état chrétien calviniste à Genève au temps de Théodore de Bèze* (Geneva, 1902), 203–12, esp. 203; Beza, *Correspondance* 4:138, 140; Vogler, *Vie religieuse en pays rhenan,* 976; Ridley, *Knox,* 417; K. M. Brown, "In Search of the Godly Magistrate in Reformation Scotland," *Journal of Ecclesiastical History* 40 (1989): 568–69; Graham, *Uses of Reform,* 175; Davies, "Law and Order in Stirlingshire," 104–20; Thomas, "Puritans and Adultery," 257; Hsia, *Social Discipline,* 145; Richard van Dülmen, *Theatre of Horror: Crime and Punishment in Early Modern Germany* (Cambridge, 1990), 55 and appendices.

47. Pfister, "Reformierte Sittenzucht," 307–14.

48. Schilling, "Calvinism and the Making," 58–59; Roodenburg, *Onder Censuur,* 342–43, 354–61; Graham, *Uses of Reform,* 267, 290–98; K. M. Brown, *Bloodfeud in Scotland 1573–1625: Violence, Justice and Politics in an Early Modern Society* (Edinburgh, 1986). Other studies that reach a similar conclusion are Estèbe and Vogler, "Genèse d'une société protestante"; Labrousse-Goguel, "Eglise réformée du Carla," esp. 234ff., but cf. Gregory Hanlon, "Les rituels de l'aggression en Aquitaine au XVIIe siècle," *Annales: E.S.C.* 40 (1985): 249–50, which questions the consistory's success in reducing violence but credits it with effectively promoting sobriety. Schmidt, *Dorf und Religion,* likewise finds little evidence of increased control of violent impulses.

49. See above; Davies, "Law and Order in Stirlingshire," 87; Mitchison and Leneman, *Sexuality and Social Control,* esp. 147; Brown, "In Search of the Godly Magistrate," 569, 580. Schmidt, *Dorf und Religion,* again questions the extent of change in this domain. More studies of consistorial discipline need to complement their investigation with parish register evidence in order to allow us confidently to gauge the intensity and efficacy of consistorial oversight more confidently.

50. Schmidt, *Dorf und Religion;* Estèbe and Vogler, "Genèse d'une société protestante."

51. Christian Tümpel, "Die Reformation und die Kunst der Niederlande," in Werner Hoffman, ed., *Luther und die Folgen für die Kunst,* exhibition catalogue (Munich, 1983), 317; id., "Jordaens, a Protestant Artist in a Catholic Stronghold: Notes on Protestant Artists in Catholic Centres," in *Jordaens (1593–1678),* exhibi-

tion catalogue, 2 vols. (Antwerp, 1993), 1:31–37; Volker Manuth, "Denomination and Iconography: The Choice of Subject Matter in the Biblical Paintings of the Rembrandt Circle," *Simiolus* 22 (1993–94): 240; Philip Benedict, "Calvinism as a Culture? Preliminary Remarks on Calvinism and the Visual Arts," in Paul Corby Finney, ed., *Seeing beyond the Word: Visual Arts and the Calvinist Tradition* (Grand Rapids, 1998), 19–45, esp. 36; *Masters of Light: Dutch Painters in Utrecht during the Golden Age,* exhibition catalogue (Baltimore, 1997), 71, and catalogue entries 8, 19; Chareyre, "Consistoire de Nîmes," 571–72.

52. Benedict, *Faith and Fortunes,* 199–202.
53. Siegfried Müller, "Die Konfessionalisierung in der Grafschaft Oldenburg—Untersuchungen zur 'Sozialdisziplinierung' einer bäuerlichen Gesellschaft in der Frühen Neuzeit," *Archiv für Reformationsgeschichte* 86 (1995): 195.
54. Benedict, *Huguenot Population,* 95–99. While it is also tempting to compare illegitimacy rates and statistics about prenuptial conceptions between countries of different religions, broader comparisons of this sort are likely to mislead because it is known that in early modern Europe variations in local courtship patterns and differing attitudes about when it was appropriate for engaged couples to begin to engage in sex made for great regional disparities in these statistics that appear to be unrelated to the religious affiliation of the region in question. See here Peter Laslett, Karla Oosterveen, and Richard M. Smith, eds., *Bastardy and Its Comparative History: Studies in the History of Illegitimacy and Marital Nonconformism in Britain, France, Germany, Sweden, North America, Jamaica and Japan* (Cambridge, Mass., 1980); Martine Segalen, *Love and Power in the Peasant Family* (Chicago, 1983), 21–24; Jan Kok, "The Moral Nation: Illegitimacy and Bridal Pregnancy in the Netherlands from 1600 to the Present," *Economic and Social History in the Netherlands* 2 (1990): 7–36. For some anecdotal evidence of greater moral uprightness among the Huguenots, see Chareyre, "Consistoire de Nîmes," 424.
55. Schaab, "Obrigkeitlicher Calvinismus," 75–76; observations about Amiens based on ongoing research by the author.

CHAPTER 15. THE PRACTICE OF PIETY

Bibliographical Note   The literature on Reformed devotional life and religious culture is extremely uneven. The abundance of Puritan diaries, the exceptionally rich tradition of Puritan studies launched in the United States by Perry Miller's still rewarding *The New England Mind: The Seventeenth Century* (New York, 1939), and the inspiring example of anthropologically informed history provided by Keith Thomas's monumental *Religion and the Decline of Magic* (New York, 1975), have combined to generate a rich literature about English and North American religious life, especially that of the godly. Within this literature, Charles E. Hambrick-Stowe, *The Practice of Piety: Puritan Devotional Disciplines in Seventeenth-Century New England* (Chapel Hill, 1982); Paul S. Seaver, *Wallington's World: A Puritan Artisan in Seventeenth-Century London*

(Stanford, 1985); Charles L. Cohen, *God's Caress: The Psychology of Puritan Religious Experience* (Oxford, 1986); Kaspar von Greyerz, *Vorsehungsglaube und Kosmologie: Studien zu englischen Selbstzeugnissen des 17. Jahrhunderts* (Göttingen, 1990); David D. Hall, *Worlds of Wonder, Days of Judgment: Popular Religious Belief in Early New England* (Cambridge, Mass., 1990), Ronald Hutton, *The Rise and Fall of Merry England: The Ritual Year 1400–1700* (Oxford, 1996); and David Cressy, *Birth, Marriage and Death: Ritual, Religion and the Life-Cycle in Tudor and Stuart England* (Oxford, 1997), stand out as innovative and illuminating works about worship and belief among the mass of the population. Collinson, *The Religion of Protestants,* mentioned above, chapter 8, is also fundamental. Two excellent recent studies have begun the exploration of Scottish religious culture: Marilyn J. Westerkamp, *Triumph of the Laity: Scots-Irish Piety and the Great Awakening, 1625–1750* (Oxford, 1988), and Leigh Eric Schmidt, *Holy Fairs: Scottish Communions and American Revivals in the Early Modern Period* (Princeton, 1989), while the old work of G. D. Henderson, *Religious Life in Seventeenth-Century Scotland* (Cambridge, 1937), remains illuminating on that subject. David George Mullan, *Scottish Puritanism, 1590–1638* (Oxford, 2000), is a major contribution that reached me too late to be extensively cited.

For Europe's other Reformed churches, the literature is far spottier, a consequence of the absence of as rich a set of autobiographical documents and of the Reformed tradition's paucity of those kinds of voluntary religious practices that leave behind copious traces for the historian and have sparked so much of the excellent recent work on Catholic popular religion. Three noteworthy exceptions of fundamental importance exist: Bernard Vogler, "Vie religieuse en pays rhénan dans la seconde moitié du XVIe siècle" (Lille: Service de Reproduction des Thèses, 1974), the relevant chapters of van Deursen, *Bavianen en Slijkgeuzen* (see chapter 10), and significant portions of Henri Vuilleumier's vast and authoritative *Histoire de l'Eglise réformée du pays de Vaud sous le régime bernois,* 4 vols. (Lausanne, 1927–33). Marie-Louise von Wartburg-Ambühl, *Alphabetisierung und Lektüre: Untersuchung am Beispiel einer ländlichen Region im 17. und 18. Jahrhundert* (Bern, 1981); R. A. Houston, *Scottish Literacy and the Scottish Identity: Illiteracy and Society in Scotland and Northern England, 1600–1800* (Cambridge, 1985); Engelina Petronella de Booy, *Kweekhoven der Wijsheid: Basis- en vervolgonderwijs in de steden van de provincie Utrecht van 1580 tot het begin der 19e eeuw* (Zutphen, 1980); and Margaret Spufford, *Small Books and Pleasant Histories: Popular Fiction and Its Readership in Seventeenth-Century England* (Athens, Ga., 1981), are important studies of schooling, book ownership, and reading practices. Certain of the essays in Benedict, *Faith and Fortunes of France's Huguenots* (see chapter 11) attempt to work outward from patterns of book ownership and the literature of piety to capture broader elements of religious experience. Other recent studies that illustrate the potential of work in this mode include Marianne Carbonnier-Burkard, "Les manuels réformés de préparation à la mort," *Revue de l'Histoire des Religions*

217 (2000): 363–80, and the relevant essays in Bruce Gordon and Peter Marshall, eds., *The Place of the Dead: Death and Remembrance in Late Medieval and Early Modern Europe* (Cambridge, 2000).

1. Jurieu, *Traité de la dévotion* (Rouen, 1675), 184.
2. *Passevent parisien, Respondant à Pasquin Romain: De la vie de ceux qui sont allez demourer à Genève, et se disent vivre selon la réformation de l'Evangile* (Paris, 1556; repr. Paris, 1875). On this work, see also Vuilleumier, *Histoire de l'Eglise réformée du Pays de Vaud* 1:323; Charles Lénient, *La satire en France, ou la littérature militante au XVIe siècle*, 3d ed., 2 vols. (Paris, 1886), 1:185–88, 229–31.
3. *Passevent parisien*, 26–28
4. Ibid., 74–75.
5. Ibid., 11–13.
6. Ibid., 70–71.
7. Ibid., 72–73.
8. Quoted in Cressy, *Birth, Marriage, and Death*, 128.
9. Beza, *Correspondance* 12:195.
10. Hollweg, *Augsburger Reichstag von 1566*, 104–05; Abels and Wouters, *Nieuw en ongezien* 2:171–2; Evenhuis, *Amsterdam* 3:118–27; Münch, "Reformation of Life," in L. Laeyendecker et al., eds., *Experiences and Explanations*, 46–47; above, 469–70; Hall, *Worlds of Wonder*, 58–60; Gaberel, *Histoire de l'Eglise de Genève* 3:45–47; *Farel*, 615.
11. Hall, *Worlds of Wonder*, 167–72, esp. 167; Hambrick-Stowe, *Practice of Piety*, 100–02; de Félice, *Protestants d'autrefois* 1:156–74.
12. Vuilleumier, *Histoire de l'Eglise réformée du Pays de Vaud* 1:329–40; Murdock, "International Calvinism and the Reformed Church of Hungary," 176ff.; Laura L. Becker, "Ministers vs. Laymen: The Singing Controversy in Puritan New England, 1720–1740," *New England Quarterly* 55 (1982): 82–96.
13. Chevalier, *Prêcher*, 47; T. C. Smout, "Born Again at Cambuslang: New Evidence on Popular Religion and Literacy in Eighteenth-Century Scotland," *Past & Present* 97 (1982): 123; "Extrait du journal manuscrit ou diaire autographe du ministre Jacques Merlin, pasteur à La Rochelle," in Gaberel, *Histoire de l'Eglise de Genève* 2:154. C. A. van Swigchem, T. Brouwer, and W. van Os, *Een huis voor het woord: Het protestantse kerkinterieur in Nederland tot 1900* (The Hague, 1984), reproduces a number of paintings of sermons in progress.
14. Van Swigchem, Brouwer, and van Os, *Huis voor het woord*; M. D. Ozinga, *De Protestantsche Kerkbouw in Nederland van Hervorming tot Fransche Tijd* (Amsterdam, 1929); George Hay, *The Architecture of the Scottish Reformation* (Oxford, 1957); Georg Germann, *Der protestantische Kirchenbau in der Schweiz von der Reformation bis zur Romantik* (Zurich, 1963); Finney, ed., *Seeing beyond the Word*, 49–82, 133–62, 301–42, 429–504; T. J. Saxby, *The Quest for the New Jerusalem: Jean de Labadie and the Labadists, 1610–1744* (Dordrecht, 1987), 107.

NOTES TO PAGES 497–502

15. *Registres de la Compagnie des Pasteurs* 4:181; de Félice, *Protestants d'autrefois* 1:40–50; Vuilleumier, *Histoire de l'Eglise réformée du Pays de Vaud* 2:331–32. Richard Gough organized his *History of Myddle,* ed. David Hey (London, 1981), around the story of the families in the village and organized it in the order of the pews in which they sat in church. It is unclear whether or not seating by status appeared in the other Reformed churches.

16. Archives Communales de Sumène, GG 13; Saxby, *Quest for New Jerusalem,* 112.

17. Vogler, "Vie religieuse en pays rhénan," 650–67; Leah Leneman, "'Prophaning' the Lord's Day: Sabbath Breach in Early Modern Scotland," *History* 74 (1989): 229.

18. David Beck, *Spiegel van mijn leven; een Haags dagboek uit 1624,* ed. S. E. Veldhuijzen (Hilversum, 1993); Chevalier, *Prêcher,* 24.

19. *Registres de la Compagnie des Pasteurs* 1:14; Watt, "Reception of the Reformation in Valangin," 95; Vogler, "Vie religieuse en pays rhénan," 656–67; Foster, *Church before the Covenants,* 177; van Deursen, *Bavianen en Slijkgeuzen,* 169; Schmidt, *Dorf und Religion,* 114; de Félice, *Protestants d'autrefois* 1:98.

20. Fundamental texts in Irmgard Pahl, ed., *Coena Domini I: Die Abendmahlsliturgie der Reformationskirchen im 16./17. Jahrhundert* (Freiburg, 1983). See also Yngve Brilioth, *Eucharistic Faith and Practice: Evangelical and Catholic* (London, 1930), 157ff.; Vuilleumier, *Histoire de l'Eglise réformée du Pays de Vaud* 1:343–45; Sipallyo, *Akta Synodów Rózniowierczych w Polsce* 3:40; Buscay, *Geschichte des Protestantismus in Ungarn,* 111; Murdock, "International Calvinism and the Reformed Church of Hungary," 165ff.

21. Fills, *Lawes and Statutes of Geneva,* 14v, 15; Vuilleumier, *Histoire de l'Eglise réformée du Pays de Vaud* 2:101, 417–18, 453; Henderson, *Scottish Ruling Elder,* 45–55; Frank Delteil, "Institutions et vie de l'Eglise réformée de Pont de Camarès," in Michel Péronnet, ed., *Les églises et leurs institutions au XVIe siècle* (Montpellier, n.d.), 106; Brilioth, *Eucharistic Faith and Practice,* passim; Pettit, *The Heart Prepared;* Benedict, *Faith and Fortunes,* chap. 7; J. C. Wolfart, "Why Was Private Confession so Contentious in Early Seventeenth-Century Lindau?" in Bob Scribner and Trevor Johnson, eds., *Popular Religion in Germany and Central Europe, 1400–1800* (New York, 1996), 140–65; Hans-Christoph Rublack, "Lutherische Beichte und Sozialdisziplinierung," *Archiv für Reformationsgeschichte* 84 (1993): 127–55; Beza, *Correspondance* 14:264.

22. Vuilleumier, *Histoire de l'Eglise réformée du Pays de Vaud* 1:313, 2:416; Schimdt, *Dorf und Religion,* 114; Evenhuis, *Amsterdam* 2:52; Abels and Wouters, *Nieuw en ongezien* 1:209; Illyés, *Egyházfegyelem a magyar református egyházban,* 92; Foster, *Bishop and Presbytery,* 140–41; McMillan, *Worship of Scottish Reformed Church,* 190–97; Horton Davies, *The Worship of the English Puritans* (London, 1948), 206, 213–14; Pruett, *Parish Clergy,* 121–22; Gerraint H. Jenkins, *Literature, Religion and Society in Wales, 1660–1730* (Cardiff, 1978), 69–71.

23. Garrisson-Estèbe, *Protestants du Midi,* 243; Philip Benedict, "La pratique religieuse huguenote: Quelques aperçus messins et comparatifs," in François-Yves Le

Moigne and Gérard Michaux, eds., *Protestants messins et mosellans, XVIe–XXe siècles* (Metz, 1988), 94; van Deursen, *Bavianen en Slijkgeuzen,* 135; Bardgett, *Scotland Reformed,* 158; Vuilleumier, *Histoire de l'Eglise réformée du Pays de Vaud* 2:444; Vogler, "Vie religieuse en pays rhénan," 738ff.; J. P. Boulton, "The Limits of Formal Religion: The Administration of Holy Communion in Late Elizabethan and Early Stuart London," *London Journal* 10 (1984): 135–54; Donald A. Spaeth, "Parsons and Parishioners: Lay-Clerical Conflict and Popular Piety in Wiltshire Villages 1660–1740" (Ph.D. diss., Brown University, 1985), 50–53; Jenkins, *Literature, Religion and Society in Wales,* 71; Arnold Hunt, "The Lord's Supper in Early Modern England," *Past & Present* 161 (1998): 41–45.

24. Schmidt, *Dorf und Religion,* 138; Mentzer, "Marking the Taboo," 119; Carter, *English Reformed Church in Amsterdam,* 186; Spaeth, "Parsons and Parishioners," 57–70; Vogler, "Vie religieuse en pays rhénan," 738, 748–49; Isaac Casaubon, *Ephemerides* (Oxford, 1851), passim.

25. Westerkamp, *Triumph of the Laity,* esp. 24–36; Schmidt, *Holy Fairs,* esp. 27–44, 124–26, 155.

26. This was done in the Church of England except during the Puritan interlude from 1645 to 1660, in the Hungarian churches, in Scotland prior to 1638, and in Amsterdam's church briefly after 1578. Roodenburg, *Onder Censuur,* 161–62; Cressy, *Birth, Marriage, and Death,* 101–03; Murdock, "International Calvinism and the Reformed Church of Hungary," 160; Donaldson, *Making of the Scottish Prayer Book,* 77–78. On the pre-Reformation beliefs, see Jean-Claude Schmitt, *The Holy Greyhound: Guinefort, Healer of Children since the Thirteenth Century* (Cambridge, 1983); John Bossy, *Christianity in the West 1400–1700* (Oxford, 1985), 14–15.

27. Duke, *Reformation and Revolt,* 263; Evenhuis, *Amsterdam* 2:51–52; van Deursen, *Bavianen en Slijkgeuzen,* 140–43; de Félice, *Protestants d'autrefois* 1:182–86; Garrisson-Estèbe, *Protestants du Midi,* 247–48; Gueneau, "Protestants du Centre," 262; Mitchison and Leneman, *Sexuality and Social Control,* 118; Benedict, *Huguenot Population,* 24–26; Cressy, *Birth, Marriage, and Death,* 101. There is evidence of parents waiting as long as five or ten years before baptizing their children in the Netherlands.

28. D'Huisseau, *La discipline des Eglises Reformées de France,* 77; Jacobus Koelman, *De Pligten der Ouderen om Kinderen voor God op te Voeden,* quoted in Jonathan N. Gerstner, *The Thousand Generation Covenant: Dutch Reformed Covenant Theology and Group Identity in Colonial South Africa, 1652–1814* (Leiden, 1991), 130; Cressy, *Birth, Marriage, and Death,* chap. 7, esp. 161–62.

29. David Hackett Fischer, "Forenames and the Family in New England: An Exercise in Historical Onomastics," *Chronos* 1 (1981): 76–111.

30. Benedict, *Huguenot Population,* 80–90; Foster, *Church before the Covenants,* 119; Perrenoud, *Population de Genève,* 383–85; G. J. Mentink and A. M. van der Woude, *De demografische ontwikkeling te Rotterdam en Cool in de 17de en 18de eeuw* (Rotterdam, 1965), 140; van der Woude, *Het Noorderkwartier* (Wageningen, 1972), 791. In England, an initially strong tendency to avoid marriages during

Lent gave way to increasingly frequent weddings during this period, without the Lenten dip ever entirely disappearing from curves of the seasonality of marriage prior to 1800. Wrigley and Schofield, *Population History of England,* 198–300; David Cressy, "The Seasonality of Marriage in Old and New England," *Journal of Interdisciplinary History* 16 (1985): 1–21.

31. *First Book of Discipline,* 200.

32. Carbonnier-Burkard, "Manuels réformés de préparation à la mort"; id., "L'art de mourir réformé: Les récits de 'dernières heures,' aux XVIIe et XVIIIe siècles," in *Homo Religiosus: Autour de Jean Delumeau* (Paris, 1997), 99–107; Bruce Gordon, "Malevolent Ghosts and Ministering Angels: Apparitions and Pastoral Care in the Swiss Reformation," in Gordon and Marshall, eds., *Place of the Dead,* 87–109, esp. 103; Hall, *Worlds of Wonder,* 206–10; Jean Jacob Salchli, *Recueil des dernieres heures de Messieurs De Mornay Du Plessis, Gigord, Rivet, Du Moulin, Drelincourt, et Fabri* (Lausanne, 1759).

33. Keith Luria, "Separated by Death? Burials, Cemeteries, and Confessional Boundaries in Seventeenth-Century France," *French Historical Studies* 24 (2001): 185–222, esp. 197–200; Susan Amanda Eurich, "Religious Frontiers and Resistance to the Reformation in Sixteenth-Century Béarn," *Proceedings of the Western Society for French History* 24 (1997): 359. Note the absence of this issue in Watt, "Reception of the Reformation in Valangin"; Chareyre, "Consistoire de Nîmes,"; Duke, "Reformation of the Backwoods"; Roodenburg, *Onder censuur.*

34. Quoted in Jenkins, *Literature, Religion and Society in Wales,* 33.

35. De Félice, *Protestants d'autrefois* 1:110–17; Leroux, "Église réformée de Bordeaux," 201; Gueneau, "Protestants du Centre," 296, 298; Brandt, *History of the Reformation in and about the Low Countries* 3:30, 34; Volger, "Vie religieuse en pays rhénan," 794; Houston, *Scottish Literacy,* 150; Parker, "Success and Failure," 78n; Henderson, *Religious Life in Seventeenth-Century Scotland,* 12.

36. Houston, *Scottish Literacy,* 5; Enno van Gelder, *Getemperde Vrijheid,* 195; Elliott, "Protestantization," 436; Sipallyo, *Akta Synodów Różniowierczych w Polsce* 3:41, 83; Donaldson, *James V to James VII,* 264; James Scotland, *The History of Scottish Education,* vol. 1, *From the Beginning to 1872* (London, 1969), 52.

37. De Booy, *Kweekhoven der Wijsheid,* 42–45; Margaret Spufford, "First Steps in Literacy: The Reading and Writing Experiences of the Humblest Seventeenth-Century Spiritual Autobiographers," in Harvey J. Graff, ed., *Literacy and Social Development in the West: A Reader* (Cambridge, 1981), 125–50; Houston, *Scottish Literacy,* 126–27; Odile Martin, *La conversion protestante à Lyon* (Geneva, 1986), 287–88; Ruth B. Bottigheimer, "Bible Reading, 'Bibles' and the Bible for Children in Early Modern Germany," *Past & Present* 139 (1993): 79–81.

38. *Acts of the Parliament of Scotland* 3:139; Cowan, *Scottish Reformation,* 142; Henderson, *Religious Life in Seventeenth-Century Scotland,* 4; Sipallyo, *Akta Synodów Różniowierczych w Polsce* 3:24–25; von Wartburg-Ambühl, *Alphabetisierung und Lektüre,* 164; Gilmont, *Le livre et la Réforme,* 129, 169; John Morgan, *Godly Learning: Puritan Attitudes towards Reason, Learning*

and Education, 1560–1640 (Cambridge, 1986), 157; Henderson, *Religious Life in Seventeenth-Century Scotland,* 5.

39. Anjubault and Chardin, *Recueil,* 17; Abels and Wouters, *Nieuw en ongezien* 1:319; de Félice, *Protestants d'autrefois* 2:46; Münch, *Zucht und Ordnung,* 158; Houston, *Scottish Literacy,* 133; Henderson, *Religious Life in Seventeenth-Century Scotland,* 8; George I. Murray, *Records of Falkirk Parish* (Falkirk, 1887), 151; Stauffenegger, *Eglise et société,* 308; Chareyre, "Consistoire de Nîmes," 725.

40. Vogler, "Vie religieuse en pays rhénan," 790–99; Zschunke, *Konfession und Alltag in Oppenheim,* 93; Wiebe Bergsma, "Een achttiende-eeuwse kroniek van de dood," *Nederlands Archief voor Kerkgeschiedenis* 73 (1993): 82–83.

41. Henderson, *Religious Life in Seventeenth-Century Scotland,* 5; Houston, *Scottish Literacy,* 56, 104.

42. In addition to the data in table 15.4, see Christian Desplat, "Notes pour une approche des rapports entre Réforme et culture populaire en Béarn du XVIe siècle au XVIIIe siècle," in *Arnaud de Salette et son temps: Le Béarn sous Jeanne d'Albret* (Orthez, 1984), 74 (nearly identical rates); de Booy, *Kweekhoven der Wijsheid,* 273–75 (signature rates roughly 15–20 percent higher among Protestant artisans and farmers, but on the basis of evidence from 1818).

43. Furet and Ozouf, *Lire et écrire* 1:175, 309; T. C. Smout, "Born Again at Cambuslang: New Evidence on Popular Religion and Literacy in Eighteenth-Century Scotland," *Past & Present* 97 (1982): 122.

44. Müller, "Konfessionalisierung in der Grafschaft Oldenburg" 304, 308ff.; Egil Johansson, "The History of Literacy in Sweden," in Graff, ed., *Literacy and Social Development,* 176–79.

45. Von Wartburg-Ambühl, *Alphabetisierung und Lektüre,* 129; Henderson, *Religious Life in Seventeenth-Century Scotland,* 4; Smout, "Born Again at Cambuslang," 123.

46. Benedict, *Faith and Fortunes,* 163; Hall, *Worlds of Wonder,* 247–49; Peter Clark, "The Ownership of Books in England, 1560–1640: The Example of Some Kentish Townsfolk," in Lawrence Stone, ed., *Schooling and Society: Studies in the History of Education* (Baltimore, 1976), 99; François Gronauer, "Livre et société à Genève au XVIIIe siècle" (Mémoire de licence, University of Geneva, 1969), 11. The Amiens evidence is based on as-yet-unpublished research by the author and rests on a sample of fifty Protestant inventories.

47. Van Deursen, *Bavianen en Slijkgeuzen,* 181–82; Richard Baxter, *Autobiography,* ed. N. H. Keeble (London, 1974), 4, 7; Spufford, "First Steps," 138; Vuilleumier, *Histoire de l'Eglise réformée du Pays de Vaud* 2:612.

48. *Journal de Jean Migault,* ed. P. de Bray (Paris, 1854), 76.

49. Martin, *Conversion protestante à Lyon,* 224; *Diary of Sir Archibald Johnston of Wariston 1632–1639,* ed. G. M. Paul (Edinburgh, 1911), 10; *The Life of the Reverend Mr. George Trosse,* ed. A. W. Brink (Montreal, 1974), 52.

50. Etienne François, "Les protestants allemands et la Bible: Diffusion et pratiques," in Yvon Belaval and Dominique Bourel, eds., *Le siècle des Lumières et la Bible* (Paris, 1986), 54–56.

51. Etienne François, "Livre, confession et société urbaine en Allemagne au XVIIIe siècle: L'exemple de Spire," *Revue d'Histoire Moderne et Contemporaine* 29 (1982): 355.

52. Seaver, *Wallington's World,* 3–5.

53. The most outstanding studies within this abundant literature are listed in this chapter's bibliographical note. The following paragraphs are based primarily on these works and on such classic Puritan autobiographies as Baxter, *Autobiography;* John Bunyan, *Grace Abounding to the Chief of Sinners,* ed. Roger Sharrock (Oxford, 1962); *Life of Trosse.*

54. Seaver, *Wallington's World,* 24; Macdonald, *Mystical Bedlam,* 220, 224; also Wallace, *Puritans and Predestination,* 75; Hill, *World Turned Upside Down,* 137; Margaret Spufford, *Small Books,* 208–10.

55. Seaver, *Wallington's World,* 20, 214.

56. Ibid., 39; Elisabeth Bourcier, *Les journaux privés en Angleterre de 1600 à 1660* (Paris, 1976), 326.

57. Seaver, *Wallington's World,* 31–36; also Hambrick-Stowe, *Practice of Piety,* 206–18; Pettit, *Heart Prepared.*

58. Hambrick-Stowe, *Practice of Piety,* 89.

59. Zaret, *Heavenly Contract,* 114; David D. Hall, "Religion and Society: Problems and Reconsiderations," in Jack P. Greene and J. R. Pole, eds., *Colonial British America: Essays in the New History of the Early Modern Era* (Baltimore, 1984), 336; Collinson, *Religion of Protestants,* 230.

60. Collinson, *Religion of Protestants,* 191.

61. Nicholas Tyacke, "Popular Puritan Mentality in Late Elizabethan England," in Peter Clark, A. G. R. Smith, and Tyacke, eds., *The English Commonwealth 1547–1640* (Leicester, 1979), 77–92, esp. 89; Martin Ingram, "Religion, Communities and Moral Discipline in Late Sixteenth- and Early Seventeenth-Century England: Case Studies," in K. von Greyerz, ed., *Religion and Society in Early Modern Europe 1500–1800* (London, 1984), 177–93; Collinson, *Religion of Protestants,* 239–41; Seaver, *Wallington's World,* chap. 5. Cf. Keith Wrightson and David Levine, *Poverty and Piety in an English Village: Terling, 1525–1700* (New York, 1979), esp. chap. 7.

62. "The Wills of Thomas Bassandyne and Other Printers, etc. in Edinburgh, 1577–1687," *The Bannatyne Miscellany* (Edinburgh, 1836), esp. 192–202, 242–43, 251.

63. Gordon Marshall, *Presbyteries and Profits: Calvinism and the Development of Capitalism in Scotland, 1560–1707* (Oxford, 1980), 74–77; *Diary of Johnston,* passim; "Memorial or Diary of Mr Francis Borland, minister of Glassford, 1661–1722," Edinburgh University Library MS; "Part of the Diary of the Revd. Mr Thomas Hog," Edinburgh University Library MS; National Library of Scotland MS 34.5.19 (a collection of autobiographies by Covenanters); "Diary of Mr James Murray," National Library of Scotland MS 3045; "The Memoirs of Walter Pringle" and "The History of Mr. John Welsh, Minister of the Gospel at Ayr," in W. K. Tweedie, ed., *Select Biographies* (Edinburgh, 1855). Mullan, *Scottish Puri-*

tanism, contains much further evidence of the similarity between Scottish and "Puritan" piety in this period.

64. E.g., "Diary of the Experiences of James Nasmyth," Saint Andrews University Library MS DA 804.IN2.

65. Murdock, "International Calvinism and the Reformed Church of Hungary," 153; John Dury, *The Earnest Breathings of Foreign Protestants . . . for a Compleat Body of Practicall Divinity* (London, 1658), B 1–2; Hartmut Kretzer, "Die Calvinismus-Kapitalismus-These Max Webers vor dem Hintergrund französischer Quellen des 17. Jahrhunderts," *Zeitschrift für historische Forschung* 4 (1977): 425n. For the count of editions of *The Practice of Piety,* I searched the major library catalogues and national bibliographies, e.g., *The National Union Catalogue,* the *Deutsches Gesamtkatalog,* the catalogue of the British Library, and also relied upon W. J. op 't Hof, "Everhardus Schuttenius (ca. 1595–1655)" in Brienen et al., *Figuren en thema's van de Nadere Reformatie* 2:30; Georges Ascoli, *La Grande-Bretagne devant l'opinion française au XVIIe siècle,* 2 vols. (Paris, 1930), 2:312; Imre Bán, "Die literatur- und kulturgeschichtliche Bedeutung des ungarischen Puritanismus des 17. Jahrhunderts," in Peter F. Barton and László Makkai, eds., *Rebellion oder Religion?* (Budapest, 1977), 77.

66. Breward, ed., *Works of Perkins,* 613–32, which also lists 173 English editions and 41 in Latin; K. Koltay, "Two Hundred Years of English Puritan Books in Hungary," *Angol filolaogiai tanulmanyok* 20 (1989): 61–62.

67. Cornelis Willem Schoneveld, *Intertraffic of the Mind: Studies in Seventeenth-Century Anglo-Dutch Translation* (Leiden, 1983); W. J. op 't Hof, *Engelse pietistische geschriften in het Nederlands, 1598–1622* (Rotterdam, 1987), esp. 562, 576, 636, 642; C. Graafland, "De invloed van het Puritanisme op het ontstaan van het Gereformeerd Piëtisme in Nederland," *Documentatieblad Nadere Reformatie* 7 (1983): 1–24.

68. J. van Voorst, "De Nadere Reformatie van een leesgierige vrouw? Sporen van Nadere Reformatie in een zeventiende eeuwse boekenlijst," *Documentatieblad Nadere Reformatie* 16 (1992): 36–37; F. A. van Lieburg, "De receptie van de Nadere Reformatie in Utrecht," *De Zeventiende Eeuw* 5 (1989): 121–25; id., "Piëtistiche Egodocumenten in 18de-Eeuws Nederland," *Spiegel Historiael* 25 (1990): 320–24; W. van 't Spijker, "Jacobus Koelman (1632–1695)," J. van Genderen, "Wilhelmus à Brakel (1635–1711)," and id., "Herman Witsius (1636–1708)" in Brienen et al., *Nadere Reformatie,* 127–218; [Mattheus du Bois] *Godts Wonder-werck, voor en in de Weder-gheboorte* (Amsterdam, 1680).

69. F. A. van Lieburg, *Levens van vromen: Gereformeerd piëtisme in de achttiende eeuw* (Kampen, 1991); James H. Tanis, *Dutch Calvinistic Pietism in the Middle Colonies: A Study in the Life and Theology of Theodorus Jacobus Frelinghuysen* (The Hague, 1967), 140–42; Enno van Gelder, *Getemperde vrijheid,* 67.

70. Kretzer, "Calvinismus-Kapitalismus-These," 425; Benedict, *Faith and Fortunes,* chap. 6; *Life of Trosse,* 52–53.

71. Hermann Beck, *Die religiöse Volksliteratur der evangelischen Kirche Deutschlands in einem Abriss ihre Geschichte* (Gotha, 1891), 177ff.; Udo Sträter,

Sonthom, Bayly, Dyke und Hall: Studien zur Rezeption der englischen Erbau-
ungsliteratur in Deutschland im 17. Jahrhundert (Tubingen, 1987), esp. 5–11,
41–43; Johannes Wallmann, "Johann Arndt und die Protestantische Frömmigkeit:
Zur Rezeption der mittelaltlichen Mystik im Luthertum," in D. Breuer, ed.,
Frömmigkeit in der Frühen Neuzeit: Studien zur religiösen Literatur des 17.
Jahrhunderts in Deutschland (Amsterdam, 1984), 53, 57; Gottfried Mai, *Die*
niederdeutsche Reformbewegung: Ursprünge und Verlauf des Pietismus in
Bremen bis zur Mitte des 18. Jahrhunderts (Bremen, 1979), esp. 77–88, 96–
97; Tanis, *Dutch Calvinistic Pietism,* 19–22; Vuilleumier, *Histoire de l'Eglise*
réformée du Pays de Vaud 3:235–36.

72. Beza, *Correspondance* 13:136, 144.

73. For the rarity of such cases in the first years of the French Reformed churches,
see Graham, *Uses of Reform,* 324–32.

74. "Pierre Lézan, secrétaire du consistoire de Saint-Hippolyte 1663–1700: Extraits
de ses mémoires," in Clément Ribard, *Notes d'histoire cévenole* (Cazillac, 1898),
543–61.

75. Eurich, "Religious Frontiers and Resistance to the Reformation in Sixteenth-
Century Béarn," 359.

76. Maltby, *Prayer Book and People.*

77. Detailed studies identifying those texts and practices of early modern devotion
that reached across confessional lines and those that were distinctive to each
one have yet to be undertaken. My remarks here are based on an admittedly limited reading of widely reprinted Catholic and Lutheran devotional works and on
such studies of the Catholic and Lutheran devout as Patrice Veit, "Le dévotion
domestique luthérienne: Instructions, images et pratiques," *Revue de l'histoire*
des religions 217 (2000): 593–606; and Barbara Diefendorf, "Exemplary Lives:
Pious Women and Their Biographers in Catholic Reformation Paris," paper delivered to the American Society of Church History/American Historical Association
meeting, Boston, January 2001.

78. Charles Bost, "Poésies populaires huguenotes du Vivarais (du XVIe siècle à la fin
de la révolte camisarde)," *Bulletin de la Société de l'Histoire du Protestantisme*
Français 89 (1940): 201–36, 317–40; above, 477, 506. See also Philippe Joutard,
"Protestantisme populaire et univers magique: Le cas cévenol," *Le Monde Alpin*
et Rhodanien 5 (1977): 145–71.

79. Wiebe Bergsma, "'Slow to Hear God's Holy Word'? Religion and Everyday Life in
Early Modern Friesland," in Laeyendecker et al., eds., *Experiences and Explana-*
tions, 67–68. Jancz.'s diary has been edited and published by P. Gerbenzon, *Het*
aantekeningenboek van Dirck Jansz. (Hilversum, 1993).

CONCLUSION TO PART IV

1. Schilling, *Konfessionskonflikt und Staatsbildung.*

2. Max Weber, *Economy and Society,* ed. G. Roth and C. Wittich (Berkeley, 1978),
1208; James Hastings Nichols, *Democracy and the Churches* (Philadelphia,
1951), 29ff.

3. De Tocqueville, *Democracy in America* (New York, 1945), 33, cited in David Zaret, "Religion and the Rise of Liberal-Democratic Ideology in 17th-Century England," *American Sociological Review* 54 (1989): 166; McNeill, *History and Character of Calvinism,* 411–18.

4. Brian M. Downing, *The Military Revolution and Political Change: Origins of Democracy and Autocracy in Early Modern Europe* (Princeton, 1992); Thomas Ertman, *The Birth of Leviathan: Building States and Regimes in Medieval and Early Modern Europe* (Cambridge, 1997).

5. Bethel, *The Present Interest of England Stated,* 24, 22.

6. Münch, "The Thesis Before Weber," 56, 64–66; J. Maarten Ultee, "The Suppression of *Fêtes* in France, 1666," *Catholic Historical Review* 62 (1976): 181–99.

7. Jan de Vries and Ad van der Woude, *The First Modern Economy: Success, Failure, and Perseverance of the Dutch Economy, 1500–1815* (Cambridge, 1997), 617.

8. Jan de Vries, "The Industrial Revolution and the Industrious Revolution," *Journal of Economic History* 54 (1994): 249–70.

9. De Vries and van der Woude, *First Modern Economy,* 165–72; de Vries, *The Economy of Europe in an Age of Crisis, 1600–1750* (Cambridge, 1976), 176–92; id., "Between Purchasing Power and the World of Goods: Understanding the Household Economy in Early Modern Europe," in John Brewer and Roy Porter, eds., *Consumption and the World of Goods* (London, 1993), 85–132.

10. Benedict, *Faith and Fortunes,* chap. 3.

11. Jean-Louis Thireau, *Charles du Moulin (1500–1566): Etude sur les sources, la méthode, les idées politiques et économiques d'un juriste de la Renaissance* (Geneva, 1980), 354–56; Noonan, *Scholastic Analysis of Usury,* passim, esp. chap. 18; René Taveneaux, "L'usure en Lorraine au temps de la Réforme catholique: Les controverses sur le prêt à l'intérêt," *Annales de l'Est,* 5th ser. 27 (1974): 187–216; id., *Jansénisme et prêt à intérêt* (Paris, 1977); Bartolomé Clavero, *La grâce du don. Anthropologie catholique de l'économie moderne* (Paris, 1996); and especially Henri Lapeyre, *Une famille de marchands, les Ruiz* (Paris, 1955), 126–35.

12. Tyacke, "Popular Puritan Mentality," 189; Chadwick, *The Reformation* (Harmondsworth, 1964), 184; Jean Lejeune, "Religion, morale et capitalisme dans la société liégoise du XVIIe siècle," *Revue Belge de Philologie et d'Histoire* 22 (1943): 125–27.

13. See above, 317–29, 520–26. One important recent work of sociological history, Gordon Marshall, *Presbyteries and Profits: Calvinism and the Development of Capitalism in Scotland, 1560–1707* (Oxford, 1980), claims to offer empirical verification of Weber's theory. The book convincingly demonstrates both that concern with making one's election sure came to the fore within Scottish Calvinism in the generations after 1560, and that entrepreneurs grew more rational in their attempts to calculate profitability within Scotland's developing economy; but it fails to prove that these contemporaneous developments were linked.

14. Berger, *The Desecularization of the World,* 16. For a different, ground-level view
of evangelical Protestantism's relatively ephemeral effects in a single Andean
village, see Nathan Wachtel, *Gods and Vampires: Return to Chipaya* (Chicago,
1994). Especially noteworthy here are the findings of Sherman, *Soul of Development,* esp. 86–93, whose survey research findings within a work shaped
powerfully by Weberian assumptions reveal that the group she labels orthodox
Catholics exhibit the same patterns of behavior as evangelicals, although both
differ from those contemporary Guatemalans whose worldview is magical and
"Cristo-Pagan."

INDEX

Zurich (*continued*)
Poland, 262, 269; seventeenth-century
theology, 348–49, 351; literacy in
countryside, 514. *See also* Bullinger;
Zwingli
Zweibrücken, 222, 381, 500
Zwilling, Conrad, 15

Zwingli, Huldrych: early life and formation, 22–24; theology of, 24–25, 28,
33–34; work in Zurich, 25–32; disputes with Luther, 34–35; influence
beyond Zurich, 36–48, 53, 84–85, 130,
180; diffusion of writings, 59, 63